The Train Robbery Era

The Train Robbery Era
An Encyclopedic History

Richard Patterson

PRUETT PUBLISHING COMPANY
BOULDER, COLORADO

Printed in the United States of America

First Edition
1   2   3   4   5   6   7   8   9

Library of Congress Cataloging-in-Publication Data

Patterson, Richard M., 1934–
    The train robbery era : an encyclopedic history / by Richard Patterson.
        p.   cm.
    Includes bibliographical references.
    ISBN 0-87108-807-X : $39.95
    1. Train robberies – United States – History – Handbooks, manuals, etc. I. Title.
    HV6658.P38   1991
    364.1′552′0973 – dc20   91-2291
                                                                CIP

To Wynonia, with love.

PREFACE

Anyone who has produced a book of this length knows the tedium that comes with long hours of research and writing. But with this book I was fortunate to have encouragement along the way from an unexpected but most welcome source: the reference librarians and historical society researchers who so graciously helped me with my task. Almost to a person, they applauded my effort, mainly because they agreed with me that the train robbery era was a segment of America's past that almost no one had attempted to chronicle. Believe me, encouragement like that—from persons whose job it is to preserve and pass on our history—kept me at the word processor long into the night.

Why the present interest in the train robbery era? There has long been a fascination with crimes and criminals, and that has not changed. If a report of a bank robbery appears on the front page of your local newspaper, won't that be the first story you read? But more than that, I think the interest stems from America's enchantment with the railroads.

In today's high-tech environment it is difficult to imagine that life in most of the United States was once dominated by something as simple (at least by modern standards) as the railroads. "Railroad iron is a magician's rod," Ralph Waldo Emerson wrote in the 1840s, "in its power to evoke the sleeping energies of land and water." From the end of the Civil War to the 1920s, the railroad industry reshaped the nation and touched the life of nearly every citizen. Fortunes were made and lost overnight, and many towns would thrive or die, depending upon the route of the rails.

The railroads were a means of livelihood, and sometimes prosperity, for many Americans. Usually this was achieved through hard work or investment, and occasionally through speculation or just plain luck. But there were some men who saw in the rail cars not wealth to be earned, but treasures to be taken at gunpoint.

Train robbery flourished in the American West, but it was not confined there. It is generally accepted by outlaw historians that the first peacetime express car robbery occurred in Seymour, Indiana, in 1866. Incidents of the crime then moved south, first to Kentucky and eventually to most of the southern states. The

Atlantic coast also had its share of robberies, and the New York Central Railroad in upstate New York was a favorite target of robbers. Eventually, however, the crime became almost endemic to the frontier, where the rails outdistanced the ability to defend them, and desolate miles of track were made to order for banditry. This book, I hope, has preserved that period of history.

Many persons deserve thanks for helping me with this work. Foremost is Roy P. O'Dell of Cambridge, England, member of the English Westerners' Society and a dedicated and tireless researcher and writer on outlaw and lawmen history. Thank you Roy—I owe you much. Also, in alphabetical order, my thanks go to: Gary Avent, Reference Librarian, Elko County Library, Elko, Nevada; The Ballard/Carlisle County Historical-Genealogical Society, Wickliffe, Kentucky; Clay County Department of Parks, Recreation and Historical Sites, Kearney, Missouri; Robert Bruce Clifton, La Conner, Washington; Barry B. Combs, Union Pacific Railroad, Omaha, Nebraska; the Dalton Museum, Coffeyville, Kansas; Jim Davis and other members of the staff, Microfilm Division, Indianapolis-Marion County Public Library, Indianapolis, Indiana; Jim Dullenty, Rocky Mountain House, Hamilton, Montana; Charles B. Eames, Reference Librarian, Okefenokee Regional Library, Waycross, Georgia; Betty L. Elliott, Ballard-Carlisle Historical-Genealogy Society, Paducah, Kentucky; Mrs. M. Frank, Reference Department, Joliet Public Library, Joliet, Illinois; Friends of the James Farm, Kearney, Missouri; Richard E. Gannaway of Clarksville, Tennessee; Pam Gee, Vicksburgh-Warren County Public Library, Vicksburg, Mississippi; Everett R. Huffer, Cedar Rapids, Iowa; the Kansas State Historical Society, Topeka, Kansas; David V. Lewis and other members of the staff of the Indiana State Library, Indianapolis, Indiana; Ken Long, Research Specialist, Union Pacific System, Omaha, Nebraska; Connie Mills, Kentucky Library Supervisor, Western Kentucky University, Bowling Green, Kentucky; Walter H. Murphy, Director, Flint River Regional Library, Griffin, Georgia; Jean Nichols, Librarian, Clarksville-Montgomery County Public Library, Clarksville, Tennessee; Marion C. Parker, Goodland, Kansas; Capt. & Mrs. Michael R. Patterson, Ft.

Campbell, Kentucky; W. James Patterson, Glendale, Arizona; Pinkertons, Inc., New York, New York; the staff at Purdue University Libraries, Lafayette, Indiana; Bill Robertson, formerly of the Public Relations Department, Southern Pacific Railroad; the late William A. Settle, Columbia, Missouri; Nancy Thomas, Librarian, Goodnight Memorial Library, Franklin, Kentucky; the staff at the Union Pacific Railroad Museum, Omaha, Nebraska; the University of Texas, Austin, Texas; the staff at the Wabash College Library, Crawfordsville, Indiana; Dave Walter, Montana Historical Society Library, Helena, Montana; the staff at Wells Fargo Bank History Room, San Francisco, California; and the staff at the Western History Research Center, University of Wyoming, Laramie, Wyoming.

A

ACQUIA CREEK, VIRGINIA. It was the biggest train robbery in the East, if not in amount stolen, at least in excitement generated. On October 12, 1894, two masked men jumped into the locomotive cab on a Richmond, Fredericksburg & Potomac northbound express near Acquia Creek, Virginia. The engineer, Frank Gallagher, was ordered to stop the train; when he didn't, one of the intruders grabbed the throttle from him and applied the brakes. The train was brought to a halt, and while one of the masked men guarded the engineer and fireman, the other one headed for the express car. The Adams Express Company messenger, Percy Crutchfield, gave this account:

Charles Searcey. *Pinkertons.*

> [Only] one robber entered the car. He was heavy build, [*sic*] and was dressed like a farmer, but he seemed thoroughly to understand his business. He had a red handkerchief over the lower part of his face. When the train was stopped, I opened the door of my car. The robber fired at me. I dodged back and closed the door.
>
> "Open the door," he shouted. I didn't do it. "Open the door, or I'll blow the whole car to pieces with dynamite." Then he threw a stick of dynamite, which struck the door and shattered it and the casing. The force knocked me off my feet.
>
> I then opened the door. The robber came in and made me open the safe. He took everything. There was one package which he must have thought contained only papers, for he threw it back into the safe. It contained $6,000. Then he said: "Open that other safe."
>
> "That is simply a deadhead safe," I said. "The ——— it is," he said. "Show me your waybill for it."
>
> I started to get the bill, and he said: "Keep your hands up. Show me the paper. I'll get it."
>
> He looked at the bill, and he was satisfied that the second safe contained nothing, which was true. The man was very cool all the time. We had seven or eight through express pouches, each containing packages of money; how much I can't guess. The man cut a slip in each pouch, and took every package.

The train had left Richmond at 7:00 P.M. and was stopped by the robbers at approximately 9:30. The robbers chose their spot well: a rugged stretch of wilderness between Brooks Station and Wide Water. It was believed that they climbed aboard the blind baggage area between the tender and front end of the express car when the train made the required stop before it crossed the bridge over Acquia Creek.

Although only two bandits were involved, in the excitement the train crew and passengers reported seeing as many as seven or eight. Besides the express messenger, only one trainman showed courage. The conductor, M. A. Birdsong, who was back in a rear passenger coach, went looking for a gun. He found one, a tiny lady's pistol, and charged forward to the front platform of the first coach. Throwing open the door, he shouted to the robbers that he would kill the first man who attempted to enter a coach. The robbers, one busy guarding the engine crew and the other trying to gain entry to the express car, ignored him, and several passengers managed to drag him back into the car and quiet him down.

After the robbers finished their work, they uncoupled the locomotive and climbed into the cab. After traveling a mile or so, they leaped out. The engine, with throttle still open, hurtled toward Quantico, where the

Charles Morganfield.
New York Times.

RF&P's southbound *Atlantic Special* was standing at the station. A quick-thinking yardman at Quantico saw the danger, however, and switched the unmanned engine onto a siding and up a grade to a coal dump, where it came to a stop after crashing into a string of coal cars.

Railroad officials believed that the robbers made their escape by boat across the Potomac River into Maryland.

It was first estimated by the Adams Express Company that the bandits got at least $150,000, but as further audits were made, this figure was reduced. The car's manifest showed a total express shipment of $182,000, but much of this was in bonds and other securities.

On October 14, the Adams Express Company's office in Washington, D.C., released the name of a suspect, George Carter, a former railroad engineer who had recently escaped from prison in New York. Carter roughly matched the description of the robber who blasted his way into the Adams Express car. Also, Carter had once lived in the area where the robbery occurred.

Three days later an arrest was made, but it was not Carter who was charged. Charles J. Searcey, said to be from Kansas, was picked up at the Baltimore & Ohio Railroad station at Cumberland, Maryland. A policeman at the station noticed that Searcey, who was carrying two satchels, seemed to be acting "nervous." When the officer approached, Searcey ran. The policeman caught him, and on being searched, the suspect was found to be carrying two revolvers and forty-three cartridges, a set of muddy shoes and clothes that appeared to be a disguise, and $1,552.53 in cash stuffed into two woolen socks.

Baltimore & Ohio station at Cumberland, Maryland. Charles Searcey was captured here five days after the robbery. *Smithsonian.*

On the same day Searcey was arrested, the Adams Express Company reported that several of the stolen packages that were thought to contain cash and negotiable securities actually contained drafts upon which payment could be stopped. This discovery, the company said, reduced the amount of actual loss to approximately $20,000.

The next day, October 18, a second suspect was arrested in Cincinnati, Ohio. He said his name was Charles A. Morganfield. He was found lying near the tracks of the Cincinnati, Hamilton & Dayton Railroad with a broken leg. He claimed he was injured trying to board a train. The suspect said he was from Tennessee, but the authorities reported that he had a pronounced Virginia accent.

Buried in the dirt near where Morganfield was found was a Colt 44 revolver and a pocket knife. He was carrying $432 in cash in his pockets, and hidden in his undershirt was a roll of bills totaling another $760. He also was carrying a valise that contained a brown slouch hat and a shirt similar to those worn by one of the robbers. Hidden behind the band of the hat were a $100 draft drawn on the Bank of Commerce of Baltimore and a $50 draft on the First National Bank of Camden, N.J., both of the type stolen in the robbery.

Morganfield, who was also found to have gone by the name Charles Morgan, was brought to trial in February 1895. Percy Crutchfield, the Adams Express Company messenger, and a second messenger, Harry Murray, both identified Morganfield as the man who entered their car. When told of this testimony, Searcey decided to turn state's evidence and confess. The jury deliberated only ten minutes before finding Morganfield guilty, and he was sentenced to seventeen years at the state penitentiary at Richmond. In return for his guilty plea, Searcey received a ten-year sentence. (Sources: Pinkerton, *Train Robberies*; *St. Louis Globe Democrat*, 13, 16, 18, 19, 24, 30 October, 16 November, 22, 27 December 1894, 11, 19 January, 22, 23 February 1895; *New York Times*, 14, 15, 18–20 October 1894, 21–23 February 1895.)

ADAIR, IOWA. The wreck and robbery of a Chicago, Rock Island & Pacific Railroad passenger train on July 21, 1873, near the town of Adair, Iowa, is sometimes mistakenly called the first train robbery in the United States; in fact, a marker placed near the site in 1954 made such a claim. (It was later corrected.) The Adair robbery was, however, probably the first holdup of a train by Jesse James and his gang.

The town of Adair is about sixty miles west of Des Moines, in Adair County just below the Guthrie County line. The site of the wreck, about three miles west of the Adair station, was well chosen for purposes of a robbery; at the time there was no habitation within two miles.

Rock Island depot at Adair. *Everett R. Huffer Collection.*

The train was eastbound, due in Des Moines at 10:15 P.M. At around 7:00 P.M. the robbers, using a rope, jerked away a loosened rail and sent the engine, tender, and express and baggage cars off the tracks and into the ditch. The front trucks of the first passenger coach were derailed, but the coach itself stayed on the track.

The engineer, John Rafferty, saw the displaced rail; he applied the brakes and simultaneously threw the wheels into reverse, but it was too late. As the engine left the track, Rafferty was dashed against the side of the cab and died almost instantly from a broken neck. The fireman, Dennis Foley, survived the crash and dragged his dead companion from the wreckage. He also managed to reach a relief valve on the boiler and open it, no doubt averting an explosion.

The robbers, not satisfied with derailing the train, fired repeatedly at the engine cab as it toppled and ground to a halt. (When the engineer's body was examined later, a bullet was found in his thigh.) Before the dust had settled on the crash, the robbers, the exact number of which was never determined, rushed to the express car and smashed their way in.

According to the Wells, Fargo messenger, whose

name was Burgess, the robbers demanded to know where the bullion was located. The car did contain bullion, both gold and silver bricks—nearly three tons neatly stacked on the floor. Messenger Burgess even pointed to it, knowing that there was no way the robbers could carry away more than a few bricks. The robbers, however, were not interested. Apparently they thought "bullion" meant bags of coins, and they kept insisting that Burgess unlock the express company safe. Burgess complied, and the bandits took what money was contained inside: about $1,700 and a sealed Wells, Fargo bag, the contents of which were not known. According to the messenger, apart from the gold and silver bricks, the amount of money he carried in his safe that night was far less than usual, the smallest amount he had carried in months.

When the robbers had finished, they saddled up and rode south. The following month, authorities in St. Louis issued a press release that they believed the robbers to be from western Missouri—the same ones who robbed a bank in St. Genevieve, Missouri, the previous May, as well as banks in Russelville, Kentucky, and Gallatin, Missouri, two years earlier. They listed their names as Jesse and Frank James, Bill Sheppard, Cole Younger, and McCoy.

Whether the James-Younger bunch were responsible for the Adair robbery has never been positively established, although most researchers believe they were. The Pinkerton's National Detective Agency officially named them as the culprits, listing them individually as Jesse and Frank James; Frank, Cole, and Jim Younger; plus Clell Miller, Bob Moore, and Comanche Tony. The Pinkerton files also contained reports that following the robbery the gang members rode southeast to Ringold County, Iowa, just above the Missouri line, where they were "given supper and later that evening sat on the porch of the farmhouse discussing numerous subjects including farming and religion." (Sources: Settle, *Jesse James Was His Name*; *St. Louis Democrat*, 12 September 1873; *New York Times*, 23, 26 July, 8 August 1873.) *See also* **The James-Younger Gang**.

ADAIR, OKLAHOMA. The robbery of an express car on the Missouri, Kansas & Texas Railroad at Adair on July 15, 1892, was the last committed by the famous Dalton gang and it was nearly a disaster. According to Emmett Dalton, who later gave an account of the affair, the gang had planned to rob the train ten miles to the south, at Pryor, but the outlaws' camp was discovered that morning by a farmer, and they were afraid he might have notified the authorities.

Adair is in Mayes County, northeast of Tulsa. Apparently, the plan was to take command of the depot first and then wait for the arrival of the train. This was accomplished, but just before the bandits moved out to attack the train, gunfire broke out from a shed near the tracks. Three lawmen and a railroad guard had spotted the outlaws at the station and had opened fire. With the air full of lead, the bandits had to change their plan of attack. While part of the gang held off the men in the shed, three of the outlaws worked their way around to the opposite side of the train, away from the lawmen's guns, and forced their way into the express car. Once in the car, the robbers quickly blew the safe and grabbed the contents, reported to be about $40,000 (although this was never verified).

Although the men in the shed were troublesome to the robbers, they were not well situated to keep up the attack. The shed was thin-walled and offered little protection. In minutes, all four men inside were hit, one seriously. Also, it was a bad day for innocent bystanders. Several stray bullets shattered the window of the town drugstore where two doctors were sitting at a table. Both were injured, and one, W. L. Goff, later died.

When the men in the shed could no longer fight, the outlaws completed their work and departed with their loot. According to witnesses, they made their escape toward the rugged Dog Creek Hills. (Sources: Preece, *The Dalton Gang; New York Times*, 16 July 1892.)

ALLEN, TEXAS. Sam Bass has been credited with this robbery. After holding up a Union Pacific express car at Big Springs, Nebraska, the previous September, Bass returned to Texas and hid out in nearby Denton County. Bored with hideout life, Sam first robbed a couple of stagecoaches west of Fort Worth, and then, probably because of slim pickings, once again tried trains.

On February 22, 1878, Bass and four companions overpowered the station agent at Allen, which is just north of Dallas, a few minutes before the Houston & Texas Central passenger train was due in. When they descended on the Texas Express Company car, however, they met stiff resistance from the messenger, James Thomas. Several shots were exchanged, and Thomas

might have wounded one of the attackers. Eventually, he gave in, and the bandits took between $1,200 and $2,500 from the safe.

The gang introduced a new twist to train robbery at Allen. To keep the passengers in line, one of the bandits raced through the coaches shouting that a robbery was in progress and that the robbers numbered "between 50 and 60." Needless to say, none of the passengers ventured forward to find out if this was true. (Sources: Gard, *Sam Bass; New York Times*, 24 February 1877; *Galveston News*, 23 February 1877.) *See also* **Sam Bass**.

ALTOONA, PENNSYLVANIA. The lone bandit who robbed an express car on the Pennsylvania Railroad near Altoona in 1909 had to be one of the dumbest robbers in the history of the crime.

Shortly after midnight on August 31 of that year, on a lonely stretch of track along the Juniata River just outside Altoona, the engineer and fireman of the Pennsy's eastbound Pittsburgh Express were startled by an explosion under the big locomotive's wheels. At first the engineer, Sam Donnelly, thought they had run over a railroad torpedo, the signal used by railroaders to warn an engineer of trouble ahead on the track. But the second blast was much too strong for a torpedo, and the third explosion rocked the engine back and forth, smashed its headlight, and sent a section of a rail end-over-end down the embankment. Fearing another blast would cause a derailment, Donnelly eased off the throttle and brought the engine to a halt.

As Donnelly and his fireman, G. D. Willis, started to climb down to check the track ahead, they heard a noise in the underbrush, and out stepped a man with a revolver in each hand and a burlap mask over his face. "Are there any mail cars on this train?" he asked.

"No," answered Donnelly.

"Any express cars?" asked the masked man.

Donnelly told him there was an express car, and the man ordered the two trainmen down to the ground and told them to march ahead of him, because that was where they were going.

As they neared the express car, the messenger, John W. S. Harper, opened the door and peeked out. The masked man saw him and ordered him to open the door all the way. If he didn't, said the robber, he would toss in a stick of dynamite. Harper opened up.

In his report filed after the robbery, messenger Harper said that there were five bags of coin and bullion in his car. Without getting into the car, the robber ordered Harper to throw out the five bags. This Harper did. The first bag contained more than $5,000 in gold bullion. The next two bags held $100 each in Lincoln pennies, a fourth bag contained $100 in silver dollars, and the last bag, ten silver dollars. As Harper tossed the bags out on the ground, the robber ordered engineer Donnelly to put them into two larger bags which he apparently had brought with him.

When the two large bags were filled, the robber ordered Donnelly back into the locomotive cab, and told Harper and Willis to pick up the two bags and march ahead of him down the track. After about 200 yards he told them to start up the mountainside. After a few hundred more yards, he told them that was far enough, and that they could return to the train. As they turned to go, the robber bid them "goodbye and good luck."

Engineer Donnelly rushed the train to the next station and sent word of the robbery to the authorities. By dawn, railroad officials and police had converged on the scene. The robber's route led nearly straight up the mountain and was easy to follow; all the pursuers had to do was to follow a trail of bullion and coins.

Apparently the robber had underestimated the difficulty of the climb, or his own stamina, because before long the pursuers found one of the two large bags, and in it was $5,000 in bullion. A little further along they found a second bag, one of the bags of pennies, and then a little later, the second bag of pennies. Eventually, they began finding loose coins. All in all, the detectives picked up all but $65 of the stolen money.

The detectives were at a loss as to why the robber discarded all of the bullion. He had several hours' head start and he was not being rushed. As heavy as the bullion was, he could have carried some of it. And if he did have to discard the bullion, why did he not take time to hide it so he could come back for it later? Of course, it was possible that he did not know its value. Another theory was that he intentionally dropped the bullion and kept the shiny new pennies, thinking they were gold coins; when he saw they were not, he discarded them. (Source: *New York Times*, 1 September 1909.)

ALVORD, BURT. While sheriff of Willcox, Arizona, Burt Alvord engineered the robbery of a Wells, Fargo express car at Cochise Junction in September 1899. He was arrested for the robbery, but with the help of fellow gang member Billy Stiles he escaped, and he and Stiles rode the outlaw trail in southern Arizona for several years, later joining up with bandit Augustin Chacon. Alvord turned himself in to the authorities in 1903 and was eventually convicted of the robbery. The stolen loot was never recovered. *See* **Cochise Junction, Arizona**.

AQUA ZARCA (SONORA), MEXICO. In 1888 Aqua Zarca was a dusty little station on the Sonora Railroad about twelve miles south of Nogales, Arizona. The village is probably still there, but it disappeared from most maps long ago. On May 12, 1888, a southbound train consisting of two passenger coaches, a combined baggage-express car, a mail car, and five freight cars left Nogales at 9:00 P.M. An hour and one-half later, as the engineer, James Gray, slowed for the Aqua Zarca siding to take on wood, rifle bullets and shotgun pellets began bouncing off the side of the locomotive cab. Engineer Gray, who was sitting in the cab window, dived to the floor. The fireman, whose name was Forbes, was in the passage between the locomotive and the tender; he was struck in the abdomen by a load of buckshot.

As the train slowed to a stop, the attackers rushed for the baggage-express car. The messenger, Isaac Hays, apparently slid open the door to see what was happening. He was immediately hit by two bullets, one in the head and one in the side, and he fell back into the car and crumpled to the floor. The conductor, Lewis Atkinson, who was at the open side door of the baggage end of the car, was also hit, as was one of the passengers, W. H. French, who stepped out onto the platform of the second-class passenger coach.

The robbers, who numbered six and were all masked, climbed into the express end of the car. Messenger Hays lay on the floor, nearly unconscious but still alive. One of the bandits turned him over and took his keys, hoping to unlock the small iron box that served as the express company safe. When the keys would not work, they picked up the box and threw it out of the car. In the meantime, several curious passengers had come forward, but they were quickly discouraged from making trouble by more shots from the outlaws.

About a half-mile north, eight Mexican customs guards were encamped near the track. They heard the shots and came running, but by then the robbers had fled.

Engineer Gray cut the freight cars from the train and immediately rushed back to Nogales, hoping to get the injured men to a doctor in time, but the fireman died on the way, and conductor Atkinson died shortly after they arrived.

A posse was formed and began riding south in the belief that the bandits intended to return to Nogales. There was some speculation that the gang might have been from the lower part of Sonora, but most of the authorities placed the blame on some of the criminal types that hung out on both the American and Mexican sides of the border.

The local press assumed the robbers were Mexican because "they followed Mexican [bandit] policy of killing first and robbing victims afterwards." During the afternoon two Mexican customs guards were brought to Nogales for messenger Hays to identify, but he failed to recognize them. The Mexican authorities vowed that they would arrest every man south of the border "who could not give a wholly satisfactory account of himself" at the time of the robbery.

The posse found the empty box the bandits had taken from the express car. According to messenger Hays's records it had contained only $130. None of the express shipments along that road were very large. However, the day before the robbery, the paycar for the railroad had arrived in Nogales and was to be attached that night to the 9:00 P.M. train. At the last minute, however, the railroad officials scheduled it for a later run.

Several days later, an Arizonian named J. J. Taylor was arrested while buying a hat in Nogales. The rumor was that he was replacing a hat that had been found by the posse at the scene of the robbery. Taylor denied taking part in the robbery, but did mention that he believed that the gang that committed the crime was led by Conrad Rohling (or Rolling). Later, under further questioning, Taylor implicated himself in the affair, admitting that the robbery had actually been planned in his house.

Rohling was picked up by the authorities and on June 12 he and Taylor were handed over to Mexican authorities. It was expected that the suspects would be dealt with swiftly. (Train robbery was a capital offense in Mexico, and when a killing was involved in a robbery, punishment could come quickly and surely.) On December 9, 1889, word came from Guaymas that Taylor had been executed by a firing squad. (Sources: *St. Louis Globe Democrat*, 13, 14, 19 May, 12 June 1888, 10 December 1889; *New York Times*, 13 May 1888.)

ARMER, FRANK. Frank Armer, a cowboy from the Salt River Valley area of Arizona, was convicted of being one of three men who robbed a Wells, Fargo express car at Maricopa, Arizona Territory, on October 1, 1894. It was believed to be the three robbers' first attempt at a train holdup, and it was an amateurish job. The bandits got only $160 in the robbery, and were easily tracked by local peace officers. See **Maricopa, Arizona**.

ARMORED RAILWAY CARS. Not long after the first express car robbery in 1866, it became obvious that the express cars were not built to withstand assaults by bandits. Over the next thirty years, the railroads and express companies toyed with the idea of constructing defensible armored cars, but it never became a reality. The feeling was that an armored express car could be derailed as easily as an ordinary express car, or as one observer stated: heavier, so-called robber-proof cars "will fall just as far through a sawed bridge and be just as undesirable to be in while rolling down an embankment owing to the absence of a rail from the track as any other style of cars." Express cars were eventually strengthened, however, and by the end of the 1890s, many were able to withstand assaults except when the attackers made liberal use of explosives. (See **Express Cars**.)

During the 1880s the United States Post Office Department also considered ordering armored cars for its railway mail service, but it, too, eventually opted for merely strengthening the cars. However, in 1924 following the $2 million robbery at Rondout, Illinois, during which eight bandits broke into three railway mail cars and gassed the clerks with formaldehyde (see **Rondout, Illinois**), the Post Office Department ordered the construction of a bulletproof and gas-proof armored car capable of withstanding all but the most severe onslaught.

The new postal car had bulletproof windows reinforced with wire mesh. The sides were steel and equipped with "loopholes" through which clerks could fire rifles. On both sides of the car were two special holes through which the clerks could insert flares. When these were lighted, the entire area around the car became bright as day. The most ingenious device, however, was an iron cone situated below the floor of the car. Through a hole immediately above it, a clerk could fire a "riot gun" and the cone would deflect the shot laterally in all directions. Any would-be robber standing on the ground near the car would have his legs riddled with buckshot.

On August 20, 1924, at Brewster, New York, a prototype of the car was put to a test during a mock holdup by six "armed" bandits. It passed with flying colors, and the Post Office Department immediately put in an order for 3,000 units. (Sources: *New York Times*, 17, 21 August 1924.)

ARMSTRONG, OSCAR. Oscar Armstrong, a dishonorably discharged soldier and suspected small-time thief, was convicted of participating in the robbery of a Wells, Fargo express car near Maricopa, Arizona Territory, on October 1, 1894. In the annals of train robbery, the holdup was considered an amateurish job, and Armstrong and his two companions were easily tracked by peace officers. *See* **Maricopa, Arizona**.

ASKEW, HARRISON. Harrison Askew tried his hand as a train robber with the Rube Burrow gang but failed in his first holdup attempt. Claiming to be an ex-convict, Askew arrived at Rube Burrow's ranch looking for work in the fall of 1887. When he learned that Rube also robbed trains, he was eager to join the gang.

In the early morning hours of January 23, 1887, the gang held up a passenger train on the Texas & Pacific line near Gordon, Texas. Askew's role was to hide along the track with fellow robbers Jim Burrow and Nep Thornton while Rube Burrow and another gang member overpowered the engineer and fireman and brought the train to a halt. They succeeded in stopping the train, but when the express messenger refused to open the express car, and Rube attempted to change his mind by threatening to kill the engineer, Harrison Askew suddenly decided that he was not cut out for robbing trains. He disappeared into the night, never to be heard from again. (Source: Breihan, *Rube Burrow*.) *See also* **Rube Burrow; Gordon, Texas**.

ATHOL, IDAHO. Few men have successfully robbed a passenger coach single-handedly. On September 22, 1900, in western Idaho, a lone bandit robbed two Pullmans and almost added a day coach before escaping in a running gun battle with the conductor.

The bandit boarded the westbound Northern Pacific express at Sandpoint, in Bonner County. Around one o'clock in the morning, shortly after the train pulled out of Athol, the intruder – who "was a little over five feet in height, of slight build, had a light mustache, and wore a dark suit of clothes, a mask, and a slouch hat" – went to work on the first Pullman car. He went from bunk to bunk, waking up sleepers and demanding their money and valuables while threatening them with his revolver. A newspaper reporter who interviewed the victims later wrote "[t]he robbery was evidently carefully planned and was executed with a cool deliberation which showed the robber thoroughly understood his business." Until he left the train, "few of the passengers realized that only one man was in [on] the plot."

After cleaning out the first car, the bandit entered the second and easily completed the job there. The third car was a day coach, and he might have succeeded again, but for several women passengers whose screams brought the conductor.

On seeing the conductor, the robber made a hasty exit. The train was just pulling into Rathdrum, which is in Kootenai County, Idaho, just east of Spokane, Washington. The robber jumped off onto the station platform. As he did, the conductor fired two shots, both of which missed. The bandit returned the fire. According to witnesses, he fired three shots, none of which struck the conductor, but one bullet clipped a piece of leather off one of the conductor's shoes.

A posse was formed immediately, and it tracked the bandit to a point three miles south of Athol, where he stole a horse and disappeared. (Source: *New York Times*, 23 September 1900.)   □

B

BALLARD, WASHINGTON. In October 1905 the Great Northern's *Oriental Limited*, on a run from Seattle, was halted near Ballard by two masked men. The men had slipped aboard as the train was pulling out of the Ballard station and climbed on between the tender and the express car. After the train picked up speed, they crawled over the coal pile and down into the cab, where they ordered the engineer to put on the brakes at a specified spot. Another bandit was waiting there beside the tracks, and the three of them marched the engineer and fireman back to the express car, all the while firing shots alongside the coaches to keep curious passengers from venturing out. When the express company messenger refused to open up, the bandits blew the door of the car off with dynamite and emptied the safe of nearly $50,000.

Because of the size of the loss, rewards were posted immediately and bloodhounds were dispatched to the scene. A tip led to Bothell, Oregon, and dogs were put on a trail there, but a rainstorm erupted and they lost the scent near Bitter Lake.

At the time, P. K. Athearn, General Superintendent of the Pinkerton National Detective Agency's Seattle office, suspected the leader of the three-man gang was the notorious "Old Bill" Miner who had been operating in the Pacific Northwest off and on for several years. It was later discovered that Miner, who was then hiding out in British Columbia, did "come into some money" about the time of the robbery. In subsequent Pinkerton reports, however, Miner was never definitely connected with the crime. (Sources: Pinkerton, *Train Robberies*; Rickards; "Bill Miner—50 Years a Hold-up Man.") *See also* **Bill Miner.**

BARDWELL, KENTUCKY. Western Kentucky seemed to be fertile ground for train robbers in the 1890s. On November 11, 1893, the Illinois Central's northbound Train No. 22 was about to leave Bardwell—which is in Carlisle County, just across the Mississippi River from Cairo, Illinois—when three masked men climbed down from the coal pile on the tender and ordered the engineer, whose name was Clark, to "pull out as soon as

you can." When he did not move fast enough, one of the robbers grabbed the engineer's left arm; another put a revolver under his ear and informed him that either he did what he was told or he would be killed. This was too much for the fireman, who scrambled out of the cab and scurried forward along the catwalk to the front of the engine.

Once the fireman was gone, one of the robbers grabbed the shovel and began throwing on coal. The engineer was ordered to move out and stop only when he was told to.

When the train reached the Mayfield Creek trestle, a little more than two miles north of Mayfield Junction, the robbers told the engineer to halt. The gang then quickly descended on the American Express car, forcing the engineer to march in front of them. At the engineer's order, the express messenger, whose name was McNeil, opened up.

A freight was due out of Bardwell in a few minutes, and the engineer asked if he could have a flagman to go to the rear of the train to warn it. The robbers allowed him to go, then began work on the safes in the express car. When they had finished, they returned to the locomotive and had the engineer proceed to Port Jefferson, where they jumped off.

The American Express Company reported a loss of slightly more than $7,000. Posses were rushed to the scene from Bardwell and Fulton. According to the trainmen, all the robbers "wore soft hats and masks of black cloth completely covering their heads, with only the holes cut in for seeing and breathing." Two of the bandits were "spare-built men" and the other was "heavy and tall, and wore blue overalls." One of the spare-built men was "well-dressed, but the clothes of all were covered with mud." All carried "fine double-barreled shotguns, besides their revolvers."

The American Express Company and the Illinois Central Railroad offered a joint reward of $1,500 for the arrest and conviction of the three robbers. The following April a man named William Brown was arrested and eventually confessed, naming as his confederates William O'Bryan and James E. Breckenridge. (Sources: *St.*

Louis Globe Democrat, 12 November, 14 December 1893; 26 April, 3 May 1894; *New York Times*, 12 November 1893.)

BARNES, SEABORN. Seaborn Barnes was a member of the Sam Bass gang during their reign of stagecoach and train robberies in and around Denton, Texas, in 1877–78. On April 10, 1878, he was shot in both legs during the holdup of an express car at Mesquite, Texas, but escaped. He was killed at Round Rock, Texas, when the gang was ambushed by Texas Rangers. *See* **Sam Bass; Mesquite, Texas**.

BASS, SAM. Sam Bass, originally from Indiana, grew up in Denton County, Texas. In his early teens he was considered industrious and frugal, but later he turned to gambling, brawling, and racing horses. In 1876 he and a Dallas saloon keeper, Joel Collins, drove a herd of cattle north to Nebraska. From there they drifted up to Dakota where they tried their hand at gambling and then in rapid succession they invested in a bawdy house, a quartz mine, and a freighting operation. After all of these ventures failed, they organized a gang and began robbing stages.

By the fall of 1877 the law had begun closing in, and Bass and Collins rode south. On September 18 of that year, at Big Springs, Nebraska, they and four other men robbed an express car on the Union Pacific Railroad of $60,000.

Following the robbery, the gang split up. Collins and fellow gang member Bill Heffridge headed for Kansas, but they were spotted at the Republican River near the Nebraska-Kansas line. Kansas authorities were alerted, and the two outlaws were intercepted by a squad of soldiers from Fort Hays and local peace officers at Buffalo Station, a lonely whistle-stop on the Kansas Pacific Railroad. A shootout followed, and Collins and Heffridge were killed.

Another member of the gang, Jim Berry, headed for Missouri, his home state. In the little town of Mexico, in Audrain County, Berry visited three banks and exchanged $9,000 in gold coins from his share of the loot for currency. The banks sent some of the coins to the depository at St. Louis, and within days they were identified as part of the stolen money. Berry was picked up by the local sheriff and was shot when he tried to escape. He died two days later.

Sam Bass. *University of Texas.*

Sam Bass rode back to Texas following the robbery, but because he was known to be an acquaintance of Joel Collins, Bass's name was on wanted posters almost before he arrived at Denton. During the first few weeks he hid out in Cove Hollow, a cave-studded canyon wilderness in the northwestern corner of Denton County. Later he formed a new gang and roamed the wooded marshes of Hickory Creek south of Denton, occasionally robbing stages.

On February 22, 1878, Bass and three companions overpowered the station agent at Allen, in Collin County, and robbed $1,200 from the express car on an incoming Houston & Texas Central passenger train. The following month Bass and two men repeated the effort at Hutchins, in Dallas County, but the messenger had time to stash away most of the treasure, and the bandits got less than $500. Two more tries at Mesquite and Eagle Ford in April garnered even less.

Bass and his fellow outlaws played hide-and-seek with the authorities throughout the spring and summer of 1878, engaging in several chases and gun battles, one of which was at Pilot Knob, about six miles southwest of Denton. Other shootouts occurred at Bullard's Mill, several miles east of Pilot Knob, and Warner Jackson's farm, about a mile and a half from Bullard's Mill. Three of the gang members were wounded at Jackson's but they all escaped.

On June 13, 1878, a combined force of Texas Rangers and local possemen surprised the gang while they were camped on Salt Creek near Cottondale, Texas, in Wise County. One of the outlaws, Arkansas Johnson, was killed. Another, Henry Underwood, was wounded but managed to ride off. The remaining four gang members, including Bass, hid in a cave until night and slipped away in the darkness.

The end finally came for Bass the following month. On July 18, he and three companions rode into Round

Rock, in Williamson County, intending to rob the bank. Ordinarily such a holdup would have been easy for the gang, but there was now a spy in the outfit, Jim Murphy, who had told the Texas Rangers where the gang was heading.

On arriving in town, Bass and fellow outlaws Frank Jackson and Seaborn Barnes were supposed to head for a general store owned by a man named Henry Koppel, which was near the bank. Murphy was to check out another store on the other end of town. If both ends of town looked clear, they were to meet at Koppel's and then head for the bank. But as they rode in, a deputy sheriff named Maurice Moore thought he noticed the bulge of a six-gun under Bass's coat. He told fellow deputy A. W. Grimes, who followed the three strangers into the store. Apparently neither Moore nor Grimes recognized Bass and his companions as the outlaws they were looking for. Grimes walked up and placed his hand on Bass's coat, and asked him if he was carrying a pistol. Startled, Bass whirled, drew his weapon, and fired. So did Jackson and Barnes. Grimes stumbled backward and collapsed near the door. Moore, who had waited outside, put a bullet through Bass's right hand, nearly amputating his middle and ring fingers. The outlaws rushed out of the store, firing as they ran. Moore was hit in the chest, but continued shooting.

There were Texas Rangers all over town, and they immediately converged on the scene. Bass was hit again as he neared his horse, which was tied in an alley beside the livery stable. The bullet, believed to have been fired by Ranger George Harrell, struck the outlaw about an inch to the left of his spinal column. Bass stumbled and went down. Seaborn Barnes, running at his side, took a slug in the head and died instantly. Frank Jackson, still unscathed, helped Bass to his feet and onto his horse, all the time returning enough fire to keep the Rangers from closing in.

Bass and Jackson rode north out of town, toward Georgetown, then turned west into a dense oak woods. About three miles from town, Bass became too weak to go on and slipped to the ground. Jackson, after binding his companion's wounds, rode on. The following morning Bass crawled about a third of a mile to a newly constructed spur of the International & Great Northern Railroad, where section hands found him later that day. He was weak but still alive. He died at

Round Rock the next day, July 21, his twenty-seventh birthday. His body lies today in the Round Rock cemetery near his fellow outlaw, Seaborn Barnes. (Sources: Gard, *Sam Bass*; Spring, *The Cheyenne and Black Hills Stage and Express Routes*.) *See also* **Allen, Texas; Big Springs, Nebraska; Eagle Ford, Texas; Hutchins, Texas; Mesquite, Texas**.

BASSETT, TEXAS. A railway mail car robbery that occurred in transit between Bassett and Texarkana on December 14, 1900, is known in railroad annals as the "Mysterious Case of the Uncoupling Cars."

When the northbound *Cotton Belt Express* pulled away from the water stop at Bassett, the passenger coaches did not follow. Somehow, the express and mail cars had become uncoupled from the rest of the train. Trainmen recoupled the cars, and the train started up again. Twice more, however, during the thirty miles between Bassett and Texarkana, the cars became uncoupled. Each time they were reconnected and the train proceeded.

Upon arrival at Texarkana, the transfer clerk for the Railway Mail Service knocked at the door of the mail car for the clerk, John N. Dennis, to open up. When there was no response, postal officials forced open the door and found the clerk unconscious on the floor with a severe head injury. Nearby were several registered mail pouches that had been torn open and the contents removed. A doctor was called, and Dennis was rushed to the hospital. Two hours later he revived sufficiently to tell his story.

After collecting mail at Bassett, Dennis said he returned to find two men had entered his car. Before he could give the alarm, he was hit over the head with a fire shovel. He said he knew nothing more until he awakened at the hospital in Texarkana.

Railway mail officials returned to the car and conducted a careful inspection, concentrating on how someone might have entered the car in the clerk's absence. All doors were locked and windows barred. The only other openings into the car were small trapdoors in the floor at each end that were used to reach a crank for uncoupling the car in an emergency. The officials measured the dimensions of the opening, and to their surprise, found that they were just large enough for a small person to squeeze through.

With regard to the mysterious uncouplings during

the run from Bassett, the officials speculated that it was the work of the robbers from inside the car, and that somehow it had figured in their plans in carrying off the robbery. Just how, they did not know, except that when the engineer brought the train to a halt the second time to go back to pick up the detached passenger coaches, the robbers probably took advantage of the opportunity to make their escape. (Source: *New York Times*, 14 December 1900.)

BAXTER, CHARLES. By 1900 U.S. railroads and express companies had been battling train robbers for more than thirty years and appeared to be losing the war. In just the last decade of the nineteenth century there had been more than 200 robberies of express cars and passenger coaches in the United States. It seemed that the robbers had the upper hand and would keep it. Express companies tried to encourage underpaid and overworked express company messengers to stand up to bandits, but most of them saw little wisdom in laying their life on the line for the sake of their company's reputation. The industry's morale was at a new low. It needed something to show that the battle was not lost. It got it—on the night of October 3, 1900, about three miles south of Council Bluffs, Iowa.

Two masked men boarded a Chicago, Burlington & Quincy passenger train at the Union Pacific transfer south of Glenwood. Quickly they climbed over the tender and placed guns in the ribs of the engineer and fireman just as the train was crossing the Mosquito Creek Bridge. While one of the men guarded the engine crew, the other uncoupled the express car from the rest of the train.

The engineer followed the orders the bandits gave him and pulled the train another half mile down the track. The bandit who had uncoupled the cars then returned to the express car. "Open up," he shouted to Charles Baxter, the messenger, but Baxter was in no mood to cooperate with a bandit. The robber was prepared for a rebuff and he quickly stuffed a stick of dynamite in the handle of the side door. In the meantime, however, Baxter grabbed his shotgun and slipped out the other door.

While the bandit at the express car was setting the fuse, Baxter sneaked forward along the side of the tender toward the engine. The blast knocked the door off its slide, and the bandit at the express car shouted

for his companion to bring the engineer and fireman back. Meanwhile, Baxter crept around in front of the engine. As he peered around the boiler, he could see the bandit standing guard over the engine crew—a perfect target. Baxter took careful aim and fired. The bandit crumpled and fell.

The other bandit, who was just about to blow the safe, panicked and ran.

Baxter's courage in thwarting the robbery was no greater than that showed by many express messengers, but it came at just the right time to put new life into the railroad and express people. The four railroads running in and out of Council Bluffs—the Burlington, Union Pacific, Rock Island, and Northwestern—all announced that they were providing the express messengers on their trains with new Winchester "pump" shotguns and "in other ways are preparing to exterminate the first road agent band that attempts to hold up one of their trains." The courageous Mr. Baxter had provided the impetus the industry needed to renew the fight. (Sources: Harlow, *Old Waybills*; *New York Times*, 5 October, 4 November 1900.)

BEARMOUTH, MONTANA. Bearmouth, Montana, was situated on a lonely stretch of track in the rugged Rocky Mountains east of Missoula. It was an ideal place to bing a train to a halt, ransack the express car, and escape on one of the winding mountain trails.

On the night of June 16, 1904, train robber George Hammond and at least one confederate silently took control of the Northern Pacific's *North Coast Limited* about a mile and a half from the water tank at Bearmouth. The details differ on just how the train was stopped. One report said the bandits held up the engineer and fireman while they were on the ground at the tank, though another said the robbers slipped aboard as the train was pulling away and took charge farther down the line.

The engine crew was marched back to the express car, which was blown open with dynamite. The safe, too, was blasted open. Early reports suggested as much as $65,000 was taken, but later express company officials claimed "nothing of great value was secured." Train robber Hammond, when interviewed the following month, said he and his companion got $3,500 in cash and "about 400 small diamonds." Some of the contents of the safe may have been destroyed in the explosion. According to witnesses, the safe was blown nearly forty feet by the blast.

A passenger on the train, a man named Annaweldt from Butte, Montana, claimed that there were more robbers involved. He said that when the two bandits left, he followed them down the track and heard them talking to others in a nearby woods where they apparently had left their horses.

A posse was dispatched to the scene, and bloodhounds were put on the trail. They led the pursuers to the bank of the Hell Gate River where the robbers had stashed a rowboat. After searching the shoreline for several hours, the possemen abandoned the chase.

The following month, George Hammond was arrested in Spokane, Washington, and charged with the crime. Apparently, on arriving in the city he had become acquainted with a lady to whom he revealed his secret, and she later went to the authorities. Under questioning, he confessed to the holdup and told where he had hidden some of his share of the loot. He led them to a cache near Coeur d'Alene, Idaho, where they recovered 350 diamonds and $225 in cash.

Hammond identified the man who helped him rob the express car as John Christie. Both men were convicted and sentenced to prison, Hammond for fifteen years and Christie for seven. According to some sources, Hammond was also involved in the 1902 robbery of a Northern Pacific train at nearby Drummond, Montana.

In the 1930s, a story circulated in western Montana that an old prospector had discovered part of the loot in an abandoned cabin near Maxville, south of Bearmouth, but what first appeared to be a stack of rotting bank notes turned out to be a bundle of worthless stock certificates. (Sources: Block, *Great Train Robberies of the West*; *New York Times*, 18 June, 27 July 1904.)

BELLEVUE, TEXAS. Bellevue, Texas, on U.S. Highway 287 about thirty miles southeast of Wichita Falls, was the site of the first train robbery by Rube Burrow, who eventually became known as the "King of the Train Robbers."

The date was December 1, 1886. An eastbound Ft. Worth & Denver passenger train had stopped at the water tank about 300 yards west of the Bellevue station. It was 11:00 in the morning, hardly a customary time for a train robbery, but Burrow was new at rob-

The Bellevue depot. *Everett R. Huffer Collection.*

bing trains and probably was short on good judgment. With Rube was his brother, Jim, and two of the Burrow ranch hands, Nep Thornton and Henderson Bromley.

Compared to most train robberies, the Bellevue holdup was a daring affair. The station was filled with travelers and station employees. If Burrow considered this at all, he must have counted on getting in and out in a hurry without attracting attention. Approaching the locomotive cab from the side opposite the station, the robbers, with their faces covered by bandanas, informed the engineer and fireman that they had better do as they were told. Nep Thornton climbed up into the cab and held a gun on the two crewmen, while Rube, Jim, and Bromley walked back to the first passenger coach.

In traditional fashion, the bandits moved up and down the aisles, ordering the passengers to empty their pockets. But since it was broad daylight, and the passengers had plenty of warning that a robbery was in process, most of them probably stashed much of their money and valuables away in the seats and in other hiding places before Burrow and his men entered the cars. The gang's total take was a measly $300.

The bandits completely ignored the express car. Some writers blame this on Rube's inexperience as a train robber; nonetheless, to have attempted to enter the express car with the train so near the station would have been foolhardy.

The Bellevue robbery came close to being Burrow's last. In the last car of the train, three soldiers were escorting several prisoners to Ft. Worth. The troopers chose not to put up a fight and even allowed themselves to be relieved of their weapons. Their conduct resulted in stiff disciplinary action from their superiors. Later it was reported that they had been prepared to fight but were persuaded not to by several frantic women passengers. (Sources: Agee, "Rube Burrow"; Breihan, *Rube Burrow*.) *See also* **Henderson Bromley; Jim Burrow; Rube Burrow; Nep Thornton**.

BENBROOK, TEXAS. Benbrook (sometimes spelled Ben Brook), Texas, which is now a Ft. Worth suburb, is notable in the annals of train robbery because it appears to have been the first time a railroad trestle was used by the robbers to make their job easier. On the night of June 4, 1887, Rube Burrow and Henderson Bromley, their faces covered with burnt cork, climbed aboard behind the tender of a Texas & Pacific express as it was pulling out of the Benbrook station. After getting the drop on the locomotive crew, Burrow ordered the engineer to stop the train on the far side of a trestle over a deep gorge, so that only the locomotive, tender, and express car were on solid ground. The robbers' theory was that any of the train crew or passengers in the rear of the train who might be inclined to come forward to interfere with the robbery would be discouraged from doing so because of having to walk the narrow trestle.

Rube's brother, Jim Burrow, and another gang member, Bill Brock, were waiting in the underbrush beside the track with horses. After the train came to a halt, the engineer and fireman were ordered down and marched back to the express car. Jim and Brock stationed themselves at the rear of the car to prevent anyone from coming forward through the end door of the first passenger coach.

The express messenger refused to open up, but Rube ordered the engineer to force the door open with a crow bar. Once inside, Rube and Bromley helped themselves to less than $2,500 from the express company safe. Minutes later, the four robbers were saddled up and heading for the open prairie. As if planned, a sudden summer storm broke loose and obliterated their tracks.

The robbery had gone so smoothly that Rube decided to hit the same railroad again. On September 30, 1887, the same four robbers stopped the same train at the same trestle. Even the same train engineer and fireman were on board. The hapless trainmen knew exactly

what they were expected to do. This time the robbers took slightly more than $2,700 from the express company safe. Shortly after the outlaws rode off it began to rain, once again washing out their tracks.

The September assault on the express car at Benbrook was the fourth successful robbery for Rube Burrow and his pals within just ten months. Rube would go on to commit a total of eight train holdups throughout Texas, Arkansas, Mississippi, and Alabama, and would become known as the "King of Train Robbers." (Sources: Agee, "Rube Burrow"; Breihan, *Rube Burrow*.) *See also* **Rube Burrow**.

BERRY, JIM. Jim Berry was from Mexico, Missouri, a small town in Audrain County between Columbia and St. Louis. During 1876–77 he rode with the Sam Bass-Joel Collins gang when they preyed upon stage coaches in Dakota's Black Hills. Berry also was along in September 1877 when the gang robbed an express car on the Union Pacific Railroad of $60,000 in gold coins at Big Springs, Nebraska.

Following the Big Springs robbery, Berry returned to Missouri to spend some of his share of the loot. He arrived in Mexico on October 5, a Friday, carrying his gold pieces—nearly $10,000 worth—in a pair of worn saddlebags. The next morning, he did a very stupid thing: As soon as the town's three banks opened, he traded in $9,000 of the coins for currency. As was their practice, the banks immediately shipped part of the coins to a St. Louis depository. The following Monday St. Louis informed the banks that the coins were probably from the Big Springs robbery. By Tuesday, Union Pacific detectives were in town conferring with Audrain County sheriff Henry Glasscock.

A search of Berry's family home failed to turn up the outlaw. However, the next Saturday a man from nearby Callaway County walked into a Mexico department store and presented a claim check for a suit of clothes Berry had ordered the previous week. The man, R. T. Kasy, said Berry had told him he could have the suit if he paid the balance due on it. Having no better lead, Sheriff Glasscock staked out Kasy's home, near the town of Shamrock, and began scouting the area. Sunday morning a posse found Berry hiding in a woods about a mile away.

When Berry spotted the lawmen he ran, but Sheriff Glasscock brought him down with a load of shotgun pellets in the legs. Berry, resigned to his fate, pleaded with Glasscock to finish him off rather than make him stand trial. The sheriff declined and took him back to town. Berry got his wish, however; he did not have to stand trial. His wounds became infected, and he had lost much blood. His condition rapidly worsened, and in two days he was dead. He was buried on October 17 in the local cemetery, next to his aged mother who had preceded him in death by only a few hours—some say from a broken heart over learning that her son was an outlaw. (Source: Gard, *Sam Bass*.) *See also* **Sam Bass; Big Springs, Nebraska**.

BIG SPRINGS, NEBRASKA. The holdup at Big Springs on September 18, 1877, stands out in the annals of train robbery because of the amount stolen, $60,000, probably the record as of that date, and because it launched the notorious Sam Bass's career as a train robber. The so-called Bass gang is credited with the robbery, although it is believed that Joel Collins, Bass's partner in crime, was in charge of this affair.

Big Springs is located on U.S. Highway 30 in the southwestern part of the state, just north of Julesburg, Colorado. The Union Pacific's westbound No. 4 was due that day at 10:48 P.M. The outlaws, six in all (some excited witnesses reported as many as thirteen), arrived shortly after 10:00. The station agent, George Barnhart, was alone. When he saw pistols pointed at him from all directions, he quickly complied with the order to put his telegraph key out of commission. Next, the robbers forced him to hang out a red signal to stop the train.

No. 4's engineer, George Vroman, could not ignore the stop signal, and he brought the big engine to a halt. But when he saw that he had been waylaid by gunmen, he became enraged and began throwing coal at the outlaws. The robbers discouraged this with a few shots, then headed for the express car.

The express messenger, George Miller, opened up, and the robbers immediately knocked him to the floor of the car. He pleaded with his attackers that the through safe had a combination lock that could only be opened by selected express agents along the line. The robbers seemed to accept this and began rummaging through the express packages. After only a few minutes they found three wooden boxes, each containing $20,000 in freshly minted gold pieces. There

were also U.S. Mail sacks in the car, but they were left untouched.

The robbers dragged the boxes out onto the station platform, but they were still not satisfied with their haul. They proceded to go through the coaches, ordering passengers to hand over their money and valuables. They even tried to enter the sleeping cars, but found them locked. They did not injure the passengers, except for one man, Andrew Riley of Omaha, who was grazed in the forehead by a bullet when he failed to follow the robbers' orders.

As they were finishing up in the coaches, the robbers heard the whistle of an approaching train. They sent the conductor down the track to warn it; while he was gone, they saddled up and rode off.

At first it was thought the James gang had committed the robbery, but eventually it was attributed to Bass and his bunch. (Sources: Gard, *Sam Bass*; *New York Times*, 20 September 1877.) *See also* **Sam Bass**.

BLACKSTONE SWITCH (OKLAHOMA). Thanks to the preservation of several eyewitness accounts, outlaw historians have a pretty good description of the robbery at Blackstone Switch on November 13, 1894.

Blackstone Switch was near Wybark (sometimes called Wybank), in eastern Indian Territory on the Missouri, Kansas & Texas Railroad about eight miles north of Muskogee. The bandits struck about 10:00 P.M. Their plan was to throw the switch and send the northbound Katy No. 2 onto the siding. However, the engineer, Joe Hotchkiss, saw the switch light in time and brought the big locomotive to a halt.

The bandits had received a tip that there was a large shipment of money in the express car. This tip might have been intentionally planted, because instead of the big shipment, the express car held four federal officers: United States deputy marshals James F. "Bud" Ledbetter, Paden Tolbert, Sid Johnson, and Frank Jones. All were crack shots and all were itching to get a bead on the gang of train robbers that had been plaguing the Indian Territory in recent months.

Engineer Hotchkiss knew full well the procedure that usually followed the halting of a train: the bandits would climb aboard the locomotive cab and order the engineer and fireman back to the express car where they were often used as hostages to force the express messenger to open up. Hotchkiss, knowing what was waiting for bandits in the express car, wanted out of the way, so as the engine rolled to a stop, he jumped down from the cab on the opposite side from the outlaws and ran for cover in the darkness of the underbrush. According to one account, his fireman thought that was a good idea, and he quickly followed.

As expected, when the bandits approached the express car they got a good surprise. One of the passengers, Muskogee merchant Samuel Sodheimer, gave this version of what happened next:

> Ledbetter ordered all [express car] doors opened. A deputy appeared in each of these, pumping lead, and drove the robbers back. But the outlaws had plenty of nerve. They were Texas Jack, Buz Luckey and Will Smith, Negroes, and Tom Root, a bad Cherokee. For nearly an hour they fought, even threatening to throw dynamite into the cars, but Bud and his men stuck to their posts and kept using their rifles.
>
> During the excitement, Jack [Texas Jack] slipped under cover of some ties piled along the track past the express car. He entered the front of the first passenger coach, carrying a gunnysack and wearing false whiskers, and while the firing was still hot outside, [he] passed through the entire train. As he entered each coach he shouted, "Everybody drop his valuables in this sack or be killed."
>
> I saved my watch and diamond ring by sliding them across the aisle under the skirts of a lady passenger. I hid part of my money in a cuspidor and the rest under a seat cushion.
>
> Ledbetter caught one short glimpse of Jack as he was leaving the last coach. That was all Bud needed to crack down on him. Jack fell, badly wounded. Buz Luckey, a big, strong man, picked him up and carried him to his horse. After a few more shots, Smith and Root rushed to their horses, and all rode away. The engineer crawled from hiding, backed the train onto the main line, and proceeded to Gibson station to await orders.

Texas Jack, whose real name was Nathaniel Reed, later gave his own account of those moments in the passenger coach when Deputy Ledbetter nearly brought his train robbery career to an end:

> I was taking up this Sunday School collection, had $460, eight watches and three pistols in the sack, and things were going well until Ledbetter jumped in on me with a gun in each hand. He got me through both hips then and there, and I'm still a cripple from the wounds he gave me.

Despite his wounds, Texas Jack jumped from the coach and escaped.

The American Express Company praised Ledbetter and his fellow deputies for their "valiant stand against these desperadoes in defense of the property in their charge" and offered a $250 reward for each robber captured and convicted.

On December 5, U.S. Deputy Marshal Newton LaForce, an Indian police officer, and six possemen found Tom Root and Buz Luckey hiding at Root's home at a settlement called Broken Arrow in the Creek Nation. It was early in the morning and foggy, and in the ensuing gunfight, LaForce was killed. Root took a bullet in the thigh, but both outlaws escaped. Luckey was captured several weeks later near Muskogee, and Root surrendered the following August.

Texas Jack Reed remained on the loose for three months, but his wounds bothered him considerably, and he finally gave himself up. Will Smith, the fourth robber at Blackstone Switch, was never heard from again. (Sources: Shirley, "The Bungled Job at Blackstone Switch"; *New York Times*, 15 November 1894; *Ardmore State Herald* [Oklahoma], 22 November 1894; *Vinita Indian Chieftain* [Oklahoma], 15 November 1894; *Fort Worth Gazette*, 14 November 1894.) *See also* **Nathaniel "Texas Jack" Reed**.

BLANKSTON, ALABAMA. Blankston, which was the scene of two turn-of-the-century train robberies, is in the southeast corner of Fayette County, about forty miles east of Columbus, Mississippi.

On the night of December 17, 1896, three bandits stopped Southern Railway's westbound No. 5 at a deep cut near Blankston. The locomotive engineer, Graham Jones, was ordered to accompany one of the bandits back to the express car and smash the door in with a sledgehammer. He begged off, however, complaining of a recently injured arm. The robber then smashed in the door himself.

As the robber entered, the Southern Express Company messenger, A. L. Buffington, hit him on the head with a lantern. As the men were scuffling, a brakeman at the rear of the train ran to get help. A third bandit, hiding near the track, fired a shot at him but missed.

Once inside the express car, the bandits tried to gain entry to the through safe but could not open it. They had to settle for the contents of local safe, about $500, and several express packages. They also took several jugs of liquor.

Buffington said he shot at the robbers as they rode away, but apparently missed. The countryside was scoured by a local posse, but no trace of the outlaws could be found. It was speculated that the robbers were "residents of that part of the country [and] well acquainted with its nooks and corners."

Robbers struck again on January 21, 1897, presumably the same three men. This time the victim was Southern Railway's Train No. 35, which had left Birmingham at 4:00 P.M.

It is believed the men slipped aboard the front end of the combined express-baggage car at Berry Station. Because of the earlier robbery, the express messenger, Wert, and baggagemaster, Falkner, were well armed and well warned to keep on the lookout for another attack.

As before, the robbers climbed over the tender and took command of the locomotive. The engineer was forced to stop at the bridge over the North River. When the train came to a halt, Falkner, who was new on the line, unwisely opened the door of the baggage compartment to see why the train had stopped. What he saw were two shotguns pointing at his face.

While one of the robbers stayed with the engineer and fireman, the other two entered the car and emptied the contents of the local safe, about $200. They did not bother the larger through safe. The robbers jumped off and the engineer was ordered to move on. The whole affair took only twelve minutes.

This robbery was especially embarrassing for the railroad. Not only had the express messenger and baggageman been teamed together, fully armed and warned to watch out for robbers, but also the supervising route agent for the road, W. C. Agee, was on board in one of the passenger coaches.

Agee immediately called for a special train of detectives from Birmingham to pursue the bandits. Also, several bloodhounds were secured from a nearby prison. The night air was cool and moist, ideal for tracking. The robbers' trail was picked up and followed north to Eldridge in Walker County. There two of the bandits were captured. One man refused to give any information, but the other identified himself as John Calhoun Ward, twenty-six, who claimed to be the son of a well-to-do rancher near Pembroke, Texas. Ward said he had been in Alabama for only two weeks, but a witness was found who testified that he had seen him in Eldridge as early as December 18, 1896, which also made him a suspect in the earlier robbery near Blankston. Further investigation revealed that under the name

of George Hutchinson, Ward also was wanted by the authorities in Vicksburg, Mississippi. (Sources: *St. Louis Globe Democrat*, 19 December 1896, 22, 23, 24, 26 January, 13 February 1897; *New York Times*, 19 December 1896, 22 January 1897.)

BLIND BAGGAGE. The blind baggage was the windowless platform area at the front end of an express or baggage car, just behind the tender, so named because a person hiding there could not be seen from the locomotive. For years the spot was the favorite boarding place for tramps and train robbers. The blind baggage became so popular among train robbers in the 1890s that the editors of the rail industry periodical *Railway Age* urged car builders to abolish the front platform on baggage and express cars. The idea was resisted. All railway cars had front and rear platforms to allow trainmen to move freely from one end of a train to the other. In 1895, however, the U.S. Post Office Department adopted the idea for some railway mail cars.

An alternative to solving the blind baggage problem was to install a window in the front end door. This idea was not new. In the 1870s there were such cars on the Oregon & California Railroad, but the idea did not catch on, possibly because glass could be broken too easily, allowing bandits, even if the window was barred, to shoot into the car. (Source: Patterson, *Train Robbery*.)

BLUE CUT (MISSOURI). The Blue Cut, sometimes called the Rocky Cut, was a slice carved out of a thirty-foot hillside in Jackson County about two miles west of Glendale Station (in what is now the eastern suburbs of Kansas City) to accommodate the tracks of both the Chicago & Alton Railroad and the Missouri Pacific line. In the 1880s and 1890s the cut—remote and inviting—was a perfect spot for a holdup, and in the annals of train robbery it holds the record for the site most often chosen by the bandits who preyed on express cars.

The first robbery at the Blue Cut occurred on the night of September 7, 1881. Warning lanterns were displayed to halt the train, and rocks and logs were stacked on the track in case the engineer failed to stop. The robbers broke open the doors of the express car while the passengers were kept in line by occasional rifle shots alongside the coaches. Once in the express car, however, the intruders found the pickings slim, and they vented their anger by viciously beating the express

Unlike most express cars in the 1870s, the car shown in this photo of an early Oregon & California train had a window in the front. Because many did not, the area between the express and the tender became known as the blind baggage, a favorite place for train robbers to sneak aboard while the train was pulling away from a station. *Southern Pacific Railroad.*

messenger on the head with their revolvers. (A rumor that circulated claimed that if they had waited for the next train they would have found $100,000 in the express car safes.)

Fortunately, the holdup resulted in no further casualties, and a tragedy was narrowly avoided, as well. A freight train was following behind the halted express, and a brakeman, Frank Burton, made a heroic dash down the tracks to flag the freighter to a stop.

Although disappointed with the amount of the loot, the leader of the gang, in a departing act of bravado, saluted the engineer of the halted train and gave him two silver dollars from the stolen cash, with instructions to use it to "drink to the health of Jesse James." However, doubt was cast on the James gang's role in the robbery when in the following weeks several local suspects were charged with the crime. One reportedly confessed and named three companions, none of whom belonged to the James gang. But later, two members of the James gang were caught, and both placed Jesse and Frank at the scene of the crime.

Fifteen years passed before the next Blue Cut robbery. On the evening of October 23, 1896, Chicago & Alton's westbound No. 48 was slowed to a halt by a red lantern. Armed men converged on the locomotive from trackside, and the engineer, B. V. Meade, and fireman, Arthur Post, were taken captive. The robbers cut the express car from the rest of the train, helped themselves to the contents of the local safe – about $300 and some jewelry – and then commandeered the engine for a half-mile ride toward Kansas City. At an obviously preselected spot, the bandits stopped the engine and disappeared into a nearby woods.

Later, two local farmers, James Flynn and George Bowen, and a former Southern Pacific Railroad engineer named Jack Kennedy, were charged with the crime. None of the three, however, were ever convicted.

Two months later, on December 23, 1896, the Chicago & Alton's westbound No. 49 was hit at nearly the same spot. Three robbers slipped aboard at Independence and hid in the blind baggage area at the rear of the tender. As the train neared the cut, they took over the engine cab, which again was in the command of engineer B. V. Meade, and ordered him to halt. The train was uncoupled behind the Pacific Express car; two of the robbers climbed in and took the express messenger, A. J. Frier, prisoner. The remaining bandit returned to the engine with Meade and the fireman and ordered Meade to pull ahead to the bottom of the grade west of the cut.

Back in the express car, the bandits demanded that messenger Frier turn over the keys to the safes. When he refused, they threw him to the floor and, with a kit of tools, tried to open the large through safe themselves. When they were unsuccessful, they went to work on Frier again, and he reluctantly turned over the keys to the small safe. They opened it and took out a number of packages of ten- and twenty-dollar gold pieces, which Frier later said ran into "the thousands."

When Frier finally convinced them that he could not open the large safe, the bandits resorted to dynamite. They blew the door off and helped themselves to the contents, which Frier described as "more money and valuables than usual." Later, unofficial reports listed the loss at anywhere from $4,000 to $30,000.

After finishing with the large safe, the robbers went through Frier's pockets and took all of his money. When he complained, one of the robbers gave him back two dollars and told him: "Get yourself a drink for a Christmas present."

The robbers finally decided they were running out of time. Before they left, however, they cut the engine loose from the tender and express car, ran it ahead a mile or so, and disabled it.

Engineer Meade said he thought the robbers were the same bunch that held up his train the previous October. James Flynn was again picked up, and this time he confessed. Jack Kennedy was also arrested and tried, but he got off with a hung jury. He was later retried, but was acquitted.

Another robbery occurred at Blue Cut on the night of November 12, 1897. This time the victim was the Missouri Pacific's Mail Train No. 8 out of St. Louis. Once again a red lantern was used to stop the locomotive, and the bandits, this time wearing shapeless women's "Mother Hubbard" gowns to hide their clothing, went away nearly empty-handed. At least this was the official statement released by the railroad, which reported the loss was only $2.85. (Sources: Burton, "John F. Kennedy of Missouri"; Settle, *Jesse James Was His Name; New York Times,* 24 October, 25 December 1896.) *See also* **The James-Younger Gang; Jack "Quail Hunter" Kennedy**.

BLUE SPRINGS, MISSOURI. An in-transit robbery in 1885 that occurred near Blue Springs, Missouri, is sometimes mistakenly identified with the series of express car holdups near the Blue Cut (see **Blue Cut**).

On the night of September 2, 1885, four men approached a Chicago & Alton passenger train at the depot in Blue Springs, which is twenty-two miles east of Kansas City, and started to enter the smoking car. The car was crowded, however, and a number of passengers were standing outside on the rear platform. The four men walked on by and went to the next car in line, a day coach. There they split up; two of the men stopped before the front platform of the car and the other two headed for the rear. The dim light of the station was now behind them, and their faces were mostly in shadows. As the train began to pull away, the men stepped on board and all four reached under their collars and quickly slipped on handkerchief masks, covering everything but their eyes and foreheads.

With revolvers drawn, one man stood guard at each end of the coach while the other two started down the aisles. On command, each passenger was forced to turn over his money. No requests were made for jewelry. When the two robbers reached the middle of the aisle, one of them pulled the bell cord to signal the engineer to stop the train. When it had slowed, the four intruders leaped off and disappeared.

Although witnesses said the robbers appeared nervous, the affair was accomplished quickly and surely, in what could almost be described as a military fashion. The intruders had come and gone almost before the passengers knew what was happening to them. In fact, the passengers in the adjoining cars did not know of the robbery until the conductor informed them at the next stop. (Source: *New York Times,* 3 September 1885.)

BOSTON, MICHIGAN. During the 1890s the upper peninsula of Michigan was not unlike the western frontier. The land was windswept and rugged, and between the sparsely populated towns there were remote areas well-suited to miscreants, including train robbers.

Houghton County, on the eastern end near the northernmost tip of the peninsula, was copper mine country; the Calumet & Hecla Mine was one of the area's biggest producers. Twice a month the C & H's payroll was transported by express car on the Mineral Range Railroad. This was not exactly a secret; in fact it was well-known to anybody connected with the mine or the railroad.

On September 15, 1893, at 9:30 A.M., the train carrying the payroll was stopped by four bandits near Boston, about halfway between the towns of Calumet and Hancock. The express company messenger, Edward Hogan, complied with bandits' orders to open up the car; without resistance he unlocked the safe, which contained nearly $75,000. The robbers quickly transferred the money to a bag they were carrying and fled. It was believed they had horses tied nearby, and that they rode from the scene of the robbery to the shore of Lake Superior where they took a boat north to Canada.

Later in the day, however, peace officers of Houghton County picked up three suspects who were seen leaving the area about an hour after the robbery. They were identified as John King, Jack Kehoe, and John Chellew. Information on King and Kehoe was lacking, but Chellew was a saloonkeeper in nearby Negaunee, Michigan. According to the Houghton County Sheriff's office, the descriptions of two of the robbers "almost tallied" perfectly with those of Kehoe and Challew. Later, Kehoe was also identified as the man who purchased the cloth from which the gang made their masks.

Additional arrests were made over the next several days. George Liberte, a former fireman on the Duluth, South Shore & Atlantic Railroad, was picked up in Marquette, Michigan, and under questioning he "made a clean breast of the affair." Implicated were A. S. Cannon of Hancock, a "young man of good family" whose trunk was used to carry away the loot; two brothers, Michael and John Shea, who operated a saloon in Marquette; Ed Hogan, also a Marquette saloonkeeper; and W. Shlope, a hack driver. Named also were Tom Winters, a baggage man on the Mineral Range Road and, perhaps to no one's surprise, Edward Hogan, the messenger whose car was robbed.

Approximately $30,000 of the stolen payroll was recovered from Liberte, and another $14,000 was found at the Shea brothers' saloon. Liberte told the authorities that the rest of the loot was in A. S. Cannon's trunk, which had been left alongside the tracks. But when the trunk was found, it was empty. Liberte said he suspected that the money was taken by Ed Hogan's brother, who knew about the holdup. (Sources: *New York Times*, 15, 19 September 1893.)

BRACKENRIDGE, TEXAS. Railroaders in southern Texas never took kindly to having their trains invaded, nor did their passengers, as three would-be robbers discovered on a warm afternoon in June 1893. In Wilson County, about thirty-five miles southeast of San Antonio, a San Antonio & Arkansas train was slowly rounding a curve south of the tiny village of Brackenridge when a man aboard the tender shouted to the engineer and fireman in the cab to "throw up your hands!"

The man had a revolver in each hand and he appeared to mean business. The engineer, Mike Tierney, did as he was told, but the fireman, F. F. Martin, made a move toward a box under his seat. The man on the tender fired, and Martin toppled forward off the engine gangway and under the wheels of the train.

The man on the tender and two companions had slipped aboard as the train was pulling out of Brackenridge. The other two bandits were on the front platform of the baggage car. When they saw the fireman fall under the wheels of the train, they panicked and jumped off, apparently having no taste for killing.

The train rolled to a stop, and the passengers in the coach behind the express car came running forward. In 1893 in Texas, a man seldom traveled a long distance without a gun, and most of the passengers were armed. When they saw the two would-be robbers running for the bushes, they gave chase.

The man on the tender, however, was made of sterner stuff than his confederates. He still had his mind set on taking the train. He leaped down from the tender into the cab and ordered engineer Tierney to run the train forward to the Indian River Bridge. Tierney, however, was in no mood to cooperate. Instead of giving the engine the throttle, he locked the air brakes.

The bandit grabbed the throttle and tried to pull ahead, but the big locomotive would not move. Disgusted, he jumped out of the cab and began running forward along the track.

Just then the conductor came running up. Seeing the fleeing outlaw ahead on the track, he quickly ran back and uncoupled the tender from the remainder of the train. The engineer threw the throttle wide open and the engine leaped forward.

The bandit was trying to reach the Indian River Bridge, where three more confederates waited. But when he glanced back and saw the big engine catching up with him, like his companions he headed for the woods.

It now became a three-way gun battle. The conductor, who was armed, jumped out of the cab and ran after the bandit, firing as he went. The bandit's three companions on the bridge saw the conductor and began firing at him. The engineer and messenger, in turn, began shooting at the men on the bridge.

The conductor caught up with the bandit just inside the woods. The outlaw's guns were now empty and the conductor quickly disarmed him. The three outlaws at the bridge guessed what had happened and fled.

The captured bandit said his name was J. D. May, and that he was from Dallas, but the authorities said they believed this was an alias. He would say little else that could be believed, except that he and his fellow bandits had planned to rob both the express car and the passengers. A wire was sent to the authorities, and a U.S. marshal and several deputies soon arrived by special train. It wasn't a minute too soon. The train crew, angered over the death of the fireman, were just about to lynch May when the lawmen arrived. He was quickly hustled off to Brackenridge for safekeeping. (Sources: *New York Times*, 29, 30 June, 2 July 1893.)

BRISCOE STATION, KENTUCKY. On October 11, 1866, several men, possibly four, unfastened a rail on the Louisville & Nashville Railroad track near Briscoe Station, Kentucky, which is about five miles north of Bowling Green. The rail was left in place and attached to a long wire that led to a dense grove of underbrush near the track; the rail could be quickly jerked out of line as a train approached.

The train wreckers' target was the L&N paycar, which was due in a few minutes. It was broad daylight (for safety's sake, the paycar never traveled at night), and the engineer had a good view of the track ahead. Although there had never been an in-transit robbery of a paycar on the Louisville & Nashville Railroad, an engineer was always especially watchful when pulling the road's paycar, and he easily spotted the loose rail. He immediately applied the brakes and threw the locomotive in reverse, but it was too late: the front trucks left the tracks and the engine, tender, and paycar toppled over on their sides.

The robbers instantly descended on the wrecked paycar. Inside, the conductor, whose name was Church,

lay stunned on the floor; he had been struck in the head by a large water bottle. The paymaster, G. W. Craig, was not injured and, suspecting that they were about to be robbed, he frantically searched for a place to hide the payroll. He succeeded in stashing away a little more than $6,000 before the robbers broke in. They wasted little time in scooping up the remainder, about $8,000, and disappeared in the underbrush that bordered the right-of-way.

A posse was formed to hunt down the robbers but it was unsuccessful. The authorities speculated that the robbers might have been John James and Newt Guy of Allen County, and two brothers, Henry and Seaton May, who had recently escaped from jail in Bowling Green. (Sources: Herr, *The Louisville & Nashville Railroad 1850–1963*; *Louisville Daily Journal*, 17, 19 October 1866.)

BROCK, BILL. Bill Brock was a member of the Rube Burrow gang. He joined the outfit in May 1887 and participated in the two express robberies on the Texas & Pacific line at Benbrook, Texas, on June 4 and September 20. On December 9, 1887, Brock and the two Burrows, Rube and Jim, robbed a Southern Express car on the St. Louis, Arkansas & Texas Railway at Genoa, Arkansas. Following the robbery, the three outlaws split the loot and headed their separate ways: the Burrows for their childhood home in Alabama, and Brock for Texas.

Prior to the Genoa robbery, the Burrow brothers and Bill Brock had met at a hotel in Texarkana to plan the holdup. The Burrows had used fictitious names when they signed the register, but Brock had signed "W. L. Brock." The Pinkertons, during their investigation of the robbery, checked all hotels in the area and made a list of all the names contained on the registers.

Bill Brock. *Pinkertons.*

Also, the three robbers had left their raincoats and a hat at the scene of the holdup. Through a manufacturer's mark, the Pinkertons traced one of the coats to a store in Alexander, Texas, where a clerk remembered selling it to a local cowboy named Bill Brock. A store clerk's description of Brock matched the description of one of the train robbers. The clerk also remembered the two men who were with Brock when he purchased the coat. These descriptions roughly matched the descriptions of the other two robbers.

Local law enforcement officers converged on Brock's family home and arrested him. On being taken to Texarkana and identified by one of the crewmen on the train that had been robbed, Brock realized that it was hopeless. He confessed his part in the robbery and identified the other two participants as Rube and Jim Burrow, which eventually led to the arrest of both men. (Source: Breihan, *Rube Burrow*.) *See also* **Rube Burrow; Genoa, Arkansas**.

BROCK, LEONARD C. Leonard C. Brock, also known as Lew Waldrip and Joe Jackson, briefly accompanied the "King of the Train Robbers," Rube Burrow, during his robbery spree in Mississippi in 1888. Brock, not to be confused with Bill Brock, an earlier member of Burrow's gang, hailed from somewhere in Texas and for a short while had worked on Burrow's ranch as a wrangler. According to one account, Burrow became impressed with Brock when he saw him disarm a knife-wielding bully in a saloon brawl. Later, Burrow persuaded Brock to join him in an unsuccessful attempt to rescue his brother, Jim Burrow, who had been captured following a train holdup at Genoa, Arkansas, in 1887.

Brock assisted Burrow in the robbery of a Southern Express Company car on the Illinois Central line at Duck Hill, Mississippi, in December 1888, and again on the Mobile & Ohio Railroad at Buckatunna, Mississippi, in September 1889. Following the Buckatunna robbery, Burrow hid out in Florida. Brock, however, sought refuge in Lamar County, Alabama—Burrow's boyhood home, where Brock thought he had friends among Burrow's relatives. However, the Burrow clan was curious as to why Brock and Rube had split up, and they did not go out of their way to protect Brock from the law as they had previously when he had hid out there with Rube. The authorities picked up Brock's trail,

and on July 15, 1890, he was arrested without a struggle at Columbus, Mississippi. He confessed to his part in the Buckatunna robbery and was sentenced to the state prison at Jackson, Mississippi, where he committed suicide in November 1890. (Sources: Agee, "Rube Burrow"; Breihan, *Rube Burrow*.) *See also* **Buckatunna, Mississippi; Rube Burrow; Duck Hill, Mississippi**.

BROMLEY, HENDERSON. Henderson Bromley was a member of Rube Burrow's gang. Bromley, one of Burrow's ranch hands, was in on Rube's first robbery, a daylight holdup of passengers on the Ft. Worth & Denver line at a water tank at Bellevue, Texas, on December 1, 1886. Bromley also participated in an express car robbery of an eastbound passenger train on the Texas & Pacific line at Gordon, Texas, on January 23, 1887, and in assaults on express cars on the same line on June 4 and September 20, 1887, both at Benbrook, Texas. After the second Benbrook robbery, the robbers split up for a while to spend their loot. When Rube summoned the gang for another job at Genoa, Arkansas, the following December, Bromley did not show. It was a wise move on Bromley's part. Mistakes made at the Genoa robbery would eventually lead to the break-up and capture of the gang. (Source: Breihan, *Rube Burrow*.) *See also* **Bellevue, Texas; Benbrook, Texas; Rube Burrow; Gordon, Texas**.

BROWN, JOSEPH C. A young man calling himself Joseph C. Brown was convicted of robbing a postal car on the Southern Pacific Railroad near Conklin, California, on April 16, 1910. Brown, who never revealed his real name to avoid embarrassment to his family, claimed to be the son of a prominent Texas state official. He was sentenced to forty-five years in Folsom Prison, but escaped on May 11, 1917. He was never heard from again. *See* **Conklin, California**.

BROWNING, SAMUEL. Sam Browning was killed by a county sheriff while attempting to rob passengers on a Southern Pacific train at Reed's Crossing, California, on March 30, 1895. Browning's companion, Henry Williams (real name, Henry Ury), killed the sheriff and escaped on a bicycle. *See* **Reed's Crossing, California**.

BROWNSTOWN, INDIANA. Shortly before 10 P.M. on July 9, 1868, five men boarded a westbound Ohio &

Mississippi passenger coach at Seymour, Indiana. But as the train pulled out of the station, and the conductor asked for their tickets, they told him that they did not have the money to purchase any. As expected, the men were put off the train at the first stop, Brownstown, ten miles out of Seymour.

It was all part of a plan. Several weeks earlier, local members of the Reno gang had approached an Ohio & Mississippi locomotive engineer, James Flanders, with a deal that would allow them to rob the express car on one of his trains in return for paying him a share of the loot. Flanders agreed to the deal, but went immediately to officials of the railroad and reported the incident. After a brief deliberation, the officials told him to pretend to go along with the plan, and a scheme was promptly devised to lay a trap for the would-be robbers.

The train the robbers chose was an eastbound that would pass through Brownstown around 2:00 A.M. on July 10. Although the train was not scheduled to stop at Brownstown, Flanders was instructed to pretend to need water. The five men would be waiting to slip out of the shadows. One would board the cab and the others would go immediately to the Adams Express Company car and separate it and the locomotive from the rest of the train. Their plans were then to pull the express down the track for a few miles where they would empty the contents of the Adams company safes.

Flanders brought the locomotive to a halt and the men rushed toward the train as planned. The Adams express messenger had rehearsed his lines carefully. When he heard the would-be robbers' command to open up, he shouted back that he would comply, but only if he could be allowed to leave unharmed. The bandits agreed, and the messenger slowly eased open the wooden door, jumped down to the station platform, and raced for the safety of the station.

The apparently abandoned express car now stood open before the bandits, inviting them to step in and take its treasures. No one wondered why the messenger had doused the lights before he left. Had they been more curious, the night would have gone better for them.

Inside the express car the jittery Pinkerton agents had become impatient. Stiff and sore after more than an hour of confinement, their nerves twitched for action. When the first of their targets appeared at the thresh-

old of the door, they fired hastily without taking aim. Only a few shots reached their mark. The bandits scattered and ran down the track toward the underbrush where a sixth member of the gang was holding their horses. Having no horses ready with which to follow, the Pinkertons had to wait until morning to pick up the trail.

Only one of the would-be robbers was captured: the man who had boarded the locomotive cab. His name was Volney Elliott, a member of the local Reno gang, perpetrators of the first peacetime train robbery in the nation's history, near Seymour, Indiana, in October 1866. On hearing the gunfire, Elliott started to leap from the cab, but was felled by a bullet from George Flanders, brother of the engineer, who had been hiding on the opposite side of the engine as it pulled in. A second later, however, George Flanders himself was shot in the knee by a Pinkerton who mistook him for one of the fleeing bandits.

The ambush had been pretty well botched, but the holdup had been foiled. It was not a total victory, but it was decisive. For the first time train robbers had been met squarely and defeated.

Within forty-eight hours, two more suspects were in custody: Charlie Roseberry, who had been wounded in the fusillade, and Theodore Clifton, the sixth bandit, who had been holding the gang's horses. Later, the remaining three gang members were picked up: Henry Jerrell, Frank Sparks, and John Moore. None of the robbers would see a jury, however; all six were eventually taken from the authorities by angry citizens and lynched. (Sources: Boley, *The Masked Halters*; *Seymour Democrat*, 15 July 1868.) *See also* **The Reno Gang**.

BUCKATUNNA, MISSISSIPPI. On September 25, 1888, Rube Burrow, at one time known as the "King of the Train Robbers," and two companions, Leonard C. Brock and Rube Smith, robbed a Southern Express Company car and a U.S. Mail car on a southbound Mobile & Ohio passenger train. Two of the men, their faces covered with red bandanas, slipped aboard the blind baggage area behind the tender. They quickly climbed forward and covered the engineer, Seak Therell, and the fireman, Thomas Hurt, with their revolvers.

About two miles south of town, Burrow ordered Therell to stop the train with the express and mail cars just across a trestle that spanned the Buckatunna River.

The third robber, who had been hiding beside the track, joined them. The engineer and fireman were marched back to the express car, where the messenger, J. W. Dunning, was forced to open up. While Brock and Smith held guns on the train crew, Burrow ordered the messenger to dump the contents of his safe, about $2,700, into a canvas bag. In his haste, Burrow overlooked packages containing a U.S. Treasury shipment of $70,000 in currency that were stacked near the door.

In the postal car immediately behind, the mail clerk, W. C. Bell, suspected that a robbery was taking place. He picked up an armload of registered packages and headed for the rear door, intending to hide them in the baggage car. Burrow, however, anticipated his move and intercepted him at the door. The robber took the packages, twenty-four in all, and the registered pouch.

In the meantime the conductor, Billy Scholes, grabbed a lantern and a Winchester rifle and started forward along the edge of the trestle. Two pistol shots from the robbers, however, sent him hustling back. The robbers then finished up quickly, and after ordering the engineer to return to his locomotive and pull ahead, they disappeared into a woods. A posse was quickly formed by the Wayne County sheriff, and bloodhounds were called out, but the robbers threw them off the scent by spreading red pepper on their trail.

When the engineer was questioned later, he said the leader of the robbers had told him that he had read that because of the fear of robbery, train crews on the Mobile & Ohio were being armed with rifles and told to use them if attacked. As far as he was concerned, said the robber, this was a "standing challenge to hold up the train." (Sources: Breihan, *Rube Burrow*; *Birmingham Weekly Herald*, 2 October 1889.) *See also* **Leonard C. Brock; Rube Burrow; Rube Smith**.

BULLARD, CHARLEY. In 1869 Charley Bullard (alias "Piano Charley") and a partner, "Big Ike" Marsh, boarded a northbound Hudson River Railroad passenger train at the depot in New York City. They quietly concealed themselves in the coach next to the Merchants Union Express Company car. When the train was well under way, just before it crossed into Westchester County, New York, they broke into the express car and bound and gagged the messenger.

According to the files of the Pinkerton National Detective Agency, the car was carrying nearly $100,000,

and the robbers took it all, which set a record for an amount stolen during a train robbery up to that time. Bullard and Marsh were later arrested in Canada and returned to White Plains, New York, for trial, but with the help of a confederate, "Billy" Forrester, they escaped and headed north again.

The Hudson River Railroad robbery was Bullard's only express car robbery. In the annals of train robbery, Bullard's name probably would never be noticed except that he probably was the most educated of any nineteenth-century hard case who ever raided a rail car. He could speak German and French fluently, and was a skilled pianist. Charley's problem was that he could not keep his hands off other people's money. After escaping from the Massachusetts State Prison at Concord, where he was serving twenty years for a Boston bank robbery, he was arrested for burglary in Canada. He served five years for that crime and then headed for Europe, where he was arrested in the act of robbing a bank in Viveres, Belgium. He died in a Belgium prison in 1890. (Source: Pinkerton, *Train Robberies*.)

BUNCH, EUGENE. Eugene Franklin Bunch did not rob enough trains to become famous in that endeavor, perhaps because his deeds were at times confused with another robber, Rube Burrow, who operated at the same time and in the same general area. But in recent years Bunch has received more attention by outlaw historians and is now being given a more appropriate role in the history of the era.

Bunch was born in Noxubee County, Mississippi, in 1843. He was a bright boy and apparently did well in school. When he was fifteen, his family moved to Washington Parish in eastern Louisiana. Three years later, when the Civil War broke out, he enlisted in the

Eugene Bunch. *Pinkertons.*

Fourth Louisiana and probably fought at Shiloh and Vicksburg. He was captured at the fall of Vicksburg and paroled in July 1863. While in the service of the Confederacy he was considered a capable soldier, but somewhat troublesome because of a tendency to drink and gamble.

Following the war, Bunch taught school for a brief period in Amite in Tangipahoa Parish, but was discharged – probably because of his bad habits. Sometime in the late sixties he married and moved to Dexter, Texas, north of Gainesville, where he taught school again and farmed with his brother, James, who lived nearby. He apparently led a respectable life, acquired some property, and in 1876 was elected County and District Clerk. Within the next five years, however, he piled up considerable debts, possibly from gambling, and in the early 1880s he had to sell off his holdings. His reputation suffered, and he was defeated for reelection to the Clerk's office in 1884.

A beaten man, Bunch left his wife and ten-year-old son the following year and headed for Wichita Falls, Texas, and a job on the *Wichita Herald*. Later, he may have opened a real estate agency. This lasted for two years; in 1887 he moved to Fort Worth and returned to gambling. It was during this period that Bunch's name first came in connection with train robbery.

During 1886 and 1887 there were several train robberies in northeastern Texas, later attributed to Rube Burrow and his brother Jim. At the time, however, Eugene Bunch was a suspect; possibly because of his reputation of being a crack shot and always going around heavily armed.

In June 1888 Bunch moved to New Orleans under an assumed name, Captain J. H. Gerald. Five months later, on November 3, it is believed that he committed his first train robbery.

The victim was New Orleans & Northeastern's southbound Train No. 5 out of Cincinnati. About sixty miles north of New Orleans, just south of Derby, a man suddenly entered the combined express and baggage car, locked the door behind him, and ordered the baggage clerk and express manager to raise their hands. The bandit was tall and thin, his face was covered with a red bandana, and he carried a revolver. At first the men thought the train crew was pulling a joke on them, but then they saw that the stranger was serious. The messenger was forced to open the express company safe,

take out the money, and place it into a sack. When this was done, the robber ordered the two men to put sacks over their heads and draw the drawstrings tight. He then pulled the bell cord, and when the train slowed, he exited by the end door and disappeared into a dark woods. When the train finally stopped, it was about one and a half miles north of Lacy's Station at a place called McClure's Switch.

The robber had planned this job well. When the conductor and brakeman started forward to see why the cord had been pulled, they found the door of the smoking car – which was immediately behind the baggage-express car – locked, which forced them to get off the train and go around the outside to reach the revenue car. When told the intruder had entered the end door of the car from the rear of the train, the conductor went through the coaches, asking if any of the passengers had departed. He found none of the passengers missing.

Why Eugene Bunch became a suspect in this robbery is still a mystery. Possibly the authorities already had him under surveillance. Whatever the reason, something led them to an associate of Bunch's, Leon Pounds of St. Tammany Parish, whom the police probably also were watching. Under questioning, Pounds implicated Bunch in this robbery.

Believing they had enough evidence on Pounds to make an arrest, the police swore out a complaint charging him with conspiring with Bunch to rob the United States mails. He later made bail and was released. Bunch, in the meantime, made himself scarce.

From November 1888 to early 1892 Bunch kept on the move. He was reported to have been seen in Texas, Tennessee, Louisiana, New Mexico, Mississippi, Alabama, California, Mexico City, Vera Cruz, and Monterey. Whether he was robbing trains during this period is not known. He was a suspect in robberies in Mississippi and Alabama that were later attributed to Rube Burrow. Sometime in early 1892 Bunch did turn up in Marion County, Mississippi, where he made an acquaintance with a farmer named Edward Scanlon Hobgood. The two then went on a spree of burglaries and robberies in eastern Louisiana. Around this time they also recruited a third man, Henry Carneguay.

On April 13, 1892, Bunch, Hobgood, and Carneguay robbed a Southern Express car on the Illinois Central Railroad at Tangipahoa, Louisiana, but they got only a few hundred dollars, some jewelry, and a handful of lottery tickets.

The authorities received a tip that both Bunch and Hobgood were involved in this robbery. Also, they received word that a shady character named Henry Sherling might know something about it. The story was that Bunch had tried to recruit Sherling for the gang, but Bunch was turned down. Sherling was brought in, and a deal was made. He would receive part of the reward being offered for Bunch if he could make contact and lead the authorities to him. Sherling did make contact, but apparently Bunch became suspicious. On August 6, 1892, Sherling was found shot to death in Amite, Louisiana.

Believing that Bunch was hiding somewhere in the area, a posse was formed on August 14 in Osyka, Mississippi, just across the Louisiana line. Their first stop was Marion County, Mississippi, and the farm home of Edward Hobgood. He was nowhere to be found, but they got a tip on Henry Carneguay. Carneguay was located, and after a mock hanging (a rope was placed over his head in an attempt to make him believe he was being lynched) and a vicious blow to the stomach from a deputy's rifle butt, Carneguay confessed that he, Bunch, and Hobgood had indeed committed the Tangipahoa robbery.

The following week the posse formed again and returned to Hobgood's house. Hobgood was not at home, but his brother, Robert, was. Robert denied any knowledge of his brother's whereabouts, but by now the possemen were losing their patience. They informed Robert that either he divulge his brother's hideout or they would kill him. Robert obliged, after extracting a promise that his brother would not be killed. He said Hobgood and Bunch were hiding in a farmhouse about sixteen miles east of Franklinton, Louisiana.

The posse found the house, but it was empty. There was evidence, however, that it had been recently occupied. The possemen decided to make a careful search of the surrounding area. It was a wise decision: about 400 yards from the house, in a shallow ravine, they came across the two outlaws. Bunch was taking a nap and Hobgood was standing guard. Apparently, they had become uneasy about the safety of their hideout and had decided to camp out for the night.

When Hobgood spotted the possemen, he threw up his hands and surrendered. Bunch, however, made a run for it, turning and firing his Winchester as he ran. A short distance away was a thick grove of trees. If he could make them, he had a chance. But the men who made up the posse that night were southern woodsmen—all crack shots. Five shots rang out and five bullets pierced the body of fleeing Eugene Bunch. As he fell, he tried once more to raise his rifle, but the weapon discharged harmlessly into the ground. (Source: O'Dell, "Bunch & Hobgood.") *See also* **Edward S. Hobgood; Tangipahoa, Louisiana**.

BURIED LOOT. As farfetched as it may seem, even today one might still uncover buried loot from a train robbery. Depending on where they were heading and how far they had to ride, many train robbers would not risk carrying stolen loot in their saddlebags. If a posse caught them with the proceeds of a holdup they were usually finished. Outlaws did, on many occasions, hide the loot with the intention of recovering it later, but often they were killed or captured before they could return.

And seldom did anyone else know where the loot was buried. It was common for a gang to split up after dividing the plunder of a major robbery. Although the outlaws often rode off in pairs, they usually went off by themselves if they were going to hide their cache. A wise outlaw didn't bury his share of the booty in front of a witness who could come back later and dig it up.

Where a train robber hid his loot often depended upon the remoteness of the area where the robbery occurred. The more populated the area, the more likely the loot would be hidden nearby; the robber would have to hide it quickly if there was a good chance he would encounter a posse rushing to the scene.

Coins and bullion were, of course, the most difficult to carry away from a robbery, and were the most likely booty to be buried. There is speculation that part of the proceeds from one of the first train robberies in the West, the 1870 holdup of an express car on the Central Pacific Railroad near Verdi, Nevada, still lies hidden somewhere near the scene of the crime. (See **Verdi, Nevada**). The unrecovered money was in $20 gold pieces, at the time worth about $3,000. At the current price of gold, it has been estimated that today the cache would be worth over $500,000.

It is believed the most money ever buried by train

robbers came from an express car holdup near Colorado Springs, Colorado, in October 1881. The robbers got over $100,000 in cash and $40,000 in jewels and other valuables. Most of the loot might still be hidden today along the banks of the Bear River near Corinne, Utah. (See **Colorado Springs, Colorado**.)

The haul from a Wells, Fargo express car robbery in October 1894, which consisted of around $50,000 in gold pieces, greenbacks, and coin, might still be hidden somewhere near the scene (see **Sacramento, California**), although a story has circulated that the money was found by a tramp somewhere around the turn of the century. According to the tale, the tramp used part of the money to live a life of luxury for a couple of years, until word got back to Wells, Fargo officials who went to the site and recovered what was left. The story could not be verified because the records of Wells, Fargo & Company were destroyed in the 1906 San Francisco earthquake and fire.

There may be treasure buried in western Montana. Two train robbers supposedly buried much of the loot from an express car holdup on the Northern Pacific Railroad in 1904. After his capture, one of the robbers told where the money was hidden, but there is no evidence that it was ever found. (See **Bearmouth, Montana**.)

It is rumored that part of a $30,000 shipment of gold coin and bullion stolen from a Wells, Fargo express car in September 1899 lies buried somewhere in Cochise County, Arizona, probably not too far from the town of Willcox, home of Burt Alvord, who engineered the robbery. (See **Cochise Junction, Arizona**.)

Some evidence has turned up that suggests Butch Cassidy might have buried loot from some of his robberies in the Wind River Mountain area of Wyoming, perhaps near the town of Lander. The amount has been estimated as high as $30,000.

While it is possible that much money was hidden during the years that train robberies flourished in this country, it is also very likely that much of it was found and never reported. It is not difficult to imagine the deals that might have been struck on lonely mountain trails between captured train robbers and underpaid peace officers. But it couldn't all have been dug up. And what better way is there to spend a sunny Sunday afternoon than skimming the wooded edges of an old Rock Island right-of-way with a metal detector?

(Sources: Block, *Great Train Robberies of the West*; Pointer, *In Search of Butch Cassidy*.)

BURROW, JIM. Jim Burrow, originally from Lamar County, Alabama, was the younger brother of Rube Burrow, who was sometimes called the "King of the Train Robbers." Rube and Jim began robbing trains in December 1886 with a daylight holdup of passenger coaches on the Ft. Worth & Denver line at Bellevue, Texas. With the help of two or three other gang members, Rube and Jim also robbed express cars on the Texas and Pacific line at Gordon, Texas, on January 23, 1887, and at Benbrook, Texas, on June 4 and September 20, 1887.

The gang's next holdup was Jim's last. On December 9, 1887, the Burrows struck an express car on the St. Louis, Arkansas & Texas Railway at Genoa, Arkansas. Raincoats and a hat left near the robbery scene eventually led to the identification of the gang. Rube and Jim were arrested in Montgomery, Alabama, in 1888. Rube escaped while being taken to the police station, but Jim was taken back to Arkansas to await trial for the Genoa robbery.

In September 1888 Rube attempted to rescue Jim while he was being transferred from the Little Rock, Arkansas, jail to Texarkana, but the attempt failed. Just before his trial, Jim, who had decided to plead guilty, changed his mind and wanted to plead not guilty. His

Jim Burrow. *Pinkertons*.

lawyer, taken by surprise, asked for a continuance. Jim was returned to Little Rock to await a new trial date. Shortly thereafter, Jim became ill and developed a high fever, probably from pneumonia. He slipped into a coma and died about a month later. (Source: Breihan, *Rube Burrow*.) *See also* **Bellevue, Texas; Benbrook, Texas; Rube Burrow; Genoa, Arkansas; Gordon, Texas.**

BURROW, RUBE. Although less famous today than many of the outlaws who plundered express cars in the 1880s and 1890s, Reuben "Rube" Burrow, at the peak of his career, proudly carried the title of "King of the Train Robbers." Before his death in a gunfight with authorities in October 1890, Rube's confirmed train robberies totaled eight, which placed him near the front, if not at the head, of the pack.

Rube Burrow. *Pinkertons.*

As a lad of eighteen, Burrow migrated to Texas from Lamar County, Alabama, in 1872. With the help of an uncle he learned to punch cows, and by branding strays off the prairie he eventually became the owner of his own modest spread on the outskirts of Ft. Worth. He married and started a family, and from appearances, seemed satisfied with the rewards of honest effort. But after their second child, Rube's young wife died, which may have had some effect on the course his life would eventually take.

Some say Rube worked for the railroad for a while,

probably the Ft. Worth & Denver or the Texas & Pacific, which also may have given him the idea to try his hand at robbing trains. For whatever reason, in the end he gave up cattle for express cars.

Burrow's career as a train robber began in December 1886 with a foolhardy midday robbery of passenger coaches of an eastbound Ft. Worth & Denver express while it was taking on water about 300 yards from a busy depot at Bellevue, Texas. But after this shaky beginning, Burrow quickly honed his skills and began a reign of express car assaults throughout the South and Southwest.

Rube's first gang, the one that earned its spurs at Bellevue, consisted of his brother, Jim, and two of his own ranch hands, Nep Thornton and Henderson Bromley. A month after the Bellevue robbery, they struck an express car on an eastbound Texas & Pacific passenger train at Gordon, Texas. At Gordon, Burrow developed a robbery pattern that would vary little during the rest of his career. He and another gang member would slip aboard the blind baggage area behind

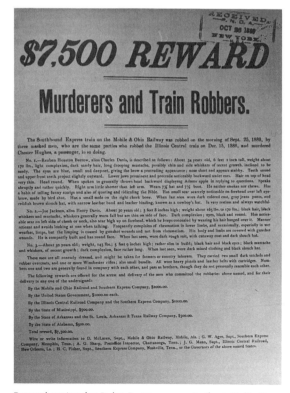

Reward notice for Rube Burrow gang. *Author's Collection.*

the tender as a train was pulling out of a station. A mile or so out of town another member of the gang would be waiting. The robbers would shove guns into the ribs of the engineer and fireman and order the train to be halted at the selected spot. The engineer and fireman would be marched back to the express car and the messenger would be forced to open up.

After the holdup at Gordon, the Burrow gang robbed the Texas & Pacific two more times, on June 4 and September 30, 1887, at the same location: just outside Benbrook, Texas. At the first of these, Burrow introduced what may have been the first "trestle robbery"—the practice of ordering the train to stop with the revenue cars just off the forward end of a trestle. This trick made it difficult for the train crew and the passengers to come from the rear of the train to interfere.

Following the second Benbrook holdup, Rube and Jim returned to their boyhood home in Lamar County, Alabama, where Rube showered friends and relatives with gifts bought with the stolen loot. In return, the Burrow clan and their neighbors provided the outlaw brothers with a secluded hideaway in the hill country of Lamar County, which Rube made use of during much of his brief outlaw career.

When the money began to run low, Rube and Jim, with the help of another Texan, W. L. "Bill" Brock, robbed an express car on the St. Louis, Arkansas & Texas Railway at Genoa, Arkansas. But raincoats foolishly left at the scene of the holdup led to the identification of all three men, and in January 1888 Pinkerton agents and express company detectives traced the outlaws to the Burrow homestead in Lamar County.

Thanks to their network of informers, Rube and Jim were warned that the authorities were closing in and they managed to slip away. They headed south on foot and when they thought it safe, they boarded a Louisville & Nashville southbound train for Montgomery. But by sheer chance, the conductor on their coach recognized them from a wanted poster the Pinkertons had quickly printed up, and when they departed the train at Montgomery, the police were waiting for them.

Rube tried to convince the police that he and Jim were timber men in town on business, but the police insisted on taking them to headquarters for further identification. Figuring they had little to lose, when they arrived at the door of the police station, the Burrows made a break for it. Luck was with Rube; as he dashed

for freedom, the officer who was guarding him got his coat caught on the doorknob and could not reach his gun. Jim was not so lucky. He was wrestled to the ground and quickly subdued.

Since Rube had not yet been placed under arrest, he still had his gun. As he ran, he glanced back and saw someone he thought was a pursuer. He fired two quick shots, and the man staggered and fell. The man was a local newspaper reporter named Neil Bray. He struggled near death for several weeks but eventually recovered.

Rube was in excellent physical shape. Despite the past several months of the easy life with his family in Lamar County, the long hard days on the Texas ranch had conditioned him well. Reared in hill country and unfamiliar with cities, he immediately headed for the outskirts of town and the terrain he knew: one of southern Alabama's dense woods. By noon the following day he had put five miles between himself and Montgomery.

It was the beginning of a two-year run from the law. Hiding by day and traveling by night, Rube worked his way north to safety in the backcountry of friendly Lamar County. When the law eventually closed in, he hightailed it south toward Florida, where he got jobs at lumber camps.

In September 1888 Rube and a fellow Texan, Leonard C. Brock (no relation to Bill Brock), made plans to rescue Jim from the authorities in Arkansas, but the plan fell through. Not long after, Jim took sick and died in jail.

While eluding his pursuers, Rube robbed three more trains. On December 15, 1888, he and Brock held up an express car on the Illinois Central at Duck Hill, Mississippi. And on September 25, 1889, Rube, Brock, and a new recruit named Rube Smith, a cousin of Burrow's, struck a Mobile & Ohio express on a trestle just south of Buckatunna, Mississippi. They gathered up $2,500 from the express car, and probably about the same amount from the mail car, but in their haste they overlooked $70,000 in packkages of new treasury currency that had been stacked near the express car door.

Rube's final robbery was on September 1, 1890, a single-handed holdup of an express car on the Louisville & Nashville line on a trestle over the Escambia River in northwestern Florida, just across the line from Flomaton, Alabama. Following this robbery, Rube's luck ran out. On September 29 detectives for the Southern Express Company, who had joined forces with Louisville & Nashville detectives, received a tip from an informer that Rube was seen near Repton, Alabama, a tiny farm community about seventy-five miles northeast of Mobile. From that day on, the authorities were never far behind Rube Burrow. The manhunt continued until October 1890. On the seventh day of that month, Rube was captured in a cabin near the Tombigbee River, just west of Myrtleville, Alabama.

Rube was shackled and taken to nearby Linden, Alabama, the county seat. But when he and his captors, two deputy sheriffs named John McDuffie and J. D. Carter, arrived, they found the jail locked and the sheriff out of town. An office next door was open, and Rube was placed inside, shackled to an iron ring that was bolted to the floor.

During the night, Rube began complaining that he was hungry. When he was told that there was no food to be had in town at that hour, he reminded the deputies that the sack that he had with him when he was captured had gingersnaps and candy in it. Deputy McDuffie had checked the sack and remembered that it did have food in it. The sack was brought in and McDuffie, without checking it again, gave it to Burrow. Rube reached in and pulled out a handful of gingersnaps. Then he reached in again and pulled out a pistol.

McDuffie's revolver was lying on the table out of reach. There were two other men in the room, but neither was armed. Burrow ordered one of them, a man named Jesse Hildreth, to unlock his shackles, lock up the other two men, and then take him to where the other deputy, J. D. Carter, was sleeping. Carter had taken Rube's Marlin rifle, and Rube wanted it back. Carter was found in the back room of a nearby store,

and Rube ordered Hildreth to call to him, and tell him that McDuffie wanted him at the jail.

When Carter came out the door, Rube, who was hiding behind a tree, called out that he wanted his rifle. Carter went for his pistol, and Burrow fired; his shot struck Carter in the shoulder just above the heart. Carter also fired, and the two men exchanged several more shots. On Carter's fourth shot, Burrow was seen to "leap into the air" and fall to the ground. He writhed on the ground "like a snake" said a witness, and after several violent gasps, he died.

On October 9 a train carrying Rube Burrow's body arrived at the Sulligent station in Lamar County. Waiting there were several members of the Burrow family. The Southern Express Company officials who were in charge of the body during its final trip tossed the box out the door onto the station platform: a supreme gesture of contempt for the outlaw who had embarrassed their company and made life miserable for the firm's express messengers. (Sources: Agee, "Rube Burrow"; Breihan, *Rube Burrow; Birmingham [Alabama] Weekly Age Herald*, 10 October 1890.) *See also* **Bellevue, Texas; Benbrook, Texas; Buckatunna, Mississippi; Duck Hill, Mississippi; Escambia River Bridge (Florida); Genoa, Arkansas; Gordon, Texas.**

BURTS, MATT. Burts was a member of a gang led by Burt Alvord, sheriff of Willcox, Arizona, who engineered the robbery of $30,000 from a Wells, Fargo express car near Cochise Junction, Arizona, in September 1899. Three of the four members of the gang were arrested for the holdup, but Burts escaped and was not heard from again. The stolen money was never recovered. *See* **Cochise Junction, Arizona.**   □

C

CAHABA RIVER BRIDGE (ALABAMA). On December 27, 1896, robbers wrecked a passenger train on the Birmingham Mineral branch of the Louisville & Nashville Railroad near Gurnee Junction in Shelby County, south of Birmingham. A rail was displaced on the bridge over the Cahaba River, and when the locomotive struck it, the bridge collapsed, and the train plunged 110 feet into the water below, killing more than twenty passengers and crew members. Several more passengers were severely injured, and some were reported missing. On final count, the death toll reached twenty-seven.

Witnesses told of seeing three "rough-looking" men sneak out of a nearby woods immediately after the wreck and go through the cars, robbing the dead and dying. The robbers were "poorly clad and wore big pistols," witnesses said, and "they did their work of robbing in a very few minutes and then fled to the woods, paying no heed to the cries of the wounded passengers."

It was later learned that the governor of Alabama, Joseph F. Johnston, was on a Southern Railway express that was to cross the bridge just before the ill-fated train. His train, however, was delayed, which probably saved his life.

The Louisville & Nashville and the Southern Railway dispatched a small army of detectives to search the area. From the description of the bandits, it was believed they were the same gang that robbed a Southern Railway express car at Blankston, Alabama, ten days earlier. The L&N and the Southern Railway announced a joint reward of $10,000 for the arrest and conviction of the guilty parties. (Sources: *New York Times*, 28, 29 December 1896.)

CALERA, ALABAMA. Calera is in Shelby County, twenty-eight miles south of Birmingham. Shortly before midnight on March 9, 1897, two masked bandits carrying Winchesters and dynamite sneaked aboard the Louisville & Nashville's Fast Mail No. 4 at Calera. They quickly climbed forward over the tender and ordered the engineer, Sam Orr, to stop the train about two miles out. The express messenger was forced to open up his car and the robbers helped themselves to the contents of the safe. When they had finished, the bandits rode off on horses that had been hitched nearby.

According to Southern Express Company officials the two men got over $14,000. They said the robbers were tracked fifty miles east to Pell City in St. Clair County, where they then took a train to Georgia.

On July 3, 1897, a man named George Hall, a.k.a. Gus Hyatt, who gave his home as Sandoval, Illinois, was arrested in Kansas City and charged with the robbery. Four days later he confessed to the Calera hold-up and several others. On August 19, Thomas N. Lowe was arrested in Rockville, Indiana, and charged with being the second man in the Calera robbery. Hyatt

was imprisoned in a Tennessee penitentiary in Nashville for a crime in that state, but on August 5, 1902, he escaped by blasting his way through a wall with dynamite. (Sources: *San Francisco Chronicle*, 5 August 1902; *St. Louis Globe Democrat*, 11 March, 14 April, 7, 8, 13 July, 21, 22 August 1897.) *See also* **Gus Hyatt**.

CANADIAN, TEXAS. An attempted train robbery with an unusual twist occurred at Canadian, Texas, on the night of November 24, 1894. Canadian is in the Texas Panhandle, on the Canadian River, about twenty-five miles west of the Oklahoma line.

As the Santa Fe's southbound passenger train arrived at the depot, all hell seemed to break loose. A gang of outlaws had ridden down from the Wichita Mountains and were waiting in the shadows near the station. When the train stopped rolling, the bandits let out a whoop and, in a fusillade of gunfire, laid siege to the Wells, Fargo express car. A rumor had been circulating in Canadian for several days that this particular express car was carrying a package containing $25,000 in currency, and the outlaws were apparently after it.

When the shooting started, Hemphill County Sheriff Tom McGee was not far away; he rushed to the scene, only to be nearly cut in two by the outlaws' Winchesters. But other townsmen came, and were soon peppering the bandits; this encouraged the Wells, Fargo guards inside the car to keep up a steady stream of gunfire of their own. Eventually, the attackers realized there was no hope of getting into the car, and they ran for their horses and rode off.

Sheriff McGee's body was taken to the town undertaker, and things began to quiet down. While the Wells, Fargo messenger and the Santa Fe conductor were making out their reports, somebody suggested that they take a peek at the package that apparently had caused the ruckus. The messenger was called over, and the package was opened. To everybody's astonishment, they found that it contained only a few hundred dollars, which had been neatly placed on top of a stack of blank paper.

Eventually the secret came out. A local cattleman, George Isaacs, had shipped the phony package to himself from Kansas City. He was in cahoots with the would-be robbers. They were supposed to have stolen the package, and he was to file the loss with the insurance company and share the proceeds with the gang.

Four suspects were later arrested in connection with the affair. Two were identified as Jim Harbold and Jake McKinzie, both of whom were believed to be riding with the Bill Doolin gang of train robbers. There was also some mention of Doolin gang member "Red Buck" Waightman being involved. (Source: Shirley, *West of Hell's Fringe*.) *See also* **Bill Doolin**.

CANEY, KANSAS. Some students of western outlaw history believe that a robbery of an express car on the Missouri Pacific line at Caney, Kansas, on October 13, 1892, was part of a hoax perpetrated by Dalton gang member Bill Doolin on the neighboring town of Coffeyville in retribution for the slaying of the Dalton bunch by Coffeyville citizens eight days earlier.

Doolin's plan, they think, was to make everybody believe the gang would descend on Coffeyville when in fact they had their eye on the train at Caney or one of the other nearby towns. The day before the Caney robbery, John J. Kloehr, one of the principals in the Coffeyville shootout, received a letter signed by the "Dalton Gang" promising revenge on the town for the "killing of Bob, Grat and the rest." Coffeyville town fathers, expecting an outlaw invasion, called for help from the surrounding towns. This left Caney and other towns in the vicinity vulnerable to a raid.

The robbers at Caney, presumably led by Doolin, boarded the Missouri Pacific locomotive as it was leaving the depot. They quickly climbed over the tender and covered the engineer and fireman with Winchesters. After ordering the engineer, whose name was Eggleston, to pull two miles out of town, the gang uncoupled the express car from the passenger coaches and then had the engineer pull ahead another half mile.

Back in the express car, the messenger, J. M. Maxwell, blew out his light and prepared for the onslaught. It came as expected, and almost immediately his arm was shattered by a bullet. The injury took the fight out of Maxwell, and he opened up his car. The outlaws then forced open the safe and took the contents, which the express company claimed was a smaller than average shipment, possibly even as little as $100.

Despite the small haul, the robbery launched Doolin as a gang leader in his own right. Over the next several years he and his companions would ravage many a train and town. (Sources: Shirley, *West of Hell's Fringe*;

Kansas City Star, 14 October 1892; *New York Times*, 14 October 1892.)

CANEY, OKLAHOMA. They were all fairly new at train robbery; in fact, it probably was the first train any of them had ever held up. They so enjoyed the experience that they hung around for two hours, laughing and joking and relishing the attention. And before they left, they presented the engineer with a gift: a diamond ring and a flashy shirt stud they had stolen from one of the passengers.

Caney is in southern Oklahoma, in Atoka County, about thirty miles north of the Texas line. In those days it was still part of the Choctaw Nation.

The date was August 13, 1901. It was a hot, breezeless night. Caney Switch, as it was called then, was not a regular stop for the southbound Missouri, Kansas & Texas passenger train, but the engineer was given the proper signal, and the switch was open to take the train onto the Caney siding, so he gave a blast on the whistle that said he was coming in. As the big engine rolled to a stop, two masked men appeared at the side of the cab.

There were six robbers in all. While two kept watch over the engineer and fireman, the other three attended to the express car. When the messenger would not open up, they blew the door off with dynamite. It was wasted effort, however, because when they finally blasted their way into the through safe, they found only $1.50. A large money shipment had been placed on the train, but it had been taken off at Muskogee.

The railway mail car was next. The robbers, evidently in no hurry, went through every pouch, carefully selecting pieces that appeared valuable. When they had finished, they ordered the mail clerk, whose name was Tulley, to pick up one of the sacks and go with them to the passenger coaches. Unlike most train robbers, this gang did not separate the express and mail cars from the rest of the train. Later, officials surmised that the bandits probably had intended to rob the passengers from the beginning.

Still without any attempt to hurry, the robbers went through the coaches, gathering up what money and valuables the passengers had not been wise enough to hide. They seemed to be amused during the entire affair; only once did they lose their sense of humor, when one of the passengers refused to give up his possessions. After a few whacks with a pistol barrel, he changed his mind.

Even after finishing with the passengers, the robbers still seemed reluctant to go. They sat around, laughing and joking, as if they had all the time in the world. Two hours had passed since they had taken control of the train; probably a record for a train robbery in Indian Territory, perhaps even in the entire Southwest. Finally, they got up and rode off—toward the east—into the dense bottom timber of Caney Creek.

In the end, the joke would be on them. The following day all six men were arrested at their homes near Caney. Their names were E. C. Richmond; Bob Alford, George Brown, John Gibson, Tom Edwards, and Jack Barr. A report from J. B. Davis, U.S. Deputy Marshal at Colbert, said: "Within two hours after the robbery was committed, bloodhounds had trailed these men to their homes. We found wet clothing identified by passengers as that worn by the robbers. We also found three masks, and in the firebox of the cookstove [in the home of one of the men] were the shoes of the men arrested. The tracks were measured and fitted the shoes exactly." (Source: *New York Times*, 14 August 1901.)

CARLISLE, WILL. Will "Bill" Carlisle was one of the last of the "lone bandits" to prey on trains. Carlisle's first robbery was on February 4, 1916, when he held up pas-sengers on the Union Pacific's eastbound *Portland Rose* near Green River, Wyoming. Witnesses described him as a dashing figure in a white bandana, haughty and brash as he strutted down the aisle with his six-gun in the ribs of the Pullman car porter whom he forced to pass the hat.

Carlisle struck again on April 4, another UP passenger train, this time near Laramie. With this second robbery, the newspapers began playing up the story of this colorful robber as a throwback to the days of Butch Cassidy. Carlisle became giddy over the publicity, and boldly wrote an anonymous letter to the *Denver Post* in which he announced that he planned "to hold up the next Union Pacific train west of Laramie." To prove that he was the robber in question, he enclosed a gold watch chain taken during the second holdup.

The authorities refused to believe that he would make good his threat, but he fooled them. He robbed another UP passenger train the following day, a few miles west of Laramie, just as he said he would. But his flair for the dramatic cost him dearly. The newspaper repro-duced his letter on the front page, and a rancher near Cheyenne recognized the handwriting as that of a for-mer wrangler named Will Carlisle.

Carlisle's next robbery was a week later, on an east-bound near Walcott, Wyoming. Becoming increasingly bolder, this time he bought a ticket, rode part of the

Bill Carlisle (in handcuffs). *Wyoming State Archives, Museums, and Historical Department.*

way with the passengers, then slipped on his mask when nobody was looking. After helping himself to the money and valuables, he leaped off the train at Walcott. But as he landed, he severely sprained his ankle. Conspicuous because of his limp, he was spotted the next day and picked up by a sheriff's posse. After a speedy trial he was sentenced to the Wyoming State Penitentiary.

For three years, Carlisle was a model prisoner. Then one day he slipped into a packing crate in the prison shirt factory and had himself shipped to freedom. A week later he was back in business, but his first choice of trains was an unfortunate one. The date was November 21, 1919, and the trains still occasionally carried soldiers returning from the war. Carlisle happened to pick one. When he saw his mistake, he refused to take any loot from the servicemen, but he did pass the hat among the few civilians in the car, telling the doughboys "Keep your money boys, I don't want it."

When the train slowed for Medicine Bow, Wyoming, Carlisle made a dash for the rear vestibule, intending to jump off. But as he stepped through the door, he was grabbed, and his gun discharged. The bullet ripped through his hand and wrist. The soldiers spilled out of the car after him, but he escaped by running through a line of sheep corrals that bordered the tracks. Weak from his wound, he was forced to seek help from local residents. The law closed in, and several days later he was found hiding in a miner's cabin above Estabrook, a mountain resort. When Will appeared at the door, the sheriff ordered, "Hands up." Because of his wound, however, Carlisle could not raise his right arm. The sheriff, thinking he was reaching for a gun, raised his rifle and fired, striking Will in the chest.

Carlisle lived and was returned to prison. Again, he became a model prisoner. Following his release, he opened a cigar store in Kemmerer, Wyoming, and later bought a gas station and cafe outside of town near the junction of U.S. highways 30 and 189, which he operated until his retirement in the 1950s. (Source: Patterson, *Wyoming's Outlaw Days*.)

CARNEGUAY, HENRY. Henry Carneguay, believed to be from either southern Mississippi or eastern Louisiana, participated in one train robbery on April 14, 1892, at Tangipahoa, Louisiana. Picked up as a suspect, Carneguay named his two confederates in the robbery,

Eugene Bunch and Edward S. Hobgood. For Carneguay's part in the crime (some say he only held the horses), he received five years at hard labor. He was released after two years and was killed in a domestic squabble with his brother-in-law in 1899. (Source: O'Dell, "Bunch & Hobgood.") *See also* **Eugene Bunch; Edward S. Hobgood; Tangipahoa, Louisiana**.

CASSIDY, BUTCH. *See* **Robert LeRoy Parker**.

CENTRALIA, ILLINOIS. As the number of express car robberies increased during the 1880s and 1890s, the express companies armed their messengers and encouraged them, at least officially, to resist attackers. When a messenger did put up a good defense, he was rewarded handsomely. Off the record, however, company officials seldom blamed the messenger who chose to save his own skin when faced with near certain death at the hands of a robber.

A single messenger rarely could hold off an attack, but when an entire train crew joined in on the fight, a bandit gang could be in for a long night. Just such a night occurred in September 1893, when three would-be robbers bent on emptying the contents of an American Express Company safe on the Illinois Central's southbound *New Orleans Limited* found that they had clearly chosen the wrong train crew with which to tangle.

The train left Chicago at 2:00 P.M. on September 20. All went well until 11:00 that night, during a stop at Centralia. As the train pulled away from the depot, three heavily armed men sneaked aboard behind the tender.

The lights of the city streets had hardly disappeared when the engineer, Ben Young, heard a noise on the coal pile behind him. He turned and saw two men with revolvers scrambling down toward the cab. "Keep your mouths shut and stop the machine, or we'll shoot," said one of the men.

Guns or no guns, Young and his fireman, whose name was McDowell, were not going to turn over their train to a couple of bandits. Young let the throttle go and McDowell grabbed his shovel, and together they rushed their attackers head-on. It was an admirable but foolish act. The bandits each fired once, and both trainmen staggered and fell to the floor of the platform separating the locomotive from the tender. With no hand on the throttle, the engine slowed to a stop.

In most train robberies, after the robbers stopped the locomotive, they would jump to the ground and head back to the express car. These bandits, however, scrambled back over the tender and climbed to the roof of the express car. Using grappling hooks which they fastened to the center of the roof, they lowered themselves over the edge, and began smashing at a side door with a sledgehammer. Inside, the American Express messenger and the conductor, both well armed, commenced firing through the door.

Had the bandits been attacking the car from the ground, the fusillade from inside might have ended the assault at that moment. But the messenger and the conductor, not realizing the attack on the door was coming from above, were aiming too low.

Under the heavy blows from the sledge, a portion of the door gave way, giving the attackers an opening into which they could shoot. Inside, the messenger and conductor hurriedly stacked crates and boxes for protection.

Back among the passengers was an Illinois Central brakeman, P. J. Sanders, who was deadheading his way home. From somewhere he obtained a pistol and rushed forward to help. Despite being shot at from the third bandit, who had positioned himself forward of the express car, Sanders took careful aim and put a bullet into one of the attackers hanging from the roof of the car. On seeing their comrade fall, the other two bandits decided they had better give it up, and they fled.

The injured bandit had been shot above the left eye but was still conscious. He gave his name as George Jones, and without hesitation he named his companions, whom he said were Martin Nichols and James Hardin. On learning that the engineer and fireman had been severely wounded, there was some talk among the passengers about lynching Jones right on the spot. And by the time the train arrived back in Centralia, where word had quickly spread about the shootings, several of the townspeople were carrying ropes. Local officials, however, discouraged any such action.

Later, George Jones, who eventually was identified as L. B. Jones of Kansas City, gave the authorities the name of a fourth man who had been involved in the planning of the robbery: Charles O'Dwyer of Centralia. (Source: *New York Times*, 22 September 1893.)

CERES, CALIFORNIA. In Stanislaus County, about four miles south of Modesto, just off Highway 99, is the site

of the famous Ceres Holdup, an attempted robbery of a Wells, Fargo express car on Southern Pacific's Train No. 19.

The date was September 3, 1891, and the attack was the fourth in a series of train holdups first attributed to the Dalton gang and then to California renegades Chris Evans and John Sontag. The methods used in all the holdups were virtually the same.

At Ceres, two masked men apparently slipped aboard behind the tender as the train pulled away from the Ceres water tank. A mile south of town the engineer was ordered to stop, and he and his fireman were forced to walk back to the express car. The Wells, Fargo messenger, U. W. Reed, was ordered to open his car but he refused; he and his helper, whose name was Charles, doused their lanterns and prepared for an assault.

The Southern Pacific depot at Ceres. *Everett R. Huffer Collection.*

The outlaws had come equipped with dynamite and they blew a sizable hole in the side of the car. Then they handed the fireman a lighted lamp and forced him to climb through the hole. Messenger Reed, however, was not so easily persuaded; he promptly told the fireman to crawl back outside or he would shoot him. The fireman, apparently fearing Reed more than the bandits, crawled back outside.

The bandits countered by tossing a lighted stick of dynamite into the car, but it failed to go off. By now, two Southern Pacific Railroad detectives who had been riding in one of the passenger coaches had become curious about the delay. When they saw what was happening they opened fire on the bandits. The bandits ducked beneath the car and returned the fire. One of the detectives, Len Harris, was hit in the neck. The bandits, however, had had enough for the night. They ran to their horses and rode away south, toward what is now the town of Newman. (Source: Glasscock, *Bandits and the Southern Pacific*.) *See also* **Evans and Sontag**.

CHAMBERS, CHESLEY. Chambers was a respectable southern Indiana livestock buyer whose life was ruined when he was wrongly convicted of robbing an express car and shooting an express messenger and baggage clerk near Harrodsburg, Indiana, in April 1885. Although Chambers had an alibi for the night of the crime, he closely resembled the real culprit. Worse still, in his hotel room the authorities found currency with needle holes punched in it that were similar to the holes made by express company clerks in packaging bills for shipment. When he could not explain to the satisfaction of the jurors how he came to obtain these bills, they sent him to prison for two years. Later, after Chambers had served his time, the real guilty parties were identified. (Source: Rainey, *Demise of the Iron Horse*.) *See also* **Harrodsburg, Indiana**.

CHAPMAN, JOHN T. John T. Chapman was a respectable Reno, Nevada, citizen and former Sunday school teacher who suddenly turned to train robbery in 1870. In November of that year he recruited a five-man gang of local hard cases who robbed a Wells, Fargo express car of $40,000 in gold at Verdi, Nevada. It was the first train robbery committed west of the Mississippi. *See* **Verdi, Nevada**.

CHICAGO, ILLINOIS. Even the bustling urban center of Chicago was not immune to train robbery during the height of the era. On the night of February 15, 1894, two masked men attempted to rob passengers on a Ft. Wayne Railroad coach shortly after it departed Chicago's Union Station. The train had left the station at 11:30 P.M. Just before it was about to cross the bridge at Sixteenth Street, where the engineer was required to run at a slow speed, two men jumped aboard the platform on the forward end of one of the day coaches.

The robbers, possibly amateurs, attacked the nearest passenger, who was in a seat near the door. One of the intruders was carrying a stick, and he hit the passenger in the head, as the other attacker grabbed the man's coat and a watch from his vest pocket. A melee then erupted. Nearly a dozen other passengers came to the victim's assistance. The robbers quickly backed toward the door. One of them carried a gun and he fired into the ceiling of the car. It was a grave mistake. The shot brought out several weapons among the passengers, who also commenced firing, and it is believed that one of their bullets wounded one of the robbers.

The robbers immediately retreated, but the one who held the passenger's coat did not let go, which later led to some speculation that the robbers knew that it contained something of value.

Later the same year Chicago was the scene of a second train robbery, which this time involved a killing. On August 24 two men forced their way into a caboose on a Chicago, Milwaukee & St. Paul freight train while it was taking on water at Deerfield, now a Chicago suburb just north of Northfield. The men flashed large revolvers in the face of the conductor, whose name was Sargent, and ordered him to hand over his gold pocket watch. Just then a CM&StP detective, Patrick Owens, entered the car. The robbers shouted for him to throw up his hands, but he went for his pistol instead. Both robbers fired, killing him nearly instantly. The two men then jumped off the train and caught a southbound freight that was passing by.

The conductor of the southbound freight spotted the two men boarding, and when the train stopped at the northern Chicago suburb of Mayfair, he informed the station agent, Fred Marshal, and another CM&StP detective, Patrick McGrath. Marshal and McGrath found the men hiding in a coal car. When McGrath tried to climb into the car, the men fired two shots at him, striking him in the arm and the side. The two men then climbed out of the car and ran toward Milwaukee Avenue.

As they ran north on Milwaukee Avenue, the men encountered a farmer bringing vegetables to market. They ordered him down, seized his wagon, and headed west on Higgins Road. The farmer ran to the nearest police station and reported the theft. The police, who were already on the lookout for the men, gave chase.

The two men continued west for three miles, across cornfields that now border the northern edge of Chicago-O'Hare International Airport. Thinking they had lost their pursuers, they stopped at a farmhouse and ordered the occupants to fix them breakfast, but before they could eat the police arrived. With seconds to spare, the fugitives raced out the back door and escaped into a nearby woods riding double on the farmer's horse.

The end came near Elk Grove. Surrounded by nearly 100 policemen, the men made a last-ditch effort to shoot it out and were both wounded. Finally they surrendered.

As they were being put in irons, the two men identified themselves as William Lake and H. F. Gorman, both of San Francisco. The authorities later learned that Gorman's real name was Harry D. Griswold, and that both he and Lake had been living in Chicago for more than two years. Griswold was a pressman at the Rand-McNally Company, and Lake was a member of the American Railway Union who had been working recently as a coffin trimmer. They confessed to killing detective Owens but claimed he had drawn on them first. (Sources: *New York Times*, 16 February, 26 August 1894.)

CHICKASHA, OKLAHOMA. By 1897 train robbery in Indian Territory had developed into a continual battle of wits between the outlaws and federal authorities. Nearly all trains had extra guards, and posses were scouring the territory, but the outlaws still held the upper hand. At Chickasha the robbers probably prevailed because they boldly struck at midday, an unusual time to hold up a train.

Chickasha is about thirty miles southwest of Oklahoma City, and in 1897 it was a major stop on the Rock Island line. Near the end of September a rumor had spread that bandits were planning to hit one of the Rock Island trains somewhere in the Chickasha area. Extra guards were put on all trains running at night. The southbound day train, however, was not considered threatened, and no special effort was made to protect it.

The attack came at a siding just outside Chickasha. As the train approached, the engineer could see four section hands beside the track. One of them was giving the signal to stop. Since nothing looked out of the ordinary, the engineer probably figured that the crew had spotted a loose rail and did not have time to repair it. He was sadly mistaken. Just out of sight was a gang of five masked outlaws, their guns trained on the railroaders.

Under the cover of Winchesters and six-shooters,

the train crew, express car messenger, and all the passengers were forced to climb down and line up along the track. One by one they were searched and their money and valuables taken. Only one passenger, James Wright of Mincot, showed any resistance, and the robbers promptly shot off a piece of his ear. There was no more trouble.

After the crew and passengers were thoroughly plucked, the robbers went to work on the express and railway mail cars. The registered mail pouches were ripped open and emptied, but the through safe proved too tough to crack, even with dynamite.

When they had finished, the robbers rode off to the west, toward what is now Caddo County. (Source: *New York Times*, 3 October 1897.)

CHILLICOTHE, IOWA. Although the 1890s were the peak years of train robbery in the United States, with a robbery occurring somewhere in the nation on an average of every two weeks, a few express messengers still left the doors of their cars unlocked in transit. On January 12, 1895, just as a Chicago, Burlington & Quincy passenger train was leaving the depot at Chillicothe, two men, who had been hiding in the shadows behind baggage carts, raced across the station platform toward the tracks, reached up and slid back the side door of the express car, and jumped in.

In a matter of seconds they overwhelmed the surprised express messenger, the baggage man, and the railway mail clerk, and proceeded to tie them up. Next, they quickly emptied the express company safe of $4,000 and, as the train slowed for a crossing at the edge of town, they leaped off and fled.

In reporting the robbery, the editors of *Railway Age*, obviously critical of the messenger's carelessness, described the affair as "one of the neatest jobs on record—no shooting of engineer, no bother of detaching cars and running ahead with them, no dynamite, no killing of messengers, no breaking open of safe, no alarming of passengers. An unlocked door gave the opportunity, and nerve and a little cord did the business." (Source: *Railway Age*, 18 January 1895.)

CHRISTIAN BROTHERS. Robert "Bob" and William "Will" Christian were small-time outlaws who mainly engaged in stealing horses and peddling whiskey until sometime in 1894 or 1895. The records are far from exact, but it is believed that around that time they graduated to more serious crimes. In April 1895 they were involved in the killing of a deputy sheriff, William C. Turner, in Pottawatomie County, Indian Territory. The following month they were captured and taken to jail in Oklahoma County, but on June 30 they escaped.

From then on the brothers' trail becomes difficult to follow, thanks mainly to their liberal use of fictitious names. Reports placed them in Indian Territory, Arizona, and New Mexico during the rest of 1895 and in 1896.

During those years they formed a gang, known by some as the High Fives and by others as the Black Jack gang. Either Will or Bob became known as Black Jack. Most writers believe it was Will, but no one knows for sure. Their specialty seemed to be store robberies or break-ins, mostly in and around Indian Territory.

On October 2, 1896, it is believed that the Christians and their followers, riding as the Black Jack gang, struck an Atlantic & Pacific eastbound train near Rio Puerco, New Mexico. But they came away empty handed, thanks to a stubborn express messenger named L. J.

Bill Christian. *Author's Collection.*

Kohler and an aggressive United States deputy marshal named Will Loomis, who was riding in the first passenger coach. The gang did, however, manage a successful escape. A string of robberies followed: stages, post offices, and railroad depots were their favorite targets.

Some researchers believe that Will Christian, riding as Black Jack, was killed in a gunfight with a posse near Clifton, Arizona, on April 28, 1897, at a place called Cole Creek Canyon. Others suggest it was some other member of the gang. In any event, the gang apparently held together and continued their operations including, it is believed, the robbery of the Atlantic & Pacific's eastbound Train No. 2 at Grants, New Mexico, about ninety miles west of Albuquerque, the first week of November 1897.

Following the Grants holdup, the robbers, with Bob Christian riding under the name of Tom Anderson, rode south to Mexico, crossing the border on November 23. They were later spotted in Fronteras, Sonora, and for a while they may have been in the custody of the Mexican authorities. A telegraph message reported their capture, and Arizona peace officers and Wells, Fargo detectives rushed to Fronteras, but found the outlaws gone. This was the last that was heard of Bob Christian.

The identity of the members of the Christian brothers' gang remains pretty much a mystery even today, mainly because of their penchant for aliases. The list of hard cases who possible saddled up with Will and Bob Christian as part of the High Five or Black Jack gangs includes: John Champion, Cole Harris (alias Cole or Code Young, Cole Estes), Samuel Hassells (alias Bob Hayes or Hays), Theodore James, West Love, Sid Moore, George West Musgrave (alias Bob Cameron, Jeff Davis, Jesse Johnson, Ed Mason, Bob Steward, Jesse Williams), Van Musgrave (alias Bob Lewis), Dan "Red" Pipkin, and Bill "Slim" Traynor. (Source: Burton, "Bureaucracy, Blood Money and Black Jack's Gang.") *See also* **Grants, New Mexico; Rio Puerco, New Mexico**.

CIMARRON, KANSAS. A robbery on Santa Fe's California Express No. 3 near Cimarron on June 9, 1893, was the work of Bill Doolin and his followers, successors to the Dalton gang.

Cimarron is in Gray County, about sixteen miles west of Dodge City. The outlaws flagged down the engineer with a red lantern—the danger signal. He and the fireman were then forced to walk back to the express car. Inside, Wells, Fargo express messenger E. C. Whittlesey was probably saying to himself, "why me?" Just a year before, at Red Rock in Indian Territory, he and an assistant messenger had the fight of their lives trying to defend their car against an attack by the Daltons.

The accounts of what happened next differ. It is believed the bandits forced the engineer to batter in the door with a sledgehammer. Whittlesey, of course, could not shoot for fear of hitting the engineer. Also, the robbers fired many shots into the car and may have used dynamite on the door. Whittlesey was hit in the arm. Once inside, however, the outlaws were unable to open the through safe, which on that run carried $10,000. They had to settle for the contents of the way safe, which held between $1,000 and $2,000.

The gang fled southeast, crossing Clark County near Ashland. In northern Oklahoma they encountered a posse, and Doolin was shot in the foot. (Sources: Shirley, *West of Hell's Fringe; New York Times*, 11 June 1893.) *See also* **Bill Doolin**.

CLARKSVILLE, TENNESSEE. The day after this robbery the *Clarksville Leaf Chronicle* proclaimed that "Jesse James would be proud of such a hold-up." He probably would have, because it is doubtful that Jesse ever would have considered robbing a train single-handedly.

Depot at Clarksville. *Author's Collection.*

The robbery occurred on June 22, 1897, shortly after 9:30 P.M. Just before the Louisville & Nashville's northbound Train No. 102 pulled out of the Clarksville station, a man in his early thirties wearing a blue suit and a slouch hat quickly boarded the steps of the first passenger coach. There was nothing to distinguish him from the other passengers, except that as soon as the train began to move, he got up from his seat and headed for the front door of the car, the door that led to the Southern Express Company car immediately ahead.

Inside the express car, messenger L. C. Brannon was at the safe, which was open, sorting through his money packages. With him in the car were four others: T. O. McCaddon, the L&N baggage clerk; a baggage helper; an Illinois Central conductor who had hitched a courtesy ride; and Brannon's cousin, J. S. Williams, a passenger on the train who had come to the express car to visit with his cousin. When the men heard a knock on the door, McCaddon, who was near the rear of the car getting a drink of water, walked back and opened the door. It was the man in the blue suit; he now wore a black mask and held a shiny, silver-plated revolver in each hand.

At first, McCaddon thought somebody was playing a joke, and he tossed the cup of water at the intruder. "Quit this damn foolishness," the man in the blue suit said. "I mean business. Throw up your hands!"

McCaddon's act of opening the door without having the person identify himself was especially careless that night, because two weeks earlier, Louisville & Nashville officials had been warned that there might be a robbery attempt somewhere on the line. For the past ten days, conductors and brakemen had been checking the blind baggage area of their trains as they pulled away from stations and water tanks to make sure nobody slipped on board, and L&N detectives had been riding among the passengers, watching for suspicious persons.

Because of the warning about a robbery attempt, messenger Brannon had been keeping his pistol close by him in the express car. When the man in the blue suit entered, the gun was lying on the messenger's desk, just out of reach. Brannon started for it, but the intruder saw it, too, and he ordered the messenger and everyone else to the far end of the car. After placing one of the revolvers in his pocket, with one hand he picked up the money from the safe and stuffed it into a sack that he had tied over his shoulder, all the time keeping the five men covered with his other revolver. When he had finished, he walked up to the conductor, plucked the man's gold watch from his vest pocket, and tossed it into the sack. Then he turned and pulled the bell cord (the signal to the engineer to stop). When the train did not slow down, he pulled again. Still the train sped on. Swearing, he jerked it a third time. This time the brakes were applied, and when the train had slowed sufficiently, he backed toward the rear door, out onto the vestibule, and jumped off.

Site near Clarksville where Gus Hyatt jumped off the train. *Author's Collection*.

Apparently, the engineer had heard only two signals from the express car. On being interviewed later, he said that the first signal on the bell cord was incorrect and he thought it had probably been pulled by accident, so he did not stop. The next signal was proper, however, and since the train was nearing the station at St. Bethlehem, he concluded that one of the passengers had decided to get off there. The robber jumped off a few hundred yards short of the station and ran into the underbrush. (In some reports, this robbery is referred to as occurring at St. Bethlehem.) A posse was organized but by the time it reached the scene the culprit's tracks had been washed away by rain.

An investigation by local authorities revealed that the railroad had been aware that a man had been travel-

ing up and down the line acting in a "suspicious manner." They did not say just what the man was doing to make his actions suspicious, but his description matched that of a man who had been waiting around the Clarksville station the night of the robbery, and roughly matched the descriptions given by the five men who had been present in the express car. On June 24, two days after the robbery, this man was identified as Gus Hite, believed to be from Earlington, Kentucky.

Hite was picked up by police in Kansas City, Missouri, on July 3. His arrest was pure luck. He had gone to a Turkish bath and while he was taking the bath somebody went through his clothes and stole his wallet, which contained $1,000 from the robbery. Hite had been drinking heavily and when he discovered his money was gone he caused a row with the manager of the bath, and the police were called. When they found Hite's two revolvers, they took him to headquarters. There they discovered his close resemblance to the description of the suspect in the report they had been sent about the Clarksville robbery.

Hite was returned to Clarksville and on July 12 he pleaded guilty to the express car robbery. During the investigation, it was discovered that his real name was Gus Hyatt, that he was twenty-six years old, that he was originally from Cherokee, North Carolina, and that he also was wanted for murder in DeKoven, Kentucky, and had participated in a train robbery at Calera, Alabama, the previous March.

Hyatt was sentenced to fifteen years at the state penitentiary in Nashville. On August 4, 1902, he and fifteen other prisoners escaped by blowing a hole in the prison wall. (Sources: *St. Louis Globe Democrat*, 7, 8, 13 July 1897; *Clarksville Leaf Chronicle* [Tennessee], 23–25, 26, 28 June, 12, 13 July 1897, 4 August 1902.) *See also* **Gus Hyatt**.

CLIFTON, "DYNAMITE DICK." Although it is generally believed that Dynamite Dick Clifton got his nickname from blowing up express car safes, a better source credits it to an idea he once had during his early outlaw days that he could give his cartridges explosive power by hollowing out the points and filling them with dynamite. His companions probably had a good laugh at his expense, and the name stuck.

Dick Clifton's background was stealing horses and peddling whiskey. He was a "heavy-set man, well muscled, and of fair intelligence" who was once described as a shrewd and dangerous criminal. Yet, like the "dynamite bullet" incident, there were apparently moments of utter stupidity that no doubt rankled his leader, the cautious Bill Doolin, who took him into his gang in 1892.

Nearly topping the exploding bullet trick was Clifton's mail order gun incident shortly after he joined the Doolin gang. While hiding out between train robberies, Clifton decided he needed a new pistol, so he ordered one by mail from a firm in Tulsa. He directed that it be sent by express to the railroad station at Ingalls, Kansas, the town nearest to the gang's hideout. This in itself was not so bad, but Dick used his real name on the order. The U.S. marshal's office was tipped off and staked out the station. Despite Clifton's carelessness in placing the order, the authorities did not think he would be foolish enough to try to pick up the gun during the day, so they only halfheartedly guarded the station from dawn to sunset. This was their mistake. Clifton boldly rode into town one afternoon at two o'clock, paid the startled station agent for the package, and rode out without the deputies recognizing him.

Clifton rode with the Doolin gang on and off for four years. When the gang finally broke up in 1896, Clifton drifted around, picking up change wherever he could find it. One day while peddling whiskey in Indian Territory, he was arrested and thrown into jail. He was using an alias, Dan Wiley, and the arresting officer, a Texas lawman, did not recognize him. The sentence for illegally selling whiskey was only thirty days, and Clifton sat quietly in his cell waiting for his time to be up. He almost got away with it, but two local deputies happened by and noticed that Dan Wiley the whiskey peddler matched the description of Dynamite Dick Clifton the train robber. A scar on Clifton's neck, picked up in the Doolin gang's narrow escape at Ingalls several years earlier, confirmed the identification, and the next day Dynamite Dick was on his way to Guthrie, Oklahoma, to stand trial for train robbery.

At the jail at Guthrie, Clifton was housed with his old gang leader Bill Doolin, who was already in the process of planning an escape. On the night of the breakout, Clifton tagged along, and both outlaws were again on the loose. Doolin, however, was killed by law officers in August 1896 at Lawson, Oklahoma.

Clifton and one remaining Doolin gang member,

"Little Dick" West, tried to put together another outfit. In 1897 they came across two ex-lawyers, Al and Frank Jennings, who had decided to try their hand at train robbery. Another pair of brothers, Morris and Pat O'Malley, were added, and the Clifton-Jennings gang was formed.

The new outfit did not work out too well, and Clifton pulled out after a few months. While riding alone one day about ten miles west of Checotah, Oklahoma, Clifton came upon a pair of U.S. deputy marshals. They recognized him and ordered him to surrender, but he would have no part of it. He reached for his Winchester, but he was too slow. A bullet shattered his arm and knocked him from his horse. He scrambled for the brush, and for a while it appeared that he might escape, but a short time later he was cornered in a nester's cabin. He was offered a chance to give up, but it was not in his nature. He kicked out the door and rushed out with his gun blazing. He got only a few steps. (Sources: Patterson, *Train Robbery*; Shirley, *West of Hell's Fringe*.) *See also* **Bill Doolin**.

CLIPPER GAP, CALIFORNIA. An attack on a Wells, Fargo express car at Clipper Gap in 1888 holds a special place in the annals of train robbery for the unusual method the robbers used to enter the car.

Clipper Gap was a water stop on the old Central Pacific line about five miles north of Auburn in Placer County. The assault occurred on Christmas Eve. The two bandits, Harry L. Gordon and his brother, George, crept onto the roof of the express car while the train was standing at the station. Each man carried a six-gun and a rope ladder, and one of them carried an axe.

As the train pulled out, the bandits fastened the rope ladders to the edge above the side doors and dropped

George Gordon. *Pinkertons.*

the ladders over the edge. When the train was well under way, they climbed down the ladders, smashed open the transom windows above the doors and slipped inside.

Before the startled Wells, Fargo messengers, Robert Johnson and A. M. Carpenter, could figure out what was happening, the Gordon brothers had them covered with their pistols. The robbers quickly removed $5,000 from the express company's safe and stuffed it into two grain sacks. After tying the sacks to their belts, they climbed back out the windows, and as the train slowed for the grade near New England Mills, they dropped to the ground and disappeared.

When Johnson and Carpenter reported the robbery, they were met with disbelief, and a rumor soon spread that the messengers had concocted the story after taking the money themselves. The express company's top investigators, however, Chief Detective James B. Hume and Special Officer Jonathan N. Thacker, proceeded with the investigation on the presumption that the messengers were telling the truth, and before long they found a man who had assisted the Gordon brothers in preparing for the robbery. After questioning by the detectives, the man—who lived just four miles from the spot where the bandits jumped off the train—admitted supplying the axe and helping the Gordons to obtain the material and construct the rope ladders. The man said he was willing to talk because the robbers had treated him shabbily, giving him only $30 for his help.

Using the description of the bandits given by their accomplice, Hume and Thacker traced them from New England Mills to Sacramento and from there to Reno, Nevada. At Reno, Hume was called off the case and sent East to handle another investigation. Thacker stayed on and learned that the robbers had taken an eastbound train for Kansas, where their father owned a farm near Olathe. There, on February 22, 1889, the detective found Harry Gordon and arrested him for the robbery. Gordon denied any knowledge of the holdup, but on searching him, Thacker found $2,000 of the stolen money. Harry Gordon was returned to Placer County to stand trial for the robbery; he was convicted and sentenced to ten years at San Quentin. At first he refused to name his accomplice, but eventually he admitted that his helper was brother George. George, however, was never captured. In 1894 Thacker learned that he had been killed during a holdup attempt in

the East. (Sources: Boessenecker, "John Thacker: Train Robbers' Nemesis"; Dillon, *Wells, Fargo Detective*.)

COCHISE JUNCTION, ARIZONA. Cochise Junction is in southeastern Arizona, on the Southern Pacific tracks between Tucson and the New Mexico line, about ten miles west of Willcox. On the night of September 11, 1899, two masked men boarded a westbound Southern Pacific passenger train at Cochise while the locomotive was taking on water. They forced the engineer and fireman to uncouple the Wells, Fargo express car from the rest of the train and pull ahead about a mile. There the bandits forced their way into the express car, and while one man held a gun on the messenger, the other man packed dynamite around the iron safe. The door blew completely off, and the robbers hastily scooped up the contents, rumored to be almost $30,000 in gold coins, most of which were recently minted and uncirculated. When they had loaded their loot onto their horses, the two bandits rode off quickly, disappearing into the darkness of the Arizona desert.

The engineer threw the locomotive into reverse and returned to the passenger coaches at Cochise, but when he arrived he found that the telegraph wires had been cut. A horse was finally found, and a rider was dispatched to Willcox to alert the authorities. The Willcox sheriff, Burt Alvord, was notified and he quickly formed a posse and rushed to the scene, but no trace of the robbers could be found.

Locally, the robbery was nearly forgotten, but a month or so later an uncirculated gold coin turned up at a Willcox saloon. Wells, Fargo detectives and the Arizona Rangers were notified and they identified it as one stolen in the robbery. After a few questions, the coin was traced to a local hard case named Bob Downing. Although witnesses had seen Downing spend the coin, he denied any knowledge of it and claimed that on the night of the robbery he had been playing poker with the sheriff, Burt Alvord, in the back room of Schweitzer's saloon. At first it seemed the investigation had come to a standstill, but one of the Arizona Rangers, Burt Grover, became curious about the poker game that provided Downing with an alibi.

There were four players in the game that night: Sheriff Alvord, Bob Downing, and two of their friends, Billy Stiles and Matt Burts. Downing, Stiles, and Burts were occasionally employed by Sheriff Alvord as special deputies; most of the time, however, he kept them around as personal bodyguards, which he claimed he needed because he had made many enemies over the past few years. Although Stiles and Burts did not have as bad a reputation as Downing, who some say once rode with train robber Sam Bass, they were tough characters and were known locally as gunslingers.

Ranger Grover was pretty well convinced that Downing had passed the stolen coin, and that all four men were involved in the robbery, so he went to work on Billy Stiles, whom he considered the most gullible of the bunch. Grover told Stiles that he had heard that Alvord and Downing were planning to pin the crime on him and then kill him. Stiles went for the ruse and confessed to Grover what had happened. The four men had planned the poker game as an alibi. During the evening Stiles and Burts slipped out the back, committed the robbery, and returned. No one saw them leave, except a waiter who brought drinks during the game, and Alvord had bribed him to strengthen the story.

Matt Burts left town before he could be picked up, but Alvord and Downing were arrested and put in jail in Tombstone. Before long, however, Stiles figured out that he had been fooled and he refused to sign a confession or agree to testify against Alvord and Downing. Downing was released in hopes that he would lead the authorities to the hidden loot. He didn't. Alvord was kept in jail, but Wells, Fargo officials promised him they would ask for a light sentence for him if he would turn over the money. Stiles was promised the same if he could convince Alvord to talk. Stiles made the authorities think he was going along with their plan, but on April 8, 1900, during one of his visits to the Tombstone jail, he engineered Alvord's escape.

For three years Alvord and Stiles roamed Arizona rustling cattle and robbing mine payrolls. They eventually hooked up with a notorious outlaw, Augustin Chacon. In 1903 Alvord, in failing health and wanting to make some kind of deal, sent word that he might give himself up. The Arizona Rangers responded by offering him a light sentence if he would help them bring in Augustin Chacon. A deal was made, and with Alvord's and Stiles's assistance, Chacon was captured. Alvord and Stiles were returned to Tombstone and stood trial for the robbery at Cochise Junction. Although one of the Arizona Rangers testified on the two out-

laws's behalf, the trial ended in a hung jury. Alvord and Stiles concluded that they had been tricked, and they broke jail once more. A posse overtook them near the Mexican border, and both men were wounded. Stiles escaped, but Alvord was returned for a second trial. He was sentenced to seven years at Yuma prison. His health worsened, and after two years he was released, At this point he disappeared. Some say he returned to Willcox and dug up the hidden loot, but there is no proof of this. It is more likely that he retrieved the money years earlier when he and Stiles were riding the outlaw trail.

Billy Stiles escaped to Mexico, then headed for the Philippine Islands, where he may have served in the army. He later returned to the United States and settled down in Nevada, where he became a deputy sheriff under the name William Larkin. He was eventually killed by the brother of a rustler whom he killed during an arrest. (Source: Dillon, "Arizona's Last Train Robbery.")

COLBERT, WASHINGTON. A railway mail car robbery on the Great Northern Railroad at Colbert, Washington, on May 15, 1909, differed little from numerous other mail car holdups that were plaguing the nation's railroads at the time, except for a deadly new twist, a feature that railroad officials prayed would not catch on with other robbers.

The robbers climbed aboard the tender at Colbert, which is about fifteen miles north of Spokane, apparently while the engine crew was busy with switching duties. Shortly after the train pulled out, they descended on the cab and shoved guns into the backs of the engineer, Bill Miller, and the fireman, John Hall. In the traditional method practiced by train robbers for nearly four decades, the bandits ordered the train uncoupled behind the mail cars and then had the engineer pull ahead a few miles, thus putting distance between the passenger coaches and the robbers while they worked.

The bandits entered the mail car and quickly went through the registered mail, taking anything that appeared valuable. When they finished, their next move ws the departure that set this robbery apart from the hundreds that had preceded it. Instead of heading for their horses and riding off, as most robbers did, one of the bandits climbed into the engine cab—which was sitting at the top of a slight grade—released the brake, and started the engine up in reverse, toward the cars filled with sleeping passengers at the bottom of the grade.

Down at the cars, conductor C. L. Robertson, who was standing on the front platform of the first Pullman coach, saw what had happened. Shouting to a brakeman and several porters to come help him, he jumped down and ran toward a stack of crossties beside the track. Together the men threw as many ties as they could across the rails, hoping to slow the momentum of the oncoming engine and mail car. The crossties helped, but did not stop the engine and mail car, which by then were traveling at almost twenty-five miles per hour. The mail car hit the ties, jumped off the rails, but continued to roll. When it telescoped into the first Pullman, the passengers were thrown from their seats and sprayed with shattered glass. Twelve passengers were injured, several seriously, but thanks to the quick action of conductor Robertson there were no fatalities.

Later, railroad officials could not decide whether the robbers had sent the engine and mail car down the track out of sheer meanness or whether it was intended to create a diversion to allow them more time to escape. In either event, they hoped and prayed that this feature would not catch on with future train robbers. Fortunately, it didn't. (Source: *New York Times*, 18 May 1909.)

COLFAX, CALIFORNIA. Although the Southern Pacific Railroad would be struck by bandits more than fifty times before the end of the train robbery era, there was an unusual lull in attacks on the SP during the 1880s, especially in California. There seems to be no logical explanation, other than that word got around that Wells, Fargo & Company was hiring hard-nosed messengers who would not turn over their express cars to bandits, even on the threat of death. A good example of this boldness was set near Colfax, California, in 1881.

On the night of August 31 of that year, three would-be robbers tore up a section of rails and waited for the big double locomotives drawing a long SP passenger train to go careening off the track. They did, and took the tenders and the Wells, Fargo express car with them.

The bandits no doubt counted on the messenger, if he was still conscious, to be so shaken that he would readily open up his car and give them access to the safes. They guessed wrong. When his car finally rolled

to a stop, the messenger, whose name was Chadwick, got to his feet, stumbled his way over scattered crates and express packages to the doors, made sure they were locked, and then sat down with his revolver and waited for his attackers. The bandits were not prepared for this. Realizing that before long the wreck would draw a crowd, the bandits gave up in disgust and left. They were later captured. One escaped while awaiting trial; the other two were identified as George Steingell and George Shinn.

Colfax was the scene of another robbery on Christmas Eve 1922. The Southern Pacific's *Daylight Special*, Train No. 31, was approaching Colfax during a mountain snowstorm. Snowdrifts were piled high along the right-of-way. It was 11:00 P.M., and the train was running behind schedule.

Just before he was to give the first whistle for the station, engineer Jim Simpson saw a stack of railroad ties ahead on the track. He slammed on the brakes and the train jerked, then began to roll to a stop. Back in the coaches, conductor Mike Malone and brakeman Sim Spaw stepped out onto the platform between the cars to see what had caused the unscheduled stop. They were met by two armed, masked men who ordered them to put up their hands.

When the train had come to a full stop, one of the bandits headed for the locomotive, while the other ordered Malone and Spaw to march to the baggage car. Daylight No. 31, on a short-run schedule, did not carry a safe, and the bandit ordered Malone to climb inside and open it up. Malone explained that the safe was secured with a combination lock that could be opened only by the station agent at Colfax. The bandit, unconvinced, hit Malone over the head with his revolver. When Malone still resisted, the bandit went into a fury. Grabbing an axe off the wall, he began smashing every package in sight. When he came to several small boxes strapped with iron, out rolled a handful of recently minted $20 gold pieces, part of a payroll shipment from San Francisco to the silver mines in Colfax.

The bandit, now joined by his partner who had returned with the locomotive crew, tossed the boxes off the car onto the ground. One of them left briefly and then returned with two horses that apparently had been tied up nearby. As one of the men guarded the prisoners, the other broke open the boxes and stuffed the sacks of coins into large pouches that he draped over their saddles. When he was done, the robbers rode off into a thick, snow-covered woods.

On arriving at Colfax, the trainmen spread the news, and a posse was hastily formed. Although the robbers' tracks were rapidly being covered by a new snowfall, the possemen, led by Placer County Sheriff John Bradberry, managed to follow them a short distance. They began in a northwesterly direction, but then appeared to turn south. It was too dark to see the trail clearly, however, and the possemen gave up for the night.

The next morning the trail was picked up by two of the posse members who had ridden off alone. This time the tracks led northeast. After a few miles, the two trackers found where the bandits had burned the gold sacks. After another eight miles, they found one of the masks used by the bandits. The trail eventually led to the town of Emmigrant Gap, where the trackers found a merchant who had sold the bandits some flour, bacon, and clothing. The men had paid with a $20 gold piece taken during the robbery. The trackers were now close behind and late that afternoon they spotted their quarry. One of the trackers kept on the trail, while the other rode back to find the main posse.

The bandits' route was now southwest, toward Dutch Flat. On arriving there, they made the mistake of talking to the Southern Pacific station attendant, who became suspicious. As soon as they left, he notified other stations along the line and Southern Pacific officials that he believed that he had seen the robbers.

Placer County Sheriff John Bradberry and five heavily armed deputies arrived at Dutch Flat by special train and within an hour they picked up the two mens' tracks, which, after a few miles, separated. One trail led to a ranch near Cisco owned by a man named Nat Stockton. The posse followed this one and on arrival at the ranch found Stockton's father-in-law, Thomas Fulcher, bedding down a horse that had recently been ridden hard and long. Fulcher, age fifty-six, matched the description of the older of the two robbers. Fulcher was questioned, but denied any knowledge of the robbery.

The posse then backtracked and followed the other trail. This led to another ranch where they found another Fulcher, Sidney, age twenty-four, Thomas's son. Staked out in an adjacent canyon was another exhausted horse. Bradberry was fairly certain they had their robbers, but when he found out that the Fulchers

were well-respected cattlemen in the area with many friends, he elected to move slowly.

Before long, however, the evidence began to pile up against the suspects. The older of the two robbers had used a fancy silver-plated, pearl-handled revolver. Thomas Fulcher owned such a revolver. The older of the two robbers also appeared to have a bad right arm. Thomas Fulcher had a partially paralyzed right arm. Then came the clincher: Sidney Fulcher had served in the army during the World War. Thus, his fingerprints were on file. A copy was obtained and compared with a set taken from the raincoat left in the locomotive cab. They matched perfectly! Icing was added to the cake when a neighbor of the Fulchers reported to Bradberry that they had asked him to swear that he was with them the evening of the robbery.

The Fulchers were indicted by a federal grand jury on five counts involving robbery of a mail train plus a charge for assaulting the conductor, who had been "jostled" during the robbery. The defendants hired a good defense lawyer, and the case dragged on nearly four years. Finally, in April 1926, a jury returned verdicts against both men on all counts, and they were sentenced to twenty-five years at the United States Penitentiary at Fort Leavenworth, Kansas. The gold, which the authorities believed was buried somewhere near Dutch Flat, was never found. (Sources: Block, *Great Train Robberies of the West*; DeNevi, "Holdup of the Santa Claus Special"; *Virginia City Enterprise* [Nevada], 2 September 1881.)

COLLERAN, MICHAEL. Colleran was one of four men who robbed an Adams Express Company car on the Ohio & Mississippi Railroad near Seymour, Indiana, in October 1867. On being questioned about the robbery, he drew a knife and tried to escape. He later pleaded guilty and was sentenced to five years in the Indiana State Prison. *See* **Seymour, Indiana**.

COLLINS, JOEL. Joel Collins was a Dallas, Texas, saloon keeper when he met up with Sam Bass around 1876. After driving a herd of cattle to Nebraska, the two men headed on north to seek their fortune in Dakota's Black Hills where the gold rush was on. Following the failure of several honest ventures, Bass and Collins formed a gang and tried holding up stages. In September of 1877 they rode south to the Union Pacific Railroad at

Big Springs, Nebraska, and robbed an express car of $60,000 in gold coins.

The outlaws split up, and Collins and fellow gang member Bill Heffridge headed for Kansas. They were spotted as they crossed the Republican River near the Nebraska line, and since trails at that time were sparse, the authorities had a pretty good idea of their course. When word of their whereabouts reached Hays, Kansas, the Ellis County sheriff and ten soldiers from Fort Hays boarded a train heading west. They estimated the route of the outlaws and guessed they would cross the Kansas Pacific Railroad somewhere close to Buffalo Station, Kansas (now called Park), so the sheriff and soldiers chose that town as their base of operations. At the time, Buffalo Station consisted of little more than a depot, a water tank, and a section house, all maintained by a man named Jim Thompson.

Collins and Heffridge rode into Buffalo Station early on the morning of September 25. There was a heavy fog, and they did not see the sheriff and soldiers camped on a small ridge near the section house. Nor did the soldiers see the outlaws. The two men rode up to the station and asked the telegraph operator, Bill Sternberg, about purchasing supplies. They told him they were Texans who had come north with a herd of cattle and were on their way home. Sternberg took them up to the section house.

While the men were paying for their grub, Sternberg noticed an envelope sticking out of Collins's pocket with Collins's name on it. He recognized it as being mentioned in connection with the Big Springs robbery.

By the time Sternberg reached the sheriff on the ridge, the two outlaws had ridden on. The sheriff and several of the troopers caught up with them about a mile south of the station. Seemingly unperturbed, Collins and Heffridge readily agreed to ride back to the station so the sheriff could check out their story. But as soon as it appeared to the outlaws that their pursuers had relaxed, they went for their guns. The troopers, however, were ready for them. The crack of gunfire echoed across the silent prairie, and the two train robbers toppled from their saddles, both dying as they struck the ground. (Source: Gard, *Sam Bass*.) *See also* **Sam Bass; Big Springs, Nebraska.**

COLLIS, CALIFORNIA. *See* **Kerman, California.**

COLORADO SPRINGS, COLORADO. In October 1881 the biggest train robbery in Colorado history occurred a few miles north of Colorado Springs. The northbound express of the Colorado & Southern Railroad had barely gained speed for the long haul up to Denver when it was jolted to a stop by a stack of crossties on the track. Three masked men sprang out of the darkness and ordered the engineer and fireman to raise their hands. With near military precision, the outlaws forced the two trainmen to march back to the express car.

The engineer pleaded with the express messenger to open his door, claiming that a refusal could mean death for them all. Just then the conductor and several curious passengers stepped down from the first coach, but a volley of shots from the robbers sent them scurrying back to safety. The gunfire also won over the messenger, who slid open his door.

The bandits took only a few minutes to blow open the safe and clean out its contents—$105,000 in cash and about $40,000 worth of jewelry and other valuables. After tying the bags of loot to their horses, the robbers rode north into the darkness.

The engineer backed the train into Colorado Springs, and the conductor sent word along the line about the robbery. A posse was quickly formed; after tracking the bandits for several miles they found the gang's horses, which apparently had been replaced by a fresh team. The tracks then led northwest, toward the mountains, where the pursuers soon lost them on the rocky slopes.

The robbers, later determined to be George Tipton, Gene Wright, and Oscar Witherell, rode northwest across the Rockies to the Idaho line near Bear River, then south into Utah. At Corinne, Utah, which today is just west of Interstate 84 about seven miles northwest of Brigham City, the three bandits apparently began attracting attention and decided to leave the trail and hide the stolen loot. It is believed they buried all but a few hundred dollars at a spot on the bank of the Bear River where the river "made a bend against a low timbered hill."

The robbers used the money they didn't bury for a good time in Corinne, then a wide-open town catering to prospectors, stockmen, and soldiers. But before long they encountered trouble. Out of money, Wright and Witherell tried to pawn a watch stolen out of one of the express packages. This roused the suspicion of the local marshal. He challenged them, and a gunfight erupted. Wright was wounded, and in the confusion, Tipton, who had been standing on the sidelines, was hit in the leg by a stray bullet. Wright and Witherell were hustled off to jail, but Tipton was not arrested.

Wright and Witherell were charged with participating in the Colorado robbery and, in hopes of making a deal with the authorities, they admitted that the loot was buried along the Bear River. The deal did not work out, however, and they did not reveal the exact location of the buried money.

Wright and Witherell were sentenced to prison at Cañon City, and Tipton, biding his time, remained in Corinne, probably waiting until things cooled down so he could recover the buried loot. His wound did not heal properly, however, and infection set in. His condition worsened and eventually his leg had to be amputated. Probably suspecting that the authorities were on to him, he left town one night, heading north toward the Idaho line. His stump had now become infected, and he made it only as far as a rancher's cabin just across the line. By then gangrene had set in and two days later he was dead. Before he died, however, he told the rancher, whose name was Lafe Roberts, about the hidden loot. But Roberts, thinking the story was the product of a feverish man's imagination, did not follow up on it. Only years later did he get around to visiting the river bank. When word got around that Roberts might be searching for stolen treasure, Wells, Fargo officials, who had never closed the file on the robbery, questioned the rancher, but apparently got nothing out of him.

It is not believed that Roberts found the loot. As time passed, interest in the treasure lessened, and eventually the story was nearly forgotten. In recent years, however, the Bear River site has been listed in several treasure hunter's books. (Source: Kildare, "Bear River Loot.")

CONKLIN, CALIFORNIA. The date was April 16, 1910. The Southern Pacific's Train No. 10 had pulled out of Benicia, California, on the southeastern edge of San Pablo Bay, at 10:17 P.M., bound for Sacramento, approximately forty-five miles away. Unknown to the locomotive crew, before the train had gathered speed, two masked men had climbed aboard behind the tender and were hugging the coal pile. Just beyond Goodyear Station they climbed down toward the cab and

pointed guns at the engineer, George Marsh, and fireman, Ben Blakely.

One of the intruders shoved Marsh aside and took control of the throttle. Expertly, he eased it forward until the train was traveling nearly seventy miles per hour. Marsh, concerned by the rate of speed, shouted a warning that the locomotive was old, and he was not sure it could stand up under the strain. The bandit, however, paid no attention.

Just before the station at Conklin, near the center of Solano County, the bandit at the throttle yelled for his companion to apply the air brakes. He did, and the train, with its fourteen passenger coaches, ground to a halt. The outlaw at the throttle then turned to Marsh and asked: "Now, which one's the express car?" The engineer replied that there was no express car, that there was only a postal car. After a few curses, the bandit ordered the two trainmen to climb down from the cab and follow him. The second bandit fell in behind.

In the postal car, the mail clerk, H. J. Black, saw the bandits through his window. In an instant he made the decision to stand his ground. The solidly built car should withstand an assault, he thought. But when he reached the door, one of the bandits shouted: "Open that door or we'll kill both the engineer and fireman, and blow the hell out of you and the other passenger cars." Black thought for a minute and then threw open the door and tossed out three sacks of second class mail. The bandit took one look at the bags and yelled: "What the damn hell do you take us for? Throw out that registered mail. That's what we're going to get, or there's gonna be some dead people around here!" Black knew he had played his last card and he and his helper quickly threw out the ten bags of registered mail. The bandit ordered the engineer and fireman to start loading the bags into the locomotive cab. When they had, he told them to cut the engine away from the rest of the train.

After the bags were on board the locomotive, the bandit who had been doing all the talking ordered Marsh and Blakely to jump off and he and his partner climbed into the cab. An instant later, the locomotive was rolling down the track, leaving the engine crew staring after them in the darkness.

One of the train crewmen ran to a nearby farmhouse. The owners had a telephone, and a call was placed to the local sheriff, who in turn wired ahead to Tolenas.

The robbers, however, had abandoned the engine before it reached the town. It was later found smashed into a freight car on a siding.

A search of the track along the way turned up the mail bags. Only one had been opened. Also found were forty-one sticks of dynamite near where the train had been stopped, and a sawed-off shotgun with a belt and twenty shells. And in the locomotive cab, the robbers had left behind a long, black overcoat.

Railroad police and local lawmen covered the surrounding area the next day, working their way south toward Benicia. In questioning local residents, they learned that for several weeks two strangers had been occupying a deserted cabin on what was known as the Frazier Ranch, several miles south of Benicia on the outskirts of the town of Martinez, on the south shore of Suison Bay. Neighbors had become suspicious of the men because all they did all day was row about the Carquines Straits in a skiff. They did not fish, just rowed about. And one of the men, said a local farmer, had been wearing a "long, black overcoat." The skiff was eventually found, and hidden under a floorboard were several sticks of dynamite matching those found along the SP tracks. Also in the skiff, officers found two cards used by the mail clerk to cover several registered letters that had been in the stolen bags.

The trail led no further. A check with officials in Martinez, however, did turn up a report that the shotgun found near the scene had been stolen with a number of other guns in a recent burglary. The Southern Pacific put out a reward of $5,000 for the suspects via circulars containing what information had been collected, including the serial numbers of the gun stolen in the Martinez burglary.

Three months went by with no more leads in the case. Then, on July 15, a Sacramento constable named Michael Judge spotted two men on a hay wagon a few miles south of the city. There was something about them that "aroused his suspicions," Judge later said, and he searched the wagon. On the bottom, underneath the hay, were two guns with serial numbers matching those of the weapons stolen at Martinez.

The two men said they were Joseph C. Brown and Charles B. Dunbar. They denied any knowledge of the Southern Pacific mail car robbery and claimed that a farmer had hired them to drive the hay wagon to a nearby town. Eventually, however, on being told that Marsh, the SP engineer, said that he could identify the bandits if he saw them, the man calling himself Brown suddenly announced that he was "ready to talk."

Brown admitted committing the robbery and said that Dunbar helped him. Dunbar continued to maintain his innocence for several days, but finally he, too, broke down and confessed. They said the robbery was a disaster, that they got only $17.50 from the mail bags before they had to abandon them beside the track.

The two men were tried and convicted and were each given forty-five years in prison. Brown was sent to Folsom Prison and Dunbar to San Quentin. Since no backgrounds could be found on either man, the authorities were sure the names Brown and Dunbar were aliases. Before sentencing, both were asked to reveal their real names, but both refused, claiming that it would embarrass their families. Brown said that he was the son of a prominent state official in Texas, and Dunbar claimed to be a member of an influential family in Connecticut.

On May 11, 1917, Brown escaped from Folsom and was never heard from again. Dunbar was paroled in 1919. (Source: DeNevi, "Train Robbers of Suison Bay.")

CONNERS, JIM. Conners was a member of "Old Bill" Miner's gang. On September 23, 1903, he was shot and killed by an express messenger during an attempted holdup of the Great Northern's Oregon & Washington Train No. 6 just east of Portland, Oregon. The gang blew the door off the express-mail car with dynamite, but the messenger, F. A. Korner, met the bandits at the doorway with his Winchester. One of his first shots struck Conners in the chest, killing him instantly. (Source: Rickards, "Bill Miner—50 Years a Hold-up Man.") See also **Bill Miner; Portland, Oregon.**

COOLIDGE, KANSAS. Although fully aware of the possibility of a robbery at any time, many express messengers, especially those on night runs, considered it a traditional privilege to catch a catnap whenever the opportunity presented itself. On a Santa Fe run through Kansas in 1883, one such messenger, Samuel Patterson, woke up from his nap to find a robber standing over him, ready to put him in a coffin.

Coolidge is in western Kansas, in Hamilton County, about two miles from the Colorado line. On September 29 at around 2:00 A.M., messenger Patterson had

Coolidge depot. *Everett R. Huffer Collection.*

just put off some mail and had stretched out near the depot side of the car on one of his express boxes to catch a few winks. Santa Fe's No. 4 had a twenty-minute layover at Coolidge, just enough time to give the passengers a chance to grab a bite to eat at the station.

Patterson was not alone in the car: the baggage man, Johnston, was seated at the rear door, facing the outside platform. Nor was Patterson totally oblivious to his responsibility to protect his employer's shipments. He had taken his .41 caliber double-action Colt revolver out of its scabbard and placed it by his side, within easy reach.

The twenty minutes had nearly passed when Patterson awoke to the sound of a voice. "Come out of there, you damned sonofabitch!" It was Greeley, the conductor, and he apparently was talking to somebody in the car. Patterson glanced down toward his feet and saw a man standing over him with a pistol. Before he could move, the man fired. The bullet missed, but just barely; Patterson could feel the fire from the muzzle burn his face. The man then whirled and fired out the door toward the conductor.

Afraid that the man would turn back to him, Patterson's first thought was to make him think he had killed him. He lay perfectly still. When the man turned and looked toward the rear of the car, apparently trying to see what had happened to the baggage man, Patterson slipped his hand down toward his own revolver. As the man turned and began to walk away, Patterson grabbed the gun and jumped up. The man heard him and turned and fired, but he missed. Patterson also fired and thought his shot struck home, but the man turned and ran out the rear door. Just as he fired, Patterson saw a second man appear at the side door, but he quickly darted back out of sight.

Thinking that his attackers would return at any moment, Patterson hurriedly began stacking boxes and

crates near the door to provide some protection. Then, about thirty seconds later, he heard several shots from the front of the train. Three minutes after that, conductor Greeley appeared at the door. "Have they gone?" Patterson asked, and Greeley answered that they had.

The conductor went forward and found the engineer and fireman had both been shot. The engineer, John Hilton, was dead from a bullet in the heart, and the fireman, George Fadel, also shot in the breast, was in very bad shape.

Several known outlaws in the area were picked up and questioned about the killing, but all had to be released for lack of evidence. (Sources: *New York Times*, 30 September, 1 October 1883.)

COPLEY, CALIFORNIA. Copley was a tiny station on the Southern Pacific line in Shasta County, northwest of Redding. On March 31, 1904, at around 10:30 in the evening, a Wells, Fargo car was attacked near Copley by three bandits in an attempt to rob the express car. In the process, the messenger was killed.

The killing was senseless and uncalled for. The Southern Pacific engineer, B. F. Joessink, had brought the train to a halt as ordered. But when messenger William J. O'Neill—a veteran of fifteen years of service with Wells, Fargo—opened the door of the express car, one of the bandits, without warning or reason, shot him in the head.

The bandits, who were experienced criminals and should have known better, then committed a second stupid act. In attempting to break into the two safes the car carried, they used a stack of dynamite sticks "the size of a man's derby hat." When the charge went off, it shook the entire train. According to witnesses "the small safe was converted into thin air, and the large one [was] so badly bent and shattered that its contents were rendered worthless to the robbers, even the greenbacks being ripped to shreds." After this blunder, the frustrated outlaws ordered the engineer to proceed south to Keswick, where they left the train at a bridge about 200 yards on the far side of the station.

Witnesses described the man who killed the messenger as "the smallest robber, a quick little man, who made himself remembered for his masterly flow of profanity."

On May 7, Wells, Fargo and Southern Pacific detectives announced that he had the identity of the robbers: George and Vernon Gates of Alameda, California, and James Arnett of Alturas, in Modoc County. The Gates brothers were well known to law enforcement authorities. George had committed his first crime in 1902 when he tried to rob a general store in Jackson, California. It was also believed that he and brother Vernon, and possibly Arnett, participated in an attempted express car robbery near Trinidad, Colorado, in November 1902. Following the Trinidad incident, it was believed the Gates brothers and Arnett robbed several stagecoaches, stores, saloons, and possibly trains, in California, Oregon, and Washington.

Immediately after the Copley robbery, George Gates' trail was picked up in Portland, Oregon, but it also ended there. A general manhunt was launched in northern California and Oregon, but it also was unsuccessful.

Although it is quite possible these three outlaws were responsible for some of the many train robberies that occurred throughout the Far West during the following year, they were not connected to any particular holdup.

According to the files of Pinkerton's National Detective Agency, the end came for George and Vernon in Lordsburg, New Mexico, on March 15, 1905. Surrounded by officers who were attempting to arrest them for a series of local robberies, both brothers committed suicide rather than surrender. (Sources: Pinkerton, *Train Robberies*; *San Francisco Chronicle*, 1 April and 7, 8, 10–12, 19, 31 May 1904.)

CORETTA SIDING, OKLAHOMA. Although many train robberies resulted in death or injury to the participants, and even more often to trainmen or express messengers, the passengers in the coaches and Pullman cars usually were fairly safe. Outlaws who struck trains preferred the treasures the express cars held, and only occasionally invaded the coaches—and when they did, the passengers were seldom harmed. A notable exception occurred in northeastern Oklahoma (then Indian Territory) in 1894.

On October 21 of that year, at about ten o'clock in the evening, robbers struck the Kansas & Arkansas Valley branch of the Missouri Pacific line, about seven miles east of Wagner. (The exact spot where the attack occurred, Coretta Siding, is now near the eastern shore of the Fort Gibson Reservoir.) To stop the train, the MP's No. 223, the bandits threw the switch, sending it onto the siding and into a row of unoccupied cars and coaches.

There were either four or five bandits involved, and they may have suspected a trap, because almost immediately they began shooting at the windows of the coaches. The Missouri Pacific trains in northwestern Indian Territory at the time were all heavily guarded because of numerous robberies. Although details were sketchy, newspaper accounts reported that at least four or five passengers were injured. The man who was most seriously injured was Jack McHara, an advance agent for the McHara minstrel show; he was shot in the forehead.

Because of the gun battle, the robbers could not spend much time in the express car. While no official report on the loss was released by the express company, it was believed that only the local safe was opened and the amount taken was small. (Source: *New York Times*, 22 October 1894.)

COTOPAXI, COLORADO. On the night of August 31, 1891, seven masked men forced a flagman to halt the Denver & Rio Grande's eastbound passenger Train No. 4 near Cotopaxi, Colorado. Cotopaxi is on the Arkansas River, about twenty miles west of the Royal Gorge.

The engineer and fireman were forced to march back to the postal car where the bandits broke through the doors. They did not find anything they wanted in the registered mail, however, and they proceeded on to the combined baggage-express car.

The express messenger, whose name was Angel, suspected a robbery when the train was stopped, and he was waiting for the intruders when they approached his car. He fired several shots through the glass portion of the car door, but was not sure if he hit any of the attackers. Realizing that his condition was hopeless, he finally surrendered.

The robbers took $3,600 from the express company strong box and a gold watch from the fireman, but they did not bother the passenger coaches. When they finished, they rode off on horses that had been tied nearby, heading in the direction of West Mountain Valley.

A local posse took up the chase the following morning. The robbers' trail led south up Sand Gulch to where they mingled their horses with ranch stock to hide their tracks.

When it appeared that local authorities were not making any headway with the investigation, the railroad sent in two Pinkerton agents. One of these was the famous Tom Horn, who had recently joined the agency after a career as an army scout. The other was Doc Shores, a former Gunnison County sheriff with a reputation as a manhunter. After several months of persistent detective work, they arrested Robert "Pegleg" Eldredge and Bert Curtis, members of the notorious McCoy gang. Other arrests followed, including Tom McCoy, Frank Hallock, William Parry, and two brothers named Price.

William Parry confessed and agreed to testify against the others. His testimony established Eldredge and Curtis as the principals in the crime and they were tried separately. In January 1892 both were convicted in the U.S. District Court in Denver and sentenced to Michigan's Detroit House of Correction. Parry was already wanted for breaking out of jail in Cañon City and he was returned to serve out his sentence there. The remaining defendants were tried later and acquitted for lack of evidence. (Sources: Miller, "The McCoy Gang"; *New York Times*, 2 September 1891.)

COUNCIL BLUFFS, IOWA. On October 3, 1900, two men tried to rob an express car on the Chicago, Burlington & Quincy Railroad about three miles south of Council Bluffs. The express messenger, Charles Baxter, killed one of the bandits and chased off the other one. Baxter's courage was no greater than that displayed by many messengers, but it came at a time when railroad and express officials were facing what appeared to be a losing battle against train robbers, and it provided the impetus that the industry, and especially the express messengers, needed to continue to stand up to attacks by these outlaws. *See* **Charles Baxter.**

CROWE, PATRICK. Pat Crowe was a dapper, professional criminal who operated in Colorado, Missouri, and Nebraska. He was connected with several crimes, including kidnapping a millionaire's son in Omaha and committing a large diamond robbery in Denver. And while confined to jail in Milwaukee, Crowe confessed to several train robberies in western Missouri in 1894 — perhaps to avoid extradition to Colorado for the diamond robbery. However, when questioned by the Pinkertons and officials of the Chicago, Burlington

Patrick Crowe. *Pinkertons.*

& Quincy Railroad, his stories did not ring altogether true.

Apparently it was a stalling tactic, because before he could be arraigned on the train robbery charges, he escaped from jail. Later he wrote William Pinkerton that his statements regarding the Missouri robberies were a lie.

Crowe was eventually picked up in Cincinnati and was taken back to Missouri. Again he pleaded guilty and was sentenced to three years in the Missouri State Prison at Jefferson City. On his release he was extradited to Colorado, but managed to avoid a conviction in the Denver diamond robbery.

Crowe later wrote a book about his exploits and claimed that he was going to launch a tour around the country "to atone for all the crimes he ever committed by demonstrating to the young the folly of criminal life." According to the Pinkerton files, however, he may have fallen back into his old ways, because he was later accused of robbery in Council Bluffs, Iowa. (Source: Pinkerton, *Train Robberies*.)

CUMMINGS, JIM. Jim Cummings was the name used by train robber Fred Wittrock in posing as an Adams Express Company employee in order to hold up an express car on the St. Louis & San Francisco Railroad on a run out of St. Louis on October 25, 1886. Wittrock, who used forged papers signed by Adams officials to gain entry to the car, got nearly $90,000 in loot. The "Jim Cummings" case made national headlines for more than two months, mainly because of charges against the Adams Express Company messenger, David S. Fotheringham, who was suspected of being involved in the plot. *See* **Fred Wittrock.**

CURRIE, GEORGE. He was known as "Flat Nose" George Currie (or Curry). A wanted poster tacked up in Butte County, South Dakota, in June 1897 described him this way: "George Currie—about 5 feet 10 inches, weight 175 pounds, age 27 years, light complexion, high cheek bones, flat forehead, flat pug nose, big hands and bones, stoops a little, long light mustache, probably clean shaven."

His nickname, Flat Nose, suited him well. Either by nature or a childhood injury, George Currie's nose resembled that of the classic prizefighter's: nearly boneless, with the upper portion plastered back against his face. Wyoming lawman Joe LeFores once said: "George's nose was so flat between his eyes that standing at his side, one could see his eye lids standing higher than the bridge of his nose."

George Currie was a Canadian by birth. His father was a stern Scottish Presbyterian. Like Butch Cassidy, young George had rebelled against his early religious training and had struck out on his own while still a teenager.

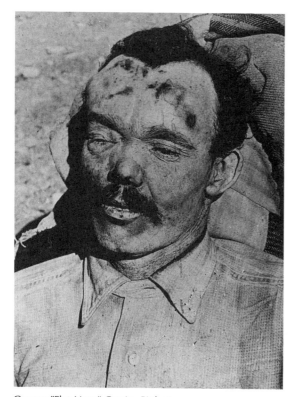

George "Flat Nose" Currie. *Pinkertons.*

Despite his appearance, Currie was a likeable sort. When once asked why he had turned to a life of outlawry, he laughed and replied: "Oh, I don't know, just for the fun of it I guess, just the fun."

Before joining the Wild Bunch and becoming a train robber, Currie had been a charter member of Wyoming's Hole-in-the-Wall crowd of outlaws and perhaps was even in on the discovery of the famous hideout itself. In the 1880s Currie rode with a gang of rustlers led by Sanford "Sang" Thompson, who supposedly was the first to come upon the "Hole," a natural gateway through a red canyon wall on Buffalo Creek near Kaycee, Wyoming, that formed a nearly perfect hideaway.

Currie had once led a gang in himself, but his forte was rustling and he left the more complex jobs of planning and leading train robberies up to those who were better equipped to do so. During his days with the Wild Bunch, he occasionally was confused with Kid Curry (Harvey Logan), which has troubled some outlaw researchers in placing him at the scene of some of the gang's holdups. He is believed to have been in on the Southern Pacific robbery at Humboldt, Nevada, in July 1898 and the Union Pacific robbery at Wilcox, Wyoming, in June 1899.

Soon after the Wilcox robbery Curtis parted company with the Wild Bunch's inner circle. Most of the gang members headed south to New Mexico and Arizona, while Currie remained in Wyoming. Eventually he drifted back into rustling.

On April 17, 1900, a posse out of Vernal, Utah, came across a lone rider camped on the bank of the Green River. The lawmen were out after a local rustler named Tom Dilly and when they saw the man at the river bank they thought he was their outlaw. The posse opened fire, and the man scrambled behind a pile of boulders. Seeing no movement after waiting nearly an hour, the lawmen cautiously approached. They found the man dead, a bullet hole in his forehead, just above his puggish, flat nose.

Currie's body was eventually taken to Chaldron, Nebraska, where it lies today in the town cemetery. Why the outlaw was taken to Chaldron is not known; probably the body was claimed by a relative who was living there at the time. (Sources: Patterson, *Train Robbery*; Pointer, *In Search of Butch Cassidy*.) *See also* **Humboldt, Nevada; Wilcox, Wyoming.**

CURTIS, OKLAHOMA. Curtis is in northwestern Oklahoma, in Woodward County, just east of the panhandle. On September 12, 1895, a westbound Santa Fe express was stopped by a stack of crossties on the rails in a deep cut two and one-half miles out of Curtis. Federal marshals believed the culprits were led by "Red Buck" Waightman, a former member of the Bill Doolin gang of train robbers. Waightman's companions on the raid were thought to be two Texas outlaws, Joe Beckham and Elmer "Kid" Lewis, and possibly a man named Charlie Smith.

The assault, which took place about 3:15 in the afternoon, was not successful. As the engineer slowed the big engine to a halt, the quick-thinking Wells, Fargo express messenger, whose name was Kleaver, locked his safes and hid in the baggage car. The bandits had not brought along explosives and when they could find neither the messenger nor his keys, they took his revolver and some shells and departed, riding northeast toward the Glass Mountains. (Source: Shirley, *West of Hell's Fringe*.)   □

D

THE DALTONS. There were ten Dalton brothers in all, but only four—Grat, Bob, Emmett, and Bill—became outlaws. Perhaps it was in their bloodline. They were the cousins of the Younger brothers who rode with Jesse and Frank James, and as children they boasted of this proudly. And in rural Cass County, Missouri, where the Dalton brothers were born, the name Younger was held in reverence.

In 1883, the year after Jesse James was killed, the Dalton family left Cass County and headed west, eventually settling in Indian Territory. Two of the boys, Frank and Grat, by then in their early twenties and eager for excitement, hired on as special Indian police whose main job it was to keep white squatters off tribal land. Frank excelled at the work and soon earned a commission as a United States Deputy Marshal under Judge

Isaac Parker at Fort Smith, Arkansas. Grat went with him as his posseman-helper. And when Frank was killed in November 1888 by a whiskey runner, Grat moved up to take his job. He, in turn, hired brother Bob, then nineteen, as his aide. But Bob was too independent to remain a deputy's helper and he transferred to the Osage police department, where he soon rose to chief. As chief, one of Bob's first acts was to hire brother Emmett as his sergeant.

To be a good law enforcement officer in Indian Territory required nerve, common sense, and a willingness to work hard for low pay. The Daltons had the first two qualities, but none were willing to live on a peace officer's meager wages. Soon they all were earning more from crooked dealings than they were from their jobs. Finally, in June 1890, they gave up their work as lawmen and went into the stolen horse business.

Their specialty was Indian ponies, which they would steal from the Cherokees and drive up to Kansas and sell. Things went well at first, probably too well, because they became careless. That winter Grat was arrested and thrown into jail at Fort Smith. The evidence against him was strong: he had been caught with two stolen ponies in tow and he had accepted a check in his own name as payment for several other horses. However, the case against him was dismissed. Some say it was because he had built up a few favors at the United States Attorney's office when he was a deputy marshal; others say that he was turned loose with the

Bob Dalton. *Pinkertons.*

Grat Dalton. *Pinkertons.*

tered on the railroads, especially on charges of rate-gouging and questionable land dealings on the part of the Southern Pacific. Politicians were forced to declare which side they were on, and Bill Dalton was clearly antirailroad. In fact, locally he was something of a thorn in the side of the Southern Pacific, and Will Smith, the railroad's craggy Chief of Detectives, made it a practice to keep a wary eye on Bill.

Detective Smith was particularly interested in Bill's house guest, brother Grat, who he had heard was a hell-raiser and was once wanted by the law back in Indian Territory. Grat did not disappoint Smith. Soon after his arrival he began making a name for himself around Fresno as a heavy drinker and gambler—a hard case who just might bash in the head of a loser who does not pay his gambling debts.

Word also reached Smith that two more Dalton brothers had arrived on the scene. Thus, when Southern Pacific's Atlantic Express was held up at Alila, California, on February 6, 1891, Smith came looking for the Daltons. What followed has never been made clear. Grat Dalton was arrested but released for lack of evidence. Bob Dalton and Bill McElhanie, whom the authorities apparently mistook for Emmett, could not be found. Some say they avoided arrest by hiding in Bill's attic. Then, a week later some stirrups were found in an abandoned camp thought to have been occupied by the Alila robbers. These were later identified as having been borrowed by Bill Dalton and used by his brothers. This evidence was quickly taken to the Tulare County grand jury, and an indictment was issued for

hope that he would lead the law officers to the rest of the gang. It probably was the first reason, and quite likely as part of the deal he had agreed to leave the territory, because immediately after his release he headed for California, where his brother Bill had married and settled down in the ranching business.

Brothers Bob and Emmett were also wanted by the law for their involvement in the same transaction. That presented them with three choices: they could turn themselves in and try for a light sentence; they could leave the territory like Grat; or they could become full-fledged outlaws and go for the big dollars. They opted for the third choice and spread the word among close associates that they wanted to form an outfit. Three recruits were soon chosen: George "Bitter Creek" Newcomb, Bill McElhanie, and Charles Bryant.

The new gang got off to a bad start. They rode west, into the Territory of New Mexico, and robbed the operators of a Silver City faro parlor. They came away with a bundle of cash, but also with a band of Mexicans in pursuit. A shootout followed, and Emmett Dalton was wounded in the arm. Perhaps unnerved, the new outlaws decided to split up until things cooled off. Emmett headed east for the hill country, to lie low until his wound healed. Bob Dalton and Bill McElhanie struck out for brother Bill's ranch near Paso Robles, California, where Grat was then staying.

Bill Dalton had married a straightlaced woman who had kept him from joining his wilder brothers on the wrong side of the law. Although probably as adventuresome as the rest of the clan, he had instead channeled his energies toward ranching and politics. He even had an eye on a seat in the state legislature at Sacramento. Political squabbles within the state at the time cen-

Dalton gang following Coffeyville raid. *Dalton Museum, Coffeyville, Kansas.*

all four Dalton brothers. By this time Bob and McEl-hanie were on their way back to Indian Territory, but Grat was rearrested and so was Bill.

The authorities thought they could make a case against Grat, at least as an accessory. Bill was a different story; he had led a respectable life as a rancher and had friends in the area. In an interview with a reporter for the *Fresno Expositor*, he was quoted as saying "The truth is, I am like Paddy Miles' boy—no matter what goes wrong, or what depredation is committed, Bill Dalton is always charged with same."

The cases against both men were weakened somewhat when another robbery of the Southern Pacific occurred on September 3, 1891 at Ceres. At the time, Grat was in jail and Bill was 120 miles away. But James Hume, Chief Special Officer for Wells, Fargo, believed that Emmett and Bob were still around. Shortly after the Ceres holdup, he wrote his wife that "Bill Dalton and Riley Dean [a Dalton acquaintance] are not the men who robbed, or attempted to rob the train on the 3d. Bob and Emmet [sic] Dalton are the fellows."

Bill was eventually cleared of the Alila robbery, but Grat was found guilty. Whether either was actually involved in the robbery has never been settled. Emmett Dalton, years later, denied that any of the Daltons were involved, claiming that the gang's first train robbery took place at Wharton, Oklahoma Territory (now Perry, Oklahoma) in May 1891, shortly after he and Bob returned from California.

Following the Wharton holdup, Emmett, Bob, and their companions in the affair, Bitter Creek Newcomb and Charley Bryant, hid out near Beaver Creek, about ten miles south of town. They had planned to make it only a stopover and were intending to move on early the next day, but they spotted an enticing herd of broncs grazing on a nearby ranch and they decided to cut out the ten best. The owner noticed the loss almost immediately, and the Daltons were slow getting away. A handful of ranchers caught up with them, and in the resulting gunfight, one pursuer was killed and another wounded.

Later that summer, they lost gang member Charley Bryant. For some time Charley had been nursing an advanced case of syphilis. Finally the disease got unbearable and he had to seek treatment. He sought out a doctor in the town of Hennessy, was recognized, and was later killed trying to escape.

Bryant was replaced with a former horse thief, Bill Doolin, and two more members were added to the gang, bringing the total to seven. Their next target was an express car on the Missouri, Kansas & Texas Railroad at Leliaetta, Indian Territory. They had picked up a tip that a large shipment of cash, the proceeds of a large Texas cotton crop, was being sent south. This time the affair went off as planned, and the getaway was clean. A problem occurred later, however, when it came time to divvy up the loot. An argument erupted over shares, and an angry Bob Dalton announced that he was dissolving the gang, that each man could just ride off in his own direction.

The Dalton story might have ended there, but for Grat. Shortly after his conviction in California, he escaped from jail. After hiding out the winter in the hills of Tulare County, he headed back to Oklahoma Territory, set on rejoining the gang and resuming operations. Bill Dalton, too, became fed up with California and returned to Oklahoma. But he still preferred to maintain an honest front and set himself up as a land dealer in Bartlesville, hoping to cash in on the rush to buy up Indian land.

Grat, Bob, and Emmett resumed operations in June 1892. Their target was the Santa Fe night express at Redrock, a little town on the Otoe Indian Reservation. But as the train approached, one of the gang members noticed that there were no lights in the first coach behind the express car. It was too early for the passengers to be asleep, so they let the train pull up, take on water, and depart. They were about to leave when they heard another train coming. As it turned out, the first train had been a decoy, and the second carried the express shipment. They raided the express car, but only got $1,600 because they could not open the through safe.

The Daltons's next victim was another Missouri, Kansas & Texas train, at Adair, Oklahoma Territory. They arrived early and took the station agent by surprise. But just as they were about to make their move on the train, gunfire broke out from a shed near the tracks. Three lawmen and a railroad guard had spotted them. Working their way along the opposite side of the train, three of the gang members forced their way into the express car while the rest peppered the shed with their rifles. The shed was thin-walled and offered little protection. In minutes, all four men inside were hit, one seriously.

Also, several shots went wild and shattered the window of the town drugstore where two doctors were sitting at a table. Both were injured, and one, W. L. Goff, later died.

The killing and wounding of the innocent bystanders, plus the shooting of the lawmen and railroad guard, sent the Dalton gang to the top of the wanted list. Peace officers from miles around vowed to track down these vicious outlaws and put an end to their reign. The gang, however, knew the hill country well, and the men were nowhere to be found.

Fred Dodge, Special Officer for Wells, Fargo & Company suggested forming a special "Dalton posse"—a team devoted solely to killing, capturing, or driving the gang out of business. Dodge sought out the general managers of the four railroads that had fallen victim to the gang: the Southern Pacific, the Rock Island, the Santa Fe, and the Missouri, Kansas & Texas, plus the St. Louis & San Francisco, the tracks of which ran through some of the most vulnerable stretches of Indian and Oklahoma territory. To these were added the other two express companies that operated in the area: the United States Express Company and the Pacific Express Company. The plan was for the companies to foot the bill for outfitting and maintaining a hand-picked posse that would stay in the field until the Dalton problem was solved. To offset their expenses, it was agreed that the backers would share in any rewards that might become payable on the death or arrest and conviction of the outlaws. (This was a novel arrangement, perhaps adopted mainly to pacify stockholders; since the bulk of the rewards out on the gang were offered by the same eight companies, they would merely be getting their own money back.)

For the money they were investing in the crusade, the sponsors naturally wanted the best manhunters available, and Dodge did not disappoint them. His first choice was Heck Thomas, United States Deputy Marshal out of Fort Smith. Thomas had prowled the Oklahoma and Indian territories for years and knew the arroyos and washes nearly as well as the men he would be chasing. Next, Dodge selected his close friend, and one of the best trackers in the Southwest, Burrell Cox. Cox had served Dodge as a posseman on many trips into Indian country, but more importantly, Cox's wife was Creek and had many contacts among her people and neighboring tribes who could deliver up-to-date information on any white man traveling through tribal land.

The remainder of the posse was left pretty much up to Dodge and Thomas, with few questions asked. By agreement, the names of the rest of the possemen would remain unknown to the sponsoring companies. Some would be hired gunfighters with whom the company officials would prefer not to be connected. Others, perhaps, would be outlaws themselves who may have made deals with Thomas to ride after the Daltons in return for favorable treatment by the government for past crimes.

The Dalton posse was to ride in three groups: in front were two scouts, both white men from the territory who, like Cox, had married Indian women and who thus could mix with the locals and gather information. Next came Dodge and Thomas. They were to remain as inconspicuous as possible and be reaady to ride off and wait beside the trail if necessary. Both were well known in the area, especially Thomas, and it would do no good for them to be seen with a posse. Several miles behind rode the main body: a small group of hard-nosed gunmen led by Cox.

The Daltons's ability to avoid capture was due mainly to a network of friends and paid informants. A posse could not ride ten miles into Dalton territory without the alarm being sounded. Back in Fort Smith, however, Judge Isaac Parker, the "Hanging Judge," had an idea on how to neutralize this network. Parker wanted Heck Thomas and Fred Dodge to seek out all suspected Dalton friends in the posse's path and immediately place them under arrest. Following up would be a bevy of United States deputy marshals ready to hustle them back to Fort Smith. Parker's theory was that once word spread of the roundup, the Dalton network would break down.

Using this approach the Dalton posse began cutting a swath across central Oklahoma. They had been out about a month when word reached them that the gang was set to pull another major robbery and then pack up and leave the country for either Mexico or South America. The informant was a reliable one, the brother of one of the posse members. He did not know where the Daltons would strike, but from what few details he had picked up, Dodge and Thomas believed the target would be the Santa Fe again, or perhaps a bank in one of the northeastern towns,

Muskogee or Vinita, or maybe across the Kansas line at Coffeyville.

To be on the safe side, Dodge sent a warning to the Wells, Fargo offices in all three towns. The posse itself would head for the Santa Fe tracks and be ready to go either direction on short notice. As it turned out, the target was Coffeyville.

According to the tip, if the Daltons raided Coffeyville, they might try to hit both of the town's banks: the First National on the east side of Union Street, and the C. M. Condon & Company Bank just across the street on the north side of the plaza. A meeting of town officials was quickly called, and a plan was drawn up whereby the two banks could be defended by volunteers at a few minutes' notice. Arrangements were made to store weapons at the Isham Brothers & Mansour Hardware next door to the First National. From the front of the hardware store, one could also command a good view of the Condon & Company Bank. Guns also were made available at Coffeyville's other hardware store, A. P. Boswell & Company, across the plaza.

The Dalton gang rode into Coffeyville on the morning of October 5, 1892. Although they wore an assortment of fake whiskers and mustaches, several townspeople recognized them immediately. Word spread quickly, and the minute Bob and Emmett Dalton entered the lobby of the First National, a dozen townsmen headed for the arsenals at the hardware stores.

Over at the Condon & Company Bank the scene was much the same. Grat Dalton and gang members Bill Powers and Dick Broadwell ordered the bank's co-owner, C. T. Carpenter, and cashier Charles M. Ball, to fill their grain sacks with cash. Ball tried to stall for time by telling the outlaws that the time lock on the vault would not open for another ten minutes.

At the First National, Bob and Emmett had their money and were heading out the front door when two shots rang out from Rammel Brothers' Drug Store immediately north of the bank. Wisely, they hurried back inside. The bank had a rear entrance and they rushed toward it. Outside, only one townsman had been assigned to guard it, Lucious Baldwin, a clerk at the Read Brothers' General Store. Before he could take aim, one of the Daltons put a bullet in his left breast, and the two outlaws ran through the alley to Eighth Street, the first street north. They turned west, toward Union Street, which ran along the east side of the plaza.

As Bob and Emmett crossed Union Street they spotted George B. Cubine standing in the doorway of Rammel Brothers. Although nearly forty yards away, the outlaws hit him with three bullets. Fellow townsman Charles Brown ran to his body, picked up his rifle, and turned toward the robbers, now almost across Union Street. Four more shots rang out and Brown fell to the sidewalk. An instant later, Tom Ayres, the cashier at the First National, leaned out of the doorway of Isham's Hardware and took a bullet below the left eye.

Meanwhile, across Union Street on the north end of the plaza, Grat Dalton, Bill Powers, and Dick Broadwell were fighting for their lives. At least a dozen guns were blasting away at the plate glass windows and two sets of double doors. Most of the firing was coming from Isham's store, where Henry Isham, a carpenter named Anderson, and a third man, Charles Smith, manned shiny new Winchesters. A fourth man, hardware clerk Lewis Dietz, was keeping the barrel of a six-gun hot. All four men had unobstructed views of the route the three outlaws would have to take if they tried to reach their horses, which were tied up more than a block to the west, in what has now been labeled Death Alley. Also, probably another half-dozen townsmen were positioned in various doorways on the south and west sides of the plaza, all with guns trained on the Condon & Company Bank's front doors.

It was a shooting gallery. With guns blazing, the three robbers kicked open the door on the southwest side of the building and ran out into Walnut Street, which bordered the plaza to the west. Grat Dalton and Bill Powers were hit before they went twenty yards. Witnesses said they could see dust flying from their clothes as the bullets struck. But somehow they kept running. Grat found cover under a wagon about a third of a block down the alley. Powers tried to duck into a doorway but found the door locked. He then raced back into the alley, took another bullet in the back, and fell dead. Grat ran from his hiding place to the rear of a barn that jutted out into the alley, which for the moment provided him with cover from the deadly fire coming from the east. Broadwell had been hit but was still on his feet, running zigzag toward the horses. He found his horse, climbed on, and spurred the animal west toward Maple Street. When he reached Maple, he turned north, which would put him out of range of the blazing rifles, but as he did, he took two more hits.

City Marshal Charles Connelly had worked his way north from Ninth Street through a vacant lot to the alley. Thinking Grat Dalton was west of him, he stepped out into the alley with his gun ready and turned left. Grat, only a few yards away to his right, had only to raise his rifle hip-high to put a bullet in Connelly's back.

Meanwhile, Bob and Emmett had reached the alley from the north and emerged from a driveway near the middle of the block, across from the rear of Slosson's Drug Store. Bob spotted F. D. Benson at the window of the store and took aim. But as he fired, Bob stepped out into the alley, and a rifle bullet sent him staggering across the alley into a pile of curbstones near the building that was serving as the town jail. As he struggled to reach his feet, he saw John Kloehr, owner of the livery, inside the fence near Slosson's store. He fired at Kloehr, but missed. Kloehr stepped back, but did not run. Bob then made it to his feet and hugged the rear of the barn to the west of the jail, trying to clear his head. Kloehr moved in and put a bullet into the outlaw's chest.

Down the alley to the west, Grat Dalton, bleeding and limping, had almost reached his horse. But Kloehr spotted him, took careful aim, and shot him in the throat, breaking his neck.

Somehow, Emmett Dalton, as yet uninjured, had worked his way along the north edge of the alley and was almost across from where the horses were tied. But as he tried to cross, he was hit in the left hip and the right arm. Even then, he managed to mount, and for an instant it appeared that he might escape, but as he spurred his horse, townsman Carey Seamen emptied both barrels of his shotgun into Emmett's back.

Of the five gang members who rode into Coffeyville that day, only Emmett Dalton survived. After serving time in prison, he headed west to Los Angeles where he tried to capitalize on his reputation in the motion picture industry. He set up his own production company, Southern Feature Film Corporation, but the company produced only one film, *Beyond the Law*, which retold the story of the Dalton gang. Emmett wrote the script and played the lead. The film was amateurish, even for its day, and Emmett was no actor. He toured with the picture, giving a "law and order" sermon with each showing. The picture did not do well, and the company folded. Emmett then tried the construction business, and thanks to the building boom in the Los

Angeles area, he was moderately successful. Occasionally he would return to the studios where he would pick up a writing assignment or a small part. He died peacefully on July 13, 1937. (Sources: Dillon, *Wells, Fargo Detective*; Lake, *Under Cover for Wells, Fargo*; Preece, *The Dalton Gang*; Steele, "The Dalton Family Found in California.") *See also* **Adair, Oklahoma; Leliaetta, Oklahoma; Perry, Oklahoma; Redrock, Oklahoma**.

DANVILLE, ILLINOIS. Rare double-header train robberies occurred at Danville early on the morning of November 3, 1883. As a westbound Indianapolis, Bloomington & Western passenger train was nearing town, four men who had boarded somewhere in Indiana entered one of the passenger coaches and, with drawn revolvers, ordered the passengers to hand over their money and valuables. According to an inventory taken by the conductor after the robbers departed, they obtained about $1,200 in cash and a negotiable check in the amount of $1,700.

The robbers leaped off the train when it arrived at the Danville station, but instead of fleeing into the city, they immediately boarded an eastbound Wabash, St. Louis & Pacific train and shortly thereafter robbed the passengers in a day coach on that line, this time collecting around $800.

The four robbers, none of whom attempted to hide their faces, were described by witnesses as large men and extremely well-dressed. (Source: *New York Times*, 4 November 1893.)

DAVENPORT, IOWA. Railroad officials called this robbery "the straw that broke the camel's back."

The date was November 21, 1902. The robbers struck just after 11:30 P.M., about three miles west of Davenport, just past the village of Rockingham on the outskirts of the Chicago, Rock Island & Pacific Railroad yards. (In some reports this holdup is known as the Rockingham robbery.) The victim was a westbound Rock Island passenger train.

The engineer spotted a red lantern on the track and eased to a stop. Immediately the train was surrounded by a gang of bandits, perhaps as many as twelve to fifteen. The train was separated behind the express car, and the engineer was ordered to pull ahead to a "heavily timbered" area two miles west of Rockingham. After smashing their way into the United States Express

Company car, the outlaws blew open the safe with dynamite. They made their escape by uncoupling the locomotive and riding it westward along the northern edge of the Mississippi River to a small station called Buffalo where they disappeared.

No trainmen or passengers were injured in this holdup, and it was estimated that the amount stolen was less than $1,000, but this robbery was the latest of a recent rash of holdups occurring in the four-state area of Illinois, Iowa, Missouri, and Nebraska. Angry railroad and express company officials announced that they had "had enough." Despite the small loss, the Rock Island line and the United States Express Company announced a joint reward of $5,000 for information leading to the arrest and conviction of the Davenport robbers. In addition, the Chicago, Burlington & Quincy Railroad, which also had recently fallen victim to bandits, made it known that it wanted to see "some dead train robbers." On November 24, Burlington general manager F. A. Delano issued the following statement to the newspapers: "We have given all our trainmen to understand that a dead train robber is worth $1,000 to any of them. All of our conductors and trainmen carry revolvers, and we are encouraging them to do so, and to learn to shoot straight. I am in favor of a concerted action on the part of the railway managements and express companies which shall have for its object the hounding of train robbers to the ends of the earth."

Officials of the Chicago, Milwaukee & St. Paul, the Illinois Central, and the Chicago & Alton railroads immediately endorsed the Burlington statement and declared that they would bear their share of "any burden brought about by the concerted movement to eradicate this evil."

Just how much effect this strong action had upon the problem is not known, but during the next twelve months the rate of train robberies nationwide decreased by nearly two-thirds. (Sources: *New York Times*, 23, 24 November 1902.)

THE DeAUTREMONT BROTHERS. On October 11, 1923, three brothers—Roy, Ray, and Hugh DeAutremont—attempted to rob the mail car on a Southern Pacific train at Siskiyou Station, Oregon. The attempt failed, but the would-be robbers killed the engineer, fireman, and a brakeman. The brothers were identified by scientific analysis of articles left at the scene and eventually arrested. *See* **Siskiyou Station, Oregon.**

DESLYS, JEAN. Jean Deslys, alias Jimmy Barry, was a small-time forger. He and Jean LaBanta, a more experienced train robber, robbed a mail car on the Southern Pacific line on January 10, 1914, as it was leaving the San Jose rail yards. Deslys was arrested soon after, apparently from an anonymous tip. He pleaded guilty and was sentenced to five years at San Quentin Penitentiary. (Source: DeNevi, *Western Train Robberies*.) *See* **Jean LaBanta.**

DIABLO CANYON STATION, ARIZONA. Diablo Canyon had once been a thriving end-of-track town, but by the late 1800s it was reduced to a lonely station, a warehouse, several loading pens, and a trading post. On March 21, 1889, it was the scene of one of Arizona's most interesting train robberies—carried out by four bored cowboys who had never before committed a crime.

The four cowboys were John H. Smith, John "Long John" Halford, Daniel M. Havrick, and William D. Starin. They had decided to rob the train without any planning and they had no idea how much, if any, treasure was on board.

When the Atlantic & Pacific's eastbound No. 2 stopped to pick up wood at Diablo, the four cowboys moved quietly out of the shadows. The engine crew's first warning came when the fireman, who was lean-

Diablo Canyon Posse. Buckey O'Neill is second from right. *Sharlot Hall Museum.*

ing over to check something under the locomotive's giant boiler, felt a hand on his shoulder. Thirty seconds later the fireman and the engineer were being marched back to the express car.

At the express car, the cowboys found the messenger unusually cooperative, almost jovial. Expecting a trap, John Smith cautiously entered the car, but no one else was inside. About that time a handful of curious passengers came walking forward, led by the conductor carrying a lantern. A few shots over their heads sent them back to the safety of their coaches.

The jovial messenger now informed the would-be robbers that he could not open the large through safe, that it was time locked. The cowboys seemed to understand this and ordered him to open the local safe instead, which he did. Its contents were quickly emptied into three heavy cotton sacks. After tying the sacks to their horses, the four cowboys rode off toward the south. After riding five miles, they reined up at a grove of cedars and made camp. Once their fire was hot and their beans were boiling, they emptied the sacks and divided their loot. Years later, when Havrick told of that night, he said the haul was around $7,000 in cash and some jewelry. The express company, however, reported a loss of $40,000, but its accounting was vague. According to Havrick, almost all the jewelry was buried, along with the gang's rifles.

Before breaking camp, the cowboys decided to split up and meet later. Havrick and Starin headed for the San Francisco Peaks and the Black Falls of the Little Colorado River. Halford and Smith rode off for the river north of Diablo Canyon, toward Navajo country.

In those days, Diablo Canyon Station was part of Yavapai County, and within the jurisdiction of Sheriff William Owen "Buckey" O'Neill, an ambitious peace officer. With deputies Jim Black and Ed St. Clair, and two railroad detectives, Carl Holton and Fred Fernoff, Sheriff O'Neill picked up Halford's and Smith's trail on the Navajo reservation. Riding at a furious pace, the posse gained a little on the outlaws each day. By the time they crossed into Utah two weeks later, they were finding warm campfires. Also, somewhere in Utah, they discovered that the tracks now showed four riders, suggesting that the two pairs of fugitives had rejoined.

O'Neill and his possemen caught up with the bandits near Wah Weep Canyon, a Mormon settlement near Cannonville. In the resulting gunfight, O'Neill's horse was killed and as it fell, the animal pinned the sheriff to the ground. Holton, however, pried O'Neill loose, and after another five minutes of fighting, the outlaws surrendered. (Sources: Kildare, "Arizona's Great Train Robbery"; Walker, "Buckey O'Neill and the Hold-up at Diablo Canyon.")

DODGE, FRED. Fred Dodge was a Wells, Fargo & Company detective from 1879 to 1895. In his early days with the company he worked as an undercover agent, mostly in and around Tombstone, Arizona. Beginning in 1890, he served as a special officer, mainly in Oklahoma, Texas, and Kansas, and was involved in pursuing the Dalton and Doolin gangs.

Perhaps because of habits picked up during his early years in undercover work, throughout his later career Dodge shunned publicity and was a tight-lipped investigator. Whenever there was a train robbery, newspaper reporters always wanted as many details as possible from Wells, Fargo representatives, but they obtained little from Dodge. As a special officer investigating express car holdups, he prided himself as being "known among reporters from New York to San Francisco as the man who could not be interviewed." In describing Dodge's success in avoiding the limelight, a newspaperman later wrote: "His nature and his job required that he be just off the stage of tumult but never out of action; he was the prompter in the wings, the conductor in the pit, the scrim man high in the flies."

But while Dodge avoided discussing his work as he performed it, he realized the value of preserving a first-hand account of some of the frontier's most exciting days. He quietly kept detailed journals and notes of his investigations, probably with the intention of someday seeing them published. In 1928 Dodge wrote a letter to Stuart Lake, biographer of Wyatt Earp, saying that he was constantly receiving letters from authors who wanted information about his days as a Wells, Fargo detective. He refused to comply because, in his words, he was "quite liable" to use the material for himself.

But as so often happens, Dodge kept putting off doing anything about his files until it was too late. He died in 1938 at age eighty-four without his story seeing print. But by then he and Stuart Lake had become good friends, and Dodge's wife, Jessie, sent Lake all of her husband's material. Lake, however, wanted to tell a more complete story than was contained in Dodge's papers, and much of the material he felt he needed had been destroyed along with other Wells, Fargo records in the San Francisco earthquake and fire of 1906.

Fred Dodge's story was finally published in 1969, by Stuart Lake's daughter, Carolyn, who found Dodge's files in her father's littered office following his death in 1964. (Source: Lake, *Under Cover for Wells, Fargo*.)

DONOVAN, JOHN. John Donovan, an ex-convict who served time in New Mexico and Arizona prisons, was a suspect in the robbery of a Wells, Fargo express car near Maricopa, Arizona Territory, on October 1, 1894. The holdup is considered to be one of the most amateurish jobs in the annals of train robbery. Two of the robbers, Frank Armer and Oscar Armstrong, were captured and convicted. Donovan, who also used the aliases John O'Bryann and John Bryant, was never apprehended. *See* **Maricopa, Arizona.**

DOOLIN, BILL. William "Bill" Doolin was twenty-three when he left his home in Johnson County, Arkansas, and headed west, where it was said there were great opportunities in store for young men bent on adventure.

Bill was a typical Arkansas farm lad: slim and strong, good with a saw and an axe, and an accurate shot with a rifle. Bill's first job was as a helper on a freight outfit running out of Fort Smith. One day on a trip to Caldwell, Kansas, he met a rancher who offered him a job building shacks and corrals on his spread near the Oklahoma line. Bill took the job, and when the work was done there, he moved on to other ranches in the area, taking whatever work was available. Eventually, he became an accomplished cowhand.

Sometime in 1890 or 1891, Bill crossed paths with the Dalton brothers, and evidently through them he developed an itch to try his hand at train robbery. He joined the gang officially in September 1891, in time for the robbery of an express car on the Missouri, Kansas & Texas Railroad at Leliaetta, Indian Territory.

Doolin was well suited for outlawry. Unlike the Dalton brothers, he had no particular grudge against railroads and had no chip on his shoulder. As Oklahoma historian Glenn Shirley observed, Doolin "had no wrongs to avenge [and] no persecutions that drove him into crime." He merely had "tasted the fruits of victory in gunfights and known the excitement and glow that came in train robberies." Bill Doolin stormed express cars for the pure pleasures and treasures they offered.

Doolin soon established himself as a regular with the Dalton gang. Although basically he was a cautious sort, he performed well in tight situations and early on won the respect of his fellow long-riders. After only a few raids, it was obvious to many of the men that Doolin would make a better leader than any of the Daltons, but Bill generally kept in the background. He preferred not to challenge the Daltons's authority, until the day that he decided that Bob Dalton was not sharing the stolen loot honestly.

The rift came shortly before the Daltons's ill-fated raid at Coffeyville, Kansas. Some say that this is why Doolin did not ride along that day. Another version is that he started out on the raid, but that his horse went lame before the gang reached the town. Whichever version is true, Doolin missed the affair, and lived to gather up the pieces.

Doolin showed his cunning immediately after Coffeyville. While the town fathers were still in a daze over the bloody battle, Doolin wrote them a threatening letter in which he vowed on behalf of the remaining members of the Dalton crew to avenge the slain outlaws' deaths. The citizens of Coffeyville were furious and they raced about preparing for another attack. The mayor of the town hurriedly wired for reinforcements, including extra rifles and ammunition. A Missouri, Kansas & Texas railway car, loaded with armed guards, was dispatched to the town. A huge bonfire was built on the town plaza and was kept lighted from evening till dawn to eliminate shadowy corners and alert the citizens of any strangers that might come riding in.

They reacted just as Doolin had hoped. While nearly the entire county braced for another raid on Coffeyville, Doolin and two Dalton gang left-overs, "Bitter Creek" Newcomb and Charlie Pierce, plus a newcomer, Bill Raidler, rode on by the town and attacked an express car eighteen miles south at Caney, Kansas. Smug over their triumph, the four outlaws then rode back north to Spearville, Kansas, annd on October 21, 1892, robbed that town's bank.

With the loot from these two robberies, Doolin and his companions spent the winter lying low. But on June 11, 1893, they saddled up and hit an express car on the Santa Fe a half mile west of Cimarron, Kansas.

At the Cimarron robbery, Bill Doolin ran into trouble

for the first time. The Wells, Fargo safe held $10,000, but Bill could not get into it. He scooped up about $1,000 from the local safe and headed for hill country. Within an hour, however, a posse was on the outlaws' trail. Lawmen and volunteers came from everywhere, and by morning the countryside was dotted with possemen. Doolin and his men were overtaken, and in a running gunfight, Bill was shot in the foot. It was a painful injury, with the bullet entering the heel and tearing along the arch, shattering bone as it went. Although dripping a trail of blood from his wound, somehow Doolin managed to escape and he made his way to Ingalls, Kansas, a little town where two months earlier he had secretly married a local woman named Edith Ellsworth.

Doolin's companions also straggled in, and for a while Ingalls became the gang's safe haven; however, word eventually reached the authorities that the Doolin bunch was hiding out there. Around midnight on August 31, 1893, two white-topped wagons arrived on the outskirts of town. Each appeared to carry only a single driver, but carefully hidden inside were six deputies. A battle soon erupted, but luck was with the outlaws. Doolin escaped as did most of the gang. Three of the deputies were killed.

Flushed with victory at Ingalls, the gang romped unhindered for nearly two years. Bill Doolin became famous, achieving a notoriety matched only by the Daltons. Then, Doolin's luck turned sour. It began on April 3, 1895, on the Rock Island line near Dover, Oklahoma, about ten miles north of Kingfisher. The through safe contained nearly $50,000 – payroll money bound for army troops stationed in Texas – but the express messenger convinced Doolin that the safe had been locked in Kansas City. After failing to drill open the box, the gang stormed through the passenger coaches and then rode off.

By dawn a posse led by famed manhunter U.S. Deputy Marshal Chris Madsen had picked up the outlaws' trail. At noon, Madsen split the posse into two groups. Taking five men, Madsen headed southwest, hoping to cut off Doolin and his gang somewhere near the Cimarron River. The other group, led by Deputy Marshal William Banks, followed the outlaws' tracks as they zigzagged in a westerly direction. Late that afternoon, Banks came upon the gang carelessly napping in a grove of blackjack trees with only one guard posted.

The guard spotted the lawmen as they started to close in. The outlaws carried more Winchesters than their adversaries, but the lawmen were better positioned. During a battle that lasted nearly three-quarters of an hour, more than 200 shots were fired, but only one man was hit: outlaw William "Tulsa Jack" Blake. The fight ended in a standoff, and when night fell, the rest of the gang escaped in the darkness.

Doolin was seldom heard from for the rest of the year. On December 26, 1895, however, the *Perry Democrat* reported that the outlaw had sent word that he wanted to turn himself in. According to U.S. Deputy Marshal Steve Burke, Doolin had said: "If I could give up and know I'd get a light sentence, I'd do it tomorrow. I want to get rid of this business. . . . I've done some meanness, but some other fellows have done much of which I am charged." The story generated excitement but within days it was declared a fake, believed to have been concocted by Burke to gain publicity for himself.

However, through an attorney, Doolin had been in touch with the local U.S. marshal, E. D. Nix, and had offered to surrender if allowed to plead guilty only to a charge of robbery. Nix rejected the offer, according to an article in the *Guthrie Daily Leader*, because Doolin had "laid low" some of his best men, and because the marshal had spent more than $2,000 of his own money trying to apprehend him. Nix, according to the article, proposed to make Bill Doolin "pay the penalty."

It is possible that at the time Doolin's attorney was conveying the outlaw's offer, Marshal Nix had something up his sleeve: a tip that Doolin might be hiding out in one of the hot spring spas in northwestern Arkansas, taking treatments for his rheumatism. In January 1896 a deputy marshal was sent to search all the spas, and, sure enough, Doolin was found lounging in a bathhouse in Eureka Springs. Taken by surprise, he calmly accepted his fate and surrendered without a fuss.

Bill Doolin, train robber and killer, suddenly became a charming and cooperative celebrity. To the newspaper reporters who crowded around his cell in Guthrie, he proclaimed that he was misunderstood, that he was hardly the desperado the authorities claimed him to be, and that he was glad to have the opportunity to prove his innocence. Before long he even took in his captors; pleading that his dark and damp cell was affecting his health, he was given the run of the bullpen during the day. It was, of course, all a ruse. On July 5, 1896, he and fellow prisoners overpowered a guard and escaped.

Bill Doolin was free once more, but not for long. On August 4 deputies captured one of the prisoners who had escaped with Bill. In return for favorable treatment, he revealed that Doolin had told him that as soon as he could pick up his wife and child, who at the time were living with his wife's mother in Lawson, Oklahoma, he was going to flee the territory. The authorities immediately staked out his mother-in-law's home, and on August 25, lawmen were waiting when liverymen arrived with a wagon to load up the outlaw's family's belongings.

The deputies let the men load the wagon, figuring they would follow it to find where Doolin was hiding, but to their surprise, Doolin himself soon appeared. The following account of what happened next was taken from an article in the *Oklahoma State Capital*:

> He [Doolin] came with the rein for his fine riding horse on one arm, and the other holding a Winchester. When he was within reach, the marshals cried out to him to throw up his hands. Instead of doing so he wheeled about and lifted his Winchester. At the same moment the marshals on the other side cried, "Stop, throw up your hands!" He turned in the direction of the last voices and fired his Winchester once, and dropping it, followed up with three shots from his revolver. A volley of Winchesters from the marshals on both sides and the emptying of a double-barreled shotgun razed him to the ground.

The following day Bill Doolin's wife composed a poem about her husband, which she had printed on cards and sold with his picture for twenty-five cents. Included was a note that the proceeds would be used for burial expenses. They did not sell well. When Bill was finally buried, a twisted, rusty buggy axle was driven into the ground for a marker. (Sources: Patterson, *Train Robbery*; Shirley, *West of Hell's Fringe*; *Oklahoma State Capital*, 26 August 1896.) *See also* **Caney, Kansas; Cimarron, Kansas; The Daltons; Dover, Oklahoma; Leliaetta, Oklahoma**.

DOVER, OKLAHOMA. Dover is northwest of Oklahoma City in Kingfisher County, on the old Rock Island tracks between Enid and El Reno. On April 3, 1895, the Rock Island's southbound passenger train No. 1 was taken over by bandits as it neared the water tank at Dover.

It is generally agreed the outlaws were members of the Bill Doolin gang, although Doolin himself was probably not along. Likely present were "Bitter Creek" Newcomb, Charlie Pierce, William "Tulsa Jack" Blake, Bill Raidler, and "Red Buck" Waightman.

The bandits' target was the express car, but here they ran into trouble—a stubborn messenger, J. W. Jones, who refused to open up the door. The attackers riddled the car with bullets, wounding Jones in the wrist and leg, but he still resisted. Finally, when they threatened to kill the entire train crew, Jones gave in.

Once inside the express car, the bandits encountered more bad luck. The mail pouches contained nothing of value, nor did the way safe. The through safe did hold $50,000—a payroll destined for federal troops in Texas—but messenger Jones, still defiant despite his wounds, convinced the outlaws that the safe had been locked in Kansas City and could be opened only by the express agent at Fort Worth.

The bandits had brought along a brace and bit, but they had not anticipated the hardness of the steel, and after struggling for an hour, they abandoned the idea of drilling into the safe. Instead, they headed for the passenger coaches. But here they were still unlucky. Because they had taken so long in the express car, the passengers had plenty of time to hide away their money and valuables. One man slid his expensive gold watch under the stove, and another stuffed a $500 roll of bills into a crack in the seat cushions. All told, the bandits' earnings that night consisted of only about $450 in cash, seven or eight watches, and some miscellaneous jewelry valued at about $1,000.

On leaving, one of the bandits apologized to the passengers for having to take money from them, explaining that "times were hard." (Sources: Shirley, *West of Hell's Fringe*; *New York Times*, 5 April 1895.)

DOWNING, BOB. Bob Downing was a member of a gang led by Burt Alvord, sheriff of Willcox, Arizona, who engineered the robbery of a Wells, Fargo express car of $30,000 near Cochise Junction, Arizona, in September 1899. It was rumored that Downing also once rode with Sam Bass. Downing was arrested for his part in the robbery but was released for lack of evidence and with the hope that he might lead the authorities to the stolen loot, which was never recovered. *See* **Cochise Junction, Arizona**.

DRUMMOND, MONTANA. Dan O'Neill had been with the Northern Pacific Railroad longer than any other engineer. He had a comfortable house in Missoula, a loving wife, and five children; no one expected him to risk his life to prevent one of his trains from being taken over by a gang of outlaws.

It was October 23, 1902, a Thursday night, and O'Neill's eastbound Northern Pacific passenger train had cleared Missoula shortly after 10:30 P.M. He was pulling a long train: mail, baggage, and express cars, and nine coaches.

No Northern Pacific engineer was without an occasional thought about what he would do if ever confronted by train robbers. The Northern Pacific had been hit only a few times. The Great Northern, Montana's other major railroad, had been less fortunate; only the previous year it had fallen victim to the Wild Bunch at Wagner, Montana. But neither road was taking the beating the southern lines were taking, especially the Southern Pacific, which by then had been struck by robbers more than thirty times.

Maybe O'Neill was thinking about this when, at around midnight, he saw a red lantern being waved ahead on the track. The train at that point was two miles west of Drummond, Montana, which was a little more than midway between Missoula and Deer Lodge. Whatever O'Neill's suspicions were, he had no choice but to obey the signal. He eased off the throttle and prepared to stop.

Just then he turned, probably to say something to his fireman, and he saw a man behind him on the tender. The smart thing to do would have been to stop, but he didn't. Instead, he pulled open the throttle and gave the big engine all it would take. It was the last conscious act of Dan O'Neill's life. The man on the tender fired, and Dan fell dead on the floor of the cab.

The train eased to a stop, and the bandit ordered the fireman to take the throttle and pull ahead to a point two miles on the other side of Drummond. On the way, he boasted that this was not his first holdup, that the previous year he had taken part in the robbery of a Southern Pacific train in Oregon.

Witnesses believed that there were at least eight bandits in all. In short order they rifled both the express and mail cars, collecting an undetermined amount of cash and valuables. A posse was immediately dispatched from Deer Lodge, but the only clue found was a mask worn by one of the robbers; it was found on a mountain trail about two miles from the scene. (Source: *New York Times*, 25 October 1902.)

DUCK HILL, MISSISSIPPI. On December 15, 1888, Rube Burrow and a confederate, Leonard C. Brock, who at times was also known by the aliases Lew Waldrip and Joe Jackson, robbed a Southern Express Company car on a northbound Illinois Central express headed for Chicago.

Just after 10:00 P.M., Burrow and Brock climbed aboard behind the tender as the train was leaving the station at Duck Hill. They scrambled over the tender and pointed guns at the engineer and fireman. About a mile north of town the engineer was ordered to apply the brakes. The engineer and fireman were marched back to the express car and the messenger was told to open up. He offered no resistance, and Burrow emptied the safe of about $2,000 in cash, which he dumped into a grain sack.

This was the sixth train robbery for Rube Burrow. In each holdup, the victims had cooperated without putting up a fight. This night it would be different. As Burrow was filling his sack with the stolen loot, the train conductor, who had guessed what was happening, enlisted the help of a passenger, Chester Hughes of Jackson, Tennessee, and with borrowed Winchesters the two men climbed to the roof of the first coach. In the darkness, they could only see shadows beside the express car, but they opened fire anyway. Brock saw the flash of their rifles and returned their fire. Burrow, still inside the express car, heard the shots and raced to the door. From his higher elevation, he had a clearer shot and put three bullets into the courageous Hughes. The conductor, seeing the passenger was badly wounded, laid his rifle down to help him. Burrow and Brock took this opportunity to make their escape. (Sources: Agee, "Rube Burrow"; Breihan, *Rube Burrow*.) *See also* **Leonard C. Brock; Rube Burrow**.

DUNBAR, CHARLES B. A young man calling himself Charles B. Dunbar was convicted of robbing a postal car on the Southern Pacific Railroad near Conklin, California, on April 16, 1910. Dunbar, who never revealed his real name to avoid embarrassment to his family, claimed to be a member of an influential Connecticut family. He was sentenced to forty-five years in San Quentin Penitentiary and served until 1919, at which time he was paroled. *See* **Conklin, California**.

DUNN, WILLIAM "SHORTY." Shorty Dunn, who also at times used the aliases John Grell and William Grell, was a confederate of train robber "Old Bill" Miner. Dunn, Miner, and a man named Lewis Colquihoun held up the Canadian Pacific's *Transcontinental Express* on May 9, 1906, at Furrer, British Columbia, about twenty miles east of Kamloops. Mounties tracked the robbers to their camp near Douglas Lake. Dunn tried to make a run for it and was shot in the leg. Dunn and Miner were sentenced to life imprisonment, and Colquihoun to twenty-five years. All three were sent to New Westminister Penitentiary.

According to the files of the Royal North West Mounted Police, before being taken off to prison, the good-natured Dunn thanked the Mounties for the way they had cared for his injured leg, and the treatment he had received generally. He added: "You may think it funny coming from me, but I certainly admire the way you boys do your work."

Always a model prisoner, Dunn's sentence was reduced from life to fifteen years, and in May 1915 he was paroled. An American by birth, he later applied for Canadian citizenship which, despite his conviction for train robbery, was granted. A few years later he drowned during a canoe trip near Tatsa River Forks. (Source: Rickards, "Bill Miner—50 Years a Hold-up Man.") *See also* **Furrer, British Columbia; Bill Miner**.

DUVAL, TEXAS. A robbery in 1893 on a northbound International & Great Northern express train in central Texas could have been called "the case of the forgetful train robbers."

On December 11 of that year, a half-dozen masked bandits sidetracked the train at Duval, which is about seven miles north of Austin, and immediately began shooting off their six-guns, apparently to intimidate the passengers. After ransacking the express car, from which they took one package containing $600, the gang entered the coaches to see what they could pick up there.

Three robbers entered the first coach; one of them was carrying the package taken from the express car. The robber carrying the package also carried a large cloth sack, which he intended to use to collect the money and valuables from the passengers. As he unfolded the sack, he laid the express package down on a seat, and the other two bandits went to each end of the car to stand guard. By the time the bandit passing the sack had reached the opposite end of the car, the passengers had become unruly. This seemed to unnerve the bandit, and when he took the money from the last passenger, he hurriedly slipped out the door and jumped to the ground. The other two bandits quickly followed. None of them remembered to pick up the package containing $600 on the seat in the coach. (Source: *New York Times*, 12 December 1893.) □

E

EAGLE FORD, TEXAS. The robbery of an express car on the Texas & Pacific Railroad at Eagle Ford on April 4, 1878, was the third in a series of train holdups by Sam Bass and his gang following Bass's return to Texas the previous winter.

The Eagle Ford robbery, which occurred about six miles west of downtown Dallas, was unspectacular and gained the outlaw band little in the way of loot. The two earlier Bass gang express car robberies in the Dallas-Fort Worth area (*see* **Allen, Texas**, and **Hutchins,** **Texas**) had put the Texas & Pacific Railroad and the Texas Express Company on guard. When possible, valuable money shipments assigned to the express company were being sent by special messengers who rode inconspicuously among the passengers in the day coaches. Bass apparently had not caught on to this and did not disturb the passenger coaches.

Even though the Texas Express Company was using this device to protect its money shipments, it still expected its messengers and express car guards to put up a fight when assaulted by train robbers, and when it was discovered that the messenger and guard at Eagle Ford did not resist the Bass gang's attack with the fervor the company expected, it promptly fired them. (Source: Gard, *Sam Bass*.) *See also* **Sam Bass**.

EARLIMART, CALIFORNIA. The town of Earlimart, formerly called Alila, is located on the Southern Pacific tracks about forty miles north of Bakersfield. On the night of February 6, 1891, two men slipped aboard the blind baggage of a train as it was pulling away from the Alila station. After about a mile, they drew their guns and ordered the engineer to halt.

When the bandits beat on the door of the express car, the Wells, Fargo messenger, C. C. Haswell, refused to open up, and the attackers fired into the car through the slats in the door. Haswell, although nearly blinded by blood streaming down his face from a scalp wound, returned their fire repeatedly. During the attack, the fireman, whose name was Radcliff, was shot in the stomach.

Haswell continued to fight, and the attackers realized they were running out of time. They finally gave up and fled.

The messenger expected to be proclaimed a hero for his stubborn defense, but instead the local authorities sought to bring charges against him for shooting the fireman. Although the case was obviously weak, Haswell was indicted by a Tulare County grand jury, possibly because at the time there was much hatred for the Southern Pacific Railroad on the part of local citizens because of high freight rates and disputed land rights.

To nearly everyone's surprise, the case went to trial. In his defense, Haswell argued that there were in fact three robbers instead of two, and the third man, who the messenger said was stationed on the opposite side of the express car, must have shot Radcliff. Haswell's attorney found several witnesses to support this claim. He also introduced medical evidence that the bullet that hit Radcliff was ranging "slightly upward," and thus could not have come from the gun of the messenger, who was firing down through the grating in the lower part of the express car door. Despite a clearly unfavorable jury, Haswell was acquitted. (Source: Glasscock, *Bandits and the Southern Pacific*.)

EDMOND, OKLAHOMA. Edmond is just north of Oklahoma City. An unsuccessful attempt to rob a southbound Santa Fe express near Edmond on August 16, 1897, was probably the work of the Jennings gang.

Al Jennings and his brother, Frank, were both lawyers who turned to crime, mainly train robbery, in the 1890s. At the time of the Edmond robbery, they were relatively new at the art, but "Dynamite Dick" Clifton and "Little Dick" West were thought to be along, and they had ridden with the Bill Doolin gang in 1894 and 1895. Also, the fifth and sixth members of the gang that night were probably the O'Malley brothers, Pat and Morris, described as two "wild Irish boys" always looking for a fight.

Several versions of the holdup have been told. According to the conductor, whose name was Beers, three men got on board as passengers at Ponca City. They rode as far as Edmond, perhaps to see if there were any federal marshals on the train. They got off at Edmond, but as the train was pulling away from the station, they apparently slipped back on, probably hiding in the blind baggage area between the rear of the tender and the front of the express car.

After working their way forward over the wood pile, the bandits put guns in the backs of the locomotive crew and ordered the engineer to stop the train about three miles south of town. There three more outlaws were waiting in the tall brush beside the tracks. After firing several shots alongside the coaches to frighten the passengers into staying put, the bandits forced their way into the Wells, Fargo express car, which was occupied by messenger W. H. May. Once inside the car, however, the bandits could not get the safe open, even after two attempts to blast it open with dynamite. Disgusted, the gang jumped off the train and ordered the engineer to return to the locomotive and proceed on his way. (Source: Shirley, *West of Hell's Fringe*.) *See also* **"Dynamite Dick" Clifton; Al Jennings; "Little Dick" West**.

ELBURN, ILLINOIS. By 1899 congested areas such as Chicago sprouted tentacles of railroad tracks. To handle increasing traffic, the major roads constructed switch towers from which yard masters and tower operators could control the routing of trains over divided tracks, sidings, and junctions with other lines.

On the evening of October 14, 1899, the operator of the Chicago & Northwestern Railroad's Tower W at

Elburn, Illinois, about forty-five miles west of downtown Chicago, was routinely performing his duties when four men entered the tower and asked him the number of the next train going west. He started to tell them when they pulled revolvers out of their coats and told him that if he made a move they would kill him on the spot. In minutes, they had him bound, gagged, and secured to the floor of the tower.

The Northwestern's westbound No. 9 was the Chicago-to-Council Bluffs leg of the transcontinental Fast Mail, and because it had to average a mile a minute on its run, it had priority through the entire state of Illinois. It had left the Chicago depot on time and was running on schedule through the small towns that bordered Chicago's western edge. But as it approached Tower W at Elburn, the engineer, whose name was White, noticed that the tower was not giving him a go-ahead signal. Fearing a stalled train on the mainline, White slowed, hoping the signal would change, but when it didn't, he closed the throttle, applied the brakes, and brought the train to a standstill. Suddenly, two masked men jumped up on the steps of the cab and ordered White and his fireman to throw up their hands.

While the train was stopped, four more bandits boarded near the rear and overpowered the conductor. They also tried to take one of the brakemen captive, but he jumped off the train and disappeared in the darkness.

Engineer White was ordered to pull forward two miles. He did as he was told, and when the train stopped again, the bandits in the rear ascended the American Express Company car. The bandits ordered the express messenger, Frank Hobson, to admit them

Chicago & Northwestern depot at Elburn. *Everett R. Huffer Collection.*

to his car. He hesitated at first, but after several shots whizzed past his ear, he changed his mind and opened up. Hobson was ordered to open both safes, but he replied that he carried keys only to the small local safe. The bandits seemed to anticipate this. They immediately withdrew dynamite from their pockets and began packing it around the door of the through safe. The charge blew the door off, and the robbers helped themselves to the contents, around $25,000 in cash and some jewelry.

Meanwhile, the brakeman had raced back along the track to Geneva and had wired the Northwestern officials that a robbery was in progress. A wire was dispatched to the conductor of eastbound freight No. 118, which was then about four miles east of Elburn, to stop and back up to Tower W.

The crew of No. 118 arrived at the tower and found the operator still bound and gagged. When he told them what had happened, they climbed back on board and headed west. When they reached No. 9, they found the conductor, engineer, fireman, and messenger all securely tied up in the express car. The robbers had made a clean escape. (Source: *New York Times*, 15 October 1899.)

ELKHART, INDIANA. Robbers seldom tried to assault a train unarmed, but in northern Indiana, in a bizarre incident on the Lake Shore & Michigan Southern Railroad in 1893, eight unarmed men tried to commandeer a Lake Shore freight train and use it to wreck a Chicago-to-New York fast express so they could rob it.

The first section of Lake Shore's freight No. 60 pulled out of Elkhart at 10:23 P.M. with orders for a run via Goshen to Ligonier, a distance of just less than twenty-five miles. About a mile out, the conductor, John Hickok, and his two brakemen were suddenly pounced upon by eight men.

Railroad brakemen in those days were made of fairly stern stuff. Besides handling the duties of a dangerous job, they were expected, when necessary, to be able to quickly rid a freight car of up to a half-dozen tramps without calling for the engineer to "slow her down." Thus, the eight men who chose to try to take over No. 60 that night found they had their work cut out for them.

At first the fight went in favor of the intruders, and they managed to get the train stopped, their purpose being to block the track in order to derail the incoming express. But when the engineer and fireman discovered what was happening, they ran back and joined the fray, which evened the odds considerably.

The train crew won the first bout, and the would-be bandits, apparently thoroughly thrashed, were deposited in a car for safekeeping. The engineer and fireman returned to the cab, and the train got under way. But five miles out of Goshen, the attackers once again jumped the conductor and brakemen, and the battle was on again.

As the train pulled into Goshen, the fists were still flying, and the engineer gave a signal to railroaders at the yard that there was trouble on board. Not knowing exactly what kind of trouble had occurred, the reception committee at the yard was slow to act, and six of the eight attackers fought their way out of the car and escaped. Two, however, were captured a short time later.

The express targeted for robbery was Lake Shore's No. 12, the same train that was robbed at Kessler just two months before. Lake Shore officials estimated that if the gang had been able to carry out their plan, which was to send No. 12 crashing into the stalled freight cars, it could have resulted in the loss of many lives. (Source: *New York Times*, 27 November 1893.)

ELLIS JUNCTION, WISCONSIN. Passengers on a Milwaukee & Northern Railroad train were robbed near Ellis Junction, Wisconsin, in May 1889 by a lone bandit whom newspapers called "Black Bart of Wisconsin." The robber, who was later connected to numerous holdups in Wisconsin and neighboring states, was eventually captured in August 1889 at Republic, Michigan. He was identified as Reimund Holzhay of Pulsifer, Wisconsin, who, the authorities claimed, "took to the life of a robber as the result of reading dime novels." *See* **Reimund Holzhay.**

ESCAMBIA RIVER BRIDGE (FLORIDA). The Louisville & Nashville trestle over the Escambia River, just below the Alabama line in northwestern Florida, was the site of the last express car holdup by Rube Burrow, the "King of the Train Robbers." Burrow, out of friends and running from the law, committed the robbery single-handedly, a feat seldom attempted by even the boldest train robbers.

On September 1, 1890, around 10:00 in the evening, Burrow, dressed as a railroad worker, climbed aboard the locomotive of an L&N southbound as it was leaving Flomaton, Alabama, a few miles above the Florida line. The engineer and fireman, busy getting under way, did not notice him until he shoved his two pistols into their ribs. His orders were explicit. "Pull ahead and don't stop the train with the express car on solid ground or I'll blow you to hell." The engineer did as ordered.

When the train halted, Burrow ordered the engineer and fireman to climb down to the ground. The fireman, terrified by the thought of dying from a bandit's guns, dashed for a wooded area near the track. Burrow now had only the engineer to deal with. A veteran of six successful train robberies, Rube knew his next move was vital: he must keep the rest of the train crew and the passengers in the coaches. Quickly, he fired nine shots back along the side of the cars—five on one side and four on the other—to give the impression that the train was being assaulted by a gang and not just a lone bandit.

Meeting little resistance from the Southern Express Company messenger, Burrow ordered him to open the safe and dump the contents into a sack. The take was paltry, a mere $256.19. Burrow accused the messenger of hiding the rest of the money, but the messenger swore that it was all he carried. Convinced, Burrow leaped from the car and disappeared into the night. (Sources: Breihan, *Rube Burrow*; Larck, "The One-Man Holdup.") *See also* **Rube Burrow.**

EVANS AND SONTAG. The names of Chris Evans and John Sontag (also known as John Contant) began appearing in California newspapers during the investigation of the robbery of a Wells, Fargo express car on August 3, 1892, at Collis, California.

Chris Evans's background was never clear. At times he gave both Vermont and Canada as his place of birth. He claimed to have served in the Civil War in what must have been some very interesting battles (he claimed to have fought not only "the Confederates" but also the "Sioux and Cheyennes," yet no service records were ever found for him nor did he ever apply for a pension). He also said that he had worked for the Union Pacific Railroad during its expansion westward and, later, for the Central Pacific out of Stockton. Some writers have said that Evans settled on unoccupied

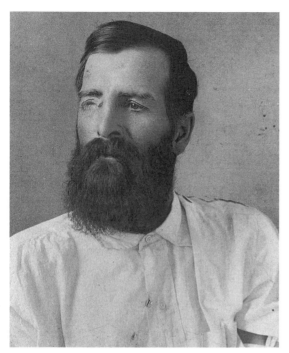

Chris Evans, following his capture. *Wells Fargo Bank History Room, San Francisco.*

railroad land in Tulare County and was thus involved in the later broken promises and "price gouging" by the Southern Pacific Railroad, but this has been disputed. Others have said that he did have a hatred of the Southern Pacific, but that probably it was the result of the railroad overcharging him for shipping farm products to market.

John Sontag was from Minnesota and had worked for the Southern Pacific as a brakeman. In 1887 he was injured while coupling cars and suffered a wrenched back, broken rib, and possibly a broken ankle. Ap-

John Sontag. *Pinkertons.*

parently he got into an argument concerning his treatment by company doctors and later disputed their evaluation of his fitness to return to his former duties. He was not rehired.

At the time of the investigation of the Collis robbery, Sontag, still unemployed, was staying at the Evans household, as was Sontag's brother, George, who had arrived from Minnesota on the train that had been robbed. Apparently George Sontag had been frequenting the saloons of Fresno and Visalia and had been talking a lot about the robbery. When it seemed that he knew too many details, somebody tipped off the authorities. It was discovered that he had a police record back in the Midwest, and that he, his brother, and another man (possibly Evans) were suspects in a train robbery back there. This was enough for the authorities, and on August 5 George Sontag was arrested in a Visalia saloon by Tulare County Deputy Sheriff George Witty and Southern Pacific detective Will Smith.

Later in the day, Witty and Smith rented a horse-drawn cart and rode out to Evans's home. As they pulled up, they saw a man they believed to be John Sontag enter the house through the back door. They went to the front door, and were greeted by Evans's sixteen-year-old daughter. When she told them John Sontag was not there, Smith called her a "damned little liar," and she yelled for her father.

A moment later Evans and Sontag appeared, and both were armed. Witty and Smith made a hasty retreat, and Evans and Sontag ran after them, firing as they ran. Witty was wounded in the shoulder, and Smith took several shotgun pellets in the back. Neither, however, were seriously injured. Evans and Sontag climbed into the officers' cart and rode off.

There are other versions of the encounter. Evans's daughter later claimed that Witty and Smith fired first, and there are still local residents around Visalia who will tell you that Evans and Sontag were innocent and ran from the lawmen only from fear of rough treatment.

A posse was organized, but no trace was found of the fugitives. The house was staked out by possemen, and that night, shortly after midnight, the two men returned, apparently to get provisions. They were discovered in the barn, and a gunfight erupted. A deputy sheriff, Oscar Beaver, was killed, and Evans and Sontag once again escaped unharmed.

Visalia was only a half-day's ride from the high country, and Chris Evans was a mountain man, so there was little doubt where the two would hide out. A posse was organized the following morning, but they could not pick up a trail. Wells, Fargo announced that a generous reward would be given for the capture of the two men, and posses were sent into the mountains off and on for the next month, but with no success. Southern Pacific and Wells, Fargo detectives from out of state were called in to help in the search, as well as expert Indian trackers from Arizona. Also, freelance manhunters from across the West joined in the quest.

On the morning of September 13 the main posse, which included Southern Pacific detective Will Smith and Tulare County Deputy Sheriff George Witty, came across an isolated shack in the mountainous area of what is now the Sequoia National Forest. To the tired and hungry manhunters, the shack, known locally as Young's cabin, looked like a good place to stop and have breakfast. Although the posse members knew that the two fugitives could be anywhere in the area, they did not dream that with lawmen on their trail they would be so careless as to be hiding out in the cabin. They were wrong.

While the posse tied their horses, two of the members, Southern Pacific detective Vernon Wilson and Stanislaus County Deputy Sheriff Andrew McGinnis, headed for the cabin to check out the fireplace. As they neared the door, Evans and Sontag, hiding inside, opened fire with their rifles. Both men died almost instantly. The rest of the posse, taken off guard, raced for cover. Evans and Sontag ran for a nearby woods, shooting as they went. The luckless Deputy Witty, who had only recently recovered from his earlier wound, was hit again.

A search for the bandits turned up nothing, and after two more months of scouring the mountains, the authorities, faced with early winter weather, gave up the hunt until spring.

The fugitives spent the winter hibernating on deer meat, nuts, and berries in a cozy notch carved out of a cliff above Dry Creek, a few miles southeast of Camp Badger near Eshorn Valley. Detective Will Smith, now clearly obsessed with capturing the two killers, spent the winter spreading the word that come spring, California would see the greatest manhunt in its history.

In the meantime, George Sontag was taken to Fresno County and tried for being a participant in the Collis

George Sontag. *Pinkertons.*

robbery. He was convicted and sentenced to Folsom Prison. The following year he would confess not only to the Collis robbery, but also to earlier holdups on the Southern Pacific at Pixley, Goshen, and Ceres, and name his brother and Evans as his accomplices.

When the spring thaws came, the high country virtually overflowed with bandit chasers. But by now Chris Evans, who had for years prospected in the area, had been in contact with enough mountain friends to develop an efficient early warning network of informers. Although posses scoured the ridges and passes, the renegades were never spotted. So successful were the two fugitives in eluding the hunters, Evans was able to make several trips back to Visalia to visit his wife.

In April 1893 Evans and Sontag ventured out of hiding long enough to stop a stagecoach near Camp Bridger. They forced the passengers to line up for a search, assuring them that if they were all "working men," nothing would happen to them. They were, they said, looking for manhunters, or "blood hunters" as Evans called them. Finding none on board, the renegades left. It was later suggested that they were probably looking for their old nemesis Will Smith who was supposed to have been on board. He was not; he had changed his

Chris Evans's barn. *Southern Pacific Raliroad.*

plans at the last minute. As the fugitives rode off, Sontag was heard to call out that they had "never robbed a person of a cent, and never robbed a train." This remark revived a feeling among many residents in the area that the two men were unjustly accused. This view was later strengthened when the *Fresno Expositor* published a maudlin letter from Evans to his wife lamenting on how lonely she must be, and asking her to "kiss the babies for papa."

The chase finally came to an end during the second week of June 1893, at a site known locally as Stone Corral, a circular hog pen built out of boulders on the lower southeastern slope of Stokes Mountain. In the valley just below the corral was a vacant cabin known as Widow Baker's place. Apparently the renegades had been using the cabin at night.

A posse had arrived in the valley during the day while the outlaws were away. After checking out the cabin, they went inside to rest. When Evans and Sontag returned around dusk, they did not spot the posse's horses, which had been tied on the opposite side of the cabin. It was the reverse of the situation involving the shootout the previous fall. The outlaws calmly came walking up the path leading to the cabin, never suspecting that it was occupied. Had trigger fingers been less itchy, it would have all been over in seconds, but Fred Jackson, a federal officer called in from Nevada, squeezed off a rifle shot while the outlaws were still at least seventy-five yards away. The bullet caught Evans in the left arm, and he and Sontag dashed for the only cover available, a large pile of straw and manure.

The manure pile kept the posse from getting a clear shot, but it offered little protection. More bullets reached their marks. Sontag took a hit in his right arm, rendering it useless. Minutes later another slug ripped into his side. Evans raised up to check his wounded

partner and a bullet creased his back. Sontag, now bleeding badly, pleaded with his comrade to put him out of his misery. Evans declined. Seconds later, Evans took another hit, this time in his right arm, and almost instantly he was hit again by three shotgun pellets in the face, one of which tore his right eye out of its socket. Clearly, the outlaws were finished, but the posse had no way of knowing this, and they kept firing—until it was too dark even to see the manure pile.

At daybreak the lawmen closely watched the pile for movement; they saw none. Considering the number of bullets fired, there was little chance that either man survived. Yet, during the night, they had heard two shots from the pile. They waited almost another hour before they cautiously moved in.

They found one man behind the manure: Sontag, sitting upright and nearly covered with straw and manure. During the night he had tried twice to end his own life, but was too weak to take proper aim. He had merely given himself two more flesh wounds. Evans had escaped.

Despite his loss of blood and severe shock, Chris Evans had managed to crawl six miles to a ranch in Wilcox Canyon, where a family named Perkins took him in and summoned the authorities. Tulare County officials took him to Fresno where his wounds were treated. Slowly, he recovered, but his left hand had to be amputated. Sontag hung on, but developed tetanus, and was soon in agony. Jail officials reported that his jaw locked so tightly that they had to remove one of his teeth to insert a straw to feed him. His mother was summoned from Minnesota to care for him. He lived three weeks.

Evans was convicted of first degree murder for the

Jim Young's cabin. *Southern Pacific Railroad.*

killing of Vernon Wilson. The jury recommended life imprisonment, and he was sent to Folsom.

The story might have ended there, but on December 28, 1893, with the help of a gun smuggled in by a hero-worshiping ex-convict named Ed Morrell, Evans escaped Folsom and once again headed for the mountains. A posse eventually picked up the trail, and on February 5, 1894, Evans and Morrell were found at a ranch about twenty miles east of what is now Dinuba in Tulare County. A shootout followed, but once again Evans and his companion escaped. Their trail was followed to near Camp Badger where they were spotted again and shot at, but not apprehended.

If Evans had headed east, he may have escaped permanently, but once more he headed for his home in Visalia. Morrell, unwisely, went along. The Evans' residence ws still being watched by the local authorities, and on February 19, 1894, Evans was spotted. The house was quickly surrounded and Evans knew he had no chance. He sent a note to Tulare County Sheriff Eugene Kay that he would surrender. He and Morrell came out peaceably and were taken into custody.

On his return to Folsom, Evans became a model prisoner. On April 14, 1911, he was paroled with the understanding that he would settle in Portland, Oregon. He died in 1917 at age seventy.

Both George Sontag and Ed Morrell, who were re-

Bullet-riddled body of John Sontag. *Wells Fargo Bank History Room, San Francisco.*

leased from prison within a week of each other in 1908, later "wrote" books about their experiences. Morrell's, entitled *The Twenty-Fifth Man*, is believed to have been ghosted by Jack London. (Sources: Edwards, "Chris Evans—The Ready Killer"; Glasscock, *Bandits and the Southern Pacific*.) *See also* **Ceres, California; Collis, California; Goshen, California; Pixley, California**.

EVANS, CHRIS. *See* **Evans and Sontag**.

EVANSTON, MISSOURI. The successful use of dynamite in robbing express cars naturally depended upon how much experience the outlaws had with explosives. Former miners were fairly successful. Cowboys-turned-highwaymen had little such experience, however, and were a danger to themselves and their captives.

A holdup on a Chicago & Alton train on October 6, 1897, at Evanston, Missouri (now a Kansas City suburb), could easily have resulted in many deaths. At first it appeared the bandits were a polished, experienced gang. They stopped the train by placing railroad torpedoes on the track, a signal that no engineer could ignore. They took command of the locomotive, separated it and the express car from the passenger coaches, and had the engineer pull forward a safe distance.

All seemed to be going well until the time came to blow the two safes carried in the express car. As the astonished express company messenger and engine crew watched, the bandits placed *twenty-four* sticks of dynamite on top of the large through safe and then lifted up the smaller local safe and placed it on top of the dynamite. Although it was not mentioned in the report of the holdup, one can almost be sure that somebody among the trainmen suggested that the would-be robbers were using too much explosive. If so, the warning was ignored.

One of the bandits put a match to the fuse and waited. Nothing happened. For fear that the charge could go off at any time, they were afraid to try to relight it. After waiting a few minutes more, they gave up and rode off. Had the fuse worked, it is likely there would have been no one around to tell what happened. (Source: *New York Times*, 8 October 1897.)

EXPRESS CARS. Once train robbery became popular, it was apparent that the express cars were poorly designed for protection against intruders. The cars were

Although some railroads began building steel express and baggage cars in the late 1890s, this wooden model was still in use on the Southern Pacific as late as 1909, and was a frequent target of robbers. *Union Pacific Railroad Museum Collection*.

wooden and could be pierced by rifle bullets or burned. The doors on the end were a particular problem; even if chained, they could be opened with a simple "jimmy tool."

Yet, improvements were slow in coming. By 1878 a few cars were being built on heavier frames, and some railroads—such as the Missouri, Kansas & Texas—began building express cars with end doors plated with boiler iron; however, the feeling among some railroad officials was that stronger cars were not the answer. The general manager of one western railroad, when asked why his line was not considering sturdier express cars, answered: "Why should we do that, when anyone may buy a quarter's worth of dynamite, and blow to pieces the strongest metal ever put together?"

Some railroad and express company officials delayed ordering the construction of stronger cars because of the expense. As late as 1894, Charles L. Loop, general auditor of the Southern Express Company, pointed out that the low rates then being received by the express companies for transporting money would not cover the cost of manufacturing bulletproof cars. Others sug-

gested that stronger express cars might encourage robbers to wreck the trains to gain entry. In a letter to the editor of *Railway Age*, a reader wrote that heavier, so-called robber-proof cars "will fall just as far through a sawed bridge and be just as undesirable to be in while rolling down an embankment owing to the absence of a rail from the track as any other style of cars."

There were, however, those who supported the idea of stronger cars. In 1893, Wade Hampton, then Commissioner of Railroads, suggested that every express car should have, in addition to its ordinary sliding side door, "an independent one made of strong iron grating, which could remain closed should the outer door be broken in." Such a device, said Hampton, should present a "serious obstacle" to the robber and should "repel any attack save by the use of dynamite," especially if backed up by extra guards armed with "repeating shotguns" and "seven rounds of buckshot cartridges" which would be a match "for four times their number" in train robbers. To Commissioner Hampton, it was simple: "Should an attack be made on any express car, and the outer door be broken in, the first man showing himself in front

A combination U.S. Mail, baggage, and express car used by the Union Pacific Railroad shortly after the turn of the century. These "combo" cars fared slightly better against bandits than the solo express cars since they carried a mail clerk and baggage clerk in addition to the express messenger. *Union Pacific Railroad Museum Collection.*

of the iron grating could be shot down, while the men inside could be behind cover. A few such receptions," said Hampton, "would bring the [train robbery] business into disrepute."

Hampton's idea did not impress the editor of *Railway Age*, who commented that the iron grating and extra guards "would doubtless bother the robbers until they had blown a hole in the side of the car and blown into fragments the occupants, by means of dynamite."

By the late 1890s many ideas were being proposed to repel robbers, among them globular steel cars, cars with gun slits or "loopholes" from which messengers could pick off bandits, cars with revolving turrets, cars equipped with Gatling guns and searchlights, and cars

with an impregnable "steel stronghold" in one end where the express messenger could make a stand. One letter writer to the *New York Times* suggested a device whereby the messenger, just before he jumped out and turned his car over to bandits, could throw a switch and fill the entire car with steam.

Another enthusiast, a man named George Dubrow, urged Wells, Fargo to equip its express cars with tubes projecting through the roof through which the messenger could fire skyrockets and parachute flares that would attract the attention of lawmen and citizens who could ward off the attack.

Wells, Fargo did not go to such extremes, but in 1892 the company did introduce a reinforced express car

This baggage-express car, in use on the Union Pacific line in 1910, was heavily reinforced with steel. Side widows were eliminated, as was the wire-mesh ventilator grating on the side door, a frequent means of entry for bandits. *Union Pacific Railroad Museum Collection.*

An express car demolished by dynamite. *Wells Fargo Bank History Room, San Francisco.*

touted as a "tough nut to crack." This was proven to some extent on August 3, 1893, near Kerman (then Collis), California, when dynamite charges placed by bandits on both doorsills only twisted the ironwork and splintered the car's planking. But the bandits did manage to blow two small holes in the doors and finally entered by prying the doors open.

While express cars were eventually built stronger and heavier, at the peak of the train robbery era there was much more interest in strengthening the safes that held the money. The editors of *Railway Age,* in December 1893, urged the express companies to make a safe so strong "that it can only be opened after the expenditure of a great deal of time," since "train robbers have not the advantage of what is known in the safe trade as burglar's time—i.e., thirty-six hours, or from Saturday evening till Monday morning." Such a safe, they suggested, could be "dynamite-proof to the extent that it couldn't be shattered without destroying the contents." On the other hand, the same publication reminded the express companies that if they eventually prevented robbers from emptying the express car safes,

would not the robbers turn toward the passengers with possibly disastrous results?

Cars were strengthened and safes were strengthened, but it is questionable how much this had to do with the eventual decline in express car robberies. Holdups of express cars declined after the turn of the century, but by then there was less money being carried by the express companies. It became cheaper to ship money and valuables by registered mail, and soon the train robbers were redirecting their attacks to the railway mail cars. (Sources: Dillon, *Wells, Fargo Detective*; Hampton, "Brigandage on Our Railroads"; Harlow, *Old Waybills*; *New York Times*, 20 November 1891, 20 November 1893; Patterson, "The Fine Art of Robbing Trains"; *Railway Age*, 25 August 1893, 2, 9 November and 14 December 1894, 15 March 1895.)

THE EXPRESS COMPANIES. In the United States the business of transporting money, packages, and goods other than heavy freight began in New England sometime in the 1780s. By 1829 there were stagecoach lines running out of Boston. By 1832 the number had increased to 106. When the railroads came along, the larger bankers and brokers in New York, Boston, Philadelphia, and Baltimore employed messengers to carry bonds, money, and other valuables between these cities. Two of these messengers, brothers B. D. and L. B. Earle, formed Earle's Express sometime in the mid-1830s, which may have been the first express service to operate exclusively by railroad.

Notwithstanding the efforts of the Earle brothers, the pioneer of the U.S. express industry is generally considered to be a former railroad conductor and ticket agent named William F. Harnden. In February 1839 Harnden ran an advertisement in the Boston newspapers that he would: "run a car through from Boston to New York and vice versa four times a week, commencing on Monday, the 4th of March. He will accompany the car himself for the purpose of collecting drafts, notes and bills. Orders of all kinds promptly attended to. He will take charge of all small packages of goods, bundles, etc., that may be entrusted to his care, and see them safely delivered and attend to forwarding merchandise of all descriptions."

Although in mentioning running a "car," Harnden was voicing a future hope—the first few months he carried all of his customers' packages in a medium-sized valise—the fledgling Harnden's Express Company did break the ground for those that followed.

As the rails spread across the nation, so did the express companies. Most railroads eventually entered into long-term contracts with one of the major express companies: Adams, American, Southern, or Wells, Fargo for the exclusive right to handle express shipments on that line. By the 1870s only in sparsely populated areas of the West—the domain of Wells, Fargo—were express shipments still being made by stagecoach.

Under the typical contract, an express company would pay the railroad a lump sum for the contract plus a fixed amount, usually adjusted annually, for the right to operate an express car on a given route. On the smaller lines, where the traffic was light, the express company might only buy space in the baggage car. And on some lines, a car might be shared by an express company and the government's Railway Mail Service.

An express car was operated by an express messenger, sometimes called an express agent. In especially hard times it was a job to be coveted, but it was backbreaking and dangerous work, and the pay was modest. Even in the 1890s a messenger for one of the major express companies, depending upon his length of service, earned only about $40 to $70 a month. For this sum he was supposed to lay his life on the line for shipments that might exceed a half-million dollars. Despite the amounts carried, the messengers were often blasé about their responsibilities. As Alvin Harlow said in his history of the express industry: "An outsider in those silver-dollar days would have been startled at seeing two or three hundred canvas bags containing a thousand silver dollars each, stacked in the end of a car like so much salt; but to the messenger it was a humdrum, common experience."

The express companies' first encounter with train robbers was in 1866 with the holdup of an Adams car on the Ohio & Mississippi Railroad near Seymour, Indiana. With that robbery a war began between the companies and outlaws that would last more than fifty years.

The express business, as it was conducted by separate privately and publicly held corporations under contracts with the railroads, came to an end in 1918. That year the four major express companies (Adams, American, Southern, and Wells, Fargo), weakened by competition from the Post Office Department's parcel post service and by government control of the railroads during World War I, were taken over by the government and consolidated into what would become the American Railway Express Company. (Source: Harlow, Old Waybills.)

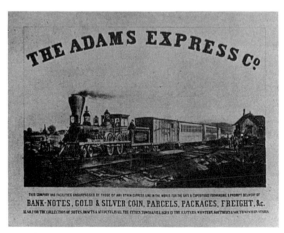

An Adams Express Company advertising poster, circa 1860. Author's Collection.

Adams Express Company

Adams Express Company, founded as Adams & Company by Alvin Adams in 1839, began with a route between Boston, Worcester, Norwich, and Stonington, Massachusetts. From there it would spread with the railroads south and east until it became, for a while, the largest express company in the nation.

The first prosperous year for the company was 1843, when it took over an established route between Philadelphia and Washington, D.C. Two years later, the company entered into a contract with the partially completed New York & New Haven Railroad, paying $1,000 per month per car for space on express trains. This was an exorbitant amount for the times, but growth followed immediately, and the contract established the company firmly. Adams and the New Haven would be together for the lifetime of the company.

In 1845 an editorial in the *New York Herald* described the Adams company as "the Great Eastern, Southern and Southwestern forwarders [that have] one or two hundred men in their employ, who work on an average twelve hours a day, and are remarkable for their energy and enterprize."

Adams's early expansion was in the north central states, which rails had not yet connected. The company carried westbound cargo from New York by water to South Amboy, New Jersey, then by rail on the Camden & Amboy Railroad to Philadelphia. From Philadelphia it shipped via the Ohio River to Cincinnati, Louisville and Cairo, Illinois, and by the Mississippi River to St. Louis. The entire trip took at least ten days, depending

Early headquarters of the American Express Company at Jay and Hudson streets, New York City, circa 1860s. *American Express Company.*

on the weather, but merchants were generally satisfied. When Adams contracted with the Ohio & Mississippi Railroad, which was completed from Cincinnati to East St. Louis in 1857, time in transit was reduced to six days. It was this route that would secure a permanent place in the annals of train robbery history. Eleven years later the first peacetime train robbery in the United States would occur in an Adams express car on the Ohio & Mississippi line, just outside Seymour, Indiana.

The year 1854 would be an important one for the Adams company. That year the Pennsylvania Railroad completed its difficult Horseshoe Curve, linking Philadelphia and Pittsburgh. Over the years, as the Pennsy spread its tracks west, the line would become, as one observer wrote, Adams's "Rock of Ages." Also in 1854, Adams & Company acquired three smaller express firms: Thompson, Livingston & Company; Kinsley & Company; and Hoey & Company; plus a steamship company. With these acquisitions, Adams clinched its hold on the southeastern states. It then reorganized as Adams Express Company with capital of $1.2 million and, through board member Johnston Livingston—already a prominent official in the American and National Express Companies—established an interlocking directorship that launched an interesting tangle of interrelationships that would continue throughout the history of the express business in the United States.

Adams also was one of the first express companies to see the advantage in linking up with California following the discovery of gold there in 1849. By 1851, the "Adams & Company's Express and Banking House" was offering to forward gold dust, insured or uninsured, to any part of the United States or England, and to receive deposits and make drafts in Boston, New York, Philadelphia, Washington, or London. In September of that year, Adams was advertising to pay $17 an ounce for "good, clean gold dust."

By the mid-1850s the Adams Express Company controlled the majority of the express business of southern New England, New York City, New Jersey, Pennsylvania, the Ohio and Mississippi rivers, the southwestern states, and the southern Atlantic and Gulf seaboards. The growth of the company can be best described by a popular joke told over and over at minstrel shows in the mid-1850s: "For what purpose was Eve created?" a black-faced jester would ask. The answer, which always got a roar from the audience, was "For Adam's express company."

As the Adams Express Company grew, so did the threat of theft and robbery. Adams was the first express firm to retain pioneer detective Allan Pinkerton to investigate losses. In April 1858 Pinkerton was called in to investigate the disappearance of money shipments between Montgomery, Alabama, and Atlanta, Georgia. Pinkerton and his operatives soon found the culprit: the Adams agent in Montgomery. On two occasions the agent had pocketed customers' packages. The first incident involved $10,000 that arrived in a locked pouch from Atlanta. The agent, Nathan Maroney, a handsome, likable fellow who liked high-living and betting on horses, simply removed the package, destroyed the waybill, and claimed to his superiors that nothing was in the pouch when he opened it. A week later, when asked to place four packages containing $40,000 in an Atlanta-bound pouch for a local customer, Maroney instead slipped them behind the counter. Maroney was Pinkerton's first suspect, and he had his men watch him and his wife day and night. Several of the operatives became good friends with the couple, who one day mentioned how they had hoodwinked Maroney's employer. Most of the loss was recovered, and Maroney was sent to prison for ten years. Pinkerton's young detective agency was put on permanent retainer by appreciative Adams officials.

In addition to handling numerous small investigations, in 1864 Pinkerton operatives solved a $90,000 theft in the Adams company's Baltimore office. And two years later, Pinkerton was called in to solve the largest theft in Adams's history, a break-in of an express car on the New York & New Haven's New York City-to-Boston run.

But for a legal technicality, this theft would have been the first peacetime train robbery in the United States, and little Seymour, Indiana, would have lost its place in railroad history as the site of the birth of a brand new crime. In the New York case, the theft was from an unoccupied express car. Legally, therefore, it was a *burglary* and not a *robbery*, which requires the presence of at least one human victim during the commission of the act.

On the New York City-to-Boston run, the Adams express car routinely carried shipments for Hartford, Connecticut, and Springfield and Worcester, Massa-

chusetts. In between these stops, the Adams express messenger made it a habit to ride in the adjacent baggage car and visit with the baggage clerk. After each stop, whether or not there was an express shipment for that city, the messenger was supposed to check the doors of the express car to see if they were still securely padlocked. This eventually became a nuisance for some of the messengers, and they frequently neglected this duty.

On January 6, 1866, a Saturday evening, the Adams car was carrying, along with expressed freight, three company safes containing nearly $750,000. The train had left New York City at 8:00 P.M., and the Adams messenger had checked the padlocks prior to departure. He did not check them again until the train stopped at Bridgeport, Connecticut, and then he checked only the locks on the side next to the station platform. Later, when the train arrived at New Haven, the conductor noticed that one of the doors was slightly ajar. On entering, the messenger found two of the three safes battered open and nearly $700,000 gone.

Allan Pinkerton sent his operatives to work in the towns along the line questioning anyone who might have seen or heard something suspicious on the weekend of the theft. One of the operatives found a livery stable owner at Stamford, Connecticut, who remembered two men who had wanted to rent a horse and buggy Saturday night. The operatives distributed the men's descriptions to nearby hotels and rooming houses, and found where they had spent the night. They also found that they had taken a train out of Stamford Sunday night. They were traced to Norwalk, where

American Express railroad cars being unloaded at Hudson Street building, New York City, circa 1860s. *American Express Company.*

one of them was identified as a brakeman on the New York & New Haven. Further questioning led to the name of a third man, an acquaintance of the other two who had been seen on Monday morning carrying a heavy parcel aboard a train bound for New York City. This man had a niece who lived on the city's lower East Side, and on searching her apartment five days later, police found $100,000 of the stolen money.

Further investigation revealed that eight men were involved, and all were eventually rounded up. Persistent questioning disclosed that the brakeman had discovered which of the Adams express messengers was the most careless about checking the padlocks on the car doors, and the gang had waited until his turn on the run. Three men had hidden in the railroad yards in New York City where the train was shunted for final makeup. There, shielded by darkness and the noise of other locomotives, they had pried off a lock and en-

tered the car. The rest of the gang members were waiting in a deserted area north of the Harlem River. The plan was for the trio in the car to pull the bell rope and slow the train, then jump off with the safes. But the bell rope did not work, so the men battered open two of the safes, stuffed the money in two bags, and left the train at Cos Cob, Connecticut. They hid one bag near the station in a pile of lumber and the other behind a stone wall about a mile west of the bridge across Cos Cob inlet. They walked into Stamford, spent the night, and returned the following evening to retrieve their loot.

When Allan Pinkerton closed the case for the Adams company, he saw to it that every detail of the crime was stored in his agency's files. Pinkerton knew that criminals followed patterns. Stealing from an express car on a moving train was a unique form of crime because the express business on railroads was relatively new, but he knew a pattern would develop; there

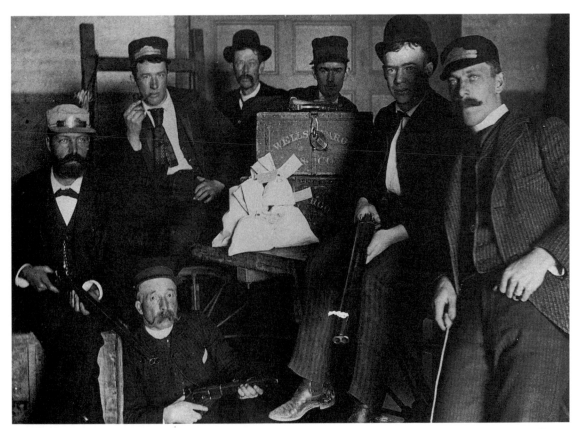

To stem the tide of robberies, express companies added extra armed guards and equipped them with the latest and most effective weapons. *Wells Fargo Bank History Room, San Francisco.*

would be more such mischief. He did not have long to wait. Nine months later the Adams Express Company would wire him again with a loss to investigate, the holdup of an express car near Seymour, Indiana, the crime that would launch the train robbery era in the United States. (Source: Harlow, *Old Waybills*.) *See also* **Reno Gang; Seymour, Indiana.**.

American Express Company

The American Express Company was formed in 1850 in Buffalo, New York, and immediately secured a contract to handle express shipments on the Hudson River Railroad. Soon thereafter the new firm also obtained contracts with the New York & Erie Railroad, Michigan Central Railroad, and Little Miami Railroad. Where there were no railroads, the firm shipped by canal, and, of course, the Great Lakes. The company was an immediate success, earning in the first four months of operation enough revenue to pay a dividend of 10 percent to its stockholders.

The company, which was capitalized originally at only $150,000, suffered a serious loss in its third year of operation. On August 19, 1852, the steamer *Atlantic*, en route from Buffalo to Detroit, sank with more than $50,000 in the safe, all of which was entrusted to the care of the American Express Co. American spent more than $3,000 for divers in an attempt to salvage the safe, but it was all in vain.

In 1855 the company suffered its first major loss of a shipment made by rail. That year the American Express agent in Dubuque, Iowa, accepted two boxes represented to contain a total of $50,000 in gold for shipment to the Assistant Treasurer of the United States in New York City. The shipment arrived without incident, but when the boxes were opened in New York, instead of gold they were found to contain lead bullets. Officials of American were convinced that the bullets had been in the boxes from the beginning, but since their agent in Dubuque had accepted them as being full of gold, the company had to write a check to the government for $50,000.

Despite the losses, profits continued to climb. In 1855 the company picked up a route contract with the Lake Shore Railroad from Buffalo to Toledo. By 1858, with the company having spread its routes over most of the north central states, more than $2 million a day was being carried by American Express. By 1862 the company was maintaining 890 offices in ten states, had a payroll of 1,500, and was running express over 9,200 miles of railway each day.

The war years brought in huge profits, and the post-war years were even better, until the company began to feel the effects of the United States Post Office Department's new "money order," which reduced considerably the amount of cash being shipped by express. Then, in 1867, the upstart Merchants Union Express Company out of New York City cut into American's business and turned a $100,000 monthly profit into a $250,000 loss. But the battle for customers cost Merchants, too, and to survive the two companies merged into what would become for six years the American Merchants Union Express Company. The company climbed back to a stable position and in 1882, once more under the banner American Express Company, it brought out its own money order.

In 1883 the company introduced the special American Express Train on the New York Central line between New York City and Buffalo. In describing this innovation, an observer wrote:

> Every weekday evening the express station was a scene of apparently frantic confusion and hurry. With their wide doors standing open, the express cars, consigned to all parts of the West, stood alongside the loading platform while the express wagons drove up and burly expressmen transferred packages, boxes and crates, containing everything from Paris hats to pedigreed pups, to the train. At 8:15 p.m. the doors began to slam shut, and promptly at 8:20 p.m. steam hissed into the cylinders of the racing Atlantic-type locomotive, and with her doleful bell clanging its warning she pulled across the maze of switches at the start of her flying run to Buffalo. The American Express Special beat the time of the fastest passenger train from New York to Buffalo by *four hours and fifty-five minutes.*

Although by the 1890s American Express was looking abroad for expansion of its business—especially the travel business with the American Express Travelers Cheque—it would continue to maintain a generous portion of the railway express business thanks to its longstanding contract with the New York Central Railroad and new contracts with Missouri, Kansas & Texas and the Illinois Central railroads. In 1918 the company's railway service was separated from the other business aspects of the firm and became the American Railway Express Company, Inc. (Sources: Harlow, *Old Waybills*; Hatch, *American Express*.)

Southern Express Company

The Southern Express Company was a product of the Civil War. In 1857, when it appeared that a conflict between the northern and southern states was inevitable, Henry B. Plant, superintendent of the southern division of the Adams Express Company, informed the Adams board of directors that if a Southern Confederacy were established, all northern-owned property, including the express routes and assets of the Adams company, would be confiscated. He suggested that to avoid this, the southern division should be sold to him. Some of the directors later said that Plant went further than just issue a warning. By their account he had made it clear that if he was not given control of the southern routes, he was prepared to organize a company of his own and take over the routes under the authority of the Confederacy.

The Adams directors complied, and almost immediately a new dummy express company came into being, quietly assuming all the Adams contracts in Alabama, Arkansas, the Carolinas, Florida, Georgia, Louisiana, Mississippi, Tennessee, Texas, and Virginia. Then on April 8, 1862, just four days before the attack on Fort Sumter, it was made official. Henry Plant and several southern associates purchased the Adams contracts. On May 1 all the Adams signs came down from the express offices and signs of the Southern Express went up.

During the war, the Adams and Southern companies formed the only practical, if imperfect, means of communication by letter or transportation between the North and the South. As the armies advanced, so did the companies, taking "enemy" express offices as they went. When General Lee or General Bragg surged northward, the Southern Express followed and Adams fell back. Toward the end of the fighting, when the Confederacy began its retreat, Adams retook its lost ground, almost before the smoke of battle had cleared.

At the close of the war, Adams restored to Southern its routes along the Mississippi River and business on all railroad lines in the South with the exception of the Mobile & Ohio Railroad and a few lines in Kentucky. Adams continued to operate on the Mobile & Ohio until late 1866.

During the postwar years the Southern Express Company thrived along with its sister companies, Adams, American, and Wells, Fargo. Probably because of the impoverished conditions in the war-torn South, however, it was among the first to fall victim to train robbers. (Source: Harlow, *Old Waybills*.)

Wells, Fargo & Company

Wells, Fargo & Company was formed in 1852 to compete for the express business in gold-rich California. The official announcement in the May 20, 1852, edition of the *New York Times* reported that the company ws "ready to undertake the general forwarding agency and commission business; the purchase and sale of gold dust, bullion and specie, also packages, parcels and freight of all description in and between the City of New York and the City of San Francisco, and the principal cities and towns in California." A similar notice, which appeared about the same time in the *Alta California*, boasted of "energetic and faithful messengers furnished with iron chests for the security of treasure and other valuable packages."

While Wells, Fargo was not the first express company in California, it soon became the greatest and most powerful of them all, thanks mainly to the influential American Express Company back East with whom it shared several of its founders and directors.

With its own stagecoach lines and a lucrative transcontinental mail contract, Wells, Fargo sat at the top of the heap for nearly two decades, but its officials underestimated the progress of the railroads in their attempt to link the nation. In October 1868 Wells, Fargo received its last intercontinental mail contract from the government. Facing the loss of $1.75 million in revenue a year, the company began selling off the stage lines, retaining only the right to transport express over each line sold.

When the Union Pacific and Central Pacific rails joined at Promontory Point, Utah, in 1869, both railroads were ready with their own express companies: the UP's United States Express and the CP's Pacific Union Express. Wells, Fargo, which once could boast of nearly all the express business west of the Mississippi, was in trouble. Charles Crocker and Lloyd Tevis, owners of the Central Pacific Railroad, quietly watched the value of Wells, Fargo stock fall, then stepped in and offered to sell Pacific Union Express for $5 million. With the deal would come a ten-year contract to carry express over the Central Pacific Railroad. Wells, Fargo had no choice but to accept; it was either grab the opportunity or wither and die. To swing the deal, Wells, Fargo had to recapitalize, and Lloyd Tevis acquired enough of the new stock to control the company. Wells, Fargo's stagecoach days were nearing an end, and its future now lay with the rails.

Wells, Fargo prospered. When its ten-year contract with Central Pacific expired, it would renew for a fifteen-year period, and also enter a similar contract with the Southern Pacific Railroad, which would eventually merge with the CP. To pay for these contracts, Wells, Fargo would merely issue more stock, which it would sign over to the two railroads. For the actual operation of express business, it would pay the railroads a specified amount per ton. Since Wells, Fargo was the only express company that could transport by rail in and out of California, it could charge its customers a rate high enough to earn a tidy profit.

The overall growth of Wells, Fargo was continuous. Its 156 agencies in 1863 became 573 by 1880 and 2,830 by 1892. Between 1872 and 1902 the company never paid less than a 6 percent dividend to its stockholders, and often as much as 12 percent.

Beginning in 1852 Wells, Fargo competed with the United States government in delivering the mails in the West. The company even erected its own private mailboxes on San Francisco streetcorners and provided a rapid intracity mail system for messages and small parcels.

Wells, Fargo was the preeminent express company in the West from 1855 to 1917. Thus, it was natural that one of its revenue cars would fall victim to the first train robbery west of the Mississippi River. In November 1871 a former Sunday school superintendent, John T. Chapman, engineered the robbery of a Wells, Fargo express car on Central Pacific's Train No. 1 at Verdi, Nevada. It was the first encounter between train robbers and Wells, Fargo in a war that would last nearly half a century.

Armed robberies, however, were nothing new to Wells, Fargo. Highwaymen had plagued the company's stagecoaches for years. As a result, when the first express car was assaulted, the company already had a sizable detective force on hand to tackle the problem. The company's policy was to make good to shippers instantly all losses in transit and to trust its detective force not only to catch the culprits but to recover

Express messengers checking their weapons. *Frank Leslie's Illustrated Magazine, 1877.*

enough of the stolen loot to keep the net loss at an acceptable figure.

For more than twenty-five years, Wells, Fargo detectives, led by their capable chief, James B. Hume, would work hand-in-hand with railroad police and local law enforcement authorities to track down train robbers. And they would be kept busy. Before the last train robber was put behind bars, the Central Pacific and Southern Pacific would be hit over fifty times, more than any other line, and it was the Wells, Fargo express cars that took the brunt of the attacks. (Sources: Dillon, *Wells, Fargo Detective*; Hungerford, *Wells, Fargo*.) *See also* **James B. Hume; Verdi, Nevada**.

EYLAU SIDING (TEXAS). A popular saying among lawmen during the train robbery era was that "railroaders make the best train robbers." There was much truth to the statement. In more than half the outlaw gangs that preyed on express and railway mail cars during the 1880s and 1890s, you probably could have found at least one former railroader. Of greatest value to a gang was a member who could operate a locomotive. After flagging down or overpowering the engine crew, the robbers could cut loose the express and mail cars from the passenger coaches and take off with the treasure, leaving the engineer and fireman behind, thus eliminating two captives who would have to be guarded while the loot was being extracted.

Also, being able to drive the locomotive could give a bandit gang a decided head start on escaping. After cracking the treasure cars, the gang could cut loose the engine and tender, pile into the cab, and head for a preselected escape route far up the track. If they also snipped the telegraph wires, it might be hours before the abandoned train crew spread the alarm.

A holdup on the Cotton Belt line south of Texarkana on September 3, 1901, was a good example of how easy it could be to rob a train with an experienced hand at the throttle of the locomotive. The southbound passenger train left Texarkana at 9:25 P.M. Four miles out, the engineer had to stop for the junction with the Texas & Pacific tracks. When he did, six masked and armed men climbed aboard and took control.

The express and mail cars were cut loose, and the engineer, whose name was Henderson, was ordered to head for the siding at Eylau, a few miles down the track. Working methodically, the outlaws forced their way into the express and blew open the safe. They loaded up the contents into two large sacks and returned to the locomotive.

One of the bandits, obviously a former trainman himself, turned to the engineer, and in railroad jargon, said: "We will just shell road you here [put him off the train]. You're not the only engineer in this crowd, and I guess we can run the machine without your assistance. When you locate your wagon [locomotive], figure the run in on your mileage, as we won't put in time for the run we make." Putting out the headlight, the bandit engineer opened the throttle and gave it full steam.

Engineer Henderson hiked his way to the nearest section shack, borrowed a handcar, and started after his engine, hoping he would not have a long trip. He didn't; the robbers had left it in a densely wooded area at the bottom of a grade near Redwater (then called Red Water), about eight miles out. They had arranged for an ideal escape. There was no way to tell where they had actually jumped off the cab. They could have departed anywhere from the top of the grade to the bottom and let the engine slow to a stop on its own. Later, when interviewed, express and railroad officials had to admit that it was a "perfect job." (Source: *New York Times*, 5 September 1901.)   □

F

FAIRBANK, ARIZONA. Most western train robberies occurred on lonely stretches, usually far enough away from the nearest town to give the robbers plenty of time to ransack the express car, and maybe the passengers coaches, and disappear over the nearest ridge. Thus, the robbery attempt on the Southern Pacific at Fairbank on February 15, 1900, was unique; it took place at the station in the midst of a crowd.

Fairbank is in Cochise County, in the southeastern corner of Arizona. The outlaws' plan was to hit the express car as the messenger was unloading it at the station, using innocent bystanders as shields.

To the misfortune of the outlaws, they picked a night when the messenger on duty was Jeff Milton, a former lawmen and Texas Ranger. It was speculated that the bandits, knowing of Milton's reputation, tried to pick a night when he was off duty, but that night he had substituted for another manager.

When a voice from the station platform shouted "hands up," Milton thought it was a joke and continued unloading packages. But the next command was "throw up your hands and come out of there," followed by a shot that knocked off Milton's hat. Milton had left his pistol on the desk inside the car. A sawed-off shotgun was near the door within his reach, but he was afraid to use it for fear of hitting bystanders.

By now the bandits probably recognized Milton and decided they had better put him out of commission.

Their next shot struck him in the left arm, knocking him to the floor of the car. His attackers, thinking that he was finished, rushed the door, but by then Milton had his scattergun. His first blast put eleven pellets into the nearest robber, Jack Dunlap. A twelfth pellet hit a second outlaw, Bravo Juan Yoas. It wasn't a serious wound but it took the fight out of him, and he headed for his horse.

The three remaining bandits riddled the interior of the car with their Winchesters. Milton, although weak from loss of blood, pulled the keys to the safe from his pocket and threw them into a corner behind some packages. Then he passed out. The bandits entered, but were unable to find the keys. Since they had not come prepared to blow open the safe, they picked up their wounded comrade and rode off.

It was speculated that the bandits were led by Burt Alvord, a former peace officer at Willcox, Arizona. (Source: Haley, *Jeff Milton.*) *See also* **Burt Alvord**.

FARRINGTON BROTHERS. In the fall of 1871 the Southern Express Company engaged Pinkerton's National Detective Agency to track down a gang of suspected train robbers who operated along rail lines near the Mississippi River. Their specialty was express cars, and on completing a robbery, they would escape by way of the river using a skiff, which they would later scuttle.

William Pinkerton, son of the agency's founder and then in charge of investigating train robberies, went to work with Patrick Connell, special agent for the Southern Express Company, and one of his assistants, a man named Bedlow. They scoured the banks of the river without success until they received a tip from local residents about a "party of strange men in a swamp" near Lester's Landing, in Fulton County, Kentucky. According to a report later filed by Pinkerton, they found that the men they were looking for were operating a small general store at the landing "to cover their real business of train robbery."

"We surrounded and attacked," said Pinkerton, and in the ensuing gunfight one of the suspects, Henry (also called George) Bertine, was killed. Two others, later identified as Hilary Farrington and William Barton, escaped. Pinkerton was shot in the side; Connell, in the stomach. According to one account, after the battle was over, Pinkerton—bleeding profusely himself—

removed the bullet from Connell's gut with a corn knife.

Further investigation revealed that the gang was led by Hilary Farrington and his brother, Levi. Both were dirt farmers from near Gilliam Station in western Tennessee and both had developed "murderous natures" during bloody raids with Quantrill's guerrillas during the Civil War. A fifth member of the gang was William Taylor, also from west Tennessee.

Following his escape from Lester's Landing, Hilary Farrington fled to western Missouri where, several months later, he was located hiding in a farm house near Venita. He refused to surrender, and local authorities had to set fire to the place to flush him out. A few days later, Levi Farrington was spotted in Farmington, Illinois. According to one report, he got drunk and "shot up the town square, challenging one and all to a duel." The local town marshal overpowered him and dragged him off to jail, where he was identified as the

William A. Pinkerton (seated) and two special agents of the Southern Express Company—Pat Connell (left) and Sam Finley (right). This photo was taken during the hunt for train robbers Levi and Hilary Farrington in 1871. *Union Pacific Railroad Museum Collection.*

wanted train robber. He was later arrested by Robert Pinkerton, William's brother. In the meantime, gang member William Barton was picked up, as was William Taylor.

Neither Farrington would ever see a courtroom. While being returned by steamboat to Tennessee to stand trial, Hilary got into a scuffle with his guards, "fell" overboard, and was crushed to death by the boat's stern paddle. Robert Pinkerton managed to get Levi Farrington back to Union City, Tennessee, where he was to be tried. Before the trial, however, a friend of Farrington's, a man named Toler, attempted to rescue the outlaw. In doing so, he shot and killed the Union City assistant city marshal and wounded a railroad watchman. Irate citizens formed a vigilance committee and stormed the jail. Barton and Taylor were being kept in a local hotel, and the Pinkertons were able to hustle them out of town. Levi Farrington and Toler were not so fortunate. The vigilantes overpowered the authorities guarding the two prisoners. Farrington was shot and killed, and Toler was lynched. (Sources: Nash, *Bloodletters and Badmen*; Patterson, *Train Robbery*; Pinkerton, *Train Robberies*.)

FERRELL, CHARLES. It was called the Wedding Present Robbery, a tragic story that involved the death of an express messenger at the hands of a former friend.

On the night of August 12, 1900, the Pennsylvania Railroad's eastbound Train No. 4 from St. Louis arrived at the Union Station at Columbus, Ohio, at 11:40 P.M., only a little behind schedule. The Adams Express Company transfer agent, whose name was Sheldon, noticed that the express car door was still closed. At the end of a long run, the messengers were always in a hurry to get home—seldom did Sheldon have to wait for a car to be opened up. Sheldon waited a few seconds, probably thinking that the messenger had fallen asleep. Finally, he pushed open the door. A wave of nausea nearly overcame him: on the floor lay the messenger, Charles Lane, in a pool of blood.

Twenty-eight-year-old Charles Lane, married and the father of a young child, had been shot eight times. The local safe was unlocked, and the contents were gone. There was a sign of a struggle inside the car, but there was no evidence of the car having been broken into.

Pennsylvania Railroad and Adams Express Company detectives concluded that messenger Lane had either let the killer in or had carelessly left one of the doors, probably the rear door, unlocked, and the intruder had entered and surprised him. A check with members of the train crew established that the latter was probably the case; Lane, contrary to company rules, did not always keep the rear door locked.

Since the killer or killers had to have left the train before it arrived at Union Station, the next morning investigators were dispatched back along the line to interview station agents and anyone else who might remember something of value. When nothing turned up, the investigation was extended to rooming houses and hotels. This step immediately brought results. At Plain City, the second stop before Columbus, the desk clerk at a hotel reported that a man had checked in the night before without registering. Fortunately, his room had not been cleaned. The detectives could not believe their luck. Under the mattress, they found a .38 caliber Smith & Wesson revolver. (It appeared that Lane had been killed with a .38.) Also, on the floor near the bed they found several Adams Express Company waybills.

Several of the detectives suggested that the search should begin with Adams employees and former employees: persons with whom the dead messenger was acquainted. Although the report of the crime did not specify why, their suggestion probably stemmed from the observation that most robbers will not commit murder unless there is a reason, and frequently that reason is that the victim, if allowed to live, could identify them.

A list of names was obtained from the Adams company and dozens of employees and ex-employees were questioned as to their whereabouts on the night of the murder. Suspicion immediately fell upon one man: Charles R. H. Ferrell, a friend of Lane's who had been discharged by the company three months earlier. Ferrell had no alibi for August 13, he had not obtained another job, and he needed money desperately because the next day, August 14, he was getting married.

Ferrell was picked up at the home of his fiancée, Lillian Costlow of Columbus, the daughter of a Pennsylvania engineer. Under questioning, Ferrell at first denied the charge, but in doing so, he assumed what the detectives felt was a suspicious "nonchalant demeanor." They were pretty sure they had their man, and finally, with more pressure, he confessed. He admitted entering the car and shooting his friend, Charles

Lane, eight times. His only reason was that he needed the money. When asked what he did with the money he stole, he said he gave it to Miss Costlow. The detectives returned to her home, and found the money. (Sources: *New York Times*, 12, 13 August 1900.)

FLATONIA, TEXAS. Nameless, faceless train robbers were always the bane of journalists who strived to give life to their news stories. It is surprising, therefore, that somebody didn't come up with "Captain Dick and his candy stick" in writing up the robbery of a Southern Pacific passenger train near Flatonia, Texas, on June 18, 1887. The leader of the gang was indeed "Captain Dick," or at least that was what his confederates called him during the holdup. And, sure enough, during the whole affair he sucked on a stick of candy.

Flatonia is in Fayette County, about midway between Houston and San Antonio. As the eastbound train pulled away from the station, two men with revolvers slipped aboard behind the tender, climbed over the coal pile, and ordered the engineer, B. A. Pickens, to keep going until he was told to stop. He did as he was told, and after a short distance the bandits ordered him to stop at a bridge near where a large bonfire was burning beside the track. In the light of the fire he could see four or five more armed men waiting to board the train.

Nothing was overlooked: the express car, the mail car, and the passenger coaches were all ransacked. In most train holdups, if the robbers invaded the express or mail car, they usually left the passengers alone, but not this bunch. There were no official figures given out on the total loss, but some estimates placed it as high as $10,000. More would have been taken from the coaches, but for engineer Pickens's daring. While the robbers were not looking, he slipped away to the first coach, told the passengers what was happening, and urged them to pass the word on back and hide as much of their money and valuables as possible.

In the express car, Wells, Fargo & Company messenger Frank Folger tried to hide some of his money packages in the belly of the stove, but the bandits caught him in the act and gave him two or three blows on the head as punishment. Then, when they discovered that he had tossed the key to the safe out the door, they slit his ears with a knife and told him that there was more coming unless he went out and found it.

These particular robbers were especially brutal. A young Englishman in the sleeping car was caught attempting to hide his money, more than $1,000, and was beaten soundly, as were two drummers who apparently just did not move fast enough. And, possibly for the first time in the history of train robbery, a woman passenger was struck for being too slow in turning over her pocketbook.

Among the passengers was an officer in the Mexican army, a Colonel Quintas. When he heard why the train had been halted, he called for someone to bring him his pistol and said he would "kill all the robbers." But by the time the bandits reached the colonel's car he had second thoughts, and when Captain Dick informed him that he was not particularly fond of Mexicans, and that "I'd just as soon kill you as eat my breakfast," the colonel quickly handed over his pouch containing $400.

The brutality shown by the outlaws enraged the public. Texas Governor Lawrence S. Ross issued an official declaration that "[t]rain robbery is to be a fighting business and attended with almost certainty of failure and detection." He announced that from then on "[t]here will be five to ten well armed fighting men on each train," and to show that he meant what he said, he authorized commissions for 390 new Texas Rangers. (Sources: Dillon, *Wells, Fargo Detective*; *New York Times*, 19 June 1887.)

FONDA, NEW YORK. Most people connect the crime of train robbery with the American West and are surprised to learn that the first such robbery (except for raids conducted during the Civil War), actually occurred in Indiana. (*See* **Seymour, Indiana.**) Many are even more surprised to learn that even before the first train robbery was committed in the West (*see* **Verdi, Nevada**), eastern roads had already fallen victim to this new crime.

Early on the morning of August 11, 1869, three men forced their way into a combined express and baggage car on the Central Railway at Fonda, New York, bound the messenger and baggage clerk hand and foot, and helped themselves to the contents of the safe. The car was not taken without a struggle, but the attackers had brought along three pacifiers—chloroform, cayenne pepper, and a large club.

These robbers did not want for boldness. While they

were ransacking the car, the train made a routine stop at Schenectady, and one of the bandits quickly tossed several bags out onto the station platform and slammed the door shut. The station baggage agent thought such abruptness was unusual, and some of the owners of the bags complained, but no one suspected that the car was in the process of being robbed.

It was never determined when the robbers made their escape. When the train arrived at Albany, station attendants found the messenger and baggage clerk still tied up, their faces bruised, heads cut, and eyes red and watering from the cayenne pepper. (Source: *New York Times*, 12 August 1869.)

FOTHERINGHAM, DAVID S. David Fotheringham was an Adams Express Company messenger accused of conspiring with Fred Wittrock, a.k.a. Jim Cummings, to rob his own express car on October 25, 1886. Using forged papers from Adams officials, Wittrock posed as a new express messenger to gain entry to the car and got away with nearly $90,000. The case made headlines nationally for more than two months. Wittrock, who as "Cummings" claimed to be a former member of the James gang, was eventually arrested and pleaded guilty. Wittrock testified that Fotheringham was not involved, but the Pinkerton's National Detective Agency and the Adams Express Company continued to press charges against him. When his case was finally dismissed, Fotheringham brought a civil suit against the Adams company and collected $20,000 in damages. *See* **Fred Wittrock**.

FRANCIS, JAMES. James Francis (alias J. S. Francis and S. C. Francis) was a member of Marion Hedgepeth's outlaw gang. He was in on the robbery of an express car on the St. Louis & San Francisco Railroad at Glendale, Missouri, a St. Louis suburb, on November 30, 1891, and an express car robbery on the Missouri Pacific line at Lamar, Missouri, on January 22, 1892. He was killed following the Lamar robbery during a shootout at Pleasanton, Kansas.

Although few details are known of Francis's criminal career, he may have ridden with the Hedgepeth bunch for several years. In the files of the Pinkerton's National Detective Agency, Francis was considered a "notorious" western outlaw, but the Pinkertons used such descriptions liberally.

At the time of the Lamar robbery, Francis's wife and child were living in Kansas City, Kansas. With his share of loot from the Glendale robbery, Francis had bought a farm for the family near Kansas City. The authorities had the place staked out at the time of his death.

When the report of Francis's death reached the newspapers, a rumor spread that he was a cousin of Governor David R. Francis of Missouri. Apparently there was a physical resemblance, but the governor's family immediately issued a press release that there was no truth to such a tale. (Sources: Pinkerton, *Train Robberies*; *New York Times*, 24, 30 January 1892.) *See also* **Glendale (St. Louis County), Missouri; Lamar, Missouri; Marion Hedgepeth**.

FRANKLIN, KENTUCKY. On November 8, 1866, at 2:00 in the morning, a southbound Louisville & Nashville passenger train was thrown from the track in Simpson County, three and one-half miles from Franklin. The engine struck a pile of rails that had been placed on the track, and it, the tender, express car, baggage car, and smoker all plummeted over an embankment, nearly killing the engineer, Jim Stewart. The wrecked express car caught fire from its overturned stove, and the Adams Express Company messenger barely escaped with his life.

The robbers, possibly twelve in all, had not counted on the express car catching fire and they were unable to enter it and ransack the safe. They did manage to get into the baggage car and rifle some of the valises. Afterward they headed for the coaches, taking money and jewelry from the passengers, who were too stunned and shaken to resist. The amount taken was never calculated, but one man reported a loss of $1,700. When the robbers finished with the passengers, they raced to their horses, which had been tied nearby, and rode off toward the east.

By then the fire had spread to the baggage car and smoker; only a courageous effort by the train crew and passengers in uncoupling and backing up the rest of the train, which was still on the track, saved it from being engulfed in flames.

An armed posse arrived at the scene before dawn, and a troop of cavalry was called up from Nashville but they had little success picking up the culprits' trail.

Then, on November 14, word came that L&N detectives, with the help of citizens of Franklin, had captured six members of the gang, and that one of the captured men, Stephen Conwell, age twenty, had made a full confession, including a recital of the details of the robbery. According to Conwell, the idea for the holdup came to several of the men on hearing about the attack on an L&N paycar near Briscoe Station the previous month. They thought that if three or four men could rob a paycar, a dozen or so could ransack a whole train. (Sources: *Louisville Daily Journal*, 9, 15 November 1866.)

FULCHER, THOMAS. Thomas Fulcher, age fifty-six, and his son, Sidney, age twenty-four, were respectable cattlemen in Placer County, California. In April 1924 they were convicted of having robbed a mail car on the Southern Pacific *Daylight* of $87,000 in gold coins near Colfax, California, on December 24, 1922. The coins were never recovered. It is believed the robbers buried them along the tracks somewhere near Dutch Flat in Placer County. *See* **Colfax, California**.

FURRER, BRITISH COLUMBIA. This is the robbery that led to the end of the career of famous "Old Bill" Miner, longtime stagecoach and train robber, and subject of the much-acclaimed 1983 Canadian film, *The Gray Fox*. The victim of the attack was the Canadian Pacific Railroad's crack *Transcontinental Express*. Around 1:00 A.M. on May 9, 1906, Miner, who apparently had climbed aboard the tender at Kamloops, ordered the engineer to halt the train near Furrer, not far from the twenty-mile post. When the train was brought to a stop, two

more bandits stepped out of the darkness from beside the tracks. The train was uncoupled behind the first car, and the engineer was ordered to pull ahead a mile.

When the robbers entered the car, they found an express messenger and a postal service clerk, but no express packages — only mail. On this run, the mail car had been placed ahead of the express car, which was now a mile down the track with the rest of the train. The flustered old outlaw rummaged through the mail for a few minutes, then called it quits. The robbers rode off with a measly $15.50.

Despite the small loss, the Canadian Pacific Railroad immediately offered a generous reward for the capture of the suspects. Several local posses were quickly formed, and dozens of Indians from Kamloops took up the hunt. Five days later Miner and his two companions were captured in a camp near Douglas Lake. (Sources: Pinkerton, *Train Robberies*; Rickards, "Bill Miner — 50 Years a Hold-up Man.") *See also* **Bill Miner**.   □

Reward Notice following Furrer robbery. *Provincial Archives of British Columbia*.

Site of the Furrer robbery. *Provincial Archives of British Columbia*.

G

GADS HILL, MISSOURI. The robbery of the express car, mail car, and passengers on the Arkansas branch of the Iron Mountain Railroad at Gads Hill (also called Gadshill) in 1874 was Missouri's first train holdup. Many such holdups would follow, thanks mainly to the James-Younger gang, which eventually resulted in Missouri becoming known nationally as the Train Robbery State, a nickname of continual embarrassment to the state's law-abiding citizens.

The Gads Hill robbery, which was attributed to the James-Younger bunch, was not that gang's first train robbery. According to most outlaw historians, that honor goes to a Rock Island train that was wrecked and robbed at Adair, Iowa, on July 21, 1873. (See **Adair, Iowa.**)

Gads Hill was a small Wayne County town of around thirty inhabitants about 130 miles south of St. Louis. On January 31, a Saturday afternoon, five masked men rode into town and, without firing a shot, took control of the tiny railroad station. (This method of operation would become something of a James-Younger trademark.) On the arrival of the southbound Little Rock Express, which they detoured to the Gads Hill siding with a flag on the main line, the outlaws swiftly overcame the engine crew. Using the crew as hostages, they went through the entire train—express car, mail car, and passenger coaches. Just how much was taken was never determined; reports have ranged from as little as $2,000 to as much as $22,000.

The robbery infuriated the citizens of the area, and a posse was immediately formed at Piedmont, about eighteen miles south of Gads Hill, to hunt the robbers. Later, when word was announced that rewards totaling $17,500 were offered for the arrest and conviction of the guilty parties, the hills around the scene of the holdup were suddenly overflowing with amateur man-hunters. Thanks to this abundance of trackers, the suspects' trail was picked up; when it clearly led westward, toward the home county of the Jameses and Youngers, the authorities were fairly certain who was involved. (Sources: Morse, *Cavalcade of the Rails*; Settle, *Jesse James Was His Name*; *St. Louis Times*, 19 March 1874;

New York Times, 14 February and 23 March 1874.) *See also* **The James-Younger Gang**.

GAGE STATION, NEW MEXICO. The eastbound Southern Pacific passenger train was five miles east of Gage Station, New Mexico, about an hour out of Deming. The date was November 24, 1883, and dawn was still almost three hours away. The engineer, Theo Webster, was working with his gauges, and his fireman was watching the track ahead in the bouncing headlight. Suddenly, the fireman shouted "my God, there's a hole in the track!" The engineer reached for the brakes, but it was too late. The front trucks under the stack buried themselves into the ballast where the rail had been removed, and the first three cars followed the locomotive and tender off the tracks and onto the roadbed.

Fearing the steaming boiler was about to burst, the fireman leaped from the cab. Webster started to follow him, but as he stepped up on the ledge to jump, a rifle exploded from underbrush beside the track, and the engineer fell head-first onto the ground, a bullet lodged in his heart.

Charles Gaskill of Chicago, a passenger in the first coach, jumped to the ground and ran forward to help. Immediately behind him was Zach Vail, the conductor. Neither man knew the train was being robbed until a voice from the shadows ordered them to throw up their hands. Both were quickly relieved of their money and valuables. The conductor, who was carrying the cash he had received by late-boarding passengers, had to turn over nearly $200.

In the Wells, Fargo express car, the stunned and bruised messenger stood by helplessly as the robbers battered in the door and helped themselves to the contents of the safe, about $1,800. The robbers then moved on to the postal car, but on rummaging through the registered mail, they found nothing of value. When they finished there, they mounted their horses and rode off to the north, toward what is now Grant County.

After checking the passengers to see if there were any injuries, conductor Vail ordered the brakeman, Tom Scott, to start back to Gage Station and wire for help from Deming. Shortly after 7:00 A.M., a special train arrived with an armed posse.

There were several able trackers in the posse, and the robbers' trail was easily picked up; however, the outlaws had chosen their route of escape well and their tracks were soon lost in a rolling ridge of hard rock.

Nearly everyone in the posse had a theory about who the robbers might be. Some thought the culprits were a gang of rough-edged cowboys from San Simon, Arizona Territory; the engineer would have recognized some of the members, which would explain why he was killed. Others suspected the so-called lower Gila gang, also called the Cliffton gang, from along the Gila River near Pima, Arizona.

Despite a reward of $2,550 offered jointly by the Southern Pacific Railroad and Wells, Fargo, no leads were uncovered for more than three months. Then, the first of March 1884, four suspects who roughly matched the descriptions of the robbers were picked up and taken to Silver City. They were George Washington Cleveland, Frank Taggert, Mitch Lee, and Kit Joy. Cleveland, Lee, and Joy had been captured near Socorro, New Mexico, and Taggert at Porte Canon de Agua Frio, near St. Thomas, Arizona.

All four suspects were taken to Silver City because the jail there was supposed to be better equipped to handle them. As it turned out, this was not the case. On March 10 the four suspects, plus two other prisoners—Carlos Chavez and Charles Spencer—managed to overpower the jailer and two guards, remove their leg shackles, and escape armed with pistols, a shotgun, and a rifle. They did not remain free for long, however. A local resident, John C. Jackson, saw them leave town and followed them out the Fort Bayard road and then north toward the Pinos Altos Mountains. The fugitives could not make good time because when they picked up horses at the local livery stable, George Cleveland selected a bronc. The horse threw him, and he had to double up with another rider. A posse of townsmen led by Silver City deputy sheriff F. C. Cantley soon caught up, and the fugitives were forced to make a stand.

In a fierce gunfight, Cleveland and Spencer were killed, along with a posseman named Lafferr; Mitch Lee was seriously wounded. Frank Taggert and Spencer surrendered, but Kit Joy managed to escape. Furious over the death of Lafferr, the possemen quickly voted to hang Taggert and Lee from the nearest tree. Cantley

objected, but the townsmen ignored him and went looking for a suitable branch. But just then a U.S. deputy marshal named Jensen rode up, and the townsmen had to put their plans on hold. The townsmen, however, got rid of Jansen by suggesting that he ride to Fort Bayard and consult with the commanding officer to find out what should be done with the prisoners. He rode off, and the townsmen resumed their search for a tree. Deputy Cantley again protested, and this time he was promptly relieved of his guns.

A tree was found, nooses were tied, and Frank Taggert and Mitch Lee were invited to say their last words. Taggert admitted participating in the robbery, but denied any part in shooting the engineer. Mitch Lee, he said, did the killing. At first Lee protested, but as the noose was being tightened, he made his peace with his creator and confessed the shooting.

Four days later a coroner's jury at Silver City officially held that "the deceased came to their death by gunshot wounds and other injuries inflicted by the sheriff's posse and citizens while in pursuit and endeavoring to recapture the prisoners." (Source: Caldwell, "New Mexico's First Train Robbery.")

GARDNER, ROY. Roy Gardner was born in Trenton, Missouri, in 1886. A bright boy, he graduated from high school at age sixteen. He probably could have succeeded in several professions, but he was adventurous and began to drift. He worked in the silver mines in

Roy Gardner.
Southern Pacific Railroad.

Arizona for a while and eventually joined the army. Somewhere at this point in his life Gardner developed a tendency toward bad judgment. In 1906, with only two months left on his enlistment, he committed some minor infraction and deserted.

For the next three years Gardner led the life of a soldier of fortune. In 1909 he was arrested in Mexico for smuggling ammunition to revolutionaries and was thrown in jail. He escaped, however, and found his way back across the border. After a few months back at mining, he turned to prizefighting and won several bouts in and around Oklahoma City.

In December 1910, after a short up-and-down career at honest work in San Francisco, he was arrested for robbing a jewelry store and sent to San Quentin. By 1912 he was out, however, having received an early parole for coming to the assistance of the guards during a prison riot.

It appeared that Gardner was a changed man; for eight years he led an honest life, during which time he married and started a family. But in April 1920, after a business failure and a series of drinking bouts and visits to the gambling tables, he robbed a San Diego mail truck. He was arrested and sentenced to the federal penitentiary at McNeil Island, Washington, for twenty-five years. But prison was not in the cards for Roy Gardner this trip. On June 5, 1920, while on the train to Washington, Gardner jumped the two federal marshals who were guarding him and four other prisoners and escaped out a drawing room window.

Gardner was on the loose for almost a year, traveling throughout the West and Midwest as a welding equipment salesman, a trade at which he had become proficient during his honest years. In May 1921 he was almost captured when he tried to arrange a meeting with his wife who was then living in Napa, California.

On May 19, 1921, it is believed that Gardner and another man stole two sacks of registered mail from a storage car on the Southern Pacific's eastbound Train No. 10. Gardner's connection with this crime, however, was never verified. But on the following night, May 20, Gardner, working alone, held up railway mail clerk Ralph Decker on the Southern Pacific's Train No. 20 as it was leaving Roseville, California. After tying Decker's hands together with a leather strap, Gardner helped himself to the contents of the registered mail pouches. After selecting the packages he wanted, he

stuffed them into a mail sack. When the train reached the west end of the yards at Newcastle, he pulled the emergency cord, kicked the sack out the door, and jumped off. It was assumed that he then disappeared into the nearby mountains.

This time the authorities got lucky. Photographs of Gardner were distributed in and around Roseville, and the proprietor of a local cafe recognized him as a man who had been a regular customer there during the month of May. The area was stacked out, and several days later Gardner was captured while playing poker at a nearby hotel.

Mail clerk Decker identified Gardner as the man who robbed him; Gardner pleaded guilty. Twenty-five years were added to his previous sentence, and he was once again put on a train to the federal penitentiary at McNeil Island. This time, he was heavily manacled, fitted with a fifty-pound "Oregon Boot," and placed under the guard of two U.S. marshals in a private drawing room.

But again Gardner was not destined to reach prison. Shortly after the train left Vancouver, Washington, he asked his guards to remove his handcuffs so he could use the toilet. While in the toilet he pulled out a .32 caliber pistol that he somehow had managed to conceal. When he returned, one of the marshals was asleep. He quickly got the drop on the other one, and with the help of a second prisoner, Morris Pyron, who had been put on board at Dunsmuir, California, he tied up the marshals and escaped through a window when the train stopped for water at Castle Rock, Washington.

Neither man remained free for long, however. Morris Pyron was captured near Kelso, Washington, on June 12, and Gardner was picked up four days later at a Centralia hotel. Immediately after the escape, the area was flooded with photographs of Gardner; to disguise himself, he had covered his face with bandages. When someone would ask what happened, he would tell them that he had been injured in a fire. A Centralia police officer became suspicious, however, and took Gardner down to the station. His face was unwrapped, and once again he was in custody.

This time Roy Gardner made it to McNeil Island, but it was not to be for long. Being athletic, he won a place on the penitentiary baseball team. On September 5, 1921, during a game, Roy and two other prisoners cut their way through the wire fence that surrounded the outfield. Roy made it through first and reached a patch of underbrush about fifty yards from the fence. The other two prisoners were cut down in a barrage of gunfire from the guards. No man had ever escaped from McNeil Island, but Roy Gardner did.

On September 26 the *San Francisco Call* received two letters signed by Roy Gardner. One detailed his escape from McNeil Island, and the other was an appeal to President Warren G. Harding for leniency so that he might "make good" for his wife and daughter. A close inspection of the handwriting convinced the authorities that the letters were indeed from Gardner. Unfortunately, the postmarks on the envelopes were illegible.

The second letter was forwarded to Harding, who did not reply. Later, the Postmaster General issued a statement that the government would not compromise with criminals.

Nothing more was heard from Gardner until November 14. On that day he attempted to rob a railway mail car at Phoenix, Arizona. Gardner ordered the mail clerk, Herman Inderlied, to lie down on the floor of the car while he sorted through the registered mail pouches. Inderlied, however, saw a chance to catch Gardner off guard, and he grabbed his gun. The two men wrestled on the floor. Gardner, with his athletic build and experience as a boxer, probably should have prevailed, but Inderlied apparently was the more determined. When help arrived, the clerk was sitting astraddle the robber.

During his trial, Gardner's attorney tried to establish that he was insane, but it did not work; on December 18, 1921, he was sentenced to another twenty-five years in federal prison, this time at Leavenworth, Kansas.

In 1925, after being involved in several escape attempts, Gardner was transferred to the federal penitentiary in Atlanta. He remained there until 1934, when he and numerous other federal prisoners, considered to be dangerous or escape-prone, were transferred to Alcatraz Island.

On being paroled in 1938, Gardner settled down in a cheap hotel in San Francisco's Tenderloin district and got a job as barker at the Treasure Island Exposition. Not long after he ended his life in his bathroom by inhaling potassium cyanide, after leaving a note for the maid not to enter because she might accidently breathe some of the deadly fumes. (Source: DeNevi, *Western Train Robberies*.)

THE GATES BROTHERS. George and Vernon Gates, residents of Alameda, California, were believed to have committed at least two, and possibly many, train robberies between the years 1902 and 1905.

George Gates, who also traveled under the alias of Guy Williams, Guy Endicourt, and Bruce Van Drake, was born in 1882. The Southern Pacific Railroad's and Wells, Fargo & Company's files on George listed him as: "height, five feet eleven inches; weight, about 185 pounds; hair, black; eyes, brown; and complexion, dark." He also had a "round face," was smooth shaven, and had a short neck and square shoulders. Also, the index fingers on both hands were "bent or stiff." He was well versed in the mining business and was once a prizefighter. He could, however, be "gentlemanly and quiet-mannered" when necessary.

Edwin Vernon Gates, alias Ed Lee, Edwin Wallace, Ed Williams, and Arthur Reed, was born in 1886. His file listed him as five feet two inches tall, 145 pounds, brown hair "with a gray streak on top of middle," gray eyes, a light sallow complexion, round face, smooth shaven, and slender build. Also, an eye tooth on the right side was gold:

The two men were definitely connected with the Wells, Fargo express car robbery at Copley, California, on March 31, 1904, and they may have been involved in the Trinidad, Colorado, attempted express car robbery in November 1902. It is quite possible that if the descriptions given by witnesses to other train robberies in the Far West between 1902 and 1905 were checked against the descriptions of George and Vernon Gates, there would be some matches.

According to the files of Pinkerton's National Detective Agency, the trail ended for the Gates brothers at Lordsburg, New Mexico, on March 15, 1905, when they committed suicide rather than submit to arrest for several local robberies. (Sources: Pinkerton, *Train Robberies*; *San Francisco Chronicle*, 1 April, 7, 8, 10–12, 19, 31 May 1904.) *See also* **Copley, California; Trinidad, Colorado**.

GENOA, ARKANSAS. This train robbery near Genoa, Arkansas, on December 9, 1887, was the fifth and last committed by the Burrow brothers, Rube and Jim, as a team. Mistakes made in connection with this robbery led to the capture of both outlaws. It was the end of Jim Burrow's career as a train robber; Rube would commit several more holdups in the South while eluding the authorities.

By the winter of 1887 the Burrows's cash was running low. Rube called for a gathering of his outlaw companions for another robbery, but only three of the gang members would take part: Rube, Jim, and a relative newcomer, Bill Brock. The Burrows's first four holdups had taken place in Texas, 200 miles to the west. Why Rube chose Genoa, a small stop six miles southeast of Texarkana on the St. Louis, Arkansas & Texas Railway, for his next job was never determined, except that Rube may have felt that he had pushed his luck in Texas, and Arkansas was safer.

On December 3 Rube and Jim checked into the Cosmopolitan Hotel in Texarkana to await the arrival of the other gang members. The hotel guest book would later show that the two outlaws registered under the names of R. Houston and James Buchanan. Brock was the only other member to arrive. For some reason, he signed the book in his own name, W. L. Brock, a mistake that would eventually lead to his capture.

After scouting the area, the three men chose December 9 as the night of the robbery. It is not known why they waited six days; perhaps they had a tip about an especially large shipment of cash. If so, the tip was wrong.

The three outlaws knew better than to hang around town for six days and attract attention, so they took a train back to Alexander, Texas, Brock's hometown. The weather was cold and rainy, so while in Alexander they purchased rubber raincoats. They probably arrived back in Texarkana by train on the morning of the ninth. They may have considered renting horses for the ride to Genoa, but dismissed the idea as too risky; it would be too easy for the livery owner to give their description to the law. Possibly they chose not to take the train for the same reason. In the end, they walked the six miles to the robbery site.

That night, as the train pulled out of the Genoa station, Rube and Brock slipped aboard the express car and the tender. Jim was already hiding down the track at a deep wooded cut. As the train picked up speed, the two outlaws worked their way forward to the locomotive cab, where they thrust their guns into the backs of the engineer and fireman. Rube ordered the engineer to halt the train. They separated the express car from the cars behind, and then had the

engineer pull the express car up to the cut where Jim was waiting.

At first the Southern Express Company messenger proved stubborn. For half an hour he resisted the outlaws' orders to open the express car door. Finally, when Rube loudly told the engineer to get an oil can and start a fire under the car, the messenger opened up. Once in the express car, the outlaws quickly broke into the safe, which held around $2,000.

After stuffing their loot into sacks, Rube ordered the engineer to get up steam and pull away. As the train disappeared in the distance, the outlaws began walking northwest along the tracks toward Texarkana. Possibly Rube believe that the authorities would never suspect that the robbers would be on foot and walking into town. For all the train crew knew, the robbers had horses hidden near the track and would be riding hard on one of several roads that led away from Genoa. But Rube had guessed wrong. The local sheriff had quickly formed a posse in Texarkana, and took the shortest distance out to Genoa: along the track. The posse and outlaws nearly met head-on. Only at the last second were the three robbers able to reach the safety of the underbrush. The posse opened fire, but could not get a clear shot in the darkness. By crouching low and dashing from shadow to shadow, the outlaws managed to reach Texarkana and a hideaway they had selected earlier. They divided the loot and split up.

While the Burrows's first four train holdups had left the authorities scratching their heads over the identity of the robbers, the Genoa affair was doomed from the start. The gang had left two of their new rubber raincoats and a hat at the scene. Inside the coats were the letters "K.W.P." In the hat was the mark of the manufacturer, a hatmaker in Dublin, Texas. Southern Express Company officials immediately wired the regional office of the Pinkerton National Detective Agency, and two days later the agency's top investigator, Assistant Superintendent William McGinn, arrived in Texarkana to take charge of the case.

Standard Pinkerton procedure included questioning all local hotel and livery stable operators for the names and descriptions of all transients in the area just prior to the crime. Included in the list of names collected from Texarkana's Cosmopolitan Hotel were the names "R. Houston," "James Buchanan," and "W. L. Brock." Next, McGinn sent an agent to Dublin, Texas, to question the hatmaker about the hat found at the scene. The hat was a standard model, and many had been sold. The detectives had better luck with the raincoats. The letters "K.W.P." were identified as a pricing code used by a merchant in Alexander, Texas. On being questioned, a clerk at the store remembered that one of the purchasers was a local cowboy named Bill Brock. The agent checked the name against the list of Texarkana transients and found "W. L. Brock" from the register of the Cosmopolitan Hotel. The store clerk was questioned further and remembered that when Brock bought the coat, there were two strangers with him who also bought coats, and they roughly matched the descriptions of two of the robbers.

Further checking revealed that Bill Brock had recently made a trip to Texarkana, and that even more recently he had been seen in Waco spending large sums of money. He was found at his home on December 31 and surrendered without a struggle. On being taken to Texarkana and identified by the engineer as one of the robbers, Brock realized that his only chance was to confess and hope for a reduced sentence in return for his cooperation. He admitted his part in the Genoa robbery, and an earlier holdup at Benbrook, Texas, and identified his partners in crime as Rube and Jim Burrow. (Sources: Agee, "Rube Burrow"; Breihan, *Rube Burrow*.) *See also* **Bill Brock; Jim Burrow; Rube Burrow.**

GLENDALE (JACKSON COUNTY), MISSOURI. There were two Glendales in Missouri: one in Jackson County, just east of Kansas City, and the other in St. Louis County, just west of St. Louis. There were train robberies at both locations, and the two are often confused.

The robbery at the Jackson County Glendale occurred on October 8, 1879, and the victim was the Chicago & Alton Railroad.

The outlaws rode in at sunset, probably expecting the town to be deserted. It was not; several farmers were gathered on the board sidewalk in front of the general store. They eyed the strangers as they rode up, which apparently made them nervous, because they drew their weapons and ordered the entire bunch to march down the street to the train depot.

At the depot the outlaws promptly destroyed the telegraph key and forced the station agent to change the signal from green to red, which would halt the southbound express which was scheduled to arrive at 8:00.

When the train rolled to a stop, the United States Express Company messenger suspected trouble and began stuffing money from his safe into a valise. Having done this, he tried to climb out one of the windows, but the outlaws spotted him. Angered by his attempt to flee, they knocked him in the head with a pistol butt.

Apparently the messenger did not manage to hide all the money. An early report estimated the loss at $40,000, but later this was reduced to about $6,000 in cash and an undetermined amount of nonnegotiable paper.

Soon after the robbery a story made the rounds that the robbers had left a note at the scene. It read: "We are the boys who are hard to handle, and we will make it hot for the boys who try to take us." At the bottom were the names of Jesse and Frank James plus six companions.

Whether the note was genuine was never positively determined. There were rumors that Jesse James was spotted in Kansas City in the weeks preceding the robbery, and there were witnesses at the scene of the robbery who claimed they recognized him as the leader of the gang. The general manager of the United States Express Company, which offered a reward of $15,000 for the arrest and conviction of the robbers, released a statement the following day that the James gang was not involved.

The following year, however, an outlaw named Tucker Bassham was arrested and charged with participating in the robbery. He testified that the group was led by Jesse James. A second suspect, Dick Liddil, told substantially the same story. (Sources: Settle, *Jesse James Was His Name; New York Times*, 10 October 1878.) *See also* **The James-Younger Gang**.

GLENDALE (ST. LOUIS COUNTY), MISSOURI. On the night of December 30, 1891, an express car on a westbound St. Louis & San Francisco passenger train was assaulted near Glendale, and the safe was robbed of from $25,000 to $50,000. The express messenger's name was Mulrennan.

The four robbers, Marion Hedgepeth, James Francis, Adelbert D. Sly, and L. D. "Dink" Wilson gained entry to the car by blowing the door off with dynamite. Francis was killed a month later, following an express car robbery at Lamar, Missouri. Hedgepeth, the leader of the gang, was captured in February 1892 in San Francisco. *See* **James Francis; Marion Hedgepeth; Lamar, Missouri**.

THE GOLD TRAIN. The largest shipment of gold to be transported by rail during the train robbery era was in 1892. Dubbed the "Gold Train," the shipment consisted of $20 million in bullion and coins transferred from the United States Mint in San Francisco to the subtreasury in New York City.

The shipment was made near the height of the train robbery era, and the U.S. Post Office Department's Railway Mail Service went to great lengths to protect the treasure. Fifty armed guards were used, carefully selected from among Railway Mail Service personnel who had military experience in the Civil War or on the western frontier. Each guard was armed with a Winchester rifle and a Colt revolver.

To hide the true nature of the trip, the bills of ladings listed the cargo as "silk from the Orient." To maintain secrecy, during the trip James E. White, general superintendent of the Railway Mail Service and the man in charge of the shipment, used an elaborate code to communicate with Post Office and Treasury Department superiors in Washington.

On the morning of departure, a letter was intercepted by railroad officials in San Francisco suggesting that a robbery might be attempted; however, it turned out to be a false alarm. Two more false alarms occurred during the trip when the nervous guards first mistook a band of tramps, and later a railroad section gang, for bandits.

Twice on the steep western slope of the Sierra Nevadas, couplers broke and nearly caused a wreck, but the engineer had wisely ordered safety chains installed between cars which prevented the heavy train from careening down the mountain out of control. Other equipment failures caused delays at several points, but five days after leaving San Francisco, the Gold Train pulled into New York City with its treasure intact. (Source: White, *Railway Mail Service*.)

THE GORDON BROTHERS. Harry Gordon and his brother George committed a daring robbery of a Wells, Fargo express car at Clipper Gap, California, on Christmas Eve 1888. Using rope ladders, the two men climbed down from the roof of the car and smashed in the transom windows above the side doors. They quickly covered the startled messengers and escaped with $5,000. Harry was captured the following February by Wells, Fargo detective Jonathan Thacker at the Gordons's father's farm near Olathe, Kansas. George eluded capture but was later killed in a robbery attempt in the East. *See* **Clipper Gap, California**.

GORDON, TEXAS. This was the site of the Rube Burrow gang's second train robbery. The town of Gordon, a tiny hamlet in southern Palo Pinto County, was a brief stop on the Texas & Pacific line about midway between Ft. Worth and Abilene. About 2:00 A.M. on January 23, 1887, Burrow and gang member Henderson Bromley slipped aboard an eastbound passenger train as it pulled away from the Gordon station. As quickly as possible, they scrambled over the tender and down into the locomotive cab, where they put the muzzles of their revolvers into the necks of the surprised engineer and fireman. The engineer was ordered to stop at a pre-

Captain James White: in charge of the "Gold Train." *Author's Collection*.

selected spot down the track where Rube's brother, Jim Burrow, and two more robbers, Nep Thornton and Harrison Askew, lay waiting.

As the engine sat idling, the engineer and fireman were forced to alight from the cab and march back to the express car. At the car door, Rube Burrow pounded loudly and ordered the messenger to open up. Just then the conductor stepped out onto the platform of one of the passenger coaches and wanted to know why the train had stopped. Jim Burrow and Nep Thornton gave him his answer with a volley of shots. On hearing the gunfire, the express messenger doused his lanterns. When the messenger refused to open up, Rube put his pistol at the engineer's head and ordered him to tell the messenger that if he did not cooperate, he, the engineer, was a dead man. The messenger still held fast.

Furious, Rube riddled the car with bullets, but still the messenger held out. Finally, on Rube's threat to set the express car on fire, the messenger gave in. On entering the car, the robbers forced the messenger to open the safe and they scooped out just less than $3,000. Minutes later, the same procedure was followed in the U.S. Mail car, which was immediately behind the express car, where the robbers took $2,000 from the registered mail sack.

After firing a final round of shots in the air to discourage passengers from leaving the coaches, the gang rode north for several miles, then backtracked. Another turn took them over a rocky stretch where they left few tracks. After another couple of miles they headed for the open prairie. A posse was formed, but lost the trail after several hours. (Source: Breihan, *Rube Burrow*.) *See also* **Harrison Askew; Henderson Bromley; Jim Burrow; Rube Burrow; Nep Thornton**.

GORIN, MISSOURI. An attempted holdup of an express car near Gorin, Missouri, in 1894 holds a special place in the records of the Atchison, Topeka & Santa Fe Railroad, for it was one of the few times an ambush of would-be robbers was successfully carried out.

On September 18, 1894, the Santa Fe's Train No. 5, the *Utah & Colorado Express*, was stopped by bandits waving a red lantern at the end of a deep cut about a mile north of Gorin, which is Scotland County, about twenty miles southwest of the Iowa state line. Although the engineer, William "Dad" Prescott, brought the train to a halt as ordered, the four masked bandits, com-

manding both sides of the track, viciously opened fire at the locomotive cab. Prescott was hit, but his wounds were not serious.

The would-be robbers suspected nothing until they reached the express car. Hiding inside and in the adjoining coach were a dozen Santa Fe detectives and special agents. The bandits never had a chance. Charles Abrams, the leader of the gang, went down immediately, and he would later die of his wounds. "Link" Overfield managed to escape, but he was captured a few hours later at Memphis, Missouri. The remaining two bandits did escape, and bloodhounds were put on their trail.

The plot to rob No. 5 was hatched three weeks earlier. Unknown to Abrams and his confederates, an undercover detective, whose name was not revealed in the report of the holdup, had infiltrated the gang and passed the word along to Santa Fe officials. (Source: *New York Times*, 19 September 1894.)

GOSHEN, CALIFORNIA. Goshen is in Tulare County, on Highway 99, about forty miles south of Fresno. The town's contribution to the annals of train robbery occurred on the night of January 20, 1890.

As Southern Pacific passenger Train No. 19 was pulling away from the station, two masked men swung aboard behind the tender, the blind baggage area so popular with train robbers. A little more than two miles out of town, they climbed over the coal pile and down to the locomotive cab, where they ordered the engineer, S. R. DePue, to stop the train. DePue and his fireman, W. G. Lovejoy, were then marched back to the Wells, Fargo express car, and the messenger was ordered to open his door and throw out his strongbox.

The messenger did as he was told, and as the robbers were preparing to leave, a tramp who had been riding under the express car chose that moment to drop to the ground and run. One of the robbers raised his gun and fired, striking the tramp squarely between the shoulder blades.

When the robbery was reported, Southern Pacific and Wells, Fargo detectives converged on the scene. A dozen suspects were picked up over the next several days, but all were released for lack of evidence.

Although the exact figure was never revealed, the two bandits reportedly got away with $20,000 for their night's work. Irate Southern Pacific and Wells, Fargo

Goshen station. *Southern Pacific Railroad.*

officials announced that the guilty parties were to be caught regardless of the cost.

Eventually the robbery was blamed on the notorious Chris Evans and John Sontag, who during the following three years would lead law enforcement authorities and volunteer bounty hunters on one of the largest manhunts ever conducted in the state of California. (Source: Glasscock, *Bandits and the Southern Pacific.*) *See also* **Evans and Sontag.**

GOTHENBURG, NEBRASKA. By 1895 bandits in the West were following an almost identical pattern in robbing express cars. The train would be stopped either by signaling the engineer with a red lantern (the universal signal for trouble ahead on the track) or by slipping aboard unnoticed behind the tender. The train would be separated behind the express car, and the engineer would be ordered to pull ahead a mile or so. The engineer and fireman would then be marched back to the express car, which would be entered either by intimidating the messenger to open up or by blasting the door off.

If the above plan was followed, the robbery usually was a success. A variation, however, could cause trouble, as a handful of bandits discovered on a dark night in 1895.

It was shortly after midnight on August 21, and the Union Pacific's eastbound Flyer No. 8 was about thirty miles east of North Platte. About midway between the towns of Brady's Island and Gothenburg, a red lantern being swung at trackside brought the big locomotive to a halt. Following the usual pattern, the bandits cut the train apart behind the express car. After the front

section was pulled ahead, the engineer was ordered to open the express door with a crowbar. When this failed, the bandits blew off the door with dynamite.

It was at this point the robbers got careless. They ordered the engineer to accompany them to the express car, but they left the fireman unguarded in the locomotive cab. While the robbers were busy working on the safe, the fireman fired up the boiler, uncoupled the locomotive from the tender, and took off at full steam for Gothenburg. As the robbers watched the locomotive disappear down the track, they apparently realized that a posse would soon be on the way and they hurried to finish their work.

Although express company officials would not release the actual amount of the loss, they commented that the fireman's bold action probably resulted in the bandits overlooking "much valuable express matter." (Source: *New York Times,* 22 August 1895.)

GRANTS, NEW MEXICO. During the 1890s New Mexico was plagued by the famous Black Jack gang, thought to be led by the outlaw Bob Christian. One of the express car robberies attributed to the gang occurred at Grants, New Mexico, about ninety-five miles west of Albuquerque on November 6, 1897; it almost resulted in the loss of the entire train.

The Atlantic & Pacific's eastbound No. 2 had stopped at Grants for water. While the engineer, H. D. McCarthy, and the conductor, whose name was Aldrich, were standing on the station platform, a sudden fusillade of gunshots erupted and several masked men climbed into the cab of the locomotive. The fireman, Henry Abel, was still in the cab. At the point of a cocked revolver, the intruders ordered him to pull the train ahead a short distance to a row of stock pens just beyond the edge of town. As the train pulled away, McCarthy and Aldrich jumped on the platform of one of the rear coaches.

On reaching the stock pens, the bandits uncoupled the train behind the Wells, Fargo express car and ordered the fireman to pull ahead once more and stop a mile or so down the track. There, the outlaws used dynamite to blast their way into the express car. The first two charges failed to do the job, but the third blew the entire end out of the car and set it smoldering.

Once inside the car, the bandits used more dynamite on the safe and soon had it open. After loading the contents into sacks, they headed for their horses, which they had tied nearby.

When the robbers had gone, the fireman, Abel, figured he needed help to try to save the baggage and remaining express packages from the now burning express car, so he threw the train into reverse and began backing toward Grants. The express car, ho·"ever, was now completely ablaze, and apparently it blocked Abel's view, because he failed to stop in time. The express car rammed into the train still standing at the stock pens, telescoping it into the first and second coaches, and setting them on fire. Luckily, the passengers had left the coaches and had started back to the station; otherwise many would have been killed in the crash.

It was clearly a day the crew of eastbound No. 2 would be glad to forget. (Sources: Burton, "Bureaucracy, Blood Money and Black Jack's Gang"; *New York Times*, 8 November 1897.) *See also* **Christian Brothers**.

GREENWOOD, KENTUCKY. An unsuccessful attempt to rob the express car on Train No. 3 of the Cincinnati Southern Road (part of the Queen & Crescent System) near Greenwood resulted in two of the would-be robbers being shot dead and a third, severely wounded.

On the night of March 27, 1895, the train had just emerged from Tunnel No. 9, two miles north of Greenwood, where the track runs through a deep cut with a steep ravine on one side, when a man appeared on the track waving a lantern. The engineer, whose name was Springfield, pulled to a stop, and a tall, bearded "country-looking" fellow of about forty-five years swung aboard the steps of the locomotive and thrust a pistol in the engineer's face. Three other men, all wearing "broad-brimmed slouch hats and homemade clothes," scrambled into the baggage car, which they apparently mistook for the express car. The baggage man, J. Donovan, did not resist and was not molested.

While the three intruders began sorting through the baggage looking for valuables, back in the smoking car three Queen & Crescent detectives, Thomas Griffin, Will Eddie, and Will Altgood, decided they had better check out the trouble. With Altgood in the lead, they left the car and started forward to see what was going on. When Altgood reached the steps of the baggage car, one of the bandits ordered him to throw up his hands. Instead, the detective pulled out his revolver and commenced firing.

The bandit's companions immediately came to his assistance, but so did Altgood's fellow detectives. A furious shootout erupted. One of the robbers was shot through the heart and died nearly instantly. Another was hit in the lung and lived only two hours. A third received near mortal wounds.

It was later learned that one of the gang had tipped off the authorities that a robbery would be attempted, which explained why the three railroad detectives were on the train. The informer, Sam Fraser, was not one of the men in the baggage car, but was back in the woods, tending to the gang's horses. The dead men were identified as Jesse Morrow and his son, Tom. The wounded man turned out not to be one of the robbers, but a tramp named Martin. The man who escaped was thought to be Mose Morrow, a brother of Tom. (Sources: *St. Louis Globe Democrat*, 28, 29 March 1895; *New York Times*, 27 March 1895.)   □

H

HAMMOND, GEORGE. George Hammond and a partner, John Christie, were convicted of robbing an express car on a Northern Pacific Railroad near Bearmouth, Montana, on June 16, 1904. Hammond was arrested in July 1904 at Spokane, Washington. He named Christie as his accomplice and also assisted in the recovery of some of the stolen loot.

Some sources say Hammond was also involved in a similar robbery at Drummond, Montana, in October 1902. During that holdup, the robber confessed to the fireman that he also was wanted for robbing a Southern Pacific train in Oregon.

It is doubtful that Hammond would have admitted being connected with the Drummond robbery, because during that holdup the engineer, Dan O'Neill, was killed. Hammond's name might have come up in connection with the earlier holdup because of a story that circulated that at both the Bearmouth and Drummond robberies, one of the robbers gave a cigar to a trainman to light the fuse to the dynamite used on the express car. (Source: Block, *Great Train Robberies of the West*.) *See also* **Bearmouth, Montana; Drummond, Montana**.

HAMMOND, WALKER. Walker Hammond was one of four men who robbed an Adams Express Company car on the Ohio & Mississippi Railroad near Seymour, Indiana, in October 1867. Injured while escaping, Hammond was arrested shortly after the crime and later pleaded guilty, which resulted in a six-year sentence in the Indiana State Prison. *See* **Seymour, Indiana**.

HANFORD, JAMES. James Hanford, a native of Royal, Nebraska, participated in the last robbery engineered by "Old Bill" Miner. Miner, in his sixties, and a man named Charlie Hunter recruited Hanford sometime in late 1910 or early 1911. It probably was Hanford's first attempt at train robbery. He later said that it took Miner two weeks to persuade him to join the gang. Hanford, said Miner, "was an unusual person and had an unusual personality. He could persuade almost anyone."

On February 18, 1911, they struck an express car on Southern Railway's Train No. 36 near White Sulphur, Georgia. The bandits had trouble dynamiting the through safe, however, and had to settle for $1,500 from the messenger's local safe.

Using bloodhounds, a posse tracked the robbers to their hideout and all three were captured. Hanford and Hunter readily confessed and received fifteen years in the Newton County, Georgia, work camp. Hanford was a model prisoner and was cited by prison officials on at least one occasion for helping recapture escaped convicts. In 1918, after serving seven years, he was paroled and a year later he was granted a full pardon. (Source: Rickards, "Bill Miner—50 Years a Hold-up Man.") *See also* **Bill Miner; White Sulphur, Georgia**.

HANS, FREDERICK M. Fred Hans was a turn-of-the-century bandit hunter for the Northwestern Railroad. Mild mannered and pleasant looking, with a "care-

less smile," Hans looked more like a traveling salesman than a manhunter.

The Northwestern Railroad's main route ran from Omaha, Nebraska, to Deadwood in the Black Hills, over which the prosperous Homestake Mine sometimes shipped as much as $100,000 in gold a month. The shipments were seldom troubled by robbers, and many believed that Fred Hans was the reason.

It was said that Hans carried a "considerable number of bullet wounds on his person," souvenirs of several gunfights with some of the worst of the West's renegades. A story circulated in the late 1890s that in one battle near Custer, South Dakota, Hans, riding alone, was ambushed by five members of a gang whom he had been chasing. If the story is true, it was one of the most spectacular exhibits of shooting ever performed by a western lawmen.

According to the tale, as the outlaws closed in, one of their shots killed Hans's horse. Using the animal for a shield, Hans drew his two revolvers and carefully took aim at his attackers. His first shot struck the nearest outlaw in the chest, killing him instantly. His next shot dropped a second bandit's horse. His third shot hit another bandit in the head, killing him, and his fourth bullet wounded still another outlaw in the abdomen. The remaining attacker surrendered.

With this kind of reputation, one can understand why outlaws hesitated to take on Fred Hans. (Source: *New York Times*, 4 November 1900.) *See also* **Wilcox, Wyoming**.

HARRISON, JEFF. Jeff Harrison, originally from the mountain country of northeastern Alabama, was possibly one of the South's most prolific train robbers. He was positively identified as being responsible for two holdups, yet various railroad and law enforcement authorities suggest that he might have been involved in at least a half-dozen others.

On October 31, 1892, Harrison, his younger brother Dick, and James Brown held up an East Tennessee, Virginia & Georgia train near Piedmont, Alabama, and robbed the express and railway mail cars. All three were arrested. Brown and Dick Harrison pleaded guilty; Jeff Harrison was convicted following a week-long trial. He was sentenced to life imprisonment at the federal reformatory at Anamosa, Iowa, but received a presidential pardon in 1901 after serving only eight years.

Although there is no sound proof, it is believed by some authorities that by 1910 Harrison was again leading a gang of southern train robbers and preying upon express and mail cars from Alabama to Texas. He was, however, connected with only one such holdup: an express car robbery of $100,000 on the Baltimore & Ohio Railroad near Central, West Virginia, on October 8, 1915.

Following the West Virginia robbery, Edmund Leigh, head of the B&O's police force, dispatched fourteen railroad detectives throughout the countryside disguised as tramps, peddlers, and underworld characters. After talking to hundreds of local residents, they found a woman who lived near Central who had given water to a man the day before the robbery. As she described the incident, it appeared that he and others were camping in the woods near her house. She provided a good description of the man, which matched that of a known train robber out of St. Louis. The detectives searched the woods and found a jacket which they later traced to Parkersburg, West Virginia. An investigation there revealed that the robbers had lived in a camp south of town for six months before the holdup.

While this investigation was going on, some of the money taken from the express car turned up in San Antonio, Texas. This was traced to a Mr. Harrison who operated an automobile repair shop. Detectives sent a description of Harrison back to West Virginia where one of the railway mail clerks said it matched that of one of the robbers. Harrison's shop was searched, and the police found $50,000 of the stolen bills.

Harrison was convicted of the robbery and sentenced to twelve years in the federal penitentiary in Atlanta. (Sources: *St. Louis Globe Democrat*, 1 November 1892; *New York Times*, 23 December 1916.) *See also* **Central, West Virginia; Piedmont, Alabama**.

HARRODSBURG, INDIANA. Known in Indiana as the Monon robbery, this holdup occurred on April 29, 1885. Around 10 P.M. a northbound passenger train on the Louisville, New Albany & Chicago Railroad, which would later be known as the Monon Line, had stopped for water about two miles north of Harrodsburg, a small town in Monroe County about twelve miles south of Bloomington. As the train was pulling away, a man entered the unlocked rear end door of the express car, which was also used for baggage and mail. The baggage clerk, George K. Davis, was taking a nap on a pile of mail sacks and did not see the man enter. Without hesitating, the intruder bashed in Davis's head with a club. The express messenger, Peter Webber, tried to draw his revolver, but the bandit knocked the gun from the messenger's hand. Webber and the intruder grappled for the weapon, and it discharged, striking Webber a glancing blow on the head. The bandit then turned and shot the baggage man.

After helping himself to the contents of the express car safe, which totaled several thousand dollars, the bandit pulled the bell cord, the signal to the engineer to stop the train.

As the train slowed, the robber leaped off the car into the darkness. The wounded men were rushed to Bloomington for medical attention. Webber quickly recovered, but Davis's brain was severely damaged, and he remained mentally disabled the remainder of his life.

Monroe County authorities converged on the scene, as did railroad and express officials. The only clue found was a shoeprint—size nine. On questioning the passengers, it was discovered that several had been looking out the window at the time, and they said that they thought they saw some men, possibly three, in the woods near where the train had stopped. Also, several passengers in the coach immediately behind the express car said they saw a man with a blond mustache enter the vestibule between the two cars just before the robbery occurred.

The investigation continued without further results. Then, several weeks following the holdup, the messenger, Peter Webber, was walking along a street in Bloomington when he saw a man who closely resembled the robber. He told the authorities, and the man was picked up. His name was Chesley Chambers, a well-respected southern Indiana livestock buyer. A search of Chambers's hotel room turned up some currency with holes punched in it, similar to the tiny needle holes the express company clerks made in the center of bills to tie them together for packaging. On the strength of this evidence and Webber's testimony, Chambers was arrested.

Apparently Chambers could not account for the bills in question, and the railroad and express company pushed for trial. Despite excellent character witnesses and a strong alibi for the night of the crime, the case went to the jury. The jurors, confused over the conflicting evidence, could not decide. Six voted for conviction and six for acquittal. When they could not break the deadlock, the judge dismissed them and rescheduled the case. The second time around, the jury came in with a guilty verdict; however, probably as a compromise, they settled on a sentence of only two years in prison.

Chesley Chambers, a broken and ruined man, served his time. Then, several years later, as the result of a dying man's confession to a minister and a notary public, three others were named as the guilty parties. According to one of Chambers's attorneys, H. W. East, the real culprits were three small-time crooks, Charles Dock, Jim Nason, and Ben Mercer. Dock, according to attorney East, was the one who did the shooting. (Source: Rainey, *Demise of the Iron Horse.*)

HEDGEPETH, MARION. Marion Hedgepeth's early years are not well documented. It is believed that he was born in Cooper County, Missouri, but there is no record of the year. At age fifteen he headed west to become a cowboy. Some say he became proficient with a revolver, but that was said about almost every westerner who turned to crime.

Known as a fancy dresser, Hedgepeth usually appeared all in black with a large wing collar, a cravat bearing a diamond stickpin, and a derby hat. Perhaps it was his way of compensating for an otherwise rough appearance. He was large, rawboned and gangling, with enormous ears and a classic "horse face."

Hedgepeth began as a small-time criminal in the early 1880s—break-ins, small robberies, safecracking, and the like—in and around Kansas City. In 1883 he ran afoul of the law and was sent to the Missouri State Penitentiary at Jefferson City for seven years. He was released in 1890 and likely robbed his first train sometime that year.

On November 30, 1891, Hedgepeth and three others robbed an express car on the St. Louis & San Francisco Railroad at Glendale, Missouri, a suburb of St. Louis. The amount of the loss was never reported officially, but unofficial reports listed it at anywhere from $25,000 to $50,000. Hedgepeth's accomplices in the robbery were Adelbert D. Sly, James Francis, and L. D. "Dink" Wilson.

Following the holdup, Hedgepeth and his wife went to St. Louis, where they rented a small house in a quiet neighborhood. Not wanting to leave his large collection of guns lying around where somebody might spot them, he buried them under the dirt floor of an old shed in the back yard. To protect them, he stuffed them in several large envelopes he had picked up during the Glendale holdup. After a week or so, Hedgepeth and his wife, Maggie, decided to move to another house. Either he forgot about the guns or he decided to abandon them; in any event, shortly after he moved, a neighbor girl was playing in the shed and dug them up. She showed them to her parents, and they called the police.

Leaving the guns was bad enough, but worse still, Hedgepeth and Maggie had used their real names when they rented the property. It didn't take the police long to connect him to the train robbery. In the meantime, Hedgepeth and Maggie had gone to Oakland, California. Before leaving, they made arrangements to have their trunk shipped at a later date. When Maggie called at the Wells, Fargo office in Oakland to pick up the trunk, the police were waiting for her.

Maggie Hedgepeth was not a strong person and she soon broke down and admitted that her husband was the Glendale train robber. She did not, however, reveal where he was hiding. But Marion Hedgepeth's horse face was difficult to conceal, even in large cities. On February 10, 1892, he was picked up in San Francisco.

This time Hedgepeth was sentenced to twelve years at Jefferson City. While in prison, he developed tuberculosis. When he was released in 1908, possibly because of his ill health, it is believed he tried to form a new gang somewhere in the western states, but there is little evidence of this.

Sometime in late 1909, Hedgepeth, his lung condi-

Marion Hedgepeth.
Pinkertons.

tion worsening, headed back east. On January 1, 1910, while celebrating New Year's Day in a Chicago saloon, he apparently ran out of money and decided to help himself to the bartender's cash drawer. But just at that moment, a policeman walked by the front window and saw Marion with his pistol drawn. The cop burst in the door and shouted to Hedgepeth to surrender. Marion, thin and weak, coughed several times and managed to spit out "never!" Both men shot at the same time. Marion, no longer accurate with a gun, if indeed he ever was, missed completely. The policeman, however, did not miss. The bullet struck Marion in the chest, apparently puncturing his aorta. With blood spurting everywhere, the old outlaw was too weak to raise his weapon a second time. He squeezed off his remaining rounds into the sawdust floor, sunk to his knees, and pitched forward dead. (Sources: Nash, *Bloodletters and Badmen*; Patterson, *Train Robbery*; Pinkerton, *Train Robberies*; *New York Times*, 25, 30 January and 11 February 1892; *Railway Age*, 4 December 1891.) *See also* **Glendale (St. Louis County), Missouri; Lamar, Missouri**.

HEFFRIDGE, BILL. Bill Heffridge was a member of the Sam Bass-Joel Collins gang that robbed an express car on the Union Pacific Railroad at Big Springs, Nebraska, in September 1877. Following the robbery, Heffridge and Collins rode south to Buffalo Station, Kansas, where they were intercepted by the Ellis County, Kansas, sheriff and a squad of soldiers from Fort Hays. Both men were killed trying to escape. *See* **Joel Collins**.

HEYWOOD, EVERETT B. Conductor Everett Heywood was in his sixties, a gray-haired man who did not seem like someone to be feared. At least this was the opinion of one train robber who, much to his dismay, found out otherwise.

The date was November 25, 1904, a Sunday night. The train had left Kansas City at 9:00 P.M. It was an eastbound combination: a single train pulling cars of both the Chicago & Alton Railroad and the Chicago, Burlington & Quincy Railroad. From Kansas City to Mexico, Missouri, it would use the tracks of the Rock Island line. At Mexico it would split, with the Alton heading for Chicago, and the Burlington for St. Louis.

About 100 miles out, at the tiny village of Slater in Saline County, a man jumped aboard the platform of the smoker as the train was pulling away from the station. His name was Claude Randall, and the late boarding was intentional. Just before he stepped inside the car, he slipped on a mask.

None of the passengers resisted, not when they saw the revolver in the man's hand. One by one, as he went up the aisle, they meekly turned over their money and valuables. When he had finished in the smoker, Randall went onto the next car, a day coach, and repeated the process.

Bandits who robbed train passengers seldom stripped more than two cars—it just took too much time. But Randall was brazen and he was no newcomer to the business; he was calm and methodical.

The third car was a sleeper, and Randall stuck his gun in the face of a porter and told him to go to each passenger and collect his money. Halfway down the aisle, Randall saw conductor Everett Heywood and he shouted for him to help the porter with the collections. Heywood nodded, and without hesitation, went to the nearest passenger and asked for his wallet.

The conductor looked old and gray, so Randall saw no reason to fear him; when Heywood handed him the wallet, Randall carelessly let his gun-hand drop as he stuffed the passengers' money into his belt. It was the opportunity that Heywood was waiting for. In one quick move the conductor grabbed the bandit's gun, jammed his thumb between the hammer and the breech, and jerked the weapon out of Randall's hand.

Now facing his own gun, Randall made a dash for the door. Heywood ran after him and caught his coat collar just as he was about to leap off the train. The two men struggled violently on the platform between the cars. The younger man was clearly the stronger, but Heywood had the gun and he used it efficiently on Randall's head.

The next stop on the line was Armstrong, and Randall, tied hand and foot, was deposited in the care of the town marshal. As he was being taken off the train, the robber berated the passengers for their cowardice, declaring that the conductor was the only man among them with any nerve. But the passengers were too busy to hear—they were arguing over the distribution of the money the bandit had taken from them. (Source: *New York Times*, 27 November 1904.)

HOBGOOD, EDWARD S. Edward Scanlon Hobgood,

also known as "Curnell" and "Colonel" Hobgood, was a farmer from Marion County, Mississippi, whose one venture in train robbery came through an association with Louisiana renegade Eugene Bunch.

Hobgood and Bunch first got together sometime in early 1892. Bunch, a known hard case and suspected robber, had whetted his appetite for railway express cars during an in-transit robbery on the New Orleans & Northeastern Railway in November 1888. Hobgood, apparently new at the business of crime, joined Bunch for a spree of store burglaries and robbeies in eastern Louisiana. Shortly thereafter they added a third member to their gang, another Mississippian named Henry Carneguay, and they took on their first train at Tangipahoa, Louisiana, on April 14, 1892.

The men made a grave mistake in robbing a train so close to home. Gossip soon reached the authorities that Bunch and Hobgood were involved, and deputies converged on Hobgood's brother, Robert, who was forced to tell them where Bunch and his brother were hiding out. The two robbers were surprised near a farmhouse outside of Franklinton, Louisiana, and Bunch was killed. Hobgood surrendered without a struggle.

While Hobgood was sitting in jail, a rumor spread that he had made a deal with the authorities, and that it was he who had killed Bunch, not the possemen. He was eventually cleared of this charge, but was tried for the Tangipahoa robbery. He was found guilty, but the verdict was overturned on a technical error. He was not retried.

Hobgood lived until 1921. In October of that year he was found stabbed to death in Madison Parish, Louisiana, apparently in a fight over a woman. (Source: O'Dell, "Bunch & Hobgood.") *See also* **Eugene Bunch; Tangipahoa, Louisiana**.

HOEHN, CHARLIE. Charlie Hoehn was a member of train robber "Old Bill" Miner's gang. On September 23, 1903, he was shot by the express messenger during an attempted robbery of the express-mail car on the Great Northern Railroad's Oregon & Washington Train No. 6 just east of Portland, Oregon. The gang blew the door of the car off with dynamite, but the messenger, F. A. Korner, met the robbers with his Winchester blazing. Miner called off the attack, but as the gang was retreating, Korner fired off a final shot, striking Hoehn. With Miner's help, Hoehn escaped, but he was weakened by his wound and was captured a short time later. (Source: Rickards, "Bill Miner—50 Years a Hold-up Man.") *See also* **Bill Miner; Portland, Oregon**.

HOLLYWOOD TRAIN ROBBERIES. A train robbery was chosen for the plot of one of the milestones of the pioneer motion picture industry. While the 1903 epic *The Great Train Robbery* was not, as some movie historians proclaim, the first film using a story plot or the first western film ever made, it was responsible for an array of movie firsts and it established the direction and tone of the early western films, and films generally, for years to come.

The Great Train Robbery was produced and directed for Thomas Edison's turn-of-the-century film company by Edwin S. Porter, one of the most prominent innovators in U.S. cinema during the industry's formative years. With its cast of forty characters, the picture was an "epic" of its day. And it was lengthy for 1903 films— an unheard-of twelve minutes long. Its success was phenomenal: it remained the industry's most famous and profitable motion picture until D. W. Griffith's *The Birth of a Nation* in 1915.

The plot was a natural for a motion picture. The interiors were set in a railway depot and an express car, and the climax was a scrambling outdoor gunfight on horseback. In 1905 two Pittsburgh theater managers, John P. Harris and Harry Davis, used the picture to open the first Nickelodeon in the United States.

The film was based on a stage play written by Scott Marble during the peak of the real train robbery era. The play was first performed in October 1896 at the People's Theatre in New York City and ran for eight performances. The following February it ran for eight more performances at the Columbus Theater. It was revived two more times: in September 1897 at the Peoples, and again in February 1898 at the Star Theater.

Train robberies continued to make exciting plots for films during the heyday of western movies. While film equipment and techniques improved over the primitive standards in use in 1903, the robberies themselves as portrayed by Hollywood were often unrealistic. To begin with, the train robberies in the movies usually occurred in the daytime, mainly because it was much cheaper to film the scene during the day. Real train robberies almost always were committed at night, usually around midnight or later.

Another glaring error in movieland train robberies was the frequent scene in which the outlaws come dashing out of the woods and ride along the side of the train, then leap from their saddles to the steps or platforms of the passenger coaches. In hundreds of reports of real train robberies in the United States during the years 1866 through 1934, this feat is never described. It just was not attempted. Under ideal conditions it probably could have been accomplished—at least a few Hollywood stuntmen could pull it off with special running boards for the horses—but in real life it was not worth the risk.

One reason is because the roadbeds were constructed with ballast—crushed rock or gravel used to hold the crossties in place and the rails in line. Once settled, ballast tamps down well, drains well, and resists the growth of weeds, but it offers very poor footing for a galloping horse. Also, to get close enough to a moving train for a rider to leap aboard a platform, his horse would encounter the ends of the crossties, which would easily trip the horse. Of course, it is quite possible that a few outlaws tried to board a train in this manner and never lived to tell about it.

HOLZHAY, REIMUND. He was known as Black Bart of Wisconsin, a lone bandit who preyed on railroads and stage coaches. Law enforcement officials were never sure just how many robberies Reimund Holzhay was responsible for. He definitely was connected to two: the holdup of a Milwaukee & Northern train near Ellis Junction, Wisconsin, in May 1889, and a stagecoach robbery at Lake Gogebic in August 1889, during which a passenger was fatally injured.

It was the passenger, Mr. Fleischbein, who gave a description of Holzhay that later led to his capture on August 31, 1889, at Republic, Michigan. It was pure happenstance. The Republic city marshal, whose name was Globe, was walking down the steet near the railroad station when he saw a man who fit the robber's description. The man, Globe later said, was "dressed roughly and apparently [was] anxious to escape attention." The marshal stepped in front of him and said "I want you."

The stranger "whipped his hand to his hip pocket," but before he could draw his gun, Marshal Globe hit him over the head with his billy club. He was taken to jail, and upon being searched, was found to be carrying three revolvers, three gold watches, and four pocketbooks. One of them belonged to the deceased stagecoach passenger, Fleischbein.

Holzhay had arrived in Republic the previous evening and had rented a room in the Republic House Hotel. During a routine check of strangers in town, a Republic police officer had noticed that Holzhay matched the description of the robber, which had been distributed throughout the Midwest, and he had been put under surveillance almost immediately.

Faced with the incriminating evidence, Holzhay admitted the Ellis Junction and Lake Gogebic robberies, but at first he refused to discuss any others. Finally, under lengthy questioning about a long list of holdups, he did say: "It is generally supposed that one man has done them all, and I think that is so." According to the police, he then "entered into a detailed statement of his various crimes." Among them was a holdup of passengers on the Central Wisconsin Railroad the previous month.

Holzhay came from Pulsifer, Wisconsin, and a newspaper article at the time of his capture gave the following additional information: "Black Bart is a German boy twenty-two years of age. He was born in Germany. He is polite and pleasant in his manners and is of square build. He always carries a knife and a revolver. He took to the life of a robber as the result of reading dime novels, over a hundred of which were at one time found in his room."

After his capture, Holzhay was described as "sullen and defiant," and was overheard to say to the officers who held him "If I had my guns and was free, you fellows wouldn't be so anxious to get close to me." (Sources: *New York Times*, 1, 2 September 1889.)

HOMERVILLE, GEORGIA. Homerville is located in southeastern Georgia's Clinch County, about midway between Valdosta and Waycross. About 1:30 A.M. on June 26, 1894, as Savannah, Florida & Western's No. 6 was pulling out of the Homerville station on its nightly run from Thomasville to Savannah, six masked and armed men stormed the engine and tender and took control of the train. With a pistol in his back, the engineer, who was named Jenkins, was ordered to halt about one and one-half miles north of town.

The train carried two Southern Express Company cars; the first one was occupied by a messenger named

Crawley, and the second, a messenger named Reynolds. Reynolds saw the bandits approaching, quickly locked his car, and left by the rear door for the safety of the adjacent passenger coach. Messenger Crawley refused to open his car, and the robbers blew the door open with a charge of dynamite. The explosion knocked the messenger unconscious. The robbers then used dynamite to blast open the express company safe.

The robbery took about a half an hour, during which time several of the robbers entered the passenger coach and reminded the passengers that they had better stay in their seats. Apparently, the robbers did not notice express messenger Reynolds among the passengers. They did not try to enter the second express car.

When the robbers had finished, they ordered the fireman to cut the locomotive and tender loose from the rest of the train. They then climbed aboard the locomotive and sped away. Later that morning, the locomotive was found abandoned north of the town of Argyle, about fourteen miles from the scene of the robbery, near a road leading into the Okefenokee swamp, which at that point was about two miles away.

A posse of nearly fifty men, many armed with Winchesters, was quickly organized; and special trains were sent to neighboring towns for talented bloodhounds. By 7:30 A.M. the dogs were put on the robbers' trail. The dogs managed to track the robbers for

a while and determined that they turned back to the south toward Homerville, but the dogs eventually lost the robbers' scent.

The amount taken in the holdup was not reported by the Southern Express Company. Unofficial estimates placed it anywhere from $100 to $10,000. (Sources: *Waycross Herald* [Georgia], 30 June 1894; *St. Louis Globe Democrat*, 27 June 1894.)

HORSE CARS. Horse cars, also called posse cars, were the Union Pacific Railroad's converted baggage cars filled with mounted possemen (frequently called ranger posses) who were dispatched to the scene of a train robbery on lightning-fast special trains. The practice began in 1898, when E. H. Harriman took over as president of the railroad and vowed that express car robberies would not become one of his headaches.

Harriman quickly surveyed the problem as it existed in Wyoming, a hotbed of holdups, and came to the same conclusion that Butch Cassidy did when he got into the train robbing business: "success lay in horseflesh." Harriman knew horses, and knew that a bandit's chance for escape was usually only as good as the mount he was straddling. Harriman immediately ordered the Union Pacific's Wyoming division to find horses that could go "one hundred miles in a day." Next, he ordered the UP's officials to find the best men avail-

A horse car and Union Pacific posse. *Union Pacific Railroad.*

Union Pacific tracks near Medicine Bow, Wyoming: Wild Bunch country patrolled by the UP's horse car posses. *Union Pacific Railroad.*

able to pursue bandits. For this job, the railroad selected famed Wyoming lawman Joe Lefores and the equally experienced T. T. Keliher. To these two manhunters were added an expert guide and tracker, Sam Lawson.

Using the horse cars, the railroad put together a crack mounted posse that could be transported to the scene of a robbery in an hour or less—often much less. The plan was simple and effective, and once it was in operation, train robberies ceased to be a serious problem for the Union Pacific.

The idea of a standing force of mounted pursuers was not new. As early as 1891 observers were pointing out how effective mounted police were in handling crime in the western Canadian provinces. And in 1894 the editors of the popular industry journal *Railway Age* were pleading with the railroads and law enforcement agencies to consider such a move to combat train robbers. "Mounted police are what is wanted for the robber-cursed regions of Kansas, New Mexico, Indian Territory, Texas and where ever railway trains are being plundered without protection or redress from the government," said the *Railway Age* staff. "This remedy is worth more than all the devices for protection that have been

suggested." Eventually, the Union Pacific's E. H. Harriman proved them right.

On witnessing the success of the Union Pacific's horse cars, Pinkerton's National Detective Agency began rushing its operatives to robbery sites by flat car. Soon United States deputy marshals copied the procedure. Going a step further, some railroads began keeping single locomotives with attached horse cars in readiness on sidings at strategic locations. This proved of double value because any persons injured in a holdup could be whisked away for medical attention. (Source: Patterson, *Train Robbery*.)

HOWARD, WILLIAM. Early in the morning of December 24, 1891, a westbound Chicago & Northwestern limited passenger train, carrying Christmas travelers, left Eau Claire, Wisconsin, bound for Minneapolis, Minnesota. At the first stop, a small station just outside Eau Claire, a man boarded. He was more than six feet tall and had a black beard (later believed to be false). He wore a slouch hat, dark sack suit, and heavy boots. He also wore a heavy seal ring on the little finger of his left hand.

The train had hardly started on its way when the man walked forward to the smoking car. He stood for a few seconds at the smoker's glass door, watching the conductor and brakeman who were sitting inside chatting. He then walked back to the door of the coach, took a cushion off a seat, and jammed it against the lock on the door. Then he turned toward the passengers, pulled two large revolvers from under his coat, and announced to everyone in the car: "Throw up your hands."

The bearded intruder ordered the passengers to get up, one by one, and file to the front of the car, where they were to deposit their cash and valuables in a sack. Obediently, they complied.

About this time the conductor, William Howard, decided to begin his trip through the coaches to punch tickets. When he reached the door of the coach and saw what was happening, he immediately returned to the smoker. He calmly informed the brakeman, Frank Lane, that a robbery was occurring, and that he should try to get a pistol from one of the passengers, because they would have to break it up. He told Lane that at the next stop, which was only a few minutes away, he would leave the train, go back to the rear coach, get his revolver, and come back up through the aisles.

When he reached the rear door of the first coach, he would attract the robber's attention, and at that point Lane was to force his way through the blocked door.

When the train pulled into the stop, Howard did as he said he would. On reaching the rear coach, he got his gun and began working his way forward. When he reached the first coach, he made sure the robber saw him, and then ducked down behind one of the rear seats. The robber saw the conductor's gun and fired off a shot, but it missed. Howard returned one shot, but it also missed.

As the shots were fired, brakeman Lane, who had found a revolver, put his shoulder to the front door of the car and shoved, but it would not budge. One of the passengers, however, jumped up and removed the seat cushion that was jamming the lock. Lane barged into the car and fired his gun. He missed, and the robber turned to shoot him. As he did, conductor Howard fired again, this time striking the robber in the shoulder. The robber charged toward Howard, who again ducked behind the seat. Instead of attacking Howard, however, the robber, with his injured arm dangling at his side, lunged into the lavatory and locked the door, leaving behind his loot and his two revolvers.

At first it appeared that he was trapped, but within seconds he had the lavatory window open and leaped off the train. (Source: *New York Times*, 26 December 1891.)

HUMBOLDT, NEVADA. During the late 1890s the Wild Bunch was the first outlaw gang blamed for almost every robbery within riding distance of their favorite hideout, the Hole-in-the-Wall country of Wyoming. While the Wild Bunch probably was guilty of committing a fair share of these crimes, it has always been difficult to determine just which ones they were responsible for, and what gang members were present at the time.

Humboldt, Nevada, is just off Interstate 80 about 140 miles east of the California line. A holdup of an express car on the Southern Pacific Railroad outside of Humboldt on July 14, 1898, which according to the engineer was committed by "two white men and a negro," is now thought by outlaw researchers to have been the work of Wild Bunch members Harry "Sundance Kid" Longabaugh, Harvey "Kid Curry" Logan, and "Flat Nose" George Currie.

Humboldt, Nevada. *Frank Leslie's Illustrated Magazine, 1877.*

Shortly after 1:00 A.M., three masked men, who apparently had slipped aboard as the train was leaving the station, climbed down from the tender and ordered the engineer to stop the train about a mile northeast of Humboldt. The engine crew was forced to walk back to the Wells, Fargo express car, where the bandits ordered the messenger, whose name was Hughes, to open the car or they would blow the door off its hinges with black powder.

While one of the bandits fired his pistol alongside the coaches to keep the passengers from getting curious, the other two blasted the car's two safes and rode off with between $20,000 and $26,000. (Source: Kirby, *The Rise and Fall of the Sundance Kid*.) *See also* **Harry "Sundance Kid" Longabaugh.**

HUME, JAMES B. Jim Hume probably was the most capable of the many express company detectives who matched wits with train robbers during the last half of the nineteenth century. As Chief Special Officer of Wells, Fargo & Company from 1873 to 1904, Hume was responsible for putting dozens of the worst offenders behind bars, including the notorious Black Bart (whom the Pinkertons believed was both a train robber and stage robber).

Hume came to Wells, Fargo with experience in apprehending criminals. As former sheriff of Eldorado County, California, he had participated in many investigations of stagecoach robberies, particularly robberies of Wells, Fargo treasure boxes. Although thoroughly courageous and tough as nails, Hume differed from many of his contemporaries in that he was a strictly professional law officer who believed in an orderly arrest, trial, and conviction of a guilty party rather than a shoot-out. For this, he gained the respect of many of the criminals he put behind bars. He would often joke that nowhere was his personal standing higher than among the residents of San Quentin and Folsom prisons.

From the beginning, and especially after he took over the Wells, Fargo detective force, Hume diligently trained himself in the science of crime detection, at the time in its infancy in the western United States. The story is told that in 1878 Hume dug buckshot out of a dead horse, one of the victims of a Wells, Fargo stage-coach robbery, and later matched them with those taken from a suspect's shotgun, thus becoming an early practitioner of ballistics evidence.

In his early years with Wells, Fargo, Jim Hume's greatest asset as a detective was a penchant for single-mindedness during an investigation. Once on a case he would exhaust every clue and pursue the culprits tenaciously. Later, however, when nearly the whole continent became his beat (in 1888, when it acquired the Erie Express Company, Wells, Fargo reached New York City and became the first true transcontinental express company), Jim's workload became overwhelming, and

James B. Hume. *Wells Fargo Bank History Room, San Francisco.*

at times he reluctantly would have to give up on one investigation to undertake a more important one.

As a detective with an interstate express company, Hume could roam at will across jurisdictions, something akin to today's FBI special agents. And unlike many express company and railroad detectives of the day, he also enjoyed the close cooperation of most local law enforcement officers, mainly because he was not interested in advancing his own reputation and would let the local officers make arrests and take the credit.

Jim Hume remained active as chief of this company's detective force until April of 1897, when he was stricken with severe pains in his shoulder, neck, and behind his left ear, possibly a case of meningitis. During the first month of his illness he became nearly addicted to pain killers. In May he was taken to a sanitarium at Paso Robles, California, where he rested, took baths and waters, and was weaned off the drugs. The following month he was able to return to his office in San Francisco, but his health was never the same. His trips by rail to robbery sites became less frequent, and he turned many of his cases over to subordinates. By 1903 Hume, then seventy-six, still held the title of Chief Special Officer but what little work he did was out of his home in Berkeley. He died on May 18, 1904, after six months of steadily failing health. On May 20, the *San Francisco Chronicle* paid the following tribute to Jim Hume.

This country has produced few men who have made such a remarkable record in the persistent and successful pursuit of that class of robbers who prey specially on the express and transportation companies. . . . He was instrumental in running down some of the worst criminals the country ever produced. It has been the policy of the express company never to abandon or relax the pursuit of anyone who has committed a criminal offense against it. In some instances, the pursuit has extended over a series of years and been carried abroad to remote countries. The policy has proved to be a wise one, for it has acted as a deterrent as well as a punishment of crime. . . . Whenever Hume started on the trail of an offender against the corporation in whose service he was employed, the pursuit was never given up until his capture was effected. For more than a generation his name has been terror to stage and train robbers. They learned to know him as a keen, intelligent, officer who was as untiring and relentless as the United States Government in following and punishing offenders.

(Source: Dillon, *Wells, Fargo Detective; San Francisco Chronicle,* 20 May 1904.)

HUNTINGTON, WEST VIRGINIA. On December 12, 1892, four masked men tried to bring a touch of the old West to the hills of West Virginia by robbing a passenger coach. But they chose the wrong coach; the passengers were not in the mood to be robbed that day.

About 11 P.M., as the eastbound Chesapeake & Ohio passenger train was midway between Hunting and Guyandotte, the would-be robbers burst into the coach with guns drawn. In traditional fashion, they started down the aisle, intent on collecting the passengers' money and valuables. The first passenger who decided otherwise was Henry Zelcher of Cincinnati, Ohio. Zelcher reached up, grabbed one of the men, and tried to wrestle away his gun. The bandit jerked the gun free and shot Zelcher in the abdomen.

As the men grappled, passenger Peter Lake went to Zelcher's assistance, and he was shot twice. A third passenger, however, Sam Matthes, managed to knock the gun out of the bandit's hand. Meanwhile, the conductor, whose name was Zingley, secured two pistols of his own and began firing at the other gunmen. He wounded two of them, and they all turned and ran.

As the would-be robbers limped away through a nearby woods, they no doubt wondered if all those accounts of successful train robberies out West were indeed true. (Source: *St. Louis Globe Democrat*, 14, 15 December 1892.)

HUTCHINS, TEXAS. Hutchins, Texas, is now a southeastern Dallas suburb. On March 18, 1878, it was the scene of the Sam Bass gang's second holdup in a series of train robberies committed by the gang in the Dallas–Fort Worth area following Bass's return to Texas the previous fall.

As in their first Texas robbery (see **Allen, Texas**), as well as in the earlier $60,000 Nebraska holdup for which Bass became famous (see **Big Springs, Nebraska**), Sam and his comrades overpowered the Hutchins station agent and were waiting on the depot platform for the arrival of the next train, in this case, the Houston & Texas Central Railroad's No. 4.

Number 4 pulled in around 10:00 P.M., and the robbers sauntered over to the locomotive cab, raised their pistols, and ordered the engineer and fireman to climb down with their hands in the air. The Texas Express Company agent, Heck Thomas, and the railway mail service clerk, whose name was Terrell, both saw what was happening and began to hide away packages containing money; Thomas stuffed his in the express car's potbellied stove.

Messenger Thomas, who was no pushover (he was the Heck Thomas who later became the famous United States deputy marshal), also briefly put up a fight, taking minor gunshot wounds in the neck and face, but eventually he had to give in when the robbers made the fireman stand at the edge of the station platform in his line of fire.

Thanks to the quick work of Thomas and Terrell, the outlaws' haul was meager, less than $500 (one report said only $89). All in all it was a foolish robbery and hardly worth the risk. By attacking at the station and by not cutting the revenue cars away from the rest of the train before going after the loot, the robbers invited trouble from the passengers, which is exactly what they got. The conductor and a brakeman ran through the coaches soliciting help from the male passengers, and eventually gathered up a small armed contingent who peppered the outlaws from the coach windows. This undoubtedly hastened their departure and prevented them from finding some of the hidden packages.

On leaving, the robbers rode off in an easterly direction toward the Trinity River, probably to mislead any followers. They soon doubled back and headed northwest toward Denton County and their hideout on Hickory Creek. A posse was quickly formed but lost the robbers' tracks on the hard turf. (Source: Gard, *Sam Bass*.) See also **Sam Bass**.

HYATT, GUS. A newspaper article described Gus Hyatt's single-handed robbery of an express car near Clarksville, Tennessee, in June 1897 as a holdup "Jesse James would be proud of."

Gus was born in Cherokee, North Carolina, in 1871. Practically nothing is known of his early years, but they might have been hard years, because in 1897, at age twenty-six, he looked to be "in his early thirties" and "dissipated" from alcohol, with a "coarse, rough cast" to his face and a "wrinkled" forehead.

How many train robberies and other crimes Hyatt was connected with will never be known. In July 1897 he was arrested in a Kansas City Turkish bath and charged with the Clarksville robbery (see **Clarksville, Tennessee**). The arrest was pure luck on the part of the Kansas City police. Hyatt had left his clothes in another room to take the bath. When he returned, he found that his wallet had been stolen. Since it contained $1,000 (part of the loot taken in the Clarksville robbery), he complained to the manager. Hyatt had been drinking heavily, and he started a row. The police were called, and when they found that he was carrying two pistols, he was taken downtown to headquarters. There they found that his description matched that of the suspect in the Clarksville robbery, and he was put in the "sweatbox."

The sweatbox worked, and Hyatt confessed not only to the Clarksville robbery but also to an earlier express car holdup in Alabama. (See **Calera, Alabama**.) He also admitted to at least one murder, a member of a posse in DeKoven, Kentucky, in April 1897.

On returning to Tennessee, Hyatt pleaded guilty to the Clarksville holdup and was sentenced to fifteen years at the state penitentiary in Nashville. On August 4, 1902, he and fifteen other prisoners escaped by blowing a hole in the prison wall. (Sources: *St. Louis Globe Democrat*, 7, 8, 13 July 1897; *Clarksville Leaf Chronicle*, 23–25, 26, 28 June, 12, 13 July 1897, 4 August 1902.) □

I

IRON MOUNTAIN CROSSING (ARKANSAS). During the early years of the train robbery era, bandits occasionally used gunpowder (then called black powder) to blast their way into an express car. Later on, they switched to dynamite, which became very popular. In the interim, a few tried nitroglycerin, which sometimes was an unwise choice because of its unpredictability.

Nitroglycerin was introduced in the 1870s by Central Pacific Railroad construction crews blasting their way through the Sierra Nevadas. As a rule of thumb, nitro was considered five times more powerful than black powder, but its reputation of exploding on the slightest impact undoubtedly discouraged most outlaws from experimenting with it. Also, it was difficult to come by and usually was available only from the larger mining companies. In theory, nitro could be brewed at home, but this was especially foolhardy; it had to be kept on ice during its reaction period and carefully washed and deacidified before being used. Dynamite was more easily available and, while not free of risk, was much safer to work with.

By the turn of the century, train robberies became so common that many investigative reports no longer contained details such as what kind of explosive was used in blasting into a car or safe. Apparently, however, nitro was used at least as late as 1901.

On April 23 of that year a Choctaw, Oklahoma & Gulf passenger train was held up at Iron Mountain Crossing, about four miles west of Memphis, Tennessee. Shortly before midnight, four bandits boarded the train at Bridge Junction, Arkansas, and hid on the platform between the express car and baggage car. When the express company messenger, C. T. Meader, came out of the baggage car, they overpowered him and forced him to open up the express car.

The train had to stop at Iron Mountain Crossing; when it did the bandits took control of the locomotive and forced a porter, Sidney Drew, to uncouple the express and baggage cars from the rest of the coaches. When he didn't move fast enough, they shot him and finished the job themselves. The engineer was then ordered to pull ahead a few miles and stop.

During all this ruckus, one of the bandits had been gingerly carrying a bottle of nitroglycerin, which he attached to the express car safe. How he detonated it was not reported, but when the charge went off, the door of the safe was blown completely through the express car wall and into a tree twenty yards from the track. When the dust and debris finally settled, the bandits climbed back into the car and picked through what was left of the contents of the safe, which more than likely was not enough to have made the night's venture worthwhile. (Sources: Barber, "Gunpowder and Its Successors"; Patterson, *Train Robbery*; *New York Times*, 24 April 1901.) □

J

JACKSON, FRANK. Frank Jackson was a member of the Sam Bass gang during its reign of stagecoach and express car robberies in and around Denton, Texas, in 1877–78. He was present at Round Rock, Texas, when Bass's career came to an end at the hands of Texas Rangers in July 1878. *See* **Sam Bass**.

JAMES, JESSE EDWARDS (JESSE JAMES, JR.). Jesse Edwards James, often called Jesse James, Jr., was the son of the famous outlaw Jesse Woodson James. Young Jesse was seven years old when Bob Ford ended his father's career with a bullet in the brain at St. Joseph, Missouri, in 1882.

Jesse, Jr., was born while his parents were in hiding in Nashville, Tennessee. At the time, the elder Jesse was using the name Howard and posing as a farm produce trader and wheat speculator, a "job" that required being out of town for long periods of time. Young Jesse was named after his father's friend and supporter, John Newman Edwards, the radical St. Louis and later Kansas City newspaperman who staunchly defended the renegade Jesse and his brother, Frank, throughout their criminal careers.

On Jesse, Sr.'s death in 1882, his wife, Zee, took young Jesse and his younger sister, Mary, to Kansas City where she hoped the family could lose itself in the anonymity of a large city. Although quite poor, the family managed to survive. At fifteen, Jesse went to work running errands for a Kansas City law firm. At seventeen, he left that job for better paying work as a "stock-taker" at a meat packing company. Then in 1896 he obtained a political patronage job of managing the cigar and confection concession at the Kansas City branch of the county courthouse.

The new job paid well, but it had a bad side. Young Jesse, now twenty-one, became associated with what was considered a rough crowd, among whom was an unsavory character named Jack "Quail Hunter" Kennedy.

Jack Kennedy had been a suspect in several holdups in and around Kansas City, and had once been tried for train robbery. Apparently he and young Jesse be-

Jesse James, Jr., at age nineteen. *Carl Breihan Collection.*

came close friends. The reason for this association is not known, but it has been speculated that Kennedy had developed a fascination with the history of the James gang and had dreamed of someday leading such a group of his own. Some observers suggest that Kennedy believed that it would prove that he was a big-time outlaw if he could persuade the son of the famous Jesse James to join his gang. Whatever the reason for the relationship, it set the stage for the event that would alter the course of Jesse Edwards James' life: the robbery of a Missouri Pacific train at Leeds, Missouri.

On Friday, September 23, 1898, around 10:00 P.M., five or six armed men climbed aboard the Missouri Pacific southbound as it slowed for the Belt Line Junction near Leeds, about five miles southeast of Kansas City. After taking control of the locomotive, the robbers forced their way into the express car and dynamited the two safes. But after scooping up the contents, about $2,000, they did a curious thing; they left the following note: "We, the masked knights of the road, robbed the M.P. train at the Belt Line Junction tonight. The supply of quails was good. With much love we remain, John Kennedy, Bill Ryan, Bill Anderson, Sam Brown, Jim Redmond."

At the bottom of the note the bandits added "We are ex-compact to," which the law enforcement authorities eventually determined to be an attempt to write *ex conspectu*, Latin for "out of sight."

Local law officers assumed the name "John Kennedy" on the note referred to Jack "Quail Hunter"Kennedy, whose given name was John. Also, the reference to a "supply of quails" seemed obvious. The name "Bill Ryan" likewise was familiar: in 1881, a small-time criminal and associate of Kennedy's named Bill Ryan had been convicted of participating in a train holdup. There was no "Bill Anderson" on local police blotters, but in one of the earlier robberies in which Jack Kennedy was a suspect, a witness had testified that the name "Anderson" had been used, presumably as an alias, by one of the suspects. The remaining names, "Sam Brown" and "Jim Redmond," meant nothing.

The authorities were stumped: if Kennedy and Ryan were in on the Leeds robbery, why would they draw attention to themselves with such a note? Both men were picked up and questioned, but both produced witnesses who were ready to testify that they were elsewhere on the night of the holdup.

Two days later, Jesse Edwards James also was named a suspect in the Leeds holdup. The locomotive engineer who was forced from his cab at gunpoint told the authorities that he thought he recognized one of the bandits as a man named Bill Lowe, a former fireman on the Missouri Pacific line. Lowe was picked up, and when the officers searched him, they found two pieces of paper in his pocket. Both were notes to himself asking for a meeting; one was signed "J. F. Kennedy," and the other, "Jesse James."

The authorities wasted no time in picking up young Jesse. His friendship with Kennedy was well-known down at police headquarters, but moreover, the previous December, Jesse had been one of several witnesses who had supplied Kennedy with an alibi when he was accused of killing a Kansas City grocer during an attempted robbery.

Jesse James, Jr., at the homestead grave in Clay County, Missouri. *Carl Breihan Collection.*

When the news spread that Jesse was going to be tried for train robbery, dozens of prominent Kansas City citizens rallied to his support. There was still much sympathy in western Missouri for Jesse's father, and as far as anyone knew, young Jesse had led a clean and respectable life.

With the familiar name of Jesse James in the headlines again, the story attracted nationwide interest. As the trial date neared, out-of-town reporters converged on Kansas City to cover the case. Young Jesse enjoyed

John Newman Edwards, fiery newspaper editor whose editorials were used by Jesse James, Jr.'s lawyer to defend him in court. *Carl Breihan Collection.*

the attention and readily made himself available to the newspapermen, in one instance, even to the point of inviting a reporter out to Clay County for a tour of the family homestead.

When the case finally came to trial in February 1899, spectators packed the courtroom. At first the charge against Jesse looked weak. The sole witness against him was his fellow defendant Bill Lowe, who confessed his part in the holdup and named Jesse as a participant. Furthermore, Lowe testified that not only was Jesse involved in the plot, it was he who more or less set the date of the robbery. According to Lowe, the gang had planned to rob the train on an earlier night, but Jesse asked that it be postponed because his uncle Frank James would be in town, and in view of Frank's past record, Jesse was afraid he might be suspected of taking part in the affair.

Also, Lowe testified that one of the robbers at Leeds was a man named Charles Polk, and Polk, it was revealed, had once worked with Jesse at the meat-packing plant.

Even with all of the above, Jesse's lawyers were not too worried, because it is always difficult to get a conviction solely on the testimony of one accused criminal against another. But then the prosecutor announced that he had further evidence. Several members of the train crew would testify that they believed that young Jesse was indeed one of the men who robbed the train that night.

Jesse's best defense was an alibi. He had witnesses who would swear that he was elsewhere on the night of the holdup. His next best defense was a long line of character witnesses who would testify that the idea of this fine young man being involved in a train robbery was unthinkable.

On cross-examination, Jesse's lawyers hammered away at the trainmen, challenging them to show how they could identify masked attackers in the dark of night. The lawyers suggested to the jury that the witnesses had been pressured by the railroad and the express company to obtain a conviction no matter what. (Jesse had claimed from the beginning that his arrest had been the result of a conspiracy between the railroad and their detective agency, the Furlong Secret Service, to obtain a quick conviction regardless of the cost in order to serve as a deterrent to further robberies.)

The defense's aggressive cross-examination no doubt was effective, as was Jesse's alibi and character witnesses, which gave the jurors, if they so wished, an opportunity to disregard completely the state's eyewitness testimony. But it was a rousing summation to the jury by Jesse's lawyer, a talented Kansas City trial practitioner named Frank P. Walsh, that is remembered by reporters who were in the courtroom.

Walsh vigorously attacked the state's evidence, pointing out the obvious motives behind Bill Lowe's testimony and the probable motives of the train crew. Then he reminded the jury of the darkness of the night and the fallibility of eyewitness testimony under such circumstances. For his concluding remarks he saved his best punch, the fiery prose of an editorial of young Jesse's namesake, newspaperman John Newman Edwards, condemning the state of Missouri for the wrong done the senior Jesse James. Taking full advantage of the Robin Hood legend that hung to the memory of the James brothers, and carefully molding Edwards's familiar phrases into the facts of the case at hand, Walsh left the jurors with these eloquent words to take with them to the jury room:

> What a spectacle! Missouri, with all her order, progress and development. Missouri, with every screw and cog and crank and lever and wheel of her administrative machinery in perfect working order. Is it possible that this great commonwealth had to ally itself with hired detectives, with paid bloodhounds of the law, that the majesty of this law might be vindicated?
> This trial means more than the mere fate of this boy. If you convict him we might as well tear the two bears from the flag of Missouri, and put thereon, in place of them, as more appropriate, the leering face of a detective and the crawling, snake-like shape of an informer!

The jury returned a verdict of not guilty. Most persons who have studied the case agree that young Jesse was innocent, that Bill Lowe, Charles Polk, and several others probably committed the robbery and left the note at the scene to throw suspicion on Kennedy and Ryan. Eventually, however, the indictments against all remaining suspects were dismissed.

The trial had a profound effect on young Jesse. Perhaps fascinated by the drama of the courtroom and impressed by the talented lawyers involved in the case, Jesse got the urge to become a lawyer himself. He studied law at the Kansas City School of Law and in time was admitted to the Missouri Bar. He practiced in Kansas City for twenty-five years.

Jesse never tried to hide the fact that he was the son of the famous outlaw, and he proudly used the name Jesse James, Jr., rather than his true name, Jesse Edwards James. Not long after the trial, probably with the help of a professional writer, he came out with a book entitled *Jesse James, My Father*. In 1939 one of his four daughters, Jo Frances, helped write the screenplay for the Twentieth Century Fox motion picture, *Jesse James*, starring Tyrone Power and Henry Fonda.

Jesse Edwards James lived to be seventy-five. He died in 1951 at his home in Los Angeles where he and his wife, Stella, had moved after he retired from practicing law in Kansas City. A grandson, Jo Frances's boy, followed in his grandfather's footsteps and became a superior court judge in Orange County, California. (Sources: Burton, "John F. Kennedy of Missouri and His Circle of Train Robbers"; Garwood, *Crossroads of America: The Story of Kansas City*; Patterson, "The Trial of Jesse James, Jr.") *See also* **The James-Younger Gang; Jack "Quail Hunter" Kennedy; Leeds, Missouri**.

JAMES, FRANK. *See* **The James-Younger Gang**.

JAMES, JESSE WOODSON. *See* **The James-Younger Gang**.

THE JAMES-YOUNGER GANG. It is difficult to trace the activities of Frank and Jesse James with any accuracy. These two outlaws, natives of Clay County, Missouri, often used assumed names and seldom remained in one place for any length of time. The few persons privy to their coming and going kept their mouths shut. In fact, whether Frank and Jesse actually took part in many of the robberies with which they have been credited may never be known. It has been fairly well documented, however, that the James boys raised a lot of hell before they robbed their first train, which discredits to some extent the notion that they turned to a life of crime because of a hatred for the railroads.

Accompanying Jesse and Frank on many of their escapades were the Younger brothers, also products of rural western Missouri. There were four Youngers in all. The best of the bunch probably was Cole, a big, likeable man who charmed the ladies and possessed what many would call a kind streak. The worst was undoubtedly John: hard drinking and troublesome, he killed his first man when he was only fifteen. And then

there was Jim Younger, who was easy-going and who probably took to outlawry only because his brothers did. Bob, the youngest, was more dedicated to a career in crime and would likely have led a gang of his own one day had he not been killed at the early age of twenty-three.

The Youngers and Jameses had long been friends: Cole had seen service in the Civil War with Frank James, and Jim and Jesse had fought side by side for the Confederacy.

Jesse and Frank's first train robbery is believed to have been on July 21, 1873, at Adair, Iowa. A rail was yanked from under the drivers of a Chicago, Rock Island & Pacific locomotive, which sent it careening into the ditch. While the stunned train crew tried to rescue the engineer, who died in the crash, the robbers calmly helped themselves to the contents of the express car and then went through the passenger coaches.

Most authorities think the James's next robbery was at Gads Hill, Missouri, on January 31, 1874, this time with the help of several of the Youngers. Just before dark, five masked men walked into the depot serving the Iron Mountain Railroad and ordered all present to stand in the corner with their hands up. When the train arrived at 5:40, the gang ordered the conductor off at gunpoint and methodically went through the passenger coaches, taking money and valuables. Next, they forced their way into the express car and emptied its safe and mail bags.

The Gads Hill robbery is remembered because of a note left at the scene; the first of several attributed to the James-Younger bunch. It read:

The most daring on record – the southbound train on the Iron Mountain Railroado was Robbed here this evening by seven heavily armed men, and robbed of ——— dollars. The robbers arrived at the station some time before the arrival of the train, and arrested the station agent and put him under guard, then threw the train on the switch. The robbers were all large men, none of them under six feet tall. They were all masked and started in a southerly direction after they had robbed the train. They were all mounted on fine blooded horses. There is a hell of an excitement in this part of the country.

On the outside of the note was written: "this contains an exact account of the robbery. We prefer this to be published in the newspapers rather than the grossly exaggerated accounts that usually appear after one of our jobs."

Frank James. *The Kansas State Historical Society, Topeka, Kansas.*

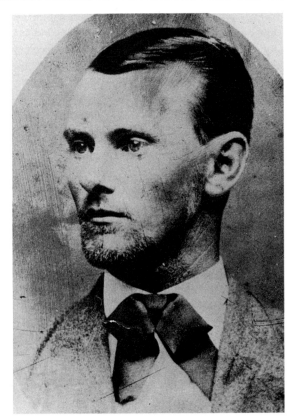

Jesse Woodson James. *The Kansas State Historical Society, Topeka, Kansas.*

Infuriated by the audacity of the outlaws, Missouri Governor Silas Woodson offered a $2,000 reward for each of the robbers. The United States Postal Department added $5,000, and the governor of Arkansas kicked in another $2,000.

At the request of the express company, the Pinkerton's National Detective Agency took up the chase. The agency sent one of its most ambitious young operatives, John W. Witcher, to western Missouri. He immediately picked up a warm trail, but it would be the last he would ever follow. A month later his body was found at the side of a road in Jackson County. He had been shot in the head, shoulder, and stomach, and half of his face had been eaten by wild hogs.

The Pinkertons were convinced that Jesse James and a fellow outlaw named Clell Miller were responsible for Witcher's death, and the detective agency launched an all-out campaign to bring in the entire gang. Several days later, two Pinkerton agents, Louis Lull and

John Boyle, and a former deputy sheriff, Edwin Daniel, came upon John and Jim Younger at a farmhouse near Monegaw Springs, in St. Clair County, Missouri. According to an account given by Jim Younger to the owner of the farmhouse, Theodrick Snuffer, a friend of the Youngers, the outlaws got the drop on the three man-hunters and ordered them to unbuckle their gun belts. Boyle spurred his horse and got away, but Lull and Daniel complied and tossed their guns on the ground. As the outlaws were picking up the guns, however, Lull drew out a concealed Derringer and shot John Younger through the neck. As Younger was falling, he got off a shot that struck Lull, knocking him from his saddle. Daniel then made a break and Jim Younger shot him. John Younger and Daniel died at the scene, and Lull died weeks later.

The remainder of the James-Younger gang immediately disappeared from the area; however, during the next year the Pinkertons picked up rumors that Jesse and Frank were occasionally returning to their family home near Kearney at night to visit their mother and young step-brother, Archie, and in some instances, to rendezvous with gang members in a nearby wooded area. On January 26, 1875, a group of men, believed to be Pinkertons, converged on the house, thinking that Jesse and Frank were hiding inside. To drive the outlaws out of the house, they tossed in incendiary devices made of oil-soaked cotton wrapped around pieces of metal. Apparently the purpose was to smoke out the bandits, but when the objects came crashing through the window, the James's brothers' step-father, Dr. Reuben Samuel, kicked them into the fireplace. On coming in contact with the flames, the second device exploded, killing young Archie and severely injuring his mother. The tragedy infuriated local residents and a Clay County grand jury indicted Allan Pinkerton for the boy's death. Sympathy for the family spread throughout the state, and a resolution was introduced in the state legislature recommending amnesty for Jesse and Frank. It failed on a split vote. The Pinkertons were now stymied. Feelings ran so high against them in western Missouri that they dared not send in any more agents.

It is believed that the next James-Younger train robbery occurred near Muncie, Kansas, on December 8, 1875. Five men forced section hands to pile ties across the track and the Kansas Pacific train was halted by a robber waving a red scarf. Approximately $30,000 was taken from the express car. Jesse James may or may not have been along on this holdup; he was at the time hiding out in Nashville, Tennessee, where three weeks later his wife, Zee, would give birth to their son, Jesse Edwards James.

Just who was riding with the James and Youngers at this point will never be known for sure. Names mentioned in the Pinkerton files included Bill Anderson, Clell Miller, John Miller, Charles Pitts, Bill Chadwell, Jim Cummings, and Dick Liddel.

Most authorities think the gang's next holdup was at Rocky Cut, near Otterville, Missouri, on July 7, 1876. The victim was the Missouri Pacific Railroad.

In September 1876 the James-Younger bunch attempted their fateful bank robbery at Northfield, Minnesota. Citizens of the town took up the fight and killed Bill Chadwell, Clell Miller, and Charley Pitts. Jesse James and Bob and Jim Younger were wounded. Several days later, Cole, Jim, and Bob Younger were captured. There

is evidence that Jesse, with the help of Frank, fled into Dakota, where they stole a skiff and escaped via the Missouri River.

Cole, Jim, and Bob Younger were all sentenced to long terms at the state prison in Minnesota. Jesse and Frank disappeared. There is some evidence that during the summer of 1878 Frank may have been involved in an attempted holdup of a Union Pacific train near Carbon, Wyoming, by the "Big Nose" George Parrot gang. According to the story, a UP section foreman noticed a rail that had been loosened by the outlaws and he flagged down the train.

There is also a story that Frank was joined by Jesse in Wyoming later that year, and the two spent the winter of 1878–79 in the southwestern part of the state. It seems unlikely, however, that Jesse, a devoted father and husband, would have left his family, then living in Tennessee, for such an adventure.

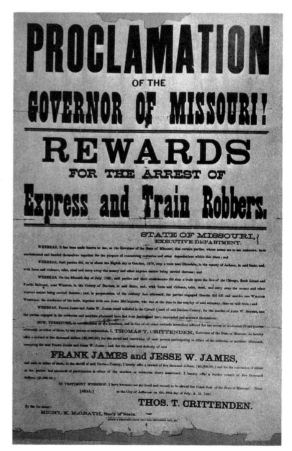

Reward notice for Frank and Jesse James. *Author's Collection*.

The James brothers were mentioned off and on throughout 1878–79 in connection with holdups, but it was early October 1879 before there was strong evidence tying them to another train robbery. On the eighth of that month a gang of robbers took over the depot at Glendale, in Jackson County, Missouri, and robbed the express car of a Chicago & Alton passenger train which arrived a short time later.

The following month a rumor spread that Jesse James had been killed. The man claiming credit was a crusty former Civil War guerrilla named George Shepherd, who had once ridden with the gang. According to a newspaper account, Shepherd had turned on Jesse in return for favors from the authorities. Shepherd was supposed to have set the gang up to be ambushed during a bank robbery at Short Creek, Missouri, a small town near Joplin, but Jesse had called off the raid when he spotted an extra guard at the bank. Shepherd then decided to shoot Jesse while the two were riding outside Galena, Kansas. According to Shepherd, he and Jesse drew at the same time but he got his shot off first, striking Jesse in the head. At first the tale was labeled a hoax, but it began to gain credence when Cole Younger, interviewed in prison, said he believed it. A week later, an unverified report appeared that gang member Jim Cummings said Shepherd had told the truth. A rumor then spread that Jesse's body had arrived at Kearney, Missouri, by train from Kansas City, and had been buried somewhere in Clay County.

The Pinkertons, however, refused to believe the story. On being sought out by reporters, Robert Pinkerton

An aged Frank James playing host to James Farm visitors. *Clay County Department of Parks, Recreation and Historical Sites.*

released this statement: "No one should know more about Jesse James than I do, for our men have chased him from one end of the country to the other. His gang killed one of our detectives, who tracked them down, and I consider Jesse James the worst man, without exception in America. He is utterly devoid of fear, and has no more compunction about cold-blooded murder than he has about eating his breakfast. I don't believe Shepherd would dare to shoot him."

It was eventually determined that Jesse had not been killed, and that the story had been concocted by Jesse and Shepherd.

The gang returned to robbing trains on July 15, 1881. The victim was the Rock Island line near Winston, Missouri. Two men were killed in the affair: the conductor and a passenger. Some say this robbery may have sealed Jesse's fate. Missouri Governor T. T. Crittenden, influenced by public outcry over the killings, announced a total of $55,000 in rewards for the outlaws. On April 3, 1882, in St. Joseph, Missouri, a fellow gang member, Bob Ford, presumably for the reward, picked up a .45 caliber Smith & Wesson handgun and put a bullet in Jesse's brain.

Jesse's death took the heart out of Frank James. Once described as not having the "quarrelsome and rowdyish tendencies" of his brother, Frank soon found that emptying express car safes no longer appealed to him. On October 5, 1882, Frank walked into Governor Crittenden's office in Jefferson City and gave himself up. (Sources: Breihan, *The Escapades of Frank and Jesse James;* Pinkerton, *Train Robberies;* Settle, *Jesse James Was His Name.*) *See also* **Adair, Iowa; Gads Hill, Mis-**

James Farm, Kearney, Missouri, now under restoration. *Clay County Department of Parks, Recreation and Historical Sites.*

souri; Glendale (Jackson County), Missouri; Muncie, Kansas; Otterville, Missouri; Winston, Missouri.

JENNINGS, AL. Al Jennings was one of the most enigmatic train robbers in the history of the western frontier. Some wonder if he ever really robbed a train. He probably did, but when and where is still in doubt. The problem is that most of the information we have on Jennings's outlaw career came from Al himself, and he had a tendency to stray from the truth.

Jennings was a not-too-successful lawyer practicing in Woodward, Oklahoma. As an attorney, Al had no special talent except, perhaps, a penchant for imagination and dramatization. Also, he was cursed with a violent temper. On October 8, 1895, Al's brother, Ed Jennings, also a lawyer, got into an argument in court with a fellow member of the bar, Temple Houston, son of the famous Sam Houston. Ed questioned the admissibility of certain testimony, and Houston mumbled something about Ed being "ignorant of the law." Ed jumped up from the counsel table and rushed at Houston. He was restrained by others in the courtroom, and tempers cooled.

That evening the two attorneys happened to meet in a local saloon, and the argument was renewed. This time guns were drawn, and when it was over Ed Jennings lay dead, and another Jennings brother, John, was seriously wounded. Houston and a friend, Jack Love, who was also involved in the shooting, were charged with murder but both were acquitted.

Al Jennings and another brother, Frank, also a lawyer, were bent on revenge, but after thinking over the consequences, they chose instead to leave town, thus avoiding, in Al's words, what would be a "continual temptation" to kill Houston.

Al and Frank drifted a while, then joined up with outlaws and, according to Al, became train robbers. It is here the story of Al Jennings becomes murky. Just what he and his brother accomplished during their crime career is open to question. They may have been involved in an attempted holdup of a southbound Santa Fe passenger train near Edmond, Oklahoma, on August 16, 1897. Shortly thereafter Al claimed they tried to stop a Kansas & Texas passenger train near Muskogee, Oklahoma, by piling a stack of crossties on the track, but the engineer chose to slam his way through, leaving the would-be robbers staring in disbelief. And there

was another attempt at a Santa Fe express car near Purcell, Oklahoma, but they had to call it off when they saw a posse in the distance.

According to Al, they finally struck paydirt in southern Oklahoma, about twenty miles north of the Texas line, but he gave few details about the robbery, except that it was a Wells, Fargo express car and he came away with $30,000. After this robbery, Al claimed that he and Frank took a vacation to Honduras. On returning, it is believed they ransacked a mail car on the Rock Island line on October 1, 1897, at what is now Pocasset, Oklahoma.

The Jennings brothers' criminal career came to an end the first week of December 1897. On November 29, federal officers received a tip that the gang was spotted about twenty-five miles northeast of Tulsa. The following night a posse surrounded them at a farmhouse near the town of Claremore. Near dawn the officers moved in. A lengthy gun battle erupted and Al was wounded, but both he and Frank escaped. They next showed up at a ranch owned by Sam Baker on Carr Creek, near Bond, Oklahoma. The story goes that Baker offered the outlaws refuge and told them that he could arrange for their escape out of the territory. Actually, however, Baker informed the authorities that the fugitives were hiding at his ranch. Federal officers closed in, and Al and Frank, together with gang member Pat O'Malley, surrendered without a fight.

While in prison, Al developed a friendship with a chubby convict named William S. Porter, a former newspaper reporter who had been convicted for em-

Lawyer-turned-train robber Al Jennings, recreating his outlaw days. *Curtis Publishing Co.*

bezzlement while working at a bank. Porter would later become famous as the short story writer O. Henry. During their days in prison, Jennings supplied Porter with many fanciful tales of the outlaw West, some of which the writer later turned into published stories. Among them was "Holding up a Train," which Porter sold to *Everybody's Magazine* in 1901 as a piece based on information supplied by "an expert in the business."

The article was written in the first person and was introduced by this note: "The man who told me these things was for several years an outlaw in the Southwest and a follower of the pursuit he so frankly describes. His description of the *modus operandi* should prove interesting, his counsel of value to the potential passenger in some future 'hold-up,' while his estimate of the pleasures of train robbing will hardly induce any one to adopt it as a profession. I give the story in almost exactly his own words. O. H."

The article, which runs nearly 4,500 words, probably was written as a rough draft by Jennings and polished by Porter. It is set in Oklahoma in 1890 (five years before Jennings became a train robber) and begins with what purports to be the writer's first train robbery. From there it quickly spans the writer's career and general philosophy on robbing trains for a living. It reeks of bravado ("I never knew officers to attack a band of outlaws unless they out-numbered them at least three to one.") and exaggeration ("I jabbed my six-shooter so hard against Mr. Conductor's front that I afterward found one of his vest buttons so firmly wedged in the end of the barrel that I had to shoot it out."), but also contains some thoughtful observations ("I saw one of the bravest marshals I ever knew hide his gun under his seat and dig up along with the rest while I was taking toll. He wasn't afraid; he simply knew that we had the drop on the whole outfit. Besides, many of those officers have families and they feel that they oughtn't to take chances; whereas death has no terrors for the man who holds up a train. He expects to get killed some day, and he generally does.")

Jennings eventually was released from prison and returned to Oklahoma where he managed to get reinstated to practice law. The celebrity bug had bitten him, however, and he thoroughly enjoyed his reputation as a former train robber. The wilder his tales, the more his audiences loved it, and he was soon adding new chapters to his story. In 1913, with the help of profes-

sional newspaperman and writer Will Irwin, he published a autobiography of his outlaw days, an outrageous account of derring-do. He would later retell his story as a serial in *The Saturday Evening Post*, and in a second autobiography in which he elaborated on his prison days and his friendship with O. Henry, who had by then become world famous. Eventually, Jennings's imagination knew no bounds. He told of how, during the height of the Civil War, his mother had borne him "in a fence corner in the snow" while she lay "in a fainting collapse" after a five-day flight from Yankee invaders who had burned the family's Tennessee plantation; and how he had run away from home at age eleven to become a cowboy; and how he killed his first badman at age fourteen.

When western movies became popular, Al drifted to Hollywood, where he tried his hand at writing, directing, and acting. He had moderate success for a while, and eventually made Los Angeles his home. In his later years he supported himself by giving long-winded speeches to local groups about his outlaw days. Always of boundless energy, he was still going strong well into his eighties. Eventually, however, his outlandish tales became a pitiful joke. For example, in 1948, before a meeting of the National Rifle Association, he told his audience: "There was no faster gunman in the world than me. . . . I could hit a fly at twenty feet every shot, and do it so fast you couldn't see me draw my gun." He followed with disjointed stories about riding with the James and Youngers, and hobnobbing with Bat Masterson, the Earp brothers, and Doc Holliday, and how he turned down an invitation from the Daltons to join them at their ill-fated venture to Coffeyville, Kansas.

Al Jennings's one claim to fame was that he probably outlived every other nineteenth-century train robber. He lived until 1961, dying peacefully at age ninety-eight. (Sources: Echols, "Old Al Jennings"; Jennings, *Through the Shadows with O. Henry*; Patterson, "The Trial of Al Jennings"; Shirley, *West of Hell's Fringe*; Wellman, *Dynasty of Western Outlaws*; Jennings v. United States.) *See also* **William Sidney Porter (O. Henry)**.

JOHNSON, ALVARADO. Alvarado Johnson was a San Fernando Valley rancher who turned to train robbery in 1895. In December of that year he and one of his ranch hands, a former South Dakota cattle rustler and horse thief named William H. "Kid" Thompson, robbed Southern Pacific Train No. 20 at Roscoe Station, about two miles north of Burbank, California. The following February they robbed the same train at the same site, this time wrecking it by leaving a switch open. Both men were captured and sent to prison. *See* **Roscoe Switch (California)**.

JOHNSON, ARKANSAS. Arkansas Johnson was a member of the Sam Bass gang during their reign of stagecoach and train robberies in and around Denton, Texas, in 1877–78. He was killed in a shootout with lawmen at Cottondale, Texas, on June 13, 1878. *See* **Sam Bass**.

JOLIET, ILLINOIS. In 1896 three train robbers tried to stage a western-type holdup on a Rock Island passenger train near Joliet, but got more than they bargained for from a mysterious stranger.

The date was March 9. About two miles west of the city, three men boarded one of the passenger cars of a westbound train as coal was being loaded into the tender. They drew revolvers and quickly marched down the aisle, ordering the passengers to hand over their money and valuables. Their take, however, appeared to be extremely light, and they proceeded through the end door to the next car.

As the men entered the second car, one of them shouted: "Hold up your hands!" Most of the passengers complied, or meekly crouched down behind their seats, hoping not to be noticed until they had stuffed their cash and jewelry into boots or crevices in the uphol-

Rock Island station at Joliet. *Everett R. Huffer Collection.*

stery. One passenger, however, neither threw up his hands nor crouched down. On hearing the robber's command, this passenger—a tall man near the front who wore a slouched, western-type broad-brimmed hat—smoothly whipped out two six-shooters from under his coat and snapped off five quick shots. Apparently he did not try to hit the bandits, but it wasn't necessary. The three intruders turned and dashed out the door. At the last glimpse, they were seen disappearing on the far side of the coal bins.

Several of the stunned passengers ventured forward to thank the man who had just spared them the loss of their cash and valuables. When they reached his seat, they found him calmly reloading his pistols. One of them later told a reporter that there was something in the stranger's appearance that suggested that he did not carry two revolvers merely for pleasure, and that they probably seldom left his side, asleep or awake. (Sources: *Joliet Daily Republican*, 9 March 1896; *St. Louis Globe Democrat*, 9 March 1896.)

THE JONES BROTHERS. It was a hot, nearly breezeless night, which was unusual for the gently rolling wheat country of eastern Colorado. The date was August 4, 1900, and the Union Pacific's eastbound No. 4 had just passed through Hugo, a tiny produce center on the Big Sandy River in sparsely populated Lincoln County. The time was shortly after midnight, and everyone in the Pullman section was asleep, everyone, that is, except Wilson, the conductor.

Wilson was wide awake. He had seen the shadow of a man on the vestibule between the first and second cars. Thinking it was a tramp, he opened the door to order him off at the next stop, but when he stepped outside, he found himself facing two masked men with guns. Motioning him back inside, one of the men said: "Take this sack and pass down the aisle and wake up the passengers one at a time. Tell them to shell out their pocket-books and jewelry and they won't be hurt. The first man who resists I'll kill. I'll be with you and I'll have a gun in each hand. Bill here, my partner, will stand back in the door. If I don't get the fellow who doesn't do as you tell him to, Bill will. And first turn up the lights."

The conductor took the sack and started down the aisle. After turning over their money and valuables, the passengers were ordered to stand in the center of the aisle where the robber in the rear could watch them. Every passenger was rousted out, men and women.

Everything went smoothly until the conductor reached the last passenger, sixty-six-year-old W. J. Fay of Anaheim, California. Fay was a former prospector, a rugged veteran of California's gold rush days, and he had seen his share of hard cases. He was not the kind to be intimidated by a brash bandit with a couple of pistols. When Wilson called upon Fay to "shell out," Fay reached under his pillow, pulled out his own revolver, and shoved it in the robber's face. But the bandit at the end of the car was quicker, and he sent a bullet through Fay's head. Fay dropped the gun and rolled out of his berth onto the floor. One of the robbers pulled the bell cord, and as the train slowed, both leaped from the car into the darkness.

Sometime during the hours before dawn, north of Boyero, Colorado, the fleeing bandits stole two horses from a rancher and headed east, toward the Kansas line. By late morning local authorities had formed a posse, and by that afternoon a detachment of the Union Pacific mounted special agents had been rushed to the scene by horse cars.

The bandits rode hard until their horses were ready to drop, then they roped two more they found grazing on the range. These animals were ridden hard too, until they both fell from exhaustion. The posse found both mounts dead on the trail. Finding no more horses, the robbers boarded an eastbound Rock Island train. Probably fearing that notice of the robbery and murder would be telegraphed to all stations in the area, the two bandits rode only as far as Goodland, Kansas, about eighteen miles from the Colorado line.

The burning of the Bartholomew home, and the end of the Jones brothers. *M. C. Parker, Goodland, Kansas.*

Outside of Goodland, the two men stopped at a farmhouse owned by a family named Bartholomew. They said they were travelers from Iowa heading for California, and the family invited them in for food and rest. Assuming they were safe for the present, the robbers decided to hang around for awhile.

But news of strangers who are in no hurry to move on traveled fast in a rural community such as Goodland, and when the local sheriff, William Walker, learned that the Bartholomews had out-of-town guests, he passed the word along the the Union Pacific agents, who had guessed that the bandits were following the Rock Island tracks eastward. On August 10, Walker and two deputies rode out to the house, pretending to be cowboys with a herd of horses. Behind them, out of sight, was the Union Pacific posse.

The bandits, who had become edgy over the past several days, were out in the field when Walker and his deputies came riding down the road. On seeing the riders, the two men raced for the house. The lawmen opened fire, and so did the bandits. One of the deputies was hit in the belly. A few minutes later, a bullet from a lawman's Winchester split the skull of one of the bandits. In the confusion, the Bartholomew family fled to safety. The remaining robber retreated to the second floor of the house where he could command a good view of his attackers.

Word spread throughout the area that a battle was in process, and hundreds of people came out to the farm to watch. Some who had brought rifles tried to crawl close enough to take potshots at the second-story windows. Late in the afternoon, rather than let his men get picked off, Sheriff Walker decided to set the dwelling on fire. The Bartholomews were consulted, and the county, or the railroad, or both, agreed to reimburse the family for the loss. Three possemen crawled close enough to the house to lob railroad torpedos into the windows, and soon the structure was in flames.

The trapped robber never came out. At 10:00 that night the lawmen found his body. He apparently had shot himself before the flames reached him. In his pockets were the two masks used in the holdup, and a watch belonging to one of the passengers. Papers identified him as John Jones, hometown unknown. The other bandit was believed to be his brother, Jim. (Sources: Porter, "The Hold-up at Hugo"; Steel, "The Jones Boys.") □

K

KANSAS CITY, MISSOURI. Around Kansas City they were calling it "another brilliant achievement" for the train robbers that continuously plagued western Missouri during the 1890s. This time the victim was the Kansas City, Pittsburg and Gulf Railroad, which with great embarrassment had to report that the robbers managed to ransack the express car and escape even before the train had left the city limits.

The date was January 4, 1898. At 6:40 P.M., the southbound *Port Arthur Express* had just left the downtown depot when two men, who apparently entered the express car as it was pulling away from the station platform, overpowered the messenger and bound and gagged him. Working rapidly, they opened the local safe, emptied it of its contents, and jumped off the car when it slowed for the crossing at Air Line Junction near the southeastern edge of the city. Nobody even knew of the robbery until a porter entered the car a short time later and found the messenger still tied up.

The express company reported the loss at only $200 to $300, but the Kansas City police believed the figure was probably closer to several thousand dollars. (Source: *New York Times*, 5 January 1898.)

KENNEDY, JACK "QUAIL HUNTER." His full name was John F. Kennedy, but he was from Missouri, not Massachusetts. His birthplace is believed to have been somewhere in Jackson County, probably just east of Independence. His year of birth was 1868 or thereabout.

On reaching adulthood, Kennedy drifted to Texas, where he went to work for the Southern Pacific Railroad out of Houston, first as a fireman on a locomotive, and then as an engineer. He was fired, however, as a result of his participation in labor union efforts.

In September 1896 Kennedy returned to Missouri. He is believed to have been one of three men who robbed an express car the following month on the Chicago & Alton Railroad at Blue Cut, about two miles west of Glendale Station in Jackson County. The robbers did not bring dynamite and, according to Pacific Express Company records, they were able to empty only the local safe, which contained around $300 and some jewelry.

Two months later, on December 23, 1896, another Chicago & Alton train was struck at the same site. This time the robbers, believed to be the same three, brought dynamite to blow the through safe, but did not need it. According to newspaper accounts, the local safe was carrying between $20,000 and $30,000, although the Pacific Express Company admitted to losing only $4,000, which in this case was probably closer to the truth.

An investigation of the two robberies turned up Kennedy as a suspect, partly from local gossip and partly because one of the robbers had shown proficiency in handling the locomotive after cutting the express and baggage cars away from the rest of the train. Kennedy was arrested on December 30, and the following week a second man, Jim Flynn, who was known to associate with Kennedy, was also picked up. Flynn, considered something of a dimwit, immediately confessed to the December robbery, but then repudiated the claim. Later, undoubtedly after a lawyer got hold of him, he confessed again, but this time in return for the prosecutor's promise that the case against him would be dismissed.

There were two other witnesses against Kennedy, but both were weak on credibility: one was something of a local character, a known perjurer of doubtful mental stability, and the other was a school marm whom Kennedy had recently spurned.

The case against Kennedy for the December robbery went to trial in April, but the evidence against him was weak. In addition, the rural Jackson County jurors did not consider stopping and robbing a train of the arrogant Chicago & Alton Railroad much of a crime, especially if one of their own boys was a suspect. As a result, Kennedy's lawyer managed to lock up the jury without a verdict. (Also, there were rumors that some of the stolen money had been spread around to the right people.)

Kennedy was retried for the December robbery the following October, this time without the testimony of the spurned school marm, whom the prosecution probably felt did more harm than good. By now, three of Kennedy's cronies were found who testified that he was with them the night of the holdup. Also, the prosecutor hurt his case by implying that the jury in the first case had been bribed. Much to the disgust of the judge, who clearly wanted to see Kennedy put away, this jury returned a verdict of "not guilty."

Despite the hung jury and then the acquittal, the authorities knew they had a train robber in Jack Kennedy, and they wanted to keep a short leash on him. To do this, the Jackson County prosecutor refused to dismiss the indictment against him for October 23, 1896, holdup. He could not bring this case to trial, becaue he knew he would lose, so he kept asking for continuances, which the judge, also convinced of Kennedy's guilt, kept granting. Thus, Kennedy was still technically under arrest and was free only on bond.

On November 12, 1897, less than a month of Kennedy's second trial, another express car robbery occurred at Blue Cut, this time on the Missouri Pacific, whose tracks crossed those of the Chicago & Alton at the cut. The details of the holdup were similar to those of the earlier two robberies, but the express company claimed the robbers came away nearly empty handed, with less than $3, because they chose to rob a mail train out of St. Louis that never carried much money. The authorities naturally wanted to know where Jack Kennedy was that night, and he was picked up for questioning. Later, newspaper reporters cornered Kennedy and also asked him about the holdup. He was quoted as answering: "If I had been going to hold up a train, I wouldn't have chosen one with only $2.85 on board."

Jack's answer was typical of his sense of humor, which, in January 1898, acquired for him his sobriquet "Quail Hunter." On the evening of the twenty-eighth of that month Kennedy set out on horseback from his home in Kansas City. Tied to his saddle or strapped to his belt were a shotgun, a revolver, ammunition for both, several sticks of dynamite, several dynamite caps, a red lantern, false whiskers, and two masks. It would have been obvious to anyone who knew him where he was headed. But the weather was bad that night. The streets were icy, and Jack's horse, probably unbalanced by the load, slipped and fell, throwing Jack onto the street and knocking him unconscious.

There were several bystanders, and one of them called a doctor who lived nearby. To Jack's bad luck, the doctor happened to be the Kansas City police surgeon. When he saw Jack's paraphernalia, he called for a police wagon. Later, when Jack was questioned about the equipment he was carrying, he smiled and answered that he was going "quail hunting." A stringer for a St. Louis newspaper was standing nearby, and the incident became a snippet of local police history. From then on, Jack Kennedy, who by now had become something of a celebrity, was known as "Kennedy the quail hunter."

Kennedy's next encounter with the law occurred in September 1898. On the twenty-third of that month, southbound Missouri Pacific Train No. 5 was struck by five bandits at an intersection of tracks called Belt Line Junction, near Leeds, Missouri, now a Kansas City suburb. This robbery had several confusing aspects. Foremost was a note left at the scene of the crime. It read: "We, the masked knights of the road, robbed the M.P. train at the Belt Line Junction tonight. The supply of quails was good. With much love we remain, . . ." This was followed by five names, the first of which was "John Kennedy."

Kennedy, of course, was a prime suspect. But then again, would he have been so stupid to leave a note bearing his name? Also, he had a ready alibi for the night in question: the testimony of friends and relatives that he was at the time in Glendale, Missouri.

The Leeds robbery became Missouri's most famous train holdup of the decade, but it was never pinned on Kennedy. Indirectly, he may have been involved, but this was never proved. In addition to the note, his name came up because of his association with Jesse Edwards James, son of outlaw Jesse Woodson James, and a suspect in the holdup. Young James was arrested and tried for the crime, but was acquitted. Most observers believed at the time that neither young James nor Kennedy were involved, and that the holdup was committed by others who tried to place the blame on them.

The law finally did catch up with Quail Hunter Kennedy the following year. On January 3, 1899, a Southern Express Company car on the Kansas City, Ft. Scott & Memphis Railroad was robbed at Macomb, Missouri, about five miles west of Norwood in Wright County. In rounding up suspects, local authorities discovered that Quail Hunter had arrived in the area just a few days before the robbery, the first train holdup ever to occur in Wright County. This fact became especially interesting when the train crew reported that one of the robbers was undoubtedly an experienced locomotive engineer. Further investigation turned up a witness who identified Kennedy as the man who purchased the dynamite used to blow the express company safe.

This time Kennedy did not have the benefit of a friendly jury. He was convicted and sentenced to seventeen years in the state prison. But it is possible that Quail Hunter once again escaped punishment for his crime. According to Jeff Burton, a British author and impeccable researcher on the American frontier West, Kennedy may have walked free shortly after the trial, possibly as the result of confessions made by other participants in the robbery. This is doubtful, however. Kennedy may have been released, but if so, it probably was only during the pendency of his appeal to the Supreme Court of Missouri. The Supreme Court heard that appeal, and on January 23, 1900, issued an opinion affirming the conviction.

At this point Quail Hunter's records were lost. Burton has evidence that a John Kennedy, possibly Quail Hunter, was convicted of train robbery in Virginia, and later may have been killed following a jailbreak. (Sources: Burton, "John F. Kennedy of Missouri"; Garwood, *Crossroads of America: The Story of Kansas City*; Patterson, "The Trial of Jesse James, Jr."; State v. Kennedy.) *See also* **Blue Cut, Missouri; Jesse Edwards James; Leeds, Missouri; Macomb, Missouri.**

KERMAN, CALIFORNIA. On August 3, 1892, the fifth in a series of express car robberies on the Southern Pacific Railroad occurred thirteen miles west of Fresno near Kerman, then called Collis. Two bandits stopped the train around midnight just east of town by sticking guns in the ribs of the engineer, Al Phipps, and the fireman, Will Lewis. It is believed the bandits slipped aboard as the train was pulling away from the station.

The bandits handed the engineer a charge of dynamite and told him to place it against the left cylinder of the locomotive. He did as he was told, and the blast crippled the engine. Loaded with more dynamite, the bandits then headed for the Wells, Fargo express car, where they encountered a stubborn messenger in George D. Roberts. The first blast did not faze him; nor did the second or the third. But after six blasts, Roberts lay dazed and bleeding, unable to defend his car.

The bandits had wasted much time trying to enter the express car and they drew the attention of a team of threshers camped in a field near the tracks. Two of the threshers, J. W. Kennedy and John Arnold, decided to harass the bandits and began taking potshots at them from the field. In the darkness, however, the snipers' aims were bad, and the robbers managed to empty the express car safe and escape with the contents.

The exact amount of the loss was never officially revealed. Some reports had it as high as $30,000 to $50,000, but serious researchers doubt these figures and have suggested that the bandits probably could not even open the triple time-locked safes Wells, Fargo was using at the time. Also, one source says the money being carried that night was mostly in Peruvian coins. According to the messenger and the fireman, both of whom were forced to help carry the money sacks down to the robbers' wagon, the total weight was probably around 125 pounds.

At first the Dalton gang was blamed for the robbery, especially after several witnesses said that they believed there were additional robbers stationed along both sides of the tracks to prevent the passengers from wandering up from the coaches. But later, attention was directed toward Chris Evans and John Sontag, the notorious renegades who hated Southern Pacific and would later lead the authorities on one of California's greatest manhunts. (Source: Glasscock, *Bandits and the Southern Pacific*.) *See also* **Evans and Sontag**.

KESSLER, INDIANA. According to statistics compiled by Pinkerton's National Detective Agency, during the train robbery era the average outlaw gang numbered about five to eight members. This figure may have been a little high; during a robbery, excited train crews and passengers tended to see more robbers than were actually on the scene.

If witnesses' accounts were accurate, the record for the largest number of participants in a train robbery goes to a gang that struck a Lake Shore & Michigan Southern train at Kessler Siding, Indiana, on September 11, 1893. On that night, the Lake Shore trainmen who fell victim to the assault said they were besieged by at least *twenty* bandits.

At Kessler, the train—an eastbound that had left Chicago at 7:45 P.M.—was given a red light that indicated that the switch was open, and that it would be shifted to a siding. The engineer, James E. Knapp, knew this was a mistake, and he applied the brakes. As the train rolled to a stop, the bandits rushed the locomotive and took command. (Much to engineer Knapp's chagrin, he later learned that the switch itself had not been thrown, but only the light had been changed. If he had ignored the signal he could have passed by unmolested.)

When the bandits took charge of the engine cab, the fireman obediently held up his hands. Engineer Knapp, however, was not so cooperative; he attempted to grab the throttle and move on, but one of the intruders shot him in the shoulder.

Two of the intruders held the engine crew at bay while the rest attacked the express car. They blasted their way into the car and in a few minutes drilled open the safe. The exact amount taken was not released by the express company, but unofficial reports suggested that it was an "unusually large sum." This fact, and evidence that the safe was opened by an expert, led the authorities to believe that the robbery was the work of real professionals.

Byron H. Hamblin, the assistant express messenger, gave the following details of the holdup:

> M. M. Weist, the express messenger on the run, and myself had just about finished checking up our way bills. It was nearly midnight and we had just passed the little town of Kessler when we felt the train first slow up and then stop. Just then there came heavy pounding on the door of our car, which was closed. Thinking something had happened about which the conductor desired to inform us, I opened the door. As I did so, I saw two men standing on the ground beside the car. One of them yelled, "Throw up your hands!" and before I could move he pointed a rifle at me and fired.
>
> I saw the motion of the gun, and threw myself to one side, and the flash from the gun almost blinded me. I managed to slam the doors shut, and bolted them. Then some one on the outside commenced smashing the doors with a sledge. He kept this up for a minute or two, and then stopped. Suddenly there came an explosion that seemed to us inside as if a bomb had been thrown against the door. A moment later there was another explosion that blew the door to bits, almost threw the car from the track, and knocked Weist and me down, piling baggage all over us. Before we could extricate ourselves several men wearing masks had climbed into the train. One fellow covered me with a Winchester rifle. Another fellow kept Weist covered in the same way.
>
> They searched Weist and me for keys to the safe, but could not find any, and they seemed to believe us when we told them that the safe was opened by men from the office at the end of the run. Then they set to work to open

the safe. With a sledge they knocked the knob off the door, and then they began to drill holes in it. They talked but little. A small, stout man, who seemed to be the leader, directed the work. Finally they got through drilling and forced the door open. The man who seemed to be the leader of the gang took the money packages and handed them to a fellow who stood outside of the car, and who ran into the woods when he got the money.

> The fellows who had charge of us told us not to move, and then they backed to the door and leaped out. The rest of the gang that had been around the engine and back by the passenger coaches also ran away, firing their guns as they went. I saw probably twenty men altogether, but I do not know that they all belonged to the gang. The explosion smashed the car door to bits and almost tore the bottom out of the car.

> The robbers missed the most valuable article on the car. Behind a coffin which was in the car and covered up by a lot of express matter were two strong boxes, which are in reality small safes, which had been transferred at Chicago from some Western road. These boxes were filled with gold being shipped East, and while I do not know just how much was in them, it must have been a large sum.

Because of the size of the loss and the number of robbers reported to be involved, officials of the United States Express Company and the Lake Shore line dispatched at least 100 detectives from offices in Buffalo, Pittsburgh, Cleveland, Toledo, Detroit, Indianapolis, Chicago, and St. Louis. It was believed that the robbers headed for one of the several swampy areas in northern Indiana, and posses were sent out in all directions from the scene.

The Lake Shore immediately ordered 2,000 posters distributed throughout the Midwest that offered a reward of $1,000 for the capture and conviction of the robbers. Similar advertisements were placed in all major newspapers along the line from Elkhart, Indiana, east to Toledo.

Nearly a year later, August 7, 1894, the Lake Shore & Michigan Southern was again the victim of a robbery attempt at the Kessler siding. Just before daybreak, the train, which was carrying $20,000 in gold in the express car, struck a pile of crossties as it was approaching the station.

The powerful locomotive pushed the obstruction aside, and the engineer, whose name was Buntin, opened the throttle to full speed. As he did, two shots were fired at the cab from trackside, but neither the engineer nor the fireman were hit. Seconds later, however, the locomotive was jerked off the main track onto the siding. The engine stayed upright, but only barely.

Then, seconds later, it struck a second pile of crossties. Engineer Buntin no doubt considered stopping at this point, but again he kept on the throttle, hoping that the switch at the end of the siding was set to throw the train back onto the main line. It was, and the train proceeded onward, leaving the would-be robbers standing dejectedly beside the track. Had the switch not be thrown, the train no doubt would have derailed. (Sources: *New York Times*, 13 September 1893, 8 August 1894.)

THE KETCHUM BROTHERS. Sam and Tom Ketchum were fairly well-known outlaws, but not famous train robbers; at least there is not much of a record on them as train robbers. Both men at times were called Black Jack, which has led to much confusion over which brother did what and when. Both apparently rode with Wyoming's Wild Bunch and probably participated in several train robberies. Later, they struck out on their own, sometimes in the company of Wild Bunch member Elzy Lay.

According to Pinkerton records, Sam Ketchum was wanted for killing two United States marshals in New Mexico. He was picked up and jailed in 1899 but died from blood poisoning in a Santa Fe prison before he could be tried.

Tom Ketchum was unstable (described by some as a "drunk" and by others as a "bit crazy"), and it is believed that most of the Wild Bunch members wanted no part of him. On one occasion it was said that after being rejected by a girlfriend, he threw a fit and began "beating himself alternately with a pistol and a lariat."

Tom Ketchum.
Author's Collection.

Others said that he had a chronic habit of such conduct; that apparently he was something of a psychopath and often "beat himself over the head with a gun butt or lariat for punishment when anything went wrong and he discovered that it was his own fault."

Tom Ketchum's career as an outlaw also came to an end in 1899 following an attempt to rob a train single-handedly near Folsom, New Mexico. Ketchum shot the express messenger in the jaw and also wounded the conductor, but as the conductor was hit, he unloaded a barrel of buckshot that shattered Tom's arm. Tom escaped, but by morning he knew he would bleed to death if he did not get help; he flagged down a freight train and surrendered to the crew. He gave his name as Frank Stevens, but Pinkerton agents identified him, and he was taken to Santa Fe to await charges.

Ketchum was wanted in several states for several crimes, and a rope was finally put around his neck in Clayton, New Mexico, on April 25, 1901. Full of bravado to the end, as he was being marched up the steps of the gallows, he taunted his executioners with "I'll be in hell before you start breakfast, boys." Then, once the rope and hood were in place, Ketchum gave the order himself: "Let her rip," he cried.

Most hangmen in those days prided themselves on not letting a condemned man suffer because of a "short fall" on the rope, that is, allowing him to strangle to death instead of coming to a quick end from a broken neck. In Ketchum's case, the hangman did his job too well. When Ketchum reached the end of the rope, the noose severed his head from his torso, and his head went skittering across the ground. A witness to the gruesome scene, Trancito Romero, brother-in-law of the sheriff, said he was not sure what actually caused the decapitation. "Perhaps the scaffold was too high, the noose too tight, or perhaps the rope was too slender to hold so heavy a man." (Sources: Horan, *Desperate Men*; O'Neal, *Encyclopedia of Western Gunfighters*; Romero, "I Saw Black Jack Hanged.")

KILPATRICK, BEN. Ben Kilpatrick, a handsome outlaw who went by the nickname "The Tall Texan," rode with Butch Cassidy and the Wild Bunch. He undoubtedly was in on many of the robberies committed by the gang in Wyoming and Montana, although just who was at what holdup has been difficult to establish. He was with the gang at Wagner, Montana, on July 3, 1901, when

Ben Kilpatrick. *Pinkertons.*

they struck the Great Northern *Coast Flyer*, which is believed to have been the Wild Bunch's last train robbery before splitting up to go their separate ways.

The following November Kilpatrick was arrested in St. Louis, Missouri. At the time, he was carrying a number of unsigned bank notes of the National Bank of Montana and the American National Bank of Helena, which were later identified as part of the loot stolen at Wagner. Back at his room at the Laclede Hotel, police also found Kilpatrick's girlfriend, Laura Bullion, with $40,000 more of the bank notes in her handbag.

Kilpatrick and Bullion were both convicted and sentenced, he for fifteen years at the penitentiary at Columbus, Ohio, which then housed federal prisoners, and she for two years and six months at the Missouri State Penitentiary at Jefferson City.

Kilpatrick was released early and he wasted no time in returning to train robbery. On March 13, 1912, he and two companions tried to rob a Wells, Fargo express car on the Southern Pacific's *Sunset Limited* near Sanderson, Texas. While Kilpatrick was sorting through the express packages, the Wells, Fargo messenger, David Trousdale, smashed him in the head with an ice mallet. (Sources: Pointer, *In Search of Butch Cassidy*; *New York Times*, 14–16 March 1912.) *See also* **Robert LeRoy "Butch Cassidy" Parker; Sanderson, Texas; David Trousdale; Wagner, Montana**.

KINCAID, CHARLES. For express messenger Charlie Kincaid, it was "just one of those days." Kincaid worked for the United States Express Company that handled shipments on the St. Louis, Kansas City & Northern

Railroad. On December 18, 1875, Charlie reported for work, ready to take the eastbound run from Kansas City to St. Louis. On checking the car, however, he noticed that one of the steel staples that held a lock and chain on the rear door had been pulled out.

Charlie Kincaid was a cautious man, and he was well aware that express cars had become popular targets for robbers, especially in Missouri, where the Jameses and Youngers were operating. He inspected the safe and the interior of the car thoroughly and also did a quick check of his packages against his waybills. Everything seemed in order. Apparently, nobody had gained entry while the car sat locked at the station.

The train pulled out on time, and the run began as usual. Even though it was a night run, which train robbers always favored, once they were fifty miles or so out, Charlie began to relax. He figured that if bandits had their eye on the car, they would have struck by then.

The train was scheduled to arrive at St. Louis at 6:15 A.M. The last stop for express packages was Mexico, in Audrain County, which was still 100 miles from the end of the run. Since there was nothing left to do, it was customary for the messenger to catch an hour or so of sleep before arrival. Charlie saw no reason why he should not take his nap. But just to be on the safe side, he padlocked the door with a chain and slid a heavy trunk against it.

Charlie did not know how long he had been asleep when he was awakened by a heavy hand on his shoulder. He turned his head and saw a masked man holding a pistol. Before he could speak, he was grabbed from behind by the collar, lifted over to a large crate, and dumped inside. The lid was closed over him and he could hear the click of a padlock. A few minutes later, he heard the safe being opened. He did not hear his attackers leave and knew nothing more until he was released from the box on arrival at St. Louis.

On inspecting the safe, express company officials found that $8,000 was missing. Charlie's story naturally raised a few eyebrows from local detectives, but he had a reputation for truth and honesty, and it was taken at face value. (Sources: *New York Times*, 19, 21 December 1875.)

KINSLEY, KANSAS. Apart from bungled attempts at train robbery by amateurs, some holdups simply failed out of bad luck. If records were kept of such things, probably the prize would go to the bandits who attacked an express car on the Santa Fe Railroad in January 1878 at Kinsley, a small town northeast of Dodge City at the junction of what is now U.S. Highways 183 and 56.

The outlaws were no amateurs; they were led by Mike Rourke, a seasoned bandit. It was just a matter of things not going their way. To begin with, the plan was to hold up the train at the water tank two miles west of Kinsley, but the train did not stop. Having run low on water early, the engineer had taken some on at Dodge City. Disappointed but undaunted as they watched the train steam on by, the outlaws leaped into their saddles and raced for the next stop, Kinsley, hoping to catch it there.

When the gang arrived at the Kinsley depot, they found only the night operator, a young lad named Andrew Kinkade. Not wanting to pass up any loot, Rourke drew his guns and ordered the boy to hand over all the money in the station. Young Kinkade, a courageous lad, jerked open an empty money drawer and announced "I have no money here."

Rourke pointed to the company safe standing in the corner and demanded that the boy open it. Kinkade answered that he did not have a key, that the day operator had it, and he was in his room at the hotel. While the outlaws were pondering this fact, they heard a whistle in the distance. But the whistle came from the wrong direction—from the east, not the west—which meant that the train they had planned to rob had already come and gone.

In the meantime, two men came walking up the steps of the station platform, apparently intending to board the westbound train. Kinkade saw them first and shouted that he was being robbed. To keep the two strangers from spreading the alarm, the outlaws ran out of the station to grab them. As they did, Kinkade slipped out of Rourke's grasp and also ran out onto the platform.

The westbound train, slowing to a stop, had almost reached the depot. Kinkade jumped off the platform in front of the engine and ran across the track. Racing alongside the locomotive on the opposite side from the depot, he shouted to the engineer that there were six armed robbers at the station. To Kinkade's delight, the big engine steamed and kept on moving. At first Kinkade thought the engineer had heard his warning but

he later learned that the brakes were faulty and the engineer had difficulty stopping the train.

The train coasted to a stop about a hundred yards beyond the station. The robbers ran to the engine, and Rourke and another of the gang members climbed into the cab. Pointing his revolver at the engineer, Rourke ordered him to start up again and "take her out of town." But the engineer, possibly faking, claimed the steam was too low to get started again.

Back in the express car, the messenger, armed with a shotgun, had seen what was happening and was ready when two of the outlaws approached his door. He caught the first one with a blast in the face. On hearing the shot, Rourke and his comrade jumped down from the cab and ran back to the express car. The engineer immediately threw the throttle forward and gave the big engine all the steam he had. Rourke and his gang could only stand and watch the train pull away.

It was not the end of the Rourke gang's bad luck. Four days later, Bat Masterson, who had recently been elected sheriff of Ford County, captured two of the outlaws at a cattle camp on Crooked Creek, about fifty miles southeast of Dodge. A little more than a month later, two more were picked up by Bat's brother, Ed Masterson, then a Dodge City marshal. The following October Mike Rourke himself was arrested after being turned in by one of his own gang. He confessed to the robbery attempt at Kinsley and was sentenced to ten years at hard labor. (Source: Vestal, *Queen of Cowtowns: Dodge City.*)

KNIGHT, LT. JONATHAN T. In 1894, near the peak of the train robbery era, Lt. Jonathan T. Knight, a young army officer, wrote an article for the *North American Review* that contained a plan to protect railway express cars from robbers. Knight suggested that the makeup of the trains be changed. The express car, said Knight, should be put at the end of the train instead of immediately behind the tender, as was the usual practice. Since most robbers stopped a train by taking control of the locomotive, under Knight's plan the bandits would be required either to march past all the passenger coaches to reach the express or divide their forces. Also, said Knight, alarms could be placed in the coaches and sleepers to alert passengers if either the locomotive crew or the express messenger came under attack.

A reverse train, as suggested by Lt. Jonathan T. Knight. *Southern Pacific Railroad.*

Weapons could be stored in glass cases in each coach for use by passengers willing to help.

Knight believed that a train so defended would require so many robbers to pull off a successful holdup that it would reduce the take in the average robbery to the point where most holdups would be unprofitable. And, added Knight, if the bandits did increase the size of their gangs, "the greater number of accomplices or principals, the greater the chances of a capture and the possibilities of some one turning 'state's evidence.' "

In placing the express car last, Knight admitted that the bandits would be tempted to cut it loose from the rest of the train while it stood idle, for example at a lonely water stop. But this threat could be eliminated by putting a vestibule (observation) car immediately in front of the express car, thus providing a place from which attackers could be seen and repelled. Knight pointed out that armed guards *outside* the express car could successfully defend it, while guards *inside* the car were usually helpless, especially if the bandits brought dynamite.

Several railroads may have experimented with reverse trains. At least one photo exists of a train made up in such fashion. However, the idea did not catch on. (Source: Knight, "How to Repel Train Robbers.")

KORNER, F. A. F. A. Korner was a stubborn express messenger who stood off the "Old Bill" Miner gang during a robbery attempt on September 23, 1903. The attack occurred a few miles east of Portland, Oregon. Miner and three companions had halted the Great Northern's Oregon & Washington Train No. 6, and had blasted the express-mail car door off. Korner, however, met the robbers with his Winchester rifle blazing. One of his first shots struck robber Jim Conners in the chest, killing him instantly. Korner then barricaded himself behind trunks and express packages, prepared to make an all-out stand. Miner, seeing the situation was nearly hopeless, called off the attack. During the gang's retreat, Korner wounded another robber, Charlie Hoehn, who was captured by the authorities a short time later. (Source: Rickards, "Bill Miner—50 Years a Hold-up Man.") See also **Bill Miner; Portland, Oregon.**   □

L

LaBANTA, JEAN. Jean LaBanta was a specialist at robbing postal cars in transit.

On October 14, 1913, LaBanta, wearing a mask and armed with a revolver, entered the side door of a mail car of a Southern Pacific express as the train was leaving the station at Burlingame, California. LaBanta ordered the two mail clerks, Pete Scott and Bruce Titus, to lie down on the floor at the front of the car and pull mail sacks over their heads while he sorted through the registered mail.

LaBanta had not finished his sorting when the train slowed for the South San Francisco station. The robber, well versed in the railway mail service's routine, boldly slid open the side door and let the station baggage man throw in a full sack of mail. He quickly finished his work, pocketed the envelopes containing cash and valuables, and jumped off the train at the Mariposa Street crossing in San Francisco. The only description the clerks could give of the robber was that he was "well dressed, about 32 years old, five feet ten or eleven inches tall, weighing about 180 lbs, and had a fashionable green fedora hat."

LaBanta's next job was on November 17, 1913, at the railroad yards at San Jose. This time he was dressed in dirty overalls and gave the appearance of a yard worker. As the SP's Train No. 77 pulled out, he swung aboard the mail car and slipped into the side door. As before, the mail clerks were forced to lie on the floor while the intruder ransacked the registered mail. After removing the envelopes that appeared to contain money and valuables, he jumped off the car near the Burlingame station.

Not far from where LaBanta jumped, police found the overalls he had been wearing. Merchants in the area were questioned, but no clue to the owner was found.

Expecting more such robberies, the Southern Pacific placed armed guards on passenger coaches immediately behind the mail cars on all runs between San Francisco and San Jose. LaBanta may have noticed this, because his next robbery occurred just north of Los Angeles.

On January 10, 1914, the Southern Pacific's Train No. 9 was scheduled to leave Los Angeles for San Francisco at 10:15 P.M. About two miniutes before departure, just after the last mail bag had been thrown on board from the station platform, a well dressed man wearing a mask entered the side door of the mail car. The two mail clerks, A. G. Wendland and D. W. Perry, were busy at work and did not notice him. "Hey," the intruder shouted to the clerks, "Throw up your hands. Put empty mail sacks over your heads!"

Jean Deslys.
Southern Pacific Railroad.

The clerks did what they were told, and as they did, a second man climbed aboard the car. As the train picked up speed, the clerks, their faces covered, could hear the two men slashing open the bags containing the registered mail. This continued for about fifteen minutes, until the train reached Tropico crossing, just south of Burbank. As the engineer slowed the locomotive down, a routine maneuver at this point to test the air brakes, the two bandits leaped out of the door.

This time the authorities were in luck. Several days after the robbery, they picked up a clue to the identity of one of the bandits, apparently from an anonymous tip. The suspect's name was Jean Deslys, alias Jimmy Barry, a local forger who had recently been released from San Quentin. Deslys was arrested and charged with the crime. Although the evidence was not strong, he was indicted by a federal grand jury on February 10, 1914. He denied any guilt, and it is likely he could never have been convicted, but suddenly, on February 17, he changed his plea to guilty. He admitted taking part in the January robbery, but denied being involved in the two earlier robberies. He was taken before the federal judge in Los Angeles and sentenced to five years in prison.

Deslys's sudden confession came as a surprise, until it was learned that LaBanta, his companion in the January 10 robbery, was already in custody. Apparently Deslys had learned of this and decided that it would be in his best interest to be the first to confess.

The capture of LaBanta was mainly luck. During the second week of January, a woman calling herself Mrs. Downing walked into the Southern Pacific's baggage claim department in San Francisco's Ferry Building and tried to retrieve several pieces of baggage without a claim check. The baggage agent refused to give her the baggage. Several days earlier, he had been informed by San Francisco detectives that the baggage in question was believed to be the property of a forger who was wanted by the sheriff of Placer County, California. The baggage agent told the woman to come back later, and he informed Southern Pacific officials.

When the woman returned several days later, she was questioned and she readily admitted that her husband was in fact wanted by the authorities. Not only that, she said she wanted him arrested because he had "left her for another woman." She said that his name was Jean LaBanta, and she told the authorities where he could be found.

Jean LaBanta was indeed wanted for forgery in Placer County, and officials from that county were immediately dispatched to San Francisco, where they found him and put him under arrest. On the way back, however, LaBanta began boasting that he was not just an ordinary forger, that he had been involved in "much more classier crimes." Suspecting that the man might be telling the truth, the Placer County sheriff arranged for an informer to be placed in the same cell with him. Two weeks later, LaBanta let it slip to the informer that he had committed the three mail car robberies on the Southern Pacific.

LaBanta was taken before the mail clerks on duty during each of the robberies, and they all identified him as the robber. Faced with this evidence, he confessed. After a plea of guilty he was sentenced to twenty-five years at San Quentin. (Source: DeNevi, *Western Train Robberies*.)

LA JARITA (NUEVO LEON), MEXICO. The town of La Jarita lay on the boundary line between the states of Nuevo Leon and Tamlaulipas, Mexico, about 25 miles south of Laredo, Texas. On November 20, 1883, about 4 miles south of La Jarita, in Tamlaulipas, Mexican National Railroad's Train No. 10 was derailed and attacked by twenty or more bandits.

The attack came in late morning. The bandits loosened the fishplates and drew the two rails toward the center of the track. When the engine's front wheels struck the gap, it and most of the cars left the rails, toppled over, and buried themselves into the embankment. The fireman, whose name was Festler, was thrown under the boiler and killed outright, and the engineer, Madden, was seriously injured.

As the stunned crew and passengers slowly climbed out of the toppled cars, the robbers converged on them from both sides. While part of the gang harassed the passengers to keep them in line, the rest forced their way into the express car.

When the express messenger could not produce a key to the safe, the robbers went at it with an axe. When this failed, they sought out the conductor and under the threat of death ordered him to get it open. He pointed out that the smashing had so battered the hinges and lock, that opening it was next to impossible. Somebody suggested getting through from the bottom, and the robbers climbed underneath the car and unbolted the safe from the floor. They dragged the box over to the door and pitched it out. Still they could not get in and they finally gave up.

Hoping to salvage something from the affair, the robbers started through the passenger coaches. The conductor was forced to open up the passengers' trunks, but aside from a few silver bars, very little was taken. The robbers, apparently all Mexicans and unusually gallant, seemed almost embarrassed that they were forced to steal from the passengers, especially the ladies.

The robbery was taking longer than expected. Even though the bandits had cut the telegraph line, time was running out. They became uneasy and suddenly mounted and rode off.

Word had already spread along the line that Train No. 10 was probably in trouble. When it did not arrive at Sanchez, the next stop on the route, and when it was discovered that the telegraph line was down, a special train filled with soldiers and armed railroaders was dispatched northward from Ciudad Victoria. This train had reached Sanchez and was taking on water when several of No. 10's exhausted passengers straggled in. The robbery scene was thoroughly searched, but no trace of the bandits was found.

The following month, a rumor circulated throughout Nuevo Leon that Pablo Quintana, Mayor of Nuevo Laredo, was involved in the affair. On December 9, 1883, Quintana was arrested by the military and charged with complicity in the robbery. However, Mexican President Gomez intervened, and Quintana was released. (Sources: *New York Times*, 2, 20 December 1893.)

LAMAR, MISSOURI. On a cold January 22, 1892, the passengers and train crew on a southbound Missouri

Pacific run from Nassau Junction to Lamar probably had the most exciting night of their lives. The train was taken over twice: first by a gang of vigilantes bent on lynching a murderer, and then by robbers who ransacked the express car.

The train had hardly picked up steam on leaving Nassau Junction when a lynching party took possession of the coach carrying a Nevada, Missouri murderer, Robert Hepler. The peace officers accompanying Hepler were quickly overcome and there was little doubt that the killer's fate was sealed. Only the choice of time and place for the hanging remained to be decided.

While plans were being made for Hepler's demise, the occupants of the Pacific Express Company car were having their own troubles. Twelve miles east of Lamar, which is in Barton County about twenty-five miles from the Kansas line, the engineer spotted a red lantern, the danger signal for railroaders, and he had to bring the big locomotive to a halt. When he did, two masked men ascended on the express car and quickly took the occupants, baggage man Hall and messenger Houck, prisoner. The robbers, however, had chosen the wrong night for a holdup. When Houck, under the threat of death, opened the express company safe, the outlaws found only $75.

In the meantime, back in the first passenger coach the lynchers had decided to hang their victim when the train stopped at Lamar. For the robbers, it was a golden opportunity to make their escape. Apparently word had reached Lamar that the vigilantes had Hepler, and when the train arrived, the station was packed with onlookers. The robbers merely slipped out of the express car and disappeared in the crowd. A few minutes later they climbed aboard a northbound freight heading for Fort Scott.

The robbers, however, had been seen, and a wire was sent ahead to the stations along the line. When the train arrived at Fort Scott, the police were waiting. A shootout erupted, and a policeman, S. B. Olemore, was killed. The robbers raced back to the station just as the same northbound freight was pulling out. The bandits climbed inside a box car and thumbed their noses at the pursuing lawmen. An effort was made to signal the engineer to stop, but it was unsuccessful.

As the northbound freight was leaving Fort Scott, the passenger train that had been robbed pulled in from

the south. When informed of what had happened, a United States Deputy Marshal named Mapes and a Missouri Pacific detective named Chester climbed aboard the locomotive cab and ordered the engineer to "catch that train." Joining them at the last minute was a Fort Scott marshal named Abbott.

The passenger train overtook the freight at the Mound City junction, just south of Pleasanton. Mapes, Chester, and Abbott jumped off and raced for the freight as it was pulling away. At the last second they managed to climb aboard the car immediately behind the box car containing the robbers. The robbers saw them, however, and opened fire. A vicious gunfight developed between the two cars.

The engineer of the freight train still did not know that he was carrying train robbers. When he pulled into Pleasanton, however, he could see lawmen crowding around the station. As the train slowed to a halt, the box car containing the robbers was immediately surrounded. The robbers were trapped, but they would not give up. The battle lasted for nearly an hour. Finally, a posseman's shot struck one of the robbers in the head and killed him. Shortly thereafter, the other robber surrendered.

The captured outlaw gave his name as Charles Myers of Kansas City. He refused to identify the dead outlaw. It was later determined that the second man's name was James Francis, also of Kansas City, a former member of a gang led by Marion Hedgepeth. (Source: *New York Times*, 24 January 1892.) *See also* **James Francis; Marion Hedgepeth.**

LA SALLE, WYOMING. On August 18, 1892, three masked men tried to hold up a Denver Pacific passenger coach as it was leaving La Salle for Cheyenne. A young easterner, S. J. Payne, thwarted the robbery attempt, frightened off the bandits, and became an instant hero. *See* **S. J. Payne.**

LAY, ELZY. William Ellsworth Lay was born in Mount Pleasant, Ohio, in 1868. When he was four, his family moved to Illinois and then to Creston, Iowa, where Elzy spent his formative years and secured a brief, yet apparently sound, education. In 1887, when Elzy was nineteen, the family moved to eastern Colorado, between Wray and Laird, where they took up homesteading. Elzy soon tired of the hard work this life entailed,

Elzy Lay. *Pinkertons.*

and he and a friend, William D. McGinnis, packed up and headed further west. On reaching Denver, however, McGinnis got cold feet and returned home; some say because Lay nearly beat a man to death and almost landed in jail. The story may be true because when his friend headed back home, Lay took his name. From that day on, Elzy Lay would often ride as William McGinnis and eventually he would even go to prison using that name.

Lay continued west and settled for a while in northern Utah near Fort Duchesne, in a lawless, federally controlled area called the Strip, where he soon developed a reputation for gambling, hard drinking, and womanizing. It was here he probably first became associated with the outlaws that would later lead to his joining the Wyoming Wild Bunch. He probably met Butch Cassidy, the Wild Bunch's leader, sometime in the early 1890s.

There is some record of Lay getting into minor trouble with the law in Lander, Wyoming, in January 1893. According to a local jeweler, Lay and another man tried to cheat him in a deal to trade a rifle. Lay and his companion were picked up by the sheriff but talked their way out of the trouble. It is believed that Lay's introduction to big time outlawry came in August 1886 when he helped Cassidy and others rob a bank at Montpelier, Idaho. Most Wild Bunch historians believe that Lay and Cassidy robbed a mine payroll at Castle Gate, Utah, in April 1897.

The robbery that Lay is best known for was the holdup of an express car on the Colorado & Southern line at Folsom, New Mexico, on July 11, 1899. Participating in the affair were Tom Ketchum, also a Wild Bunch member, and a third man who was never identified. Some say the trio may have picked up over $50,000 in the haul. A posse was soon on the outlaws' trail and it caught up with them at Turkey Creek Canyon in northeastern New Mexico on July 16. In the shootout that followed, Lay is believed to have killed a member of the posse, a sheriff from Colorado named Edward J. Farr. Another posse member was also mortally wounded, and Lay and Ketchum were both wounded. However, all three outlaws escaped. Ketchum was captured two days later and eventually was hanged. Lay remained at large until August 16, when he was captured in Eddy County, New Mexico.

To avoid embarrassment to his family, Lay was still using the name William McGinnis. Under that name he was taken to Raton, New Mexico, where he was tried and convicted of murdering Farr and sentenced to life imprisonment in the territorial penitentiary in Santa Fe. Territorial Governor Miguel Otero took a special interest in Lay's case. After Lay had served only six years of his sentence, Otero gave him a pardon; allegedly because he had personally quelled a riot in which fellow convicts had taken the warden's family hostage.

On leaving prison, Lay tried to get in touch with members of the old gang but was unsuccessful. By that time Butch Cassidy had fled the country for South America and the other members of the Wild Bunch had gone their separate ways. It has been suggested that Lay may have returned to the Folsom area and uncovered the hidden loot, but if so, he did not use it to live high. There is some evidence that he worked for a newspaper for a while in Vernal, Utah, and then went to work for a rancher named Kirk Calvert in the Little Snake River area of Wyoming. He married Calvert's daughter, Mary, and tended bar part-time in the town of Baggs. He later studied geology and was involved in developing oil and natural gas fields in Wyoming and Utah, but the ventures never made him wealthy.

In later years Lay became a heavy drinker and eventually left his wife and two children. A friend spotted him on a skid row street in Los Angeles and got in touch with his wife. She packed up the family, moved to Los Angeles, and helped him recover. He became watermaster for the Imperial Valley Irrigation Company but had to give up the job because of a heart condition. In the early 1930s Lay became acquainted with western writer Zane Grey who offered to write his biography, but Lay declined. Later, however, probably because of failing health, Lay changed his mind, and on November 7, 1934, he got word to Grey that he was ready to tell his story. But by then it was too late; three days later Elzy Lay died. He is buried in Los Angeles's Forest Lawn Cemetery.

Some have said that Elzy Lay and Butch Cassidy were much closer than Cassidy and the Sundance Kid (Harry Longabaugh). According to Lulu Parker Betenson, Butch Cassidy's sister, Lay and Cassidy had much in common. "Both had been brought up in good homes by parents who loved them and exposed them to religious training." She said that one day she asked Butch who was his best friend, and he answered: "There were a lot of good friends, but Elzy Lay was the best, always dependable and level-headed." In fact, according to Mrs. Betenson, most of the episodes in the popular 1969 film *Butch Cassidy and the Sundance Kid* actually involved Elzy Lay rather than Sundance, but, said Mrs. Betenson, "who would go to a movie titled *Butch Cassidy and Elzy Lay?*" (Sources: Betenson, *Butch Cassidy, My Brother*; Dullenty, "The Farm Boy Who Became a Member of Butch Cassidy's Wild Bunch"; Pointer, *In Search of Butch Cassidy*.)

LEECH, M. F. M. F. Leech was a self-proclaimed hero who liked to boast that, nearly single-handedly, he was responsible for the capture of the Sam Bass-Joel Collins gang following the Big Springs, Nebraska express car robbery.

Leech, interviewed in February 1895 by a reporter for the *New York Times*, claimed that in September 1875 he was on a hunting trip near Big Springs when the robbery occurred. He was at the time employed by the Union Pacific Railroad as a telegraph operator and was on a vacation. He said he was an experienced tracker and before joining the railroad he had at one time worked for the government as a scout. When he learned of the robbery, he volunteered his services to the Union Pacific to take a handful of detectives and track the robbers. He said he was turned down.

Undaunted, he claimed he struck out alone after the suspects. He said after several days he caught up with them and followed them at a distance. On two occasions he crawled near their camp at night, getting close enough to hear them talking. Once he was spotted and barely escaped with his life by hiding in a brush-filled canyon.

Leech claimed that despite his narrow escape, he continued to trail the gang until they split up near the

Nebraska-Kansas line; after that he followed Joel Collins and Bill Heffridge to Buffalo Station, Kansas, where he arrived shortly after they were killed by local lawmen and a squad of soldiers. He then got back on the trail of gang member Jim Berry and followed him to his home in Mexico, Missouri, and participated in his capture and eventual killing.

Having done away with Berry, Leech said he "traced" Sam Bass to Texas "where he was robbing trains and there [he, Leech] got one of his gang to betray him [Bass] for $2,500, when they were about to rob a bank at Round Rock."

After Round Rock, Leech said he went looking for the last two members of the gang, "Jack" Davis and Tom Nixon. He claimed he not only caught up with them, but was present when they were both killed by lawmen: Davis at Benita, Indian Territory, and Nixon in Manitoba, Canada.

Of the $60,000 stolen at Big Springs, Leech claimed he was personally responsible for recovering $37,000. "There was a reward of $10,000 offered for the recovery of the money," he said, but "I got none of it, as I was working for the railroad company on a salary."

There were many who didn't believe his story. (Source: *New York Times*, 24 February 1895.) *See also* **Sam Bass; Jim Berry; Joel Collins**.

LEEDS, MISSOURI. In 1898 Leeds, Missouri, was a small community about five miles southeast of what is now downtown Kansas City. It has by now been swallowed by the city's suburban sprawl. Near Leeds was the Belt Line Junction, where the Missouri Pacific line met tracks that circled the city not unlike our urban interstate belts of today. On September 23 of that year, around 10:00 P.M., five or six armed men climbed aboard a Missouri Pacific southbound as it slowed for the junction. One of the intruders scrambled into the locomotive cab, shoved aside the engineer, took control of the train, and brought it to a stop. The other men quickly dropped off to the ground, uncoupled the train behind the express car, and gave the man in the locomotive a signal to go. The man at the throttle then pulled ahead to a dark and remote spot about two miles further south of the junction.

When stopped once more, the intruders hurried back to the express car, where Ed Hill, the messenger, offered little resistance. The bandits entered the car, stuffed seven sticks of dynamite between the two express company safes, and set off a blast that was heard as far away as downtown Kansas City. After picking up what money they could find among the scattered contents of the safes, a sum the express company eventually reported to be slightly more than $2,000, the robbers left.

But before he departed, the leader of the gang did a strange thing; he left the following note: "We, the masked knights of the road, robbed the M.P. train at the Belt Line Junction tonight. The supply of quails was good. With much love we remain, John Kennedy, Bill Ryan, Bill Anderson, Sam Brown, Jim Redmond."

At the bottom of the note were added the words: "We are ex-compect to," which later was determined to be an attempt to write *ex conspectu*, Latin for "out of sight."

The authorities assumed the first name listed referred to Jack "Quail Hunter" Kennedy, whose given name was John, a local criminal and a suspect in earlier train robberies. The second name, "Bill Ryan," also was familiar. In 1881 a small-time criminal and associate of Kennedy named Bill Ryan had been convicted of participating in the holdup of a train. There was no "Bill Anderson" on local police blotters, but in one of the earlier robberies in which Kennedy was believed involved, a witness had testified that the name "Anderson" had been used. The remaining names meant nothing to the police or railroad detective.

Because of the mysterious note, the crime became more than just another train robbery. And as the days passed, the incident grew to receive national headlines, eventually going down in history as the most celebrated express car robbery in the Kansas City area. The following week, local newsboys were shouting from the street corners that Jesse James had been arrested for the crime—not the famous outlaw Jesse Woodson James, who had been killed by Bob Ford more than fifteen years earlier, but his son, Jesse Edwards James, also known as Jesse James, Jr. *See* **Jesse Edwards James; Jack "Quail Hunter" Kennedy**.

LELIAETTA, OKLAHOMA. Like the James brothers, the Daltons had their supporters. To die-hard sympathizers, the Daltons were simply good-hearted rascals who robbed the rich mainly for the benefit of the poor. One of the stories that formed this legend arose from the robbery of an express car at Leliaetta in 1891.

The tiny town of Leliaetta, which then could be found in eastern Indian Territory (now Oklahoma) about midway between Pryor and Muskogee, is no longer on most maps. On the night of September 15, 1891, the Dalton gang, wearing masks of red flannel, stopped a Missouri, Kansas & Texas southbound passenger train at Leliaetta and forced their way into the express car. The express companies doing business by rail in Indian Territory had begun locking their through safes at the beginning of the run and not giving the messenger the key. When the messenger convinced the Daltons that such was the case, the outlaws dragged the smaller way safe over to the door, pushed it out on the ground, and broke it open; they extracted a little more than $2,500.

According to the legend, while the gang was riding along the tracks toward Leliaetta before the robbery, they came across a hobo and his wife camped at a siding. The hobo was rummaging along the right-of-way, looking for coal for his nightly campfire. Bob Dalton was supposed to have told him that if he would wait a little bit, he would find some coal "after the express passed."

As the rest of the story goes, following the ransacking of the express car safe, before the gang rode off into the woods, Bob Dalton walked back up to the locomotive and told the fireman to "heave off a few shovels of coal" when the train passed a certain siding up the track a way. Whether the fireman did so is not known, but it makes for a good tale. (Sources: Preece, *The Dalton Gang; New York Times*, 17 September 1891.) *See also* **The Daltons**.

LIDELL, DR. F. F. Dr. F. F. Lidell was a graduate of Memphis Medical College and a trained Birmingham physician who chose a life of crime over the practice of medicine. Having already served a five-year sentence for burglary in New Orleans in 1880, Lidell, with the help of an accomplice, held up a Georgia Pacific train and robbed the mail car near Weems, Alabama, in March 1892. The following May he was killed while attempting to burglarize a Birmingham jewelry store. *See* **Weems, Alabama**.

LINCOLN, NEBRASKA. Although eastern Nebraska was a web of railroad lines by the turn of the century, the state did not experience the rash of train robberies that plagued its sister states, especially Missouri and

Illinois. Nebraska's most famous express car robbery was the $60,000 Big Springs holdup in 1877 that launched the train robbery career of the notorious Sam Bass. Less well known is a 1902 holdup on the Chicago, Burlington & Quincy Railroad near Lincoln, which netted the bandits almost as much, and showed some real ingenuity on the part of the culprits.

By 1902 train robberies in the West and Midwest were occurring in epidemic proportions, and it was not unusual for railroad and express company officials to receive tips, usually from small-time criminals in return for favors, about forthcoming holdups. In the fall of 1902 the Burlington line received such a tip about an express car robbery that was to take place on a southbound runout of Lincoln near dawn on Saturday, October 11 at St. Joseph, Missouri. The information seemed sound, and since a large shipment of gold coin was to be on board that night, extra detectives were called in and preparations were made to ambush the would-be robbers.

The shipment of gold coin never came close to reaching St. Joseph. At 2:00 A.M., on the crest of a small hill only four miles out of Lincoln, the engineer, A. L. Clayburg, saw a red lantern being waved on the track ahead. Since he could not ignore the universal signal to stop, he drew the big locomotive to a halt, and in seconds he and his fireman were facing three masked men with revolvers.

In the traditional manner, the express car was cut away from the rest of the train and Clayburg was ordered to pull ahead. The robbers riddled the express car door with bullets until the messenger, William Lupton, opened up. Wasting no time, the bandits, described by the trainmen and the messenger as "cool, talkative, and apparently experts," blew open the safe with dynamite and extracted fourteen packages of coins, later estimated by express officials to be worth nearly $50,000. (Source: *New York Times*, 12 October 1902.)

LINDEN, CALIFORNIA. An express car robbery just north of Linden on the night of February 10, 1889, marked the end of train robber Pete Skaggs. The authorities were never sure how many robberies on the Southern Pacific were the work of Skaggs and his gang. The Southern Pacific was struck more than fifty times during the train robbery era, and many of the robberies went unsolved.

Thanks to an account by John Ellis, the engineer of the Southern Pacific's southbound passenger train No. 12, the details of the Linden robbery have been well preserved. According to Ellis, three masked men thrust pistols in his face and that of his fireman, Tom Clark, about three miles north of Linden. One of the masked men said: "We ain't gonna do no harm to you if you don't rattle. Stop this junk at the crossroads coming up yonder."

Ellis did as he was told, and as the engine slowed to a stop at the crossroads, one of the bandits leaned out the window and fired three shots in the air; a signal, Ellis believed, to a confederate waiting near the road with a team of horses and a wagon.

One of the bandits handed cigars to both Ellis and Clark and told them to light up. The bandit then gave Clark a stick of dynamite with a short fuse and ordered him to attach it to the left cylinder of the engine, and use the cigar to light the fuse. After a mild protest, Clark did as he was told, and the blast broke a piston rod, but did not totally disable the engine.

The bandits then marched Ellis and Clark back to the Wells, Fargo express car. With more dynamite they blew a hole in the side door. The hole was not large enough for a person to crawl through, so they went around to the other door and blew a hole in it. That hole was also too small, so they tossed a charge just inside the door. This widened the opening large enough for a small man to enter, and the bandits chose fireman Clark for the job.

Although shaken from the blasts, Wells, Fargo messenger Oscar Bobb was prepared to stand off the attackers. When Clark stuck his head in the hole to see if the messenger was still alive, Bobb whispered to him that he had a plan. Clark was to come on in and pick up the two chests containing gold coins. He was to throw them down to the ground, and as the bandits stooped over to pick them, Clark was to drop down on the floor out of the way. "Drop to the floor," Bobb said, "and I'll start shooting. I should pick off one or two."

Clark was pretty sure he would never come out of the situation alive, but he agreed to follow Bobb's instructions. He slid the chests over to the door, and called out to the robbers: "Here's two chests, the only ones in the car. The messenger is dead. The mail bags have been torn to shreds by the blasts." Two of the robbers walked up to the car to lift the chests down. Clark dropped down out of the way, and Bobb began firing.

Engineer Ellis then gives the following account:

I made a dash into the thickets a few feet away from the track, drawing fire from another robber who had been guarding me and watching down the line for an interfering passenger. All hell broke loose. There must have been 50 shots fired, bullets whizzing every which way. I can honestly say that for the first time in my life I could easily have messed my overalls. After what seemed like a month, the firing stopped. Then I heard a tremendous explosion. Splintering, ripping, and shattering echoed my ears. . . . After that, quiet descended on the area, and within a few moments, I heard several men running along the gravel to where some horses were waiting. They mounted and with a muffled jubilant cry rode away.

I crawled from out of the thicket and made my way to the coach, which was on fire a little. Staggering from out of the ripped side of the coach (it looked like a toy gashed open on both sides by a can opener) were Tom and Oscar. Both were bleeding all about the faces, hands, and heads. Bobb was in especially painful agony. But all he could mutter was, "I think I nicked one of the snakes. They've got the chests. Maybe they dropped them getting away." Tom was just thankful to be alive and said something about retiring to a vegetable patch when he got home.

Ellis figured out later that when Bobb had started shooting, the robbers lighted another stick of dynamite and tossed it into the car, using the smoke and confusion to make their escape with the chests.

Within an hour after the train crew spread word of the robbery up and down the line, a posse of local lawmen and Southern Pacific detectives had formed to go in pursuit. Ellis agreed to ride along to identify the robbers if they caught up with them. They found the bandits' tracks almost immediately, and they appeared to be heading up into the Sierra Mountains, toward the timberline. As they started their search, the detectives told Ellis that they thought the robbery was the work of Pete Skaggs and his gang.

Ellis was a railroader and not used to being in the saddle. The ride was hard and long, longer than Ellis had expected, and a steady rain made the going much worse. On the third day, near Sonora, the posse came across two Indian trackers, whom they hired on the spot. "They took to it [the trail] like bloodhounds," said Ellis, "[b]ut as the timber became more dense, the signs were few and indistinct, even to the Indians, and the pursuit was slow."

On the fourth day the trail led to a small cabin hidden in a remote area of the Mi-Wok region. There was smoke coming from the chimney, but since it was late in the day, the possemen decided to stake the place out and wait until morning to move in.

At dawn, the leader of the posse, Sheriff Purvis of Stanislaus County, took the two Indian trackers and rode up to the front of the cabin. As he dismounted, hardly more than ten yards from the door, rifles began blazing away from within the cabin. Purvis was hit at least six times, and he sprawled on the ground in agony. The Indians ran for cover in a nearby watermelon patch. The possemen, twelve in number, opened fire.

After a few minutes a man dashed out of the cabin, firing as he ran. A bullet struck him in the head and he tumbled to the ground. Then the door opened again, and this time a woman appeared. The posse held their fire. "Don't kill us! Don't kill us!" she cried. "We're already badly hit inside. The men are out of it!" The firing stopped from inside. The possemen waited a few minutes, then two of them stood up and stepped out from behind their cover, motioning for the woman to come ahead. It was a mistake. The moment they exposed themselves, shots again rang out from the cabin, and one of the possemen took a hit above the eye.

As the firing started up again, the back door of the cabin opened and a man and woman rushed out, apparently heading for their horses tied to a line nearby. The two Indian trackers, both armed with rifles, were less than thirty yards away. They raised and fired, and killed them both.

The woman on the ground in front of the cabin was an easy target, but none of the possemen could force themselves to shoot her. Instead, they concentrated on the cabin itself, riddling it with bullets.

Finally, the front door opened again, and a man stepped into the opening. He could easily have been shot, and perhaps that was what he intended, but the possemen held their fire. He was wounded and he had tossed his rifle away. The fight was over.

As the detectives had guessed, the wounded man was train robber Pete Skaggs. He said the man and woman who were killed while trying to escape were William Maynard and Kate McClane. The other woman was not identified. After a quick trial and no appeal, Skaggs and the woman were hanged for killing the posseman. (Although hit six times, Sheriff Purvis survived.)

One of two stolen chests was found in the cabin. Skaggs said they buried the other one not far from the tracks, although he said he could not be certain of the location. A search was made, but no trace of the buried loot was found. At the end of his report, engineer Ellis commented that "I will head back to the area [where the chest was supposed to be buried] when my vacation time comes up and dig around a little. If I find that chest, you can be sure I will return it to [the] Southern Pacific." (Source: DeNevi, "The Notorious Skaggs Gang of the San Joaquin.")

LITTLE ROCK, ARKANSAS. On December 8, 1884, a cold wintery night in central Arkansas, the engineer of a southbound passenger train slowed for a switch about five miles north of Little Rock. As he leaned out of the cab, a bullet whizzed past his head, and a cry came from a grove of bushes beside the track: "Stop the train or you're a dead man!" The engineer started to throw the throttle forward, but a glance ahead told him that the switch was open, and that he might derail, so he brought the train to a halt. As he did so, five men rushed out of the bushes, all wearing white masks and all heavily armed. When they reached the locomotive, they turned and fired toward the rear of the train, obviously to discourage any curious passengers from climbing down from the coaches to find out what was happening. The only person to appear was the conductor, but several shots in his direction sent him hurrying back to safety.

The attackers split up; two of them accompanied the engineer and fireman back to the express car while the other three entered the passenger coaches and covered the panic-stricken travelers. When questioned later by the authorities, the passengers all mentioned that the robbers wore old and ragged coats, and that their trousers were wrong-side-out, apparently as part of their disguise.

In the smoking car, one of the robbers announced in a loud voice: "I'll only detain you a moment after the safe is opened; you will all be invited to contribute to the missionaries." While the safe was being opened, two of the bandits passed down the aisles and collected money and valuables in a large sack. When the last victim had been relieved of his wealth, one of the robbers said: "You will all stay here for ten minutes." When asked if they all agreed to his mandate, the passengers answered with a feeble "Yes." With that, the robbers leaped off the train and fled in the darkness.

The engineer got steam up and raced to the next town, where a posse was quickly organized and sent to the scene. An inspection of the express car revealed that around $2,000 had been taken. The passengers were questioned, and reported a total loss of nearly $5,000 in cash and valuables. (Source: *New York Times,* 8 December 1884.)

LOGAN, HARVEY. During the final days of the reign of Wyoming's Wild Bunch, Harvey Logan, also called Kid Curry, was probably the most famous train robber in the West — at the time, more famous even than Butch Cassidy. A jailbreak in 1902 propelled Logan into the

Harvey Logan. *Union Pacific Railroad Museum Collection.*

headlines. Suddenly, he was a notorious desperado. No longer just a member of the Wild Bunch, he was now proclaimed their leader. Overnight, he became one of the most feared outlaws in the West, as evidenced by the following conversation which took place in the corporate headquarters of the Union Pacific Railroad between UP president E. H. Harriman and General Superintendent W. H. Park, as related later by Park:

> In discussing one of the holdups, which in the past had been all too numerous, Mr. Harriman asked me for a detailed description of the Wilcox train robbery. At considerable length I went over the occurrence. . . . In concluding the narrative, I stated incidentally that Harvey Logan was at that time reported to be in Wyoming, either preparing to commit another robbery, or wreak vengeance upon those who had so relentlessly pursued him and the members of his gang.
> Mr. Harriman appeared intensely interested in the story, and after a few moments he turned to me, with one of his rare smiles, and said: "Mr. Park, there are just two men in these United States upon whom revolves the responsibility for the capture and reincarceration of Harvey Logan."
> "Who are those two men, Mr. Harriman?" I asked.
> Pointing his finger at me he said: "The General Superintendent of the Union Pacific Railroad, and (indicating himself with the same finger) the President of the Union Pacific Railroad."
> Knowing full well the skill of Logan with a revolver, and his delight in its use with a human being as its target, I replied: "The General Superintendent of the Union Pacific Railroad renigs [sic]."
> Mr. Harriman laughed and said: "So does the President."

Harvey Logan's outlaw connections began sometime in 1894, when he turned up at Wyoming's Hole-in-the-Wall hideout boasting that he came from Jesse James's old stomping grounds in Missouri. Logan looked the part of a mean one. Part Indian, probably Cherokee, he was dark, with a long, thin nose and black eyes that "flashed a deadly warning." He claimed he had ridden with Wyoming's famous Red Sash Gang of rustlers in the 1880s.

As did many outlaws, Logan would eventually ride under several aliases, among them Frank Jones, Tom Capehart, and most often, Kid Curry. As a member of the Wild Bunch he was one of the three gang members captured following the holdup of the Butte County Bank at Belle Fourche, South Dakota, in September 1897. During the shootout with the posse, he was wounded in the lower right arm, which resulted in a scar that would identify him throughout the remainder

of his outlaw career. He did not serve time for the Belle Fourche robbery, however; he and a handful of fellow prisoners easily overpowered their jailers at Deadwood, South Dakota, in October 1897 and escaped. According to one newspaper account of the escape, Logan showed a streak of viciousness by beating up on one of the jailer's wives.

Logan returned to ride with the Wild Bunch during whatever escapades the gang was engaged in for the next several years. In July 1910 he was a participant in the holdup on the Union Pacific at Wagner, Montana. After this robbery, he headed for Tennessee. Why he chose this state is not known, but in December he arrived in Knoxville with almost $10,000 in unsigned banknotes. Before a week was up, however, he was in trouble with the law and headed for jail.

On December 13 Logan became involved in a fight in a saloon in the Bowery section of Knoxville that resulted in a shootout and injury to two city policemen. He escaped, but was captured two days later at Johnson City, Tennessee. Once word was out that the notorious Harvey "Kid Curry" Logan was confined to the Knox County jail, Logan became a celebrity. Excited by the publicity, the sheriff even held an open house and invited the public in to see his famous guest.

On November 29, 1902, Logan was convicted in federal court in Knoxville for passing bank notes stolen in the Wagner train robbery. On the same night, however, while awaiting transfer to prison, he grabbed a guard's gun, slipped out of jail, and disappeared into the wilderness of the nearby Smokey Mountains.

Nothing was heard from Logan for nearly two years. Then, on June 10, 1904, the *Rocky Mountain News* reported that one of three men who had held up a Denver & Rio Grande train at Parachute, Colorado, was found on the trail with a bullet in his brain. It was speculated that the man was wounded in the chase, and rather than be captured, he had taken his own life.

Detectives on the scene identified the man as Harvey Logan, apparently because of a scar on his right arm identical to the one Logan was said to carry. The Pinkerton office in Denver, after examining a photograph of the deceased, proclaimed that the body was indeed that of Logan, and the outlaw was buried. But several other lawmen who were present, some of whom claimed they had once known the outlaw, said they were not so sure. To make certain, the Pinkertons obtained an order for exhumation and sent an agent, Lowell Spence, who had become acquainted with Logan while he was confined to jail in Tennessee, to identify the body. Spence said the man was definitely Logan. However, William T. Canada, a special officer for the Union Pacific Railroad who accompanied Spence on the trip, was just as positive that the body was not that of Logan.

Troubled by Canada's insistence, William Pinkerton sent agent Spence to Knoxville, Tennessee, with the picture of the dead man and instructions to show it to all of the law officers and jail personnel who had become familiar with Harvey while he was confined there. Spence returned with the affidavits of several state and federal officers confirming that the picture was indeed that of the dead train robber, and this appeared to end the matter.

But did it? Although the Pinkertons presumably closed the file on Logan in 1904, three years later, while addressing a convention of the nation's police chiefs at Jamestown, Virginia, William Pinkerton, in reciting his agency's fifty-year battle with train robbers, had this to say about Harvey Logan:

> Logan was convicted and sentenced to a term of twenty years in the United States Penitentiary at Columbus, Ohio, for uttering bank notes stolen at Wagner on which notes the signatures had been forged. On November 29, 1902, while awaiting transfer to that institution, he made his escape by "holding-up" the guards in the Knoxville jail; fleeing to the mountains on horseback. *He has not been recaptured.* (Italics supplied)

The above statement was made three years after Logan was supposed to have been killed in Colorado. Later in the same address, Pinkerton said:

> "Butch" Cassidy with Harry Longbaugh (sic) and Etta Place . . . fled to Argentine Republic, South America, where they, it is said, *have been joined by Logan.* . . . During the past two years, they committed several "hold-up" bank robberies in Argentina. . . . We advised the Argentina authorities of their presence and location, but they became suspicious of preparations for their arrest, fled from Argentine Republic and were last heard from on the Southwest Coast of Chile, living in wild open country. (Italics supplied)

The name of Harvey Logan was more or less forgotten until the late 1960s, when an Argentinian journalist named Justo Piernes, while researching an article on Butch Cassidy's escapades in South America, uncov-

ered evidence that Logan had been involved in robbery attempts in Rio Pescado and Rio Pico, Argentina, in 1909, and that some months later he was killed "by his own companions . . . in a place close to Corcovado," a tiny village on the Chilean coast.

Perhaps, however, as in the case of Cassidy and Longabaugh, we have not heard the end of the story of Harvey Logan. (Sources: Kindred, "Knoxville's Favorite Outlaw"; Pinkerton, *Train Robberies*; Pointer, *In Search of Butch Cassidy.*) *See also* **Robert LeRoy "Butch Cassidy" Parker; Wagner, Montana**.

LOGAN, NEW MEXICO. By the turn of the century many train robbers had figured out that the best way to blow open express car safes was to set the smaller local safe on top of the larger through safe and wedge dynamite between them, near the front, so that it would blow the doors loose. This procedure worked, if one used just the right amount of dynamite, but some robbers just never got the hang of this.

Logan, New Mexico, is in the eastern part of the state, about thirty miles northeast of Tucumcari. About 10:00 P.M. on the night of July 30, 1904, at the depot at Logan, between three and seven masked men boarded a Rock Island passenger train. When the conductor, John York, put up a fight, they shot him in the leg.

After uncoupling the express car from the rest of the train, they ordered the engineer to pull down the track, where they went to work on the express car safes. In traditional fashion, they placed the small safe on top of the larger one, and sandwiched dynamite between them. But when they ignited the charge, the blast blew the small safe through the roof of the car. The bandits retrieved the safe, and again placed it on the larger safe. This time the charge blew the smaller safe through the side of the car. Out of dynamite, the gang saddled up and rode off empty-handed.

Local authorities speculated that the culprits were a gang of outlaws from southern Colorado. (Sources: *San Francisco Chronicle*, 31 July, 1, 2, 4 August 1904.)

LONGABAUGH, HARRY "SUNDANCE KID." Few details were known about the Sundance Kid until the release of the popular movie *Butch Cassidy and the Sundance Kid* by Twentieth Century Fox in 1969. Almost immediately, writers of western frontier history began digging into this outlaw's past to see if he really was

Harry Longabaugh.
Pinkertons.

the interesting character actor Robert Redford portrayed him to be. Most were disappointed, not so much in what they found but in what they did not find. Sundance had covered his tracks well.

Sundance was born Harry Alonzo Longabaugh in Phoenixville, Pennsylvania, sometime in 1867 or 1868. According to family records obtained by his biographer, Edward M. Kirby, he "left home for the West" in August 1882 at age fourteen to work on a ranch in LaPlata County, Colorado. From there he drifted to New Mexico and later Utah, where he became a skilled rider and an expert at shooting at targets with a borrowed Colt revolver. It is believed that he first became acquainted with outlaws during a trip to Wyoming's Hole-in-the-Wall area in 1883 or 1884. Although not confirmed, it was reported that his first brush with the law came when he was involved in a fight between rival cattlemen near Springer, New Mexico, in 1884. Several cowboys were killed, and Longabaugh and several others fled the territory. Later, he worked for a cattle company in Wyoming and got into similar trouble there.

Longabaugh officially became an outlaw in 1887. While visiting, or possibly working, at the Three-Vee Ranch in Crook County, Wyoming, he stole a horse, saddle, and gun from fellow employees. The owner of the gun rode down to Sundance, the county seat, and complained to Crook County Sheriff Jim Ryan. Ryan traced Longabaugh up to Miles City, Montana, where he had worked on a ranch the previous year, and put him under arrest. But instead of taking his prisoner directly back to Wyoming, Ryan placed him in shackles

and the two men boarded a Northern Pacific train for St. Paul, Minnesota, where the sheriff apparently had business to conduct. During the trip, while Ryan was using the toilet at the end of the coach, Longabaugh picked the locks on his chains and escaped. He was soon recaptured, however, and eventually returned to Sundance, Wyoming, to stand trial.

Longabaugh pleaded guilty to the thefts and in August 1887 he was sentenced to eighteen months at hard labor. He was supposed to be sent to the state penitentiary at Laramie, but it was full, so he was kept in the Crook County jail at Sundance to serve out his term. It was from this experience that he picked up his nickname.

On his release from jail in 1889, Longabaugh got into trouble again. On May 17 of that year he was involved in a shooting about thirty-five miles north of Sundance at Salt Creek, during which a small-time fugitive named Bob Minor was killed. Longabaugh and another man, known only as the "Chicago Kid," were with Minor when the lawmen closed in and both were charged with threatening to kill the law officers. The charge was weak, however, and may have been drawn up merely to encourage Longabaugh and the Chicago Kid to leave town. If so, it worked, and both men said goodbye to Sundance, Wyoming. Some say the Chicago Kid may have been Elzy Lay, who later rode with Longabaugh and Butch Cassidy as members of the Wild Bunch.

Following his departure from Sundance, Longabaugh returned to northeastern Montana where he worked for several ranches near the Canadian border. He may or may not have stayed on the right side of the law during the next three years, but there is no record of him being arrested for any crimes during this period.

Harry Longabaugh's introduction to train robbery occurred on November 27, 1892, west of the town of Malta, Montana, in Phillips County, about sixty miles south of the Canadian border. Just before dawn he and two companions, Bill Madden and Harry Bass, climbed aboard a Great Northern westbound as it was pulling away from the Malta station and ordered the engineer to stop the train. A visit to the express car, however, was hardly worth the trip. The express messenger convinced the trio of robbers that the through safe could only be opened by agents at principal stations along the route, and the local safe contained less than $20 in cash and a few valuables.

This was probably the first train robbery for Madden and Bass as well, and they foolishly returned to Malta where they were picked up by the law from descriptions given by the train's conductor. Longabaugh was smarter; he headed west, but thanks to information given by one or both of his confederates, a wanted poster was immediately issued by the Great Northern Express Company offering a reward of $500 for "the arrest of Harry Longabaugh." The poster described Harry as being about twenty-five years old, five feet eleven inches tall with a dark complexion and a short, dark moustache. He also was supposed to be "slender and erect with a slight stoop in head and shoulders," and a "short upper lip exposing his teeth when talking." His teeth were described as "white and clean" but with a "small dark spot on the upper tooth to the right of center."

It is not known when Harry Longabaugh joined up with the outlaws that eventually would ride as the Wild Bunch. Longabaugh may have crossed paths with Butch Cassidy in Utah in the early 1880s or possibly the two became acquaintances in 1886 in Montana when, at least by some accounts, both were working on ranches near Miles City. Or, if the Chicago Kid was indeed Elzy Lay, maybe he introduced Longabaugh to Cassidy.

Some writers believed that the Wild Bunch that Butch Cassidy led was born in the cattle wars of Wyoming in 1892. If so, having at least one train robbery under his belt, Longabaugh probably signed on then. The outfit's activities for the next four or five years are not well documented. However, in June 1897 Longabaugh and the gang held up the Butte County Bank in Belle Fourche, South Dakota. All but one of the outlaws, Tom O'Day, escaped. Longabaugh, however, had his horse shot out from under him by Butte County sheriff George Fuller.

Three months later Longabaugh and two others, Walt Puteney and Lonie Logan, were captured near Lavina, Montana. At the time, Longabaugh was using the alias Frank Jones. The three were taken to Deadwood, South Dakota, and scheduled for trial, but on October 31, 1897, Longabaugh and Logan escaped.

It is believed that Longabaugh participated in the robbery of a Wells, Fargo express car on the Southern Pacific line near Humboldt, Nevada, on July 14, 1898. According to an account in a local newspaper, the robbers got between $20,000 and $26,000.

The next train robbery attributed to the Wild Bunch occurred on the Union Pacific line at Wilcox, Wyoming, on June 2, 1899. It is not known for sure whether Longabaugh was involved. If so, he shared in about $30,000 taken from the express company's safe.

Tipton, Wyoming, was the next site of a Wild Bunch train robbery. On August 29, 1900, it is believed that Butch Cassidy, Longabaugh, and fellow gang member Harvey Logan stopped the Union Pacific Flyer and blew apart the express car with dynamite. The amount taken was officially reported at $154, but there is some evidence that nearly $55,000 was lost, either taken by the bandits or destroyed in the explosion.

In early 1901 Longabaugh and his girlfriend, Etta Place, using the names Mr. and Mrs. Harry A. Place, boarded a ship out of New York for South America. Records show that in March of the same year a Mr. Harry A. Place deposited 2,000 pounds in Bank of England notes in the London and River Plate Bank in Buenos Aires, Argentina. It is believed the couple toured the country for the next year looking for suitable land for a ranching operation.

There is some evidence that Longabaugh and Etta Place, and possibly Butch Cassidy, operated a ranch in South America, probably Argentina, until 1905 or 1906, after which Longabaugh and Cassidy returned to the outlaw trail, concentrating mainly on banks.

In 1930 a western writer named Arthur Chapman, writing in *Elks* magazine, reported that both Longabaugh and Cassidy were killed in a shootout with Bolivian soldiers in San Vincente, Bolivia, in 1909. The information came from a friend of the outlaws, a mining engineer named Percy Seibert, who was in South America at the time. The Pinkertons accepted the story and the file on the two outlaws was closed.

Several writers have denounced the San Vincente incident as a hoax and have dug up evidence that Cassidy returned to the United States. Edward Kirby, Longabaugh's biographer, is the only writer so far to seriously suggest that Longabaugh also returned.

According to Kirby, Longabaugh came back by way of Mexico, where he may have stopped long enough to get involved with Pancho Villa in 1915. By 1918 Harry may have been in San Francisco, where his brother, Elwood Longabaugh, lived. Kirby said that Harry traveled under several aliases, including George Hanlon, Hiram Bennion, and Hiram BeBee. Kirby wrote that as George Hanlon, Harry was arrested in California on March 21, 1919, for grand larceny and sentenced to San Quentin for one to ten years. Later, sometime in the late 1930s or early 1940s, Harry may have settled in Utah under the name Hiram BeBee.

Kirby's evidence is certainly interesting but not convincing. It consists of: (1) Hiram BeBee's revelations to close friends that he was the Sundance Kid; (2) an unidentified source who said that Butch Cassidy told some of his friends that Longabaugh was going by the name Hiram BeBee; (3) the fact that the two men were similar physically; and (4) the fact that both men possessed a "tremendous ability to shoot fast and straight," both "displayed great intelligence," and "around both was wrapped an aura of mystery."

According to Kirby, Hiram BeBee lived in Rockville, Utah, and later in Spring City. Little information is actually known about the man. He was considered grouchy by his neighbors, some of whom said he was a whiskey bootlegger. There were reports that although BeBee was in his seventies, he could still draw and shoot a six-gun with the best of them. There were stories of how he could throw a can out into the street and "bounce" it along with repeated shots.

In October 1945, BeBee got into an argument with an off-duty town marshal in a saloon in Provo. The marshal grabbed the old man by the seat of the pants, ushered him outside, and dumped BeBee into his pickup truck. BeBee reached into the glove compartment of his truck, pulled out a revolver, and shot the marshal dead. He was convicted and sentenced to death, but the Utah Board of Pardons commuted the sentence to life imprisonment. He died on June 1, 1955, still confined. (Sources: Kirby, *The Rise and Fall of the Sundance Kid*; Pointer, *In Search of Butch Cassidy*.) *See also* **Humboldt, Nevada; Malta, Montana; Robert LeRoy "Butch Cassidy" Parker**.

LONG POINT, ILLINOIS. Long Point, Illinois (also at times spelled Longpoint), a water stop on the Vandalia Railroad about twenty-five miles west of Terre Haute, Indiana, had long been regarded by railroad men as a dangerous place; in other words, an ideal spot for a holdup. It was situated in a dense woods, and the closest house was more than a mile away. On several occasions during the summer of 1875, engine crews had seen "suspicious-looking persons lurking in that vicinity

at night." As a result, the engineers frequently passed up the water tank and rolled on by. On the night of July 8, 1875, engineer Milo Ames should have done that very thing. He didn't, and it cost him his life.

The bandits struck as the engine was taking on water. Two men boarded the cab and ordered Ames to "start her up." He hesitated, and one of the men said all right, "we'll run the thing ourselves," and they shot him.

The fireman, who was standing up front at the water pipe, ran for the safety of the dark woods, then headed back toward the rear of the train to warn the rest of the crew.

The bandits ran the train ahead about two miles, then stopped. By then, the Adams Express Company messenger, Jim Burke, had figured out what was happening. When he heard a voice outside his car say "Jim, let me in, quick," his answer was "get away from the door or I'll blow your brains out."

The attackers began shooting through the door. Burke later said that it seemed like there were a dozen bandits because the shots were coming from all sides. He grabbed his revolver and returned their fire.

In the meantime, the fireman had alerted the conductor, who gathered up other members of the train crew, plus two soldiers from among the passengers. Armed with a revolver and two rifles, they started forward, but by the time they reached the express car the bandits had gone. Messenger Burke, still not sure who was outside, refused to open up. On the floor of the cab, they found the lifeless body of engineer Ames. (Sources: *New York Times*, 10, 12 July 1875, *Cincinnati Gazette*, 11 July 1875.)

LOZIER, TEXAS. As train robberies increased during the 1890s, the express companies ordered stronger and stronger safes, thinking that this might be the answer. In some cases it was. Many outlaws were unfamiliar with the use of explosives and often they used either too much or too little to do the job.

Early on the morning of May 14, 1897, three bandits rode north out of Mexico and struck a westbound Southern Pacific near Lozier, Texas, about 250 miles west of San Antonio. The men sneaked aboard the train as it was leaving Lozier and shoved guns in the backs of the engine crew. They were able to force open the doors of the Wells, Fargo express car, but the safes were tightly sealed.

They packed dynamite around the doors but used too much; it blew the roof off the car and shattered the sides and floor. There was between $7,000 and $8,000 in the safes, but it was not known how much was salvaged by the robbers. The registered mail, which was carried in the express car, was virtually destroyed. (Source: *New York Times*, 15 May 1897.)

LYONS, NEW YORK. On February 21, 1892, an American Express Company messenger was attacked by a single robber while the train, a New York Central westbound, was east of Lyons, New York, between Jordan and Port Byron. The messenger, Daniel T. McInerey, bravely fought off his attacker, Oliver Curtis Perry, despite being shot three times. The assault on the express car was one of the most daring in the history of train robbery. Perry entered the car by lowering himself from the roof of the car via a homemade rope ladder. He escaped the same way when the train was halted at Port Byron. He climbed back on the train as it was pulling out of the Port Byron station and rode to Lyons, where he left the train again while the injured messenger was being taken off. He was spotted by the conductor and escaped by stealing a locomotive and tender. *See* **Oliver Curtis Perry**.   □

M

McAVOY, CALIFORNIA. It was 8:30 in the morning on June 22, 1929, and the Southern Pacific Mail and Express Train No. 36 was just about a mile east of McAvoy, which is in Contra Costa County on the southern shore of Suison Bay. Suddenly, two men who had been sitting in the rear of the single passenger coach pulled automatic pistols out of their pockets and fired several shots into the floor of the car. Their purpose was to attract the attention of the conductor. When he arrived, one of the men ordered him to signal the engineer to stop the train. As he did, the other man instructed the passengers, twelve in all, to march to the forward end of the car and stand there without moving.

When the train had stopped, the first man ran forward to the locomotive cab. From the ground he pointed his weapon at the engineer, Joe Barnes, and the fireman, Bob Jensen, and ordered them to throw up their hands. Then he began climbing up the ladder to the cab, but Barnes would have none of it. When the bandit reached the top of the ladder, Barnes grabbed for the gun. He missed, and the bandit fired. The bullet struck Barnes in the left elbow and shoulder. As Barnes fell to the floor of the cab, Jensen, the fireman, leaped to the other side of the cab, climbed out the window and crawled forward alongside the boiler to the front portion of the engine.

Once inside the cab, the bandit checked the engineer to see that he would be no further trouble to him, then he threw the engine into reverse and began backing up the track. When he reached the place he wanted, he braked. Immediately, a third bandit—who was hiding in a clump of bushes beside the track—pulled a tarp off of a machine gun and pointed it at the railway mail car.

The bandit in the cab put water on the fire in the boiler and released the steam valve. In the meantime, the bandit in the passenger coach marched the passengers out the door and into a group beside the track. As the bandit who had occupied the locomotive was jogging back to the mail car, he spotted the fireman sneaking through the underbrush. He fired one shot, and the fireman obediently halted, raised his hands, and joined the other captives beside the track.

A quick search of the combined express and mail car turned up little to the bandits' liking. The next car behind was also carrying mail; it was locked, and the mail clerk, Ralph Tyler, refused to open up. A short blast from the machine gun reduced the wooden door to kindling. One of the bandits then shouted to Tyler that he would blow his "Goddamn head off" if he did not "turn over the Pittsburg steel plant payrolls." Tyler handed the bandit a ring of keys and pointed to a pile of registered mail sacks on a special rack. The bandits entered the car, stuffed the packages into two mail

Circular No. 213

$9900.00
REWARD

Southern Pacific Mail and Express Train No. 36 was held up about 1½ miles east of McAvoy, Contra Costa County, California, 8:45 A. M., June 22nd, 1929, by two men, who boarded the train at Bay Point. After train left the station the bandits pulled guns and held up the conductor, brakeman and passengers, forcing the conductor to signal the engineer to stop the train.

When the train stopped one of the bandits got off, going forward to the engine. The engineer scuffled with the bandit for the gun and was shot in the left arm. The bandit then forced the engineer to back the train to where bandits had an old dark colored Hudson super-six seven passenger touring car, California License 7 T 50 86, parked.

Passengers were forced to detrain and were left in custody of bandit No. 2 who used what appeared to be a machine gun. Bandit No. 1 forced conductor to go to mail and express car asking clerk and messenger to open doors and come out. The bandit then entered the car and soon left with two mail pouches containing loot of $16,000.00 in currency.

At the point where bandits abandoned the Hudson automobile they left in coupe automobile which contained a woman.

DESCRIPTIONS:

No. 1   No. 2   No. 3. – Woman
Age: About 32 years   Age: About 40 years   Age: About 40 years
Weight: About 2 ft. 7 in. Height: About 5 ft. 8 in. Height: About 5 ft. 7 in.
Weight: About 145 lbs.   Weight: About 150 lbs.   Weight: About 130 lbs.
Hair: Dark   Hair: Dark Brown   Hair: Dark Brown
Eyes: Brown   Eyes: Blue Gray   Eyes: Dark Brown
Complex: Medium Dark   Complex: Medium   Complex: Medium
Wore no glasses   Wore no glasses
Supposed to have mole on cheek.   Supposed to have wart on eyebrow.

The above reward will be paid for information leading directly to the arrest and conviction of the guilty persons. United States Post Office Department $2000 each, Southern Pacific Company $1000.00 each, Railway Express Agency Inc. $300.00 each. If all three are convicted $9900.00.

Wire all information to me at my expense.

R. R. VEALE, Sheriff, Contra Costa County,
MARTINEZ, CALIFORNIA
TELEPHONE MARTINEZ 81

OR NOTIFY: C. E. Caine, Post Office Inspector in Charge, San Francisco, California.
D. O'Connell, Chief Special Agent, Southern Pacific Co., 65 Market Street, San Francisco, California.
W. C. Rutherford, Chief Special Agent, Railway Express Agency Inc., San Francisco, California.

Dated: Martinez, California, June 29th, 1929.

Reward notice following the McAvoy robbery. *Southern Pacific Railroad.*

sacks, and tossed them out the door. After ordering the captives not to move for a full ten minutes, the two bandits grabbed the sacks and raced down the track where their partner was holding the passengers. The passengers were told to start walking up the track toward the front of the train. The three bandits loaded the two mail sacks into a Hudson touring car that had been parked beside the track and drove away. Several days later, postal authorities would determine that the stolen mail contained approximately $16,000 in currency.

Later that afternoon, the Hudson car was found abandoned and burned on a back road between Bay Point and Concord. After checking with residents in the area, sheriff's deputies found witnesses who said they saw three men leave the vicinity in either a Chevrolet or Overland coupe being driven by a woman.

The robbers were eventually caught. A Bay area criminal, Frank Ellis, who was a suspect in several robberies, including a railway mail car at Nobel, California, was confronted at his home in Oakland; he was killed trying to escape. His wife was arrested, as well as two of his underworld associates, Charles Berta and James Sargert. Witnesses identified these three as being at the scene at McAvoy, and all were convicted and sent to prison. (Source: DeNevi, *Western Train Robberies.*) *See also* **Nobel, California**.

MACOMB, MISSOURI. Macomb was a tiny flag station on the Kansas City, Ft. Scott & Memphis Railroad in Wright County, about fifty miles east of Springfield. On the night of January 3, 1899, a westbound passenger train was taken over by armed men and the Southern Express Company's through safe was emptied of its contents. There was little to distinguish this robbery from the hundreds of others that occurred during the 1890s except that the robbers used an innocent passenger to stop the train.

Macomb, a small, rural station, was not a regular stop on the line, and passenger trains would speed on by unless there was a passenger on board who wanted to get off. If a passenger at Macomb wanted to catch a train, the station agent would signal or flag the engineer to stop. The day of the robbery, Oscar Ray – a local farmer who lived about three miles outside Macomb – had apparently been approached by several men with some kind of business arrangement that would take him to the town of Norwood, about five miles east of Macomb. The details of this arrangement are not known, but they were such that Ray would be returning to Macomb on the evening westbound, which meant that the train would be stopping there.

As the train pulled up to the Macomb station, five or six masked and armed men were waiting in the shadows. If the station agent was on duty that night, he probably had been overpowered and securely bound and gagged on the floor of his office. The train stopped, and Oscar Ray stepped down from the coach onto the darkened platform. In minutes, he was on his way home, unaware of the role he had played in Wright County's first train robbery.

Seeing that there were no more passengers leaving the train, the engineer started to give the big locomotive the throttle, when he suddenly was surrounded by men with guns. He and the fireman were ordered out of the cab and forced to uncouple the train behind the express car. One of the robbers entered the cab, took the throttle, and pulled the front half of the train forward about a quarter of a mile. The remaining robbers forced their way into the express car and placed guns on the messenger, Henry W. Newton. Then they blew open the through safe with dynamite. About $900 in currency and some watches were taken. The men finished and headed for their horses, which had been left about a half mile south of the track. They rode off in a southeasterly direction.

A week after the robbery, local authorities arrested three men from neighboring Douglas county: Elmer Byrum, Lewis Nigh, and Jake Fagley, Nigh's son-in-law. Later, three more suspects were picked up: Jack Kennedy, William Jennings, and Joseph Sheppard. After lengthy questioning, Byrum confessed to his part in the affair and became a witness for the state. A short time later, Jennings also confessed.

Jack Kennedy was recognized by the authorities as Jack "Quail Hunter" Kennedy, a known criminal and suspected train robber from Jackson County. He denied his guilt but was later identified by a witness as having purchased the dynamite used in the robbery. Kennedy was tried, convicted, and sentenced to seventeen years in the state prison. It is believed that the remaining defendants all pleaded guilty and received lesser sentences. (Sources: Burton, "John F. Kennedy of Missouri"; State v. Kennedy.) See also **Jack "Quail Hunter" Kennedy**.

McGEENEY, PATRICK S. Patrick S. McGeeney, a young brakeman on the Santa Fe Railroad, was credited with preventing an express car robbery on May 19, 1893, at Ponca City, Oklahoma, by voluntarily leaving his train and conversing with the robbers, Henry Starr, Bill Doolin, and Bitter Creek Newcomb, who had taken over the station and were waiting for the train to pull in. The resourceful McGeeney, with his quick wit and small talk, delayed the outlaws long enough for soldiers to arrive from the nearby Ponca Indian Agency. See **Ponca City, Oklahoma**.

McINERNEY, DANIEL T. On February 21, 1892, express messenger Daniel McInerney bravely fought off a vicious attack by train robber Oliver Curtis Perry during an in-transit attack on the messenger's car west of Syracuse near Jordan, New York. Perry broke into the car by smashing a window after climbing down from the roof on a homemade rope ladder. McInerney refused to surrender and continued to battle until shot three times by his attacker. Thwarted, Perry finally departed without taking a package and was captured the following day. McInerney survived his injuries and was honored by his employer, the American Express Company, with a promotion to an office position at Oswego, New York. (Source: O'Dell, "Oliver Curtis Perry.") See also **Oliver Curtis Perry**.

McNEILL, TEXAS. For want of a catchy phrase, the newspaper wags called it the "Jay Gould Robbery." During the 1880s Jay Gould, one of the richest men in the United States, owned more than a tenth of all the railway mileage in the nation. Among his lines were the Union Pacific, the Missouri Pacific, the Wabash, the Texas & Pacific, and the St. Louis & Northern. In accumulating his wealth he made more than his share of enemies, especially after an unsuccessful attempt in 1869 to corner the U.S. gold market resulted in a stock market crash and a nationwide business panic. Gould's enemies probably could cite numerous "robberies" on the part of this greedy speculator, but in the case of the robbery at McNeill, Texas, one of his railroads was the victim.

On May 18, 1887, a Missouri Pacific passenger train was struck by nearly a dozen bandits at McNeill, about twelve miles north of Austin. The gang had overpowered the station agent and was waiting when the train pulled in. A few passengers who had planned to get off dashed back into the coaches for safety when they saw the gunmen on the station platform. With the sound of crashing glass and bullets thudding into the ceilings of the cars, the frightened travelers dived to the floor and crawled between the seats. One passenger, traveling salesman Harry Landa, did not move to safety quickly enough, and was hit in the arm.

The robbers, however, were not interested in assaulting the passengers; they were after the contents of the express car, about $4,000. The door was forced open and the two messengers meekly raised their hands. When ordered to turn over the money contained in the safe, one of the messengers, whose name was Nothacker, reached in and withdrew only a small package. He was promptly hit over the head with a pistol barrel.

When the robbers turned toward the postal end of

the car, railway mail service clerk Robert Spaulding pleaded that he was not carrying any registered mail, that all the registered letters were went on the daytime runs. One of the bandits told him not to worry about it—they were not after "Uncle Sam's money, but Jay Gould's." With that, Spaulding said, the bandits bade him and the messengers a "pleasant good night" and rode off.

Ten years later, the tiny McNeill station again was in the headlines. On October 12, 1897, around 5:30 in the evening, as a southbound International & Great Northern passenger train was pulling away from the station, two heavily armed men boarded the rear platform of the last coach. The train had gone but a short distance when the conductor, Thomas Healy, stepped out the door to take the men's tickets. The men reached into their coats, but instead of withdrawing tickets, they each pulled out a pistol.

Healy did not need an explanation and he did not wait for one. He turned and ran as fast as he could. He made it half the distance of the car when a bullet sliced into his right arm and knocked him to the floor.

One of the gunmen pulled the bell cord, which was the signal for the engineer to stop the train. Two more men, their faces covered with masks, were waiting in the trees beside the track. As they approached, they viciously fired their guns into the coaches, an effective message to the passengers to stay in their seats and cause no trouble. One traveler was hit in the hand, and another had his shirt collar torn away by a bullet.

There were three coaches on the train. The bandits threw the doors open so that they had a view of the entire length of the aisles, and while one bandit stood at each end guarding the passengers, the other two forced their way into the express car. The safe, however, was locked, and the messenger convincingly pleaded that he did not have the combination. The two men returned and went up and down the aisles in pairs collecting money from the passengers. When they finished they went forward, uncoupled the locomotive, climbed into the cab, and sped away.

After several miles, they let the engine slow down and jumped off, leaving it to run on. The fire died down, and the big boiler eventually ran out of steam near Duval, a tiny flag station, without causing any damage. (Sources: *New York Times*, 20 May, 1887, 13 October 1897.)

TRAIN ROBBERY IN TEXAS

Four Bandits Take the Passengers' Money, but Fail to Open the Express Safe.

RAN AWAY WITH THE ENGINE

The Train Left on the Track Twelve Miles from Austin, While the Robbers Escape — The Conductor and a Passenger Wounded.

AUSTIN, Texas, Oct. 12.—This afternoon at 5:30 o'clock, within twelve miles of the limits of this city, the south-bound "cannonball" train on the International and Great Northern Railroad, consisting of mail, baggage, and express cars, and three coaches filled with passengers, was held up by four men and robbed. The conductor of the train, Thomas Healy, was shot by the robbers while resisting them, but was not wounded seriously.

The McNeill robbery. *New York Times.*

MALTA, MONTANA. The Great Northern Railroad's Train No. 23 left St. Paul, Minnesota, on November 27, 1892, bound for Butte, Montana. As it slowly pulled away from the station at Malta, a small town in Phillips County about midway between Havre and Glascow, three men silently slipped aboard between the tender and express car. It was still early morning, and in the dark no one noticed them. Before the engineer could get up to full speed, he felt a revolver in his back and was commanded to stop the train.

After the train had been brought to a halt, the engineer and fireman were marched back to the express car. On orders of the masked men, express messenger Jerry Hauert opened up, and two of the robbers climbed in. They informed him that they meant him no harm and were only after the treasure the car held.

The messenger's small safe held less than $20, which one of the robbers quickly pocketed. Turning to the larger through safe, the intruders ordered Hauert to open it. The messenger replied that the combination was known only to express company agents at St. Paul and at principal stations along the route. Disgusted, the robbers told the engineer to return to his locomotive and they jumped to the ground. Within seconds they disappeared into the darkness.

During the robbery the bandits' masks kept slipping. Despite their attempts to keep their faces covered, several of the trainmen got a good look at them. Descriptions were immediately sent out along the line. Several days later, word came from Malta that two men matching two of the descriptions had been seen hanging around Alex Black's saloon a few days before the robbery, and they were still in town. In fact, they frequented the saloon almost every night. On December 1 around 10:00 P.M. the local sheriff walked into Black's and placed the two men under arrest.

The men identified themselves as Bill Madden and Harry Bass, a couple of unemployed cowboys. When confronted by the trainmen, who positively identified them as two of the men who held them up, Madden confessed his part in the robbery. Furthermore, he named the third man, another local cowboy named Harry Longabaugh, also known as the Sundance Kid. Longabaugh, they said, did not return to Malta, but rode west after the robbery, along the river toward Havre.

Bill Madden and Harry Bass were convicted and sentenced to ten years in prison at Deer Lodge, Montana. In 1895 they were both released for good behavior. Madden disappeared. Bass rode down to Indian Territory near the Texas line where he was killed the same year. (Source: Kirby, *The Rise and Fall of the Sundance Kid*.) *See also* **Harry Longabaugh**.

MANNING, CHARLEY. Charley Manning's name has never appeared on a list of famous criminals. His claim to fame was the fact he had the foresight to execute his last will and testament prior to what was probably his first, and definitely his last, train robbery.

Few details are known of Manning's early years. His birth date is believed to have been Christmas Day 1881, and his place of birth, somewhere in Utah. For most of his life he made his home in Cokeville, Wyoming, where as a young man he worked in a cement plant. Later, he married and began raising a family. He had one known vice—gambling; there were a few rumors that at times he rode the outlaw trail, but never around Cokeville.

In the spring of 1914 Manning began planning a train robbery. He needed at least two men to help him, and he probably had little trouble recruiting two local sheepherders, Clarence Stoner and Al Meadors. In the spring of 1914 times were hard, and many cowboys and sheepherders were out of work.

To get Stoner and Meadors to go along with the holdup, Manning probably assured them that there was little danger involved and what risks they might be taking were well worth the rewards. Apparently, however, this was merely a show of bravado, because the week before the robbery Manning visited a lawyer in nearby Kemmerer, Wyoming, and had him make out his last will and testament. It was a wise move, because Manning was obviously an amateur when it came to robbing a train.

Malta, Montana. *Montana Historical Society.*

Charley Manning chose the first week of July to pull off the robbery. His target was a stretch of track in northeastern Oregon between Kamela and Meacham, on what is now part of the Union Pacific line.

Manning and his two companions boarded a west-bound train at Kamela. Foolishly, they immediately drew their revolvers and began a march through the coaches toward the express car where they assumed the safe contained a treasury of cash. They were wrong. The safe held little value. Rather than accept defeat, Manning decided to rob the passengers. After placing Stoner in charge of two conductors and several porters they had picked up on the way, Manning and Meadors headed back through the coaches, intent on emptying pockets and purses. But in one of the first cars was a deputy sheriff, George McDuffie of Heppner, Oregon. As the two bandits came down the aisle, McDuffie feigned sleep. Once they had passed by, he pulled out his six-gun and opened fire.

McDuffie's first two shots struck Manning in the back. The bandit whirled and got off a shot of his own, which hit the deputy in the chest. But it was McDuffie's lucky day. The bullet struck his breast pocket where he was carrying a deck of cards, a notebook, and a comb. He suffered only a flesh wound. Manning, however, was done for. Meadors, seeing that Manning was dying, ran toward the front of the train to alert Stoner, and the two bandits jumped off the train and disappeared in the underbrush. The next day they were picked up at Hilgard, about ten miles south of Kamela. They were tried, convicted, and sentenced to the Oregon Penitentiary at Salem. (Source: Dullenty, "Cokeville: A Rough Town in the Old West.")

MANSFIELD, LOUISIANA. Mansfield is in western Louisiana, near the Texas line, about forty miles south of Shreveport. Shortly after 11:00 P.M. on August 14, 1893, two men wearing red handkerchief masks slipped aboard the blind baggage of a westbound Texas & Pacific passenger train as it was pulling out of Mansfield. Two other men, also wearing masks, swung aboard the platform of the express car.

When the train had gone about two miles, the two stowaways climbed up on the tender, over the coal pile, and down into the cab, where they placed guns on the engineer and fireman. In traditional fashion, they ordered that the train be stopped and then marched the

The depot at Mansfield. *Everett R. Huffer Collection.*

engine crew back to the express car, where they forced the express company messenger to open the door.

The express car carried two safes, a local and a through safe. The messenger opened the local, but it held only $10.30. When ordered to open the through safe, he claimed he did not have the combination, that it was available only to selected agents along the route. Disgusted, the robbers rode off.

In October 1894 law enforcement authorities of near-by Grant Parish arrested Charles Carey at the railroad station in Pollack, Louisiana, and charged him with the robbery. Carey (a.k.a. Charles Barnett), a twenty-five-year-old blacksmith who had formerly worked at a saw-mill near Pollack, was wanted at the time for breaking out of jail at Amite, Louisiana, the previous May. (Sources: *St. Louis Globe Democrat*, 16 August 1893, 12 October 1894.)

MARICOPA, ARIZONA. The Maricopa holdup in October 1894 has been described as one of the most amateurish assaults in the annals of train robbery. The town of Maricopa, in western Pinal County about twenty-five miles due south of Phoenix, no longer appears on many area maps, but in 1894 it was a regular stop on the Southern Pacific line and busy enough to sport a depot as well as a water tank.

Near midnight on October 1, 1894, as the eastbound Southern Pacific's Train No. 19 was pulling away from the depot, two men dropped from the water tank onto the platform of the baggage car. This was the first example of amateurism. Knowledgeable train robbers usually hoisted themselves up from trackside onto the baggage or express car platform; they did not drop from a water tank where they could easily be seen.

As would be expected, the boarding did not go unnoticed; the chief brakeman, Gerald Cerrin, spotted them. Thinking they were tramps stealing a ride, he went forward to order them off. But by the time he got close enough to see their guns and masks, he was their prisoner.

A short time later, the engineer, Jim Holliday, saw a signal ahead on the track. Thinking that a freight train that was preceding him might have become disabled, he applied the brakes. But as the locomotive slowed, one of the masked intruders lowered himself from the tender and pointed two revolvers at Holliday and his fireman.

Holliday was ordered to stop. When he did, another masked man stepped out of the shadows beside the track. Here the robbers made another unusual, and obviously amateur, decision. They ordered the locomotive uncoupled from the rest of the train. (Experienced train robbers always had the train uncoupled *behind the express car*, to separate the express car from the coaches so that passengers and other members of the train crew could not come forward to interfere.) The engineer was then ordered to pull the locomotive down the track. One of the masked men accompanied him, and shortly they both returned on foot.

In the meantime, the remaining two robbers fired a few shots down the sides of the coaches to keep the passengers and crew in line. The Wells, Fargo messenger, George Mitchell, with the sound of the shots ringing in his ears, figured it would do no good to resist, and he opened the express car door. Probably he was not too worried about his cargo; the company had recently installed new locks on the through safes that could be opened only by station agents along the route.

When the robbers found they could not open the through safe, they settled for the money in the local safe, about $160. One of them suggested going through the passenger coaches, and asked Cerrin, the brakeman: "What sort of load to you have on the train?"

The brakeman wisely played down the prospects: "A very poor-looking crowd," he replied. "There are only five or six people in the Pullman car, and they don't look as though they have anything." The bandits accepted this answer and prepared to leave. As an afterthought, one of them took the express messenger's pocket watch.

As soon as the bandits rode off, the engineer and fireman ran up the track, retrieved the locomotive, and backed the train to Maricopa. Telegrams were immediately sent to Southern Pacific and Wells, Fargo officials, notifying them of the robbery.

The robbers' departure was as amateurish as the holdup. Apparently they made no effort to seek out hard rock areas in an attempt to hide their tracks. A local sheriff named Murphy and his deputy spotted three sets of fresh tracks leading from the direction of the robbery scene and followed them to about seven miles west of Phoenix. There, they found an unoccupied camp with three sweaty horses tied nearby. Two Winchester rifles and a shotgun were still strapped to the saddles (another obvious mistake). The horses' owners had apparently gone to a nearby pasture for some hay. The officers merely sat down and waited.

They had not waited long when one of the riders returned with a load of hay in his arms. When he was ordered to throw up his hands, he dropped the hay and went for his gun, but a load of buckshot quickly disabled him. The other two men, on hearing the gunfire, headed in the other direction.

The captured outlaw, identified as Frank Armer, a local cowboy, still carried the watch he had taken from the Wells, Fargo express messenger. Armer at times was known to ride with a hard case named Oscar Armstrong. Southern Pacific detectives were fairly certain that Armstrong, a former soldier who was wanted for holding up a cafe at Fort Wingate, New Mexico, was one of the two remaining train robbers. Several weeks later he was picked up, still on foot, near Tacna Station.

Armer and Armstrong were tried and convicted of train robbery, then a capital offense in Arizona Territory, and sentenced to hang. Both sentences, however, were reduced to forty years in the territorial prison at Yuma. Armer contracted tuberculosis in prison; to avoid contaminating fellow prisoners, in 1903 he was paroled and put in the care of a brother near Payson, Arizona. Armstrong received a parole the following year.

The third suspect, believed to be an ex-convict named John Donovan, who also rode under the aliases O'Bryann and Bryant, was never apprehended. (Sources: Edwards, "Robbery at Maricopa"; *Arizona Daily Gazette*, 2–11 October 1894.)

MARSHFIELD, INDIANA. Marshfield, as the name implies, was located in a wooded, swampy area known as the Muscatutuck lowlands in Scott County, about seventeen miles south of Seymour, Indiana, the site of what is generally accepted as the nation's first peacetime train robbery. (*See* **Seymour, Indiana**.)

In 1868 the town of Marshfield was little more than a watering station for the Jeffersonville & Indianapolis Railroad. On the night of May 22 that year, the northbound J&I passenger train arrived at Marshfield a little before 11:00 P.M. While the locomotive was taking on water, the engineer was working his way alongside the wheels with his oil can when a blow to the back of the head knocked him to the ground. Quickly, four men appeared from out of the darkness and uncoupled the express car from the rest of the train. One of the men climbed into the cab and threw the throttle forward. As he did, the conductor ran up and began shooting. The robbers returned the fire, but nobody was hit.

As the locomotive, tender, and express car raced through the night, three of the intruders climbed along the walk plank on the side of the express car and forced their way in through the side door. The messenger, F. G. Harkins, tried to resist but was beaten senseless with pistol butts and then thrown out the door. The robbers opened the express company safes with crowbars and emptied the contents, estimated between $40,000 and $96,000, into sacks.

About a mile from Seymour the robbers halted the train. Tracks found the following morning indicated that they had escaped on horses that had been tied nearby. The robbers were believed to be members of the Reno gang that had been operating in the area for several years. (Sources: *Indianapolis Daily Sentinel*, 25 May 1868; *Seymour Democrat*, 27 May 1868.) *See also* **The Reno Gang**.

MEDICINE HAT, MONTANA. This story circulated through Montana in 1892 upon publication of the reminiscences of an unidentified railroad telegraph operator. According to the storyteller, who did not give the date of the incident, it occurred when he was stationed at Medicine Hat on the Northern Pacific Railroad.

One rainy night he was surprised by a gang of outlaws bent on robbing an incoming express. One of the gang members, apparently a former telegrapher himself, sat down at the telegraph key and began tapping out messages along the line until he learned the loca-

tion of two oncoming trains, one westbound and one eastbound. Both trains had been thrown off schedule by the storm. Pretending to be the Medicine Hat operator, the bandit sent them instructions altering their speeds so that they would meet head-on along a single stretch of track near the Medicine Hat station. The idea, of course, was that the trains would collide, and the outlaw would then ransack the two wrecked express cars.

While the Northern Pacific telegrapher was trying to figure some way to escape and warn the engineers of the danger that lay ahead, the thunderstorm suddenly worsened. A bolt of lighting struck the telegraph pole outside the station and followed the wire inside. In a shower of sparks and smoke, the outlaw sitting at the key was instantly killed, and the building burst into flames. The rest of the gang, shaken at the sight of their confederate's smoldering body, fled in a panic. The telegrapher freed himself, grabbed a lantern, and ran down the track to warn the first of the approaching trains. By this time, however, the station was blazing away; both engineers spotted it from a distance and brought their trains safely to a stop. (Source: Russell, *Trails of the Iron Horse*.)

MERIDIAN, MISSISSIPPI. Early on the morning of June 18, 1871, an embarrassed Southern Express Company messenger awoke to find that someone had slipped into his express car and stolen his safe.

Just when the robber entered the car was not determined. The Mobile & Ohio passenger train was nearing Meridian when the messenger awoke and found his safe gone. There were footprints indicating that the robber was barefooted and had somehow managed to drag the safe over the the door of the car and pitch it out. It was found later in a woods near the track. It had been opened with an axe and the contents, about $12,000, were gone.

The local authorities had a pretty good idea who might have committed the robbery; for some time they had suspected a local gang of stealing from Mobile & Ohio freight cars. A raid on the home of one of the suspects, Wash Crosby, turned up the axe and the charred remains of some of the express company papers. An accomplice, Albert Grier, was also arrested. Crosby eventually confessed, and his portion of the stolen loot, about $4,000, was found hidden near the town of Whistler. (Sources: *Mobile Register* [Alabama], 24 June 1871; *New York Times*, 3 July 1871.)

MESQUITE, TEXAS. On April 10, 1878, Mesquite, Texas, was the site of the fourth in a series of train robberies by Sam Bass and his gang after Sam's return to Texas the previous fall. Today, Mesquite is a community of 70,000 on the eastern edge of Dallas; in 1878, it consisted of a railroad station, general store, blacksmith shop, two saloons, and a few residences.

The Bass gang, which had grown to eight members, struck the railroad station, overpowered the station agent, and sat down to await the arrival of the next Texas & Pacific passenger train. This was Bass's usual method of attack, and usually it was successful. This night, however, the outlaws would have their hands full. J. S. Kerley, the express messenger, saw what was happening and let the gang have five rounds from his revolver before he slammed his door shut. No one was hit, however.

Back in the first passenger coach was the train's conductor, Julius Alvord, a crusty Civil War veteran who seldom gave ground to any man, especially bandits. He also saw what was happening and began peppering away at them with his double-barreled derringer. The little gun had terrible accuracy at that distance, however, so Alvord went looking for a six-shooter. In the meantime, the bandits encountered still another problem. Across the tracks on a siding was a special car loaded with convicts used for construction labor. Their guards, fully armed and having a good view of the affair, also opened up on the would-be robbers.

Next, the baggage clerk, B. F. Caperton, dug out his shotgun, slid the baggage car door open a few inches, and joined in. A few minutes later, the train's candy

The depot at Mesquite. *Everett R. Huffer Collection.*

vendor borrowed a pistol from one of the passengers and began to contribute, but a few return shots from the outlaws gave him second thoughts and he climbed back into the coach, out of harm's way.

The outlaws must have thought they were in a war. Gang member Seaborn Barnes took bullets in both legs, and Sam Pipes was hit in the side. But just when the robbers were considering riding off, the firing slackened. Conductor Alvord, who had found a six-gun and was giving the bandits fits, was hit in the shoulder and put out of commission. Then the guards in the car on the siding apparently realized that they had better not use up all their ammunition, just in case the convicts decided to take advantage of the confusion and try to escape, and they ceased firing. The Bass gang took advantage of the lull and doused the express car door with coal oil. Messenger Kerley, who could smell the oil from inside the car, decided he did not want to go up in smoke and shouted that he was surrendering.

But when the bandits finally forced their way into the express car they found that they had risked their lives for very little reward; Kerley had hidden most of the money (some reports say $1,500, but others as much as $30,000) in the cold ashes in the potbellied stove. After helping their wounded comrades to their horses, the outlaws rode off with less than $200. (Sources: Block, *Great Train Robberies of the West*; Gard, *Sam Bass*.) *See also* **Sam Bass**.

MIKON, CALIFORNIA. The date was October 12, 1894. The night was cold and foggy. Around 8:00 P.M. John Kelly, a trackwalker for the Southern Pacific, was checking rails near Mikon, about three miles west of Sacramento, when he spotted a lantern on a crate beside the tracks. He stopped his velocipede handcar and was about to climb off to get a better look when a tall "broad-shouldered fellow in a soft cap" carrying a Winchester and a revolver stepped out of the underbrush. At the same time, on the other side of the tracks, out stepped "a slender, white-faced youth whose chin was buried in the depths of his coat collar and whose hands were thrust deep into his pockets." He also was carrying a rifle and a revolver. Both men wore long linen dusters and masks made of woolen drawers.

The tall man told Kelly to get off his handcar. When he complied, the man took the butt of his rifle and smashed the wheels of the vehicle. He then picked up

Southern Pacific track near Mikon. *Southern Pacific Railroad.*

the lantern from the crate, turned to Kelly, and said: "We're going for a walk."

About a quarter of a mile down the track, Kelly was ordered to stop. The tall man handed him the lantern and told him to sit down and wait. In about an hour, they saw the lights of the Southern Pacific's eastbound *Overland Express.* Kelly's instructions were to swing the lantern, the signal for the engineer to stop.

The engineer, a man named Scott, saw the signal and applied the brakes. When the big locomotive came to a stop, he and the fireman climbed down and walked back toward Kelly, intending to ask why he had signaled. But they had gone only a few yards when the two armed men appeared from out of the shadows. The taller man ordered the two trainmen and the trackwalker to head back toward the Wells, Fargo express car.

On the first demand, the express messenger refused to open up, but one of the bandits yelled that if he didn't, the three prisioners would be shot and the express car would be dynamited. The messenger slid open the door and stepped forward, his hands raised over his head.

On searching the express car, the bandits found four sacks of gold and silver coins, later estimated to contain $50,000, which they ordered the engineer to carry forward and place in the locomotive cab. The fireman, the messenger, and Kelly were told to remain in the express car, and the two bandits mounted the cab with the engineer. The engineer was ordered to pull forward. After a few miles, the bandits ordered him to stop, and when the locomotive slowed, they grabbed the coins and jumped off.

A careful search of the area by Southern Pacific and Wells, Fargo investigators failed to turn up any trace of the bandits. The Southern Pacific immediately sent out notices that a reward of $10,000 would be paid for information leading to the arrest and conviction of the robbers.

It was later discovered that the bandits had buried the loot along the tracks in a marshy area near the west bank of the Sacramento River. While they were digging their hiding place, however, they were seen by one of the Southern Pacific's numerous hoboes. The hobo, "Karl the Tramp," whose real name was John P. Harmans, kept quiet and let the robbers finish. After they left, Karl dug up the treasure, stuffed $10,000 in his blanket roll, and reburied the rest in a different spot a short distance away.

Karl caught a ride into Sacramento and began living the high life with his newly found wealth. When he had exhausted the pleasures of that city he headed for San Francisco, rented an expensive apartment on Nob Hill, and indulged himself with liquor and women. He soon attracted the attention of the police and was brought in for questioning. Before he could be arrested, however, he skipped town and returned to his hobo life. In April 1896 he was picked up again, and this time he revealed the source of his wealth. Almost $40,000 of the stolen money was recovered. (Source: DeNevi, *Western Train Robberies.*)

MINER, BILL. "Old Bill" Miner's career probably spanned more years than any other train robber. He was born in Jackson, Kentucky in 1847 and drifted west in his teens. Between 1866 and 1880 he was in and out of San Quentin three times, mostly for robbing stages. In 1880 he returned to the East and settled in Onondaga, Michigan, under the name of William Morgan. For a year he appeared to lead a respectable life, then in March 1881 he turned up in Colorado where he was arrested again for stage robbery. As he was being brought in, however, he escaped by shooting one of his captors. Soon he was robbing stages again.

Sometime in the fall of 1881 Miner returned to Cali-

Bill Miner. *Pinkertons.*

fornia. By the end of the year he was back in San Quentin on another stage robbery conviction, this time with a twenty-five year sentence. On being released in 1901, he vowed that he would never go back to prison. He was fifty-four years old and had already spent nearly half of his life behind bars.

In early 1903 Bill got a job with an oyster bed company on Puget Sound, where he quickly worked his way up to superintendent. He was remembered by those who knew him then for his courteous manners, especially to the ladies.

On September 23, 1903, a Great Northern express was held up east of Portland, Oregon. One of the robbers, Charlie Hoehn, was wounded by the express messenger and captured. He named Miner as one of the participants; however, Miner was long gone. Letters to friends the following year revealed that he had spent time in Mexico, Texas, Montana, and finally, British Columbia.

Sometime in the summer of 1904 Miner moved into a little cabin between Aspen Grove and Princeton, British Columbia, about sixty miles south of Kamloops. He told his neighbors that he was a prospector and used the name George Edwards. On September 10 of that year, he and two companions struck the Canadian Pacific Railroad at Silverdale, B.C. Their reported haul was $7,000 in currency and $250,000 in Australian bonds.

The robbery of an express car on the Great Northern's *Oriental Limited* out of Seattle, Washington, in October 1905 also is thought to be the work of Old Bill and his pals. Shortly thereafter, while still posing as George Edwards, Miner returned to his cabin in Brit-

ish Columbia from one of his "prospecting trips" and told his neighbors that he had struck it rich.

The robbery that would send Old Bill back to jail occurred on May 9, 1906, near Furrer, British Columbia, about twenty miles east of Kamloops. Miner's companions in this holdup were Lewis Colquihoun and William "Shorty" Dunn. The affair was a flop: the express car and postal car had been switched, and the robbers ended up uncoupling the mail car from the rest of the train instead of the express car. Their total take for the night was $15.50. Worse still, their trail was picked up by a local posse and five days later they were captured by Mounties while they were camping near Douglas Lake about thirty miles south of Kamloops. Shorty Dunn tried to run and was shot in the leg. Colquihoun also attempted to make a fight of it but was quickly subdued. Old Bill just shrugged and surrendered quietly.

Back at Aspen Grove, George Edwards's neighbors could not believe that their good friend was a train robber. George was a pillar of the community. It was George who would take the place of the preacher on Sunday if he was called away. And he would "preach a fine sermon, too" one of his acquaintances said. Another added that Edwards "was something of a favorite . . . particularly liked by those ranchers with large families because he was such a fatherly old fellow with the children."

The three train robbers were convicted and sentenced to New Westminister Penitentiary. Miner and Dunn drew life sentences, and Colquihoun, twenty-five years. On his arrival at prison, a local newspaper reporter described Miner as a "rather striking looking fellow, with grisled hair and moustache, erect and active [who] does not appear to be within ten years of the age which the prison records now credit him. He claims

Miner gang being brought in. *Provincial Archives of British Columbia.*

to be 63, but looks like a man of 50 and moves like one of 30. His eyes are ice blue and unwinking."

It took Miner just over a year to engineer an escape. One day in the summer of 1907, while working in the yard, he noticed that at one spot along the wire fence the view of the guards in the watchtower was obstructed by a chimney. Miner passed the word along to three of his fellow prisoners. From then on, when they worked in the yard they would each step behind the chimney and scoop out a handful of dirt at the foot of the fence. By dusk that evening, they made a hole large enough to crawl through.

Slipping under the fence was easy. There also was an outer fence, but between the two was a workshed, and inside it was a ladder. The four convicts smashed the padlock on the shed door, grabbed the ladder, and were over the outer fence before the alarm sounded. By the time the escape was discovered, the men had gotten a six-minute head start. It was not much, but the penitentiary was adjacent to a wooded area. Miner's companions, however, ran into bad luck. A small boy playing nearby saw them and told the guards which direction they went. They were soon captured; Miner, however, was not found.

Miner again disappeared for a while. Some say he robbed $12,000 from a bank in Portland, Oregon, in July 1909, but this was not confirmed. Besides, the holdup was committed by a lone bandit, which was not his style. Another account has him going to Pennsylvania and working in a sawmill under the name George Anderson, then later moving to Banks County, Georgia.

Miner did show up in nearby Hall County, Georgia, in 1911. On February 18 of that year he and two companions, James Hanford and Charlie Hunter, struck the Southern Railway's Train No. 36 at White Sulphur. They failed to crack the Southern Express Company's through safe, which contained $65,000, but did empty the messenger's local safe of $1,500. Once again, however, they left a trail. A posse with bloodhounds tracked them to a hideout near Dahlonega, and before long Miner was back in prison, this time the Georgia State Penitentiary at Milledgeville. The story is told that on being led from the courtroom after his trial, Old Bill tipped his hat to some ladies among the spectators with the comment: "When one breaks the law, he must expect to pay the penalty. I am now old, but during all my life

The trial of Bill Miner. *Provincial Archives of British Columbia.*

I have found the Golden Rule the best guide to a man in this life."

But Miner was still difficult to keep locked up. On October 18, 1911, he overpowered a guard and escaped but was soon recaptured. The following year he escaped again and was again recaptured.

In 1913 Miner decided to write his memoirs, and he dictated a 30,000-word manuscript to a friendly guard. Some parts of the account appear accurate, but others are fanciful. Not long after finishing the story, he tried once more to escape. It would be his last attempt. While eluding his pursuers in a swamp, he quenched his thirst with bacteria-infested water. He soon became feverish and too weak to continue. On being captured, he reportedly told the guards: "I'm getting a bit too old for this sort of thing." His condition worsened, and he died a short time later in the prison hospital. (Source: Rickards, "Bill Miner—50 Years a Hold-up Man.") *See also* **Ballard, Washington; Furrer, British Columbia; Portland, Oregon; Silverdale, British Columbia; White Sulphur, Georgia.**

MONROE STATION, FLORIDA. In 1892 Monroe Station, a tiny stop on the Jacksonville, Tampa & Key West Railway just north of Orlando, was the scene of an unsuccessful attempt by bandits to rob a Southern Express Company car. The aborted holdup resulted in the death of the messenger and the wounding of a Southern Express soliciting agent who was riding with him.

The holdup occurred early on the morning of May 21. The engineer of the northbound Train No. 14 saw a man waving a white station lantern on the track ahead. Thinking the man was the station agent, the engineer slowed the train; when he did, armed attackers jumped aboard the locomotive and ordered him to pull ahead to a trestle about 200 yards away and then stop.

I. M. Cox, a Southern Express Company soliciting agent riding in the express car, gave this account:

> When we had reached the little station of Monroe, just this side of Sanford, the train was waved down by a man with a lantern, whom I supposed was the agent. A man got on and we had started off slowly, when I noticed a man standing on the platform of the express car just outside of the door.
> Saunders [the messenger] and myself were sitting close together on a trunk near the door, and on seeing the man I asked Saunders who it was. He threw open the door to see, and as he did so two men jumped in, each with a revolver, and ordered "hands up."
> As the command was uttered Saunders grappled the first man, who was already in the car, and I the other. Then a terrible encounter took place. The men both had pistols and we were unarmed.
> Saunders had endeavored to get his pistol, but without success. Firing began at the outset, and they put it to us hot and heavy. We held our own, however, and I succeeded in throwing my man out and closing the door. Meanwhile Saunders had received mortal wounds, and staggered through the car to the end, where he fell. In the excitement I scarcely recognized that I had been shot.

In the next car J. S. Gilbert, the baggagemaster, heard the shots and went forward. At the door he encountered a fourth bandit who thrust a pistol in his face, saying "There's one man lying dead there and another in the car, and if you know what's healthy for you, you'll get in the express car in a hurry." Gilbert said he did as he was ordered.

Saunders and Cox's stubborn defense of their car took the fight out of the intruders, and they fled without attempting to get into the express company safe, which on that run held from $10,000 to $12,000.

Within an hour of the attack, local officials had organized two posses and were on the trail of the bandits. Word was sent to all law enforcement agencies along the route to keep on the lookout for the suspects. Four days later, two Putnam County sheriff's deputies, George Wurtz and T. H. Wigg, who had been stationed on the Buffalo Bluff Bridge over the St. John's River south of Palatka, spotted three men heading north. The men answered the descriptions of the suspects, and the deputies shouted "hands up." The man in the lead obeyed, but the other two went for their revolvers. Wigg was grazed by a bullet, but Wurtz quickly let go

with his shotgun, and one of the men dropped to the ground. More shots were fired, and a second bandit was hit in the leg. The third man managed to flee into a nearby swamp.

A posse soon arrived by special train. There was more gunfire as they went after the third robber, and it is believed that he was hit again by at least one shotgun charge. Later in the day his body was found partially hidden behind a tree, his face covered with blood. It appeared that he had shot himself in the mouth. In his last minutes of life, this robber, who was never identified, had scribbled the following note on the back of a map:

> Dear Mother: The time has come that you and I shall part, and I hope you will not grieve after me, for I have no fear. I would write more, but I have not time. Kiss the children for me and tell them to do better than I have done, and they will live longer than I have. Farewell, dear mother.
> Send this to Susan Bedgood, Aribi, Dooley County, Georgia. I never expect to give up a thing, and I ask you to send me home at Aribi, Ga. So, with this I close forever. Please send my body to Aribi, Ga.

The fourth robber, later identified as Bob Floyd, had split off from the other two immediately after the holdup attempt and had fled to the small town of Jonesville, about twenty-five miles west of Jacksonville, where he sought shelter in the home of a former employer. The man suspected that Floyd was involved in the affair at Monroe and he informed the authorities. A posse closed in on the house on Saturday night, May 28, and Floyd gave up without a fight. (Sources: *St. Louis Globe Democrat*, 22, 24–26, 30 May, 15 June 1892; *New York Times*, 22, 26, 30 May 1892.)

MONTAGUE, HORACE E. Horace Montague was a traveling passenger agent for the Southern Pacific Railroad. On the night of December 1, 1913, he was riding in a Pullman coach on the SP's westbound No. 9, the *Sunset Limited*. When the train was about twenty miles east of Los Angeles, a "youthful bandit" drew a gun and ordered the passengers to hand over their money and valuables.

Montague, a loyal employee of the railroad, apparently "found the spectacle intolerable," as one observer wrote, and he tried to grab the robber. But he was not quick enough, and the robber shot him in the forehead. As he fell, the robber panicked and fled.

In reporting this senseless killing, the newspapers praised the passenger agent's courage, and for a brief time he became a national hero. While admitting that agent Montague's impulsive act "was more brave than wise," an editor for the *New York Times* commented that "such unwisdom as his excites a thrill that the caution and discretion so often commended will never cause. It was folly, perhaps, but a fine, manly folly of the kind to which the world is vastly indebted."

The killer did not go unpunished. Three weeks after the killing, a man and his wife who had been in the coach at the time spotted the killer in a crowd in San Francisco. They notified a policeman, and the suspect, later identified as Ralph Fariss of Bakersfield, was arrested. He was searched and was found to be carrying a watch stolen from one of the passengers. (Sources: *New York Times*, 2, 4, 28 December 1913.)

MONTELLO, NEVADA. Montello, which is in Elko County about twenty-five miles northeast of Interstate 80, was the scene of "Aaron Ross's stand," a courageous fight by a stubborn Wells, Fargo messenger against bandits trying to raid his express car.

The outlaws had taken over the whole town, which was really only a tiny dot on the old Central Pacific (now Southern Pacific) Railroad route map. At the time it consisted of a rickety depot, a water tank and tank house, a wood shed, and a few dilapidated shacks.

It was 1:00 A.M. on the morning of January 23, 1883. Messenger Ross had been napping in his car when the outlaws signaled the engineer of the Central Pacific's eastbound passenger express to stop at the Montello station. When the train pulled in, Ross was greeted by an order from the depot platform demanding that he open up. Before becoming a Wells, Fargo express messenger on the Central Pacific run, Ross had driven a Concord stage in Montana and he was no stranger to holdups. Outlaws had tried to rob his stage twice, and twice they rode away empty-handed, on one occasion leaving behind dead comrades.

At first, Ross stalled for time. "Just wait till I get my boots on," he called to the bandit on the depot platform. "Never mind the boots," the bandit shouted. "Hop right out here and we will get through with you, and then you can get your boots on." When Ross still hesitated, the bandit yelled "Open up or we will burn you out and murder you."

This time Ross answered with his pistol. Guns now roared from outside the car. Ross was six-feet, four-inches tall and weighed nearly 250 pounds, and all he had for protection were his green Wells, Fargo treasure box, a package chest, and his bedroll. "They stationed one man at each corner of the car," he later said, "and five shots were fired simultaneously from different quarters, all ranging toward the centre of the car." Three of the shots hit Ross; one bullet struck him in the hand, a second sliced his hip, and a third gouged out flesh just below a rib. Although bleeding badly, the stubborn messenger continued to return the outlaws' fire.

About then the whistle of the Central Pacific's westbound Train No. 2 was heard in the distance. To prevent a collision, the outlaws pushed the eastbound onto a siding. As he drew near, the engineer of the westbound knew something was wrong and slowed to a stop, but when his conductor asked to speak to the eastbound's conductor, one of the outlaws stuck his head out of the cab and told him that he had better just get his train going again. When the conductor saw the size of the outlaw gang, which witnesses estimated to be from eight to twelve, he decided he had better do as he was told.

When his attackers realized they could not drive messenger Ross out with their Winchesters, they pulled the locomotive ahead and then backed the tender into the express car, hoping it would telescope into the end and split out the sides. But the car was too heavy and the frame too stout. Next, the outlaws tried to burn Ross out—he could hear the flames crackling and smell the smoke—but they could not get a large enough blaze going and they finally gave up. After one last barrage of gunfire, they rode off in disgust.

Aaron Ross recovered from his wounds and was proclaimed a hero by Wells, Fargo & Company. He was whisked off to the home office in San Francisco where company officials proudly touted him as an example of the sturdy stock of which Wells, Fargo messengers were made: stalwart and brave, eager to take the measure of anyone threatening the company's cargo. (Sources: Dillon, *Wells, Fargo Detective*; Harlow, *Old Waybills*; *Chicago Tribune*, 24 January 1883.)

MORGANFIELD, CHARLES. Charles Morganfield, who also went by the name Charles Morgan, and his partner Charles J. Searcey, were responsible for one of the most exciting train robberies committed in the East.

On October 12, 1894, Searcey and Morgan stopped a northbound Richmond, Fredericksburg & Potomac passenger train in a wilderness area near Acquia Creek, Virginia, and robbed the Adams Express Company car of over $20,000. Following the robbery, the bandits sent the unmanned locomotive hurtling northward toward a southbound passenger train standing at the station at Quantico, Virginia. Only the quick work of a switchman at the Quantico yards prevented what would have been a tragic crash with the loss of many lives.

Searcey was captured less than a week after the robbery when an alert policeman noticed that he was acting suspiciously at the train station at Cumberland, Maryland. Morganfield was captured the next day near Cincinnati, Ohio, when he suffered a broken leg trying to steal a ride on a train. Both men were convicted and sentenced to prison at Richmond, Virginia. *See* **Acquia Creek, Virginia**.

MOUND VALLEY, KANSAS. A holdup in 1893 on the St. Louis & San Francisco Railroad near Mound Valley could almost have been described as a light-hearted affair until it was discovered that the robbers, apparently out of anger at not being able to enter the express car, brutally shot and killed the messenger.

The date was September 3. The bandits, three in all, boarded at Mound Valley, which is in Labette County in the southeastern corner of the state. The engineer was ordered to pull ahead several miles from the station and then halt. The bandits went directly to the passenger coaches, where they went up and down the aisle.

FRISCO DEPOT 1955
MOUND VALLEY, KANS.

Mound Valley station. *Everett R. Huffer Collection.*

The chief of police of Wichita, Rufus Cone, was a passenger in the sleeping car and was eager to shoot it out with the robbers, but the conductor—a cautious man who had fled to the sleeper to hide—persuaded him to stay put.

Only one of the robbers wore a mask. Witnesses said all were medium in size and fairly well dressed. They were all described as "very cool."

One of the passengers was a veteran of the Grand Army returning east after a convention. He pleaded with the bandits that he had only $3.00. The bandits told him to keep it.

Another passenger, an "old gentleman," was sound asleep when the robbers reached his seat. They ordered him to turn over his money, but he continued to snore. One of the robbers grabbed him by the shoulders and shook him. The old man reached into his pocket, handed the outlaw two gold pieces, and told him that was all he had. In a half a minute he was snoring again.

The bandits collected about $500 and departed. Although two shots had been fired just before the bandits entered the first coach, the intruders made no attempt to terrorize the passengers. For a few whose losses were not especially heavy, it had been an exciting affair, an adventure. Several of the passengers remarked how "jolly" the robbers were. Then one of the trainmen noticed that C. A. Chapman, the express messenger, was missing. Several minutes later he was found alongside the track. The back of his head had been blown off. (Sources: Lake, *Under Cover for Wells, Fargo*; *New York Times*, 4 September 1893.)

MUNCIE, KANSAS. The robbery of an express car on the Kansas Pacific line near Muncie in 1874 was attributed to the James-Younger gang. Muncie is just west of Kansas City, in Wyandotte County.

The date was December 8. Around four o'clock in the afternoon, just before the arrival of an express from Denver, five men armed with breech-loading carbines and navy revolvers appeared at the side of the track near where a section gang was working. At gunpoint, they forced the railroaders to stack crossties and rails on the track.

When they heard the train in the distance, the bandits ordered one of the section hands to go out on the track and flag it down. As the train pulled to a halt, two of the gang covered the engine crew while the rest attacked the Wells, Fargo express car. They quickly forced their way in and overcame the messenger, Frank Webster. After threatening him with death, they compelled him to unlock the safe, which contained around $27,000 in currency and jewelry, plus a case of gold dust valued at $5,000. Also, one of the outlaws took two watches from the passengers, but the leader of the gang made him return them, with a comment that they were "not after personal property." When the robbers finished, they rode off on "handsome bay horses."

The outlaws were described by witnesses as "all large men" and "reckless and determined."

The James-Younger gang was implicated in the affair when it was reported that Jesse James and one of the Younger brothers had been seen in Kansas City a few days before the holdup. Also, not long after the robbery, Kansas City police picked up a drifter named Bud McDaniel who was known to be an associate of the James brothers. When arrested, McDaniel was carrying $1,000 in cash and several pieces of jewelry taken during the robbery. However, before McDaniel could be tried for the crime, he escaped from jail and was shot to death by a farmer near Lawrence, Kansas. (Sources: Settle, *Jesse James Was His Name; New York Times*, 9 December 1874.)

MURPHY, JIM. Murphy was a member of the Sam Bass gang during the outfit's binge of stage and train robberies in Denton and Dallas counties in 1877–78. In July 1878 it is believed that Murphy tipped off the Texas Rangers as to the gang's intention to rob a bank in Round Rock in Williams County. The rangers were waiting, and Bass was killed. *See* **Sam Bass.**   □

N

NEWCOMB, GEORGE "BITTER CREEK." George Bitter Creek Newcomb grew to manhood punching cattle in Texas. By his early twenties he had gained a reputation as a hard-working and able ranch hand, but like too many young men of his day, he did not long for the rewards of honest work. When an opportunity came along to ride the outlaw trail with the Dalton gang, he didn't hesitate.

Newcomb was never called George. Early in his career it was "Slaughter Kid" from having worked for a while for John Slaughter, the famous sheriff of Cochise County, Arizona. Later, it was "Bitter Creek," a nickname derived from his continuous singing of a popular campfire song of the day: "I'm a lone wolf from Bitter Creek / And tonight is my night to howl!"

Newcomb performed well for the Daltons during the gang's early days and he was a loyal member of the band. Although he may have believed that Bill Doolin—who eventually took over after the Coffeyville robbery—would have made a better leader than Bob Dalton, he sided with Bob when squabbles arose. This kept him in Bob's favor after other gang members had come and gone. But after the Dalton gang's near disaster at the attempted express car robbery at Adair, Oklahoma, in July 1892, the Dalton brothers got the feeling that Bitter Creek might be endangering the outfit by taking too many trips into town to "howl." This alone might not have caused him to part company with the band, but there was also unhappiness over the size of the splits handed out after several earlier raids. Whatever the reason, Newcomb left the gang sometime in the summer of 1892.

After the disaster at Coffeyville, Newcomb responded to Bill Doolin's invitation to return to the trail under his leadership. All went well until the gang's close call at Ingalls, Kansas. That night a posseman's bullet smashed Newcomb's Winchester and a jagged piece of the rifle's magazine penetrated the outlaw's thigh. Newcomb managed to get onto his horse, however, and the lawmen lost his trail in the darkness.

Newcomb survived another close call in April 1893 when he was shot by the proprietor of a general store in Indian Territory, just north of the Canadian River. The proprietor, a former U.S. deputy marshal, gave Bitter Creek a shattered arm to match his scarred leg.

Newcomb's last train robbery was the holdup on

the Rock Island at Dover, Oklahoma, in April 1895. Following the robbery, Newcomb and sidekick Charlie Pierce headed east, in the general direction of Payne County, which in the past had been a safe haven for long riders. Payne County was the home of a family named Dunn that for some time had opened their doors to the likes of the Doolin crowd. The authorities were on to the Dunns, however, and when Newcomb and Pierce rode out to the Dunn ranch that day they met trouble. What exactly happened was never determined. There have been several versions, but none can be trusted. The story can best be picked up from an account in the *Guthrie Daily Leader* the following day (May 3, 1895) which described the arrival of the bodies of the two outlaws in town the afternoon of the shooting:

> Shortly after two o'clock yesterday afternoon a covered wagon drawn by two half-famished horses pulled up on the east side of the water tower on Capitol Hill. Two men, armed with Winchesters and furtive glances, dismounted . . . one sped towards Marshal Nix's office. A few minutes later Spengel's undertaking barouche was speeding towards the hill, where two dead bodies were taken from the wagon, placed in the dead cart and hauled to the undertaking rooms. . . . They were identified as George Newcomb and Charlie Pierce by all the deputies and man killers in the capital, and a camera shot was taken of the dead outlaws stretched out on the embalming boards.

(Sources: Patterson, *Train Robbery*; Shirley, *West of Hell's Fringe*; *Guthrie Daily Leader* [Oklahoma], 3 May 1895.) *See also* **Adair, Oklahoma; The Daltons; Bill Doolin; Dover, Oklahoma.**

NEW ORLEANS, LOUISIANA. One of the reasons that train robbery was successful in the United States was because most robberies were committed in wild and rugged areas where the robbers could slip away and hide from posses. But there were exceptions. On December 13, 1900, a gang of bold bandits surprised the crew of an Illinois Central passenger train at the edge of the bustling city of New Orleans.

The IC's *Chicago Limited* was due to arrive at the downtown station at 7:15 P.M. But on the outskirts of town, an undetermined number of men (witnesses reported from one to a half-dozen) in black masks overpowered the engineer and fireman and took command of the train. The engineer was told to stop at the crossing at Carrollton Avenue. The conductor, whose name

was Kennebreu, was ordered to uncouple the train behind the express and mail cars. But when he was too slow about it, the bandits shot him. The bandits then uncoupled the cars, and the engineer was forced to pull ahead a half-mile.

It is possible that none of the outlaws were experienced with explosives. According to one account, they placed a charge under the express car, but apparently in the wrong spot. The car was badly shattered by the explosion, but the gang could not gain entry. They had better luck with the mail car, which was occupied by railway mail clerk R. F. Goldsby. While the car was not damaged extensively by the blast, the intruders were able to enter and take an undetermined number of pieces of registered mail. (Sources: *San Francisco Chronicle*, 14 December 1900; *New York Times*, 14 December 1900.)

NEW RICHMOND, MICHIGAN. On the night of August 20, 1895, a red lantern being swung on the track ahead brought a Chicago & West Michigan passenger train to a halt about one and one-half miles south of New Richmond, which is in Allegan County about eight miles south of Holland. When the engineer, George Zibbel, saw the signal, he applied the brakes and threw the wheels into reverse. It was well he did, because just beyond on the track was a pile of crossties. A moment later Zibbel and his fireman, Mike Driscoll, were facing four men with revolvers.

Two of the men stayed with Zibbel and Driscoll, while the other two headed for the express car. At first, express messenger Bernard Van Otten refused to open up, but when the attackers shot out all the windows of the car and then began smashing the door in, Van Otten decided he had put up enough resistance. After all, he had nothing to lose; there was no cash shipment on the run that night. There was a safe in the car, but it was not in use; it was being transported from the express company's Chicago office to Grand Rapids. The bandits learned this only after blowing off the door with dynamite.

Frustrated that the safe was empty, the would-be robbers proceeded to the first passenger coach, where they relieved the conductor of his gold watch and $7 in cash. They probably also considered going up and down the aisles but by now they had wasted much time and they apparently figured they had hung around long enough. As they were leaving, they spotted a flagman, Tim Murphy, signaling down the line, and one of the bandits shot him in the groin.

Chicago & West Michigan official dispatched a posse to the scene. After conversing with local authorities, it was speculated that the robbers were part of a local gang that had been robbing travelers on the highways for several weeks.

Five days later a Grand Rapids detective, George W. Powers, attempted to arrest a suspect, John Smalley, on a Grand Rapids & Indiana train as it was leaving that city. Powers was shot and killed, and Smalley escaped. The following Saturday, the twenty-fifth, Smalley was killed in a shootout with two Missaukee County deputies at McBain, Michigan.

On October 1, 1895, two more suspects in the New Richmond holdup, James Brown and Vic Taylor, were arrested near Brinton, Michigan. Both men were identified by the engineer as being at the scene. (Sources: *New York Times*, 21, 26 August, 2 October 1895.)

NEW SALEM, NORTH DAKOTA. For the miles of track within its boundaries, North Dakota experienced few train robberies. The state's severe weather possibly had something to do with this; most outlaws did not favor long treks across the prairie in bad weather. Also, unlike its neighboring states of Montana and South Dakota, whose gold rushes drew the worst of the hard cases, North Dakota was relatively free of outlaws. The really bad characters just did not venture that far into the northern grassland.

A train robbery did occur in North Dakota in June 1890, but thanks to a quick-thinking express messenger the robbers rode off with little loot. Around midnight

The station at New Salem. *Everett R. Huffer Collection.*

on June 7, about fifty miles west of Bismarck, four masked bandits took control of the locomotive of an eastbound Northern Pacific passenger train. The train had just left New Salem, and apparently the intruders had climbed aboard the blind baggage.

In traditional fashion, the locomotive engineer, whose name was Kilmartin, was ordered to halt. When he did not, a bullet was sent whistling past his ear. He then complied, and the train came to a stop. Four men appeared from the coal pile. One stayed with the engine crew while the others headed toward the express car. Several passengers got curious and left the coaches, but a few shots sent them hurrying back inside.

When the express messenger, whose name was Angevine, heard the gunfire, he guessed what was happening and quickly emptied the express company safe of its contents, about $6,000. He stashed the money under some express packages, blew out the light, jumped out of the car, and began running back down the track toward New Salem.

The robbers hit the postal car first. The railway mail clerk offered no resistance. One of the bandits rummaged through the registered mail, apparently looking for something specific. According to the clerk, the robber muttered "his disappointment at his failure to find some evidently expected mail." He then moved on to the express car.

Finding nothing in the express car safe, the robbers "vented their chagrin in oaths." In their wrath, they turned to the fireman, whom they mistook for the express messenger, and fired off another shot to "expedite his movements." When satisfied that the real messenger might have gone back to New Salem to spread the alarm, they decided that they had better call it a night.

After the robbers left, the engineer backed the train to New Salem, where the local sheriff was already forming a posse. A search of the scene turned up nothing, however. (Source: *New York Times*, 9 June 1890.)

THE NEWTON BROTHERS. There were four of them: Willis, Dock, Jess, and Joe, and they helped pull off the biggest train robbery in U.S. history.

On June 12, 1924, the Newton brothers and four others held up a Chicago, Milwaukee & St. Paul mail train near Rondout, Illinois, a railroad junction about thirty miles north of Chicago. The train, made up of only mail and express cars, was carrying bonds and currency from the Federal Reserve Bank of Chicago to banks in the Northwest. The robbers stopped the train at a crossing just south of Rondout by taking command of the locomotive. Gaining entry by tossing bottles of formaldehyde through the windows they stormed the first three mail cars. Dock Newton was shot during the robbery and while he was laid up with his wounds, Chicago police discovered his hiding place. Eventually the entire gang was captured and all served time. It was discovered later that Chicago's top postal inspector was the "inside man" on the robbery. The Newtons, who pleaded guilty, received light sentences at Leavenworth. (See **Rondout, Illinois**.)

The Newton brothers' criminal career began in 1914 in and around their home, Uvalde, Texas. Although the details are lost to history, according to Joe Newton, sole survivor of the clan, during the next ten years the four brothers netted over $4 million from robbing trains and banks. He would often boast that they stole more money than Jesse James, Butch Cassidy, Bonnie and Clyde, "and all the other famous bank and train robbers put together."

The Newtons began their robberies on horseback and finished in automobiles, preferably Studebakers and Cadillacs. Willis, who was the first to turn to crime, became the leader, and eventually they concentrated on banks, "mixing in an occasional train holdup for the fun of it and for the booty that usually rode in the baggage and mail cars."

Joe claimed that he and his brothers robbed or burglarized over eighty banks and held up six trains without killing anybody, and that they wounded "only a few." Their territory stretched from the Mexican border north to Canada, but mainly they operated in Texas and Colorado. They only ventured east of the Mississippi River once—for the robbery at Rondout—and it was their last as a team.

After their term at Leavenworth, Jess Newton settled down and lived quietly. Joe and Willis were convicted once more, for robbing a small bank in Oklahoma, for which they served another ten years. (Joe claimed they were innocent of this one.) Dock also eventually got restless, and in 1968, at age seventy-six, he broke into a bank at Rowena, Texas. The bank had no burglar alarm, but the one in a liquor store next door went off. When the deputies came, he tried to shoot it out, but was overpowered. Because of his age he was given only two years.

In 1957, Joe used money he earned from farming to buy a corner lot in downtown Uvalde and for twenty years operated a service station and cafe. In the late seventies he leased it out and retired. He was last heard from in 1984, at which time he said he spent most of his time hunting and fishing and, at eighty-three, enjoying the life of a minor celebrity as the nation's last living train robber. In the early eighties he and Willis, who was still alive then, gained national attention when students at San Antonio's Trinity University produced a documentary film entitled *The Newton Boys: Portrait of an Outlaw Gang*. The picture was shown around the country and Joe appeared on ABC's "Tonight" show. (Source: Maguire, "The Texas Terrors.")

NICHOLS, KELLOGG. Kellogg Nichols was a messenger for the United States Express Company on the Chicago, Rock Island & Pacific Railroad. On the night of March 13, 1886, when the train pulled into Morris, Illinois, while on run from Chicago to Davenport, Iowa, he was found murdered, and his express car ransacked. No one saw the robbers leave, but a baggage man in the next compartment, Newton H. Watt, claimed they entered through his compartment, and one of them kept a gun on him while the others entered the express compartment and apparently killed Nichols.

The press played up the incident as a mystery, and "The Express Car Murder" drew national attention for months. Two men were finally convicted of the crime: Watt, the baggage man, and a brakeman on the train, Henry Schwartz. See **Henry Schwartz**.

NOBEL, CALIFORNIA. As Southern Pacific's westbound Train No. 36 left the University Avenue Station at Berkeley on the morning of November 7, 1930, the rear brakeman saw a man wearing brown overalls climbing onto the tender. Figuring he was a hobo catching a free ride, the brakeman gave the matter little thought. But before the train had gone a quarter of a mile, the man had slipped a white gauze mask over his face, climbed down the coal pile, and pointed a gun at the engineer, Pete Lemery, and the fireman, H. D. O'Brien. As the train approached the next station, Nobel, the man told Lemery to bring her to a halt.

Lemery was ordered to put out the fire in the boiler and then, with O'Brien, to jump down to the ground and walk around to the front of the locomotive. As they did, four more men appeared on the scene, apparently from a dark-colored Studebaker sedan parked near the track. They all carried machine guns.

The five men went to work immediately, as if the whole scene had been rehearsed. One man stayed with the train crew and kept them covered with his gun. Two went toward the rear of the train to discourage any passengers from coming forward. The fourth went to the mail car and began pounding on the door, and the fifth man climbed up on a flat car that was parked on a siding opposite the mail car.

Receiving no response from the railway mail clerk, the bandit fired a shot into the side of the car. The clerk, John McClintock, saw that it was useless to resist and opened up.

"Where's all the money?" the bandit asked.

"What money?" McClintock replied.

"The money for Pittsburg and those other places," said the bandit.

McClintock pointed to a small bank package on a bench near a stack of registered parcels. The bandit picked it up, slit it open, looked inside, and threw it out the door to the bandit standing on the flat car. Then he reached down and scooped up several more packages of registered mail and several sacks. When he appeared to find all that he was looking for, he jumped down and joined the other bandits, and they all headed for the Studebaker sedan. As the car sped away, both Lemery and O'Brien got the license number.

Investigators scoured the area. On the ground between the flat car and where the Studebaker had been parked they found a sack containing 1,000 silver dollars, apparently dropped by the bandits in their haste. Several hours later, in Berkeley, they found other mail sacks, all empty. That night they located the Studebaker, abandoned in Berkeley at Euclid and Virginia streets. It had been stolen the previous night from an Oakland garage.

When the authorities found the stolen car in Berkeley, their thoughts immediately turned to a suspect. His name was Frank P. Ellis, a.k.a. Frank E. Smith, a local criminal who was wanted at the time for robbing a bank in Rodeo, California, in September 1929. They had a tip that Ellis had been making inquiries about payroll shipments heading for manufacturing plants in South San Francisco. Also, the stolen Studebaker had been abandoned only a few blocks from where the suspects in the Rodeo bank robbery had abandoned their getaway car.

A check with the motor vehicle department turned up a driver's license in Ellis's name. The address he had given was that of a brother-in-law. From him, the police obtained a current address. The authorities stormed the house, found Ellis at home, and also found an arsenal of weapons. In addition, they found some very damaging evidence: a notebook containing coded memoranda concerning train robberies, plus dates of payroll shipments for several large manufacturing towns in the area.

Ellis was taken by automobile to the main post office in Oakland, apparently for questioning, but as he and the postal officials were walking toward the door of the building, Ellis attempted to escape. A secret service agent fired one shot, which struck the bandit in the abdomen. He died an hour later.

Further investigation revealed that Ellis's wife had also been involved in the Nobel robbery, as well as a railway mail robbery at McAvoy, California, the previous June. Additional clues were followed up, and two more suspects were arrested: Charles Berta and James Sargert. Both men, together with Mrs. Ellis, were convicted of the McAvoy robbery and of conspiring to commit the Nobel robbery. (Source: DeNevi, *Western Train Robberies*.)

NORTH BEND, OHIO. It is generally accepted that the first peacetime train robbery in the United States occurred near Seymour, Indiana, in October 1866. However, a few railroad and outlaw historians suggest that the first was a holdup at North Bend, Ohio, the first week of May 1865. There was such a robbery, but was it a peacetime robbery or a carryover from the Civil War? There were several train robberies during the war, but few argue that these should be considered the beginning of the train robbery era, since presumably they were for military and not personal gain. But what about a robbery that occurred after hostilities had ended, but was carried out by rebel guerrillas? This seems to have been the situation at North Bend.

The site of the holdup was on the Ohio & Mississippi Railroad at a spot seven and one-half miles west of Cincinnati, between North Bend and a tiny stop called Gravel Pit Station, where the track runs very near the Ohio River. A rail had been removed, and the locomotive, tender, express car, and baggage car careened off the track. The first passenger coach stayed on the rails, but telescoped into the baggage car.

When the Adams Express Company messenger, whose name was Pierce, poked his head out of the wreckage, a voice from the side of the track warned him to stay put. Then a gang of "rough-looking" characters immediately surrounded the car and forced their way in. In minutes they broke into the through safe with an axe.

Witnesses said there could have been as many as twenty in the gang. Those that were not ransacking the express car headed for the passenger coaches. Two to a car, they went up and down the aisles, ordering the passengers to turn over their money and valuables. They carried "navy revolvers," witnesses said, and in the traditional highwaymen style, seemed "chivalrous." One of the robbers was quoted as saying "[r]ob the men, but don't hurt the ladies."

The robbers escaped by crossing the river to Kentucky on skiffs. Witnesses said they believed that they probably were rebel guerrillas, because several times they referred to one another as "lieutenant" and "captain." At the time, federal troops were still pursuing rebels believed to be operating out of Nelson County, south of Louisville. (Sources: Rainey, *Demise of the Iron Horse*; *Indianapolis Daily Sentinel*, 10 May 1865.) *See also* **Seymour, Indiana**.   □

O

OKESA, OKLAHOMA. Bill Miller, the engineer of the Missouri, Kansas & Texas Railroad's southbound Train No. 123, might have been warned that an attempt might be made to rob his train. The higher-ups knew; a tip had been received by Katy officials the previous week that a robbery might be attempted somewhere near Bartlesville, Oklahoma, but whether this information was passed on to the train crews is not known.

The attack came shortly after midnight on August 21, 1923. The train had just left Okesa, which is in Osage County, eight miles west of Bartlesville. The two men probably sneaked aboard as the train was pulling out of the station, hid in the blind baggage area just behind the tender, and then climbed over the coal pile. Miller and his fireman, B. D. Tower, first knew they had trouble when they heard the sound of feet land on the cab floor behind them.

"Stop the train" one of the men shouted. Miller and Tower spun around and stared at their two attackers. One was short and stocky, the other was tall and slender. Both were armed and had silk stockings over their heads to disguise their features. "I said stop this train," the shorter one shouted and gave Tower a staggering blow to the head with his pistol barrel. Miller immediately grabbed the brake handle and yanked hard.

When the train had stopped, Tower, bleeding from the gash in his temple, was ordered to go back and uncouple the mail car from the rest of the train. When this was done, the short man told Miller to pull ahead a short distance to a deep, brushy cut. When they reached this cut, five more bandits appeared from out of the darkness.

The attackers shouted for the mail clerks to open the door of the car; to encourage them to obey, they fired several shots into the side of the car. At first, the two clerks refused, but when the robbers threatened to blow up the car with dynamite, they gave in and unlocked the door.

The robbers worked swiftly, sorting through the registered mail until they came to a package containing $21,000 in negotiable bonds consigned to the state treasurer in Oklahoma City. Having found what they were looking for, the bandits quickly disappeared in the darkness.

Back at Okesa, Charley Carson, a section foreman for the Katy Railroad, had heard No. 123 stop and then heard the gunfire. He guessed what was happening and immediately telephoned the dispatcher at Bartlesville. In an hour Katy officials were at the scene and a search party had been formed, but no trace of the robbers' trail was found. However, in the mail car, officials found a rubber finger stall or "cot" used by doctors, which apparently had been used by one of the robbers to avoid leaving fingerprints.

A search of all the neighboring towns was made to find out where the finger stalls had been purchased. At Pawhuska, ten miles southwest of Okesa, a drugstore owner remembered selling the same kind of cots to Isaac "Ike" Ogg, a local character of questionable background. Ogg was picked up, and under "extensive interrogation" admitted that he was connected with the robbery. He had not been at the scene, but he had ridden on the train as a passenger as far as Okesa, to make sure that the train had stopped there so his two confederates could slip on board. Ogg also provided the authorities with the names of the rest of the gang: Al Spencer, Frank Nash (the two men who had boarded the train), Grover Durrill, Earl Thayer, Curtis Kelly, Riley Dixon, and George Curtis. The name Al Spencer was familiar; he was one of Oklahoma's most notorious bandits of the day, a major criminal and escaped convict who was wanted for numerous bank burglaries and robberies.

Bulletins were sent to all local law enforcement agencies and to neighboring states—with astounding success. Within weeks Durrill and Kelly were found hiding on a ranch northwest of Pawhuska, Thayer was picked up in Oklahoma City, George Curtis was found in St. Louis, Riley Dixon surrendered to the authorities in New Mexico, and Frank Nash was caught wading the Rio Grande River trying to slip back into the country from Mexico. And on September 22, just over a month after the Okesa holdup, Al Spencer was killed while avoiding arrest near South Coffeyville, Oklahoma. (Sources: Shoemaker, "Al Spencer: Transition Outlaw"; *Bartlesville Enterprise*, 21 September 1923.) *See also* **Al Spencer**.

OLYPHANT, ARKANSAS. Some trainmen accepted holdups as inevitable. Others lived in constant fear of an attack. A few, however, actually dared bandits to take control of their train. One of the last group, aging conductor W. P. McNally of the Iron Mountain and Southern Railway, often vowed that no one would rob his train while he was alive. Tragically, his prediction came true.

The town of Olyphant can no longer be found on most maps. Even in 1893 it was little more than a flag stop on the Iron Mountain line, about nine miles south of Newport, near the Jackson County line. On November 3 of that year, Iron Mountain's Train No. 1 was crowded with passengers returning from the popular Columbian Exposition in Chicago. As the train approached the stop at Olyphant, it was running behind. This was not unusual, but it always troubled conductor McNally at this point of the run, because later on, at Grand Glaise Siding, No. 1 had to take to the siding to let a northbound express pass. If No. 1 was running too late, the northbound would have to be warned, and McNally never liked to see these entries on his train's log.

The stop at Olyphant should not have taken long. There were only a few passengers getting off, and none getting on. When the last one departed, McNally swung his lantern for engineer Bob Harris to pull out. But the train did not move. Irritated, McNally started up front to see what the problem was, when a boy who was selling newspapers came running down the aisle. "Mac, there's robbers up front," he shouted. "You better get up there in a hurry!"

Both McNally and his brakeman, Charles Beehm, kept revolvers in a cubicle in the rear Pullman for just such emergencies. McNally's was an ancient breech-loading Colt and Beehm's was a newer .38 Smith & Wesson. Both men raced to the cubicle, grabbed their guns, and started forward. As they did, they heard gunfire.

With Beehm beside him, McNally stepped to the edge of the front platform of the Pullman and peered around the corner of the next car. Winchesters and shotguns were blazing near the depot. True to his word, McNally was not going to give up his train. In the next instant he was gone, on his way to join the fight.

The shooting suddenly stopped, and in the darkness, Beehm could hear men running on the cinder path that bordered the track. And then more shots, much closer, and the breaking of glass. Beehm guessed that the robbers had overcome the engine crew and whoever was in the depot and were now heading back through the day coaches, firing their weapons to terrorize the passengers. Beehm turned and raced back into the Pullman; if he was to make a stand, that was the place to do it. He took a seat and shoved his gun in the crack of the cushion.

Several minutes later three robbers burst into the car.

Beehm later said that his first thought was to tell the robbers that if they did not soon move to a siding, the northbound would be bearing down on them. But he hesitated; if they had so easily taken control of this train, they probably could just as easily take over the northbound. No doubt they would order him to flag the northbound to a stop and rob it. He decided to wait and see. If the robbers would finish their work and leave, he would still have enough time to halt the northbound.

In minutes the bandits relieved the Pullman passengers of their money and valuables. When they were done, they quickly left by the rear door. Beehm stayed seated. As he had hoped, he soon heard the sound of horses. The robbers were leaving.

Beehm next heard Bob Harris release the brakes. He was going to back up and put No. 1 on the siding at Olyphant. Beehm grabbed a lantern just as the Olyphant station agent, Charlie Land, came running up. He handed the lantern to Land and told him to signal the northbound to slow down and allow the mainline to be cleared.

No. 1 should have had enough time to get to the siding, but the fire in the boiler had gone down to the point where the engine could hardly move. Also, for some reason, the northbound did not slow; in fact, it appeared to pick up speed. No. 1 made it to safety, but only barely. The northbound sped on past as if there was no problem. Later, it was discovered that Charlie Land, the station agent, had been holding the lantern the wrong way—he had given the northbound the green signal for full speed ahead.

Conductor McNally had kept his word: the robbers had not robbed his train while he was alive. Beehm later discovered that the stubborn conductor had raced forward to the baggage car and had made his stand there. He died before he could fire a shot. (Source: Rains, "Trouble at Olyphant Depot.")

OSAGE CITY, KANSAS. A tragic train wreck near Osage City, Kansas, on September 21, 1891, could have resulted in the biggest train robbery west of the Mississippi.

One million dollars in cash was being shipped by the Mexican Central Railroad to its offices in Boston via express car on the Santa Fe Railroad. Just over the top of a grade near Osage, the robbers had removed a fishplate—which is the joint or splice bar that connects

the ends of two rails—and shifted one of the rails to the side, just far enough to cause the leading wheels of the locomotive to leave the track.

The big drivers of the locomotive dug into the crossties and ballast, sending splinters and rock in every direction. The tender and express car followed the locomotive off the tracks and down the embankment in a billowing cloud of smoke and steam, killing the engineer, fireman, and two Wells, Fargo express messengers.

The would-be robbers had done their job well—too well, in fact. The express car was so deeply buried in the tangled wreckage the bandits could not enter it and reach the money. They rode off in disgust, amid the cries of the shaken and injured passengers. (Source: Shaw, *Down Brakes*.)

OTTERVILLE, MISSOURI. The Missouri Pacific line near Otterville, Missouri, which is in Cooper County about ten miles east of Sedalia, was the scene of two nineteenth-century train robberies.

About a mile east of Otterville the tracks cross the Lamine River. On approaching the bridge from the west, the rails pass through Rocky Cut, a rugged slice in the cliffs that overlook the river. On the night of July 7, 1876, eight men hid in a nearby woods until well past sunset, then sneaked out and overpowered the watchman at the bridge. Using the watchman's red lantern, they gave the westbound express the signal to stop. As the engineer pulled to a halt, the leader of the gang shouted from the darkness that he and his men were holding up the train.

The express company safes contained over $15,000, which two of the robbers quickly stuffed into sacks. Back in the coaches, the stunned passengers sat quietly under the steady gaze of the robbers' confederates. In one of the coaches, a preacher was praying softly that the lives of all aboard would be spared.

After dividing the loot, the outlaws saddled up and disappeared into the night. Later, it was said that the posse that was formed only half-heartedly tried to pursue them, fearing, perhaps, a bullet from the blackness of the dense Missouri woods.

Not long after the holdup, peace officers in Granby, a small town south of Joplin, picked up a young drifter named Hobbs Kerry. Although Kerry was arrested more than 150 miles from the scene of the robbery, he was flashing a wad of bills believed to have been part of the stolen loot. Kerry's description was sent to witnesses in and around Otterville, and a farmer from Sedalia identified him as one of a group of strangers who stopped at his house the week before the holdup. After intensive questioning, Kerry confessed his part in the crime and named his confederates: Jesse and Frank James, Cole and Bob Younger, and three other members of the James-Younger gang.

The second robbery occurred early on the morning of August 17, 1890. The victim was the Missouri Pacific's westbound *Kansas City Express*. It was believed that two bandits climbed aboard at Tipton, ten miles to the east, and hid in the tender. Two men had been seen hanging around the front end of the train, and then they had mysteriously disappeared just before departure.

The men, both masked, covered the engine crew with their revolvers, and ordered the engineer, Frank Droyer, to "run this train to the Otterville water tank." If the engineer attempted to stop at any other point, said one of the bandits, he and the fireman were "dead men."

Droyer was ordered to bring the locomotive to a stop at just about the same spot as the 1876 robbery. When the train had come to a halt, one of the bandits ordered Droyer to march back with him to the express car while the other bandit stayed with the fireman. When they reached the express car, there were five more masked bandits waiting to join them.

The express company messenger, Samuel Avery, was ordered to open his door. He complied, and three of the bandits climbed into the car. Avery was then forced to open the express company safe, and the robbers emptied the contents into a gunnysack. In the meantime, the conductor had come forward from the passenger coaches to find out why the train had stopped. He was stopped by one of the bandits who ordered him to go back and "collect tickets. . . . We'll take care of this end of the train." The conductor hurried back and warned the passengers to hide their valuables.

When the robbers finished in the express car, they rode off into the night. The engineer pulled the train into Otterville, and the conductor notified the company officials of the holdup. A posse was quickly formed and immediately picked up the robbers' tracks, but after a few miles, lost them. The express company did not release the amount of money stolen, but a newspaper reporter who had questioned Avery, the messenger, said he believed that it was as much as $75,000, mostly currency. (Sources: Settle, *Jesse James Was His Name; New York Times*, 18 August 1890.) *See also* **The James-Younger Gang**.   □

P

PACIFIC, MISSOURI. The express car robbery at Pacific, Missouri, on May 24, 1893, differed little from other holdups during the last decade of the nineteenth century, except that the governor of Missouri and the state treasurer were both on the train when it was held up, and nobody knows for sure how many robbers were involved; witnesses say up to seven, yet the only man convicted of the holdup said he pulled off the job *alone!*

Governor Stone and State Treasurer Stephens, on their way back to the State Capital at Jefferson City, were probably preparing to retire in their compartments in the sleeping car when a man waving a red lantern brought Missouri Pacific's westbound Train No. 3 to a halt near Pacific, which is about fifteen miles southwest of St. Louis. The train had just gotten under way and was building up a good head of steam when the engineer saw the signal, which, under railroad rules, he could not ignore. As the train slowed to a stop, witnesses said six men sprang from the underbrush beside the track and surrounded the express car. And then a seventh bandit, brandishing a large revolver, climbed aboard the steps to the cab and ordered the engineer and fireman down.

As instructed by his employer, the express messenger, Samuel Hammill, refused to open the express car door to the intruders. But they were prepared for such as reception. In minutes they had dynamite packed around the door, and when the smoke cleared, there was a hole two feet in diameter in the door. One of the bandits thrust his pistol through the opening and suggested to the messenger that he reconsider. Reluctantly, he did.

Hammill was stubborn, and only after the bandit placed his cocked revolver to the messenger's head did he agree to open the company's safe. When the robber examined the contents, he probably was disappointed. There was a bag of silver coins containing about $1,000, and a $250 bag of currency. A little further digging turned up another $400 in Missouri Pacific tickets and several express packages that appeared to contain money. In all, it was not a big haul.

Calling it a night, the robbers left as quickly as they arrived. The whole affair took less than twenty minutes.

A team of St. Louis detectives was dispatched to the scene, but they failed to pick up a trail. Governor Stone personally offered a reward of $300 for information leading to the capture and conviction of the robbers.

It first appeared that the investigation was at a standstill, but not far from the scene of the robbery, the authorities found a valise bearing the name Samuel Wilson of Lebanon, Missouri. A Missouri Pacific detective, Thomas Furlong, remembered that in early 1892, Wilson had been involved in an aborted attempt to rob a train near that city. He did some checking on Wilson's whereabouts the night of the Pacific robbery, and suddenly Wilson became a prime suspect.

On being questioned, Wilson broke down and confessed to the robbery. Immediately thereafter he told reporters: "The only thing that is left for me to do now is to go into court and plead guilty and ask for the mercy of the court for a light sentence . . . and should I get a light sentence I will serve my term, and I will promise all that never again in my life will I do anything wrong."

Wilson said he decided to rob a train when he was fired from his job as a telegraph operator for a St. Louis brewery. The day after his discharge he went to a gun store and bought a .38 caliber revolver, four sticks of dynamite, and fuses. Later that day, May 23, he took a train west out of St. Louis and got off at Kirkwood, a St. Louis suburb. That evening he started walking, and around midnight he found himself at Pacific. Having never handled explosives, on the way he practiced igniting a stick of dynamite.

At Pacific he said he boarded the Missouri Pacific train as it was leaving the station. About a mile out he climbed over the tender and held up the engine crew. At pistol point, he marched the engineer and fireman back to the express car. He stuffed the dynamite sticks around the express car door and set them off. Then he fired a few shots in the air with his revolver, "not for the purpose of hitting anyone, but merely to frighten the passengers and to make it appear as if I was more than one man."

After he left with his loot, he said, the bag containing the $1,000 split open and he lost half the contents. Then he found that the express packages he stole contained only a few dollars. To top it off, he couldn't remember where he had left his valise, which he had hidden before the robbery, and which contained a change of clothes and personal effects that he had cleaned out from his desk at the brewery. Dismayed, he spent the night killing "a good old bottle of whiskey."

Despite his confession, on conviction Wilson was sentenced to fifteen years in prison, only five less than the maximum that could be given for train robbery in the state of Missouri. Although Wilson said he was alone when he committed the robbery, it was difficult to disregard the statements of witnesses who said that there were as many as seven robbers involved. The truth probably will never be known. (Sources: Murray, "Sam Wilson: Single-Handed Train Robber"; *New York Times*, 24 May 1893.)

PANTHER BURN, MISSISSIPPI. A courageous engineer on the Yazoo & Mississippi Valley Railroad prevented the robbery when he refused to honor a suspicious signal to stop.

Shortly after midnight on November 18, 1894, as Y&MV Train No. 5 was leaving the station at Panther Burn, which is about sixty miles north of Vicksburg, the engineer, whose name was Harris, saw a man on the track ahead waving a red lantern. Harris could tell by the way the signal was being given that the man was not a railroader, and he suspected a robbery attempt. Instead of slowing, as the rules required, Harris leaned on the throttle and sped on past. As he did, from two to five men (the reports differ) joined the men with the lantern and all began firing at the locomotive. Harris was not injured, but his fireman was hit in the arm and head. Neither wound, however, was serious.

Later that day, the authorities arrested a Sharkey County man named Bud Logue, who was already facing a murder charge for killing a man in a fight ten days earlier. Logue was placed in jail at Rolling Fork. He soon confessed and named two accomplices: Barney Boykin and John V. Williams. Both men were arrested and Boykin also confessed. (Sources: *Vicksburg Evening Post*, 19 November 1894; *St. Louis Globe Democrat*, 19 November 1894.)

PAPAGO, ARIZONA. On the night of April 27, 1887, a westbound Southern Pacific passenger train was halted and the express car robbed at Papago, in Pima County, eighteen miles east of Tucson. The robbery occurred about 9:30. A gang of five to eight men used a red lantern to signal the engineer, Bill Harper, to stop. As Harper brought the train to a halt, he could see that obstructions had been placed on the track to derail the locomotive if the signal was not obeyed.

Once the train was stopped, one of the bandits, carrying a pistol in each hand, boarded the engine cab and ordered Harper back to the express car. When the Wells, Fargo messenger, Charles F. Smith, refused to open up, the bandits tried prying open the door. While they were attempting this, messenger Smith quickly hid $3,500 in gold by stuffing it into the express car stove. After failing to pry open the door, the bandits placed a charge of black powder under the door and ordered Harper to ignite the fuse. Fearing that he would be blown up, Smith shouted that he would open the door.

After taking command of the express car, the robbers uncoupled it and the baggage car from the rest of the train and ordered Harper to pull forward. The bandits then put Harper off and one of them climbed aboard the locomotive cab and pulled the express and baggage cars six miles toward Tucson, near what is now the southeast corner of David-Monthan Air Force Base. During the run, the robbers in the express car went through the contents of the express and mail packages. Express officials later reported that they believed no more than $5,000 was taken; later the loss was estimated to be $3,227.60.

While the express car was being robbed, a brakeman ran back eight miles to Pantano Station to notify the authorities of the robbery. A posse was dispatched immediately, as were Indian trackers and a troop of cavalry. No clues could be found to identify the bandits, although at least one or two of them were believed to be former railroaders. Although they forced engineer Harper to tell them how to operate the locomotive, it was his opinion that "they were familiar with such work."

Wells, Fargo and the Southern Pacific Railroad offered a reward of $1,000 for each of the robbers captured.

Not long after the robbery, the proprietor of a Fort Bowie saloon, James Barrock, and two men named McCussick and Swain were arrested and jailed on suspicion. All three came up with alibis, however, and had to be released.

On August 10, 1887, the same train was hit again about a mile east of the site of the first robbery. The bandits again signaled with a red lantern and also with railroad torpedoes that had been placed on the track. This time the engineer did not stop in time, and the locomotive struck obstructions on the track and a half-opened switch, and overturned. There were several injuries, but no one was killed.

Wells, Fargo messenger Charles F. Smith was again on duty in the express car. When the robbers learned this, they informed him that his "stove racket" would not work this time. Smith once again resisted, but the bandits blew a hole in the door and sent the railway mail clerk inside to try to convince the stubborn messenger to give up. Reluctantly, he finally did.

The amount taken was not officially reported. It is believed the bandits got from $1,000 to $2,000; however, the *Arizona Daily Star* reported the loss to be nearly $70,000.

After loading up their horses with the loot, the gang rode off toward the Rincon Mountains. Again, Indian trackers and the army were put on the outlaws' trail. Virgil Earp also came over from Tombstone to assist. The gang's tracks led to a cave at Mountain Springs, about twelve miles from the scene of the robbery, but a heavy rainstorm on the night of the twelfth wiped out any further trace of the culprits and forced the pursuers to abandon the hunt.

Eventually, five men were arrested for this second robbery: Larry M. Sheehan, James T. Johnson, T. Joseph Brooks, T. J. "Dick" Hart, and Si Blunt. The first two, Sheehan and Johnson, were actually Jim and John Cravens, two brothers from Williamson County, Texas, who were wanted in that state for rustling. Of the five, the Cravens were the only two to serve any time for the holdup. (Sources: Dillon, *Wells, Fargo Detective*; Kubista, "No Headlight in Sight"; Rasch, "Train Robbery Times Four"; *Arizona Daily Star*, 11 August 1887; *New York Times*, 29 April 1887.)

PARACHUTE, COLORADO. The June 7, 1904, robbery of Denver & Rio Grande's westbound Train No. 5 near Parachute, Colorado, may have spelled the end for Harvey "Kid Curry" Logan, a member of the Wild Bunch and one of the West's most notorious outlaws. The details of the robbery have remained sketchy until this day. It is believed that from three to five men halted the train three miles west of Parachute, a small fruit station about midway between Grand Junction and Glenwood Springs. After taking control of the locomotive, the bandits dynamited the express car and took from the safe at least one sealed bag containing currency. The exact amount was not established.

Following the robbery, the bandits headed for the mountains. Shortly thereafter posses from both Grand Junction and Glenwood Springs converged on the scene and were soon hot on their trail. Two nights later, on the ninth, the suspects were cornered in a gully near Rifle, Colorado. During the ensuing gun battle, one of the robbers was heard to cry out: "I'm hard hit and going to cash in quick . . . you go on." At dawn the posses rushed the gully and found a lone dead outlaw. He had a revolver in his hand and two bullet wounds, one apparently self-inflicted.

The dead man was first identified as J. H. Ross, but that name was soon revealed to be an alias. Next, the corpse was said to be Tap Duncan, a local cowboy, but as more lawmen arrived on the scene, word spread that the body might very well be that of the notorious Harvey Logan. Thus was sparked one of the most controversial issues in the annals of western outlaw history, an issue that still has not been resolved. (Sources: O'Neal, *Western Gunfighters*; Patterson, *Train Robbery*; Pinkerton, *Train Robberies*; *New York Times*, 9, 10 June 1904.) *See* **Harvey Logan**.

PARKER, FLEMING "JIM." FLeming "Jim" Parker and another man held up a Santa Fe train near Peach Springs, Arizona, in February 1898, and robbed the railway mail car. After an all-out manhunt, he was arrested and confined to jail at Prescott. On May 9 he escaped, in the process killing an assistant district attorney. He

was again captured and tried for murder. He was hanged at Prescott in June 1898. *See* **Peach Springs, Arizona**.

PARKER, ROBERT LEROY "BUTCH CASSIDY." Robert LeRoy Parker, alias Butch Cassidy, probably was the most likable of the nineteenth-century train robbers. Although hardly the Robin Hood some of his fans have made him out to be, he certainly was not cut from the same cloth as most of his contemporaries. The average train robber in Butch's day was ignorant and mean; Cassidy was neither. He was bright, personable, and there is no evidence that he ever killed anybody, except, perhaps, during the famous (possibly legendary) shootout with Bolivian soldiers in 1909 that reportedly ended Butch's career.

But for the fact that Cassidy was an outlaw, there have been few disparaging words said about him. Even wanted posters distributed by Pinkerton's National Detective Agency described him as "cheerful and ami-

Butch Cassidy. *Pinkertons*.

able." He was a handsome man: rugged, square-jawed, but with a pleasant, almost gentle face.

Cassidy was born in Beaver, Utah, in 1866. His Mormon family had migrated to the West a decade earlier. Butch, then called Roy, was thirteen when he had his first brush with the law. On a trip to town to buy a pair of trousers at a general merchandise store, he found it closed. Rather than make another trip, he simply let himself in the building, picked out a pair of pants, and left a note that he would pay the next time he came to town. The storekeeper, however, was not amused, and complained to the sheriff.

It has been suggested that the young Mormon had no idea that he had done anything wrong, and that since his "word was his bond," he believed that the storekeeper should have known that he would have returned to pay his debt. In the words of his biographer, Larry Pointer, "The IOU was an inviolate pledge. The merchant's distrust was an unfamiliar response and, before the matter was settled, the humiliated youth was having mixed emotions over legal process and blind justice." Apologists might suggest that the incident planted the seed that eventually produced the outlaw.

Whatever the cause, young Roy was a restless youth. He soon began resisting the strict religious training traditionally imposed on young Mormon men, and several years after the store incident he took up with a drifter named Mike Cassidy who occasionally supplemented his meager ranch hand's income by rustling steers. Mike Cassidy became Roy's hero and mentor, and soon the boy was joining in on Mike's raids.

In the summer of 1884 a handful of steers carrying some of Roy's overbranding wandered back to their original herds, and the owners put the law on Roy.

Butch Cassidy's childhood home near Circleville, Utah. *Utah State Historical Society.*

Rather than witness the shame that he would bring to his family, the boy packed up and left, adopting as he did the name of his former saddlemate.

Now riding as Butch Cassidy, the boy headed east, to the mines of Telluride, Colorado, where he got a job as a mule driver hauling ore to the processing mills. Tiring of this after a few months, he struck out for Wyoming, where he drifted from ranch to ranch as a cowhand.

It is believed that Cassidy advanced from a small-time rustler to official outlaw status in 1889, when he and several friends rode into Telluride and held up the San Miguel Valley Bank. Western writer James D. Horan, however, believed that Butch may have been involved in the holdup of a Denver & Rio Grande train at Unaweep Switch, Colorado, in November 1887. According to Horan, who gleaned the information from the Pinkerton files, Cassidy played a minor role in this train robbery, which gained the robbers very little.

In the Telluride robbery, Butch and his companions made use of relay teams of horses for their escape, a practice that became a specialty with Cassidy when he turned to robbing express cars. He was said to be a perfectionist when it came to getaways. When he was in his prime, it was said that for several weeks before a robbery he would scout around for fast, surefooted horses capable of good speed for short distances. These would be used for the robbery itself. For the second leg of the relay, he would select deep-chested and long-legged thoroughbreds, the kind suited for endurance. Depending upon how much distance had to be covered, he sometimes used a third and even fourth relay team, both chosen for their stamina. Every horse selected was grain-fed and exercised vigorously before use, so it would be in top shape come time for the robbery.

Following the holdup of the bank at Telluride, Cassidy apparently returned to the range. Nothing was heard from him until 1894, when he was arrested in Wyoming for stealing horses. He may actually have been innocent of this crime, since there is some indication that he only purchased the stolen horses. But there is little doubt that he knew they were stolen. Two years later, when he was released from prison, he was said to be quite bitter over what he considered a vicious injustice. (Apologists again?) Some suggest that he vowed revenge against those who were responsible for his imprisonment, but this seemed unlike him. Whatever the motive, he was now a hardened outlaw, and he spent the next several months putting together a gang. It would eventually be known as the Wild Bunch, a name taken from Dalton days in Oklahoma and Indian Territory. Among the early members of this group was Harry Longabaugh, alias the Sundance Kid, who had recently been opening express cars on the Great Northern Railroad in Montana.

Other gang members were picked up from among the residents of the Hole-in-the-Wall, a general purpose hideout for outlaws located some sixty miles northweset of Casper, Wyoming.

The new gang's first major crime may have been a bank robbery in central Utah in early 1896, but there is little record of this holdup. Another bank robbery, at Montpelier, Idaho, in August 1896, is generally accepted as the first committed by the Wild Bunch with Cassidy participating.

The gang may have committed minor robberies during the next two years, but there is nothing in the record. Cassidy himself may have been connected with the robbery of the Pleasant Valley Coal Company at Castle Gate, Utah, in April 1897. The money, the company payroll, came in on the Denver & Rio Grande, and Cassidy supposedly shoved his six-gun into the paymaster's ribs as he was walking up to the company's office from the station. Cassidy and an accomplice, reportedly Elzy Lay, then dashed away along the track toward Price Canyon. The coal company officials tried to follow them with a locomotive, but the bandits switched to a new team of horses that had been hidden near the track, and they disappeared riding south toward the San Raphael desert.

It is believed the gang planned to hold up a Union Pacific train that spring, but word of the plot leaked out and the attempt was cancelled. Probably within the year the Wild Bunch did assault several express cars. By the end of 1898 they were being referred to by law enforcement agencies as "train robbers." In fact, while Cassidy and his crowd have never been officially linked to any holdups following the Castle Gate robbery through the end of 1898, they were undoubtedly blamed at the time for most of the mischief occurring in the Rocky Mountain area. Horan wrote of a meeting of the governors of the states of Colorado, Utah, and Wyoming in March 1898, in which they agreed to

Hole-in-the-Wall area, Johnson County, Wyoming. Hideout used by the Wild Bunch. *University of Wyoming, American Heritage Center.*

handpick a select squad of law officers from each state to go after the Wild Bunch and exterminate them once and for all. But on the announcement of the Spanish American War, the plan was canceled.

An interesting legend developed about this time. The rumor spread that Cassidy and his gang, bursting with patriotism, planned to sign up en masse to fight in the war. The story makes good reading, but may have been just wishful thinking on the outlaws' part. They may have put out feelers on such a proposal, but without an official grant of amnesty by the governors of the states where they were wanted, it is doubtful they would have risked capture by waltzing into a recruiting office. The Pinkertons believed that some of the younger gang members did go ahead and enlist under assumed names.

Some believe that Cassidy and his comrades had a major flaw in their approach to robbing trains that may have kept them from being more successful than they could have been. They, like other large gangs, would send out riders to scout gold shipments, and often they would bribe railroad employees for information. But sometimes their plans were so elaborate and complex, and so many people were involved, that the details would reach the authorities before they could put them into operation. As a result, many of the holdups never came off.

There is fairly good evidence that Cassidy personally participated in the robbery on the Union Pacific Railroad at Wilcox, Wyoming, in June 1899. The robbers garnered $50,000 but were almost captured in the chase. A hastily organized posse barely let the robbers get out of sight, and in the ensuing gunfight one of the gang, Harvey Ray, was killed.

When he eventually eluded the posse, Cassidy headed north into Montana, where after several days he hitched a ride on a train bound for Seattle. From there he caught another train to Los Angeles, where he closeted himself in a seedy sailor's hotel until the robbery was no longer in the headlines.

There is some evidence that sometime in 1900 Butch decided to give up his life of crime and try to arrange a pardon. As the story goes, he retained a lawyer to make contact with the governor of Utah, Heber Wells. The lawyer was to inform the governor that Cassidy would promise to go straight if he was forgiven for his transgressions. If the story is true, he was wasting his time. The authorities in Wyoming wanted Cassidy much worse than those in Utah, and Wells could not speak for a sister state. Perhaps, however, Cassidy felt that if such a deal was cut, he could return to Utah and his family, and at least live in peace there. Undoubtedly, part of the deal would be an agreement on the part of Wells not to allow him to be extradited to another state. According to the story as reported, Governor Wells came up with an alternative plan. If Cassidy would ask the Union Pacific Railroad to drop its charges against him in return for his promise to go straight, Wells would do what he could to persuade the railroad to accept the proposal. And to make the deal attractive to the railroad, Wells suggested that Cassidy offer to become an express car guard. Wells's thinking was that the railroad could keep an eye on him, and, further, the arrangement would persuade other would-be robbers to stay clear of the Union Pacific.

As preposterous as the plan was, according to those who support the story, the railroad officials agreed to meet with Cassidy to talk. A time and place was set. Cassidy appeared, but the Union Pacific officials were delayed en route. Suspecting a double-cross, he gave up and left.

Cassidy was now ready to rob trains again. The gang struck the Union Pacific at Tipton, Wyoming, on August 19, 1900. The robbery was a repeat of the Wilcox affair, except that this time the getaway was clean. The railroad reported a loss of only $54, but other sources place the haul closer to $50,000, some of which Cassidy may have buried somewhere in Nevada, possibly near a place called Huntington, where he occasionally hid out at a friend's ranch.

While in Nevada, Cassidy and several others may have held up a bank at Winnemucca on September 19, 1900.

Cassidy drifted about until spring. In June it is believed that he participated in a midday holdup of an express car on the Great Northern Railroad at Exeter Switch, near Wagner, Montana. Butch himself was never positively identified as one of the robbers, but it is doubtful that he would have missed the affair, since he had apparently planned to make it his last before fleeing the country.

After nearly a decade of robbing banks and trains, Cassidy decided to retire. Following the Wagner robbery, it is believed that he rode to Miles City, Montana, and boarded a train for Minneapolis. From there he headed for Canada via Duluth and Sault Ste. Marie. His next stop was Montreal, where he stayed at least for six weeks. In the spring of 1902 he went to New York and boarded a ship for Liverpool, England. Here his trail disappears. Later, the Pinkerton files place him in Buenos Aires, using the name Ryan, where land records show that he settled on "four square leagues" of government land in the province of Chubut near Cholilo, presumably with the intention of starting a sheep ranch.

Joining in this venture were "Mr. and Mrs. Harry A. Place," identified later as Harry Longabaugh and his girlfriend, Etta Place. It is believed that the trio led a quiet life until 1904 when Cassidy may have been recognized by local authorities. Perhaps using this for an excuse, Cassidy and Longabaugh resumed their criminal ways. Local records suggest that they robbed a bank at Rio Gallegos in February 1905.

Another view of the Hole-in-the-Wall area. *Jim Dullenty Collection.*

There are only sketchy reports of Cassidy's activities from then on. He and Longabaugh may have held up several more banks, and perhaps they introduced train robbery to Argentina. Several accounts have them migrating to Bolivia, where they alternated between honest work and crime.

There were several persons who say they saw Cassidy back in the United States in 1908. And in February of that year, he is believed to have written a letter to his employer at the time, C. R. Glass, manager of a South American tin mine. But from there on Cassidy's trail becomes difficult to follow, and for the most part he was forgotten.

In 1930 an article on Cassidy appeared in the April issue of *Elks Magazine*. The author, western writer Arthur Chapman, claimed that he had obtained new information about Cassidy from an American mining engineer named Percy Seibert, who had worked with the outlaw in 1908. According to Seibert, Cassidy and Longabaugh were killed in a blazing gunfight with Bolivian soldiers at San Vincente sometime in 1909. Since there was no apparent reason to doubt the story, and since nothing had been heard from Cassidy or Longabaugh for more than two decades, the story was accepted as fact. The files, including those of the Pinkerton National Detective Agency, were closed on the two outlaws.

Author Chapman gave graphic details of the gun battle that supposedly ended the two outlaws' career. Cassidy and Longabaugh had stopped at a San Vincente cantina to drink and dine and were recognized by local authorities. A troop of Bolivian cavalry was nearby and they quickly surrounded the place. A Bolivian captain entered the cantina and ordered Cassidy and Longabaugh to surrender. The two outlaws chose not to, and Cassidy whipped out his revolver and shot the captain dead. Outside, the soldiers, on hearing the shot, rushed the cantina, but Cassidy and Longabaugh blazed away at them with deadly effect. The battle raged throughout the afternoon and into the evening.

The details read like a Hollywood script. The outlaws had left their rifles and extra ammunition with their horses in the courtyard. Longabaugh, who had been drinking heavily, tried to reach them and was hit crossing the courtyard. Cassidy, in true heroic fashion, raced to his partner's side and carried him back to safety. Cassidy then made several attempts himself to reach the horses, but was driven back.

The soldiers poured a steady stream of bullets into the building well into the night. The shots from inside, however, became fewer and fewer. Morning came, and the firing from inside stopped all together. Around noon, the soldiers rushed the cantina and found the Americans dead. Cassidy had fired a bullet into Longabaugh's brain and then used his last cartridge on himself.

Chapman's story was accepted by most readers as a fitting end for the two bandits. The newspapers picked up the story and reported it as a news item: "Butch Cassidy is dead, a victim of a gun battle with Bolivian troops."

But a group of Cassidy's old friends were not so sure. They chipped in and sent one of their members to Bolivia to find out for sure. They talked to some of the Bolivian soldiers involved and apparently were convinced that the story was true. They even brought back pictures the army had taken of the dead outlaws.

Several years later, however, in July 1936, word filtered out of the little town of Lander, Wyoming, that Cassidy had been seen there. The story probably would have caused little interest except that there were still a handful of Lander residents who had known Cassidy in the old days. On being interviewed, one of these old-timers admitted that he had indeed seen Butch, and that he had told him that he was then living in Seattle, Washington, under the name "Bill Phillips." This intrigued several Wyoming historians who decided to dig more deeply. Unfortunately, however, they spent too much time verifying the accounts in and around Lander, and when they finally extended their search to Seattle, they discovered that the only William Phillips known in that city had died in July 1937.

Despite a growing number of persons who claimed to have seen Cassidy after he was supposed to have been killed, the San Vincente story was upheld by most researchers and Cassidy's name gradually disappeared from print—for almost thirty years. Then in 1969 the film *Butch Cassidy and the Sundance Kid* was released. Thanks mainly to its stars, Paul Newman and Robert Redford, the picture was a box office smash. As so often happens with successful pictures based on fact, audiences flocked to the libraries to learn more about Butch and Sundance. Many were curious as to whether the two outlaws did indeed die in the shootout with the Bolivian soldiers, and the film's poularity renewed

Posse on the way to a Wild Bunch robbery. *Union Pacific Railroad.*

interest in the Lander, Wyoming, reports about Cassidy reappearing.

In 1970 another intriguing tidbit was uncovered. During the filming of the picture, the production people discovered that Cassidy had a sister still living in Utah. Her name was Lulu Parker Betenson, and although she was then eighty-six years old, she was still active and spritely. She visited the set and became friends with Newman and Redford. But when talk came around to whether Cassidy was really killed at San Vincente, she hedged, at least publicly; apparently she preferred to let the tale remain a mystery. But in 1970 she relented and revealed in an interview with a reporter that her brother had indeed survived the years in South America, and had returned to visit his family in Utah in 1925, some sixteen years after he was reported dead at San Vincente. When asked why she had never mentioned this before, she replied: "The law thought he was dead and he was happy to leave it that way." She added: "He made us promise not to tell anyone that he was alive. And we never did. It was

the tightest family secret. He died peacefully in Spokane in 1937."

Lulu Betenson's disclosure whetted the appetites of many Western writer-historians, and some began to dig into the files on Cassidy again, but when they learned that Mrs. Betenson herself was preparing a book on her brother, most of them backed off, preferring to wait and see what she had to say. One exception was a young part-time writer named Larry Pointer who stumbled across the Cassidy story during a trip to Lander, Wyoming, in 1972. A friend of Pointer's told him how his grandmother had claimed that she had once dated Cassidy and that he had been seen in Lander as recently as the mid-1930s. Pointer became hooked on the story and began a five-year search into the mystery.

About the same time, another writer began a separate search into the possibility that Cassidy had lived in Spokane under the name Bill Phillips. Jim Dullenty, a reporter for the *Spokane Daily Chronicle*, discovered that a Spokane resident named William T. Phillips who had died in 1937 had an adopted son who was still living in the city. Dullenty interviewed the son and was nearly floored when the man readily admitted that although the fact had been a well-guarded family secret for many years, his father had indeed ridden the outlaw trail as Butch Cassidy. The son produced photographs of his father, and Dullenty compared them with those of Cassidy. Although taken at least twenty years apart, there was a definite resemblance!

Dullenty dug more deeply and found a local woman who claimed that she and her first husband, by then deceased, had been close friends of Phillips, and that he had told them that he was Cassidy. Furthermore, this woman had in her possession a copy of a manuscript written by Phillips in 1934 that purported to tell the true story of Butch Cassidy. The account was written in the third person, with no suggestion that Phillips himself was the famous outlaw. In the foreword, Phillips claimed that he had been acquainted with Cassidy "since early boyhood." The manuscript, amateurishly titled "The Bandit Invincible," was poorly written, badly organized, and difficult to follow. The woman said Phillips had tried to sell it to book publishers and as a series of magazine articles, but was turned down.

About this time, Larry Pointer's search led him to Spokane where he learned of Dullenty's work, and the two joined forces, hoping their combined efforts would lead to a book. The photographs of Cassidy and Phillips were sent to a renowned realist sculptor, Harry Jackson, who, after studying the bone structure and patterns of the faces, said that he believed that they were of the same man, and that it was quite possible that the man in the later photographs (Phillips) had undergone plastic surgery, particularly around the ears.

Pointer and Dullenty also sent samples of the handwriting of both men to an expert who reported that in her opinion the writings were by the same person.

Next, Dullenty located the son of the woman who owned the Phillips manuscript. He stated that he had helped Phillips try to sell the story and, further, he had accompanied Phillips in 1934 on one of his trips to Lander, Wyoming. He remembered quite well how Phillips had been greeted in Lander as "George Cassidy," the name that Butch was often known by. But even more interesting was a letter that the two writers found in the possession of a Casper, Wyoming, woman. It had been written in 1935 to the woman's mother who claimed she had also been one of Cassidy's girlfriends. It closed with "I am always your old sweetheart," and was signed first "Geo" and then "W. T. Phillips."

Pointer interviewed Cassidy's sister. Although she denied that her brother and W. T. Phillips were one and the same, she did admit that Butch occasionally used

Inner circle of the Wild Bunch. Front row, left to right: Harry "Sundance Kid" Longabaugh, Ben Kilpatrick, and Cassidy. Second row, left to right: Will Carver and Harvey "Kid Curry" Logan. *Union Pacific Railroad.*

the name "Phillips" as an alias during his outlaw days. In her book, which was published in 1975, she continued to reject the notion that Butch became Phillips, but she clearly debunked the story that her brother had been killed in Bolivia in 1909.

The Pointer-Dullenty joint enterprise to produce a book on Cassidy eventually faltered due to scheduling problems and other obstacles, and the two parted company, each retaining the right to use any of the material already collected as they wished. Pointer came out with *In Search of Butch Cassidy* in 1977, an excellent biography with a plausible thesis that Cassidy was indeed William T. Phillips, a Spokane businessman.

The William T. Phillips uncovered by Dullenty and Poiinter was a highly talented and innovative individual. In the 1920s he developed one of the early "adding and listing" machines similar to those later used by millions of shopowners and bookkeepers. His machine, however, never reached mass production and his company failed during the Great Depression. Nearly broke, Phillips spent his meager savings on several trips to Wyoming desperately searching for stolen loot thought to have been stashed away by turn-of-the-century outlaws. Failing to locate any of these treasures, he tried panning for gold along the Columbia River in eastern Washington, also without success.

The story he told of being an outlaw himself was shared with only a few close friends, and it may have been that he believed that he was still wanted by the law. If so, he may have been guilty of murder, since it would have been the only crime of his early days for which punishment would not have been erased by the statutes of limitation.

In 1935 during his unsuccessful attempts to sell his manuscript "The Bandit Invincible," Phillips's health began to fail. At the same time his marriage deteriorated and he began to drink heavily. According to evidence uncovered by Pointer, at one point he nearly returned to his criminal ways, through an ill-conceived plot to kidnap a local businessman for ransom. The plan was aborted, driving Phillips into even deeper despair. In a letter to an old Wyoming sweetheart in December 1935, he described his life as a series of "flops" and lamented that his only hope lay in the passage by Congress of the "Townsend Plan," a precursor of social security. In 1937, lonely and penniless, he died of cancer.

William T. Phillips.
Jim Dullenty Collection.

Cassidy may or may not have been William T. Phillips. In 1982 a story surfaced that suggests that Cassidy may have been around as late as 1939. According to a Utah woman named Joyce Warner—daughter of Matt Warner, a member of Butch's gang—a man called at her home in November of that year looking for her father. At first he would only give his name as "Frank," but Miss Warner guessed that he was Cassidy, and he later admitted as much. Cassidy told her that he had been working for a railroad in the East, had married, had two daughters, and that his family did not know his real identity. After learning that Matt Warner had died the previous year, the man spent most of the afternoon at the Warner residence, and then left about 6:00 to "catch a train." Miss Warner never saw him again, but he did correspond for a while. She said she was convinced that the man was Cassidy from the description her father had given her, and because of the man's knowledge of details that her father had told her about his days on the outlaw trail.

The account of Butch Cassidy's final days probably is yet to be told. Dullenty and others are still searching for the true story. Dullenty, once nearly convinced that William Phillips was indeed Cassidy, said that now he is not so sure. Although Dullenty praised Pointer's book, he said it omits information that would cast doubt on the conclusion that Phillips and Cassidy were one and the same.

Dullenty also said he doubts Lulu Betenson's story. During the 1970s, said Dullenty, Lulu's story kept changing. When questioned about her inconsistencies, she always claimed that she was misquoted.

But Dullenty's mind is still open. "Much remains a

mystery about Phillips," he said. "If we could just prove once and for all that he was *not* Butch Cassidy, I'd be so damn happy." (Sources: Betenson, *Butch Cassidy, My Brother*; Dullenty, "Was William T. Phillips Really Butch Cassidy?"; Horan, *Desperate Men*; Kelly, *The Outlaw Trail*; Lacey, "Matt Warner's Daughter Meets Butch Cassidy"; Pointer, *In Search of Butch Cassidy*.) *See also* **Harry "Sundance Kid" Longabaugh; Tipton, Wyoming; Wagner, Montana; Wilcox, Wyoming**.

PARROTT, "BIG NOSE" GEORGE. Big Nose George Parrott was known mostly as a cattle rustler and not as a famous train robber—in fact, he may never have successfully robbed a train. A try at stopping a Union Pacific passenger train near Carbon, Wyoming, in June 1878, might have been his first and last attempt. But that effort, which led to his grim end two years later, reserved him a prominent place in the Union Pacific history museum in Omaha, Nebraska.

The story of George Parrott is marred with errors and legends. Some western writers have confused him with one of the ubiquitous "Currys" who rode with the Wild Bunch in the 1890s (fifteen years after Parrott's death) and others have him mixed up with "Flat Nose" George Currie, another Wild Bunch member.

A tale that some writers have accepted, however, is that Parrott was riding with Frank James at the time of the attempted robbery at Carbon. According to that account, in the spring of 1878, two years after the James brothers' narrow escape in the bank robbery attempt at Northfield, Minnesota, Frank James drifted west into the Powder River region of northern Wyoming. Somehow he met up with Parrott who was leading a makeshift gang of former road agents out of the Black Hills. If the story is true, one could understand how they might decide to join up. If Frank needed cash and wanted to tackle another express car, it would be much easier to ride with an already established outfit than to recruit a new one of his own. And Parrott, a relatively minor outlaw, could benefit from learning the trade of train robbery from somebody like James.

As the story goes, Frank, who was riding under the name McKinney, chose to stay in the background, content to let Parrott act as leader. Their first robbery was to be the Union Pacific's westbound No. 3 at a site near Carbon, now a caved-in ghost town on the sun-blistered plain between Medicine Bow and Rawlins. As a pioneer

"Big Nose" George Parrott. *Union Pacific Railroad Museum Collection.*

in the art of train robbery, James had experimented with several methods of gaining access to express cars. At Adair, Iowa, in 1873, which is believed to be the James-Younger gang's first express car holdup (see **Adair, Iowa**), they had merely loosened a rail and let the locomotive drag the cars into the ditch. It had worked well then and it was simple. The fact that somebody could be killed (as was the engineer at Adair), did not seem to bother Frank.

Breaking into a section gang toolhouse for picks and shovels was easy, and in minutes the outlaws, perhaps with Frank supervising, pried loose a rail from its joint bars. But as they started to wrap a wrie around the rail in order to yank it aside as the train approached, they saw a handcar coming down the track from the west. Scrambling for cover in the tall sagebrush, they barely made it out of sight as John Brown, a crusty Union Pacific section foreman, came pumping by. An experienced track worker, Brown had a keen eye for trouble

Carbon, Wyoming. *Frank Leslie's Illustrated Magazine, 1877.*

along the line and he immediately spotted the loosened joint bars as his car passed over them. Brown was no fool; he knew the westbound was due soon, and that if the rail had recently been loosened, the culprits were nearby. Without a sideward glance, he kept pumping away as if nothing was wrong.

Later, George Parrott was to say that Frank James had wanted to put a bullet into the foreman's back before he got out of range, but Parrott stopped him, figuring that Brown had missed seeing the loose rail. Brown, of course, raced down the track and flagged the oncoming train.

When word of the attempt to wreck and probably rob the westbound was sent out along the line, posses were quickly formed at both Laramie and Rawlins and they soon converged on the scene. When the trackers could not pick up the outlaws' trail, the posses split up, one heading north along the Medicine Bow River and the other went west toward the town of Hanna. Two of the possemen, however, Henry "Tip" Vincent, a Union Pacific detective, and Bob Widdowfield, a coal mine boss from Carbon, had a hunch that the outlaws went a third direction: south toward Elk Mountain. They followed that route, and sure enough, they picked up what appeared to be tracks leading toward Rattlesnake Pass.

Vincent and Widdowfield were good trackers, but they were hardly careful outlaw hunters; when they reached the pass, they unwisely followed the tracks right in. The Parrott gang was waiting for them, and a bullet from Big Nose George's rifle split Widdowfield's skull. Vincent spurred his horse and made a dash for safety but he got less than a hundred yards before he, too, was dropped, probably by gang member Dutch Charley Burris.

After killing the possemen, the Parrott gang split up. It was rumored that Frank James headed for southwestern Wyoming and spent the rest of the year near the

Bitter Creek region, then disappeared. Dutch Charley Burris was picked up in Montana and returned to Wyoming to stand trial at Carbon. On arriving at the depot, however, an angry mob, friends of the murdered Bob Widdowfield, surrounded the train and called for a lynching. Burris figured his only hope was to confess the crime to the authorities and hope that in return they would save him from the threatening mob. He gave his confession, but instead of being placed in jail, he was taken outside and made to stand on a barrel under a telegraph pole. A rope was placed around his neck, and he was asked if he had anything to say before he met his maker. Before he could answer, Bob Widdowfield's widow stepped out from the crowd. "No, the son-of-a-bitch has nothing to say," she said, and she kicked the barrel out from under him.

George Parrott met a similar fate. The following year he was also captured in Montana and returned to Wyoming. But instead of being taken to Carbon, he was jailed in Rawlins, where the authorities believed he might be safer from a lynch mob. But they were mistaken. A short time later he was snatched from his cell and also hanged from a telegraph pole.

By then George Parrott had become famous. Following the lynching, a local physician, John E. Osborne,

Big Nose George Parrott's bones, found during excavation in Rawlins in 1950. *Union Pacific Railroad Museum Collection.*

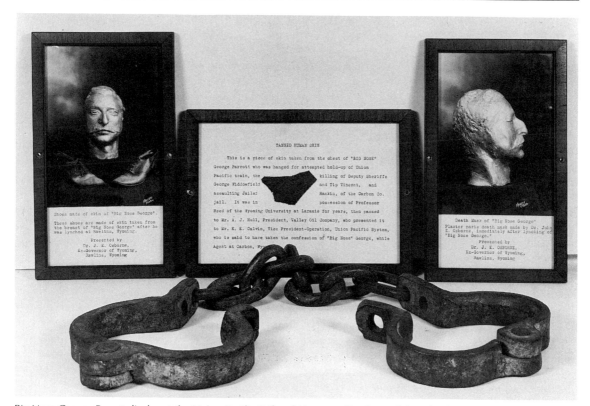

Big Nose George Parrott display at the Union Pacific Railroad Museum, Omaha. At left and right are George's death masks. In the center is a piece of his skin. In the foreground are the shackles used in his capture. *Union Pacific Railroad Museum Collection.*

made a death mask of Parrott's face, one of the few ever made of a western outlaw. But the gruesome Dr. Osborne did not stop there. Part of George's skull was removed, as well as skin from his chest and thighs. The skull was given to Osborne's assistant, Lillian Heath, as a souvenir. According to a local story, the good doctor kept the skin from the outlaw's chest for himself, and later had it fashioned into a small medicine bag, except for one piece which was given to an unknown party in Rawlins. This piece eventually found its way into the Union Pacific Railroad Museum in Omaha, Nebraska, as did the piece of skull. The skin from Parrott's thighs, it is said, was used to make a pair of shoes, and they ended up in the possession of the Rawlins National Bank.

On May 12, 1950, while workmen were digging the foundation for a new store in downtown Rawlins, they uncovered a tightly sealed whiskey barrel. Inside were a bottle of vegetable compound, a pair of shoes (regular leather), and a human skeleton. Local officials later identified the skeleton as old George's. (Sources: Block, *Great Train Robberies of the West*; Breihan, "The Outlaw Who Became a Pair of Shoes"; Patterson, *Wyoming's Outlaw Days*.)

PAYNE, S. J. The headline read "Train Robbers Beaten: a Plucky Denver Drummer Drove Them Off."

S. J. Payne was a frail young man from the East. Westerners looked upon him as "dandified," but as history would show, Payne was of sterner stuff than anyone would have guessed.

On August 17, 1892, young Payne boarded a Denver Pacific passenger train bound for Cheyenne, Wyoming. It would be his first trip as a drummer for his new employer, Evans and Littlefield of Denver. Although he came west for adventure and was excited about his new job, Payne was uneasy about traveling—especially when he had to go by train, because of the many holdups that were being reported in the newspapers. To the mild-mannered easterner, the West seemed "very wild," and on every trip he made, he "more than half expected trouble." Because of this, he had purchased a revolver and kept it with him at all times. On the night of August 17 he got a chance to use it.

As the train was pulling away from La Salle station, about sixty miles south of Cheyenne, three masked men entered the passenger coach with drawn six-shooters. After scanning the car carefully to make sure there were no lawmen on board, they announced to the stunned passengers that they were going to have to give up their money and valuables. "Everybody hands up!" they shouted, and to make their point, they fired several shots toward the ceiling.

Several of the ladies screamed, and one or two fainted. According to a witness, R. J. Ekfelt of Fremont, Nebraska, quite a few of the men passengers "dived under the seats," some of them hiding their money and others simply hoping they would not be noticed by the bandits. But not the young easterner, S. J. Payne. Payne was near the rear of the car and half asleep when the bandits commenced shooting. It took a few seconds for him to realize what was happening. By the time he had fully awakened, two of the masked strangers were heading down the aisle collecting their loot. Later, in telling the story, Payne said that all he could think about was that he did not "relish giving up [his] money and jewelry."

S. J. Payne had bought his pistol for just such an eventuality. Without another thought, he pulled it out and began firing.

Payne had no experience shooting a handgun, and most of his shots went wild, but according to one of the other passengers, it appeared that at least one of his bullets hit the mark. The witness said he heard one of the bandits "yell as in pain." Completely unnerved, the three outlaws turned and raced for the exit. The train was still moving at a slow speed, and they leaped off without looking back. As they did, they dropped their plunder bag that contained what little they had collected from the coach.

S. J. Payne spent the remainder of the trip accepting the hearty thanks of his grateful fellow passengers. (Source: *New York Times*, 8 August 1892.)

PEACH SPRINGS, ARIZONA. Peach Springs, population about 600, is in Mohave County at the southern edge of what today is the Hualapai Indian Reservation.

Six miles east, along the tracks of the Santa Fe, is a gouge in the desert landscape called Rocky Cut. There, on the night of February 8, 1897, the Santa Fe's Overland No. 1 was stopped by two masked men. The men ordered the engineer and fireman back to the express car and forced them to uncouple it and the railway mail car from the rest of the train. But while this was going on, the Wells, Fargo express messenger, Alexander Summers, and his assistant, a man named Randall, slipped out of the car. One of the robbers caught sight of Randall and drew a bead on him with his shotgun. Messenger Summers, however, had picked up his Colt 45 as he was leaving; with one shot he put a bullet through the bandit's head. Seeing a comrade killed would have unnerved most train robbers, but the second bandit, who had stayed up front near the locomotive, calmly ordered the engineer, William Daze, to keep on the throttle.

After about two miles, the bandit told the engineer to stop. The locomotive was then just short of what is now a tiny dot on the map called Nelson, then called Nelson Siding. With a gun in their backs, engineer Daze and his fireman reluctantly marched back to the express car. With the messenger and his assistant long gone, the bandit easiliy climbed in; however, the express company safe was locked, and the dynamite the robbers had brought along was stuffed in the pockets of the bandit's dead confederate.

Dejected, the bandit jumped off the express car and went back to the mail car. Whether the railway mail clerk, Albert Grant, resisted is not revealed in the report of the robbery. The bandit quickly scooped up several packages of registered mail and raced to his horse, which was tied nearby.

From a description given by the engineer, the authorities guessed that the bandit who had escaped was Fleming Jim Parker, known in Arizona as James T. Parker. He was a hard case from Utah who possibly was kin to Robert LeRoy Parker, the notorious Butch Cassidy. The dead bandit was not identified.

A sheriff's posse followed Parker's tracks for three days; on one occasion the posse came close enough to exchange a few shots with him, but eventually drifting snow persuaded the lawmen to abandon the chase. Another posse was formed, however, led by Ralph Cameron, sheriff of Conocino County, and they found Parker's horse and saddle at a cabin near Peach Springs.

Cameron was positive that Parker was now only hours ahead of them and astride a strange mount; he sent two Indian trackers out to overtake the bandit. They did and they captured him, but during the night Parker slipped out of his bounds, seized the Indians' weapons, and told them to "git"—which they did. However, the Indians' and Parker's horses ran off, and Parker was forced to strike out on foot.

Not accustomed to traveling without a mount, Parker wore out rapidly. On February 15, about twenty miles north of Peach Springs, the posse caught up with him as he was wading across Diamond Creek. His feet were badly blistered and partially frozen, and he had been without food for two days. He gave up without a fight.

Parker was taken to the county jail at Prescott, where the railway mail clerk identified him as the robber. He was not to be confined long, however, On May 9 he and two other prisoners broke out of jail by overcoming the jailer, R. W. Meador, and shooting an assistant district attorney, Lee Norris. They ran to the livery stable, snatched three horses, and rode off toward the hills.

Parker's freedom was short-lived. On May 25 a posse found him fast asleep on a trail about sixty miles north of Tuba City. He was taken back to jail, tried for killing attorney Norris, and in June 1898, hanged at Prescott, Arizona. (Sources: Rasch, "Fleming 'Jim' Parker, Arizona Desperado"; *Arizona Weekly Journal Miner*, 8 June 1898.)

PEQUOP, NEVADA. The robbery of the Wells, Fargo express car on the Central Pacific's eastbound passenger Train No. 1 at Pequop, Nevada, on November 5, 1870, was the second train robbery west of the Mississippi River. The first had occurred less than twelve hours earlier at Verdi, Nevada, and it had involved the same express car and the same messenger, Frank Marshall. (*See* **Verdi, Nevada**.)

Pequop is in northwestern Nevada, in Elko County, about thirty-five rail miles from the Utah line. (Pequop can still be seen on some maps; however, in 1870 the neighboring town of Independence, fifteen miles to the west, was slightly more prominent. In the annals of train robbery, Independence is sometimes given as the site of this robbery.)

By the time the train had reached Pequop, messenger Frank Marshall had learned a lesson: hide some of the money before the robbers force their way in. The

robbers at Verdi had overlooked between $4,500 and $8,000 (depending upon whose account you read), and Marshall had picked up several more cash express packages while crossing Nevada, including $10,000 in bagged gold coins. When the train reached Independence, there was at least $15,000 and possibly $20,000 on board. When he heard the train being stopped a second time, Marshall quickly stuffed the bags of coins behind of rack of lanterns and signal flares. As a result, the robbers got only about $4,500.

Although the procedure was similar (the robbers detached the engine and the express and mail cars from the rest of the train, and had the engineer pull them ahead), the robbery at Pequop was unrelated to the Verdi holdup. Although the Verdi affair had been well planned, the idea for the Pequop holdup was conceived on the spur of the moment by army deserters from nearby Camp Halleck. A clue to the identity of one of the bandits was found in the express car immediately after the holdup—a glove with the name "Carr" on it, which was the same name as a trooper at Fort Halleck who had recently escaped after being named a suspect in a murder of a woman on post.

A special train with a posse on board was dispatched from Elko, Nevada, and the culprit's tracks were quickly picked up. They were soon overtaken in the Independence Mountains. (Sources: Beebe and Clegg, *U.S. West: The Saga of Wells, Fargo*; Drago, *Outlaws on Horseback*; *Elko Independent*, 9 November 1870.)

PERRY, OKLAHOMA. An express car holdup on the Santa Fe Railroad at Perry, Oklahoma, on May 9, 1891, might have been the Dalton gang's first train robbery; so said Emmett Dalton, who probably was there. Perry is in the north central part of the state, in Noble County, about fifty-five miles north of Oklahoma City. In 1891 the town was called Wharton.

Technically, it may not have been the first train held up by a Dalton; Bob and Grat Dalton were suspected of robbing a Wells, Fargo express car on the Southern Pacific Railroad the previous February (*see* **Earlimart, California**), although most writers now agree that that holdup probably was the work of Chris Evans and John Sontag.

In the case of the Perry robbery, it is believed that the Daltons had information that there would be a large shipment of money on board. After stopping the train, the outlaws detached the express car from the rest of the cars and had the engineer pull ahead. Then they marched the engineer and fireman back to the express car. However, while they were doing so, the Wells, Fargo messenger was busy hiding much of the money and valuables. The gang finally got in and gathered up what they believed was a good haul, but when they stopped out on the prairie to divide up their loot, they discovered that they had been tricked. An especially enticing package, which looked large enough to hold thousands of dollars, turned out to be stuffed with canceled waybills, old telegrams, and similar worthless paper.

When Emmett Dalton reminisced about the robbery years later, he claimed that he and his companions rode away with $14,000, but other sources place the amount between $500 and $1,750. (Sources: Preece, *The Dalton Gang; Guthrie Elevator* [Oklahoma], 15 May 1891.) *See also* **The Daltons.**

PERRY, OLIVER CURTIS. Had the colorful Oliver Curtis Perry (alias Oliver Moore; James Perry) been a western train robber, he probably would have been one of the most famous; his exploits certainly were remarkable enough. But Perry operated in the East, mainly in New York state, and his deeds never made the traditional dime novels that glorified the renegades of the frontier.

Perry was born in Amsterdam, New York, probably around 1865. It was said that he was a descendant of Oliver Hazard Perry, naval hero of the battle of Lake Erie during the War of 1813. Although of a good family background, Perry was in constant trouble as a youth, and at fourteen he was sent to the state reformatory for burglary. Following his release, he headed west, where he committed numerous crimes and spent three more years in prison in Minnesota. He has been traced

Oliver Curtis Perry.
Pinkertons.

to Illinois, Nebraska, Texas, and Wyoming, during which time he worked as a wrangler, and on the railroad, possibly as a fireman on a locomotive. Some say he might have been an engineer, but this is unlikely because of his age; he was still in his twenties. While in the West, Perry may have been involved in robbing trains, although there is no record of this. His first recorded train holdup occurred after he returned to his home state of New York.

On the evening of September 29, 1891, Perry slipped aboard the express car platform of the New York Central's eastbound No. 31 at Oriskany, New York, about five miles west of Utica. Perry was alone, so it would have been difficult to take command of the locomotive, stop the train, and then attack the express car. Perry's method was more ingenious: with a brace and bit, he drilled four holes in the wooden end door of the express car, connected the holes with a keyhole saw, and lifted the loosened panel out. He could then easily reach in and unlock the door.

Because of the noise of the train, the express messenger, Burt Moore, sitting at the safe with his back to Perry, never heard a thing. The first sound he heard was a voice that said: "Keep right on working and don't make an outcry. Keep away from the bell rope. I'm after money."

Moore offered no resistance, and Perry quickly tore through the express packages. He found a package of $5,000 in small bills, and some watches and diamonds that would later be valued at about $3,000. When the lights of Utica began to show out the window, Perry pulled the bell rope to stop the train. He jumped down and disappeared in the darkness.

When messenger Moore reported the holdup, his superiors were skeptical. Undoubtedly angered, Moore probably got out of order and was placed on suspension. The Pinkerton National Detective Agency was called in, however, and conducted its usual thorough investigation. To Moore's credit, a man matching Perry's description had been spotted in the area spending large amounts of money "in the hook shops," but nothing came of it. By the first of November, Pinkerton operatives combing the transient hotels and cheap dives of Syracuse turned up the name Oliver Curtis Perry as a suspect. Perry, however, was nowhere to be found.

Then, on the night of February 21, 1892, Perry nearly accomplished one of the most daring robberies in the annals of railroad history. At dusk, as a ten-car New York Central westbound was pulling out of the Syracuse station, Perry, wearing a sandy moustache, glasses, dark clothes, and with a bag slung over his shoulder, swung aboard the express car platform. About twenty miles out, near Jordan, he donned a red flannel mask, climbed to the top of the car, and then worked his way to near the center. With a homemade rope ladder fitted with metal hooks, he lowered himself over the edge of the car and down the side until he dangled precariously outside one of the windows. With one of his two pistols, he smashed the glass.

Inside, express messenger Daniel T. McInerney heard the crash and looked up. When he saw the masked face staring at him through the window, he grabbed his revolver. "Drop that gun or I'll shoot you dead," the face shouted. McInerney answered with a shot. His aim was true, but the bullet was deflected by a bandolier of ammunition Perry wore under his coat. Perry fired, and the bullet struck McInerney's pistol, shattering it and driving pieces of metal into the messenger's wrist.

Now weaponless, McInerney reached for the overhead bell rope to stop the train. Perry shouted at him not to touch the rope and drew aim to fire again. McInerney pulled back from the rope and instead tried to kick the chimney of the oil lamp, hoping to throw the car into darkness. Perry fired, and this time the bullet struck the messenger a glancing blow on the forehead, cutting a furrow just above his left eyebrow. Dazed, McInerney staggered and fell to the floor.

When McInerney came to, he found himself over by the door, partially shielded by a pile of boxes. The light was out, and his attacker, thinking the messenger was dead, was rummaging through the express packages. Quietly, without being seen, McInerney once again tried to pull the bell cord, but Perry had tied it up in a knot. The messenger later gave this account of the next few minutes:

> Many times I brought my full weight down on the rope, which, slipping through my uninjured hand, burned the palm painfully. . . . I then began to pull the bell cord in the opposite direction, thinking to arouse the train crew in their coach at the rear of the train.
>
> I no longer ducked as I pulled — my time had come I thought. Perry fired from a distance of about six feet with both revolvers and, as I rushed to meet him, a bullet entered my right leg near the groin and another whizzed by my ear. . . .

Wild with rage, he ordered me to get over to the safe, and purposely I beat him to it. With his gaze obstructed by his revolvers and mask, in the dim light I made a quick shift and stood on as many of the money packages as possible and tried to give him the idea that there was no great amount of moeny in the car.

He then cried, "Move over," but I did not move more than a step, feigning inability because of the crowded condition of the car. The risk I was taking was tremendous, for had he stepped into my place or bended over, he would have discovered how I was foiling him.

I was then commanded to "open those envelopes" and he pointed one of his revolvers to a number of waybills which were only for the shipments in the other locked seven cars on the train. This gave me a chance to delay him more. As I removed the contents, I scattered the envelopes over the money shipments under my feet.

Meanwhile, in the first passenger coach, conductor Emil Laas thought he heard a noise up front in the express car. He went out onto the end platform and hoisted himself up until he could see through the bell cord hole in the end of the express car. From the light of the flickering oil lamp, which Perry apparently had relighted, Laas could see the intruder pawing over express packages. Laas immediately pulled the bell cord, and the train began to slow. But then, from inside the express car, came two pistol shots and a shout: "Get this train to running again or I'll blow you all to pieces." Laas, fearing the intruder would kill the messenger, did as he was told.

A few miles down the track, at Port Byron, Laas could see a freight train waiting at a siding, and he knew that there would be trainmen on the platform who could help. Inside the express car, Perry, feeling the train slowing again, decided that it was now time to leave. He quickly climbed out the window he had first entered, grabbed his rope ladder, and scrambled up to the roof.

As the train stopped, Laas shouted to the trainmen on the platform that the express was being robbed. They forced open the door, and found the messenger weak and bleeding on the floor of the car. Assuming that the robber had run off, and since the messenger desperately needed a doctor, Laas order the train to proceed on to Lyons where he could get medical help.

Oliver Curtis Perry had climbed down off the roof of the car, but instead of slipping off into the darkness, the nervy bandit waited until the train began to pull away, and swung aboard again.

The telegraph operator at Port Byron had wired ahead to Lyons, and as the train pulled in, a crowd was gather-

Reward notice for Perry. *Pinkertons.*

ing at the station. As the wounded messenger was being lifted from the express car, Perry, unnoticed, lowered himself to the ground and joined the onlookers. It was a serious mistake. Laas, on his way back to the train after filing his report of the incident, spotted him. While Laas ran for a policeman, two trainmen made a rush for the slippery bandit. Perry, however, was much the quicker. Dashing across the train yards, he ran behind the tender of a freight train that was waiting to depart. He pulled the pin from the coupler and jumped aboard the locomotive. Ordering the engineer and fireman out, he threw the throttle wide open. The drivers spun, then caught, and he was off.

His pursuers, believing it too risky to try to climb aboard and get shot at, quickly uncoupled another locomotive waiting on the adjacent track. Armed with a shotgun, they piled into the cab and took off after the wily bandit.

The trainmen's locomotive was faster, and they soon caught up. The two steaming engines sped through the night, bullets and buckshot raking the cabs. But the pursuers eventually ran out of ammunition and they gave up the chase and returned to Lyons.

Perry, unable to keep the boiler fired and the throttle open at the same time, began to lose steam. Near Blue Cut, about two miles east of Newark, he abandoned the locomotive and headed for the woods.

Moving too slowly on foot, Perry found a farmer with a plowhorse and commandeered it at gunpoint. When the animal proved too slow in constantly falling snow, he exchanged it for a faster horse and a small sleigh.

Had Perry, at this point, chosen the right roads, he might have escaped. But in unfamiliar territory, he ended up on a logging road that came to a dead end in a frozen swamp near the tiny Wayne County village of Arcadia. A five-man posse led by the Wayne County sheriff was not far behind. Perry, knowing the end was near, crouched behind a stone fence and prepared to make a stand.

"Is there an officer in the crowd?" Perry asked from behind the fence. When deputy sheriff Jerry Collins answered that he was an officer, Perry promised that he would not shoot if Collins would come forward unarmed and talk things over. The two met, and Perry's first question was whether he had killed the express messenger. He seemed relieved when told that McInerney was alive.

While the two men talked, other members of the posse slipped around behind Perry. The movement distracted the robber, and deputy Collins rushed him. Overpowered, Perry was soon subdued and handcuffed.

On May 19, 1892, at the courthouse in Lyons, New York, Oliver Curtis Perry was convicted of the attack on express messenger McInerney, plus robbery and burglary, and sentenced to the state prison at Auburn, New York, for a total of more than fifty years. In five months, however, he escaped but was recaptured in less than twenty-four hours.

After his return, Perry began to act strangely and in 1895 he was declared insane. He escaped again in April 1895, but was recaptured a month later in Weehawken, New Jersey. This time he was transferred to the state hospital for the criminally insane at Clinton, New York. His condition worsened. He tried to starve himself by refusing food and had to be forcibly fed. In 1905 he blinded himself by gouging out his eyes. He spent the next twenty-five years in madness and darkness, until death ended his misery on September 5, 1930. Before the end, in a brief period of lucidness, he remarked one day: "Nobody ever stole a train just the way I did." (Source: O'Dell, "Oliver Curtis Perry.")

PIEDMONT, ALABAMA. Piedmont is in northeastern Alabama, about forty-five miles east of Gadsden. On Halloween night 1892 several men donned masks and climbed aboard a southbound East Tennessee, Virginia & Georgia passenger train as it pulled away after taking on water just below Piedmont. The express company messenger and the railway mail clerk were ordered to raise their hands and the intruders took $705 in cash from the express car safe and several packages of registered mail. After several miles the robbers pulled the bell cord, jumped off, and quickly disappeared in a thick woods.

In January 1893, James Brown, from nearby Lincoln, Alabama, was arrested for the crime. The following month two brothers, Jeff and Dick Harrison—who were described as northern Alabama mountaineers—were also picked up. Under steady questioning by local authorities, Brown and Dick Harrison, who was only fifteen, finally confessed to the robbery. Jeff, however, continued to deny his guilt. He was brought to trial in federal court in Birmingham and was found guilty on March 31, 1893. He was sentenced to life in prison at the Anamosa Reformatory in Iowa. He served only eight years, however, and was pardoned by President McKinley in 1901. On his release he returned to a life of crime and went on to become one of the South's most wanted train robbers. (Sources: *St. Louis Globe Democrat*, 1 November, 23 December 1892, 8 February, 2 April 1893; *New York Times*, 23 December 1916.) *See also* **Jeff Harrison**.

PIERCE, CHARLIE. Charlie (also Charley) Pierce rode with the Dalton gang and was probably in on some of the train robberies committed by that bunch. In the summer of 1892, however, he parted company with the Dalton brothers, and thus avoided the disaster at Coffeyville, Kansas, in September of that year. (*See* **The Daltons**.) After the Daltons's downfall, Pierce joined up with Bill Doolin's new outfit for the express car robbery at Caney on October 13, 1892 (see **Caney, Kansas**), and probably was around for most of the rest of the Doolin bunch's raids. (*See* **Bill Doolin**.)

Charlie's best pal among the Doolin crowd was Bitter Creek Newcomb, and usually wherever Newcomb went, Pierce followed. Pierce, however, was not at Ingalls, Oklahoma, in September 1893 when Newcomb and the Doolin gang were almost wiped out by federal officers.

Pierce's career came to an end the first week of May 1895 at a ranch owned by the Dunn family near Ingalls. As usual, he was with Newcomb. The details of the two outlaws' deaths are shrouded in mystery. There are three or four versions of the story. Some say Pierce and Newcomb were ambushed by federal marshals, while others say they were killed by the Dunn brothers, John and Bill. Bill Dunn was supposedly both a bounty hunter and stool pigeon who had worked both sides of the law for years. One version of the killings has Pierce dying from a blast of Winchester as he peered out the door of the Dunn farmhouse during an early morning raid by a mysterious "special deputy" brought in from Texas. This account has Newcomb being shot as he tried to escape through a window.

Another version has the two outlaws slain as they rode into the Dunn barnyard, and still another account has them killed in their sleep—a story that stemmed from a report that the soles of Pierce's feet indicated that he had been shot with his boots off. Some later writers have created even more confusion by misreporting the date of the deaths, placing the incident in July 1895. The only sure fact seems to be that Pierce and Newcomb were killed at the Dunn ranch.

Pierce was laid to rest at the territory's expense in Guthrie, Oklahoma, at the town's Summit View Cemetery. His grave can be visited today, in the Boot Hill section, Pauper's Grave No. 65. (Sources: Patterson, *Historical Atlas of the Outlaw West*; Patterson, *Train Robbery*; Shirley, *West of Hell's Fringe*.)

THE PINKERTONS. Pinkerton's National Detective Agency was born in 1855 when the founder, Allan Pinkerton, after consulting with six midwestern railroads, created the agency in Chicago to assist the companies in investigating labor problems, thefts of property, and customer complaints.

Allan Pinkerton had arrived in America from Scotland in 1843. While operating a small cooperage business in Dundee, Illinois, about forty miles northeast of Chicago, he accidentally uncovered a camp of counterfeiters in 1847 and arranged for their arrest. Local merchants, who were suffering heavy losses from bogus currency and were far from impressed with the efforts of local law enforcement agencies, offered to hire Pinkerton on a part-time basis to watch out for counterfeiters. He soon engineered several more arrests and before long he decided that he liked detective work more than the cooperage business.

Pinkerton's work against counterfeiters eventually brought him to the attention of the U.S. Treasury De-

William A. Pinkerton.
Pinkertons.

Robert A. Pinkerton.
Pinkertons.

partment, which at the time had no detective force of its own. In 1851 and 1853 the government hired him to investigate counterfeiting cases in Illinois. This led to a special assignment from the Cook County Sheriff to rescue two kidnapped Michigan girls who had been taken to the western part of the state. Pinkerton found them in Rockford, Illinois, and shot one of the kidnappers. The sheriff saw the value in a man like Pinkerton and offered him a deputy's job. In 1855 Pinkerton opened his own detective agency.

In addition to his detective work for the railroads and other business clients, Pinkerton became a special agent for the Chicago post office. Also, through his contacts with railroads, he picked up clients among several national express companies, including the giant Adams Express Company. Adams executives recommended him to eastern railroads, and in 1861 he opened a branch office with five operatives in Philadelphia to accommodate a major new client, the Pennsylvania, Wilmington & Baltimore Railroad.

It was through his contact with this railroad that led Pinkerton to uncover a possible plot to assassinate newly elected President Abraham Lincoln on his trip from Illinois to Washington, D.C. Pinkerton assisted in getting Lincoln to Washington safely. Lincoln and his staff were impressed, which resulted in Pinkerton, personally, and later the agency, receiving lucrative contracts for secret service work during the Civil War.

Following the war, Pinkerton expanded his agency's operations, with his major clients still being railroads and express companies. Excluding thefts and burglaries, the Pinkerton agency's first contact with armed train robbery came in 1866 with the holdup of an Adams Express Company car on the Ohio & Mississippi Railroad near Seymour, Indiana. The robbery was the work

of the Reno gang of Seymour, which at the time had local authorities in their pocket. Pinkerton moved in and, with secret operatives, managed to put the gang out of business within two years.

As train robbery caught on, first in the Midwest, then the South, and finally over the whole nation, Pinkerton's National Detective Agency was in great demand by the railroads and express companies. Allan Pinkerton's two sons, William and Robert, joined the firm and proved to be as talented as their father in chasing criminals.

The agency's methods were effective. It let it be known that once it opened a file on a fugitive, it would close it only upon his death—and then, only if the death was thoroughly investigated and confirmed. It was not unheard of for Pinkerton operatives to wangle the disinterment of a corpse for a "final photographing" to establish identity. The photographs would be sent to persons who had known the deceased: prison officials, police officers, prosecuting attorneys, and even members of the jury that had convicted him. With a few exceptions (e.g., Robert LeRoy "Butch Cassidy" Parker and Harry "Sundance Kid" Longabaugh), the agency laid a file to rest only when positive proof was in.

Allan Pinkerton became obsessed with catching train robbers, most of all the James brothers, especially after Jesse's and Frank's younger brother was killed and their mother severely injured during a Pinkerton raid on the family homestead in 1875. The incident brought disgrace to the agency.

The Pinkertons never denied their participation in the raid on the James's homes, and it was not the only black mark for the agency during their fifty-year war with train robbers. More than once the Pinkertons were charged with bending the rules to catch a renegade (kidnapping, for example, in the Reno case), and when it appeared a criminal might not get what he deserved from the courts, it was rumored that the Pinkertons did not discourage a lynching.

Also, it was suggested that the agency's extreme loyalty to its clients eventually determined which express cars would be robbed. The agency was accused of letting it be known (or at least not discouraging the rumor) that while its operatives would hound to the grave a criminal who robbed a Pinkerton client, if an operative came across the path of a criminal who had robbed a victim who was not protected by the Pinkertons, he might very well look the other way. What effect this actually had on train robberies is not known, but statistics compiled by the banking industry showed that during a sixteen-year period the Pinkertons were under contract with the American Bankers' Association, losses by Pinkerton-protected banks were one-tenth that of those not so protected.

As train robberies spread west, an office was opened in Denver under the supervision of James McParland, whose undercover work in the coal fields of Pennsylvania had toppled the troublesome Molly Maguires. McParland handled most major cases, but often when a large express car robbery occurred, either William or Robert Pinkerton would rush out from Chicago to supervise the investigation.

The time-worn Pinkerton practice of flooding the countryside with inquisitive operatives was particularly effective in the sparsely populated West. Their orders always were to question local inhabitants about anything that seemed unusual during the days before and immediately after the robbery, regardless of whether it seemed relevant to the crime. It was William Pinkerton's theory that the loneliness and desolation of the prairies and mountains "emphasized the unusual" for the local residents, and that the tiniest bit of news was usually devoured and passed on to neighbors. Thus, often scattered among endless trumpery were valuable clues.

As they did in the East, the Pinkertons kept many informers on its rosters throughout the frontier: saloon owners, cattlemen, mine operators, merchants, and bankers—persons who traditionally frowned upon lawlessness and who wanted to see the criminal element eliminated. Others became informers from the money they could earn gathering information. Many were railroad employees, but these men had to be recruited with care, because bandit gangs also put railroaders on their payrolls to learn dates and times of large express shipments. It is not too difficult to imagine two railroad employees working side-by-side, one secretly passing information to robbers, and the other to the Pinkertons. The identity of all informers was always closely

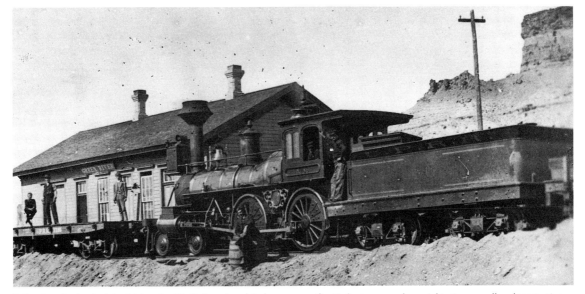

Following the lead of the Union Pacific Railroad and its horse cars, the Pinkertons used special trains, usually a locomotive, a tender, and a flat car, to rush operatives to the scene of a robbery. *Wyoming State Archives, Museums and Historical Department.*

guarded, with only code names being used in official communications.

Data on crime and criminals flowed steadily into the Pinkerton's Denver office from all over the West. Salaried operatives were under strict orders to send in reports daily. Files were established on suspects; these in turn were cross-indexed with files of other suspects, creating on paper theoretical "tables of organization" of outlaw gangs. This information was forwarded to cooperating sheriffs and town marshals who, in return, formed a network of additional sources for the agency. It was not Pinkerton policy for operatives to accept reward money, and this was used to encourage police officers who could receive rewards to participate in the agency's intelligence system.

When possible, the Pinkertons placed an undercover operative in a position to infiltrate an outlaw gang. These agents would often be given new identities, complete with fake criminal records and wanted posters. One of the more successful was Charles Siringo, a slightly built, gray-eyed Irish-Italian from Texas who cut his teeth as a manhunter at age twenty-two stalking Billy the Kid. (He said he gave up the hunt when he lost his traveling money at a poker table.) Siringo joined the Pinkertons in 1886 and spent the next twenty years on the trails of some of the West's most dangerous outlaws. He became, as one observer wrote, "an almost unshakable bloodhound."

One of Siringo's greatest accomplishments was the infiltration of the Wild Bunch in the late 1890s, during which time he tipped off the authorities about the gang's plan to rob several express shipments on the Union Pacific Railroad. But before Siringo could engineer the elusive outlaws's capture, his true identity leaked out and he had to flee for his life.

Perhaps the most famous Pinkerton operative was Tom Horn, although Horn's fame came later, when he was a free-lancer. This swaggering, broad-shouldered ex-deputy sheriff worked for the agency for four years tracking down train robbers and other miscreants before he struck out on his own as a hired gun. Although he denied that his job with the Pinkertons called for the killing of desperadoes (and there was no proof that it did), this was a special service that he would offer later when he was on his own.

But train robbers who did find Tom Horn on the trail probably wished they had chosen another line of work.

Rumor had it (but again, no proof) that Horn personally filled seventeen graves while with the Pinkertons.

A major part of the Pinkertons's success was due to their persistence. The agency claimed that it would spend $20,000 to catch a robber who stole $200. This kind of reputation was effective; in 1873 an associate of Allan Pinkerton revealed that during the agency's pursuit of the Reno gang, the outlaws sent word to the Adams Express Company that they would return the money they stole during the Marshfield, Indiana, robbery if the Pinkertons were taken off the case. Notwithstanding their methods, the Pinkertons well earned the trademark, "The Eye That Never Sleeps." (Sources: Horan, *Desperate Men: Revelations from the Sealed Pinkerton Files*; Horan, *The Pinkertons*; Jarman, "The Pinkerton Story"; Marcy, "Detective Pinkerton"; Morn, "*The Eye That Never Sleeps*"; Patterson, *Train Robbery*.) *See also* **Reno Gang**.

PIXLEY, CALIFORNIA. The robbery at Pixley on February 22, 1889, was the first in a series of holdups on the Southern Pacific line that were first blamed on the Dalton gang and later attributed to the notorious Chris Evans and John Sontag.

It was a cold, cloudy night in the San Joaquin Valley. As the Southern Pacific's southbound No. 17 slowly pulled away from the Pixley station, two masked men, each carrying a shotgun, slipped out of the shadows and swung aboard the blind baggage area behind the tender. Two miles out of town, the engineer, Pete Boelenger, felt a gun barrel in his back.

The train was halted, and Boelenger and his fireman were marched back to the Wells, Fargo express car. When the messenger, J. R. Kelly, refused to open up, the bandits stuffed dynamite under the car.

In the meantime, the conductor, James Symington, had spotted the trouble and had sought out Ed Bently, a deputy sheriff from Modesto, who was a passenger in the smoking car. Symington also summoned the brakeman, whose name was Anscon, and another man, a passenger believed to be a Southern Pacific employee named Gabert. Quietly the four men dropped to the ground from the second coach platform and, two on each side of the train, began to work their way forward toward the express car.

Just before the dynamite went off, one of the robbers spotted Anscon and Gabert, and fired a blast from

Pixley station. *Southern Pacific Railroad*.

his shotgun. The charge struck Gabert, seriously wounding him. On the other side of the car, the second robber also fired, striking Deputy Sheriff Bently. Symington and Anscon realized the robbers were more than they could handle and they hastily retreated.

Although dazed from the explosion, express messenger Kelly still refused to open up. But the robbers soon convinced him that if he didn't, they would kill the engineer and fireman. Reluctantly, he threw out the strongbox. The robbers quickly emptied it and raced to their horses, which they had tied to a nearby telegraph pole.

When the authorities arrived, they found two tramps who had been at the station at Pixley. One of them gave the following story:

We were waiting for the train to ride out to Pixley, and noticed two more men who seemed to be waiting. We went up and commenced talking to them. They acted in a very peculiar manner. It was so dark that we could not tell exactly how they looked, but [I] think both were good-sized men. Both wore overcoats and white shirts. One had clothes strongly perfumed; both had shotguns or what appeared to be shotguns. They asked us where was a good place to get on the train. We told them, and asked them where they were going. They said to Delano, to shoot jack rabbits. We asked them what was the matter with shooting jack rabbits at Pixley. One said he had a ranch at Delano. Just then the train came along and the men jumped on the front part of the engine.

The other tramp continued: "Something seemed to warn me that all was not right. As the train passed, a third man jumped out from somewhere and boarded one of the passenger cars. I felt uneasy and walked over to the station and told some one what had happened.

I was only laughed at, but it was not long before he heard what had happened."

The first tramp, who had hitched a ride on the train, then added:

The train commenced to slow up when we got a short distance beyond Pixley. When it had nearly stopped I discovered that there was trouble of some kind and jumped off. When they commenced shooting, I ran and jumped a wire fence and lay down in the field near by. I heard some one say, "My God, I am killed," when the shooting occurred, and then I heard an explosion of some kind. When the robbers had gone I slipped out and got among the passengers.

One of the men shot had his side torn all to pieces with buckshot. The train backed up to Pixley, when one of the passengers claimed that he saw a man fall at a distance from the track. The train went back, and we searched for the man. We soon found him. He had evidently been instantly killed. The shot entered near the nipple. He had a ticket in his pocket for Poso.

(Sources: Dillon, *Wells, Fargo Detective*; Glasscock, *Bandits and the Southern Pacific*; *New York Times*, 25 February 1889.) *See also* **Evans and Sontag**.

POCASSET, OKLAHOMA. Lawyer-turned-train robber Al Jennings was considered by some as an inept outlaw and by others as just plain unlucky. Unfortunately, most of the information we have on his escapades was written by Al himself and is unreliable.

On October 1, 1897, Al and his companions struck the Rock Island line at Pocasset, Oklahoma, in what a local newspaper writer called the "boldest holdup in broad daylight ever attempted in history." It really wasn't all that bold, and the fact that it occurred in daylight wasn't that important, since the robbers picked one of the most remote stretches of track on the line, a high prairie divide about eight miles south of Minco in Grady County—a perfect site for a holdup, where one could observe the countryside for miles around.

In 1897 Pocasset was nothing more than a section house and a siding. Prior to the arrival of the train, six outlaws overpowered the section gang and ordered one of them to flag down the southbound express. When the train came to a stop, one of the outlaws climbed up into the locomotive cab and covered the engineer and fireman with his Winchester. Two others took charge of the passenger coaches, and the last three forced their way into the express car.

Up to this point the affair went smoothly, but in the express car the bandits encountered trouble. Two charges of dynamite failed to blast open the stubborn American Express Company safe. This was not a new problem for the Jennings outfit; a month and a half earlier they had faced the same difficulty at Edmond and had to ride off empty-handed. (*See* **Edmond, Oklahoma**.)

When the second charge failed to blow open the door, the outlaws turned to the mail car, where they rifled the registered packages. Legend has it that Al Jennings always avoided the U.S. mail, but apparently this time he made an exception to his rule.

The mail offered only slim pickings, so Jennings and his companions headed for the passenger coaches. Rather than simply go up and down the aisles of the cars, the outlaws herded the passengers out onto the ground and forced them to line up to be searched. One by one, they were ordered to drop their money and valuables into a bag. During this procession, Jennings's mask slipped and the conductor, whose name was Day, recognized him as the former lawyer from Woodward, Oklahoma.

On finishing with the passengers, the outlaws rode off toward Walnut Creek, then doubled back, rode west through the uninhabited part of the Wichita Reservation, and then finally turned north. Jennings liked to claim that he was something of an expert at leading posses astray. Later, at a farmhouse near El Reno, the gang rested, divided up their loot, and then rode off to the northwest toward an old Dalton brothers' hideout on Cottonwood Creek southwest of Guthrie. (Source: Shirley, *West of Hell's Fringe*.)

THE POLLOCK DIAMOND ROBBERY. It was a Friday evening, November 4, 1892. As the northbound Sioux City & Pacific pulled out of Omaha, Nebraska, the smoking car carried only thirteen passengers—an unlucky number, especially for passenger W. G. Pollock of New York City, who was carrying $15,000 in uncut diamonds in a wallet in his vest pocket. And beside him on the seat were two leather satchels; one contained thousands of dollars more in mounted stones. Pollock, sitting near the middle of the car, was a salesman for one of the largest diamond merchants in the United States. Only one other passenger in the car knew this: an innocent-looking, clean-shaven young man sitting at the front, just behind the stove.

Soon after the train reached the twenty-mile marker,

the young man ducked his head down out of the sight of the other passengers, slipped on a false black beard and mustache, got to his feet, and walked back to where Pollock was sitting. He swiftly drew a pistol out of his coat, pointed it at the man, and said calmly: "Give me them diamonds." Pollock made no move to comply, and the man reached into another pocket, pulled out a "sapper" loaded with buckshot, and smacked the diamond merchant over the head. Dazed and reeling from pain, Pollock still clung to his satchel of gems. Infuriated, the man raised his pistol and fired. The shot struck Pollock in the right shoulder. The attacker then took aim at Pollock's left shoulder and fired again. As the other passengers dived for cover, the man ripped the wallet out of Pollock's pocket. Wounded and bleeding as he was, Pollock still wrestled with his attacker, until another blow with the barrel of the pistol sent him to the floor. The attacker quickly picked up one of the satchels from the seat and calmly pulled the bell cord, the signal to the engineer to stop the train. As the train slowed, the man leaped off. As he landed, he dropped his gun.

The train was only three miles south of California Junction, Iowa. Pollock was taken off there and returned by the next train to Omaha.

The diamond merchant who employed Pollock was a member of the Jewelers' Protective Union, which kept on retainer Pinkerton's National Detective Agency to investigate thefts and robberies. An exhaustive search of the countryside by Pinkerton operatives turned up no clues. To make matters worse, the passengers in the smoker could not agree on the robber's description. In the excitement on hearing the first shot, most of them hid their heads and did not look up. Only one other passenger besides Pollock thought the attacker wore a black beard. Some thought he may have worn a mustache, but others, remembering him before he donned his disguise, recalled only that he was young and clean shaven.

Since the robber obviously knew that Pollock was carrying diamonds, the Pinkertons reasoned that Pollock had been followed, and they traced his steps for the past several days. On questioning witnesses at the shop of an Omaha pawnbroker named Sonnenberg, which Pollock had visited the day of the robbery, an employee of Sonnenberg's remembered a "man in a slouch hat" had been lounging around the front of the

The Pollock robbery. *McClure's Magazine, April 1895.*

shop while Pollock had been showing his gems to two of Sonnenberg's customers. The age and general build of the man fit that of the suspect.

Since the Jeweler's Protective Union was one of the Pinkerton agency's best clients, William A. Pinkerton himself took charge of the investigation. After reviewing the case, he concluded that despite the apparent young age of the suspect, it would have taken a bold, hardened bandit to risk a single-handed robbery in a railroad coach containing thirteen men, and that the man probably was already in the agency's photo gallery of criminals. Sure enough, several of the train crew and passengers identified such a man from Pinkerton's photos, a steel-nerved Chicago burglar named Frank Bruce. On locating Bruce, however, Pinkerton discovered that he had an alibi for the time of the robbery, and on presenting him to the witnesses, they admitted they had made a mistake.

Now, with no suspect, Pinkerton went over the file again to see if he had missed anything. He had. The name of one of the customers in pawnbroker Sonnen-

berg's shop when Pollock had displayed his diamonds sounded vaguely familiar. The name was Jack Denton. On checking, Pinkerton found that it was the same name as a Salt Lake City gambler he had heard about three years earlier who was thought to have been involved in burglaries. That gambler, Pinkerton remembered, was supposed to have been working with a young thug, a "smooth-faced boy, about twenty years of age."

Pinkerton set out for Salt Lake City, where through inquiries by local agency contacts he learned that the young burglar in question had recently served a one-year term for robbery at Ogden, Utah, and had been released just a month before the Pollock robbery. On being arrested, the man had given the name James Burke, but his real identity had not been proven.

From another source, an underworld associate of Burke's named Marshall P. Hooker, Pinkerton learned that the man also sometimes was known as "Kid" McCoy. A check was run on Hooker, and it was found that on occasion he could suffer from a "loose tongue," especially when he had a few drinks in him. Pinkerton undercover operators were sent to mix in with Hooker's crowd, and eventually he was heard to say that Burke, or McCoy, had indeed committed the Pollock robbery.

All Pinkerton offices were notified to keep an eye out for Burke. In the summer of 1893, he was found in jail at Leadville, Colorado, on a charge of possessing burglar tools. Pollock and two witnesses to the diamond robbery were sent to Leadville, and they all identified him as the robber. According to a Pinkerton agent who was present, Burke "winced perceptibly" when he saw the two witnesses, and he "went fairly wild" when confronted by Pollock.

Frank Shercliffe. *Pinkertons.*

This time the suspect's background was investigated thoroughly. His real name was Frank Shercliffe, a midwesterner who began his career at age seventeen by burglarizing a safe in Aurora, Illinois, and shooting it out with officers who tried to arrest him.

Shercliffe was released by the authorities in Leadville and returned to Iowa, where he was tried and convicted for the Pollock robbery at Logan. He was sentenced to seventeen years at the penitentiary at Fort Madison, Iowa. He was paroled in 1904 and, from Pinkerton records dated 1906, was at that time leading an honest life. (Sources: Moffett, "The Pollock Diamond Robbery"; Pinkerton, "Train Robberies.")

PONCA CITY, OKLAHOMA. Ponca City is in northern Oklahoma, about fifty miles north of Stillwater and about thirty miles south of Arkansas City, Kansas. In 1893 it was usually referred to as Ponca Station and was mainly a mail and supply drop on the Santa Fe line for the nearby Ponca Indian Agency. The town's only other distinguishing feature at the time was a stockyard about a half-mile north of the station, which was used by ranchers who held grazing rights on reservation land.

On May 19, 1893, a tip had been picked up that an attempt might be made that night to hold up the Santa Fe's No. 97 southbound passenger train at Ponca. As a result, among the passengers were C. W. Stockton, superintendent of the Wells, Fargo office in Kansas City, and Deputy U.S. Marshal Heck Thomas, employed at the time by the express company as a special agent.

The tip had been correct. While No. 97 was still a few minutes out of Ponca, three strangers suddenly appeared at the door of the station, fired a rifle shot through the window of the telegraph office, and leveled their Winchesters at the seven men inside: the station agent, the station pumper, the night telegraph operator, a mail carrier, two soldiers from the Ponca Agency, and a local hanger-on who had dropped by to play cards. As they lined their surprised captives up against the wall, the intruders informed them that they were going to rob No. 97's express car, and that they, the seven captives, were to be used as shields.

Without informing Superintendent Stockton or Deputy Marshal Thomas, No. 97's engineer, Jack Regan, and the rear brakeman, Patrick McGeeney, a young man in his early twenties, had devised a plan in case they ran into trouble with train robbers that night. If any-

thing looked suspicious, Regan would stop the train north of the station. If it appeared to be a holdup he would blow the whistle three times and throw the locomotive into reverse. McGeeney, who was armed with a Colt revolver, would then hurry forward to the engine.

As the train approached the town, engineer Regan did indeed get the feeling that something was wrong. Somebody on the station platform was violently swinging a red lantern. The station agent would never do this; Ponca was a regular stop, and no red signal was necessary. Regan closed the throttle, shut off the steam, and applied the brakes. As he slowed, he gave the whistle three blasts. McGeeney, back in the smoker, checked his revolver, grabbed a lantern, jumped to the ground and ran forward.

Regan and McGeeney were joined at the engine by A. R. Glazier, the conductor. The three men stared down the track toward the station, still several hundred yards away. The man with the lantern had disappeared, and all was dark. Regan did not want to take the train in, but the railroad had a schedule to maintain. Finally, McGeeney offered a suggestion: "I'll walk down to the depot, look around, and you'll know the outlaws are there. If you see any signals, you'll know I'm compelled to give them, and that will be your cue to keep the train out of danger." The others agreed, but Glazier, the conductor, ordered the young brakeman to leave his revolver with him: "You're Irish and hotheaded," he warned. "You might try to use that gun, and I don't want you killed."

As he walked down the track, young McGeeney swung his lantern to and fro and tried to act nonchalant. As he neared the station, he noticed the smashed window in the telegraph office. The lamp was burning inside, but the office was empty. Otherwise, nothing seemed out of the ordinary. He decided to walk on by and headed for the water tank. As he reached the end of the platform, he heard the command "Hands up!" He turned, raised his lantern, and saw "three bandits holding the business end of their rifles on seven cowed victims." He recognized the three armed men as the outlaws Henry Starr, Bill Doolin, and Bitter Creek Newcomb.

Starr wanted to know why the train had stopped short of the station. McGeeney told him that the conductor thought that there might be a holdup in the offing. This seemed to satisfy Starr; then he asked if there were any armed men on the train beside the express messenger.

McGeeney saw no reason to lie: "Heck Thomas and Charley Stockton," he answered, "and both are loaded for bear."

Bitter Creek Newcomb muttered something to the effect that if he could get hold of Thomas and Stockton, he would "cut their damned throats."

The outlaws seemed unsure of what to do next, so McGeeney suggested that they let him give the engineer the signal to come on into the station. The outlaws thought that was a good idea, but Starr warned the young brakeman that the signal "had better be the right one!"

McGeeney stepped to the edge of the platform and gave Regan the "high ball" sign, knowing full well that he and conductor Glazier would ignore it. When the train did not move, McGeeney got another idea. He informed them that Train No. 37, a fast freight out of Arkansas City, was soon to arrive, and might very well crash into the rear of the halted passenger train. "Think of the position of those helpless passengers," he told Starr, "I know you don't want to kill anybody." Starr agreed that he did not want that.

According to McGeeney's account, the outlaws again must have been unsure of their next move, for it was he who suggested that they go up the track and take over the train. The young brakeman was counting on his and the station agent's lanterns protecting them and the other captives from being shot by Stockton and Heck, but his "hopes wilted" when Starr told them to leave the lanterns in the tall grass beside the tracks.

As they marched up the track, with the outlaws leading their horses, McGeeney edged toward the side, hoping for a chance to escape, but before he could do so, he heard somebody back at the station shout: "Let those men go or we'll blow your brains out!" Soldiers at the nearby Ponca Agency had heard the shot that had shattered the telegraph office window, and a sergeant and six men had come down to investigate.

The outlaws raced for their horses, saddled up, and after unloading a number of shots in the direction of the station, rode off into the darkness toward the Osage Hills.

As would be expected, brakeman Patrick McGeeney became an instant hero. He received congratulatory letters from Santa Fe officials, and Wells, Fargo & Com-

pany presented him with a new Winchester rifle. Several days later the Newton *Kansas Republican* published the following poem in his honor by a local poet, Robin Goodfellow:

Ye're a hero, Pat old feller
An' by gosh hit hain't no fun
Ter be gazin' down the barrel
Of a wicked lookin' gun.

An' the boys are layin' fur ye
An' don't ye never doubt,
They'll gun you like the dickens
If you don't watch out.

Within weeks after the Ponca robbery attempt, McGeeney accepted a commission as a U.S. Deputy Marshal for Oklahoma Territory. He remained with the Santa Fe, however, and worked for both the government and the railroad for more than ten years. In 1904 he moved to Mexico to work for the Mexican Central. He eventually returned to the United States, settling in San Antonio. He then tried his hand at writing stage plays and motion picture scripts. In 1919 he became involved with a Tulsa film company, Pan American Motion Picture Company, and a film entitled *Debtor to the Law*, starring none other than his old train robber acquaintance from Ponca, Henry Starr, who at the time was on parole from prison. McGeeney was involved in production and direction, and also played the role of a lawman, Floyd Wilson, whom Starr killed in a shootout in 1892. The picture, filmed in Stroud, Oklahoma, made money, but its investors had a falling out, with Starr later claiming he was cheated out of his share of the profits. (Sources: Hitt, "Real to Reel Outlaws"; Shirley, "Train Robbery that Fizzled.")

POND CREEK, OKLAHOMA. Students of outlaw history have called the attempted robbery of an express car on the Rock Island Railroad on April 9, 1894, at Pond Creek the work of amateurs trying to emulate the success of the Dalton and Doolin gangs.

Pond Creek is in northern Oklahoma, in Grant County, at what is now the junction of U.S. highways 60 and 81. The affair seemed to go well at first, thanks perhaps to the only experienced robber in the bunch, Bill Rhodes, who some say at one time might have ridden with the James-Younger gang in Missouri. As the train pulled away from the water tank, two masked men slipped out of the shadows and climbed aboard: one in the blind baggage area between the tender and the express car, and the other somewhere on the baggage car, probably on the roof.

At about a mile out, the engineer spotted a bonfire on the track ahead. He slowed the big locomotive down, and as he did, he and his fireman found themselves staring at six-guns. When it appeared that the members of the engine crew were not taking the incident seriously enough, one of the outlaws fired into the cab, the bullet ricocheting off the boiler into the roof.

The train was brought to a stop, and the two outlaws marched the engineer and fireman back to the express car, where they were joined by two more masked men who suddenly appeared from the shadows beside the tracks.

The express company messenger, John Crosswight, was told to open up his car. He resisted, and while the bandits were arguing with him, an express guard on the car, Jake Harmon, a former Wichita policeman, grabbed his shotgun and slipped out the rear door. About the same time a brakeman also dropped to the ground and began running back toward Pond Creek to spread the alarm.

Despite a few random pistol shots into the express car door, messenger Crosswight continued to refuse to open up, and the would-be robbers finally thrust a stick of dynamite under the door plate. When it exploded, it knocked Crosswight down and momentarily stunned him. As his head cleared, he heard his attackers shout that they were going to use two sticks of dynamite next time. Crosswight decided that he had resisted long enough.

In the meantime, Jake Harmon had slipped around behind the outlaws. He raised his shotgun and drew a bead on the nearest one. It was the leader, Bill Rhodes. Harmon's aim was true, and the charge killed Rhodes instantly. As his shocked comrades stared down at his shattered body, they heard two sounds: Harmon slipping another shell into his shotgun, and the shouts of riders coming from the rear—a posse had been quickly formed at Pond Creek and they were coming to help. The bandits called it a night and raced for their horses. (Source: Shirley, *West of Hell's Fringe*.)

POPE, E. B. As combination locks became more sophisticated in the 1880s and 1890s, the express companies sought better and more complex devices to protect the contents of their in-transit safes. In 1893 E. B. Pope, western agent for the Chesapeake & Ohio Railroad at St. Louis, designed a lock that appeared to have real possibilities.

Pope's device was in fact two locks that interlocked with one another. The outer lock could be either an ordinary key lock or a combination. It was connected to the inner combination lock by a small steel bar. When in use by the messenger, the inner lock would remain in an open position, held there by a safety mechanism that could withstand routine jarring and an accidental bump. The dial on the inner lock was also protected by a metal case that was hinged to the safe.

The idea of a double lock was to do away with the two safes then being used on express cars: the local or way safe in which the messenger kept packages destined for the smaller or local stops on the run, and the large through safe, which usually could be opened only by express agents at the larger cities. With Pope's double lock, the messenger could use one safe. He would have a key or the combination to the outer lock, and the inner lock would remain open. If trouble was encountered, the messenger could quickly "throw" the inner lock. He did not have the combination to this lock, and a prominent notice of this fact would be pasted on the door of the safe. According to Pope, his device could be constructed out of locks already on the market, and could be attached to safes then in use.

Pope applied for a patent for his invention in August 1893, and, assuming it performed as he said it would, it is likely that it was put into use at least on an experimental basis. However, as more and more train robbers turned to dynamite to blast their way into the safes, it is also likely that the device was not widely adopted. (Source: *Railway Age*, 18 August 1893.)

PORTER, WILLIAM SIDNEY (O. HENRY). At first blush, short story writer O. Henry, whose real name was William Sidney Porter, seems an unlikely entry in a book on the train robbery era. A study of Porter's career, however, suggests otherwise.

At age fifteen Porter, a native of Greensboro, North Carolina, quit school and went to work in his uncle's drug store. He took to the work and four years later became a registered pharmacist. But during those four years, Porter developed a persistent cough that gradually worsened into what his family doctor believed to be tuberculosis. The doctor suggested that it would be to young Porter's advantage to move to a drier climate.

At the time, the doctor's son, Dick Hall, was managing a sheep ranch in La Salle County, Texas, and Porter was invited to live with him. It was expected that to the extent that his health permitted, Porter was to earn his keep by working on the ranch. However, young Will was not cut out for ranch work and he spent most of his time reading and writing short stories. Occasionally he would send his stories back to Greensboro for publication by the local literary society.

In 1884 Hall gave up the ranch, and Porter moved to Austin, Texas, where he worked at a series of jobs, including pharmacist, bookkeeper, and finally draftsman for the state land office. The state job lasted until 1891, when Will took a position as a teller in Austin's First National Bank. The pay was modest, and to make ends meet, he supplemented his income by writing humorous articles for a local weekly, *The Rolling Stone*.

By now Porter had married, and things were working out fairly well. Then his luck ran out. In December 1894 Will's accounts at the bank were found to be out of balance. He was suspected of taking money and he was asked to resign. In February 1896 a grand jury returned an indictment on four counts of embezzlement.

Porter was convicted and sentenced to prison at Leavenworth, Kansas. However, because of overcrowded conditions at that facility, he was sent instead to the Ohio State Penitentiary at Columbus, which was at the time taking part of the overflow of federal prisoners. While at Columbus, Porter became acquainted with Al Jennings, the former Oklahoma lawyer who had become a train robber.

To pass the time, Porter began writing short stories under the pen name "O. Henry" and submitting them through an intermediary to New York magazines. Several were accepted and considered quite good. Jennings, too, was bitten by the "writing bug" and struggled to turn out several pieces of his own. His efforts were hopelessly amateurish, however, and he soon gave up on the idea. But Porter was intrigued by Jennings's criminal background and would get Al and other inmates to tell of their adventurous outlaw days. Porter quietly took notes and later used some of the material in his stories.

Porter was paroled from prison in July 1901. According to Jennings, who still had time to serve, six weeks after Porter's release, he wrote Jennings a letter with a proposition. Porter, who claimed he was doing fairly well as a free-lance writer, said he had been in touch with the editors of *Everybody's Magazine* and had suggested an article tentatively entitled "The Art and Humor of Holding up a Train." The editors were interested, and Porter had told them that he thought he could get the piece written by "an expert in the business"—meaning Jennings.

As Jennings later told the story, Porter's letter, in part was as follows:

> Of course, I mentioned no names or localities. He [the editor] seemed very much struck with the idea and has written twice asking about it. The only fear he had, he said, was that the expert would not put it in a shape suitable for publication in *Everybody's* as John Wanamaker (publisher of the magazine) was very observant of the proprieties.
>
> Now, if you would care to turn yourself loose on the subject there may be something in it and a start on future work besides. Of course, you needn't disclose your identity in the slightest degree. What he wants (as I thought he would) is a view of the subject from the operator's standpoint.
>
> My idea would be a chatty sort of article—just about the way you usually talk, treating it descriptively and trying out the little points and details, just as a man would talk of his chicken farm or his hog ranch.
>
> If you want to tackle it, let me know and I'll send you my idea of the article, with all the points that should be touched upon. I will either go over it and arrange it according to my conception of the magazine requirements, or will forward your original MS, whichever you prefer. Let me know soon, as I want to answer his letter.

The article was written, apparently as a joint effort, and was sold to *Everybody's Magazine* in 1901. (Sources: O'Connor, *The Legendary Life of O. Henry*; Jennings, *Through the Shadows with O. Henry*.) *See also* **Al Jennings**.

PORTLAND, OREGON. On September 23, 1903, "Old Bill" Miner and his pals struck the Great Northern's Oregon and Washington Train No. 6 just east of Portland. Miner, who has become a folk hero of sorts following a 1983 Canadian movie about his life (*The Gray Fox*), stopped the train in the classic fashion. Two men boarded earlier near Troutdale, hid in the blind baggage area between the tender and express car, then climbed over the coal pile and put guns into the backs of the locomotive crew, engineer Ollie Barrett and fireman H. F. Stevenson. Barrett was forced to halt the train at milepost 21, where two more robbers waited with dynamite.

The dynamite was fastened to two long willow poles, which were held to the door of the combined express-mail car. Inside, however, the express messenger, F. A. Korner, and two railway mail clerks were not in the mood to surrender. As soon as the smoke from the blast cleared, messenger Korner doused the lights in the car and appeared at the doorway with a rifle. One of his first shots struck robber Jim Conners in the chest, killing him instantly. The bullet passed through Conners' body and also wounded Barret, the engineer, who was standing behind him. Korner and the mail clerks then barricaded themselves behind trunks and express packages, obviously prepared to defend their car until help arrived. Miner, never one to engage in risky gunplay, called off the attack. As the three remaining bandits retreated, Korner fired off another round and hit robber Charlie Hoehn. Miner went to his aid, but Hoehn was too weak to keep up and was later captured.

Miner and the fourth bandit, believed to be a man named Harsham, escaped. (Source: Rickards, "Bill Miner — 50 Years a Hold-up Man.") *See also* **Bill Miner**.

PRICE, JAMES. Few express messengers were willing to risk nearly certain death to protect a shipment for which they were responsible, but Jim Price was.

The date was May 7, 1875. Price, a messenger for the Adams Express Company, had the eastbound run on the Pittsburgh, Ft. Wayne & Chicago's Train No. 6. After a short stop at Lafayette, Indiana, the train had just picked up speed when Price realized that he was not alone in his express car. He looked up and saw a "powerfully built and muscular" fellow standing at the far end of the car. Price was dumbfounded. The car had been locked, and there was no way anybody could have entered, but there he was — a masked man standing by the stove with a revolver in his hand.

The man quickly made it clear just exactly what he wanted: Price was to turn over the keys to the safe or he would be a dead man.

Most messengers would have complied with the intruder's demands, but not Price. Instead of reaching for his keys, Price made a dash for the other end of the car. The move was unexpected, and the bandit hesitated for a second, but when he figured the messenger might be going for a gun, he fired.

The bullet hit Price in the fleshy part of his left arm, just below the elbow. The bandit, seeing he had not hurt the messenger seriously, fired again. This time the bullet struck Price in the left cheek, tearing away a portion near his lip. But now it was Price's turn. As the bandit was trying to get off a third shot, Price grabbed his revolver and fired. The bullet hit the bandit just above the right eye, killing him instantly. Price cautiously approached the body and turned it over. Despite the shattered face, he recognized the man as Hiram Binkley, formerly a freight conductor on the Pittsburgh, Ft. Wayne & Chicago line who had recently been fired for stealing property from wrecked cars.

A later inspection of the express car revealed that Binkley had cut a hole in the end of the car, just large enough to reach in and slip the door bolt open. Price, who had been busy studying his waybills, had not heard the man enter.

Upon further investigation, evidence revealed that Binkley may have had two companions who had boarded as passengers, and who were supposed to come forward and help him sort through the express parcels once he had subdued the messenger. (Sources: *New York Times*, 11 May 1875; *Pittsburgh Telegraph*, 7 May 1875.)

PRYOR CREEK, OKLAHOMA. It was not uncommon for an express company to play down the amount of the loss in a train robbery. No company wanted to worry customers and potential customers by reporting huge losses, so the amount was frequently reduced in releases to the newspapers. This created a problem for the messengers who were held up. The messengers usually knew approximately how much the robbers got, but they also knew their employers did not want them to release this information. Some went along with their employers' wishes; others avoided interviews with reporters or just clammed up, while a few felt that regardless of the consequences, they could not lie and just told the truth.

A robbery of an express car on the Missouri, Kansas & Texas Railroad on November 24, 1889, at Pryor Creek, Oklahoma (then Indian Territory) was a good example of the finagling that went on in reporting losses.

The two masked men had concealed themselves in a clump of bushes beside the track. When the train stopped for water, one of the bandits climbed aboard the steps of the locomotive cab and covered the engineer and fireman while the other one uncoupled the Pacific Express Company car from the first passenger coach. The bandit in the cab then ordered the engineer to pull ahead about a mile and a half. While he was doing so, the bandit in the express car forced the messenger, Oscar Johnson, to open the safe.

When the messenger was later interviewed, he said that between $45,000 and $50,000 was taken. On this particular run, the express car usually carried a large amount, and this figure was well within the range of an expected loss. A short time later, however, the messenger changed his story. He said he had been mistaken, that he had managed to hide away all but around $1,000 of the amount being shipped. This $1,000, he said, was all the robbers got. Messenger Johnson was later seen in the company of Pacific Express officials, being hustled on a train bound for St. Louis.

Did the robbers get $45,000 or $1,000? Maybe neither. The following July, Thomas Turlington, a prisoner in jail at Bonneville, Missouri, confessed to the robbery, and said that he and his confederates actually obtained $15,000 at Pryor Creek. (Sources: *New York Times*, 26 November 1889, 11 July 1890.)   □

R

RAILROAD POLICE. After relying on the Pinkerton's National Detective Agency and a few other private detective firms during the early years of the train robbery era, the railroads began to beef up their security forces with their own police, or "cinder dicks" as they were often called. By the mid-1870s, several railroads had their own police force, and from then on the number began to grow steadily.

At first the departments were small and their investigative ability limited. Since the express cars, and later railway mail cars, were usually the targets in train robberies, the express companies and the railway mail service were expected to provide much of their own security and means of investigation. In most cases, the express companies and the government leased cars or sections of cars from the railroads, and although express messengers, railway mail clerks, railroad baggage clerks, as well as other members of the train crew usually worked in close cooperation, each was responsible for the property entrusted to his respective employer. Once an express car or mail car robbery occurred, however, it was common for the railroads to assist in tracking down the culprits.

On the eastern railroads, the railroad police were commonly called detectives, while in the West, the term *special agent* was popular, a better term for public relations and a carryover from stagecoach days.

As train robbery grew more popular, and the bandits more bold, railroad officials attempted to fill the ranks of their police departments with men who were tough and fearless enough to meet troublemakers on their own terms. This often resulted in a police force heavy on daring and light on tact and persistency.

Few railroad police were properly trained. According to H. S. Dewhurst, former secretary of the Protective Section of the Association of American Railroads, "it was the general custom simply to hand the newly appointed man a badge, a revolver, and a club, and send him out to work without further instructions as to the laws or how to enforce them, or even how to make an arrest." According to Dewhurst, "in some instances having no qualifications whatever other than, possibly, that of brawn . . . they were individuals hired on the spur of the moment to bring a rough and tumble situation under control. Whatever they learned they learned the hard way, if they survived long enough to do so." This practice, said Dewhurst, "caused this branch of railroad service to come into poor repute in communities and with railroad men generally." Railroad police were considered by many to be "fat and lazy," and were often the butt of jokes among local peace officers. A common saying was that a desk sergeant "would rather book the officer who brought in the box car thief than the thief himself."

Railroad police faced another problem: in many states they were seriously handicapped by lack of jurisdiction. Unless they could obtain appointments as deputy sheriffs or special peace officers, which was seldom, they had no authority to make arrests off railroad property. Cooperation with local law enforcement agencies was sometimes long in coming. The railroads argued that "a criminal is a criminal," and "just because he robs an express car today doesn't mean he won't rob a bank tomorrow." Some local authorities were won over and extended help to the cinder dicks, but others selfishly turned their backs, reasoning that as long as a bandit was successful robbing trains he would be less of a problem elsewhere.

The state legislatures, if they had wanted to, could have passed legislation giving railroad police the authority they needed. There was precedent for such action, and even a "model act" was available. Pennsylvania had passed such a law as early as 1865, but other states were hesitant to grant the railroad these powers, often because the feeling was that the railroads were already too powerful.

The railroad lobbyists kept trying, however, and Ohio passed the necessary legislation in 1867. Tennessee followed in 1870, Massachusetts in 1871, the District of Columbia in 1878, and Maryland in 1880. But in the West, where the authority was sorely needed, the idea was slow to catch on, and it was well into the 1890s before most states came around. By 1896, however, the individual railroad policemen themselves, with the support of most of the lines, had formed the Railway Association of Special Agents of the United States and Canada, which was supposed to lead to cooperation among the diverse railroad police departments and create something on the order of a functioning national railroad police network. The idea was sound, but the group was far from effective and actually accomplished little. A more or less official reason for the association's lack of success was "insufficient unity of practice and policy" among the various departments, but in simpler terms the organization suffered from the common malady of many such organizations: the members invariably took more from the group than they gave.

Despite the poor reputation of railroad police generally, there were exceptions: one was the small but effective department maintained by the Southern Pacific Railroad, headed by William "Will" Smith, a stubborn manhunter who was responsible for bringing many a train robber to justice. Another was a special

force used by the Union Pacific Railroad—the horse car posses—tough manhunters kept on standby readiness to be rushed to the scene of a robbery. There are some who say that the UP's possemen were largely responsible for the demise of Butch Cassidy's Wild Bunch, who eventually found it just too risky to rob express cars. (Sources: Dewhurst, *The Railroad Police*; Morn, *The Eye That Never Sleeps*; Patterson, *Train Robbery*.) *See also* **Horse Cars; Will Smith**.

THE RAILWAY MAIL SERVICE. It is generally agreed that the idea to "work" (sort) mail while it was being transported by rail came from an assistant postmaster named William A. Davis at St. Joseph, Missouri, in 1862. That year mail from the East began piling up at St. Joseph. Departing stagecoaches were either forced to wait for the mail to be sorted and placed in mailbags or leave without all of the mail. The problem lay in sorting. The mail arrived at St. Joseph by rail unsorted. Separate mailbags then had to be made up for the stage driver to throw off at Denver, Salt Lake City, Virginia City, and so on. After studying the situation, Davis devised a simple solution: he hired clerks to board the mail trains east of St. Joseph and sort the mail en route. By the time the mail arrived at St. Joseph, it was ready to be put on the stagecoaches.

The scheme was put into operation on the Hannibal & St. Joseph Railroad on July 7, 1862. A special baggage car was furnished by the railroad and altered to Davis's specifications. The car was lettered "U.S. MAIL—NO. 1." While the idea was new to the United States, similar systems were already in operation in Canada and Great Britain.

The idea caught the attention of other post office officials, especially George B. Armstrong, assistant postmaster at Chicago, who picked up on the scheme and was responsible for developing the plan nationwide.

The nation's first railway mail car. *Burlington Lines.*

Armstrong became so instrumental in the plan's adoption that he is generally credited as the founder of the Railway Mail Service. In fact, there is some evidence that he may have been involved in a similar experiment prior to Davis's. Davis never personally objected to being overshadowed, but in later years his heirs petitioned the Post Office Department to establish him as the initiator of the service.

The first full year of operation for the new Railway Mail Service was 1865. In the East, the service was launched on the New York & Dunkirk and Philadelphia & Pittsburgh lines. In the West, where the service was much more popular, the early lines to adopt it were the Chicago & Davenport, Chicago & Quincy, Chicago & St. Louis, Chicago & Centralia, Clinton & Boone, and the Chicago & Cairo.

In the beginning the postal cars were of flimsy wood construction, often rebuilt from coaches that the railroads had scrapped as too old. Gradually, as the value of the service was proved, the equipment was improved.

In 1875 the first Fast Mail service was established. Previous to that time there had been relatively fast service on short routes, but the value of speed over a long route was lost at connecting points. With the introduction of an exclusive New York-to-Chicago mail train over various independent lines, from twelve to twenty-four hours in transit time was saved. The initial trip, made with great fanfare, was the most publicized event in Railway Mail Service history and an important milestone in the progress of the Postal Service. The service lasted less than a year, however. In July 1876 it was withdrawn when Congress reduced all railroad mail pay by 10 percent, which made the service unprofitable. It was restored in 1881 and other Fast Mail routes followed, including the Pennsylvania's Limited Mail route from New York to Chicago and St. Louis, and the Burlington's Fast Mail route between Chicago and Omaha. Eventually, with the inclusion of the Union Pacific, the system became transcontinental.

Although railway mail cars were always subject to being robbed, the postal cars were not the favorite target of train robbers. Many bandits avoided robbing the mail because it was thought that the potential take was not worth the risk of angering the United States government. Robbing the mail was, of course, a federal offense, and the consequences were severe. Train rob-

Interior of the first railway mail car. *Burlington Lines.*

ber Al Jennings liked to tell how he scrupulously avoided taking anything from the mail sacks during a robbery, yet, ironically, he was eventually convicted of that very crime, because, he later claimed, a registered letter had turned up missing following one of his express car holdups.

Other train robbers shared his view. During an express car robbery in Texas in 1887, the express messenger inadvertently handed one of the robbers a sack of mail. The outlaw handed it back, telling the messenger that he wanted no part of Uncle Sam's money.

Occasionally, a railway mail clerk would actually prevent the loss of registered letters by reminding the robbers that they were asking for trouble from the federal government. During a robbery on the St. Louis, Arkansas & Texas Railroad in 1887, a clerk informed a gang of robbers that if they got caught stealing the United States mail, "it could go hard on them." One of the outlaws was said to have replied: "That is so," and the gang rode off.

To further discourage robbery of the mails, the Post Office Department made a point of playing down the amount of cash that was routinely sent by mail. In 1881 a series of in-transit mail thefts began on eastbound Kansas Pacific trains. The first loss was discovered on December 22, 1881, but the Post Office Department kept it quiet. When a second loss occurred on March 8, 1882, and a third on March 22, the newspapers got hold of the story. The fact that the thefts were repeated concerned postal officials deeply. It suggested that the thieves were gleaning enough cash from the letters to risk coming back for more. That the public was aware

Railway mail clerks at work. *Railway Mail Service.*

of the thefts made the situation much worse; if the crimes were being engineered from the outside, and word spread on how they were being accomplished, there could be a rash of such losses.

A break came on April 14. A Denver postal inspector announced that he had found the thief, a Railway Mail Service clerk, and that it appeared that he had been operating alone. But soon further digging by newspaper reporters revealed that the losses had been much more widespread than the postal officials had let on, that postal cars on two other railroad lines, the Missouri Pacific and the Santa Fe, had reported missing registered mail. Could this one clerk have been responsible for all the losses?

Faced now with having to report the whole story, postal officials released a statement to the newspapers in which they admitted that there had been more than "100 thefts" (they failed to say whether this meant the loss of 100 registered letters or there were 100 separate incidents of thievery), but that *very little cash*, no more than $600, had been taken. The statement went on to point out that although there were many bank drafts stolen from letters, they were practically worthless to a thief, since he could not cash them without assuming the identity of the payee, which in most cases would be extremely difficult.

Notwithstanding the usual small take in mail robberies, some bandits routinely ransacked the registered mail pouches, which on short runs were often carried in a separate section of the express car. And in later years, when most trains carried a postal car as well as an express car, bandits frequently cut both cars away from the remainder of the train during a holdup. By 1895 enough mail cars were being attacked that postal authorities began building cars without front platforms, the so-called blind baggage area that robbers favored in boarding a train.

Railway mail robberies increased slightly during the 1890s and into the twentieth century. The days of the large gold and silver shipments by express were over, so in comparison, the postal cars offered greater rewards to bandits. But the big surge in mail robberies came after World War I. Serious domestic crimes usually decline during wartime, and train robbery was no exception. Soon after the war ended, however, rash of mail robberies broke out. This new epidemic was so severe that in 1920 the Postmaster General ordered all railway mail clerks to carry weapons. Many clerks had been voluntarily carrying small side arms for some time, but it was thought the publicity that all clerks were now officially armed might discourage bandits. It did not, however; in fact, assaults on railway mail cars actually increased.

There was much speculation on why mail cars had become so popular among train robbers. Some thought it was a breakdown in respect for federal laws. A midwestern editor wrote: "Ten years ago a criminal hesitated to violate a Federal statute, while he had little compunction about trespassing on State laws. He believed, and had good grounds to believe, that he could not with impunity risk offending the Government. Today, he knows that there is less likelihood of swift punishment for violation of Federal laws, and in his desperation he is willing to 'take a chance' against the Federal authorities as well as those of the States." Another reason suggested was that the railway mail clerks hired during the war were less hardy than their predecessors, and the robbers found that assaulting the mail cars was less risky.

A more likely reason was the popularity of registered mail. By the 1920s the Railway Mail Service was carrying treasures in the registered mail sacks that made train robbers' mouths water: transfers of currency between banks, payroll shipments, gold and silver to and from the United States subtreasuries, negotiable bonds, jeweler's shipments of precious stones. Almost anything of value could be found in the registered mail. The days when a robber had to sort through a half dozen sacks of mail to find loot worth the taking were over. Also, a little prying or bribing could loosen tongues about

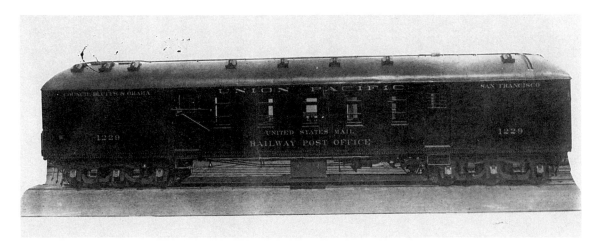

Railway mail car in use on the Union Pacific just prior to World War I. *Union Pacific Railroad Museum Collection.*

important shipments. Furthermore, railway mail schedules were well known and seldom varied.

In 1921 the problem was brought up by Postmaster General Will H. Hays during a meeting of President Warren G. Harding's cabinet. The issue was sent around the table until it reached Secretary of War John W. Weeks and Secretary of the Navy Edwin Denby. Their answer: call out the marines. In November of the same year, orders were issued for 1,000 marines to be dispatched to the use of the Post Office Department as it saw fit. And the order was not a token effort; with it came the word: "When our men go on guard over the mail, that mail must be delivered or there must be a Marine dead at the post of duty." Although a marine could not be standing guard on every run on every line, robbiong of the railway mail cars clearly became less popular.

Despite the marines, one of the most brutal train robberies in history occurred in 1923 during an attempted holdup of a mail car. On October 11 of that year three brothers, the DeAutremonts, stopped a Southern Pacific passenger train near Siskiyou Station, Oregon. After using too much dynamite to blow open the mail car doors, which resulted in the death of the clerk, the frustrated bandits methodically killed both the fireman and engineer to prevent them from identifying them. (*See* **Siskiyou Station, Oregon.**)

The greatest train robbery in history involved a holdup of a mail car at Rondout, Illinois, on June 13, 1924. The haul exceeded $2 million and the victim was the Chicago & Minneapolis Railroad. The bandits hid in the engine cab, held up the locomotive crew, and forced them to stop the train. Accomplices then shot out the windows of the mail car, drove out the clerks with gas bombs, and sped away with sixty-four sacks of registered mail. It looked like a perfect crime until an anonymous tip led to the disclosure that a postal inspector, one of the best investigators in the division, was in on the affair. (*See* **Rondout, Illinois.**)

While the Railway Mail Service was a vital means of delivering mail to the military during wartime, the need for trains to carry mail during peacetime diminished as time went by. Improvements in other means of transportation, better highways, and faster trucks and buses slowly eroded train service, and eventually the airlines began to get mail contracts. Also, by the 1930s towns were growing where there were no railroads.

The beginning of the end came for the Railway Mail

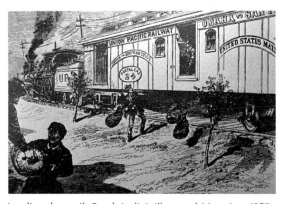

Loading the mail. *Frank Leslie's Illustrated Magazine, 1877.*

Service in 1963, when the Post Office Department introduced large mail-handling centers where mail could be sorted in stationary mechanized units, then hauled by truck to surrounding towns for delivery. Sorting mail in-transit on trains was no longer necessary. Thanks to stubborn traditionalists in the postal bureaucracy, however, the service hung on for another eight years. Then, on April 30, 1971, clerks distributed mail over the rails for the last time – with one exception – the Railway Post Office between Washington, D.C., and New York City, which was an ironical choice, because this was the most populated area in the nation, where the new sectionalized mail distribution centers were supposed to be the most efficient. (Sources: Clifton, *Murder by Mail and Other Postal Investigations*; Long, *Mail by Rail: The Story of the Postal Transportation Services*.) *See also* **The Gold Train; John Streich**.

RAILWAY TORPEDO SIGNALS. Railroaders called them "torpedoes" – small detonators that could be fastened to a rail and would explode with a loud bang and flash by the wheels of a passing locomotive. Their purpose was to alert the engine crew to danger ahead on the track: a stalled or wrecked train, a washout, an occupied crossover, a landslide, or an open drawbridge.

Torpedoes were used both day and night, usually when visual signals such as flags and lanterns were ineffective, as in a thick snowstorm or fog. Also, they were used as backup signals – when stopping a train in a hurry was imperative.

The railway torpedo was invented by an Englishman, Edward A. Cowper, around 1837. British railroads, frequently enveloped in fog and mist, were in dire need of an effective sound signal that could be activated by a moving train. Several devices had been tried, usually some kind of trackside bell or whistle, but most of these proved expensive, inflexible, or unreliable. The gunpowder-charged Cowper torpedo, which the inventor first called a "detonating bell," was cheap, portable, and when fully perfected, hardly ever failed.

It is not certain when the torpedo was first used in the United States, probably sometime in the late 1840s or early 1850s. An 1853 report on railway safety to the New York Legislature commented on the utility of torpedoes then being used by the Syracuse & Utica Railroad. Also, that year the device began to appear in advertisements in the *American Railroad Journal*.

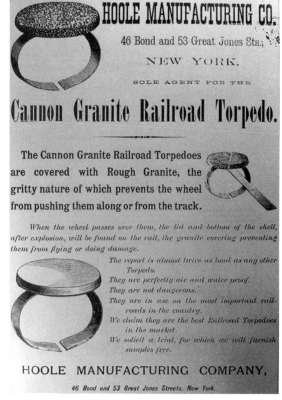

Railway torpedo. *Author's Collection*.

The torpedo advertised in the *Journal* was Wilkinson's Explosive Railway Signal, a small, circular tinplate container about two inches in diameter and one-half inch thick. Inside were several caps and ordinary gunpowder. To make it watertight, the container was covered with several coats of heavy varnish. Attached to the container were "ear" straps, made of either lead or tin, which could be bent around and fixed to a rail.

By the beginning of the train robbery era, there must have been millions of torpedoes in existence in the United States. In an article that appeared in *Scientific American* on August 6, 1870, it was noted that 35,000 of the devices were being used yearly by just one railroad, the Philadelphia & Reading. However, it is unlikely that 35,000 torpedoes were detonated on the P&R's rails every year. Undoubtedly, thousands of railway torpedoes, like railway flares of later years, were taken home by railroad employees or stolen out of tool shanties. Like dynamite caps and firecrackers, they were

Locomotive crew reacting to railway torpedo. *Frank Leslie's Illustrated Magazine.*

responsible for many a blinded eye or lost finger among careless youth of the day.

It did not take train robbers long to realize the value of torpedoes in stopping a locomotive. An engine crew might become suspicious of the looks of a bogus flagman or lantern-bearer on the track ahead, but a torpedo was a torpedo, and its sound and flash were the same, regardless of its legitimacy. And a locomotive engineer could not ignore its message.

A locomotive could always be halted if a robber's signal looked genuine. Statistics have shown that an unusually large number of train robbers were former railroad employees, and many undoubtedly were familiar with how torpedo signals were supposed to be used by trackmen, as well as how locomotive engineers were supposed to respond to them. In 1904 the following "use and placement" of torpedoes appeared in Walter M. Camp's *Tracks,* a popular railroad publication:

> The explosion of one torpedo is a signal to stop immediately; the explosion of two torpedoes is a signal to reduce speed immediately and look out for something ahead. When used by itself to stop, [the] torpedo signal is placed at the same distance from the danger point as the stop flag or stop lantern signal would be. The torpedo signal of caution (two Torpedoes) is sometimes used by trackmen and placed ¼ or ⅛ mile behind the stop signal, to call the attention of the trainmen before the stop signal is reached. . . .
>
> Torpedoes should be used in addition to flags or lights whenever, by reason of fog, storm or other unfavorable condition, there is a doubt whether the flag or light may be seen, or whenever a stop signal is left without an attendant. But some roads require the use of the torpedo signal in all cases as an extra precaution taken under the supposition that no one on the approaching train might be looking ahead at the critical time. It should be placed at such a distance behind the flag or lantern, that when

exploded, the flag or lantern may be seen from the engine or head end of the train, but not closer than 150 ft. When two torpedoes are used they should be placed 60 ft. apart. Torpedoes for signals should be placed on the engineer's side, as the train approaches, but on third-rail track they should be placed on that rail which is used by trains of either gage.

Despite advances in automatic signaling, centralized traffic control, and direct radio communication between train crews and dispatchers, railway torpedo signals never became obsolete. They are still in use today. (Source: White, "Safety with a Bang: The Railway Torpedo.")

RED ROCK, OKLAHOMA. The robbery of a Wells Fargo express car on a Santa Fe passenger train at Red Rock on June 1, 1892, has been attributed to the Dalton gang. In fact, it could easily have been the Dalton's last holdup, had the outlaws not spotted a trap.

Red Rock is in Noble County, just west of Sooner Lake, about midway between Ponca City and Stillwater. The Daltons had planned to rob the 9:00 P.M. southbound express that night, but word leaked out, and the train was packed with Santa Fe and Wells, Fargo detectives. As the train pulled into the station, one of the gang noticed that the passenger coach immediately behind the express car was dark, which was unusual for that early in the evening. Suspecting an ambush, the outlaws let the train leave without molesting it. They were about to ride away when the heard the whistle of a second train; it was the second section of the same train—the first section had been a dummy. The coaches on this train were lighted, and everything looked normal.

The gang struck just as the train started to pull out. Two of the gang climbed aboard the engine cab and ordered the engineer, Carl Mack, to pull down the track a short distance to a line of stock pens and then stop. He and the fireman, Frank Rogers, were then forced to walk back to the express car. In the meantime, five more outlaws appeared from the shadows.

When the train stopped the second time, E. C. Whittlesey, the Wells, Fargo messenger, and J. A. Riehl, an extra guard, were pretty sure they were under attack. They blew out all the lanterns in the car and prepared to make a stand.

When Whittlesey announced that he would not open the car door, the robbers began firing through the windows. Whittlesey and Riehl, well protected behind crates and packages, returned their fire. The bandits circled the car many times, trying to find openings through which to shoot. They even crawled under the car and tried to shoot through cracks in the flooring.

While the battle raged, one of the outlaws took an axe to the door, and before long, he had chopped an opening two feet wide. The bandit then grabbed the fireman and ordered him to climb through. Mack, the engineer, shouted to the messenger to tell him what was happening and pleaded with him to cease firing. Reluctantly, he complied. Once inside, the robbers used a sledgehammer and chisel to open the two safes.

After cleaning out both safes, the outlaws mounted up and rode off toward the southwest. A posse was rushed to the scene by special train. Another posse, which had been trailing the gang for weeks, arrived the following day.

Apparently there were no injuries in the express car shootout; however, a later report said that during the attack, one of the bandits returned to the depot at Red Rock and shot the telegraph operator when he found him trying to send word of the holdup.

An early report went out over the wires that the gang got $50,000 in loot, which would have been a record for the Dalton bunch. This figure was later reduced to $5,000 and eventually to less than $2,000. Years-afterward, Emmett Dalton claimed they actually picked up $11,000 that night, which may have been correct, since most express companies were hesitant about releasing accurate loss figures in robberies. Then again, Emmett Dalton, who enjoyed telling and retelling tales of his bandit years, was known to be a little careless with details. (Sources: Block, *Great Train Robberies of the West*; Preece, *The Dalton Gang*; *New York Times*, 3 June 1892.)

REED, NATHANIEL "TEXAS JACK." Texas Jack Reed probably didn't rob as many trains as he took credit for, but he robbed some, and it was while he was collecting money and valuables from the passengers of a day coach at Blackstone Switch in Indian Territory in 1894 that he received two crippling bullets in the hips that caused him to give up his outlaw career and turn to preaching for a living. (*See* **Blackstone Switch [Oklahoma]**.)

Reed was born in Madison County, Arkansas, in 1862, and lived there until 1883, when he headed west for adventure. He was a small man with "crafty eyes," and during most of his life he wore his hair long like an Indian scout. His first steady job was for a rancher named Terry in Oklahoma, where he claimed his foreman, whose name was Coffey, introduced him to train robbery.

He said he left Coffey and rode with several other outlaw gangs, but the only proof we have of this is his own account, which must be questioned. For example, he claimed that he was with the Daltons during their ill-fated raid at Coffeyville (he said he held their horses), and with Bill Doolin and his gang when they had their big shootout with federal officers at Ingalls. Serious outlaw historians deny this. Who Reed really rode with and in what robberies he participated probably will never be known. He was at the Blackstone Switch holdup, however, and took two bullets from the guns of U.S. Deputy Marshal Bud Ledbetter. He escaped and hid out while his wounds healed, but his close brush with death made him reconsider his choice of livelihood. "During the three months I hid out, wounded and suffering, I had plenty of time to think of the past and wonder what the future held for me," he later said in his memoirs, which he had published in pamphlet form and peddled on street corners for twenty-five cents a copy. In the spring of 1895 he wrote to Judge Isaac Parker at Fort Smith and arranged to surrender. He was eventually tried for the Blackstone Switch holdup and served five years.

After his release from prison, Texas Jack turned to religion and became an evangelist. And for a while, he traveled with a series of wild west shows as "Texas Jack, Train Robber." When age finally caught up with him, he settled in Tulsa, Oklahoma, occasionally preaching on street corners and peddling the latest edition of his life story, *The Life of Texas Jack: Eight Years a Criminal—41 Years Trusting in God*. He lived until 1950, when he died peacefully in bed at age eighty-seven. (Source: Shirley, "The Bungled Job at Blackstone Switch.")

REED'S CROSSING, CALIFORNIA. A robbery on the Southern Pacific's northbound *Oregon Express* on March 30, 1895, at Reed's Crossing near Wheatland Station, California, was the only known train holdup to be accomplished by bandits on bicycles.

As the train was pulling away from the depot at Wheatland Station, a quiet farm community in Yuba County about seventeen miles south of Marysville, two dark-clad men climbed onto the tender. Within minutes they donned masks, slipped down to the locomotive cab, and thrust guns into the ribs of the engineer and fireman. Their orders were "stop at the next crossing."

A trip back to the express car proved unprofitable. The Wells, Fargo through safe, which contained most of the money and valuables, was secured with a lock that could be opened only be selected station agents along the route. Rather than leave empty-handed, the two intruders motioned the crew to head for the passenger coaches.

The robbers entered the first coach, with the engineer and fireman preceding them. The trainmen were given a sack, and the passengers were ordered to drop in their cash and jewelry. One by one, they nervously complied.

Unseen by the robbers, however, the porter slipped out the rear door. He ran back two coaches where Sheriff John T. Bogard had just curled up to catch a few minutes of sleep. Without hesitating, Bogard strapped on his revolver and headed forward.

When Bogard reached the rear door of the first coach, he could plainly see one of the outlaws standing in the aisle. He did not waste time issuing a warning. He entered the coach, raised his revolver, and fired. The bandit was killed instantly. In his haste, however, Sheriff Bogard had passed the other robber, thinking he was merely a passenger. Before he could turn, the robber shot him in the back. As Bogard lay dying in the aisle, the outlaw snatched up the sack of loot and ran out the door.

Within hours posses were scouring the area for the killer. Near the crossing the officers found a bicycle. Nearby were the tracks of a second bicycle, leading down the road toward a wilderness area of thick underbrush known as Hagen Tract. There they found the second bicycle, but not the rider. An attempt was made to track him, but it was useless.

Within two weeks railroad and express company detectives identified the dead man and his companion. The slain man was Samuel Browning, an ex-convict. The missing man was believed to be Henry Williams, who also went by the name Jack Brady. Williams was

Samuel Browning.
Pinkertons.

also an ex-con, who three years earlier had served a one-year sentence at San Quentin for grand larceny. The men had been living in rooming houses in San Francisco and were believed to have been involved in several robberies and possibly two shootings in that city.

Witnesses were found who had seen the men riding around the city on bicycles. Also, two men matching their description were seen riding bicycles around Marysville several days before the robbery.

Three months went by with no trace of Williams. Then, on June 19, he was spotted near Redding. Two Shasta County deputies, George Martin and Mart Bowers, tried to arrest him. Both Williams and Martin were carrying shotguns. In an exchange of gunfire, Bowers was wounded in the hand and Williams received several pellets in the face and side. Williams's horse also was hit, but the outlaw escaped on foot.

An all-out manhunt was organized, but despite his wounds, Williams managed to disappear once again. Another three weeks passed without a sign of him. Then, on July 8, a lone bandit roughly matching the outlaw's description stopped and robbed the Redding-to-Alturas stage. By now Williams, called Brady in the

Henry Williams.
California State Archives.

newspapers, had become a celebrity, and reporters were turning in day-by-day reports on the progress of law enforcement officers in the area, most of whom stated that they expected the outlaw to be captured at any time.

The manhunt continued until July 26. On that day two lawmen found Williams hiding under a bridge near Sacramento. He surrendered without a fight.

Williams was brought to trial in August 1895 for the death of Sheriff Bogard. A jury convicted him of first degree murder, but they could not agree on the penalty. He was finally sentenced to life in prison. During the trial it was revealed that his true name was Henry Ury, that he came from Illinois, and that he had lived for a while in Virginia. He entered Folsom Prison in November 1895 where he was confined until paroled in 1913. He died on May 19, 1940. (Source: Edwards, "Bullets and Bicycles.")

REESE SIDING, OHIO. Shortly after midnight on July 25, 1895, northern Ohio was rocked by a train robbery, western style. The victim was the Lake Shore & Michigan Southern Railroad's westbound *New York & Chicago Express*, and the site was a lonely stretch of track in Fulton County known as Reese Siding, located between the stations of Archbold and Stryker, about fifty miles west of Toledo.

The robbers halted the train by placing obstructions on the track and then signaling with a red lantern. The engineer, required to obey such a signal by railroad rules, had no choice but to bring the train to a stop. The attackers quickly took command of the locomotive and then headed for the United States Express Company car.

The messenger, whose name was Nettleton, gave this account:

> I was dozing in my chair near the safe about 12 o'clock last night, and the train was making about forty miles an hour. I knew that there would not be another stop for half an hour, so I was surprised and startled when the brakes began to jar on the wheels. The train came to a stop, and I no sooner came to that conclusion than there was a shock and report under the forward part of my car. The glass in the window next to my corner was shattered into a thousand pieces.
>
> I grabbed my shotgun and stood at the door, which was unlocked and had been partly open. In the darkness I saw two men with guns pointed at me. I dodged back into the car, and raising my gun, let them have it, as I

thought, full in the face. Apparently, I did not hit them, and after that they would not stand any monkeying.

> "If you put any value on your life, you will put down that gun and let us in," one of the men said. Then I gave up, and they came in and went to work. They got into the way safe easily enough, but after exploding six charges of dynamite against the other one, they had to give it up. Three times they left me in the car while they exploded the dynamite, and three times they took me out. They kept me "covered" all the time with their guns. Two were working in the car, and two staid [*sic*] on guard outside. The men had handkerchiefs tied over their faces, and I could not recognize them. I was not frightened until it was all over.

The conductor, whose name was Darling, turned in the following report:

> I was sitting in the first-class coach when the train was stopped . . . As soon as we came to a stop I heard firing up at the forward end of the train and guessed the trouble. After sending a brakeman to the rear of the train with a lantern to protect us from anything which might be coming from behind, I went forward into the baggage car and watched what went on from there. Once I stuck my head out, but a bullet went whizzing by and I didn't try it again.
>
> There appeared to be four men in the attacking party, but it was terribly dark and we could not see very distinctly. One of the men was a short, heavy-set fellow, with a sandy beard and mustache, about forty years old. They got into the express car and opened the [way] safe, but could not get into the big safe. They made the engineer climb down from his cab, and one of the men kept him standing beside the engine in the ditch. The fireman, H. Boardman, was under guard next to the express car. After about forty minutes the robbers disappeared in the darkness. The amount taken was, I believe, about $8,000.
>
> The passengers were in a panic, but they were not interfered with. The explosions woke them, and the women began screaming and crying, while the men poked their heads out of their berths, asking what was the trouble, and getting their clothes on with all possible haste. Watches and money were tucked under mattresses and into corners, and all prepared themselves for a raid.

On examining the express car, company officials found all of the windows smashed and a board blown off the outside wall next to the through safe. The inside wall next to the safe was nothing but kindling. The small safe had been opened without much difficulty; it was nothing more than an iron-bound chest about the size of a steamer trunk. The through safe showed a "circular concave dent, about six inches in diameter," where the dial had been. The dial itself had been blown off, and fragments of it lay about the car.

Contrary to the conductor's statement, the general superintendent of the United States Express Company played down the loss, claiming that it probably amounted to no more than $150. However, a rumor spread soon after the robbery that $40,000 in jewelry had been put on board at Cleveland, and that this was known to the robbers. (Source: *New York Times*, 25 July 1895.)

THE RENO GANG. The Reno gang earned its place in outlaw history by committing what is generally considered the first peacetime train robbery in the United States. The date was October 6, 1866, and the victim was an Ohio & Mississippi passenger train out of East St. Louis, Illinois, bound for Cincinnati, Ohio. Around 6:30 in the evening, just outside Seymour, Indiana, two masked men slipped into the Adams express car and forced the messenger to turn over the key to his safes. They emptied the local safe and after pulling the bell rope to slow the train, pushed the through safe out the door to a confederate waiting in the woods. Then they jumped off the train themselves.

John Reno and fellow gang member Frank Sparks. Photo was taken in dimly lighted Seymour saloon and later touched up at Pinkerton headquarters. *Indiana State Library.*

The little town of Seymour quickly buzzed with the account of the robbery. To most, there was little doubt as to who was responsible. For several years, it was general knowledge that a local family, the Renos, had a hand in most of the serious crimes committed in the area.

The Reno family had suffered from a bad reputation dating back to the early 1860s when the clan's father, Wilkinson Reno, was accused of burning out the residents of a nearby village, Rockford, in order to buy their land. The oldest son, Frank Reno, had been arrested for robbing a post office, and the next oldest, John, was the prime suspect in the murder of a fellow gang member. None of these cases had ever been brought to trial, however, and by the fall of 1866 John and Frank, with younger brothers, William and Simeon, had accumulated a sizable band of thieves and cutthroats.

There was more than just speculation to connect the Renos with the Adams express car robbery. The Adams Express Company retained the Pinkerton National Detective Agency to ionvestigate the case, and Allan Pinkerton himself arrived on the scene to gather facts. He soon found witnesses who had seen John and Simeon Reno boarding the train at Seymour just minutes before the holdup. Also, Pinkerton discovered that footprints left at the site where the through safe was dumped off the train matched those made by boots worn by the two brothers and a companion, Frank Sparks.

Despite the evidence gathered by Pinkerton, no charges were brought against the Renos. As in the past, the gang seemed to have the local authorities under their thumbs. However, Pinkerton and his agents persisted in their fact gathering, and possibly this began to worry the Renos. One day in the summer of 1867 the whole bunch packed up and headed west. In November of that year, John Reno and gang member Volney Elliott broke into the office of the Daviess County Treasurer at Gallatin, Missouri, and rummaged two safes for around $22,000. After escaping, they caught a train for Chicago. When Allan Pinkerton learned of the crime and heard that John Reno had been positively identified at the scene, he wired the Daviess County sheriff to come to southern Indiana with a warrant for the outlaw's arrest. As expected, Reno returned to his homeground, and the Pinkertons, after luring the outlaw to the Seymour train station, whisked him aboard an outbound express, had him placed under arrest by

Frank Reno.
Indiana State Library.

the Daviess County sheriff, and in two days he was back in Missouri awaiting trial.

Thanks to further persistent detective work by the Pinkerton agency, Frank Reno and three of the gang members were later picked up in Iowa, but they escaped by punching their way through a crumbling brick wall of an ancient jail. They immediately returned to Indiana where they would commit their second train robbery. On the night of May 22, 1868, at Marshfield, Indiana, a tiny water stop seventeen miles south of Seymour, the gang struck another Adams express car. They viciously beat the Adams messenger and threw him off the train. (*See* **Marshfield, Indiana**.)

The gang's next holdup attempt was a disaster. They tried to bribe a locomotive engineer who informed the Pinkertons of their plan. On July 10, 1868, just outside the little town of Brownstown, Indiana, a few miles southwest of Seymour, a railroad car filled with detectives was waiting. As the gang approached, they were met with a barrage of gunfire. Battered and bleeding, they fled into a nearby woods. Three were later captured; none of them were Renos, but several were key members of the gang. (*See* **Brownstown, Indiana**.)

When news of the ambush reached Seymour, the town was jubilant; for the first time the arrogant Reno gang had been bested; however, there were many citizens who felt the outlaws still had too much influence on local authorities, and that they probably would never be punished. The feeling was that if justice was to be done, it would have to come swiftly, without waiting for the judicial process. In other words, the citizens themselves would have to take charge. While being returned to Brownstown for arraignment, the three captured gang members were dragged past the train

by a masked mob and hanged from a beech tree beside the track. Four nights later, three more gang members were returned to Seymour following their capture in Illinois; they fell victim to the same mob.

On July 27 the Pinkertons announced that William and Simeon Reno had been captured in Indianapolis. For safekeeping, they had been secretly hustled off to New Albany, Indiana, to the recently reinforced Floyd County jail, considered to be one of the sturdiest in the Midwest. Later the same month, word came that Frank Reno had been spotted in Windsor, Ontario.

Windsor had become a hangout for U.S. outlaws, and the Reno gang's fame had given Frank Reno a prominent place in the local criminal pecking order. But Pinkerton operatives had uncovered the outlaw's hiding place, and a week later Frank and fellow gang member Charlie Anderson were arrested and put behind bars in Canada. Under Canadian law, however, the two fugitives could not be returned to the United States without extradition, and these proceedings bogged down in international red tape. In the meantime, Frank Reno put the word out that he wanted his nemesis, Allan Pinkerton, killed. Within days, two attempts were made on the detective's life, both unsuccessful, and in both cases the would-be assassins were arrested.

Back in Indiana, when it appeared that Frank Reno's and Charlie Anderson's extradition would be delayed, a trial date was set for William and Simeon Reno. This spurred the lynch-minded Seymour citizens into action again. The night before the trial was to begin, a mob stormed the jail in Lexington, Indiana, where the case was to be tried. The Floyd County authorities had been tipped off, however, and had kept the prisoners in New Albany. The trial was postponed.

Meanwhile, the extradition proceedings involving Frank Reno and Charlie Anderson took an interesting twist. The outlaws' attorneys had made a strong argument that under the law, the new U.S. crime of train robbery was not an extraditable offense. But then word came that Canada itself had an actionable criminal charge against Frank Reno. Frank, through an intermediary, had offered the son of the local magistrate a bribe to influence his father in his decision as to whether extradition should be granted. Facing this new charge, and apparently realizing that he might have to spend considerable time in one of Canada's formidable prisons, Frank probably concluded that his chances for escape were much better back in Indiana. To everyone's surprise, especially his frustrated lawyers, Frank confessed his role in the Marshfield, Indiana, train robbery. Charlie Anderson also waived extradition, and the two fugitives were returned to Indiana.

The problem now was to keep the remaining gang members alive until they could stand trial. On October 29, 1868, Frank Reno and Charlie Anderson were turned over to Floyd County Sheriff Thomas J. Fullenlove at New Albany, Indiana, where William and Simeon Reno were still being held. Sheriff Fullenlove assured one and all that the prisoners would be safe in his facility, an impressive two-story brick structure with steel cells accessible only through a single, securely locked, heavy iron door. Allen Pinkerton was not convinced, however, and suggested the gang would be safer if kept in the jail at Indianapolis. But the sheriff was adamant, and issued a public warning that if anyone attempted to take his prisoners, they would "meet a hot reception."

The lawyers for the outlaws prepared their cases and the month of November passed without incident. By the second week of December, Sheriff Fullenlove and his deputies began to relax a little. They still guarded the prisoners day and night, but they no longer jumped at every strange sound, and visions of masked lynchmen no longer danced in the shadows. And now and then, they even forgot to lock the heavy iron door to the outer jail office. Such was the case on the night of December 11.

Shortly after midnight, eighty somber men filed out of two special passenger coaches just short of New Albany's deserted Pearl Street station. Silently, as they worked their way toward the jail, they pulled masks up over their faces. Each man carried a revolver and a large club. Five men carried brand new hemp ropes, each pre-fitted with a hangman's noose.

Floyd County Deputy Luther Whitten was warming himself by the fire in the jail office. He managed a single muffled shout before he was deposited unconscious in the corner. Sheriff Fullenlove was asleep in an adjacent room. Awakened by the noise, he dashed out into the hall and down the basement steps, hoping to reach the outside stairwell from which he could escape and summon help. He was met by men in masks. A bullet shattered his arm, and a pistol butt dropped him to the floor.

Warning to southern Indiana train robbers, December 21, 1868. *Author's Collection.*

In twenty minutes it was all over. The intruders found keys to the individual cell doors in the sheriff's bedroom. Four of the five ropes were thrown over rafters, and the outlaws' necks were placed in the nooses. The fifth noose was left dangling, as a warning to anyone who might consider following the Reno gang's path. (Sources: Boley, *The Masked Halters*; Patterson, "The Reno Gang"; Reno, *The Life of John Reno*; Volland, "The Reno Gang of Seymour.") See also **Seymour, Indiana**.

RICHLAND, MISSOURI. Although seldom mentioned in outlaw histories, what may have been one of Missouri's biggest train robberies occurred on the St. Louis & San Francisco line near Richland on April 1, 1896. Richland is in the southern center of the state, on the western edge of Pulaski County, about twenty miles east of Lebanon.

As often happened, the express company never reported the exact amount of the loss; unofficial estimates ranged between $10,000 and $100,000. It is known that in their haste, the robbers dropped one package containing $1,700.

The holdup occurred at 3:00 A.M. In traditional fashion, the train was stopped by a red lantern being waved on the track, the universal signal to an engineer to halt. As the train came to a stop, a warning bullet whizzed past the engineer's head and lodged in the woodwork of the cab. In an instant, a masked man sprinted to the cab steps and pointed a rifle at the engineer and fireman. Two more bandits stood beside the track in the shadows.

The engineer and fireman were forced to walk back to the express car and the engineer was ordered to call to the express company messenger to open up his car. At first he refused, but he changed his mind after the bandits fired several volleys at the car.

The messenger informed the bandits that he could not open the express company safe, but they had brought dynamite. They easily blew the door off the box and helped themselves to the contents. Then they uncoupled the engine and tender from the rest of the train and ordered the engineer to start up. After a mile they told him to stop. They had apparently staked their horses nearby, because several minutes later the engineer could hear them riding off.

Railroad and express company officials had no clues as to the identity of the robbers. The best description that could be obtained was that one of the robbers was a youth of not more than seventeen years of age. (Source: *New York Times*, 2 April 1896.)

RINCON, NEW MEXICO. When bandits learned of an extremely large shipment of gold, silver, or currency, they frequently would stop at nothing to get to it, including wrecking an entire train.

During the second week of April 1882, word spread that the express car on an eastbound Santa Fe train would be carrying a shipment of $200,000 in silver from nearby mines, destined for a bank in New York City. The bandits struck on the sixteenth, a Sunday night, on a desolate stretch of track in Dona Ana County near the town of Rincon. Five heavily armed bandits

placed an obstruction on the track and derailed the engine, tender, and express and baggage cars, killing the engineer and fireman, and seriously injuring the Wells, Fargo messenger.

But in the wreckage, the bandits mistook the baggage car for the express car and wasted valuable time getting in, only to find no silver. By then, the remainder of the train crew and passengers got organized and came forward to assist. The bandits, far outnumbered, fled.

The authorities failed to pick up the trail of the outlaws, whom they believed to be part of a gang that had been raiding southern New Mexico and Arizona for several months. (Source: *New York Times*, 22 April 1882.)

RIO PUERCO, NEW MEXICO. In 1896 Rio Puerco (also called Rio Purco) was a tiny station on the Atlantic & Pacific line about thirty-four miles southwest of Albuquerque. Shortly after 7:00 P.M. on October 2 of that year, eastbound Train No. 2 developed a crank pin problem just west of Rio Puerco. After pulling to a stop and inspecting the problem, the engineer, Charles Ross, thought he could make it on to the next scheduled stop, but the conductor, Sam Heady, thought otherwise. Since the conductor's word was law, Ross got out the necessary tools and began work on the pin.

Ross solved the problem with a quick adjustment and in five minutes he was back in the cab and building up steam. But before he could get up to speed, two men swung aboard—and they both had guns. A brakeman standing on the station platform spotted the intruders and shouted at them. They answered him with several shots, one of which smashed his lantern and wounded him in the hand. Ross prudently applied the brakes.

On hearing the shots, the express messenger, L. J. Kohler, locked his door and doused his lights. Back in the first coach, U.S. Deputy Marshal Will Loomis also heard the shots. He reached for his shotgun and told the train's newsboy to go fetch his shells from his baggage at the far end of the coach. In the meantime, messenger Kohler had armed himself and, on hearing the robbers outside the door of his car, "let go his shots as fast as a self-cocking revolver could send them."

Loomis leaned out the side of the rear platform of his coach and allowed his eyes to adjust to the darkness. There were men milling about two cars ahead, but he could not distinguish the intruders from the locomotive crew. Finally, one of the bandits stepped away from the others and gave Loomis a clear shot. A load of buckshot knocked the bandit, a man named Cole Young, off his feet. Although seriously wounded, Young leaped up and fired two shots at Loomis. Both missed, and the deputy took careful aim with his second barrel. Young staggered, then toppled off the track and rolled down the embankment.

Loomis, perhaps thinking the death of one of their members might scare the gang off, returned to the coach. But in a few minutes he heard the express car being uncoupled from the rest of the train. The deputy raced outside again, just in time to jump aboard the rear platform of the departing express car.

The robbers ordered the engineer to pull up to a trestle. As they slowed, Loomis jumped off. Then, possibly deciding it would be safer on the far side of the trestle, the bandits ordered the engineer to start up again. Still unnoticed, Loomis scrambled back on. Once across the trestle, the train stopped, and again Loomis jumped off.

The gang resumed their assault on the express car, but messenger Kohler still held out. Nearly three quarters of an hour had passed since they took control of the train, and so far they had nothing to show for their effort. After mumbling something about having misplaced their dynamite, and obviously uneasy over the fate of Cole Young, the frustrated bandits saddled up and rode off. The robbers were later identified as the Black Jack gang, led by either Bob or Will Christian. (Source: Burton, "Bureaucracy, Blood Money and Black Jack's Gang.") See also **Christian Brothers**.

ROACH, JOHN. Few train conductors showed more courage during a robbery than the Wabash Western's John Roach on an eastbound run out of Kansas City on the night of August 3, 1889. About 9:00 P.M., as the train pulled out of Harlem, on the outskirts of the city, two men suddenly entered one of the sleeping cars and informed the passengers that "the first one that offers resistance will be shot down by our man on the platform." One of the women fainted, and the rest of the passengers made no indication that they would give the robbers any trouble. Not so, however, for conductor John Roach.

Roach had been in one of the rear coaches and met the bandits on the platform between cars as they were coming out of the sleeper with their loot. The robber in front stuck his revolver under the conductor's nose and ordered him to hold up his hands. At first Roach thought some of his fellow trainmen were playing a joke on him. When he realized the man was serious, he became infuriated. Roach was not armed, but he was carrying his lantern. He swung it at the bandit's head, smashing the glass and dousing the light. As the bandit staggered forward, trying to gain his senses, Roach retreated through the door of the car from which he had just come.

The second bandit, caught off guard by the daring conductor's action, fired off a shot but missed. The first robber, having regained his balance, also shot and missed.

Apparently the bandits had pulled the bell cord to stop the train. It had now slowed, and the bandits jumped off. Conductor Roach, unwilling to let his adversaries get "the last tag," raced back out onto the platform and hurled his lantern after them. He said they didn't look back, but took off running down a dirt road that led back to Kansas City. (Sources: *New York Times*, 5, 6 August 1889.)

ROME, GEORGIA. An East Tennessee, Virginia & Georgia passenger train fell victim to robbers on the evening of December 3, 1891. The westbound train, which had left Rome at 10:30 P.M., was halted by a man waving a lantern about two miles west of town. As the engineer slowed to a stop, two masked and armed men swung aboard the platform of the express car. The engineer did not see the intruders; he climbed down from his cab and went looking for the man with the lantern who had fled into the underbrush.

The two bandits forced their way into the express car and ordered the messenger, a young man named Sims, to turn over the contents of the safes. In the meantime, the engineer returned to the locomotive, got an all clear from the conductor at the rear of the train, and started up again.

When the robbers had collected their loot, which the messenger claimed was only $65, but which another source reported to be $6,500, they pulled the bell cord, the signal for the engineer to stop the train. As the train slowed, the two men jumped off.

On January 21, 1892, a man named Tom Davis was picked up in Alabama as a suspect in the robbery. The following November Chester Scott was also arrested. Scott was returned to Rome and convicted of the holdup. During the summer of 1893 he escaped from jail but was recaptured the following November near Gilkerson, Arkansas. (Sources: *St. Louis Globe Democrat*, 4 December 1891, 18, 21 January, 28 November 1892, 6 November 1893; *New York Times*, 4 December 1891.)

RONDOUT, ILLINOIS. It was the nation's biggest train robbery: at least $2 million and possibly $3 million, depending upon whose figures are accepted.

On June 12, 1924, a Chicago, Milwaukee & St. Paul mail train out of Chicago was stopped by robbers near Rondout, Illinois, a railroad junction about thirty miles north of Chicago. The train, made up of only mail and express cars, was carrying bonds and currency from the Federal Reserve Bank of Chicago to banks in the Northwest.

Three robbers, who had slipped aboard behind the tender, pulled on the air brakes and took command of the locomotive at Buckley Road crossing two miles south of Rondout. Other members of the gang were waiting in automobiles near the track.

Lawrence Benson, chief of the railroad's special agents, issued this report from the scene:

> The robbers were strung about the tracks for a length of a car or two and almost at the spot where the engine stopped. Three or four of them forced the door in the first [mail] car. They were met with a rain of bullets from the mail clerks and guards in the car, but succeeded in overpowering them. One bandit, however, was shot. How badly, we don't know, although we found a pool of blood on the car platform and there was a red trail from there to Buckly [sic] Road, where his fellows carried him and placed him in an automobile.
>
> The robbers then forced their way into the second car and the third, but escaped unscathed from the rain of lead the guards and clerks fired on them, and in the first car they succeeded in overpowering the guards and clerks.
>
> The robbers did not go into any of the other cars, for they found forty pouches of registered mail in the first three cars.
>
> Although there was a crew of seventy mail clerks and guards on the train of eight cars, they were all locked in and their instructions were that in no event were they to open the doors. They were all armed and instructed to shoot to kill any one attempting to force entrance into their car.
>
> The clerks and guards from the three cars were forced

outside and lined up against the train. They were guarded by three of the bandits. As soon as the robbers had gathered their loot they piled the sacks into four automobiles parked on Buckley Road. The three bandits guarding the train crew made the crew turn away from the road as they retreated towards their cars.

A later report established that the robbers were able to gain entry to the mail cars by blinding the guards and clerks with the fumes from bottles of formaldehyde that they threw through the windows. Witnesses reportedly believed that the bandit thought to have been wounded by one of the guards had actually been accidently shot by one of his own gang.

It was obvious that the holdup had been well planned, and that the bandits knew exactly what was on board. The chief mail clerk in the second car said one of the robbers told him: "I want the Federal Reserve shipments to Milwaukee, Minneapolis, St. Paul, Helena, Butte, Seattle and Spokane." Then he added: "I also want, for my own special purposes, a sack you have consigned to Roundup, Montana."

No one at the scene was able to say exactly how many robbers were involved; there were rumors that there were as many as twenty, but this was later discounted.

As soon as word of the robbery reached Chicago, all available federal officers and railroad and express company detectives were dispatched to the scene, and they were soon joined by Lake County sheriff's deputies.

The robbers had headed west, toward Libertyville. A dispatcher at Danville Junction, about two miles from Rondout, reported seeing four automobiles speeding by in a westerly direction. He managed to get one of the license numbers, 657-616, but he did not get the state.

The following morning, sheriff's deputies found two of the automobiles used by the bandits and abandoned mail sacks along back roads leading to an area of dense forests and lakes in northwestern Lake County, which led to speculation that the robbers had a hideout somewhere in that region. Also, a theory was advanced that the robbers may have fled by an airplane. Shortly after the robbery a plane was seen to land about two miles from Rondout, and then immediately take off in the direction of Chicago. A check of local hangars revealed that no local planes were in the air at the time. Still another possibility being considered was that the robbers backtracked, headed east to Lake Michigan, and escaped by launch. This was proposed because of a report that early in the evening on the night of the robbery a launch had docked at Highland Park, and twenty men had come ashore, some of whom matched the descriptions of the robbers. Shortly thereafter, the two automobiles later abandoned by the robbers were stolen.

Because of the size of the haul, Chicago police suspected that some of the city's major criminals might be involved, and a dozen arrests were made throughout the city. Those picked up included gangsters Dean O'Bannion, Louis Alterie, and Earl Weiss. Eventually, however, they all had to be released. It was later revealed that postal authorities had received a tip several days before the robbery that a gang of criminals from Philadelphia had joined up with Chicago gangsters "for raids on the mails."

On Saturday evening, two days after the robbery, a report circulated that Chicago police cruising the city found a man lying in the front of a west side home apparently severely injured. On examining him, they discovered that he had recently been shot five times. When they found a new $1,000 bill and a new $500 bill in his pockets, they placed him under arrest. Believing that he was about to enter the house when he collapsed, they knocked at the door. When they were refused entry, they broke the door down and arrested the occupants. Later, the story was changed somewhat, to the effect that the police apparently had received a tip to check out the house, which was at 53 North Washington Avenue, and they found the wounded man hiding under a bed.

The injured man gave his name as J. H. Wayne. The other persons inside the house, two men and a woman, identified themselves as Walter McComb, his wife, Catherine, and Paul Wade. Shortly thereafter, another man arrived at the house. Not seeing the police, he entered and was also arrested. He gave his name as James Mahoney. When he was searched, the police found three more new $500 bills. The others were then searched, and over $20,000 in new bills was uncovered, most of it from Paul Wade.

At first, Wayne claimed he had been shot by a woman near Hammond, Indiana, but under further questioning, the kind Chicago police were famous for in the 1920s, he confessed that he had been in on the Rond-

out robbery and that he had been shot by the leader of the gang for "disobeying orders."

Additional checking revealed that Wade and Mahoney generally matched descriptions of two of the robbers, and that Mahoney was actually James Murray, a former Chicago political boss and part owner of a local brewery before Prohibition. Several of the railway mail guards were taken to the hospital room where Wayne was being held, and he was positively identified as the wounded robber.

By Sunday, police reported they had another suspect, James H. Watson. He had attempted to bribe several of the police officers to let him go, promising them $20,000, which he said he could obtain from a friend in Milwaukee. The police also reported that Catherine McComb admitted knowing about the robbery, and soon thereafter her husband confessed taking part in it.

The following Tuesday, June 17, an abandoned car was found near Joliet, Illinois. Inside were all but six of the stolen mail sacks. Most of the registered and insured mail was undisturbed; only the packages containing money were missing.

About the same time, police picked up a Chicago gangster named Carlo Fontano and charged him with being in on the plot. Also, they said that two more of the Rondout bandits had been identified and were being sought. They were Ernest Fontano, Carlo's brother, and Anthony A. Kisano, also of Chicago. Then, on Wednesday the eighteenth, A. E. Germer, Chief Postal Inspector, and Chicago Police Chief Morgan A. Collins announced that they had discovered that the suspects Wayne, Wade, and Watson were really three brothers from Texas: Willie "Dock" Newton, Willis Newton, and Joe Newton. Furthermore, said Germer, the last of the Rondout bandits had now been identified. They were Samuel Grant and Blackie Wilcox, both escaped convicts from the Texas State Penitentiary at Huntsville.

This brought the total number of gang members at Rondout to at least eight, and possibly nine, depending upon the participation of Walter McComb. Chicago politician James Murray, it was believed, probably only bankrolled the job and arranged to hide the wounded Dock Newton. Another gangster, Max Greenburg, was supposed to have been involved. He was said to be a member of a St. Louis gang called Eagan's Rats. According to police, Greenburg planned the robbery but did not participate.

Ernest Fontano was captured by Chicago police on June 20, and on the same day all suspects were indicted by a federal grand jury on nine counts of robbery and conspiracy to commit robbery of the United States mails. Three days later, Louise Drafke Brown was added to the list of defendants. Police said she was the friend of the Newton brothers from Milwaukee who appeared at police headquarters with $36,000 ready to put up bail for Willis Newton.

As the weeks passed, the Rondout case began to be old news, even in Chicago. But then, on August 26, another arrest was made, and the case was back in the headlines. Named as a conspirator in the robbery was Chicago's top postal inspector, William A. Fahy.

Bill Fahy was one of the foremost postal inspectors in the country. His arrest record for mail robbers was the envy of the department and he had personally solved some of Chicago's biggest cases. At first his fellow inspectors could not believe the evidence that began to accumulate against him, such as the fact that he had been seen spending more than $3,500 in one night at a Chicago speakeasy, an amount that equaled his entire year's salary. When it became clear that he was involved, word spread around the city that the underworld must have had "something on him," and had forced him to join in on the robbery.

The search continued for the suspects still at large, but the authorities had been looking for the wrong men. Three men were eventually arrested: Brent Glasscock, Herbert Holliday, and, yet another Newton brother, Jesse. All three confessed.

Background checks on the Newton brothers revealed that all four had been engaged in train and bank robberies in the West for at least ten years. Glasscock, too, was a professional criminal, and apparently was the leader at Rondout. Fahy, the others said, was the "inside man" who gave them the information on when and where to stage the holdup. James Murray was also involved, they said.

Fahy and Murray insisted on their innocence and were tried. Both were found guilty and sentenced to twenty-five years at the federal penitentiary in Atlanta. The rest of the gang pleaded guilty. All except Herbert Holliday turned over their share of the loot and testified for the government. In return they received relatively light sentences. Holliday refused to cooperate and would not reveal where his share, $100,000, was hid-

den. He received twenty-five years. (Sources: Maguire, "The Texas Terrors"; *New York Times*, 13–22, 24, 26 June, 17, 21, 27, 28 August, 18, 20, 23, 25, 30 November, 12, 21 December 1924.) *See also* **The Newton Brothers**.

ROSCOE SWITCH (CALIFORNIA). It was Christmas Eve 1893; Southern Pacific's northbound Train No. 20 had left the Los Angeles station at 10:30 P.M. A few miles north of Burbank, two men climbed over the tender, put guns into the backs of the locomotive crew, and ordered the engineer to stop at the next siding, Roscoe Switch. One of the men jumped off, opened the switch, and the engineer was ordered to pull off the main line.

The engineer and fireman were forced to accompany the two men back to the express car. When the express messenger refused to open up, the men blew the door off with dynamite. Once inside they emptied the local safe and ransacked the car for anything of value but they failed to get into the through safe. When they had finished they took the engineer a short distance away. They told him to wait there until he heard a signal; then he could return to the train. He followed their instructions, and the two robbers disappeared into a nearby woods.

By 4:00 A.M. a posse was at the scene, but rain began to fall and the bandits' tracks could not be found. Bloodhounds were brought out the next morning, but they also were unsuccessful.

On the night of February 15, 1894, the same train was struck again at the same place. This time, the bandits opened the switch to the siding. The engineer, David Thompson, spotted the open switch and applied the brakes, but a bandit was hiding in the coal pile on the tender. He shouted for Thompson to "go on," and fired a shot into the cab. The bullet struck the fireman, Arthur Masters, causing him to fall to his death beneath the train. As the engine slowed, Thompson leaped off the side and ran into the underbrush. The bandit fired at him but missed.

The train was no longer under throttle but it was still rolling; it ran off the end of the siding but remained upright. As the train came to a stop, another robber appeared on the scene. One of the robbers fired random shots down the sides of the coaches, while the other attached a charge of dynamite to the express car door. They entered but failed to open the express company through safe; however, they found a package of newly minted Mexican silver coins. Then the robbers disappeared into the night, as before.

During an examination of the scene another body was found. Apparently a tramp had been stealing a ride somewhere near the front of the train, and the bandits, thinking he was a member of the crew, had shot him.

Three weeks after the second robbery, a man named J. A. Jones was arrested in Fresno but was released. On April 8 three more men were arrested in Los Angeles. Their last names were Thorne, Comstock, and Fitzsimmons. They were brought to trial the second week in June, but the evidence against them was weak, and all three were acquitted.

The case appeared to have come to a dead end. Then, in the summer of 1894, Wells, Fargo officials received an anonymous tip that the Roscoe train robbers could be found at a ranch owned by a man named Alvarado Johnson out near the eastern edge of the San Fernando Valley. Johnson was picked up. Although he denied any guilt, and there was little evidence to go on, he was placed under arrest. While awaiting trial, Southern Pacific Special Officer Will Smith, known for persuasive measures when it came to interviewing train robbers, apparently convinced Johnson that he had better make a deal or he could hang for the death of the fireman. Johnson soon confessed and named his partner in the crime—a well-known cattle rustler and horse thief from South Dakota, William H. "Kid" Thompson, who had been working for Johnson on the ranch. Johnson said that after the second robbery, Thompson had left the area.

Thompson was at that time in Phoenix, Arizona. With him was another former Johnson ranch hand, Charley Etzler. Apparently Etzler had not taken part in the robberies but he was attracted to the reward money the Southern Pacific and Wells, Fargo were offering; he tried to turn Thompson in. When a Phoenix city marshal showed little interest in the matter, Etzler became scared that Thompson would find out what he had done, so he left town. A short time later, while working on a ranch, he told his employer about Thompson, and the employer got in touch with the local Southern Pacific special officer, Billy Breakenridge. Breakenridge summoned Will Smith from California and they went looking for Thompson.

Like Etzler, Thompson had hired on at a ranch on

Kid Thompson. *California State Archives.*

the outskirts of Phoenix, but when the two detectives rode out to arrest him, his employer told them that he had gone into town. When he returned, the rancher told him that the law was looking for him, and he quickly packed his saddle bags and rode off. A posse was formed, and he was eventually captured in a box canyon in the Four Peaks mountain range.

Thompson was returned to California and in November 1894 he stood trial for "train wrecking," which in that state could carry the death penalty. He was convicted, but because of erroneous instructions to the jury by the trial judge, on November 30, 1896, the conviction was overturned by the Supreme Court of California. Thompson was tried again, and this time the conviction was sustained. He entered Folsom Prison on April 24, 1897. Although serving a life sentence, he was paroled in December 1909. A year later he violated the terms of his parole and disappeared. Nothing more was heard from him. (Sources: Edwards, "Kid Thompson and the Roscoe Train Robberies"; *People v. Thompson.*) *See also* **Train Robbery Statutes**.

ROSS, AARON. Aaron Ross was a gritty Wells, Fargo express messenger who refused to turn his car over to bandits at Montello, Nevada, on January 23, 1883. Although wounded three times by his attackers, the stubborn Ross continued to return their fire even after they rammed his car with the locomotive and tried to set it on fire. The bandits finally rode off in disgust. Ross, who had earlier fought off outlaws when he was a messenger for the company's stagecoach division in Montana, recovered from his wounds and was given a hero's reception at the Wells, Fargo headquarters in San Francisco, where officials touted him as typical of the brave messengers the company employed. *See* **Montello, Nevada**.

ROY'S BRANCH, MISSOURI. In the long history of train robberies in Missouri, which for years carried the title "The Train Robbery State," there were few successful attempts to thwart a holdup. The one that is perhaps remembered best occurred on September 26, 1893, at Roy's Branch, which is about three miles north of St. Joseph.

The would-be robbers anticipated a generous haul—possibly from $50,000 to $100,000, because that was what the regular express car usually carried on the St. Louis to Omaha run. But on this night the bandits never got a chance at the treasure. If ever a train robber gang was doomed from the start, it was this one. The gang consisted of only six members, and three of them were working for the authorities.

One was N. A. Hurst, professional detective, an employee of the P. T. Lockis Detective Agency. The others were ordinary citizens: William Garver, a young fellow out of employment, and Charles Fredericks, a newspaper carrier. From information supplied by these three men, all of whom were present during the planning of the robbery, the officials of the Chicago, Burlington & Quincy line knew exactly when the attack was to occur and they set up a dummy train to trap the culprits.

The dummy train consisted of a baggage-mail car, an express car, and six coaches. With so much advance warning, the authorities were not going to risk the embarrassment of allowing the culprits to escape. Hiding in the express car were the Buchanan County sheriff, whose name was Garson, one of his deputies, and four St. Joseph policemen. In the baggage-mail car were a St. Joseph detective and seven policemen, and in the first passenger coach were the St. Joseph chief of police, the general manager of the Burlington line, the superintendent of the Kansas City, St. Joseph & Council Bluffs Railroad (they were using some of his line's equipment), the regional superintendent of the Adams Express Company, and three more policemen. All the officers were well armed with shotguns and Winchesters. The three unsuspecting bandits were outnumbered seven to one—if you count the three traitors in the gang, eight to one.

As the train neared Roy's Branch, a man stepped out onto the track and waved a red lantern. As instructed, the engineer slowed to a stop. Soon the man with the lantern was joined by five others, all armed and wearing masks.

In addition to the three informers, the would-be robbers included Frederick Kohler, age twenty, "steel-nerved and cool," the leader of the bunch; Henry Gleitze, a plump ex-convict and wayward son of the proprietor of a respectable St. Joseph hotel; and Hugo Engel, Gleitze's half-brother.

In traditional fashion the engineer and fireman were marched back to the express car. One of the bandits ordered the messenger to open up. He did, and Kohler entered.

Sheriff Garson, his deputy, and the policemen were well hidden behind stacks of crates and packages, but apparently the sheriff just had to take a peek. When he did, Kohler caught a glimpse of him out of the corner of his eye. Kohler immediately saw that it was a trap and he raised his gun. One of the policemen, patrolman John C. Roach, was quicker, however. Roach fired two shots and both hit their mark. Kohler toppled back and out of the car, his pistols discharging harmlessly into the roof of the car as he fell. Hugo Engel was just behind him, and a load of buckshot sent him scurrying for safety in the tall weeds beside the track.

By prearrangement, Hurst, Garver, and Fredericks all dropped to the ground, and everybody began firing. Kohler tried to crawl away but got only a few yards before he died. Engel made it to the weeds, but no farther. He lived for about an hour.

Although wounded, somehow Henry Gleitze managed to escape. He was picked up the following day in St. Joseph. He denied any involvement in the affair, but had a difficult time explaining why his pockets were full of ammunition and three fingers on his left hand were missing.

Another holdup occurred at the same site four months later. This time the robbers were successful. On January 18, 1894, a Kansas City, St. Joseph & Council Bluffs through express was again flagged down by a man with a red lantern. While three bandits sprayed the passenger coaches with bullets, two others entered the express car and forced the messenger, C. E. Baxter, to open the safe. The amount stolen was believed to be $3,000. (Sources: *New York Times*, 26 September 1893, 19 January 1894.)   □

S

SACRAMENTO, CALIFORNIA. The robbery of a Wells, Fargo express car on an eastbound Southern Pacific overland passenger train differs little from many of the holdups that occurred in the mid-1890s in California, except that the stolen loot may still be buried somewhere near the scene.

On the night of October 11, 1894, two masked men ordered the engineer, William Scott, and the fireman, F. S. Lincoln, out of the cab after stopping the train with railroad torpedoes. The engineer later said: "We were running on time, and would have been in Sacramento in about fifteen minutes. The train ran over two torpedoes. I put my head out of the window, and noticed that we were being flagged. Everything was properly done, and I had no suspicion of anything being wrong until the engine stopped, when two men with rifles sprang into the cab. They ordered fireman Lincoln and myself to dismount and go with them to the express car, which they ordered us to uncouple. They accompanied us back to the engine, and made us pull about three-quarters of a mile to a point between two trestles."

Sacramento in 1877. *Frank Leslie's Illustrated Magazine.*

The robbers meant business. While the engineer and fireman were uncoupling the car, the conductor and a brakeman came forward to see what was happening. The robbers turned and fired at them, and they scurried back to the first coach. When this happened, engineer Scott said he "knew that the robbers were determined," and he pleaded with the Wells, Fargo express messenger to open the door of the car. The messenger refused, and began firing through a window at the attackers. The robbers at first returned his fire, but then stopped, and one of the bandits shouted to the messenger that they promised not to hurt him if he opened up.

The messenger, bleeding from shards of shattered glass, accepted the offer. The robbers then ordered Scott and Lincoln to climb into the express car. The messenger turned over the keys to the express company safe, and the robbers withdrew four sacks of money. According to the engineer, two of the sacks were so heavy that one man couldn't lift them, and the robbers ordered Scott and Lincoln to carry them up front and hoist them into the cab of the locomotive. Once the sacks were loaded, the bandits told the trainmen to stand back and they climbed into the cab. One of the robbers opened the throttle, Scott said, and "the engine sprung away down the track." When the robbers reached Sacramento, they threw the throttle in reverse, jammed it open, and "sent the engine back over the track under a full head of steam." The engine struck the cars, but by then the boiler had cooled, which reduced the engine's speed, and the collision did little damage.

In addition to the engineer and fireman, two tramps witnessed the robbery; one was riding on the locomotive, and the other was on the tender. The tramp on the tender said the robbers were dressed in "close-fitting white suits" and high-peaked caps. "They looked like clowns in a circus," he said. They carried Winchester rifles, but no pistols or cartridge belts. One of them, whose mask had an especially large opening at the mouth, had a dark mustache.

From the best report available, the robbers got $51,000 from the express car. After the authorities inspected the spot where the robbers abandoned the locomotive, a rumor spread that the bandits had not taken the sacks of money with them, but had buried them somewhere in the wooded, swampy area that bordered the tracks. This theory gained support later that night when guards shot at a man who they believed

Main line east of Sacramento, as seen from an early Central Pacific locomotive. *Southern Pacific Railroad.*

was one of the robbers trying to sneak back and re-cover the loot. (Sources: *New York Times*, 13, 16 October 1894.)

SANDERSON, TEXAS. In 1912 Sanderson, which is in southwestern Texas about twenty miles north of the confluence of the San Francisco and Rio Grande rivers, lay along one of the loneliest stretches of track of the Southern Pacific's entire route. On March 13 of that year, it was the end of the line for train robber Ben Kilpatrick, the last active member of the Wyoming Wild Bunch.

Kilpatrick and a comrade climbed aboard the blind baggage of the westbound SP's *Sunset Limited* as it was pulling out of Dryden, the first stop east of Sanderson, and they took command of the engine about two miles out of Sanderson. All seemed to be going well for the bandits, so well that they committed a serious mistake for express car robbers—they split up. Kilpatrick, a veteran of many train robberies, took the No. 2 express car, which was occupied by two messengers, while his companion checked out the empty No. 1 car.

The two Wells, Fargo messengers were David Trous-dale and Jake Reagan. Trousdale, only recently promoted to messenger, was small in stature but he was not short on ingenuity or courage. As Kilpatrick was sorting through the express packages, Trousdale suggested that he check a certain small box that was "worth more than all the stuff you've got." As Kilpatrick stooped over to look at the box, Trousdale picked up a mallet and smashed him in the back of the head. As Trousdale told it later: "I saw the mallet we use for breaking up ice, and when he turned his back to me I just couldn't resist the temptation to take a crack at his head. He went down for the count the first time and when he tried to get back on his feet I batted him a dozen times until he was done."

Trousdale picked up Kilpatrick's rifle and waited for the other bandit to return to see what had detained Kilpatrick. When he entered the car, the messenger killed him instantly. A third outlaw, waiting near the locomotive with the horses, heard the shots and fled. (Sources: *New York Times*, 14–16 March 1912.)

Ben Kilpatrick, left, and partner, following robbery attempt near Sanderson, Texas. *Southern Pacific Railroad.*

SAUGUS, CALIFORNIA. The date was February 17, 1915. The Southern Pacific's Train No. 25, *The Owl*, had just left the station at Saugus, which is northwestern Los Angeles County about ten miles north of San Fernando. Unknown to the locomotive crew, two men had climbed aboard just behind the tender. Two miles out, they entered the cab and leveled guns at the engineer,

Walt Whyers, and fireman, Fred Harvey. The locomotive was halted, and the crew was marched back and forced to uncouple the train behind the mail car. When this was done, Whyers was ordered to pull ahead until told to stop again.

When the train was stopped the second time, the bandits forced the engineer and fireman to accompany them to the mail car. When the mail clerks refused to open up, the bandits fired a shot through one of the windows. Instead of complying, the four mail clerks, Sherman Gebhart, A. Brown, V. Curti, and George Wearne, extinguished the lights in the car and began piling mail sacks against the door. When they had finished, they grabbed their revolvers and went to the rear of the car and lay flat on the floor

One of the bandits shouted: "Open the damn door or we will fill you full of lead." The clerks, however, boldly refused to budge. The bandits then threatened to blow up the car with dynamite, but still the clerks resisted. Frustrated, the bandits fired a volley of shots through the windows. One of the clerks, now sensing that he and his companions might be gaining the upper hand, answered that the bandits had better "look out," because "we are going to shoot."

This apparently unnerved the bandits, and they decided to call it a night. Within seconds they disappeared into the darkness.

Posses were immediately dispatched to the scene. The following day, they picked up two tramps, Bill Miller and John Fuller, who claimed they had been riding on top of one of the sleepers when the two bandits uncoupled the train. They gave descriptions of the two bandits, whom they said they had seen earlier hanging around near the station at Saugus. Their descriptions matched those given by the engineer and fireman.

On February 24, two men answering the descriptions were picked up in Napa, California, north of San Francisco. Bill Miller was located and brought in to identify them. He stated positively that they were the men he had seen the night of the attempted robbery. The suspects were Nola Anderson and Frank Ryan, both of whom were already wanted for burglarizing the post office at Rutherford, a small town near Napa. Because the evidence against the men for the post office burglary was stronger than that for the attempted mail car robbery, they were tried for that crime and convicted. Both were sentenced to San Quentin.

Saugus was the scene of another robbery on the night of November 10, 1929. The Southern Pacific's *West Coast Limited* No. 59 was rounding a curve near Saugus when the locomotive lurched, left the rails, and viciously began digging up ties and roadbed. The engine, tender, baggage car, and smoker all toppled over. The engineer, Cyrus Ball, was severely scalded from steam escaping from the boiler.

Back in one of the Pullman cars near the rear of the train, the dazed passengers were being confronted by an unusually calm man who insisted that they return to their berths and compartments. With an air of authority, he assured one and all that very soon a special train would arrive and take them on to their destinations.

The passengers, thus reassured, returned and calmed down, only to find, several minutes later, a masked bandit at their doors demanding all their money and valuables. The bandit, who quickly escaped after he completed his collections, was described as around forty years of age, about five feet, six or seven inches tall, and weighing about 135 pounds. Witnesses who remembered him prior to his donning his mask, described him as smooth shaven, having blue eyes, and having a "very thin face and sunken cheek bones and with a sharp nose."

After interviews with the victims, it was determined that the robber got around $200. An inspection of the track revealed that someone had loosened the rails with a claw bar stolen from a nearby section tool house. Footprints were found leading from the track to the state highway. About a half-mile from the track the authorities found several articles that had been taken from the passengers, plus a man's coat. The Southern Pacific Railroad announced a reward of $5,000 for information leading to the culprit's identification and conviction.

The following day a Burbank resident named Thomas Frith appeared at the police station in that city with an interesting story. Frith said that he and his family had been driving by the scene of the wreck on their way home when a man waved them down and asked for a ride. He said that he had been a passenger on the wrecked train and that his small daughter had been injured and was being taken to the Children's Hospital in Hollywood. Frith told him to get in and he would take him to the hospital.

The man's story seemed genuine enough at first, but as they sped toward Hollywood, he changed the de-

tails some. Although suspicious, Frith dropped the man off at the hospital, and assumed that that was the end of the incident. But when he read in the newspapers the next day that some passengers had been robbed, and that the only person injured in the wreck was the engineer, he decided to get in touch with the police.

On November 29 the authorities got another break. A Los Angeles attorney named E. G. Hewitt informed the Los Angeles County Sheriff's Department that an ex-convict who had been working for him as a caretaker might have been involved in the wreck and robbery. The man's name was Tom Vernon. He had a long prison record with six felony convictions and had just been paroled from Folsom prison in August. When he was not in prison, he was known to work as a stockman and rodeo performer. Vernon's photograph was shown to Thomas Frith, who identified him as the man he had picked up at the scene of the wreck. He was also identified by several passengers as the man who had told them to return to their compartments following the wreck.

The next day attorney Hewitt received a letter from Vernon, postmarked Cheyenne, Wyoming. In it Vernon mentioned that he had left Los Angeles on the morning of November 10 by hitching a ride on a truck bound for Denver, Colorado. To both Hewitt and the sheriff's department it was a clear attempt to establish an alibi for the wreck and robbery that occurred that evening.

An investigation was launched in Denver, and it was discovered that Vernon had been registered in a hotel there under his own name. In fact, one of the hotel maids produced a note to her from Vernon, who apparently was something of a womanizer, which stated that if she ever needed his help she could get in touch with him in care of Pawnee Bill's Buffalo Ranch, in Pawnee, Oklahoma. Vernon was indeed found in Pawnee and arrested. Under questioning, he admitted that he had derailed the train at Saugus and robbed the passengers.

Extradition proceedings were commenced, and Vernon was eventually returned to Los Angeles for trial. Since train wrecking could result in a death penalty, Vernon's lawyer pleaded him guilty, hoping for a life sentence. He got it, and he was returned to Folsom where he was given his old job back, that of hoist engineer in the work area. He never saw the outside again. (Source: DeNevi, *Western Train Robberies*.)

SAVANNAH, GEORGIA. A westbound Georgia Central night express was struck by three bandits on September 11, 1891, about five miles out of Savannah. Three men boarded in Savannah as passengers, then entered the Southern Express Company car when the train stopped at a crossing. A third man is believed to have stood guard while the others ransacked the car. The robbers got $4,000 in cash and valuables from the local safe, but missed $30,000 that was contained in the through safe. When they had finished they fired several shots in the air to discourage pursuit, then they fled.

Four days later a posse led by District Superintendent C. L. Myers of the Southern Express Company arrested three former railroaders, J. M. Perkins, J. A. Turner, and J. E. Delaughter at Mosely Hall, in Madison County, Florida. On a tip that the three were hiding at Mosely, the detectives surrounded their house during the night and burst in at dawn. The suspects were still in bed, sleeping with their hands on their revolvers. They were taken to the jail at Madison, the county seat, and shortly thereafter confessed to the robbery. It was later learned that the tip as to the whereabouts of the robbers was supplied by three Savannah women with whom the men had been living prior to the robbery. The women apparently knew of the plan and were charged as accomplices. (Sources: *Madison Morning News*. 16 September 1891; *St. Louis Globe Democrat*, 12 September 1891; *New York Times*, 17 September 1891.)

SAVANNA, ILLINOIS. In the excitement and confusion that often accompanied a train robbery, many things could go wrong. With weapons cocked and nerves strained to the limit, it was not unusual to see bandits fire at shadows, and sometimes even each other. This occurred during the famous $2 million mail car hold-up near Chicago in 1924, the biggest train robbery in history. One of the robbers mistook a confederate for a mail car guard and shot him five times, and the wounded robber's trail later led to the capture of the entire gang. (*See* **Rondout, Illinois**.)

A similar incident occurred in western Illinois on the night of August 5, 1902. Eight masked bandits set off torpedoes (*see* **Railway Torpedo Signals**) under the locomotive of a Chicago, Burlington & Quincy northbound, two miles north of Savanna. When the engineer stopped, the bandits took control of the train and blasted their way into the Adams Express Company car, escaping with between $2,000 and $3,000.

After the robbers had gone, the train crew found the body of a "middle-aged, well-dressed" man near the front of the express car. He had been shot twice, once in the leg and once over the eye. He obviously was one of the gang, and at first the Adams Express company messenger, whose name was Byl, claimed that he had shot him. Later, however, the real story was uncovered.

According to the Pinkerton files, the dead man was George "Brooklyn Blackie" Gordon, a member of a known gang of "yegg" men (safecrackers and robbers), which included Edward "Conn Eddie" Estelle, William "Browney" Browning, Thomas "Pennsylvania Butch" Clark, and Johnny Bull.

On the night of the robbery, while Estelle and Clark were blasting their way into the express car, Gordon had gone forward to the locomotive. As he was returning, Estelle saw him out of the corner of his eye and mistook him for a trainman. Thinking he was about to be jumped, Estelle turned and fired, striking Gordon in the leg. Then, when they had completed ransacking the express car, and Estelle saw that Gordon was too badly injured to escape with the rest of the gang, he muttered something about not leaving him to "squeal on anybody," and he put his gun to Gordon's head and killed him.

Fearing that if the authorities found Gordon's body and identified him, it would lead to the capture of the rest of them, Estelle wanted to stuff the dead robber into the fire box of the locomotive. Clark protested, however, and they left him beside the tracks.

Estelle and Clark were convicted of felony murder and sentenced to life imprisonment at the Illinois State Penitentiary at Joliet, Illinois. None of the other gang members were picked up, but according to the Pinkerton records, William Browning was later killed at McCloud, Texas, while attempting to rob a bank. (Sources: Pinkerton, *Train Robberies*; *New York Times*, 7 August 1902.)

SCHWARTZ, HENRY. Although it was not uncommon for someone to be killed during a train robbery, the death of United States Express Company messenger Kellogg "Nick" Nichols on a run of the Chicago, Rock Island & Pacific Railroad in 1886 had all the elements of a true mystery and caught the attention of the entire nation.

The story began shortly after midnight on March 13 of that year. The westbound Rock Island passenger train had just left Joliet, Illinois, when the baggage man, Newton H. Watt, heard a knocking on his door. He opened it and was met by three masked men with revolvers. They knew he had a key to the adjacent United States Express Company express car and they demanded that he hand it over. He gave it to them, and they headed for the express car.

When the train pulled into Morris, Illinois, the next stop, the local express agent knocked on the door of the express car. Hearing no answer, he and Watt entered. The train's conductor, whose name was Wagner, gave this version of what happened next:

> As the train came to a standstill at Morris, at 1:35 this morning, I got out on the platform. About the same instant Watt jumped out of the baggage [express] car as white as a sheet and gasped out, "My God! Look in there; the safe is all gone and the papers are all over the car." I looked in with my lantern and the safe was standing open; the way bills were all scattered around and the drafts and other papers, some of them torn up, were all around on the floor. I took my key and went to the door and called "Nick, Nick," but there was no answer. As I swung my lantern into the car a horrible sight was seen. There was blood scattered around everywhere. . . . The local way bills were all covered with blood, and the legs of the chair were bloody. In the forward part of the car I found the body of Nick. His face was covered with blood and a great pool of blood was underneath him. His body was still warm. The car showed that there had been a big fight from one end to the other. Nichols lay with both hands clinched, and between the fingers of one hand he held a lock of black hair, while in the other hand was a lock of red hair."

Detectives converged on the scene and questioned the baggage man, Watt, who gave this account:

> I was sitting in the car; the chains were up on the door which went back to the train, but the door in the front part of the car was not locked, as the car ahead was the one in which was the messenger. He was checking up his runs. I sat on a trunk, and just after they had whistled for Minooka, I heard a sort of scraping around on the floor, but not much, just as though some one had rubbed his foot on the door. Before I could turn around a big gun was poked over my shoulder and a man said: "You open your mouth or move a muscle and I'll blow your brains out." I could only see the lower part of his face; it was covered with some cloth or paper. I sat looking toward the back part of the car toward the rear of the train when I heard some one at the safe, which was behind me, and

could hear the rustling and tearing of papers. This went on for a while, and the man who stood over me said to me, "If you move or stir hand or foot before the train stops at Morris that man up there will blow the top of your head off." I rolled up my eyes and there was a man's hand stuck through the ventilator [which opened to the roof of the car] with a gun in it. In about five minutes, as it seemed to me, the train slowed up for Morris and I looked up. The hand was gone, and I jumped out of the car. I heard no noise nor any shooting. The first I heard was, as I said, the man speaking to me at the same time putting the gun over my shoulder. They must have gotten into Nicols' car first and got the key to the safe before they came to me.

Doctors who examined messenger Nichols's body said there were at least thirty wounds, including three or four bullet holes. Most of the wounds appeared to have been made with a hatchet or a weapon like a hatchet. His right arm was broken at the wrist, and a blow with a more blunt instrument had crushed his skull, probably the bloody poker found hanging on the wall. A reporter on the scene wrote that the car looked like a "slaughter house. Blood was on the floor, on the walls, and on the packages. . . . Everything in the messenger's pockets had been stained with blood, even to the crystal on his watch."

United States Express Company officials at the Joliet office issued a statement that they were shocked at the death of messenger Nichols, "a brave and trusted employe [sic] . . . who had spent 20 years with the company, being one of its oldest employes running on any road out of this of this city." The company announced that it was offering a reward of $10,000 leading to the arrest and conviction of the persons responsible. The company estimated the loss at a little more than $20,000 in cash and about $5,000 in jewelry and other valuables.

Pinkerton's National Detective Agency, engaged to investigate the crime, reported that there were few clues to go on, except the hair found clutched in the dead man's fists, and a valise found the next day on the train making the return run to Chicago. The valise, which was found in a closet in the toilet on one of the coaches, contained a piece of a bank draft taken from the express car the night of the robbery. There also was strong speculation that the murderers were railroad men, because of their apparent familiarity with the baggage and express cars.

The case dragged on for months. Several suspects were picked up, raising hopes that the killers had been

Henry Schwartz. *Pinkertons.*

found, but in each case they were released for lack of evidence. Then, on December 6, 1886, it was announced that a new suspect had been found: Henry Schwartz, a brakeman for the Rock Island who had been on the train the night of the murder. The evidence against him was not strong, but did call for an explanation: (1) he had been seen in the closet of the toilet where the valise had been found; and (2) a month after the robbery he had quit his brakeman's job with the Rock Island and went to Philadelphia, where he was seen spending "considerable money," on some occasions cashing $50 bills, after which he returned to Chicago and got his job back with the railroad.

It turned out that Schwartz had been under suspicion for some time, but the authorities could not get enough evidence against him for an arrest. In January 1887 a grand jury in Grundy County, where the crime had taken place, returned an indictment for murder and robbery.

Under questioning, Schwartz's wife admitted knowledge of his involvement in the crime, but she claimed her husband was only an accessory, that the crime actually was committed by others. With her testimony alone, the case was still weak, but then the district attorney of Grundy County introduced the testimony of a cell mate of Schwartz's from the Grundy County jail. His story corroborated that of Mrs. Schwartz.

Also involved in the plot, as many suspected all along, was the baggage man, Newton Watt. Schwartz and Watt were convicted of the crime and sentenced to life imprisonment in the Illinois State Penitentiary. According to Pinkerton records, Watt died in prison. Schwartz

served until September 1896, when his sentence was commuted by Illinois Governor John Peter Altgeld. (Sources: Pinkerton, *Train Robberies*; *New York Times*, 14–20 March, 6 December 1886, 26 January, 11, 12 February 1887.)

SEARCEY, CHARLES J. Charles Searcey and his partner, Charles Morganfield (a.k.a. Charles Morgan) were responsible for one of the most exciting train robberies committed in the East. On October 12, 1894, Searcey and Morgan stopped a northbound Richmond, Fredericksburg & Potomac passenger train in a wilderness area near Acquia Creek, Virginia, and robbed the Adams Express Company car of more than $20,000. Following the robbery, the bandits sent the unmanned locomotive hurtling northward toward a southbound passenger train standing at the station at Quantico, Virginia. Only the quick work of a switchman at the Quantico yards prevented what could have been a tragic crash with the loss of many lives.

Searcey was captured less than a week after the robbery when an alert policeman noticed that he was acting suspiciously at the train station at Cumberland, Maryland. Morganfield was captured the next day near Cincinnati, Ohio, when he suffered a broken leg trying to steal a ride on a train.

Morganfield was tried first, and when the express messenger identified him as one of the robbers, Searcey, who was in jail awaiting his own trial, turned state's evidence and confessed. See **Acquia Creek, Virginia**.

SEWELL, WEST VIRGINIA. For an eastern state, West Virginia had more than its share of train robberies. Perhaps they were inspired by the state's mountainous terrain, which was not unlike that of many areas of the West. This idea might be farfetched, but in the case of an 1896 robbery near Sewell, it was not unreasonable; the robber, who carried off the affair alone, had lived in the West for some time and had returned to West Virginia only the year before.

On September 26 of that year a pay train for the Longdale Iron Company was making its way on the Short Line from Sewell to Cliff Top, about eight miles outside Charleston, when a lone bandit armed with two revolvers swung aboard the platform of the paycar. Paymaster W. L. Wilson was riding in the cab with the engineer and saw the bandit climb aboard. He drew his revolver and fired twice, but missed. The bandit returned the fire, and did not miss. Wilson crumpled to the floor of the cab, mortally wounded.

The bandit, later identified as Joe Thompson, kicked in the door of the paycar and helped himself to slightly less than $3,000. (Source: *St. Louis Globe Democrat*, 28 September 1896.)

SEYMOUR, INDIANA. October 6, 1866, was a cold and rainy Saturday. The Ohio & Mississippi passenger train was winding its way eastward through the gently rolling hills of southern Indiana. It had left East St. Louis that morning, bound for Cincinnati. At 6:20 P.M., as the cars slowly pulled away from the town of Seymour – a small, prosperous woolen mill center near the east fork of the White River – two men, each carrying a pasteboard mask, swung aboard the end platform of the Adams Express Company car. Swiftly, but carefully, almost as if they had rehearsed, they made their way along the car's narrow running board to the large sliding side door. They tested the door and found it unlocked, just as they had suspected.

Inside the express car, express messenger Elem Miller was tidying up his paper work, putting things in order for Cincinnati, the end of the run. The East St. Louis-to-Cincinnati run, and the return trip the following day, was one of the better runs for an Adams messenger. Although it meant an overnight stay, the run itself could be completed in a day, and the stations along the route were far enough apart so that the paper work could easily be completed without hurrying.

Good jobs were scarce in the years immediately following the Civil War, and Elem Miller was fortunate to have his. And it was proud work: although he worked for the express company, and not the Ohio & Mississippi Railroad, Miller was looked upon as a railroad man, which in the nation's heartland was a title that could be worn with respect, unlike further west where rail barons were soon to get fat on lush construction contracts and inflated rates.

The express carried two safes: a local or messenger's safe for shipments to and from stations along the line, and a through safe that was locked at East St. Louis and was not to be opened until arrival at Cincinnati. Both safes were the ordinary wrought iron models used by most express companies for rail shipments since before the war: 1½ feet wide by 2 feet long with rollers on the

bottom, a ring handle at each end, and a heavy strap for dragging.

The two masked intruders slid the heavy door open and slipped into the car before Miller knew what was happening. They leveled their revolvers at his head and ordered him to hand over his keys to the safes. He reached for his key to the local safe and probably tried to explain that it ws the only one he had, that the through safe could not be opened in transit. One of the masked men took the messenger's key and quickly emptied the contents of the local safe into a sack while the other man dragged the through safe over to the open door of the car. After pulling the bell rope to signal the engineer to stop the train, the robber tipped the safe over the edge and out into the night. As the train slowed to nearly a stop, he pulled the rope again, the signal to resume speed, and both men jumped out. One of them, as he landed, shouted to the engineer, "All right," and the engineer, thinking the men were passengers who had been carried past their stop at Seymour, threw open his throttle and steamed on. In less than fifteen minutes, the two robbers, with the help of a partner who was hiding in a nearby woods, had accomplished what is generally considered to be the nation's first peacetime robbery of a moving train.

In 1866 the town of Seymour, Indiana, was a spot well suited to become the birthplace of the nation's newest crime. While most small towns in America's heartland were still awaiting the arrival of a railroad, Seymour sat at the junction of two, the Ohio & Mississippi and the Jeffersonville & Indianapolis, which linked the town with four major cities: St. Louis, Cincinnati, Indianapolis, and Louisville. The railroads had brought industry, and the community prospered. But being a rail junction, Seymour became a stopping-off place for transients, especially from the four large cities at the end of the rail lines, from which it drew a steady stream of petty thieves, pickpockets, muggers, and general riffraff. By 1866 Seymour had developed a sizable criminal element.

The Adams Express Company called in the Pinkerton National Detective Agency from Chicago to find the train robbers. Once they learned of the existence of Seymour's underworld, the agency's investigators never left town. In a matter of days, the crime was traced to the worst of the local gangs, the notorious

Reno brothers, leaders of a band of hard cases that had been terrorizing the area for years.

A second train robbery occurred at Seymour the following year. At 8 P.M. on September 28, 1867, as an eastbound Ohio & Mississippi passenger train was leaving the Seymour station, four men slipped out of the darkness and boarded the platform at the front of the Adams Express Company car. Carefully, as the robbers had done during the previous robbery, they edged their way around the running board (called the "walk plank" by trainmen) to the side door and forced their way in. In minutes they had bound and gagged the messenger and, using his key, extracted between $8,000 and $10,000 from the safe.

About three miles out of town the train had to slow for an approach to a high trestle. As it did, the men leaped from the car. According to a brakeman who saw the men depart, one of the robbers injured himself as he landed, so severely that he had to be carried off by his companions.

The robbery occurred on a Saturday night. By late evening the following day, Allan Pinkerton had been summoned to Seymour to handle the case personally. Pinkerton and an assistant first inspected the spot where the men left the train. There they found one of the masks used by the robbers. Next, they scoured the town and surrounding area for persons who had recently suffered an injury. Soon the name Walker Hammond turned up. Hammond had been seen limping around town with what he claimed were bruises from falling into a thicket. His story was believable, but on being questioned, he appeared extremely nervous. In addition, a witness was found who claimed that several days earlier he had seen Hammond with a mask similar to the one found at the scene.

Pinkerton next began questioning Hammond's associates and he came up with another suspect: a former Ohio & Mississippi newspaper vendor named Michael Colleran. When informed that he was a suspect, Colleran panicked and drew a knife. He was quickly overpowered and taken to the Adams Express Company messenger who identified him as one of the robbers.

The following February Hammond and Colleran were indicted by a Jackson County grand jury for the robbery. On August 19, 1868, Colleran pleaded guilty and was sentenced to five years at the Indiana State Prison at Jeffersonville. On February 20, 1869, Hammond like-

wise pleaded guilty and was sentenced to six years at the same facility. (Sources: Boley, *The Masked Halters*; Patterson, *Train Robbery*; Volland, "The Reno Gang of Seymour"; *New Albany Weekly Ledger*, 23 October 1867.) *See also* **The Reno Gang**.

SHADY POINT, OREGON. Although the Southern Pacific Railroad, which was the victim of more holdups than any other line, ran the length of the state of Oregon, the state itself was the site of few train robberies. When a robbery did occur it was, of course, big news.

On January 29, 1897, the Southern Pacific's northbound No. 15 was struck by robbers at Shady Point, about two miles south of Roseburg in Douglas County. From their method of operation, the robbers seemed to be experienced. They stopped the train by waving a red flag. As the engineer, whose name was Morris, slowed the train, two masked men jumped on the steps of the tender. By the time the train had stopped, they were covering the engineer with their weapons.

Wasting little time, the robbers, soon joined by the man with the flag, went to the express car and demanded that the messenger open up. When he refused, they uncoupled the train between the express car and the first passenger coach, and then ordered the engineer to bump the rear cars down the track. With the express thus separated from the passengers and the rest of the train crew, the robbers attached dynamite to the door and blew it open. But when they finally entered, they discovered that the messenger had slipped out the opposite door and had fled into a nearby woods.

Again using dynamite, the intruders blew open the express company's two safes. In the process, however, the car caught fire. The outlaws then broke into the railway mail car and took a number of registered letters and packages.

By the time the robbers left, the express car was ablaze. The train crew's attempts to extinguish it were unsuccessful, and it was completely destroyed.

The amount taken in the robbery was not reported. The messenger, who returned after the robbers had done, said that they apparently were unfamiliar with the interior of the large safe, and they missed quite a bit of money contained in one of the several compartments. (Source: *New York Times*, 30 January 1897.)

SHERCLIFFE, FRANK. Frank Shercliffe (alias Frank Burke, "Kid" McCoy), a young and vicious thug, committed the "Pollock Diamond Robbery," an assault and robbery of diamond merchant W. G. Pollock in a crowded Sioux City & Pacific smoking car on the evening of November 4, 1892. In the midst of eleven witnesses, Shercliffe bludgeoned and shot Pollock, grabbed his wallet containing $15,000 worth of uncut diamonds, and leaped off the train just south of California Junction, Iowa.

Shercliffe enjoyed a short but active career as a burglar and robber, beginning at the age of seventeen with a safe burglary and shootout with police in Aurora, Illinois. He specialized in stealing from gamblers and gambling houses throughout the West and Midwest. The Pollock robbery was his biggest haul, but could have been bigger; he missed taking a satchel from Pollock that contained several thousand dollars more in mounted gems.

Pollock's firm was a member of the Jewelers' Protective Union, which had Pinkerton's National Detective Agency on retainer. The Pinkertons eventually tracked Shercliffe down through underworld associates and in 1893 he was convicted and sentenced to seventeen years at the Iowa State Penitentiary at Fort Madison. He was paroled in 1904. (Sources: Moffett, "The Pollock Diamond Robbery"; Pinkerton, *Train Robberies*.") *See also* **The Pollock Diamond Robbery**.

SILVERDALE, BRITISH COLUMBIA. On September 10, 1904, a Canadian Pacific train was flagged down at Silverdale by the notorious "Old Bill" Miner and an undetermined number of accomplices. At this robbery, Miner introduced a new trick. Prior to halting the train, Miner tapped the telegraph line and, impersonating an express company employee, told the express agent at the last stop before Silverdale not to lock the through safe because the combination had been lost. The agent complied and the robbers helped themselves to $7,000 in currency and about $250,000 in Australian bonds. (Source: Rickards, "Bill Miner—50 Years a Hold-up Man.") *See also* **Bill Miner**.

SISKIYOU STATION, OREGON. In 1923 Siskiyou Station consisted of a cluster of mountain railroad shacks at the tunnel just north of Siskiyou summit, near where the Southern Pacific tracks crossed into California. On

The dynamited mail car at Siskiyou. *Southern Pacific Railroad.*

October 11 of that year, the first section of the Southern Pacific's San Francisco-bound No. 13 slowed to a momentary halt for a routine check of the air brakes before entering the tunnel and descending into California. As the train slowed, a man jumped into the locomotive cab and pointed a gun at the face of the engineer, Sid Bates. A second man climbed aboard the tender, and a third man stationed himself at the entrance to the tunnel. The engineer was ordered to pull into the tunnel and stop just before the locomotive emerged from the other side.

The bandits' target was the mail car. When the mail clerk refused to open up, one of the men fired off a shotgun. When the clerk still refused, the man placed dynamite against the front door of the car and pushed the plunger. The charge was too strong, and the blast blew the entire front of the car apart and set it on fire. The clerk was either killed in the blast or died soon thereafter in the flames.

At this point the accounts differ on what happened. Apparently the rear brakeman, Coyle Johnson, came forward to help. According to one version, the bandit in the tunnel ordered him to uncouple the mail car from the rest of the train, and then go tell the engineer to pull forward. But when he did, he startled the two bandits at the front of the train, and they shot him dead.

By now the mail car was totally engulfed in flames, and the bandits could not enter it. Also, they may have heard the whistle from the second section of the train coming from the rear. They realized that the holdup was a failure and that they had to leave immediately, but before they fled, they calmly shot and killed both the engineer and the fireman, presumably to prevent the trainmen from identifying them.

Investigators converged on the scene. A search of the area turned up a tramp who claimed he had seen the two men climb aboard the train as it slowed for the tunnel. Also found near the scene was a .45 Colt revolver, a DuPont detonator used to ignite dynamite, a pair of greasy blue denim overalls, a satchel with an express tag on it, and pieces of gunnysacks soaked in creosote, apparently to prevent bloodhounds from picking up the bandits' scent. Near the gunnysacks were three packsacks, obviously intended to be used to carry away the loot.

An all-out manhunt was organized, with the assistance of a company of Oregon militia. Nearly every inch of the rugged mountainous area was scoured, and the searchers eventually discovered two campsites and a small cabin believed to have been used by the suspects.

The search continued for days, but nothing more was found. The evidence that had been collected was turned over to Edward O. Heinrich, a noted forensic scientist at the University of California with a Sherlock Holmes–like reputation for crime detection. Professor Heinrich lived up to his reputation. In his report to postal officials he stated: "One of the men you are looking for is a left-handed lumberjack who has worked in the Northwest recently. He is about twenty-six, has brown hair, weighs about 165 pounds, stands five foot eight inches tall, and he's rather fastidious in his personal habits."

When Heinrich was questioned about his conclusions, his answer was: "There are streaks of fresh pitch in the overalls that could have gotten there only through contact with pine trees. This suggests that the man is a lumberjack. I found Douglas fir needles in the pockets, which places him in the Northwest. A few strands

Reward notice for the DeAutremont brothers. *Southern Pacific Railroad.*

of hair on the overalls tells me his hair color and also determines his approximate age. There were worn places on the right side of the overalls but none on the left, so our man must have been standing with his right side against a tree while he swung his ax."

But the Professor saved the best for last. "I believe his name is Roy DeAutremont. I discovered a little piece of faded yellow paper jammed down in the narrow pencil pocket of the overalls. There appeared to be no writing on it, but under a microscope I detected some faint pen scratches. I brought them out under treatment in the laboratory." The scrap of paper turned to be a receipt for a registered letter mailed by Roy DeAutremont at Eugene, Oregon, on September 14, 1923. It showed that fifty dollars had been sent on that date to a Hugh DeAutremont in Lakewood, New Mexico.

A search by postal authorities in Eugene turned up

The captured DeAutremonts. *Southern Pacific Railroad.*

Cabin used by the
DeAutremont brothers.
Southern Pacific Railroad.

a barber named Paul DeAutremont who had three sons, twins Roy and Ray, age twenty-six, and Hugh, age eighteen. Roy and Ray were lumberjacks working near Silverton, Oregon, and Hugh had recently joined his brothers after graduating from high school in Lakewood, New Mexico. According to his father, Roy DeAutremont was left-handed.

In the meantime, Professor Heinrich had developed more clues. The revolver was traced to Seattle, where it had been sold to a man who had signed the receipt "William Elliot." A handwriting expert determined that the handwriting of the person who signed the receipt and samples of Roy DeAutremont's handwriting, which had been obtained from his father, were one and the same. Also, the number on the express tag attached to the satchel found at the crime scene revealed that the bag was shipped by Roy DeAutremont from Portland to Eugene on January 21, 1923.

Overalls left at the scene
of the robbery.
Southern Pacific Railroad.

When a search of Silverton, Oregon, failed to turn up the DeAutremont brothers, they were officially labeled suspects in the murders, and more than a million wanted posters were printed up and distributed to post offices and law enforcement agencies throughout the nation. When no trace of the suspects was found, the search was widened; circulars were printed in Spanish, German, French, Dutch, and Portuguese, and distributed worldwide.

Three years went by with no solid clues as to the whereabouts of the wanted men. Then, in 1926, an army corporal named Thomas Reynolds walked into the postal inspector's office in San Francisco and said that the picture of Hugh DeAutremont reminded him of a fellow soldier named Jim Price whom he had served with in the Philippines. Price was picked up in Manila and readily admitted that he was, in fact, Hugh DeAutremont, but he denied any knowledge of the Siskiyou holdup.

DeAutremont was returned to Oregon and charged with the murders. The story was given nationwide attention by the press, including pictures of the long-sought brothers, Roy and Ray. A man in Portsmouth, Ohio, wrote in, and said that he believed the two brothers were men he had recently worked with, Clarence and Elmer Goodwin. These two were picked up and were immediately identified as the missing DeAutremonts. But, like Hugh, they denied any involvement in the holdup and killings.

Hugh was tried first, and the circumstantial evidence supplied by expert witness Professor Heinrich was devastating. A verdict of guilty was returned, but the jury recommended life imprisonment for Hugh rather than the death penalty. This encouraged Roy and Ray to plead guilty, and all three brothers were sentenced to the Oregon State Penitentiary. (Sources: Clifton, *Murder by Mail and Other Postal Investigations*; Lucia, *Tough Men, Tough Country.*)

SKAGGS, PETER. Little information is known about outlaw Pete Skaggs. According to Southern Pacific detectives he was suspected of robbing several Wells, Fargo express cars during the late 1880s. In February 1889, following an express car robbery near Linden, California, Skaggs and three members of his gang, two women and a man, were tracked to an isolated cabin in the Sierra Nevada Mountains near Sonora. During a shootout with the possemen, two of the gang were killed and Skaggs was captured. A posseman also was killed, and Skaggs and the surviving gang member, one of the women, were hanged at Stockton the following March. *See* **Linden, California**.

SMITH, J. ERNEST. As train robberies in the West increased during the mid-1880s, Wells, Fargo messenger J. Ernest Smith vowed that if he were ever held up, he would make it a night the bandits would never forget. On the night of October 14, 1887, on a Southern Pacific run near El Paso, Texas, Smith got his chance.

After bandits stopped the train, they gathered outside the door to Smith's express car and ordered him to open up. He refused. The outlaws promptly shoved a charge of dynamite under the car, and with a shout "Die, damn you" to the stubborn messenger, they set it off. The blast nearly tipped the car off the tracks, but the hardy Smith was only bruised. As the smoke cleared, he placed his pistol on a ledge just inside the door, and announced that he was coming out.

Smith appeared at the darkened door with his hands held high. As he started to jump down, the bandits ordered him back in to light one of the lamps. It was just what the messenger had hoped for. Pretending to reach for a lamp, Smith grabbed his pistol, whirled, and fired. The nearest outlaw clutched his chest and fell dead. A second bandit fired, and Smith emptied his gun in his direction, then raced to the rear of the car and picked up his shotgun. It wasn't needed. Smith's second victim made it only fifty yards from the track before he staggered and died. If there were any more outlaws in on the attack, they quickly gave up the fight and fled. Smith had made good his promise; he had given them a night they wouldn't forget.

The grateful citizens of El Paso bought Smith a new suit of clothes to replace the ones ruined in the fight and also presented him with a shiny gold medal. In the hope that it would set an example for other messengers, Wells, Fargo awarded him $2,000 in cash. The Southern Pacific Railroad kicked in another $250, and the state of Texas added $1,000. In reporting the incident, the *San Francisco Chronicle* commented that "if his [Smith's] example were followed, train robbing would soon be a thing of the past."

But the J. Ernest Smith story did not end with the October 1887 robbery attempt. Four years later, at

J. Ernest Smith.
Wells Fargo Bank History Room, San Francisco.

Samuels Siding in Val Verde County, Texas, history nearly repeated itself. On the night of September 2, 1891, Smith's Wells, Fargo express car came under attack again, this time by five bandits. As before, Smith held out as long as he could, but when the attackers used dynamite to blast open the car door, Smith knew it was useless to keep resisting. No doubt it again crossed his mind to grab his gun and shoot it out with the intruders as he did in 1887, but this time he felt it was unnecessary. The large, sturdy Wells, Fargo through safe he now carried in his car was supposed to be bandit-proof, even impervious to dynamite. He meekly opened up and let the outlaws in, figuring at worst they would take the small amount of cash in the local safe and ride off. He was wrong; the bandits knew their job well, and knew exactly how to place their explosives on the "bandit-proof" safe. With little difficulty they blew off the door and scooped out the treasure.

When Smith turned in his report of the robbery he was mortified. For four years he had been a hero of the line, but now he knew his fellow messengers would tease him endlessly about losing his nerve. The more he thought about the situation, the worse he felt, and he decided his only choice was to turn in his resignation. Of course, it was not accepted, and he eventually changed his mind. (Sources: Burton, "A Tale of Two Smiths"; Dillon, *Wells, Fargo Detective*; Harlow, *Old Waybills*; *San Francisco Chronicle*, 15 October 1887.)

SMITH, RUBE. Reuben "Rube" Smith was a cousin of the notorious Rube Burrow, "King of the Train Robbers" who held up trains in Texas, Arkansas, Mississippi, and Alabama in the late 1880s. Smith, a small-time crook wanted for robbery in his home county of Lamar, Alabama, was recruited by Burrow in the fall of 1889 and participated in the robbery of an express car and mail car on the Mobile & Ohio Railroad on September 25, 1889, near Buckatunna, Mississippi.

Following the Buckatunna holdup, Smith decided to try his own hand at train robbery, and he and a friend, Jim McClung, made plans to rob an express car at Amory, Mississippi, in December 1889. The authorities were on Smith's trail, however, and he and McClung were arrested at the Amory depot while waiting for the train they intended to rob. (Source: Breihan, *Rube Burrow*.) *See also* **Buckatunna, Mississippi; Rube Burrow**.

SMITH, WILLIAM. Will Smith was the driving force behind the special agents of the Southern Pacific Railroad: a huge, brawny manhunter whose fierce determination to rid the West of every train robber was possibly brought on by his own personal misery—a nearly lifelong battle with facial skin cancer.

Smith was described by some as having a "police dog mentality," but he nevertheless solved a respectable number of major cases. Two cases, however, almost stumped him: the express car robberies at Pixley, California, on February 22, 1889, and at Goshen, California, on January 24, 1890. Smith suspected the Dalton gang and dogged them relentlessly (and most believe wrongly), until he got caught up in the chase after Chris Evans and John Sontag in 1892, who probably were actually responsible for the two robberies.

After narrowly escaping with his life while trying to arrest Evans and Sontag following the Kerman (then Collis), California, robbery in August 1892, Smith devoted nearly every waking hour to their capture. The detective and the two fugitives eventually developed a rousing hatred for one another. In April 1893 Smith again barely escaped death at their hands when, at Camp Badger, California, they waylaid a stagecoach he was supposed to have been on. (He missed the trip when urgent business took him to San Francisco.)

The vendetta came to an end two months later when Evans and Sontag were captured by lawmen in what is now Sequoia National Forest, but like the detective's skin cancer, these two outlaws would plague him for most of his life. Accused of distorting the facts at Evans's trial, Smith received much criticism for his handling of the case. Then, the detective suffered further humiliation at the hands of San Francisco theatrical promoters who portrayed him as an inept buffoon in a popular stage play based on the Evans and Sontag saga. (Sources: Glasscock, *Bandits and the Southern Pacific*; Patterson, *Train Robbery*.) *See also* **Evans and Sontag**.

SOCORRO, NEW MEXICO. In the early days of the train robbery era it was common for would-be robbers to halt a train by piling obstructions, usually rocks or crossties, on the track. In most cases the engineer, fearing derailment, would quickly apply the brakes. The bandits would then rush the cab and take control.

Occasionally, however, an engineer faced with such a situation would gamble that he could plow his way through the obstacles. Such was the case at Socorro, New Mexico, on the night of October 30, 1884.

The Santa Fe's Train No. 102 was five miles out of Socorro when the engineer, whose name was Skuse, saw a pile of rocks that stretched almost the length of a rail. Skuse did the safe thing: he threw the throttle in reverse and applied the brakes. When the big engine finally rolled to a stop, he told his fireman to climb down and inspect the track. But just then Skuse saw the real problem: five armed bandits scampering up the embankment. Skuse, in no mood to give up his train to these renegades, grabbed the throttle and pulled it wide open. The bandits, taken by surprise, fired about twenty shots at the departing locomotive, but did no damage.

The would-be robbers were local cowboys, all amateurs at train robbery. Four of the five—Punch Collins, Edwin White, J. W. Pointer, and Jefferson Kirkendall—were quickly picked up, tried, and convicted of assault to commit robbery. The fifth gang member, William Allen, managed to elude the law. (Source: Hume-Thacker Report.)

SONTAG, GEORGE. *See* **Evans and Sontag**.

SONTAG, JOHN. *See* **Evans and Sontag**.

SPENCER, AL. As far as the record goes, Ethan Allen "Al" Spencer was involved in only one train holdup. His specialty was bank robbery, but he is remembered more as a train robber than anything else.

Spencer's fame resulted from several stories, perhaps largely mythical, that grew out of that one robbery: the holdup of a railway mail car near Okesa, Oklahoma,

Al Spencer.
Author's Collection.

on August 21, 1923. (*See* **Okesa, Oklahoma**.) It was said that Spencer was a vain man who enjoyed reading newspaper accounts of his escapades, particularly his bank robberies. But in the early 1920s, robbing banks was not all that difficult, especially in small towns where there was little police protection. Also, the federal government was not yet effectively exercising its jurisdiction in such cases. Several newspaper articles allegedly mentioned this fact, pointing out that while the notorious Al Spencer might be an Oklahoma bandit in the old tradition (he was considered a "transition outlaw" because he began his career on horseback as a cattle rustler and then graduated to bank robberies and getaways in fast automobiles), he obviously lacked the real daring of his outlaw predecessors who robbed trains for a living.

Spencer was insulted by such remarks, so the story goes, and decided to pull off the Okesa mail car robbery. Furthermore, some writers believe, Al was so bent on getting full credit for a daring robbery that he invited a few trusted friends from the underworld to witness the affair. Local authorities, it is said, found a place on a hill overlooking the robbery site where the grass was trampled down and matches and cigarette butts were strewn about.

Another story that has persevered is that Spencer once rode with the famed bank robber Henry Starr. They both were Oklahoma outlaws, and Starr was only fourteen years older than Spencer, but evidence is scant that they were confederates.

Al Spencer was born December 26, 1887, on a farm near Lenapah, Indian Territory. His first arrest was in

1916, for cattle rustling, but he served no time. While out on bail he hightailed it to Kansas, where he put together a small gang to loot merchants at night. He was caught and sentenced to five years but instead of going to prison he was returned to Oklahoma for the cattle rustling charge. In 1920 he was sentenced to ten years at the Oklahoma State Penitentiary but escaped in January 1922.

Spencer immediately formed another gang and specialized in small Oklahoma banks. He quickly made a name for himself and was placed near the top of the wanted lists. In April 1923 he was almost captured at a shootout near Ochelata, Oklahoma, following a post office burglary at Pawhuska.

The Okesa mail car robbery was Spencer's last job. The following month he was traced to a hideout near South Coffeyville, Oklahoma, just below the Kansas line. On September 22, 1923, a Saturday night, he was spotted on a bridge southwest of town by a posse of federal officers and railroad detectives. He was carrying an automatic rifle and a new .38 Colt police special. He tried to make a fight of it but he was killed instantly. When he was searched he was found to be carrying ten $1,000 bonds taken from the mail car. (Sources: Shoemaker, "Al Spencer: Transition Outlaw"; Wellman, *Dynasty of Western Outlaws*; *Bartlesville Enterprise* [Oklahoma], 21 September 1923.)

ST. JOSEPH, MISSOURI. The newspapers called it an "old-fashioned robbery," referring no doubt to the exploits of the James-Younger gang in the 1870s.

The date was January 10, 1894, nearly twenty years after the James-Younger heyday. Four miles east of St. Joseph, the engineer of the Hannibal & St. Joseph Railway's Fast Mail train, nicknamed the "Ell," heard the popping of railroad torpedoes under the wheels of his big locomotive's front trucks. Torpedoes on the track were the railroader's signal that trouble lay ahead. Then, an instant later, the engineer saw a red lantern being waved – also a signal to stop.

The possibility of a robbery probably crossed the engineer's mind. Yet it was only 6:40 P.M. Robbers seldom attacked trains that early in the evening; they usually preferred to wait until at least midnight, when most of the passengers had dropped off to sleep. However, this was western Missouri, and in mid-winter it was already dark. It could be a robbery, but the engineer still had to stop. He had no choice; it was a violation of railroad rules to ignore the signal.

All doubt was removed when the engineer saw five masked men with revolvers and Winchesters surrounding the steps of his cab.

Back in the express car, messenger G. B. Wetzel was also taken by surprise. The engineer's command to open the door sounded perfectly normal to him and, again, probably because of the early hour, he did not suspect trouble. Wetzel opened up without hesitation, and seconds later his car was in the hands of the bandits.

After firing three shots in the air to warn the passengers to stay put, two of the bandits entered the express car. Wetzel turned over the keys to the through safe without resisting. When interviewed later, he would not say how much was taken, but since the train was bound for Chicago, word around town was that there was a "good deal of money" on board. The robbers moved on to the mail car, where they sliced open the registered mail pouches. Again, no figures on the loss were ever given.

In describing the two men who entered his car, Wetzel said one was "short, wore a black coat and overcoat, and a black derby hat." The other man wore a "double-breasted coat and no overcoat, and was tall and slender." A brakeman, John Ryan, who was sent back along the track to warn approaching trains, said that he saw the robbers leave in two buggies, which led the local authorities to believe that the culprits were from St. Joseph. It was speculated that they might be part of the same gang that had unsuccessfully tried to rob a Burlington train at nearby Roy's Branch the previous September. (Source: *New York Times*, 11 January 1894.)

STEWART, HENRI. Henri Stewart deserves a place in the chronicles of train robbery because he may have been the only Harvard Medical School graduate who ever robbed a train. According to outlaw researcher Wayne Walker, Dr. Stewart was the mysterious Henry Underwood who rode with Sam Bass and his gang during their train-robbing romp in and around Denton, Texas, in 1877–78.

Stewart, as Underwood, and the rest of the gang barely escaped several encounters with posses in the spring and summer of 1878. Stewart was wounded dur

ing a shootout at Cottondale, Texas, on June 13, but escaped. He made his way across the Red River and hid out with friends in the Choctaw Nation.

According to Walker, in August 1878, in Caddo, Oklahoma, Stewart got into an argument with a fellow physician, Dr. J. B. Jones. (One source suggests that Jones may have delivered the baby of Stewart's girlfriend and while doing so, learned of Stewart's outlaw connections.) On August 7, Dr. Jones was gunned down on the platform of the railroad station at Caddo, presumably by Stewart and his cousin, Wiley Stewart. Indian police were soon on their trail, and in a running gun battle several lawmen were wounded. Stewart escaped, but later, through a letter to his girlfriend at Caddo, he was traced to Monett, Missouri, where he was arrested.

In May 1879 Stewart was convicted of killing Dr. Jones, and on August 29 he died on the scaffold at Fort Smith, Arkansas. His tragic life was summed up by a brief note in the *Fort Smith Elevator*: "A sad sight to see a man of fine personal appearance, good address, possessing a good education, and just in the prime of manhood – placed in such a horrible position through his own reckless folly." (Source: Walker, "The Doctor Who Rode with Sam Bass.") *See also* **Sam Bass.**

STILES, BILLY. Stiles was a member of a four-man gang led by the sheriff of Willcox, Arizona, Burt Alvord. The gang was responsible for the robbery of $30,000 in gold coin from an express car on the Southern Pacific Railroad near Cochise Junction, Arizona, in September 1899. Stiles later helped Alvord escape from jail and the two men rode the outlaw trail in southern Arizona until 1903, when they gave themselves up. Stiles was tried for the robbery but the jury could not reach a verdict. He escaped from jail while awaiting a second trial. The loot from the robbery was never recovered. *See* **Cochise Junction, Arizona.**

STOCKWELL, INDIANA. Almost every railroad had one or more paycars that traveled the line on payday. Although usually well guarded, these cars were tempting targets for bandits. On Christmas night 1873 an engine pulling the paycar for the Indianapolis, Cincinnati & Lafayette Railroad left the Indianapolis depot for Lafayette. On board were General Paymaster Fred Lovett, Indianapolis Freight Agent Henry S. Fraser, As sistant Superintendent William Vandergrift, and a conductor, whose name was Kelly. About fifteen miles out of Lafayette, near the Stockwell station, the engineer suddenly noticed a half-opened switch. Although the train was going only twenty miles an hour, he knew it would be derailed. The only thing he could do was to throw the engine in reverse, shout a warning to the fireman, and jump.

The fireman was putting a shovel of coal in at the time. When he looked around and saw the cab empty, he also jumped. The conductor, who was standing outside the door of the paycar on the front platform, saw the engineer and fireman leave the cab, and he jumped. The three men still in the paycar felt the jolt of the engine being reversed, then the car pitched sideways and toppled off the track.

None of the men were seriously injured. The engineer came the nearest to being killed. Immediately upon landing, he got to his feet and tried to scramble back up the embankment. He slipped, however, and fell back down—which saved him from being crushed by the toppling tender and paycar. The men were fortunate that they all jumped on the high side of the track, and that the train also fell in that direction. On the opposite side was a 150-foot drop into a ravine.

Immediately before the derailment, a witness said he saw a heavily bearded men throw open the switch. The would-be robber, however, seeing that the trainmen and occupants of the paycar were not disabled, apparently lost his courage and fled.

Because it was a holiday, only a skeleton work force was on duty, and Lovett and the others had to stand guard over the payroll throughout the bitter cold night until a work train arrived the following morning.

(Sources: *Indianapolis Daily Sentinel*, 26 December 1873; *New York Times*, 26 December 1873.)

STREICH, JOHN. John Streich, a postal inspector working out of St. Paul, Minnesota, was known as the Sherlock Holmes of the Railway Mail Service. His goal in life was to catch persons stealing the United States Mail. Streich was obsessed with meticulousness. His reports were all carefully typed with a straight margin on the right as well as the left. At home, when he cut kindling for his fireplace, he would always cut the pieces precisely the same length.

Streich was responsible for several innovations having to do with mail security. For example, it bothered Streich that a thief with a key to a mailbag could open it, remove mail, and lock it up again, and no one would know that a theft had taken place. To solve the problem, Streich invented a special lock that looked like the traditional flat iron lock used on all mailbags. But on Streich's lock, one of the rivets that held the face on the lock was fake. It was attached to the mechanism so that it would turn a notch if the lock was opened. Thus, by checking this rivet one could tell if someone had been in the bag.

Another Streich invention was the "test letter," a special letter filled with marked money that would be used to trap a clerk suspected of thievery.

Inspector Streich also was known for innovative methods used to spy on suspects. In one case he had himself concealed in a coffin and placed in the express section so that he could watch the suspect, a baggage clerk, through small peepholes drilled in the sides. His scheme paid off; he actually saw the man steal some letters. (Source: Clifton, *Murder by Mail and Other Postal Investigations*.)   □

T

TAGUS SWITCH (CALIFORNIA). In March 1896 a young man walked into Tulare County Sheriff A. P. Merritt's office and informed him that there was going to be a train robbery in Tulare County sometime that month. The young man was a nineteen-year-old Texas lad named Obie Britt, who for the past six months had been working in and around Visalia as a woodcutter. According to Britt, a fellow worker, Dan McCall, and three other Visalia men, Josiah Lovern, Charles Ardell, and John Haynes, were planning to rob an express car on the Southern Pacific line in the very near future. Britt had been asked to join the group, and he had agreed, but then he had second thoughts and he decided to inform the authorities.

When Southern Pacific detectives were advised of Britt's visit, they took the information very seriously, especially when they heard the name Josiah Lovern. Four years earlier, Lovern, a Visalia saloon keeper, was suspected of being involved in the express car robbery at Collis, later attributed to Chris Evans and John Sontag. Although never arrested, Lovern was believed to have fenced through his saloon over 1,000 coins taken in that holdup.

According to Britt, the plans for the present robbery had originated with McCall. Lovern and Ardell, who was a partner in the saloon run by Lovern, were planning to wave a lantern to stop a Southern Pacific passenger train, and McCall and Britt would board the locomotive cab and cover the engineer and fireman. Haynes, Lovern, and Ardell would then fire random shots alongside the coaches to keep the passengers from interfering, while McCall and Britt would escort the locomotive crew back to the express car and force the messenger to open up. If he did not, the robbers were prepared to blast their way into the car with dynamite and blow the safe. The train selected was SP's No. 20, a northbound that would pass through the town of Tulare about 2:00 A.M. on October 19. According to Britt, the gang would stop the train at Tagus Switch, just north of town.

Sheriff Merritt's plan to thwart the robbery was simple. On the night in question, a posse would gather at Tulare, board the train, and be waiting for the robbers when they arrived at Tagus Switch. But by the evening of the eighteenth, word reached the gang from friends that something was up, that several law enforcement officers were acting suspiciously. Suspecting a trap, Lovern, Ardell, and Haynes backed out. McCall, however, was all for going ahead, with just a change in plans. He told Britt that instead of robbing Train No. 20, they would rob Train No. 19, an earlier southbound, and instead of stopping the train, they would slip aboard as it was pulling out of Goshen, about seven miles north of Tulare. It was too late for Britt to inform the authorities of the new plan, so he decided to go along with McCall and look for a chance to escape before the robbery was actually attempted.

Train No. 19 was on time arriving at Goshen. As it stood at the station discharging and taking on passengers, McCall and Britt found a dark spot beside the track near the coal bunkers where they could swing aboard as the train pulled away. But as they settled in to wait, they failed to notice two armed men step out of the shadows at the end of the station platform and head for the ladder on the side of the locomotive tender. They were Earl Doggett and Victor Reed, two Tulare County deputies on their way to join the posse at Tulare. Why they had chosen to ride in the tender instead of one of the passenger coaches was never made clear; possibly they thought the would-be robbers could have had friends watching the station, or maybe on a hunch Sheriff Merritt decided to keep an eye on Train No. 19 as well. For whatever reason, the two made themselves seats on the coal pile near the front of the tender, just behind the locomotive cab where they could take advantage of the warmth given off by the boiler.

The train pulled away from the depot just after midnight. As it passed the coal bunkers, Dan McCall grabbed the ladder on the express car platform and swung aboard. For all he knew, Obie Britt had followed him, and had boarded one of the cars behind. But Britt had found his chance to escape. While McCall was climbing aboard, Britt was dashing in the other direction toward the station. When he reached the telegraph office, he told the operator to send a wire immediately to Sheriff Merritt at the Tulare depot. The agent wired: "SHERIFF MERRITT: I AM INFORMED BY OBIE BRITT THAT MCCALL IS ON #19. LOOK OUT FOR HIM. MCCALL SUPPOSED MR. BRITT WOULD ASSIST HIM IN HOLDUP. AGENT." The sheriff, of course, could do nothing but wait, and hope that deputies Doggett and Reed were on their guard.

Doggett and Reed were not on their guard. Hunched over out of the wind and partially blinded by the glare from the firebox, the two deputies did not see Dan McCall as he came climbing over the coal from the rear of the tender. "Throw up your hands you damned sons of bitches" McCall yelled from the top of the coal pile. As the lawmen turned, McCall fired his rifle, striking Reed in the shoulder. As Reed fell, he tried to get McCall with his shotgun, but missed. McCall then shouted "Why don't you shoot? Why don't you shoot?" Apparently this was intended for Obie Britt whom McCall thought was somewhere behind him.

McCall's next shot struck deputy Earl Doggett in the chest, but Doggett also was armed with a shotgun, and he managed to get off one shot. It was low, but effective. The charge hit McCall in the groin. McCall doubled over, spun around, lost his balance, and toppled from the coal pile. He made a desperate grab for the side of the tender but missed and tumbled off into the darkness.

Deputy Doggett was rushed to Tulare for treatment of his wound. Despite a punctured lung, he survived. During a long recovery period, he became so impressed with the doctors who saved his life that he developed an interest in medicine and eventually went to medical school. He obtained his license and practiced for many years in nearby Alameda County.

Of the original gang members, only Josiah Lovern served time, probably because of his earlier reputation.

Although the express car was not actually robbed, the incident would always be known locally as the "Tagus holdup," probably because the Tagus Switch was to be the site of the holdup as originally planned, and, ironically perhaps, because the Tagus Switch was almost the exact spot where Sheriff Merritt and his deputies found the mangled body of would-be robber Dan McCall. (Source: Edwards, "Shootout on No. 19.")

TANGIPAHOA, LOUISIANA. On the night of April 13, 1892, Illinois Central passenger Train No. 2, northbound out of New Orleans, had just left Hammond, Louisiana, and was starting to build up speed when a man placed a revolver in the back of the engineer, C. C. Jarvis. The intruder's instructions were brief. When the train neared Tangipahoa, about ten miles south of the Mississippi line, the engineer was to be ready to bring it to a stop.

As the train came to a halt, two men appeared from the side of the track. The engineer and fireman were marched back to the Southern Express car where they were ordered to tell the express messenger, George Matthews, to open up. Matthews, however, suspecting that he was in for a robbery, locked the safe, hid what appeared to be packages of value, and slipped out the rear door into the coach behind. The robbers, hearing no more sounds from inside the express car, forced open the door and entered. Using the fireman's axe, they smashed open the safe and emptied the contents into a sack. A few minutes later they mounted their horses, which had been tied nearby, and were gone.

The operation had gone smoothly, but the take was not large: just less than $200 in cash, some jewelry, and a handful of lottery tickets.

Despite the small loss, railroad and express company officials converged on the scene, joining peace officers from both Louisiana and Mississippi. Bloodhounds were dispatched from the Mississippi State Penitentiary, but the bandit's trail had grown cold. Local gossip, however, mentioned several names, including Eugene Bunch, already a suspect in several burglaries and robberies in eastern Louisiana, and a Mississippi farmer named Edward Scanlon Hobgood. Through Hobgood's brother the authorities learned the suspects' hiding place, a farmhouse near Franklinton, Louisiana. On August 22 a posse surprised the outlaws camped out near the house. Bunch was killed and Hobgood was captured. The third robber, Henry Carneguay, was also arrested. Carneguay was convicted and sentenced to five years at hard labor. Hobgood was also convicted, but the verdict was overturned on a technical error, and the case was never retried. (Source: O'Dell, "Bunch & Hobgood.") *See also* **Eugene Bunch; Edward S. Hobgood**.

TEHACHAPI, CALIFORNIA. At an elevation of 3,964 feet above sea level, Tehachapi Pass, which separates the San Joaquin Valley from the great Mojave Desert, is the highest point on the Southern Pacific line. It is the site of the railroad's famous Tehachapi Loop, which, in the words of one nineteenth-century traveler, "by doubling back upon, and crossing itself, by climbing, squirming, and curving . . . gave us one of the most famous and dextrorse pieces of railroad engineering in the world."

In January 1883 a Southern Pacific express was rest-

Tehachapi Loop. *Southern Pacific Railroad*.

ing on the steep grade near the summit, just east of the town of Tehachapi, when suddenly the seven cars behind the tender broke loose and began to roll backward down the mountain.

Within minutes the runaway cars reached a speed of more than seventy miles per hour. Four miles down the grade, at the center of a long curve, the cars left the track. When the last of the bodies was removed from the wreckage, the death toll stood at fifteen. Among the victims were Mrs. John Downy, wife of the ex-governor of California, and Charles Larrabee, a former congressman from Wisconsin.

Within a week officials of the railroad announced that two of the dead passengers, neither of whom could be identified, resembled two men who had been seen at the station just before the train broke loose. From this, Southern Pacific officials speculated that the two men had intended to rob the train, their plan being to release the brakes gradually and control the speed of the cars so they could bring them to a stop somewhere down the line. (A few railroad safety critics scoffed at this idea, claiming that the railroad was simply trying to cover up carelessness on the part of the train crew in setting the brakes.) (Sources: Patterson, *Train Robbery*; Wood, *Over the Range to the Golden Gate*.)

TEMPLE, TEXAS. Over the years outlaws used many different methods to stop a train to rob it. Signaling the engineer with a red lantern was a favorite. Piling obstacles on the track, usually crossties or rocks, was another. On May 13, 1892, near Temple, Texas, which is in Belton County about sixty miles northeast of Austin, a seven-member gang of would-be robbers tried a new technique—two of them curled up on the track.

The engineer of the southbound Missouri, Kansas & Texas passenger train, which was using the International & Great Northern tracks that day, could not simply run over the men, so he applied the brakes. He was suspicious, however, and he did not come to a complete stop. When the engine was within a dozen or so feet of the men, they leaped up and dashed out of the way. The engineer immediately pulled back the throttle and gave the big locomotive full steam ahead.

Suddenly more men with Winchesters and shotguns appeared at the side of the tracks and began shooting. The express car, railway mail car, and several passenger coaches were riddled with bullets and buckshot.

Several passengers were injured by shattering glass, and a conductor for the MK&T who was deadheading in the sleeping car, was shot through the arm. (Source: *New York Times*, 14 May 1892.)

TEXARKANA, ARKANSAS. Early on the morning of June 10, 1890, a northbound passenger train on the Cotton Belt route out of Texarkana struck a pile of rocks and timber and derailed. The collision threw the locomotive off the embankment, fatally injuring the engineer. The careening engine had hardly come to rest when four armed and masked men dashed out of a pine thicket beside the tracks. The express messenger, a man named Nesbitt, saw them approaching and fired his pistol at them, possibly striking one or two. The attackers immediately returned his fire, and the messenger fell, severely wounded.

The robbers thoroughly ransacked the express car, and according to a quick estimate by express company officials, they took money and valuables worth nearly $10,000. Posses arrived within the hour, but no trace of the bandits was found. (Source: *New York Times*, 11 June 1890.)

THACKER, JONATHAN N. Jonathan Thacker was a detective for Wells, Fargo and was involved in the investigations of most of the major train robberies in California and the western states from the late 1870s to the 1890s. In July 1899, when he was past sixty and partially crippled from arthritis, he was involved in a furious shootout with remnants of the Butch Cassidy and Sam Ketcham gangs in Turkey Canyon, New Mexico.

In 1904 Thacker succeeded the famous James B.

Jonathan Thacker.
Wells Fargo Bank History Room, San Francisco.

Hume as Wells, Fargo's Chief Special Officer and held that position until his retirement three years later at age seventy. When he died at his home in Oakland, California, in January 1913, the *San Francisco Chronicle* paid tribute to Thacker as the peace officer "who struck terror to the hearts of the stage and train robbers in California, Nevada and Arizona," and who "probably captured more desperadoes than any officer in the West." (Source: Boessenecker, "John Thacker: Train Robbers' Nemesis.")

THOMPSON, WILLIAM H. "KID." Kid Thompson, a native of South Dakota, was a cattle rustler and horse thief who turned to train robbery in 1895. In December of that year he and a local rancher, Alvarado Johnson, robbed Southern Pacific Train No. 20 at Roscoe Station, about two miles north of Burbank, California. The following February they robbed the same train at the same site, this time wrecking it by leaving a switch open. They were both captured and sent to prison. *See* **Roscoe Switch (California)**.

THORNTON, NEP. Nep Thornton was an early mem-

ber of the Rube Burrow gang. He was working as one of Burrow's wranglers when Rube decided to give up ranching for train robbery in 1886. Thornton participated in the first two Burrow robberies, a daylight holdup of passenger coaches on the Ft. Worth & Denver Railroad at a water tank at Bellevue, Texas, on December 1, 1886, and an assault on an express car of the Texas & Pacific Railroad at Gordon, Texas, on January 23, 1887. When Burrow called for the return of the gang the following June for another robbery, Thornton failed to show. Apparently, it marked the end of his career as a train robber. (Source: Breihan, *Rube Burrow*.) *See also* **Bellevue, Texas; Rube Burrow; Gordon, Texas**.

TIPTON, WYOMING. Tipton is in Sweetwater County, on the Union Pacific tracks about midway between Rawlins and Rock Springs. The town's claim to fame is an express car robbery by the Wild Bunch on August 29, 1900. The robbery might have been the Wild Bunch's greatest haul or its greatest flop, depending upon which story is accepted.

The express messenger was Ernest C. Woodcock, the same messenger whose car was invaded by the Wild

Express car destroyed by the Wild Bunch at Tipton, Wyoming, in 1900. *Union Pacific Railroad*.

Bunch at Wilcox two years earlier. (*See* **Wilcox, Wyoming.**) The Tipton robbery began when one of the gang members slipped aboard unnoticed at the previous stop. He hid behind the tender, then climbed forward and halted the train at a prearranged spot marked by a raging bonfire. The rest of the gang members were waiting in the shadows, and they began firing their pistols alongside the coaches to keep the passengers in line.

Once the outlaws were sure the passengers would be no trouble, they forced their way into Woodcock's express car with threats that they would blow the car up with dynamite. Once inside, they attached dynamite to the through safe and blew it apart, which destroyed much of the car in the process.

Reports attributed to Union Pacific officials immediately after the robbery established the loss at only $54 in cash, but other sources suggested a higher amount. One unverified story had messenger Woodcock admitting a loss of $55,000, and years later, an account

$4000 REWARD

By Union Pacific Railroad Company.

Second Section Train No. 3 Held Up by Four Masked Men,

ABOUT TWO AND ONE HALF MILES WEST OF TIPTON, SWEETWATER CO., WYO., AT 8:30 P. M. AUGUST 29, 1900.

$8,000.00 REWARD!

In ADDITION to the reward of $1,000 EACH offered by the Union Pacific Railroad Company for the capture of the men, dead or alive, who robbed Union Pacific train No 3, near Tipton, Wyo., on the evening of August 29th, 1900, the Pacific Express Company, on the same conditions, hereby also offers a reward of $1,000.00 for each robber.

THE PACIFIC EXPRESS COMPANY.

Dear Sir:— **August 31st, 1900.**   Green River, Wyo., September 1st, 1900.

Our money loss is $50.40, damage to car safe and express freight will amount to $3000.00. Robbers used Kepauno Chemical Co., Giant Powder, dated September 15th, 1899. Ashburn Mo. Works, forty percent.
Yours truly,
(signed) F. C. Gentsch, Gen'l Supt.

Reward notice following Tipton robbery. *Author's Collection.*

thought by some to be written by Butch Cassidy himself (*see* **Robert LeRoy "Butch Cassidy" Parker**) gave a figure of $45,000. According to this story the outlaws buried the money soon after the holdup because it was too dangerous to dispose of at the time. Following the robbery it was believed that the gang rode west, eventually to Huntington, Nevada.

Some outlaw researchers believe that it was the Tipton holdup that firmly established the Union Pacific Railroad's commitment to its special horse car trains, which are generally credited with nearly eliminating robberies on that railroad. (*See* **Horse Cars.**) These special trains would rush an elite posse of mounted manhunters to the scene of a robbery, and within hours the posse would be nipping at the heels of the fleeing bandits. (Sources: Kirby, *The Saga of Butch Cassidy and the Wild Bunch*; Pointer, *In Search of Butch Cassidy*.)

THE "TRAIN ROBBER ERADICATOR." At the peak of the train robbery era, an express messenger for Wells, Fargo invented an ingenious device for scaring off would-be bandits. Unfortunately, the official company records detailing the story have not survived; if they ever existed they probably were destroyed along with the general files of Wells, Fargo in the 1906 San Francisco earthquake and fire. Even the messenger's name has been lost to history.

The invention consisted of a simple gas pipe fixed in the shape of an L. The messenger installed it in the floor of his car, with the lower end extending through the floor and protruding underneath. On the lower end of the pipe was a wire basket just the length and diameter of a standard railroad flare. On a dark night, if the messenger suspected trouble outside his car, he simply lighted the flare and dropped it into the pipe. When it reached the basked it flared with a brilliant white flame that illuminated the entire space under and around all sides of the car.

Thanks to the loss of the Wells, Fargo company files, there is no evidence today of the "eradicator" ever being used to discourage a robbery, but because of its simplicity it may have become popular with other messengers and it may have served its purpose quite well on several occasions. (Source: Hungerford, *Wells, Fargo.*)

TRAIN ROBBERY STATUTES. It was a crime in every state and territory to commit robbery (as well as to attempt to commit robbery), and if train robbers or would-be robbers were captured and identified, they were usually punished accordingly. Some suspects gained acquittals or successfully plead guilty to lesser offenses, depending upon the skill of their defense attorneys.

In the early days a weak spot in the law enforcement system involved outlaws who halted or wrecked a train but, for one reason or another, did not carry out the attempt at robbery. This was not an unusual occurrence. Many times a gang of outlaws would place an obstruction on the track, usually a stack of crossties, and the engineer would fail to see it or decide to smash his way through it. Sometimes bandits would succeed in derailing a train, but at the last moment chose not to attempt to rob it because the express car was heavily guarded. In a few instances, would-be robbers would cause such a tragic pileup that the express car would be buried in the wreckage and no attempt could be made to enter it. In any of these situations, even if the culprits were captured and identified, if they had skillful lawyers they often went free for lack of proof that they actually *intended* to commit a robbery.

These defendants could, of course, be sued in civil court for destruction of property or for causing personal injury to the train crew or passengers, but the injured parties could only ask for money damages. This usually was a waste of time, because the defendants in most cases were usually drifters who owned little more than a horse and saddle.

To correct this weakness in the criminal laws, railroad lobbyists in the state and territorial capitals pressured legislatures to enact special statutes that did not require proof of an intention to commit robbery to gain a conviction for derailing or wrecking (or attempting to derail or wreck) a train. But railroad lawyers supplied the wording for these laws, and they, like most lawyers of the day, were trained in the arcane verbiage of English solicitors, which often resulted in stilted and cumbersome statutes that tended to confuse rather than resolve. A typical statute produced by these efforts was the one passed by the territory of Dakota in 1887:

> Every person who maliciously, either: 1. Removes, displaces, injures or destroys any part of any railroad, whether for steam or horse cars, or any track of any railroad, or of any branch or branchway, switch, turnout, bridge, viaduct, culvert, embankment, station house, or

other structure or fixture, or any part thereof, attached to or connected with any railroad; or 2. Places any obstruction upon the rails or track of any railroad, or any branch, branchway, or turnout connected with any railroad, is punishable by imprisonment in the territorial prison not exceeding four years, or in a county jail not less than six months.

Undoubtedly the lawyers who drafted this statute thought they had covered everything. They had not. A train wrecker could simply open a switch halfway and send a flyer crashing down an embankment. His lawyer could argue that the drafters had an opportunity to include such an act in their list of prohibited conduct but did not do so.

Statutes covering train *robbery* were equally poorly drafted, and thus were occasionally thwarted. In 1896, in the California case of *People v. Thompson*, train robber W. H. "Kid" Thompson's crafty lawyer managed to get his client's conviction reversed on appeal. Thompson's conviction was based on the wording of the California statute that he "willfully, unlawfully, and feloniously threw out a switch with the intent to derail a passenger train, and he did then and there willfully, unlawfully, and feloniously board a passenger train . . . with intent then and there to rob said passenger train." Thompson's lawyer, Ben Goodrich, argued that while his client may have been seen entering the express car, no one saw him throw the switch that derailed the train. The Supreme Court of California agreed that the statute involved only *one* offense, and therefore the state had to prove that Thompson both threw the switch that derailed the train *and* entered the express with the intent to rob it, and this it had failed to do.

The wording of these statutes were frequently attacked on other grounds. In the Thompson case, Goodrich had also argued that when his client entered the express car, it and the rest of the cars were already lying by the side of the track in a shambles, and therefore there was no longer a "passenger train" to be "boarded" as stated in the statute. In another case, a train robber's lawyer contended that one cannot rob "trains," only "people," and therefore a statute prohibiting the robbery of a "passenger train" was totally ineffective. Neither of these arguments was accepted, but occasionally judges did rule in favor of the defense on technicalities nearly as ridiculous.

William Pinkerton, of Pinkerton's National Detective Agency, who spent a lifetime tracking down train robbers, believed that too many guilty defendants were going unpunished because of an uneven application of criminal justice in local courts, frequently the result of bribes and favors. Pinkerton insisted that an answer was a *federal* train robbery statute. Said Pinkerton, "If it becomes a crime against the United States government to hold up a train, it is almost certain that this class of work will soon come to an end. The government should take charge of these cases, as the robbers are not likely able to control the United States officials as they control local authorities."

Others took up the cause, and in 1892 the general managers of the major railroads drafted a resolution asking Congress to pass a federal train robbery law. Although Pinkerton knew full well that if the federal government took jurisdiction of these crimes his agency stood a chance of losing a sizable portion of its business, he eagerly assisted with the drafting.

The express companies likewise called on Congress to act, and word was leaked to the business world that they were seriously considering raising express rates so high for money shipments that the banks would have to resort to using the United States mail.

A bill was introduced in Congress in September 1893 by Ohio Congressman John A. Caldwell that provided that any person who "unlawfully and maliciously throws or causes anything to be thrown, or to fall into or strike against a railroad train, or an engine, tender, car, or truck, with intent to rob or injure a person or property on such train, engine, car, or truck engaged in interstate commerce, shall, upon conviction, be imprisoned at hard labor not less than one year nor more than twenty years."

There seemed to be genuine support for the bill; in fact, some criticized it for being too lenient. One to twenty years was not enough punishment, it was argued; the average train robber would probably risk getting caught on the chance that he could escape or obtain early parole. Henry P. Robinson, editor and publisher of *Railway Age*, urged that the crime be made a capital offense. On September 22, 1893, he wrote: "Make certain death the penalty of train robbing, whether the crime happens to result in murder or not, and the avocation will speedily be abandoned."

The *Express Gazette*, voice of the express industry, joined in: "Nothing short of hanging will check this growing evil." Robinson and the others could point to the experience in Mexico. Train holdups had become a problem there in the 1880s until the government made wrecking a train or obstructing a track punishable by death. The robbery rate fell immediately. The law was later repealed for being too harsh, and robberies increased. On the other side, anti–capital punishment groups could point to figures from California: despite a train wrecking and robbery law passed in 1891 that made the crime a capital offense, the rate of holdups actually increased.

While proponents of the Caldwell Bill argued over the appropriate penalty for wrecking a train with intent to rob it, the bill itself got lost in committee, mainly through the efforts of states' rights supporters. Fearing the measure would die in the House, the Senate began an effort to generate interest in a national law. On December 21, 1893, Senator William Peffer of Kansas introduced a resolution calling for an investigation of train robberies by the Committee on Interstate Commerce. Specifically, Peffer asked that the Committee "inquire whether and what legislation is necessary to prevent interruption of interstate railway traffic by lawless and unauthorized persons, and to punish persons guilty of robbery and murder committed on interstate railway trains." Senator Peffer's resolution was passed, but with little enthusiasm; the nation's economy had just turned sour, and Congress had more important things to worry about.

As the nation plunged into a four-year depression, Congress forgot about the problem of train robberies. Banks failed by the hundreds, and businesses by the thousands. If there was any chance to revive the train robbery issue, it was lost completely when Congressman Caldwell, the bill's sponsor in the House, took a long leave of absence and then resigned.

In 1894 the United States Post Office Department pushed for a law to better protect its railway mail service clerks from train robbers, but it likewise made no headway in Congress. The following year a senator from North Carolina named Butler introduced a bill similar to Caldwell's, but like the House bill, it garnered little support.

While the movement was meeting resistance on a national level, some of the state and territorial legislatures did manage to pass stiffer train robbery laws, especially in the West. But soon a new opponent arose: organized labor. In May 1895 a death penalty bill was defeated in Illinois by the unions, which charged that it was intended to interfere with the right of railway employees to strike. The unions objected to the language that made it a crime to put obstacles on the track, a tactic frequently employed during labor disputes.

In those states and territories that did enact the death penalty for train wrecking and robbery, the statutes were occasionally attacked on constitutional grounds as inflicting "cruel and unusual punishment." Such attacks were usually unsuccessful. While appellate courts did not hesitate to reverse the conviction of a train robber if the prosecution failed to prove its case, by the turn of the century the higher courts of the western states and territories, eager to rid the frontier of the "lawless West" image, were hesitant to throw out a law the public apparently wanted. Typical of this view was the language of the Supreme Court of New Mexico in denying the appeal in 1901 of train robber Thomas "Black Jack" Ketchum.

> Assuming, for the sake of argument, that the courts may, in extreme cases, review the discretion of the legislature in determining the severity of punishment, still we see no reason why this statute under consideration should be held to be unconstitutional by reason of its severity. The act under which the defendant was convicted was passed in 1887, and has been upon the statute books, unchallenged by the people of the territory, ever since that time. It has evidently met with the approval of the people, and has not been deemed by them cruel on account of its severity.

Efforts were not totally abandoned in Washington to obtain a national law, and bills continued to be introduced. Despite the protests of the states's rights groups, Congress finally acted in 1902. The result was the federal Train Robbery Act, which made it a federal crime to board a train within the jurisdiction of the United States with the intent to commit robbery or murder.

Just what influence the federal act had on the train robbery rate cannot be determined; as it became law several other events also were having an effect on the incidence of the crime. The West was becoming settled and train robbers were finding it more difficult to escape following a holdup. Taking a lead from the Union Pacific, railroads and law enforcement agencies were dispatching lightning-fast special trains carrying mounted posses to the scene of a robbery, which cut the bandits' escape time considerably. As western gold and silver mines played out, there was less treasure to steal. Even the passenger coaches offered less to the bandits; many passengers began carrying travelers' checks instead of cash. (Sources: Hampton, "Brigandage on Our Railroads"; Harlow, *Old Waybills*; Patterson, *Train Robbery*; Pinkerton, "Highwaymen of the Railroad"; Pinkerton, *Train Robberies*; White, *A Life Span and Reminiscences of Railway Mail Service*; Congressional Record, 53rd Cong., 16 September 1893, p. 1557, and 21 December 1893, p. 446; People v. Lovren; People v. Thompson; *Railway Age*, 22 September 1893, 19 January, 9 November 1894, 22 February, 10 May, 23 August 1895; Territory v. Ketchum.)

TRINIDAD, COLORADO. Trinidad is in Las Animas County, in southern Colorado about ten miles from the New Mexico line. On the night of November 18, 1902, four masked men flagged Colorado & Southern passenger Train No. 4 south of Trinidad. When the train slowed, the men fired a volley of shots toward the locomotive, which forced the engineer to pull to a stop. While several of the men continued to fire alongside the coaches to keep the passengers from wandering out, one of them stuffed a sack of dynamite under the express car.

When the charge had been placed, the robber ordered the engineer, John Guilfril, to light the fuse. He tried, several times, without success. One of the bandits then climbed under the car to rearrange the charge. As he did, the express company messenger, H. W. Sherwick, slid open the door, leaned out, and put a bullet into the stomach of the nearest robber. The rest of the gang, shaken by the sight of their fallen comrade, ran for a nearby woods.

The wounded bandit, identified as A. F. Hudson, a coal miner from Gray Creek, was found the next morning near the scene. He died later that day. (Sources: *San Francisco Chronicle*, 19, 20 November 1902.)

TROUSDALE, DAVID. On March 13, 1912, David Trousdale, a newly appointed Wells, Fargo express messenger, ended the outlaw career of Wild Bunch member Ben Kilpatrick on a lonely stretch of Southern Pacific track near Sanderson, Texas.

Kilpatrick and a companion halted the train just east of Sanderson and were in the process of robbing the two express cars. While the other bandit was in the car ahead, Trousdale distracted Kilpatrick by suggesting that he check one of the packages, which was supposed to be especially valuable. As Kilpatrick stooped over, Trousdale hit him in the head with an ice mallet. When the other bandit returned to see what was detaining Kilpatrick, Trousdale killed him with Kilpatrick's rifle.

When the passengers on the train learned what had happened, they took up a collection and presented Trousdale with a purse full of money. (Sources: *New York Times*, 14–16 March 1912.) *See also* **Ben Kilpatrick; Sanderson, Texas**.

TROUT, HENRY. During the train robbery era, many an express messenger became famous for thwarting a robbery attempt. Also, on occasion, a locomotive engineer or a conductor would make the headlines for an unusual act of bravery. Seldom did a brakeman or flagman have a chance to become a hero. There was, however, at least one exception.

Henry Trout was a flagman on the Union Pacific Railroad. On May 12, 1902, about four miles west of North Bend, Nebraska, Trout was set upon by a gang of would-be train robbers, apparently to obtain his lantern, which they intended to use to stop the train. They beat Trout severely, and before they left, they stuffed a gag in his mouth and tied his hands and feet to a telegraph pole.

When he regained consciousness, Trout managed to work his way free. He was too weak from loss of blood to stand, so he crawled to a nearby farmhouse. The farmer had a phone, and he called the station at North Bend and told them that there might be an attempt to rob the next train. The next train was a westbound, and it had not yet arrived at North Bend. When it did, extra guards were put on.

When the train reached the four-mile mark west of town, the guards were ready to give the outlaws a "warm reception." But no attack came. Union Pacific officials later concluded that the would-be robbers had probably returned to check on Trout and found that he had escaped. Figuring he had given the alarm, they called off the robbery.

Bloodhounds were brought to the scene, but a steady rain throughout the night had wiped out the culprits' scent. (Source: *New York Times*, 14 May 1902.) □

U

UNAWEEP SWITCH (COLORADO). In the early morning hours of November 3, 1887, about five miles east of Grand Junction, Colorado, the engineer of an eastbound Denver & Rio Grande passenger train saw a pile of rocks on the track along a curve on the Gunnison River, at a spot called Unaweep Switch. The locomotive sported the traditional heavy cowcatcher on the front, which probably would have plowed its way through the barrier, but the engineer could not take that chance on a curve with a train load of passengers. He released the throttle and reached for the brakes.

It was 3:45 A.M., and back in the postal car, Railway Mail Service clerk H. W. Grubb, with his mail pouch ready for Delta, the next stop, had been dozing. When the engineer applied the brakes, Grubb awakened, and without looking at his watch, assumed that the train was pulling into Delta. He grabbed the mail pouch and loosened the latch on the side door of the car. As the train came to a halt, he slid open the door. What he saw, however, was not the station platform, but three masked men, two with revolvers and one with a rifle, all pointed at him. Off to the side, toward the front of the train, was a fourth man holding a gun on the engineer and fireman as they climbed down from the locomotive cab.

One of the masked men asked Grubb if he was alone. When he replied that he was, he was ordered to go to the end of the car and "stand against the wall with your face toward it." The three men climbed into the car and began sorting through the mail pouches, taking out the registered letters and packages. As they worked, Grubb, at the far end, away from the car's potbellied stove, began to shiver in the cold. He complained, and asked if he could have his coat. After checking the coat for a weapon, the men let him put it on.

When the robbers had finished with the mail, they ordered Grubb out of the car and told him to join the engineer and fireman. The three masked men then walked back to the express car. Inside, express messenger Dick Williams had guessed what was happening and had grabbed his weapons, a shotgun and revolver. When he heard the order to open up, he began to weigh his chances on making a stand. To buy a few minutes of time, he shouted to the robbers that he could not open the door because there were trunks piled in front of it, and they would have to go around to the other side of the car, Williams tried to get a look at them through the end window to see how many there were, but it was too dark. Once on the other side, they again ordered him to open up. When he hesitated, they informed him that they had dynamite and would blow the door open. The word "dynamite" made Williams's decision for him. He opened up.

The express car carried two safes, a local, or messenger's safe, and a through safe. At the robbers' orders Williams opened the messenger's safe, which contained only $150. When ordered to open the larger safe, Williams answered that he could not do it, that it was opened only by station agents at the larger towns along the line, and only they knew the combination. One of the masked men then barked, "If that safe ain't opened in three minutes, I'm going to blow your head off."

Williams pleaded that he was telling the truth. At the end of three minutes he was certain that he was going to be killed. But when one of the robbers pointed his revolver at him and asked, "Shall I let him have it?" the leader of the group shrugged and answered, "No, let him go. I believe he's telling the truth."

The robbers grabbed a package that looked valuable, and a couple of letters marked "C.O.D.," then, after lining Williams and the others up against the wall, three of them returned to the postal car and ransacked it for a second time.

The train had now been stopped long enough for the conductor to guess what was happening. He went about the coaches and tried to assure the passengers that there probably was little danger, that the robbers were only interested in the express and postal cars. A young Scotchman, however, visiting America's Wild West for the first time, was not about to be calmed down. Apparently having heard the tale that western train robbers seldom bother lady passengers, he grabbed a dress from the suitcase of a woman passenger and tried to put it on. The conductor assured him that the trick would not work, and the embarrassed young man returned the dress to the owner.

About that time the brakeman and a passenger ventured forward to help, but two warning shots from the masked men sent them scurrying back to the coaches. After briefly considering whether to "pass the hat" among the passengers, the four robbers decided to call it a night and hurried off into the darkness toward their horses.

Despite the small amount taken in the holdup, the Denver & Rio Grande Express Company offered a $3,000 reward for the capture of the robbers, and the United States government kicked in another $1,000. This sum, a sizable amount for the times, caught the attention of Cyrus "Doc" Shores, noted manhunter and at the time sheriff of Gunnison County, Colorado. Shores and his brother-in-law, M. L. Allison, arrived at the scene of the robbery the next day. They hoped to find tracks, but if there were any, they had been obliterated by the hoofprints of a Mesa County posse that had raced to the site immediately after the holdup.

Shores and Allison spent the first day searching the northeast side of the track above and below the scene, making ever-widening circles as they rode. They found nothing. Then they crossed the river and searched the southwest bank. The second day they found the tracks of two men. Shortly thereafter, they found another set of two, all headed in the same direction, toward Bangs Canyon, a wild area running southwestward from the Gunnison River up to a high plateau of over 9,000 feet. On the third day, they found the two sets of tracks rejoining. They were now sure that it was the train robbers they were following.

Shores and Allison spent more than four days searching the Bangs Canyon area, returning at night to Grand Junction. Near the end of the week they took the train back to Gunnison for supplies and fresh horses, and were joined by James Duckworth, a special agent for the Denver & Rio Grande Express Company. The following day they picked up a fourth manhunter, a local cattleman named Tom Denning. They started out again, but after several days a cold and wet snowstorm set in, covering the tracks they were following. Duckworth, not used to life on the trail, took seriously ill and Shores had to take him back to town.

On rejoining Allison and Denning at Delta, Shores was ready to start out again when he picked up some interesting information. Shortly before the robbery, four strangers leading a pack horse had come into Delta on foot. They set up camp outside town and began building a boat. When questioned, they seemed friendly and said they had come from Carbondale where they had worked for the Colorado Midland Railroad. They gave their names as Jack and Bob Smith, Ed Rhodes, and Bob Wallace.

Sheriff Shores figured the chances of these four being the train robbers was a long shot, and if so, the names were probably aliases, but he sent the information over to the Pinkerton office in Denver just to make sure. In the meantime, Tom Denning became ill, and he had to give up the hunt.

Shores was about to give up the search when a report came in that four men matching the descriptions of the four they sought had been spotted at Cisco, Utah, just west of Grand Junction, catching a freight train bound for Salt Lake City. Shores immediately dispatched Allison and a Gunnison County deputy for Salt Lake City. With the help of Utah authorities, three of the four men were picked up in the Price River. They gave their names as Jack and Bob Smith, and Ed Rhodes. With but a little encouragement, they admitted taking part in the Unaweep robbery.

Sheriff Shores, desperately wanting to meet face-to-face the men he had so stubbornly tracked through the rugged Colorado Rockies, took the next train to Utah. "Well, you fellows have sure been causing me a lot of grief, tracking you all over the country," Shores said on greeting them for the first time.

"You're the damndest bloodhound I ever seen," Rhodes replied to the sheriff, "but the last couple of months ain't been no harder on you than on us. We've been living outdoors in this damned weather, freezing and starving like wild animals."

Jack Smith then added: "That's right. In a way I'm glad you finally caught up with us. I ain't been warm or had a square meal since the robbery."

For a meeting between lawman and fugitives it was a strange scene. Soon they were comparing notes on the rugged Bangs Canyon area, and how they survived the sudden winter storm. The outlaws even supplied information on the fourth man, whose real name was Bob Boyle, a resident of Paola, Kansas. Boyle was even-

tually found working on an irrigation canal near Price, Utah. Without a warrant, Shores arranged for him to be whisked away and returned to Colorado to stand trial with his comrades.

As far as anyone knows, the Unaweep Switch train robbers went straight after serving their time. Bob Smith and Bob Boyle headed for the gold fields of Alaska. Ed Rhodes got a job in Boulder, but one day he got into an argument with a coworker and was shot to death. Jack Smith settled in Whitewater, Colorado, just a few miles east of Unaweep Switch. (Source: Jessen, *Colorado Gunsmoke.*)

UNDERWOOD, HENRY. *See* **Henri Stewart**.

URY, HENRY. *See* **Henry Williams**.

UTICA, NEW YORK. While it took nerve to rob a train, it did not take an unusual amount of brains. In fact, some train robbers were incredibly stupid. Take, for example, Charles O'Rourke.

O'Rourke was what they called a high roller. He said he came from Texas and once had a large ranch there. A few months after arriving in Oswego, New York, in 1885, he married a local woman, Carrie Cotter, a refined young lady known throughout the area as an accomplished elocutionist. Not long after their marriage, O'Rourke opened a gambling house in Niagara Falls, but he got into trouble with the police and it was closed down.

What he did for the next several months is not known, but on March 30, 1887, he forced his way into an eastbound National Express Company car on the West Shore Railroad near Oneida and ordered the messenger, Charles S. Leake, to throw up his hands. Leake did not immediately respond, and O'Rourke promptly shot him in the shoulder. As the messenger fell to the floor, O'Rourke said "Now, damn you, when I tell you to hold up your hands again, you'll do it, won't you?" Leake nodded, and O'Rourke proceeded to tie his hands and feet and stuff a gag in his mouth.

Taking the messenger's keys, O'Rourke opened the safe and extracted around $3,000. When the train reached the Delaware, Lackawanna & Western junction, where it was required to stop, he jumped off, after giving a final warning to Leake that he had better keep his mouth shut or he would come back and kill him.

Messenger Leake was indeed frightened and gave only a brief report of the robbery to his superiors. He would talk to no one else, especially newspaper reporters, which led some to speculate that maybe he made up the story and had taken the money himself. But Leake had been an express messenger for more than eight years, the first six with the Erie and New England Express Company and the last two with National, and his record had always been clean.

Detectives scoured the area where O'Rourke left the train, and found empty express money envelopes, several of which had contained bank notes. In his hurry to get to the loot, O'Rourke had torn the corners off several of the notes, which were still in the envelopes.

Apparently O'Rourke had recently been down on his luck, because a few days before the robbery he had pawned his watch at a shop at Niagara Falls. Oblivious to the fact that the money could be traced, he redeemed his watch with several of the torn bank notes. Later, he paid his hotel bill at the Mansion House near Suspension Bridge with some of the same damaged money. Even as unsophisticated as small town police might have been in the 1880s, it did not take them long to pick up O'Rourke. The clincher came when he was arrested. He still had in his possession the gun and mask he used during the robbery. (Sources: *New York Times*, 1–3, 15 April 1887.)   □

V

VAIL, ARIZONA. In August 1887 the Wells, Fargo express car on the Southern Pacific line was looted by three bandits at Vail. The engineer, Jim Guthrie, and the fireman, Bob McGrath, spotted a stop signal ahead on the track, but Guthrie suspected a robbery attempt and kept on the throttle. As the locomotive ran past the signal, a rifle bullet clipped off the left side of McGrath's mustache as cleanly as if done with a pair of scissors.

Guthrie thought he had outwitted his attackers, but they had anticipated his action and had opened a switch a hundred yards down the track. The locomotive left the rails, gouged into the roadbed, and skidded to a stop. Guthrie and McGrath jumped out of the cab and ran for a dense grove of mesquite.

The three robbers, after concluding that the engineer and fireman could cause them no trouble, went directly to the express car and forced their way in. They knocked the helpless messenger in the head and threw him out of the car onto the ground. By t his time some of the train crew and passengers had come forward from the coaches, but they were persuaded not to join in by one of the bandits holding a Winchester.

After ransacking the express car, the robbers ordered the passengers to empty their pockets of cash and jewelry. When this loot was collected, they fled north,

apparently to where their horses had been tied. Pima County Sheriff M. T. Shaw hurriedly organized a posse, which tracked the culprits to a nearby cave where they found some of the jewelry. From there the trail led to the southeast and ended at Pantano, where it is believed the outlaws flagged down an eastbound train headed for El Paso. (Source: Young, "Train Robbers Mystify Sheriff and Posse.")

VERDI, NEVADA. It was November 4, 1870, and in western Nevada, near the California line, the weather was cool and crisp. In the shiny green Wells, Fargo express car the new cannonball stove glowed warmly for messenger Frank Marshall, who was trying to catch a few winks before the next stop at Reno where he would turn over the $40,000 in gold and silver coins that

John Chapman.
Southern Pacific Railroad.

John Davis.
Southern Pacific Railroad.

James Gilchrist.
Southern Pacific Railroad.

rested in the sturdy strongbox at his feet. Up front, the fireman was tossing roughly cut spruce logs into the belly of the diamond-stacked locomotive of the Central Pacific's proud Train No. 1. The engineer wanted a good head of steam when the train reached the bottom of the slope, near where the twisting Truckee River wound its way toward the next stop, tiny Verdi station. Train No. 1 had been delayed by a westbound freight that had lost a dozen cars when a shattered draft gear rammed under a set of trucks, and although the engineer was holding back a bit on the downgrade, he was still letting the train run well, maybe just a little too well for the soft ballast under the year-old track.

Up ahead at Verdi station, five darkly clad figures shuffled about nervously, straining to see No. 1's headlight in the bright, moonlit night. The leader of the five men, Jack Davis, although perhaps meek in appearance, commanded his group well; they had been thoroughly rehearsed, and he expected the assault on the Wells, Fargo express car to go smoothly.

Train No. 1 made its brief stop at Verdi and, on conductor D. G. Marshall's (no relation to the express messenger) signal, the engineer gave his locomotive the throttle and the cars slowly pulled away. As the train picked up speed, conductor Marshall, who was in the second coach, glanced out onto the platform and noticed that he had three extra passengers. At first, he probably thought they had missed his "all aboard" call and had boarded late, so he stepped to the door to collect their fares; however, three revolvers suddenly leveled in his direction told him otherwise. He was ordered back into the coach and told to sit quietly, and to see that the passengers did the same.

But D. G. Marshall, conductor of the Central Pacific's

Train No. 1, did not take orders, he gave them. As soon as the intruders turned their attention elsewhere, Marshall yanked the bell cord, the signal for the engineer to stop the train. But nothing happened. The bell cord had been cut.

In a few minutes, however, the train did begin to slow. And as it gradually rolled to a halt, the three intruders dropped to the ground and trotted forward, toward the locomotive, leaving Marshall to explain to his passengers why the train was stopping in the middle of nowhere. By now, conductor Marshall had figured out what was about to happen, and he quickly rummaged through his service box and found a battered hand axe. One hand axe against three or more guns was certainly not good odds, but Marshall was not going to stand by helplessly. Quietly, he, too, dropped to the ground and headed forward.

Before conductor Marshall reached the express car, he saw it beginning to move forward. The familiar scraping sound from the rear of the car told him that the bandits had uncoupled it from the remainder of the train, and had ordered the engineer to pull it down the track.

Up front in the locomotive, the engineer and fireman had been staring at two revolvers since shortly after leaving the Verdi station. The guns bothered them, but that was not what worried the engineer most. His concern was for the train. It had been halted on a downgrade. He had been ordered to pull the express car ahead, and he knew that soon he would be told to stop. The rest of the train, now a mile or so behind, might start rolling. If it did, and if it picked up enough speed, it could come crashing into the express car and cause serious injuries. Risking the wrath of his captors, the engineer lunged for the whistle cord and gave it two short blasts—the signal for the brakeman in the rear to set the brakes on the coach.

The engineer was eventually ordered to bring the locomotive to a halt near an abandoned stone quarry about six miles east of Verdi. Back in the express-car, messenger Frank Marshall had figured out what was happening and was pondering his fate. Should he open up or should he resist? When the order finally came, he opened up.

Moving quickly, the robbers ushered the engineer and fireman into the express car and forced them and the messenger into the postal compartment of the car, which they bolted shut. Then, turning to the safe, they made quick work of the lock with a pick, emptied the contents into sacks, and disappeared into the night.

R. A. Jones.
Southern Pacific Railroad.

On learning of the robbery, Wells, Fargo officials dispatched F. T. Burke, at the time the company's most experienced detective, and a special force of handpicked investigators. Burke's method of investigation, up to now limited to stagecoach holdups, was to flood the area with agents in the hope of picking up loose talk or spotting an unsavory character who had recently come into a large sum of money. In this case, the best place to start was Reno, at the time a thriving, boisterous town with a generous share of lawless types. It did not take long. In a few days Burke's men found a suspect, a local drifter spending an unusually large amount of cash. Soon another big spender was found, and then another. When it was discovered that all three were acquainted, the Wells, Fargo detectives were fairly sure they had their robbers.

One of the suspects was a carpenter, R. A. Jones.

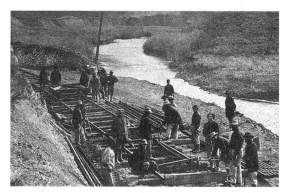

A scene often mistakenly identified as the site of the Verdi robbery. According to the records of the Southern Pacific Railroad, this photograph was actually taken in Ten-Mile Canyon along the Humboldt River in the Nevada Palisades about 432 miles east of Sacramento. It was taken by official Central Pacific photographer Alfred A. Hart in 1868. *Southern Pacific Railroad.*

Burke interrogated him personally. The detective knew his business, and before long Jones not only identified his role in the robbery but named the others.

The robbery had been planned by a rank amateur, a former Sunday school superintendent named John T. Chapman. The other members of the gang were Jack Davis, John Squires, James Gilchrist, Tilton Cockerill, and Jones. The first four were hard characters who had spent considerable time on the wrong side of the law. Jones, like Chapman, was having his first fling at crime. Davis was the worst of the bunch. A former mining

Stone quarry near site of Verdi robbery. *Southern Pacific Railroad.*

recorder from the Flowery District, he had turned to stage robbery when his wages failed to match his penchant for high living. He became so good at this work he even opened a mill in Six Mile Canyon for reworking stolen bullion. He had been caught once but got off, some said by bribing the jury.

Chapman, being a newcomer, gave himself the easiest job. He had gone to San Francisco, nosed around, and discovered when an especially large shipment of gold was being sent by rail. He then sent the necessary information to his confederates by code.

Once Jones named names, the entire gang was rounded up quickly. Detectives immediately recovered $7,000 of the loot. All except James Gilchrist stubbornly insisted on their innocence. Gilchrist backed Jones's story fully and led detectives to another $30,000 of the stolen money. (Sources: Beebe and Clegg, *U.S. West: The Saga of Wells, Fargo*; Patterson, *Train Robbery*.)

VERNON, TOM. Tom Vernon grew up on ranches in Wyoming. At times he would boast that he was the son of the notorious cattle rustlers James and "Cattle Kate" Averill. As an adult, Vernon worked as a stockman and rodeo performer, but he got on the wrong side of the law and by the time he reached his forties he had accumulated six felony convictions and had spent twenty-two years behind bars.

In November 1929, three months after being released from Folsom prison on his sixth conviction, he derailed a Southern Pacific passenger train near Saugus, California, and robbed the passengers in one of the Pullman cars. Through a letter he wrote to a former employer, he was traced to Pawnee, Oklahoma, where he was arrested and returned to California. To avoid the death penalty, which was still in effect in California for train wrecking, he pleaded guilty and was sentenced to life. *See* **Saugus, California.**

VICTOR, COLORADO. On the night of March 24, 1895, the town of Victor was shocked by the news that bandits had boarded and robbed a Florence & Cripple Creek Railroad train less than a mile and a half out of town. At 9:50 P.M., southbound Train No. 60 was pulling away from the Victor station, six miles south of Cripple Creek in Teller County, when two masked men darted out of the shadows toward the track. One slipped aboard the blind baggage behind the tender,

The station at Victor. *Everett R. Huffer Collection.*

and the other jumped on the platform of the Pullman sleeper.

The man in the sleeper immediately began waking up passengers and demanding money and valuables. As he was doing so, the man on the tender climbed over the coal pile and shoved his gun in the ribs of the engineer, issuing orders to ease the train to a stop at a point about one and one-half miles out of town. When the train had stopped, four or five more masked and armed bandits suddenly appeared at trackside. All the bandits were dressed in miner's clothes and slouch hats. The train crew described them as "jovial," but impatient, "enforcing their commands with a display of firearms." When the robber in the sleeper finished there, he went through the passenger coach. The men up front went through the express and railway mail cars.

After they had gathered their loot, the bandits ordered the engineer to move on. He first threw the engine in reverse, intending to back up to Victor, but the robbers objected and ordered him to proceed on southward. When the train reached Florence, the conductor rushed to the station and notified local authorities of the robbery.

By early morning, the Teller County Sheriff and twelve deputized possemen were on the scene but could find no tracks. They telegraphed Walsenburg and requested the use of a well-known bloodhound in hopes of picking up the culprits' trail. The dog arrived by special train at noon, and an all-out manhunt began.

By the time the trackers were ready to depart, nearly the whole town of Victor and many citizens from Cripple Creek had come out to the site of the holdup. A reporter on the scene estimated the crowd at 2,000, most of whom joined in on the hunt.

The bloodhound did his job. By late in the day he had led the posse to a mountain cabin near the Strong

Mine. At the time the cabin was occupied by a former deputy sheriff and federal marshal named Bob Taylor, and a young companion, seventeen-year-old Frank Wallace, who claimed he had arrived two weeks earlier from Oklahoma. The two men were taken to Cripple Creek where the trainmen identified Taylor as the man who went through the coaches robbing passengers. One of the trainmen also said that Frank Wallace strongly resembled one of the robbers whom the others called "Kid." (Source: *New York Times*, 25 March 1895.)

VINITA, OKLAHOMA. Train robberies did not become frequent in the territory that is now Oklahoma until the early 1890s. This 1882 robbery attempt at Vinita has nearly gone unnoticed in the annals of outlaw history.

Vinita is in the northeastern corner of Oklahoma, which was then Indian Territory, about sixty miles from Tulsa. On September 11, 1882, an Adams Express Company agent working on the Missouri Pacific line learned that an attempt would be made to rob the northbound train that was due at the Vinita station at 10:30 that night. According to the tip, the plan was for two of the bandits to slip on board at Vinita, probably by hiding in the blind baggage area behind the tender, and quietly take over the locomotive. The train would then be switched to a siding four miles north of town where the rest of the outlaws would be waiting to rob the express car, the railway mail service car, and the passenger coaches.

The Adams express agent passed the information along to the Missouri Pacific route agent, J. B. Barrett, who secured the services of Detective Erskine, then with the St. Louis & San Francisco Railroad, and several others. They immediately caught a freight train south to Chateau, which is about midway between Vinita and Muskogee. At Chateau, they waited for the evening northbound and boarded inconspicuously as passengers.

The train made the stop at Vinita, but as it was pulling away, the would-be robbers did not slip aboard the blind baggage as expected. Instead, they boarded the platform of the smoking car. There they encountered the train's conductor, whose name was Warner. It is not known exactly what happened; possibly Warner attempted to throw the men off the train. The bandits drew their guns and ordered him to put up his hands. When he did not, one of them fired. The bullet struck the conductor in the cheek, knocking him off the train.

Detective Erskine and the others heard the shot and they charged the two bandits with their guns blazing. One of the outlaws was killed instantly, and the other was quickly captured. The train was then backed up, and the conductor was taken on board and returned to Vinita for medical attention. His wound, however, was not serious. The train proceeded to the switch where the rest of the bandits were supposed to be waiting, but there was no sign of them.

The two bandits were not identified. The man who tipped off the express agent about the intended robbery was named Brown, and he was on the train at the time. He left the train later at Parsons, Kansas. (Source: *New York Times*, 13 September 1882.)   □

WAGNER, MONTANA. In outlaw chronicles this holdup has become known as the Wagner robbery, although at the time it was frequently mentioned as occurring at Havre and, sometimes, at Exeter Switch, Montana.

Wagner is in the northeastern corner of the state, about midway between Havre and Glasgow. The July 3, 1901, robbery of an express car on the eastbound Great Northern Coast Flyer, which occurred at midday, is believed to have been the last holdup by the Wyo-

ming Wild Bunch before the gang split up to go their separate ways.

Just which gang members were involved in the holdup is not known for certain—probably Butch Cassidy and Harvey "Kid Curry" Logan, and possibly Ben Kilpatrick, Bill Carver, or a newcomer, O. C. Hanks. Witnesses said there were three men involved, one of whom was a half-breed, but there could have been more.

Some say Wagner was chosen for the holdup site because of Logan's familiarity with the area. Also, some say the Great Northern Railroad was picked because the Union Pacific, the Wild Bunch's favorite target, was by then using crack teams of manhunters on horse cars, which were rushed to the scene of a robbery by special train. (See **Horse Cars.**)

The robbery actually took place at Exeter Switch, some two miles east of Wagner. Although accounts differ on how the train was halted, it is believed that one of the outlaws, possibly Kilpatrick, boarded at Malta, while another, probably Logan, slipped on behind the tender. A few miles out, Logan worked his way forward and put a gun in the back of the engineer, Tom Jones. The train was stopped at the preselected spot where another one or two outlaws were waiting. These outlaws may have used a flag to halt the train, which could explain early reports of the robbery mentioning that the train was "flagged" down by robbers.

In traditional Wild Bunch fashion, random shots were fired along the sides of the coaches to keep the passengers in line, and several persons inside the coaches were wounded slightly by ricochets. The train was then separated behind the express car, and the front section was pulled ahead. The gang broke into the express car and blew the safe, which contained around $40,000, mostly bank notes. According to the Great Northern Express Company, the bank notes were a consignment to the Montana National Bank of Helena. They were printed in sheets and all could be easily passed.

After loading the loot on their horses, the gang forded the nearby Milk River and rode south, across the trail that is now State Road 363, and then east, into what is today the Charles M. Russell National Wildlife Refuge. On July 7, four days after the robbery, express company and local law enforcement officials released the following information to newspaper reporters:

Two theories are presented. One is that the outlaws, who are far better mounted than their pursuers, have already crossed the Missouri River, and are well on their way toward the "Hole-in-the-Wall" country in Wyoming. . . . The region between the Missouri and the "Hole-in-the-Wall" is very sparsely settled. Pursuit over this wild section, according to old plainsmen, is virtually hopeless.

The other theory is that the robbers have gained the intricacies of the Bad Lands along the Missouri River, near the Little Rockies, and are there awaiting the time when the chase shall have grown cold, when they will seize a favorable opportunity to ford the river at a place where

Aftermath of Wagner robbery. *Burlington Northern Railroad.*

crossing could not be effected by men unfamiliar with the treacherous windings. Every foot of this ground is known to the robbers.

It was discovered later that several of the robbers had stopped at Miles City, in Custer County, where they spent part of the bank notes on four fresh horses. (Sources: Dullenty, "Rare Old Photos Reveal Aftermath of the Wagner Train Robbery"; Kirby, *The Saga of Butch Cassidy and the Wild Bunch*; Pointer, *In Search of Butch Cassidy*; New York Times, 4, 7 July 1901.) *See also* **Harvey Logan; Robert LeRoy "Butch Cassidy" Parker.**

Great Northern Express Co.

ST. PAUL, MINN., JULY 4, 1901.

$5000 Reward

The Great Northern Railway "Overland" West-bound Train No. 3 was held up about three miles east of Wagner, Mont., Wednesday afternoon, July 3, 1901, and the Great Northern Express Company's through safe blown open with dynamite and the contents taken.

There were three men connected with the hold-up, described as follows:

One was, height 5 feet and 9 inches, weight about 175 pounds, blue eyes, had a projecting brow and about two weeks growth of sandy beard on chin, wore new tan shoes, black coat, corduroy trousers, and carried a silver plated, gold mounted Colt's revolver with a pearl handle.

Second man, height 6 feet, weight about 175 pounds, sandy complexion, blue eyes, not very large with slight cast in left eye; wore workingman's shoes, blue overalls over black suit of clothes, had a boot leg for cartridge pouch suspended from his neck.

Third man resembled a half breed very strongly, had large dark eyes, smoothly shaven face, and a very prominent nose; features clear cut, weight about 180 pounds, slightly stooped in shoulders, but very square across the shoulders, and wore a light slouch hat.

All three men used very marked Texas cowboy dialect, and two of them carried Winchester rifles, one of which was new. One had a carbine, same pattern as the Winchesters. They rode away on black, white, and buckskin horses respectively.

The Great Northern Express Company will give $5000 reward for the capture and identification of the three men, or a proportionate amount for one or two and $500 additional for each conviction.

D. S. ELLIOTT,
Approved: Auditor.
    D. MILLER,
        President.

Reward notice following Wagner robbery. *Author's Collection.*

WASHINGTON CUT (MISSOURI). Washington Cut was a swath cut through high ground for the Chicago & Alton Railroad about six miles east of what is now downtown Kansas City. On today's maps it would be just west of the northern leg of Interstate 435.

On the night of October 6, 1897, C&A's Train No. 49 was stopped by a red lantern and a series of explosive charges from railroad torpedoes. As the locomotive slowed to a halt, the engineer and fireman were taken captive by two masked men. Other bandits (the total number was never verified; some witnesses said there were five, others said eight) raced down the track and uncoupled the train behind the mail car. The locomotive was then steamed up, and the express and mail cars were pulled ahead about a quarter of a mile.

As the train once more was halted the bandits converged on the express car, and messenger Frank Fritts was forced to open up. Once inside, the intruders stuffed more than twenty sticks of dynamite around the express company's through safe, but the fuse fizzled. As the would-be robbers fumbled with the charge, they heard the whistle of an approaching freight train. It had picked up Train No. 49's abandoned coaches and was pushing them ahead of the locomotive. The gang gave up and disappeared into the night.

When things calmed down, the total loss was estimated at no more than $55, and this came from the pockets of express messenger Fritts and two trainmen. The crime was never solved. (Source: Burton, "John F. Kennedy of Missouri and His Circle of Train Robbers.")

WATT, NEWTON H. Newton Watt, a baggage man on the Chicago, Rock Island & Pacific Railroad, was involved in the famous "Express Car Murder" of March 14, 1886. On a run from Chicago to Davenport, Iowa, United States Express Company messenger Kellogg Nichols was found brutally slain and his express car robbed when the train pulled into Morris, Illinois. After nearly a year's investigation, Watt, who claimed one of the robbers had held a gun on him while others entered Nichols's express car, was convicted of the crime, together with a brakeman on the train, Henry Schwartz. *See* **Henry Schwartz**.

WEEMS, ALABAMA. Shortly after midnight on March 31, 1892, two masked men took command of a Georgia Pacific passenger train near Weems, ten miles east of Birmingham. The locomotive had just crossed a small trestle when one of the bandits, who apparently had slipped aboard unnoticed, climbed down into the cab and ordered the engineer to stop. Back at the mail car, the second bandit fired his Winchester into the car to get mail clerk R. P. Hughes's attention. Hughes was hit but only slightly wounded. When the clerk refused to open up, the bandit broke in the door, ordered Hughes to stand against the wall with his hands over his head, and then helped himself to all of the sixty-seven packages of registered mail bound for New York.

A special train was dispatched from Birmingham and a team of bloodhounds was put on the robbers' trail. The dogs tracked the culprits up the side of a high hill that bordered the track, where the posse found one of the packages of mail and a campfire that had been abandoned less than two hours before. From there the trail turned west over hills and hollows, across Stinking Creek, and eventually to the Birmingham suburb of Irondale. There the trail was lost.

Within two weeks, however, the authorities picked up four suspects. All were eventually released, but one was kept under surveillance: a Birmingham doctor named F. F. Lidell. Lidell, although a graduate of Memphis Medical College and a trained physician, also had a criminal record, which included a conviction for burglary in New Orleans in 1880. A Birmingham detective, G. W. McDaniels, was assigned the case, and working under cover he gained Dr. Lidell's confidence. McDaniels was so successful at his job that Lidell not only admitted committing the Weems train robbery, but also enlisted McDaniels's help in planning the burglary of a Birmingham jewelry store. McDaniels notified the police, and they were waiting at the store. When the police closed in, Dr. Lidell tried to escape and was killed. (Sources: *St. Louis Globe Democrat,* 1, 6, 12, 13 April, 7, 9 May 1892; *New York Times,* 1 April 1892.)

WESTERN UNION JUNCTION, WISCONSIN. Western Union Junction was on the old Chicago, Milwaukee & St. Paul line about twenty-three miles south of Milwaukee, near the present town of Sturtevant. On November 12, 1891, the northbound midnight train out of Chicago was about half a mile south of the junction when the fireman, Edward Averill, glanced back and saw two masked men carrying shotguns and climbing down the coal pile toward him. They leveled their weapons at Averill and the engineer, Bill McKay, with the order: "Don't move an inch till we tell you to or we will blow the tops of your heads off!"

Engineer McKay was told to stop the train a mile north of the junction, where four more robbers were waiting. The trainmen were then ordered down out of the cab and back to the American Express car. By this time the conductor had come forward from the first passenger coach to see why the train had stopped, and he also was taken prisoner.

The robbers pounded on the express company door, demanding that the messenger, J. C. Murphy, and his assistant, C. H. Cook, open up. They refused, and the robbers placed either dynamite or gunpowder on the door slides and detonated it. The explosion demolished the door, but the messenger and his helper still refused to allow the men to enter. The robbers then placed a larger charge on the opposite door. This time the blast rocked the car, dousing the lanterns and knocking packages off the shelves. Before Murphy and Cook could recover, the bandits, shoving the engineer and fireman before them, entered the car and took control.

The robbers forced Murphy to turn over his keys to the local safe, which contained money and valuables destined for the smaller stations between Chicago and LaCrosse. The two through safes were secured with combination locks, however, and when Murphy convinced the robbers that he could not open them, they forced the trainmen to drag them over to the door and throw them off the car.

Several of the robbers then marched the trainmen about a quarter mile up the track. The reason for this is not clear; possibly it was to give the bandits time to discuss how they were going to transport the safes. In the meantime, some of the passengers had awakened and were peeking out their windows. They did not, however, leave the coaches.

The trainmen were eventually returned to the train, and the engineer and fireman were ordered to get the steam back up. As the train pulled away, the robbers were seen standing over the safes, as if unsure of what to do. The train stopped at Franksville, a few miles north, and telegrams were sent to stations along the line to report the holdup.

Posses and railroad police were dispatched to the scene from both Western Union Junction and Milwaukee, the latter by a special train. When they arrived,

they found the two safes still lying beside the tracks. The robbers had tried to blast them open, but apparently they did not have enough dynamite left to do the job.

An official of the railroad reported that the two through safes probably contained more than $100,000, because the train usually carried morning cash shipments from the East for Milwaukee banks. The local safe was believed to have carried about $5,000.

When the train pulled into Milwaukee shortly after 2:00 A.M., according to an observer: "The express car presented an appearance that would indicate it had been attacked by heavy artillery. Every door and window had been blown out, and the platforms and walls were shattered in half a dozen places, while the contents were piled in one indescribable heap in the center of the car. Messenger J. C. Murphy and his assistant, C. H. Cook, were found gathering up fragments of waybills." (Source: *New York Times*, 13 November 1891.)

WEST LIBERTY, OHIO. On October 2, 1890, an Adams Express Company car was robbed on a northbound Cincinnati, Sandusky & Cleveland passenger train. Soon after the train left Urbana, the seat of Champaign County about forty miles west of Columbus, two masked men carrying revolvers entered the express car and tied up the messenger, A. L. Scudder, with a rope they had brought with them. They then quickly emptied the contents of the express company safe of several thousand dollars in cash and valuables.

While the robbers were rifling the safe, a brakeman attempted to enter the car. One of the bandits shot at him, but missed, and he ran to the rear of the train, giving the alarm. Apparently somebody pulled the bell cord, and the train slowed. The robbers took this opportunity to jump off, just short of the station at West Liberty.

As the brakeman and conductor were untying the messenger, he told them that just before the robbers left, one of them tried to kill him. He placed his revolver to the messenger's head and pulled the trigger, but the gun misfired. He cocked the gun, ready to try again, but the other robber stopped him.

After a brief search of the area, the conductor gave the engineer the signal to pull on into West Liberty. The conductor wired his officials about the robbery, then ordered the train to move on. But as the train slowly pulled away from the station, the two robbers appeared once more, this time climbing aboard the engine cab. They ordered the startled engineer to put on the steam. The express messenger, who saw them board, grabbed his revolver and fired several shots at the outside of the cab, but he could not shoot into the cab for fear of hitting the engine crew. The robbers returned his fire, and several bullets nearly hit him, which caused him to duck back inside of his car.

The robbers remained in the cab for another eight miles, then, as the train slowed for Bellefontaine, they leaped off into the darkness. (Source: *New York Times*, 3 October 1890.)

WEST, "LITTLE DICK." Little Dick West joined the Bill Doolin gang sometime in 1894. Practically nothing is known of his origins. He probably was born around 1866, but even he never knew for sure. He was once reported to have said: "I was just dropped on the prairie somewhere." On his own from the beginning, young West drifted from one Texas cowtown to another, washing dishes and swamping saloons to survive. In his mid-teens, he hired on as a wrangler at a ranch in Clay County, Texas.

West was always considered strange. He was said to have had a permanent "wild look" in his eyes. Like an animal, he always ate alone, guarding his plate as if he expected somebody to steal his food. He would not sleep under a roof, even in foul weather—a trait that would make him valuable to gang-leader Bill Doolin, who could tuck the rest of his men away in a cabin hideout and post West outside as a night guard.

Although West became an accomplished hand at robbing trains, he never picked up civilized ways. Between jobs he preferred to head for remote areas where he could live unmolested by society.

Bill Doolin's death in 1896 left West and remaining gang member "Dynamite Dick" Clifton to fend for themselves. For a while they enjoyed minor notoriety for a series of store holdups in and around the Sac and Fox Reservation (now Lincoln County, Oklahoma) in the fall of 1896. Eventually, they formed another gang, joining up with renegade lawyers-turned-outlaws Al and Frank Jennings, rank amateurs at train robbery, and another pair of newcomers, Morris and Pat O'Malley. This became the short-lived Clifton-Jennings gang.

Years later, Al Jennings, in a colorful but carelessly written autobiography, credited West with teaching him the art of train robbery, which eventually led Jennings to assume leadership of the outfit. On this relationship, oulaw historian Harry Sinclair Drago wrote:

What persuaded Little Dick West, an accomplished, veteran bandit, to join a band of raw, inexperienced amateurs—and why would he permit Al Jennings, rather than himself, to become its leader? The circumstances would seem to be explanation enough. For months he [West] had lived a friendless, lone-wolf existence, hunted from pillar to post. Undoubtedly he would have associated himself with anyone who offered to take him in. Leadership was beyond him; he was not geared for it. Had it been offered, it well might have aroused his wolfish wariness and warned him of what he was letting himself in for.

West eventually tired of riding with the sometimes foppish Al Jennings, and there is some evidence, although flimsy, that he may have been involved in turning the Jennings and O'Malleys in to the authorities in December 1897. Following the breakup of the outfit, West tried to cut in on his own but was not successful. In April 1898 federal marshals got a tip that a hard case answering West's description was trying to put together a band of train robbers on a ranch outside Guthrie, Oklahoma. Deputy marshals rode out to investigate. It was West. Years later, one of the deputies described what happened in a letter to frontier historian Glenn Shirley:

As Fossett and Rinehart (members of the posse) approached the house, they saw a man step into the breezeway to look close at them. He then stepped from view, but reappeared beside a little building at the rear, walking toward the stable yard. They yelled that they wanted to speak to him, but he jerked his six-shooter, firing and running toward the wire fence enclosing the lot.
Both men fired at him as he dived under the last strand, one shot going under his right shoulder blade and through his body. He ran, I would estimate, about 150 yards beyond the fence, reloading as he ran, and turned in the act of firing when he died.

(Sources: Drago, *Outlaws on Horseback*; Patterson, *Train Robbery*; Shirley, *West of Hell's Fringe*.) See also **"Dynamite Dick" Clifton; Bill Doolin.**

WEST SIDE, NEBRASKA. In 1891 West Side, Nebraska, was a stop on the Missouri Pacific line, just beyond the western edge of Omaha, at what is now Fifty-fifth and Leavenworth streets. On November 4 of that year, an undetermined number of bandits seized control of a westbound MP passenger train as it stopped for Elkhorn Crossing, which was about a mile west of West Side.

Two of the bandits jumped into the locomotive cab and placed revolvers to the heads of the engineer and fireman. The rest of the gang forced their way into the Pacific Express car. The express messenger, S. A. Green, did not offer resistance, and the robbers took approximately $6,000 from his safe. They quickly dumped the money into a cloth bag and, leaving no trace, they disappeared into the night.

While the robbery was in process, the locomotive boiler had lost steam and now it could not be immediately moved out. To avoid being struck from behind by a following train, the brakeman and baggage man ran back toward Omaha to give warning. When the engine had built up sufficient steam, the engineer pulled ahead to Portal, placed the cars on a siding, and then returned to pick up the two trainmen. (Source: *New York Times*, 6 November 1891.)

WHARTON, OKLAHOMA. *See* **Perry, Oklahoma**.

WHITE SULPHUR, GEORGIA. In the early 1900s White Sulphur was a tiny stop on the Southern Railway in northern Georgia about seven miles north of Gainesville. Near there, on February 18, 1911, the Southern's Train No. 36 was flagged to a halt with a red signal. As the engineer, D. J. Fant, slowed to a stop, he saw three men beside the track pointing guns at him. The man who appeared to be the leader told him that a rail had been loosened up ahead and ordered him to step down to the ground. The man sent the fireman up the track (the reason for this is not known) and then he ordered Fant back to the express car. The express messenger was persuaded to open up, and Fant was sent inside, where he was forced to help pack dynamite around the safe. The bandits made three unsuccessful attempts to blow the through safe, which reportedly contained $65,000. In the end they settled for the messenger's strongbox, which held $1,500. With this pocketed, they quickly rode off.

A train robbery was practically unheard of in Georgia. Excited local authorities promptly formed a posse, and with the help of bloodhounds, they soon picked up a trail. The tracks led northwest, toward the town of Dahlonega, in Lumpkin County. The dogs did their job

and they eventually led the posse to what appeared to be a robbers' hideout. There three men were arrested: William A. Morgan, James Hanford, and Charlie Hunter; no trace of the stolen money was found.

The Pinkerton operator on the scene, W. H. Munster, sent photographs of the three suspects to agency headquarters in Chicago. There, the man who claimed to be Morgan was identified as none other than William "Old Bill" Miner, the famous stagecoach and train robber who for years had plagued the Pacific Coast.

The three men were tried. Hanford and Hunter pleaded guilty and drew sentences of fifteen years in a work camp in Newton county. The judge asked Miner if he had anything to say, and he answered, "no." The judge sentenced him to twenty years in the state penitentiary at Milledgeville, Georgia. (Source: Rickards, "Bill Miner—50 Years a Hold-up Man.") *See also* **James Hanford; Charlie Hunter; Bill Miner**.

WICKCLIFFE, KENTUCKY. On July 11, 1900, the Illinois Central's fast New Orleans-to-Chicago express was flagged down two miles south of Wickcliffe by a five-man gang of robbers. The town of Wickliffe is on the western Kentucky line, just across the Mississippi River from Cairo, Illinois. Two of the bandits held up the engine crew and pistol-whipped the fireman, J. J. Fryisch, when he tried to resist.

The bandits cut loose the express car from the rear of the train and ordered the engineer to pull ahead to the Ft. Jefferson siding about one and one-half miles away. There they forced the express messenger, K. F. Hickox, to open the express car door by threatening to blow the car up with dynamite. With the robbers inside and covering him with their guns, the messenger reluctantly opened the safe and turned over $20,000 to the bandits. When they had loaded up their loot, they mounted their horses and headed west toward the river. They crossed in a boat to the Missouri side, but in doing so dropped one of the stolen express company packages containing a little more than $700.

Two days later, two brothers, Charles W. and Channing B. Barnes (a.k.a. John Nelson), were picked up in Missouri as suspects. Charles surrendered peacefully, but Channing shot it out with the arresting officers and escaped. Charles Barnes later signed a confession admitting his part in the holdup. Channing Barnes was found in a Missouri swamp the following December with his throat cut. (Sources: *San Francisco Chronicle*, 12, 14, 16 July, 19 December 1900.)

WILCOX, WYOMING. Shortly before daylight on June 2, 1899, officials at the Union Pacific Railroad offices at Omaha, Nebraska, received the following telegram from Medicine Bow, Wyoming: "First Section No. 1 held up a mile west of Wilcox. Express car blown open, mail car damaged. Safe blown open; contents gone. We were ordered to pull over bridge just west of Wilcox, and after we passed the bridge the explosion occurred. Can't tell how bad bridge was damaged. No one hurt except Jones; scalp wound and cut on hand." It was signed, "JONES. Engineer."

Wilcox, Wyoming, which today can be identified only by a trackside sign, is about fifteen miles southeast of Medicine Bow. The robbers halted the westbound train with a red lantern at 2:09 A.M. and ordered engineer Jones to pull ahead and stop just on the other side of the bridge. When he did, the rest of the gang went to work on the express car.

Shortly thereafter there was a tremendous explosion that scattered pieces of the express car for a hundred feet in every direction. The end of the railway mail car was staved in, and several supports were knocked off the bridge. There was later speculation that the bandits heard another train coming from the east and they had tried to destroy the bridge intentionally.

Another charge of dynamite blew open the express company safe, and it took only a few minutes for the robbers to empty it. The messenger, E. C. Woodcock, had no opportunity to resist. When the robbers had finished, they signaled their confederate on the locomotive and then headed north on foot to a point behind a snow fence where they had hidden extra explosives and their horses. From there they rode almost due north, past Medicine Bow, toward Caspar.

The authorities suspected the Wild Bunch, which had been operating out of the Hole-in-the-Wall hideout in Johnson County. Just which members of the gang participated, however, has never been determined. Robert LeRoy "Butch Cassidy" Parker, Harvey "Kid Curry" Logan, and "Flat Nose" George Currie were thought to have been involved.

Posses were immediately formed, but the culprits' trail soon grew cold. A well-known outlaw hunter, F. M. Hans, who at the time was working for both the Union

$18,000.00 REWARD

Reward notice following Wilcox robbery. *Union Pacific Railroad*.

Pacific Railroad and the federal government, had been on the trail of the gang for several months. On July 8, he issued this report:

These men have made the most remarkable flight in the criminal history of the West. They have traveled over 1,500 miles since committing the crime [Wilcox robbery], and have been chased by 300 or 400 men constantly, yet they escaped. Time and again they have been surrounded by ten times their number, yet by the display of their desperate nerve and knowledge of woodcraft have managed each time to get away. They first fled to the "Hole-in-the-Wall," I found, but being so hard pressed, and having such a large reward on their heads—$18,000—they did not dare stop among their old outlaw companions for fear of being betrayed. They kept on into the Big Horn Basin, then turned back and retraced their steps through the Powder River country into the Jackson's Hole country, the wildest and most desolate stretch of mountainous country in the West. Here the Indian police under Baldwin got after them and chased them south toward the Utah mountains, and it was here that they were completely lost track of.

In the past I have hunted outlaws practically alone, as I prefer that sort of thing, but this time I found that method of little value, since the whole country was aroused and everybody was on the outlook for the men. I know George Curry very well. It is foolishness to talk of that bandit being taken alive. He and his companions will never surrender. They may be killed some day, but they have two horse loads of smokeless ammunition, and in their retreat could stand off an army. I never heard of fugitives making such a fight and flight. None but these very fellows could have done it.

Of course they had everything fixed to rush back to the "Hole-in-the-Wall," the moment the train was robbed, and they expected the chase after them to stop there, as it has in the past. They were not prepared to have the National Guard of the State called out for them. That accounts for the swift time they made.

Although the Wilcox holdup is one of the most famous western train robberies, the robbers actually got very little loot. Most of it, express company officials believed, was destroyed in the explosion. (Sources: Horan, *Desperate Men*; Pointer, *In Search of Butch Cassidy*; *New York Times*, 3 June, 10 July 1899.) *See also* **Frederick E. Hans; Robert Leroy "Butch Cassidy" Parker.**

WILLCOX, ARIZONA. Willcox is in the southeastern corner of Arizona, between Tucson and the New Mexico line. Although the ranches in the hills and valleys around Willcox were said to be notorious as refuges for fugitive gunslingers, the town itself is seldom mentioned in outlaw history. It is probably best known for the site of the killing of Warren Earp in 1900 by an old enemy, Johnny Boyer, and for the robbery of a Southern Pacific westbound overland train in 1895.

The train robbery occurred on January 30, 1895. Two men sneaked aboard the train as it was leaving Willcox and worked their way forward on the roofs of the cars. When they reached the tender, they dropped down and ordered the engineer to stop the train. At that point the locomotive was about two miles west of town. The fireman and a brakeman were forced to cut the express and mail cars from the rest of the train, and the engineer was ordered to pull ahead another two miles, where two more robbers were waiting in a culvert with horses.

The robbers proceeded to attack the Wells, Fargo express car safe with dynamite, but they ran into a problem. It took six charges to open the safe, and the

final explosion scattered much of the contents up and down the track, including 700 Mexican silver "dollars," which Wells, Fargo officials later picked up at the scene. Despite the foul-up, it was believed that the robbers got away with around $10,000.

Sheriff John Fly of Cochise County and a small posse tried to track the robbers the following morning but were unsuccessful. It was reported that a known outlaw, Grant Wheeler, was seen in Willcox the day of the robbery, and that he and another man had purchased eleven pounds of "giant powder," fifty feet of fuse, and twenty ignition caps at a local store. The storekeeper said that the man thought to be Wheeler told him that he needed the explosives for some mining he was doing in the De Cabasas area. (Source: *New York Times*, 1 February 1895.)

WILLIAMS, HENRY. Henry Williams, whose real name was Henry Ury, was sentenced to life imprisonment for killing a county sheriff during a holdup on the Southern Pacific Railroad at Reed's Crossing, California, on March 30, 1895. Williams's companion, Samuel Browning, was killed during the affair. The robbery has become a footnote in the history of train robbery because Williams escaped on a bicycle. *See* **Reed's Crossing, California.**

WILLIAMSVILLE, MISSOURI. Express car robbers seldom had to worry about trouble from the passengers; usually a few shots along the side of the coaches kept them in line. There were exceptions, however, and one occurred in 1895 on the Iron Mountain Railroad near Williamsville.

What is left of the tiny Wayne County town of Williamsville now lies surrounded by the southeastern-most section of the huge Mark Twain National Forest. Just north of the town there is a particularly lonely stretch of woods that in 1895 bordered the old Iron Mountain tracks. It was a perfect place for a train robbery if one knew the area, which the would-be robbers apparently did.

It was March 28, a cool and rainy spring night. The two men had apparently sneaked aboard in the darkness as the train was leaving Williamsville, probably at the forward end of the first day coach. When the train reached the desired spot, one of the men reached up and pulled the emergency signal for the engineer to stop the train. As the train slowed, the men slipped masks over their faces and drew revolvers out of their belts.

When the train stopped, they grabbed a porter and ordered him to jump down and uncouple the train behind the express car. When this was done they ran forward, climbed aboard the engine cab, and ordered the engineer to pull ahead a short distance. It was here the bandits made their mistake. Having the engineer pull ahead was a tactic often used by train robbers to separate themselves from the passengers while they ransacked the express car, but usually the engineer was told to go a mile or more. Apparently these would-be robbers got impatient and had the engineer stop after only a few hundred yards.

After forcing the engineer and fireman to accompany them back to the express car, the two intruders had no difficulty getting the messenger to open up. But when they demanded that the messenger open the through safe, he told them he did not have the combination. He did unlock the local safe, but it carried no money.

While the bandits were trying to decide what to do next, they heard voices down the track. The irate passengers had decided their trip had been delayed enough, and they were coming to resolve the situation. It was 1895, and the bandits knew full well that many train passengers still carried revolvers. They realized it was time to leave and they were quick about it. They leaped out of the car and ran for the woods. (Sources: *New York Times*, 29 March 1895; *Railway Age*, 5 April 1895.)

WILSON, SAM. Sam Wilson, a former railroad telegrapher, was not a well known train robber; in fact, he probably was involved in only one holdup. The facts of the case, however, are indeed interesting. If Sam's story is true, in 1893 he stopped a Missouri Pacific passenger train, robbed the express car and escaped, and in doing so left behind at least three witnesses who swore that the train was held up *by seven bandits*. See **Pacific, Missouri**.

WINSTON, MISSOURI. A rumor circulated in November 1879 that the notorious Jesse James had been killed by a member of his own gang on the outskirts of Galena, Kansas. A second rumor suggested that Jesse's brother, Frank James, was also dead. When nothing

was heard from the outlaws for more than a year, there was much speculation that the rumors were true.

Then in January 1881, an article appeared in the Sedalia, Missouri, *Daily Democrat* telling of a meeting between one of the newspaper's reporters and Jesse in Denver, Colorado, that winter. Jesse, the article said, wanted to know if some form of amnesty could be declared whereby he could return to Missouri and live a "peaceful" life.

Was Jesse James dead or alive? And if he was alive, did he want to end his career as an outlaw? On July 15, 1881, the question was answered for many Missourians with the robbery of a Chicago, Rock Island & Pacific passenger express at Winston, Missouri.

Winston is in Daviess County, just southwest of Gallatin. Around 7:00 P.M., as the train pulled out of the station, six men slipped aboard—four entered one of the passenger coaches, and two climbed up into the cab and took control of the locomotive. When the train reached a deserted area of track, the engineer was ordered to stop.

The express car was ransacked, and an undetermined amount of currency was taken (one report said only $600). Some observers, however, suggested that the attack on the express car was not the bandits' primary purpose in stopping the train. Back in the passenger coach, while the passengers were being searched for money, one of the robbers, for no apparent reason, shot and killed the conductor, William Westfall (sometimes spelled Westphal). Witnesses later testified that Westfall was not causing the bandits any trouble, and that he was standing still with his hands raised when he was killed. One of the bandits also killed a passenger in the smoking car, again for no apparent reason.

When a train robbery occurred in Missouri, thoughts immediately turned to the James brothers. This attack, however, did not follow the usual James pattern. Opinion was divided over whether the Jameses were involved, until somebody pointed out that the dead conductor, Westfall, perhaps once a family acquaintance, had been in charge of the special train that had carried Pinkerton detectives into Clay County, Missouri, on the night of January 26, 1875, which culminated in the bombing of the James family home, the killing of Jesse's and Frank's younger half-brother, Archie, and the mutilation of their mother, Zerelda Samuel.

Outlaw historians still do not agree if the Winston

affair should be credited to Jesse and Frank. Later, after Frank's surrender, he was tried for Westfall's murder and acquitted. The only evidence against him at the trial was the testimony of gang member Dick Liddil, whom the jury may have concluded was only trying to save his own neck. (Sources: Morse, *Cavalcade of the Rails*; Settle, *Jesse James Was His Name*.) *See also* **The James-Younger Gang**.

WITTROCK, FRED. Early on the morning of October 26, 1886, St. Louis' Union Station began buzzing with a rumor that sometime during the night the westbound St. Louis & San Francisco express had been held up. As the story was told and retold, it took on ghastly proportions. An early version was that the engineer and fireman had been killed; a later version was that the Adams Express Company messenger and the baggage clerk were victims. One story had the entire train being derailed. When the true story finally unfolded, it was far less tragic.

No one had been killed. The Adams Express Company car had been robbed, however. According to the messenger, David S. Fotheringham, shortly before the train was scheduled to leave Union Station, a large, well-dressed man appeared at the door of the express car with a letter addressed to the messenger. It introduced the bearer as Jim Cummings and informed Fotheringham that Cummings was a new employee, and that he, Fotheringham, was to take him on the run as far as Pierce City for training purposes. The letter was signed by W. H. Damsel, local superintendent for the Adams Express Company. Cummings then produced a second letter with similar instructions, signed by J. B. Barrett, the Adams route agent.

Messenger Fotheringham took the man on board and began instructing him on the processing of waybills. Everything seemed on the up-and-up until about ten miles out. Fotheringham turned his back on the stranger and the next thing he knew he was on the floor of the car, fighting for his life. Outweighed by many pounds, the messenger lost the struggle and was quickly bound and gagged.

As Fotheringham lay on the floor watching the man scoop up the contents of the company safe, the robber turned to him and said, "You would be surprised if I told you who I am. . . . I'm Jim Cummings, the last of the Jesse James gang. I was at the Blue Cut job, and

Fred Wittrock. *Pinkertons.*

only got $1,500 out of it. Since then, I've passed considerable time in Australia and San Francisco."

The messenger said the man went on talking about his outlaw days, and "seemed familiar with the name and doings of the various members of the James gang."

As the train pulled into the station at Pacific, in Franklin County, the robber prepared to leave. But before departing, he reached into Fotheringham's pocket and pulled out the two letters he had used to gain entry. Then, as the train slowed to a stop, he opened the door and jumped out.

At first count, it appeared that the robber had managed to get away with at least $50,000. However, this figure would later rise, several times, and would eventually reach $90,000.

When Fotheringham told his story to the Pinkertons, who were retained by Adams to handle robbery investigations, the detectives were skeptical, and they warned the Adams officials not to take it at face value. Furthermore, they suggested that the messenger should be held in custody on the chance that he might break down and confess under further interrogation.

Because the robbery occurred in transit and outside the city of St. Louis, the local police had no interest in the case. Even the St. Louis County authorities hesitated to assume jurisdiction, since the robber left the train in Franklin County. The Pinkertons, therefore, took full charge of the investigation. Their first step was to whisk messenger Fotheringham off to St. Louis' Southern Hotel and put two operatives to work trying to tear apart his story.

Fotheringham was grilled every day for a week, but for the most part held to his original account of the robbery. The investigation appeared to be getting nowhere, but then word came to the Adams officials that the *St. Louis Globe Democrat* had received a mysterious letter signed by a person claiming to be the robber, "Jim Cummings." The letter was postmarked St. Joseph, Missouri, and was dated October 31, five days after the robbery. The writer said that he was writing only to clear the name of Fotheringham, the messenger, who had nothing to do with the crime. To prove that he was who he said he was, the writer enclosed two Adams Express Company envelopes and a memorandum from a bank that had been taken from the safe.

The following week it was discovered that the writer of the letter had also written to Fotheringham's mother. He expressed his sorrow over the circumstances and enclosed $60 which he said was to be used to help pay for her son's legal expenses. When another week went by, and the Pinkertons continued to hold Fotheringham in the hotel room, the messenger's mother used the $60 to hire a lawyer to file a writ of *habeas corpus*, demanding that either he be released or any evidence against him be turned over to the grand jury.

In his letter to the *Globe Democrat* the writer gave full details of the robbery and, apparently as further proof that he was the robber, he said that he had left a package at a check stand in the Union Station containing the revolver used in the holdup. The Pinkertons found the package and the revolver. The writer also mentioned a boat that was to be used in the getaway, and camping provisions, all left near a bridge at St. Charles, Missouri. These also were found.

Despite the letter, messenger Fotheringham's credibility began to crumble. Two trainmen were found who saw him talking to the alledged Jim Cummings the night of the robbery, and their account of the scene did not jibe with his. Also, a handwriting expert stated that he would be willing to testify that, in his opinion, the "Jim Cummings" letters were in fact written by David Fotheringham. The case was given to a grand jury, and it returned an indictment against the messenger.

In the meantime, however, the search continued for "Jim Cummings," and the Pinkertons got a lucky break. The contents of the package left at the Union Station check room revealed, in addition to a revolver, several other items, including a shirt, a billy club, and several pieces of sheet music. On one of the sheets was written an address, a number on Chestnut Street in St. Louis. On calling at the address, Pinkerton agents en-

countered a landlady who, upon seeing the detectives, announced: "I know who you are. You've come here to see about the two men who were rooming here." When she described the men, one of the descriptions fit that of the man the two trainmen saw talking to messenger Fotheringham at the door of his express car the night of the robbery.

Further clues were uncovered, including the name of a lady who was keeping company with one of the suspects. She had departed recently for Chicago, and the search was begun there. On December 25, Christmas Day, the elusive Jim Cummings was arrested in a Chicago rooming house by local police and the Pinkertons. In a waistcoat in the closet of the suspect's room the authorities found $5,000 taken in the robbery. The suspect was later identified as Fred Wittrock, a former bookkeeper from Leavenworth, Kansas. Three accomplices were also picked up: Oscar Cook, William Haight, and John Weaver, all of Kansas City.

Eventually all parties except Fotheringham pleaded guilty to the crime. Cook implicated Fotheringham, whom he said knew all about the plan and was promised $10,000 out of the stolen loot. However, the indictment against the messenger was dropped.

On January 4, 1887, Wittrock and Haight were convicted and sentenced to seven years in the Missouri penitentiary. Weaver was given five years. The disposition of the case against Oscar Cook is not known. Messenger David S. Fotheringham continued to maintain his innocence, and his case was set for trial in May 1887. But public sentiment began to build in favor of the defendant, and a rumor spread that the state's case against him was weak. The charges were eventually dropped. In retaliation, Fotheringham filed a civil suit against Robert Pinkerton, head of the agency, W. H. Damsell, Superintendent of Adams Express Company, and the Adams Company itself. He charged malicious prosecution and false imprisonment. Pinkerton and Damsell were eventually dismissed from the suit, but on April 19, 1888, a St. Louis jury awarded Fotheringham $20,000 in damages against the Adams company. (Sources: *New York Times*, 27, 28, 30, 31 October, 9–12 November, 4, 26, 27, 30, 31 December 1886, 2 January, 3 May 1887, 20 April 1888.)   □

BIBLIOGRAPHY

Books and Periodicals

Agee, G. W. "Rube Burrow: King of Outlaws and His Band of Train Robbers." *Old West*. Spring 1968.

Barber, F. M. "Gunpowder and Its Successors." *The Forum*. July 1890.

Beebe, Lucius, and Clegg, Charles. *U.S. West: The Saga of Wells, Fargo*. New York: E. P. Dutton & Co., Inc., 1948.

Betenson, Lula Parker. *Butch Cassidy, My Brother*. Provo, Utah: Brigham Young University Press, 1975.

Block, Eugene B. *Great Train Robberies of the West*. New York: Coward-McCann, Inc., 1959.

Boessenecker, John. "John Thacker: Train Robbers' Nemesis." *Real West*. September 1976.

Boley, Edwin J. *The Masked Halters*. Seymour, Indiana: Grassle-Mercer Co., 1977.

Breihan, Carl. *The Escapades of Frank and Jesse James*. New York: Frederick Fell Publishers, Inc., 1974.

———. "The Outlaw Who Became a Pair of Shoes." *True West*. January 1983.

———. *Rube Burrow: King of the Train Robbers*. West Allis, Wisconsin: Leather Stocking Books, 1981.

Burton, Jeff. "Bureaucracy, Blood Money and Black Jack's Gang." *The English Westerners' Society Brand Book*. Winter/Summer 1983–84.

———. "John F. Kennedy of Missouri and His Circle of Train Robbers." *The English Westerners' Society Tally Sheet*. April/July 1980.

———. "A Tale of Two Smiths: Hero and Train Robber." *True West*. September 1984.

Caldwell, George A. "New Mexico's First Train Robbery." *NOLA Quarterly*. Winter 1989.

Clifton, Robert. *Murder by Mail and Other Postal Investigations*. Ardmore, Pennsylvania: Dorrance & Company, 1979.

Crum, Josie Moore. *The Rio Grande Southern Story*. Durango, Colorado: Railroadiana, Inc., Publishers, 1957.

DeNevi, Don. "Holdup of the Santa Claus Special." *Real West*. March 1977.

———. "The Notorious Skaggs Gang of the San Joaquin." *Real West*. January 1979.

———. "Train Robbers of Suison Bay." *Real West*. May 1977.

———. *Western Train Robberies*. Millbrae, California: Celestial Arts, 1976.

Dewhurst, H. S. *The Railroad Police*. Springfield, Illinois: Charles C Thomas, Publisher, 1955.

Dillon, Richard. "Arizona's Last Train Robbery." *Real West*. May 1977.

———. *Wells, Fargo Detective: A Biography of James B. Hume*. Reno: University of Nevada Press, 1986.

Drago, Harry Sinclair. *Outlaws on Horseback*. New York: Dodd, Mead & Company, 1964.

Dullenty, Jim. "Cokeville: A Rough Town in the Old West." *NOLA Quarterly*, Spring 1982.

———. "The Farm Boy Who Became a Member of Butch Cassidy's Wild Bunch." *NOLA Quarterly*. Winter 1986.

———. "Rare Old Photos Reveal Aftermath of the Wagner Train Robbery." *Old West*. Spring 1983.

———. "Thieves' Dynamite Tough on Express Car." *NOLA Quarterly*. Winter 1982–83.

———. "Was William T. Phillips Really Butch Cassidy?" *The Westerners Brand Book*. November–December 1982.

Echols, Lee E. "Old Al Jennings." *Frontier Times*, May 1987.

Edwards, Harold L. "Bullets and Bicycles." *Real West*. March 1988.

———. "Chris Evans—The Ready Killer." *NOLA Quarterly*. Part I, Summer 1986; Part II, Fall 1986.

———. "Kid Thompson and the Roscoe Train Robberies." *True West*. January 1988.

———. "Robbery at Maricopa." *Real West*. May 1987.

———. "Shootout on No. 19." *True West*. May 1987.

Gard, Wayne. *Sam Bass*. Norman: University of Oklahoma Press, 1960.

Garwood, Darrell. *Crossroads of America: The Story of Kansas City*. New York: W. W. Norton & Company, 1948.

Glasscock, C. B. *Bandits and the Southern Pacific*. New York: Frederick A. Stokes Company, 1929.

Haley, J. Evetts. *Jeff Milton: A Good Man with a Gun*. Norman: University of Oklahoma Press, 1948.

Hampton, Wade. "Brigandage on Our Railroads." *The North American Review*. December 1893.

Harlow, Alvin F. *Old Waybills*. New York: Appleton-Century, 1937.

Hatch, Alden. *American Express: A Century of Service*. Garden City, New York: Doubleday & Company, Inc., 1960.

Herr, Kincaid. *The Louisville & Nashville Railroad 1850–1963*. Louisville: Public Relations Department, L&N, 1964.

Hitt, James. "Real to Reel Outlaws: Badmen Who Made Movies." *True West*. June 1983.

Horan, James D. *Desperate Men: Revelations from the Sealed Pinkerton Files*. New York: G. P. Putnam's Sons, 1951.

———. *The Pinkertons*. New York: Crown Publishers, Inc., 1967.

Hungerford, Edward. *Wells, Fargo: Advancing the American Frontier*. New York: Random House, 1949.

Jarman, Rufus. "The Pinkerton Story." *Saturday Evening Post*. May 15, 22, 29, June 5, 1948.

Jennings, Al. *Through the Shadows with O. Henry*. New York: A. L. Burt Company, 1921.

Jessen, Kenneth. *Colorado Gunsmoke*. Boulder, Colorado: Pruett Publishing Company, 1986.

Kelly, Charles. *The Outlaw Trail: A History of Butch Cassidy and His Wild Bunch*. New York: Bonanza Books, 1959.

Kildare, Maurice. "Arizona's Great Train Robbery." *Real West*. September 1968.

———. "Bear River Loot." *True West*. July–August 1968.

Kindred, Wayne E. "Knoxville's Favorite Outlaw: How Harvey Logan Planned Escaped!" *NOLA Quarterly*. Fall 1985.

Kirby, Edward M. *The Rise and Fall of the Sundance Kid*. Iola, Wisconsin: Western Publications, 1983.

———. *The Saga of Butch Cassidy and the Wild Bunch*. Palmer Lake, Colorado: The Filter Press, 1977.

Knight, Jonathan T. "How to Repel Train Robbers." *The North American Review*. February 1895.

Kubista, Bob. "No Headlight in Sight." *Frontier Times*. August–September 1968.

Lacy, Steve. "Matt Warner's Daughter Meets Butch Cassidy." *NOLA Quarterly*. Spring 1982.

Lake, Carolyn. *Under Cover for Wells, Fargo: The Unvarnished Recollections of Fred Dodge*. Boston: Houghton Mifflin Company, 1969.

Larck, George. "The One-Man Holdup." *Westerner*. February 1972.

Long, Bryant Alden. *Mail by Rail: The Story of the Postal Transportation Service*. New York: Simmons-Boardsmith Publishing Corporation, 1951.

Lucia, Ellis. *Tough Men, Tough Country*. Englewood Cliffs, New Jersey: Prentice-Hall, Inc., 1963.

Maguire, Jack. "The Texas Terrors." *Southwest Airlines Magazine*. August 1984.

Marcy, R. B. "Detective Pinkerton." *Harpers New Monthly Magazine*. 1873, vol. 47, p. 720.

Milles, Victor W., "The McCoy Gang. *Old West*. Summer 1970.

Moffett, Cleveland. "The Pollock Diamond Robbery." *McClure's*. April 1895.

Morn, Frank. *The Eye That Never Sleeps*. Bloomington: Indiana University Press, 1982.

Morse, Frank P. *Cavalcade of the Rails*. New York: E. P. Dutton & Company, Inc., 1940.

Murray, David. "Sam Wilson: Single-Handed Train Robber." *Old West*. Summer 1984.

Nash, Jay Robert. *Bloodletters and Badmen*. New York: Warner Books, Inc., 1973.

O'Conner, Richard. *The Legendary Life of O. Henry*. Garden City, New York: Doubleday & Company, Inc., 1970.

O'Dell, Roy. "Bunch & Hobgood: Partners in Crime." *English Westerners' Society Brand Book*. Summer 1985.

———. "Oliver Curtis Perry: The Man Who Stole a Train." *English Westerners' Society Tally Sheet*. Summer 1983.

O'Neal, Bill. *Encyclopedia of Western Gunfighters*. Norman: University of Oklahoma Press, 1979.

Patterson, Richard. "The Fine Art of Robbing Trains." *True West*. April 1986.

———. *Historical Atlas of the Outlaw West*. Boulder, Colorado: Johnson Books, 1985.

———. "The Reno Gang." *American History Illustrated*. Summer 1982.

———. "The Trial of Al Jennings." *NOLA Quarterly*. Winter 1989.

———. "The Trial of Jesse James, Jr." *Old West*. Summer 1987.

———. *Train Robbery: The Birth, Flowering and Decline of a Notorious Western Enterprise*. Boulder, Colorado: Johnson Books, 1981.

————. *Wyoming's Outlaw Days*. Boulder, Colorado: Johnson Books, 1982.

Pinkerton, William A. "Highwaymen of the Railroad." *The North American Review*. November 1893.

————. *Train Robberies, Train Robbers, and the "Hold-up" Men*. Chicago: (Privately published) 1907. Reprinted by Arno Press, Inc., 1974.

Pointer, Larry. *In Search of Butch Cassidy*. Norman: University of Oklahoma Press, 1977.

Porter, T. R. "The Hold-up at Hugo." *The Wide World Magazine*. November 1909.

Preece, Harold. *The Dalton Gang: End of an Outlaw Era*. New York: Hastings House, 1963.

Rainey, George. *Demise of the Iron Horse*. Berne, Indiana: Economy Printing Concern, Inc., 1969.

Rains, Ray D. "Trouble at Olyphant Depot." *True West*. September–October 1977.

Rasch, Phillip J. "Fleming 'Jim' Parker, Arizona Desperado." *NOLA Quarterly*. Spring 1982.

————. "Train Robbery Times Four." *Real West*. June 1982.

Reed, Robert C. *Train Wrecks: A Pictorial History of Accidents on the Main Line*. New York: Bonanza Books, 1968.

Reno, John. *The Life of John Reno*. Seymour, Indiana: (Privately published) 1897.

Rickards, Colin. "Bill Miner—50 Years a Hold-up Man." *English Westerners' Society Brand Book*. January, April 1966.

Romero, Trancito (as told to R. C. Valdez). "I Saw Black Jack Hanged." *True West*. September–October 1958.

Russell, Don, ed. *Trails of the Iron Horse*. Garden City, New York: Doubleday & Company, Inc., 1975.

Settle, William A., Jr. *Jesse James Was His Name*. Columbia, Missouri: University of Missouri Press, 1966.

Shaw, Robert B. *Down Brakes*. London-Geneva: P. R. Macmillan, Limited, 1961.

Shirley, Glenn. "The Bungled Job at Blackstone Switch." *True West*. May–June 1966.

————. "Train Robbery That Fizzled." *Old West*. Winter 1986.

————. *West of Hells Fringe: Crime, Criminals, and the Federal Peace Officer in Oklahoma Territory*, Norman: University of Oklahoma Press, 1978.

Shoemaker, Arthur. "Al Spencer: Transition Outlaw." *True West*. March 1987.

Spring, Agnes Wright. *The Cheyenne and Black Hills Stage and Express Routes*. Glendale, California: The Arthur H. Clark Company, 1949.

Steel, Rory. "The Jones Boys." *Old West*. Winter 1982.

Steele, Phillip W. "The Dalton Family Found in California." *NOLA Quarterly*. Fall 1987.

Vestal, Stanley. *Queen of Cowtowns: Dodge City*. New York: Harper & Brothers, 1952.

Volland, Robert F. "The Reno Gang of Seymour." (Ph.D. Dissertation, Indiana University, 1948.)

Walker, Dale L. "Buckey O'Neill and the Holdup at Diablo Canyon." *Real West Annual*, 1980.

Walker, Wayne T. "The Doctor Who Rode with Sam Bass." *True West*. April 1983.

Wellman, Paul I. *Dynasty of Western Outlaws*. Garden City, New York: Doubleday & Company, Inc., 1961.

White, James E. *A Life Span and Reminiscences of Railway Mail Service*. Philadelphia: Deemer & Jaisohn, 1910.

White, John H., Jr. "Safety with a Bang: The Railway Torpedo." *National Railway Bulletin*. 1983, vol. 48, no. 6.

Wood, Stanley. *Over the Range to the Golden Gate*. Chicago: R. R. Donnelley & Sons Co., 1908.

Young, Robert. "Train Robbers Mystify Sheriff and Posse." *NOLA Quarterly*. Winter 1982–83.

Newspapers

Alabama: *Birmingham Weekly Age Herald* 1889, 1890; *Mobile Register* 1871.

Arizona: *Arizona Daily Gazette* 1894; *Arizona Daily Star* 1887; *Arizona Weekly Journal Miner* 1898.

Arkansas: *Fort Smith Elevator* 1879.

California: *Alta California* 1852; *Fresno Expositor* 1891, 1893; *San Francisco Call* 1921; *San Francisco Chronicle* 1887, 1900, 1902, 1904, 1913.

Colorado: *Rocky Mountain News* 1904.

Florida: *Madison Morning News* 1891.

Georgia: *Waycross Herald* 1894.

Illinois: *Chicago Tribune* 1883; *Joliet Daily Republican* 1896.

Indiana: *Indianapolis Daily Sentinel* 1865, 1868, 1873; *New Albany Weekly Ledger* 1867; *Seymour Democrat* 1868.

Kansas: *Kansas Republican* 1893.

Kentucky: Louisville Daily Journal 1866.

Mississippi: Vicksburg Evening Post 1894.

Missouri: Kansas City Star 1892; *Sedalia Daily Democrat* 1881; *St. Louis Democrat* 1873; *St. Louis Globe Democrat* 1888–1897; *St. Louis Times* 1874.

Nevada: Elko Independent 1970; *Virginia City Enterprise* 1881.

New York: New York Times 1866–1931.

Ohio: Cincinnati Daily Enquirer 1865; *Cincinnati Gazette* 1875.

Oklahoma: Ardmore State Herald 1894; *Bartlesville Enterprise* 1923; *Guthrie Daily Leader* 1895; *Guthrie Elevator* 1891; *Oklahoma State Capital* 1896; *Perry Democrat* 1895; *Vinita Indian Chieftain* 1894.

Pennsylvania: Pittsburgh Telegraph 1875.

Tennessee: Clarksville Leaf Chronicle 1897, 1902.

Texas: Fort Worth Gazette 1894; *Galveston News* 1877.

Other Sources

Congressional Record, 53rd Cong., 1893.

Express Gazette 1897.

Hume, James B., and Thacker, Jonathan N., *Report of Jas. B. Hume and Jno. N. Thacker, Special Officers, Wells, Fargo & Co.s Express, Covering a Period of Fourteen years, Giving Losses by Train Robbers, Stage Robbers, and Burglaries, and a Full Description and Record of All Noted Criminals Convicted of Offenses Against Wells, Fargo & Company Since November 5th, 1870.* (Privately published) 1884.

Jennings v. United States, 2 Ind. T. 670, 53 S.W. 456 (1899).

People v. Lovren, 119 Cal. 88, 51 Pac. 22 (1897).

People v. Thompson, 115 Cal. 160, 46 Pac. 912 (1896).

Railway Age 1891, 1893–1895.

State v. Kennedy, 154 Mo. 268, 55 S.W. 293 (1900).

Territory v. Ketchum, 65 Pac. 169 (1901).

INDEX